F. R Grahame

The Archer and the Steppe

Or, the empires of Scythia. A history of Russia and Tartary, from the earliest ages till the fall of the Mongul power in Europe, in the middle of the sixteenth century

F. R Grahame

The Archer and the Steppe
Or, the empires of Scythia. A history of Russia and Tartary, from the earliest ages till the fall of the Mongul power in Europe, in the middle of the sixteenth century

ISBN/EAN: 9783337245641

Printed in Europe, USA, Canada, Australia, Japan

Cover: Foto ©ninafisch / pixelio.de

More available books at **www.hansebooks.com**

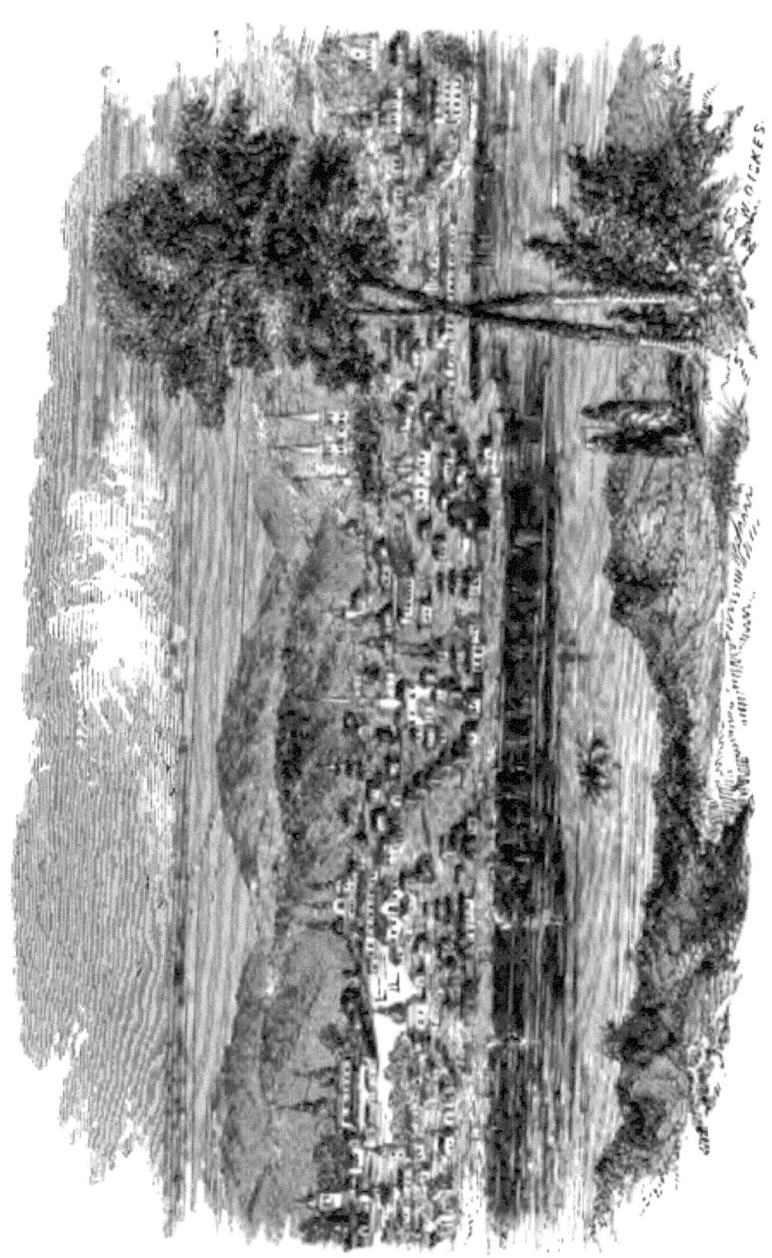

IRKUTSH, THE CAPITAL OF EASTERN SIBERIA.

THE ARCHER AND THE STEPPE;

OR,

THE EMPIRES OF SCYTHIA:

A HISTORY OF

RUSSIA AND TARTARY,

FROM THE EARLIEST AGES TILL THE FALL OF THE MONGUL
POWER IN EUROPE, IN THE MIDDLE OF THE
SIXTEENTH CENTURY.

BY F. R. GRAHAME.

> The seat
> Of mightiest empire, from the destined walls
> Of Cambalu, seat of Cathaian khan,
> And Samarcand by Oxus, Timur's throne,
> To Pekin by Sindean kings, and thence
> To Agra and Lahore of great Mogul,
> Down to the golden Chersonese, or where
> The Persian in Ecbatan sat, or since
> In Hispahan, or where the Russian czar
> In Moscow, or the Sultan in Byzance,
> Turkestan born.—*Paradise Lost.*

LONDON:
JAMES BLACKWOOD, PATERNOSTER ROW.

CONTENTS.

BOOK I.

FROM THE EARLIEST AUTHENTIC HISTORY OF SCYTHIA TO THE CONQUESTS OF THE MONGUL TARTARS.

PAGE

CHAPTER I.
Introduction 9

CHAPTER II.
Russia and her Earliest Inhabitants . . 12

CHAPTER III.
The Asiatic Scythians—The Huns—Attila 26

CHAPTER IV.
The Igours—Avars—Bulgarians—Slavonians—Chazars . . 38

CHAPTER V.
The Caucasus—Georgia . . . 40

CHAPTER VI.
The Finns—Russians—Novogorod and Kiof—Rurik—Oleg—Igor—Olga . . 61

CHAPTER VII.
Europe in the Ninth Century—Biarmaland—the Crimea . . . 80

CHAPTER VIII.—FROM 955 TO 971.
Sviatozlaf—He subdues the Chazars—Invades the Greek Empire—The Principalities—Defeat and Death of Sviatozlaf 92

CONTENTS.

CHAPTER IX.—From 971 to 1015.
Vladimir the Great—The Russians are converted to Christianity . 108

CHAPTER X.—From 1015 to 1053.
Sviatopolk—The Poles invade Russia—Jaroslaf . . . 123

CHAPTER XI.—From about 800 to 1070.
The Avars or Turks—Mahmoud of Ghizni—He invades India—The Seljuk Turks—Togrul Beg—Alp Arslan—Malek Shah—The Polotzi 136

CHAPTER XII.—From 1053 to 1078.
Iziaslaf—The Poles invade Russia—Sviatozlaf II.—Vyzevold—Novogorod . . 152

CHAPTER XIII.—From 1078 to 1125.
Vyzevold Jaroslafovitz—Sviatopolk Iziaslafovitz—Vladimir Monomachus . . . 160

CHAPTER XIV.—From 1125 to 1157.
The Poles invade Russia—Yourii Dolgorouki—Moscow founded—Kingdom of Halich 167

CHAPTER XV.—From 1157 to 1214.
Continuation of the History of Russia—Invasion of the Poles—State of Society . . 175

CHAPTER XVI.
Affairs of Poland—Esthonia—Livonia—Courland—The Teutonic Knights—Lithuania—The Ottoman Turks—The Origin of the Monguls 184

BOOK II.

FROM THE CONQUESTS OF THE MONGULS TO THE RISE OF TIMUR.

CHAPTER I.—From 1175 to 1227.
Zingis Khan—The Conquests of the Monguls 196

CHAPTER II.—From 1214 to 1246.
The Princes of Kiof—Batù Khan—He conquers Russia, and ravages Poland and Hungary—Embassy sent by the Pope to the Grand Khan—Election of Couyuk—Karacorum—Camp of Batù at Serai 214

CHAPTER III.—From 1246 to 1263.
Yaroslaf of Novogorod—Mangou Khan—Kublai conquers China—Holagou conquers Persia—The Monguls of China—Khans of Kipzak 233

CHAPTER IV.—FROM 1240 TO 1302.

Reign of Alexander Nevskoi in Russia—Noghai's Rebellion—The Monguls of Persia—Abaga—Argun—Voyage of the Chinese Princess to Persia—Kazan . . . 249

CHAPTER V.—FROM 1271 TO 1340.

Continuation of the History of Russia—Reigns of Yaroslaf, Demetrius, and Andrea—Lithuania—The Genoese Colonies—Uzbek Khan—Executions of Michael, Demetrius, and Alexander—Ivan I. . . . 264

CHAPTER VI.—FROM 1340 TO 1352.

Character of the Russians—The Black Death . . . 275

CHAPTER VII.—FROM 1352 TO 1392.

Reign of Demetrius Donskoi—Kipzak—Lithuania—Battle of the Don—Moscow burned—Monasteries—Literature—Poland—The Teutonic Knights . . . 281

BOOK III.

THE HISTORY OF TIMUR AND HIS SUCCESSORS.

CHAPTER I.—FROM 1336 TO 1404.

Timur Bek or Tamerlane—His Conquests—Toktamish . . . 295

CHAPTER II.—FROM 1398 TO 1400.

Timur invades India—The Gipsies . . . 318

CHAPTER III.—FROM 1399 TO 1403.

Timur marches against Georgia, Syria, and the Ottomans—Captures Bajazet . . . 328

CHAPTER IV.—FROM 1403 TO 1530.

Timur returns to Samarcand—Sets out for China—His Death—Troubles in the Empire—His Successors—The Emperor Baber . . . 339

BOOK IV.

CONTINUATION OF THE HISTORY OF RUSSIA, TO THE FINAL EXTINCTION OF THE MONGUL POWER IN EUROPE.

CHAPTER I.

The Fifteenth Century—Fall of Constantinople—The Monguls—Their Conquerors and Descendants—The Cossacks . . . 357

CHAPTER II.

The Horde of Toushi—Reign of Vassili, or Bazil the Blind—Manners and Customs of the Russians . . . 368

CONTENTS.

CHAPTER III.

The Reign of Ivan Vassilovitz—His Conquests—Marriage with Sophia of Byzantium—State of the Church—A new Code of Laws—War with Kipzak—Embassies to Moscow 382

CHAPTER IV.

Embassy to Vienna and Copenhagen—War with Finland . 413

CHAPTER V.

Survey of Russia—Siberia—Its Conquest—The Crimea—Her Khan submits to the Turks 417

CHAPTER VI.

War between Moscow and Poland—Coronation of Demetrius—Death of Ivan III.—Accession of Bazil IV.—Prince Glinski—Pillage of Moscow—War with Kazan—Death of Bazil—Accession of Ivan the Terrible—Capture of Kazan and Astrakhan—Extinction of the Mongul power in Europe 437

APPENDIX.

Poems describing the Places and Manners of the People, and the Country of Russia, by Master George Turberville, 1568 471
Puskin's Lay of the Wise Oleg . . 477

BOOK I.

FROM THE EARLIEST AUTHENTIC HISTORY OF SCYTHIA
TO THE
CONQUESTS OF THE MONGUL TARTARS.

> First then from hence
> Turn to the orient sun, and pass the height
> Of these uncultured mountains; thence descend
> To where the wandering Scythians, train'd to beat
> The distant wounding bow, on wheels aloft
> Roll on their wattled cottages.
> POTTER's "Translation of Eschylus."

THE ARCHER AND THE STEPPE.

CHAPTER I.

Introduction.

Oft o'er the trembling nations from afar,
Has Scythia breathed the living cloud of war.—GRAY.

DURING the century before, and that succeeding the Christian era, the whole power, influence, and civilisation of the entire known world were centred in one proud and despotic military state. Rome, by conquest and intimidation, had rendered herself mistress of all the explored and most favoured parts of Asia, Africa, and Europe; her legions held in obedience every nation, from the extremities of Greece to the British isles and the Atlantic ocean; her eagles were borne and dreaded from the sands of Egypt and Arabia, to where the barbarous Teuton, on the shores of the Baltic, encountered the rough weapons of the Goth; the wide wastes of Scythia alone were to her unknown and untrodden plains, and from Scythia her final invaders and conquerors came.

This name was the vague and general appellation bestowed by the Greeks and the Romans upon all the countries that extended from the banks of the Dnieper to the borders of the almost fabulous Cathay.* In those days they were divided by the ancients into European and Asiatic Scythia; to modern geographers they are known as Russia and Tartary.

The former, as the barrier between Asia and Europe, the theatres of present action and civilisation, and past grandeur and fame, has been agitated from time to time by the revolutions with which both have been convulsed; and over her has the first fury of every tempest rolled, that has so frequently burst forth from the centre of the greater continent, and rushed like a whirlwind over half the earth.

* The ancient name of China.

From the depths of Tartary, or Asiatic Scythia, has originally issued every torrent of invading barbarians that have overrun Eastern Europe for the last nine hundred years. Cradled on the gloomy steppes of Mongolia, where the earth for nine months remains buried under a thick bed of snow, and where the sole vegetation consists of short grass, and a few scanty tufts of heath, these hordes of martial shepherds have periodically poured down in search of a richer country and more grateful soil, and, spreading over the barren plains of Tartary and Russia, have formed themselves into moving empires, who for a few years have domineered over the surrounding trembling nations, and then vanished and melted away; leaving little other trace of their existence than the record of destruction. Such were the monarchies of the Huns, the Igours, and Avars; the Chazars, Polotzi, and Monguls; while the Ottoman Turks, who are also Scythian in origin and descent, more fortunate than their predecessors, have maintained a position in one of the finest countries of Europe for the last four hundred years.

As the most enduring, most powerful, and the most known, both in ancient and modern times, of these turbulent nations of the north, Russia occupies by far the most prominent part in the history of the Scythian empires; and I shall therefore make the annals of that country my principal subject. After tracing the origin of her people, I shall glance at the progress of the Huns, the Chazars, and the numerous other Tartar tribes, whose names were only known, by their inroads in the middle ages, to the countries and inhabitants of eastern Europe. Then, sketching the rise of the Russian monarchy, I shall proceed to the conquests of Zingis Khan and the Monguls, and the wars of his descendant, and still more formidable countryman Timur, with the short-lived domination of Samarcand.

The ancient patrimony of the Tartars is now included in the empires of Russia and China; but their conquests, which extended over India, China, Russia, Siberia, and Greece, have left upon the inhabitants of both those countries a deep impress of their long and tyrannical sway; and there is great resemblance in many of their customs * and laws, their jealousy of foreign nations, dress, appearance, and character,

---

* Amongst these may be mentioned one which prevails alike in St. Petersburg, Pekin, and Constantinople, which calls on the Emperor or Sultan, whenever a fire breaks out in the capital, to assist personally in its extinction.

and despotic patriarchal form of government. The same exclusive character, decrees forbidding emigration, rigid adherence to ancient usages, and numerous secret societies, political and religious, are alike remarkable in both; and both empires have been frequently subdued and ruled by foreign invaders and savage warlike hordes; and, exhibiting a vitality almost unknown to the nations of Europe, have risen again from their ashes, and, emancipating themselves from their conquerors, have flourished again with renewed vigour and prosperity.

But the Chinese, who since that time have once more fallen under Tartar rulers, with whom and the natives a war has long been raging, which threatens to tear in pieces the whole Celestial Empire, appear themselves to have been a Scythian people, and therefore only early settled and civilized Tartars. Their manners, says Dr. Latham, in many respects greatly resemble those peculiar to the Scythian tribes described by Herodotus; a German author has pointed out seventeen different customs which are identical in the Chinese and Turks; their language has been proved to be by no means so dissimilar to all other nations as has formerly been supposed; and the dragon, the emblem of Scythia, is used alike by the Slavonians, Chinese, and Tartars.*

About six hundred years before Christ, a horde of Scythians conquered India; and one of their tribes, the fair-haired, blue-eyed Getæ, returning towards the north, and establishing themselves in the plains to the east of the Caspian, finally settled in Scandinavia, leaving a few who are still called Jits in Hindostan,† while in Europe they became known and celebrated by the name of Goths.

* "*Encyclopædia Britannica.*"—Dr. Latham.
† Tod's "Annals and Antiquities of Rajasthan."

CHAPTER II.

Russia, and her earliest Inhabitants.

> Campestres melius Scythæ,
> Quorum plaustras vagas rite trahunt domos,
> Vivunt et rigidi Getæ,
> Immetata quibus jugera liberas.—HORACE.

UNTIL towards the latter end of the last century, when the ambition and conquests of her sovereigns had brought Russia into close contact and opposition with the other more advanced nations of Europe, she had been considered by her contemporaries of the west as rather an Asiatic than a European power, too barbarous and remote to contend with their statesmen in the cabinet, or maintain any interest or influence in common with their own; and shut out by the stormy Poland, her severe and rigorous climate, and the exclusive policy of her government, from trade or intimate connection with the rest of the continent; she had long been surely and gradually increasing both in power and extent, though hardly known and unheeded except by a few farsighted politicians, and the neighbouring states with whom she was continually at war. This isolation may be considered to have commenced in the eleventh and twelfth centuries, when a career of prosperity and conquest, which might have ended in the subjugation of the then darker and more ignorant nations of the west, was cut short by the perpetual inroads of the savage Tartar tribes who hovered on her eastern border, and the civil discords of her princes; and later, by the rapid conquests of the Monguls, under whom she was long held in slavery.

Neither history nor tradition has left us any positive information when the first colonists from Asia entered Europe; but it is generally considered that the Finns were the first inhabitants of Russia, and indeed of the whole continent, and that they were from thence driven gradually northwards to the extremities of Norway, Finland, and Lapland, where they now dwell, by the second immigration, which was probably that of the Celts. While the Finns retreated towards the north, this last people moved on to the west, being expelled from the Russian steppes by a fresh horde of invaders, the Scythians, who, scattering the inhabitants before them like chaff, precipitated themselves upon Eastern Europe. Their families and cattle encamped upon her extensive plains, which have successively pastured the flocks of the Finns, Celts, Scythians, Goths, Huns, and Monguls, the inhospitable climate denying to a people not skilled in agriculture, any other mode of supporting life than that of wandering shepherds or hunters. But since the power of the last of these invaders was overthrown, the Russian empire has continued to increase in extent and power, till it now embraces a sixth of the habitable portion of the globe, and extending from the borders of the Pacific Ocean to those of the Baltic Sea, and from the ice-bound shores of the Arctic to the sunny and fertile lands of Persia and Armenia, the greatest diversity is to be found in the inhabitants, climate, vegetation, and general aspect of the country; the former comprising nearly a hundred different nations; for the handsome Georgian, the swarthy Tartar, the fair Esthonian, the Persian of Erivan, the small and timid Lapp, the Gheber of Bakù, the fish-eating Samoyede, and the Boyard of Moscow, all alike own the sway of the Czar. In the north, where gloomy forests of pine and fir, with deep bogs and extensive marshes, cover the face of the country, till they are reduced, on the shores of the White Sea and Frozen Ocean, to scanty woods of the dwarfish birch and larch, the inhabitants are drawn in their sledges by the reindeer, and strong and shaggy Samoyede dog; while in the south, the arid steppes, overspread with grass, are traversed by the camel and araba, whose drivers, the few nomadic tribes still roaming across these sandy wastes, belong to the horde of Nogay Tartars, the peaceful and insignificant descendants of the last and fiercest conquerors of the empire.

The only mountains of any extent that break the uniformity of the level landscape in Russia, are the Urals, known to the ancients as the Ryphean chain, which divide Europe from Asia; the hills of the Caucasus, whose lofty peaks, famous in Grecian fable and Persian song, rise beyond the steppes of the Don and the Black Sea; and further south, in the kingdom of Georgia, where the vine, mulberry, and orange, luxuriantly and uncultivated, grow, lies the solitary and snow-capped Mount of Ararat, celebrated as the resting-place of the ark.

Her rivers, of which the Volga is the longest in Europe, are navigable almost to their source, and, being connected by canals, form a communication between the Black, Caspian, White, and Baltic Seas, though, from the scarcity of water in these parts, several attempts to unite the Don and Volga,* which approach to within a distance of forty miles, have failed, and they are rendered useless during many months of the year by the ice, which annually blocks up every harbour in the empire, with the exception of two or three on the Euxine; thus forming a great impediment to the commerce of Russia by sea, and causing her to carry on a comparatively larger trade by caravans with Siberia, China, and all Central Asia, than with the other nations of Europe. The limits of no empire have so frequently changed as those of Russia; her territories having spread, in the early period of her history, over nearly the same extent of country in Europe that they at present occupy; while in the beginning of the sixteenth century, when she finally emancipated herself from the Tartar rule, they had dwindled down to little more than Moscow, her capital, and a few surrounding provinces, then known as Muscovy. The kingdoms of Poland, Georgia, Siberia, Kasan, Astrakhan, and the Crimea, with a part of Armenia and the Grand Duchy of Finland, are now included within her frontiers, where, though the Slavonian is the most considerable and dominant race,† it has probably very much intermingled with the Tartar tribes, by whom it has been so frequently subdued, particularly the Monguls, its latest foreign masters, from whom a hundred and thirty noble Russian families are descended, besides many of the common people. Numerous words in the Russian language are also derived from the same source; several of their names for weights, measures, and coins, the punishment of the knout, various legal customs, habits of life, and articles of dress; with many of the forms and ceremonies at their court.‡

* They have been joined within the last few years by a tram railway.
† Professor Retzius of Stockholm, maintains that the Slavonians themselves do not belong to the Caucasian division of the human family. Dr. Latham considers that nine-tenths of the modern Russians, and inhabitants of Russia, are of the Tartar race; or, as he denominates it, the Ugrian, in which category he comprises the Huns, Fiuns, Kalmucks, and all the Tartar tribes in the empire except the Bashkirs.
‡ Article "Tartar," Penny Cyclopædia.

The Scythians are the first inhabitants of Russia of whom we have any knowledge. They peopled the north of Asia and the east of Europe, and from the most distant times frequently overthrew the thrones of Southern Asia, penetrating on one occasion even as far as Egypt, where, before the days of the Pharaohs, they founded a dynasty called the Hyskos, or Shepherd kings. In the fifth book of the Chronicles of Berosus, the Chaldean, that ancient writer informs us that Nimrod sent Assyrius, Medus, Moscus, and Magog, to found colonies in various parts of Asia and Europe, and that Moscus planted settlements in both continents. This account has given rise to the supposition, that Moscus came to European Scythia, and that from him the river Moscowa * received its name; † while Assyrius was father of the Assyrian, Medus of the Medes, and Magog of the Eastern Scythians, or Tartars. Herodotus describes these people as inhabiting a country to the westward of the Tanais, from whence they had driven the Cimmerii ‡ (a Celtic tribe), whom Niebuhr supposes retired towards the west, and emigrated from Scythia into the countries on the Danube; and, according to Sir Isaac Newton, both nations must have spread themselves over Europe and Lesser Asia before the year of the flood 1220, that is, about the time of the Israelitish judges. The Scythian hordes who came into Europe, had been expelled from the eastward of the Caspian by the Massagetæ, another of their tribes,‖ who had been dispossessed of their own country by Ninus, king of Assyria; and they appear to have carried on some commerce with the Greeks, as we learn from the historian that the caravans of Greek merchants, who traded up the Tanais or Don, towards the Ural mountains, were always accompanied by seven interpreters, speaking as many different languages. In the annals of Persia, all the country north of the Caucasus and river Oxus is called Turan, or Land of Darkness, in contradistinction to Iran, or the Land of the Sun; and their history transmits the record of perpetual wars carried on

---

* Some historians have conjectured that this name was derived from Mesech, a son of Japhet, and quote the passage from Ezekiel, which describes Mesech as supplying Tyre with staves and brazen vessels (the Tartars, from the earliest ages, have been skilful in working metals), in support of their argument.
† Sir Jerome Horsey's "Travels in Russia."
‡ Herodotus states that in his time there were still many monuments and bridges, erected by the Cimmerians, in Scythia.
‖ Pritchard's "Natural History of Man."

between the two nations from the most remote period of antiquity.*

The same manners, customs, and mode of living, appear to have prevailed among all the tribes of the Scythians, from the shores of the Euxine to where they encountered the empire of the Huns, on the borders of China, and closely resembled those of the modern Tartars. Their plains abounded in wild horses, one of which was possessed by every warrior, whose arms consisted of wooden spears or javelins, a bow and a quiver of poisoned arrows, and in passing a river † they made use of their saddles, consisting of leather sacks stuffed with straw, upon which they sat, causing their horses, whose tails they held, to swim before them, and thus float them across. When two Scythians wished to swear an eternal friendship, they were accustomed to make an incision in their bodies, and, mingling their blood in a cup, first dipped into the vessel the points of their swords, and then sucked the ends. But the geography and history of Scythia appears to have been very imperfectly known to the Greeks,‡ to whom she gave two philosophers, and who celebrated in their songs, in the days of Homer, the peace and innocence of the pastoral life as existed upon her plains, unaware of the savage manners of her people, and the frequency with which those verdant fields were stained with blood. The same custom that prevailed among the Huns, ancient Russians, Monguls, and all the Tartar tribes, of sacrificing horses and slaves over the graves of their nobles and chiefs, was also practised in Scythia; and the principal wife of a sovereign, with his cook, cupbearer, messenger, and fifty native Scythian slaves, and horses, were all strangled over the tomb of their chief, who was usually buried with great pomp and ceremony, jewels

---

* The Persian poets celebrate, in many of their songs, the glories and magnificence of Afrasib, an ancient king of the Turanians, the numbers of his retinue, and splendid court. He was the rival of their favourite hero, Roustem, whose fame has been recorded in an Iranian poem of ten thousand verses. The Turanian kings, like the Pharaohs of Egypt, were all known by the name of Afrasib.

† In 1240, when the Monguls besieged Kiof, they crossed the Dnieper in the same manner.

‡ Artemidorus of Ephesus, a geographer, who flourished about the year 100 B.C., stated that the country east of the Tanais was unexplored; and so late as after the expedition of Alexander the Great, the Caspian was believed to be a gulf of the Northern Ocean, and Pliny informs us that his contemporaries supposed the Palus Mæotis (Sea of Azof) to be connected with the Arctic Sea. The Volga was unknown to the Greeks, and is first mentioned, under the name of Rha, by the Roman writers. It is a common opinion among the most eminent geologists, that till within a comparatively recent period of the world's history, the Caspian and Black Seas were connected, and that the ocean overflowed the sandy steppes that now lie between them to the north of the Caucasus, which are still strongly impregnated with salt and shells. Herodotus speaks of the Sea of Azof as being of about the same extent as the Black Sea.

and ornaments being placed in the grave, and a fresh layer of earth raised every year over the sepulchre in which he was interred.*

Hippocrates has left us a most accurate account of the Scythians and their country. He says, "The wilderness of the Scythians, as their land is termed, is, for the most part, a plain covered with grass and destitute of trees, and moderately watered with streams.† There the Scythians dwell, who are called nomades, because they have no houses, but live in waggons. The women spend most of their time in their waggons, but the men are accustomed to ride on horseback, followed by their flocks and herds, and horses; they live on boiled meat, and drink the milk of mares."‡ The Roman writers also inform us that the Scythians covered themselves with skins, and had no cities, but continually

---

* The tumuli, which are very numerous in Southern Russia and the Crimea, are supposed to contain the tombs of the Scythian kings. Several have been opened, and found to enclose shields, bows, swords, and gold ornaments of very skilful workmanship, some of which are adorned with figures, whose dress very much resembles that worn by the Russian and Polish peasantry at the present day. In one was discovered the bones of a man of great stature, with the remains of a mitra, or Persian cap on his brow, round his neck a necklace in massive gold, upon the right arm, above the elbow, a bracelet of gold an inch wide, below the elbows two other bracelets of mixed gold and silver, one and a half inch broad, and round the wrists a third pair, finished in Persian winged sphinxes, the claws of which held the thick thread of gold that served to close the bracelet, which was of very fine workmanship. At the feet was a pile of little sharp flints, it being the custom in Scythia to tear the face and body with such instruments, and place them in the tombs as a mark of grief. In another part of the sarcophagus was the iron sword, the handle of which was covered with leaves of gold, and ornamented with figures of hares and foxes, a whip adorned with a leaf of gold, and the shield in fine gold, besides drinking-cups, lances, and several bundles of arrows; and in the same grave there appeared a second skeleton, which, from the richness of its ornaments and the mitre which it wore, was supposed to be that of the queen, whom it was the custom in Scythia to strangle over the funeral pile of her husband.—(See H. D. Seymour's "Russia on the Black Sea.")

In 1856, a tumulus eighty feet in height was opened in Southern Russia, and found to contain a travelling car, large quantities of horses' bones, every sort of gold ornament, and vessels of gold, silver, iron, bronze, and clay. Campenhausen, in his "Travels through the Russian Empire," mentions that in a tumulus he caused to be opened in the province of Ekaterinoslaf, he found the skeletons of seven men and five horses, some bows and arrows, silver buckles, and clasps of harness.

Dr. Clarke conjectured that some of the tumuli might have been antediluvian graves.

† The modern traveller Kohl, in his description of the steppes of Southern Russia, which in summer are covered with long grass, in winter with snow, observes that for hundreds of miles no break appears in these plains, which resemble a verdant ocean, "where a calf that began to graze at the Carpathian Mountains, might eat its way to the Chinese Wall, and arrive there a full-grown ox." No trees break the monotony of the apparent boundlessness of the steppes, except in some few places the acacia; but flowers are numerous, and thistles attain so great a height that they appear like trees, and a Cossack on horseback may conceal himself among them. In summer, the atmosphere is of an almost Indian heat, but the winter resembles that of the Arctic regions; and, during the late war, several battalions destined to recruit the Russian army in the Crimea, were lost in crossing these formidable plains of snow. The grass teems with animal life; spotted earth hares (as the German colonists call them) are every where to be seen, small birds, pigeons, and demoiselles abound, and eagles and vultures float high in the air. Scattered over the steppes are numberless flocks of sheep and herds of half-wild horses, who, attended by a few shepherds or herdsmen, wander from place to place over the plains in search of pasture, their attendants passing almost their whole lives on horseback, having no houses, but sheltering in their waggons, and enlivening their solitude by almost perpetual song. There are also many German colonies in the steppes, who, being allowed to frame their own local government, and exempted from taxes or conscription for a period of fifty years, are gradually bringing the steppes into cultivation.

‡ Pritchard's "Nat. Hist. of Man."

changed their habitations to procure pasture for their flocks and herds: their government was monarchical, and the deference they paid to their sovereigns was unparalleled. When the king died, his body was carried through every province, where it was received in solemn procession, and afterwards buried,* and the tumuli which abound in Southern Russia, and upon the eastern coasts of the Crimea, are supposed to have been erected by these people over the tombs of their kings. From this account, and the description of their appearance by Hippocrates, which so greatly resembles that of the modern Tartars, there appears to be no doubt that these Scythians were the ancestors of that people; and Niebuhr, in support of this argument, remarks that their custom of burning the bodies of their dead, their personal appearance, and their mode of life and customs, all point to this race of mankind. "Again," says he, "intoxication from the vapour of red-hot stones, and confined under close coverlets, is Siberian, only Herodotus confounds them with the vapour baths, which the barbarians in these parts enjoyed, and perhaps carried to a luxurious excess."† A further proof, if any were wanting, is, that the Scythians were accustomed to shave their heads from infancy, with the exception of one long tail on the crown; a practice that still prevails among the Chinese and many other tribes of Tartars.

The Scythians, in the year B.C. 624, under their king, Madyes, penetrated in vast numbers through the rocky defiles of the Caucasus, and devastating all the country on their route, overran Asia Minor, where they maintained themselves for twenty-eight years, having driven out the Medes, its former inhabitants; they also attempted to conquer Syria, and advanced as far as Egypt, but were induced to return by presents from its king, Psammetichus, and, being subsequently driven back with great slaughter, the remainder of their army was forced to retrace its steps to their own northern regions; though, among the border hills of Palestine, more than two-thirds of the invaders had found a grave. About the year 530 B.C., Cyrus the Great, king of Persia, advanced with a large army against the Scythian tribes who dwelt to the north of the Caspian Sea;

---

* Herodotus.
† For an account of the Russian vapour bath, and for the manner in which they are universally enjoyed by the people, see the last chapter of Kohl's "St. Petersburg," Custine's "La Russie en 1839," and many other works on Russia.

but he sustained a terrible defeat from their queen, Tomyris, or Zarina as she is called by Diodorus Siculus, and was himself slain in the engagement.

In the year 522 B.C., Darius Hystaspes,* king of Persia, collecting an enormous army from all parts of his empire, set out from Susa, his capital, for an expedition against the Scythians, with 700,000 men. His fleet of six hundred ships, which he manned principally with Greeks, sailed up the Danube; and, throwing a bridge of boats over the river, near the point where the stream divides, he marched his army across it, and penetrated into the wilds of Scythia. The inhabitants, on receiving intelligence of the invasion by which they were menaced, having sent their wives and children into the heart of the country, filled up all the wells, stopped the springs, and consumed the forage throughout that part of their territories over which the forces of Darius must pass. They then advanced to within sight of the enemy, not designing to come to an engagement with the numerous and well-disciplined army of the Persians, but hoping to draw them in pursuit away from the protection and support of their ships, and in a dry and sandy district, where they would inevitably suffer from want of provisions and water. Darius fell into the snare; for, seeing the Scythians each day within a short distance of his troops, in opposition to the advice of the wisest of his officers, he vainly endeavoured to overtake them, constantly expecting to succeed in giving them battle, while they perpetually eluded his pursuit. Being unencumbered with baggage, and all well mounted on their fleet and hardy steeds, the Scythians easily escaped from their more heavily laden enemies, most of whom marched on foot, and who possessed no clue† to guide them through the sandy, trackless deserts. At length fatigue, and the scarcity of forage and provisions, having greatly reduced the Persian army before they had once engaged the enemy, Darius despatched a herald with this message to the Scythian prince Indathyrus,‡—" Prince of the Scythians, wherefore dost thou fly before me? why dost thou not pause, either to give me battle if thou believest thyself able to encounter me, or,

---

* Rollin's "Ancient History." Herodotus.

† According to Herodotus, this expedition was undertaken by Darius to punish the Scythians for their conquest of Asia Minor, which was then a Persian province.

‡ Herodotus states that the Scythian kings were descended from Scytha, a son of Hercules.

if thou thinkest thyself too weak, to acknowledge thy master by presenting him with earth and water?"* The Scythian prince immediately returned this answer to the Persian monarch—"If I fly before thee, Prince of the Persians, it is not because I fear thee. What I do now is no more than what I am used to do in time of peace. We Scythians have neither cities nor lands to defend; if thou wouldst force us to engage thee, come and attack the tombs of our fathers, and then thou shalt find what manner of men we are." The further Darius advanced upon the barren and wasted plains, the greater hardships he had to encounter, while his army was threatened with famine; and at length the approach of winter rendering it probable that his troops would soon be reduced to the last extremity from hunger and fatigue, he was forced to commence an unwilling and melancholy retreat. At this juncture he received a second messenger from the chief of his enemies, who presented him with a bird, a mouse, a frog, and five arrows, which were explained in this way by one of the Persian lords, who was familiar with the habits and customs of their foes—" Unless you fly like birds, hide in the earth like mice, or swim the rivers like frogs, you shall not escape from the arrows of the Scythians." The retreat of Darius, whose original intention appears to have been to march back to Asia round by the Caucasus, was continually harassed by their unexpected and flying attacks; and the Persians only escaped complete destruction from the Scythians, having been deceived by false intelligence as to the part of the Danube which Darius intended to cross. Accordingly, they assembled in large numbers higher up the river, in order to dispute the passage of his army; while, in the mean time, the Persian king led his followers over by another point, and regained his ships in safety, with the shattered remains of his once overwhelming force.†

This expedition of Darius presents a remarkable parallel to that conducted in the same empire by Napoleon in later days—an enterprise undertaken by one of the greatest generals and the finest army of modern times, but which was even more disastrous in its result.

In the year B.C. 327, Alexander the Great took possession

---

* Herodotus.
† Rollin's "Ancient History."

of Sogdiana ; and, having made the river Jaxartes (the Sir) the boundary of his far-spreading dominions, he crossed that river with an army of Macedonians, and invaded the country of the Scythians, who had threatened his newly-founded city of Alexandria Eschate, now known as the town of Khojende. Some of the border tribes submitted to him; but Arian and Quintus Curtius relate that the renowned discipline and courage of his veterans had so small an effect upon the wild and intractable Scythians, that Alexander was forced to retire precipitately, and to turn his arms against a foe less valiant or less capable of resistance. Indeed, Curtius says that the Macedonians sustained so great a loss in one particular battle, that death was inflicted upon any person who made the least mention of its event, the abrupt manner in which the Scythians attacked, and the rapidity with which they retreated into impenetrable wastes, greatly confusing an invading army.* One of his successors, Seleucus Nicanor, afterwards attempted to unite the Don and Volga by a canal—a project which has been renewed in later times by both the Sultan Selim II. and Peter the Great, though in neither instance was it attended with success.

In the year B.C. 250, a tribe of Scythians founded the kingdom of Parthia, which existed independent and powerful for five hundred years.

But though the Scythians, from whom the country obtained its name, are the first people of Russia who were known to the ancient writers of Greece,† the Sauromatæ or Sarmatians, with whom they appear to have been frequently confounded, were in all probability the oldest inhabitants.‡ They were undoubtedly the direct ancestors of the modern Slavonians; yet historians have maintained many different opinions with regard to their origin, some asserting that they were a colony of Medes|| or a tribe of Celts, and others that they were a remnant of the Canaanites who were driven by Joshua from Palestine. Some have also supposed that they were a tribe of the Scythians, or the descendants of the Scythians, and a nation of Amazons described by Hippo-

---

* Goldsmith's "Hist. of Greece."
† Herodotus observes that all the nations beyond the Euxine, except the Scythians, were more than all others barbarous; but these appear in the western parts to have made some progress, and he mentions their town of Borysthenites, which was decorated with griffins and sphinxes, and was destroyed by lightning in the reign of the Scythian king Scyles.
‡ Latham's "Varieties of Man."
|| Diodorus Siculus maintains that they were Medes

crates, whose women rode on horseback, and used the bow and the javelin, none being permitted to marry till she had killed three enemies in battle; and Herodotus, who is the authority for this last theory, relates that the Scythians, finding themselves unable to subdue these female warriors in the field, intermarried with them, and thus the two nations became amalgamated.*

But whether or not the Sarmatians were a tribe of the Celts, they appear to have been conquered about the same time by the Scythians, and driven to the west; and it is probable that the name of Russia is derived from one of their tribes, the Roxolani, whom Strabo places at the north-eastern extremity of European Scythia, having been expelled to that barren region from the banks of the Danube, when, descending from their original home on the plains between the Volga and Don, they had invaded the border provinces of the Roman empire. Their manners and customs were very similar to those of the Scythians, perhaps having adopted them from their conquerors; and they were distinguished from their neighbours, the fair-haired Teutons, by their dark complexions and hair, and loose flowing garments, the prevalence of slaves among them, the light esteem in which they held their women, their plurality of wives, and cavalry composing their chief military force; whereas the Teutons were principally infantry, they wore clothes fitting tightly to their persons, with them slaves were unknown, and no man was allowed to possess more than one wife. Gibbon says of the former people—"Among the different branches of the human race, the Sarmatians form a very remarkable shade, as they seem to unite the manners of the Asiatic barbarians with the figures and complexion of the ancient inhabitants of Europe. According to the various accidents of peace and war, alliance or conquest, they were sometimes confined to the banks of the Tanais, and sometimes spread themselves over the immense plains which lie between the Vistula and the Volga. The care of their numerous flocks and herds, the pursuit of game, and the exercise of war, or rather of rapine, directed the vagrant motions of the Sarmatians."† Like the Scythians, their moveable camps or cities, the ordinary residence of their wives and children, consisted only of large wicker waggons drawn by oxen—a vehicle which is

---

* Herodotus.   † Gibbon's "Decline and Fall of the Roman Empire."

still in common use in Southern Russia, and among most of the Tartar tribes, by whom it is called an araba; and in the Crimea and adjacent country is generally drawn by the small two-humped camel of those parts. Their weapons of war were short daggers, long lances, and a weighty bow and quiver of poisoned arrows; and, on an expedition, they were accustomed to lead in their hands one or two spare horses,* cavalry composing their whole military strength, which enabled them to advance and retreat with a rapidity that surprised the security and eluded the pursuit of a distant enemy. From the scarcity of iron in their country, they made cuirasses of horse hoofs that were capable of resisting a javelin or sword, and, with the exception of their chiefs, burned the bodies of their dead. They possessed immense flocks and herds, and were divided into several tribes—the Roxolani, Carpi, Jazyges, Metanastœ, and Limigantes, and are first mentioned by the name of Slavonians about the fourth and fifth centuries.

The figure of a Sarmatian on the column of Trajan, is depicted in a high conical cap and full trousers, which bear great resemblance to the dress of the modern Russian peasant; and Priscus, the Roman ambassador to the court of Attila the Hun, mentions that a Scythian, or Sarmatian noble, whom he saw there, wore his head shaven in a circular form, a fashion that prevailed in Poland so late as the beginning of the present century.†

The Sarmatians worshipped the sun and moon, the air, and many inferior deities. They were a very depraved people, and are accused by their enemies and contemporaries of being the most licentious of the barbarians. They invaded the Roman empire several times during the third and fourth centuries, and Marcus Claudius sent eight thousand Jazygian horse to Britain.

Besides the Scythians, under which term the ancient writers of Greece appear to have included only the Tartar nations of Scythia, and the Sarmatians or ancestors of the Slavonians, Herodotus mentions several other kingdoms and people as in his time existing in Scythia; and among many of whom we can trace several manners and customs by which we are enabled to identify them with their descendants, who

---

* A practice that has often been made use of on forced marches by the Russian and Cossack cavalry.
† Coxe's "Travels in Russia and Poland."

inhabited the same parts at a more recent period. The Budini, who were probably Finns, he describes as being among the oldest possessors of the soil, and inhabiting that part of Russia which is now called Podolia. A Greek colony had established itself in their province, who tilled the ground, and supplied Greece with corn; and they affirmed that the Budini practised magic, and were in the habit once a-year of changing themselves into wolves, when they prowled about in this shape for a few days, and then resumed their human form.* The same charge of sorcery was constantly brought against the Finns in the middle ages; the tale of the wehr-wolf, probably derived from them, is familiar to all, and even now they have many professed magicians. The Issedones, who appear to have been the same with the Igours, Herodotus informs us, were a civilized nation, dwelling to the far east; beyond them, to the north, the country was impassable owing to the white feathers† that were continually falling, and to their right was the land of the griffins, who guarded the country of gold. Among the Scythians themselves, who were divided into many kingdoms or tribes, the same Greek writer particularly remarks upon the Melanchleni, who always clothed in black; the Agathyrsi, whose province abounded in gold, and who painted themselves, their manners being peculiar for their effeminacy; and the Argippœi, whose name was derived from the wild white horses abounding in their district, which was situated on the Volga and Don; and he observes of the whole people, that "the Scythians have not only a great abhorrence of all foreign customs, but each province seems unalterably tenacious of its own." Anacharsis, the celebrated philosopher, and the brother of their king, having visited Greece, wished, upon his return to his native land, to introduce some of her customs among his countrymen; but incurring their displeasure by this endeavour, he lost his life by the barbarous chief's own hand, and Scydes, a Scythian prince, having been educated by his mother, who was a Greek, experienced soon after his accession a similar fate for a like offence. About this period there were several wise and learned Scythians, whose names were respected even among the Greeks, and of whom Anacharsis, who was a contemporary of Solon and Decimus, appear to have been the chief; and one of the most beautiful

* Herodotus.   † It is almost needless to remark, that this was evidently snow.

of Lucian's works derives its title from the Scythian physician Toxaris.*

The Scythians adored several divinities, of whom Mars was the chief, and the only god to whom they offered sacrifices and oblations; and, with many of the wilder tribes, he was their sole deity, and was generally represented among them under the semblance of a naked sword.

* Dr. Karl Neumann, agreeing with Niebuhr, Boekh, and Grote, considers that the Scythians were undoubtedly Turanians, or, as he calls them, Mongolians. He supposes that, coming from the depths of Asia, they first settled among the Finns, on the Ural; and he has discovered in the traces remaining to us of their language, much resemblance to that of the Mongolians.

CHAPTER III.

The Asiatic Scythians—The Huns—Attila.

Shew me the rampart where, o'er many a hill,
Through many a valley, stretch'd its wide extent.
Raised by that mighty monarch to repel
The roving Tartar, when, with insult rude
'Gainst Pekin's towers he bent the unerring bow.—GLYNN.

Where furious Frank and fiery Hun,
Shout in their sulphurous canopy.—CAMPBELL.

THE general appearance of the country throughout Tartary, or Asiatic Scythia, greatly resembles the bleak and monotonous steppes of Russia. High ranges of rugged and almost impassable mountains traverse it indeed in the northern and western districts, which are frequently crowned with tall and extensive forests; but all the central part is table-land, covered in summer with little but grass and heath, and in the winter with the deep and frozen snow, the severity of the climate, in so comparatively temperate a latitude, being accounted for by its great elevation above the level of the sea. In the land of the Khalkas numerous rivers enliven the rich pastures of the plains; but in Mongolia water is rarely to be seen, as the streams are lost in the salt lakes in the deserts, and wells are dug along the most frequented routes for the convenience of caravans. Scarcely a tree is visible throughout that province, nothing but creeping briers, a few scanty tufts of heath, and the short and brittle grass; but the landscape is occasionally varied by deep rents in the earth, and rocky ravines; immense numbers of wild animals bound across the steppes; eagles and vultures, pheasants, and a variety of singing-birds, soar in the air; and in the valleys of the Altai mountains lurk the tiger and the wolf, both remarkable in these parts for their ferocity.*

The Tartars, or Turanians,† who have inhabited these

---

* Huc's "Travels in Tartary, Thibet, and China."
† Some ethnologists have designated the Turanian nations collectively as the Turks; but I have generally called them either Tartars or Turanians, both as being more usually applied to them, and also to prevent a confusion with the Ottomans, who, with the Transoxian branches of the same family (including the Seljuks, &c.), are often exclusively termed Turkomans, or Turks.

regions from the earliest ages, derive their own origin from Turk and Tata, whom they affirm were two sons of Japhet. Okhaus Han, one of their chiefs, and apparently the Madyes of Herodotus, carried his arms into Syria in the early part of the seventh century before Christ, and advanced as far as Egypt; and the Persian poets celebrate the glories and fame of the Turanian king Afrasib, the rival and enemy of their hero Roustem; and whose successors carried on many sanguinary wars with the Persians, and other nations of Southern Asia. But their early history is enveloped in the greatest obscurity; what we know of them in those times is chiefly derived from the half-apocryphal annals of the Chinese; and, though they have occasionally united in one great empire, and made considerable advances in refinement and civilization, they have never proceeded beyond a certain point, and have subsequently returned to their ancient habitations, and their wandering and pastoral life.

They early separated into many different tribes, who were constantly engaged in war with each other and the surrounding nations, and of whom the most conspicuous were the Huns, Igours, Turks, and Tartars, the name of the latter having been bestowed in the middle ages by the Europeans upon the whole people, merely from their warriors having marched in the van of the Mongul army, when, in 1224, the son of the conqueror Zingis Khan, invaded Europe. But before the Christian era, the Huns,* or Hiangnus, were by far the first and most powerful of the Turanian race. They inhabited an extensive tract of country between the north side of the great wall of China, and lake Baikal, in Siberia, and, according to the Chinese records, were governed by a sovereign whom they called Tanjou, or the son of heaven, as early as 1253, B.C., the power being hereditary in his family, which derived its source from the Hea dynasty, the third who ruled China.†

The sun was the chief object of the adoration of the Huns, and before it, every morning, the Tanjou and his people prostrated themselves on the earth;‡ and in the evening they paid

---

* Creasy says that the Huns were closely allied in origin, language, and habits with the Finns.
† Gibbon's "Decline and Fall of the Roman Empire." "Universal History." Gutslaff's "History of China."
‡ They originally made human sacrifices, but observing one year that an extraordinary oblation was followed by an unusually severe season and deep snow, they concluded that such offerings were displeasing to their deity, accordingly they were discontinued for ever. The traces that have descended to us of the language and writing of the Huns, bear strong resemblance to that of the Turks. The Hea dynasty reigned from B C., 2207, to B.C. 1767

the same honours to the moon, regarding her with almost equal veneration and respect. They frequently proved formidable to the Chinese empire and the surrounding warlike nations, most of whom they subjected to their dominion; among others the Igours, who were distinguished for their acquaintance with letters, imparted by them to the other Tartar tribes, with whom it is still in use. At last, in the year 213 B.C., after ages of hostility and warfare, the Chinese emperor Hoang Ti, caused the great wall to be constructed as a defence against their perpetual incursions, a barrier of fifteen hundred miles in length, which still bears witness to the necessity that prompted so difficult and stupendous a work. They then turned their arms against the Youei Tchi, or Getæ, who were established on the eastern shores of the Caspian, and the Hun Tanjou, Lao, slaying the enemies' chief, made his skull into a drinking-cup, and, wearing it suspended from his girdle, handed it round at the banquets with his chiefs. The Getæ, who four hundred years before had been driven by the Huns from the borders of China, again abandoned their country after this defeat, and marched southward to the banks of the Indus. They were there attacked by the Parthians, and after a long war established themselves in Bactria and Sogdiana, where they were called by the Greeks Indo-Scythians; and Strabo mentions that, instead of burning their dead, they kept dogs on purpose to devour them, a custom that prevails at this day among the Tartars in the cities of Thibet. "Hence it is," says the Greek author, "that no tombs are visible in the suburbs of the town, while the town itself (speaking of the capital) is filled with human bones.*

But the defence of the Chinese, which had been erected with so much labour and skill, proved of little avail in resisting their restless and formidable foes; and in the year 206 B.C. the Huns again invaded China, and founded the dynasty of Han, which produced several of her most celebrated and learned monarchs. The fifth of these, Vouti, in the end, proved the chief cause of their ruin; for, arming himself against the comrades of his ancestors, he repelled with dreadful slaughter a fresh inroad of the Huns, and penetrating far into their country with a well-equipped and well-disciplined force, he at length reduced their Tanjou to submission, and compelled him to pay tribute, and own the authority of

* Huc's "Travels in Tartary," &c.

the Chinese chief. They were further weakened by the division of their now humbled and impoverished tribe, one of their princes, either from fear of the enemies with whom they were surrounded, and who perpetually harassed them, since their power was no longer to be dreaded, or from love of independence and ambition of sovereign power, retiring towards the south at the head of 50,000 families, with whom he founded a separate state, leaving his countrymen to fight for every inch of their native deserts. The northern Huns continued together for about fifty years longer, when they were oppressed on every side by their enemies; and their country being exhausted by famine, their power was utterly destroyed in the first century of the Christian era, after having existed, as the Chinese chronicles inform us, for thirteen hundred years. About 200,000 men found an asylum in the empire of China, in whose military service they entered, and where they settled principally in the province of Shunchi, and 100,000 men remained in their own country; but the most warlike and powerful tribes, preferring a savage freedom in the barren and icy regions of the north, rather than submission to any foreign power, retreated beyond the Altai mountains to Siberia.* One division of this nation settled down in the plains to the east of the Caspian, where they were called the Nepthalite or white Huns, and, driving their old enemies the Getæ into Europe, founded a kingdom which existed for several hundred years, when it was overthrown by a fresh torrent of Tartar invaders; and appears at that time to have been considerably advanced in civilization.† They lived under a regular government, and were subject to one prince and a written code of laws. Gorgo, since called Carizme, was their capital, and the residence of their king, whose throne was enriched with emeralds, and his court maintained in the greatest splendour, but they retained the simple faith of their ancestors till subdued by the arms of the disciples of Mahomet. They dealt uprightly with one another, and with the neighbouring nations, and respected the faith of treaties in peace, and the dictates of humanity in war, seldom making inroads on the surrounding country except on provocation, when they proved on all occasions that they still retained their ancient valour, and extended their victorious career to

* Humboldt supposes that the Totteks or Azteks, who colonized Mexico, were a division of these people.
† Gibbon's "Decline and Fall of the Roman Empire."

the banks of the Indus and borders of Sinde. A most singular custom prevailed among them: each of their great men was in the habit of choosing twenty or more companions to enjoy his wealth and diversions during his life, and on his decease they were all buried alive in the same grave; this originating with the idea that their self-sacrifice would enable them to attend their patron in another world, where they might divert themselves with hunting and feasting, as they had done before in this.* On Perozes, king of Persia laying an unjust claim to their country, which he entered and wasted with a large force, they advanced against him, their cavalry being supported by two thousand elephants, and defeating the Persians in a great battle, in which they took prisoner the enemy's king; they released him upon his consenting to do homage, and prostrate himself before their monarch, whose feet he humbly kissed. But, on regaining his liberty, Perozes again invaded the territory of the Huns, and in this second expedition the Persian sovereign losing both his army and his life, with thirty of his sons and an immense amount of plunder, the victorious warriors overran all Persia, and held it in subjection for two years, obliging Cabades, the son and successor of Perozes, to pay them tribute. The other division of the Huns settled in the frozen deserts of Siberia, where they soon lost every trace of any of the rudiments of civilization which they had ever possessed. As late as the thirteenth century, the plains on the eastern banks of the Volga were still called Great Hungary, and the inhabitants, whose kingdom had endured till at that period it was swept away by the Monguls, still spoke their language. It is supposed that they were prompted to the invasion of Scythia by the oppression of the other Tartar nations on the outskirt of their territories; and in the year A. D. 376 they advanced with all their flocks and herds beyond the Volga, and drove out the Alani, a Slavonic nation, the remnants of whom took refuge in the Caucasus, where their descendants under the name of Ossetes still remain.† Several Gothic tribes had settled down under Christian bishops, and for many years resided peacefully and securely in well-built villages as cultivators of the soil

---

* In the southern parts of Siberia many tombs have been opened, containing the bones of men and horses, with armour, jewels, &c, many of which are supposed to be more than a thousand years old.
† Gibbon's "Decline and Fall of the Roman Empire."

in Southern Russia. Their corn-fields and habitations were burned and destroyed by the Huns, to whom it is said the use of fire was unknown, except for the purpose of desolating the countries through which they passed, and who, compelling the Ostrogoths to retreat to the Dniester, forced the Visigoths to obtain leave of the emperor Valens to settle in Thrace; their savage and frightful appearance exciting almost as much terror in the hearts of their enemies as their dreadful ravages. We are informed by the historians of the time that they were distinguished from the rest of the human species by their broad shoulders, flat noses, and small black eyes, deeply buried in the head, and that they were almost entirely destitute of beards, thus strongly resembling the modern Tartars; and the terrible report preceded them in Europe, that they were demons, or lost souls escaping from eternal punishment.* A naked sword fixed in the ground was the only object of their religious worship; they ornamented the trappings of their horses with the scalps of their enemies, and put an end to their own lives on the approach of age or disease. Jornandes says that they had no food but roots and raw meat, and always eat on horseback, scarcely ever dismounting (which in all probability induced the historian Zosimus to write that they could not walk), and had neither tents, nor houses, having such an aversion to them that they called them the sepulchres of the living, and always sleeping in the open air.

The invasion of the Huns drove the Goths upon the enervated and luxurious Roman empire, which was then little calculated to resist so great a shock; but the conquests of the barbarians were for a time suspended, and their public force incapacitated and exhausted, by the discord of their chieftains; and it was not till sixty years later, when their troubled factions were united by the firm hand and skilful policy of their celebrated chief Attila, that the Huns once more became formidable to Western Europe.

* This description of the Huns which the writers of that time have left us, bears a striking resemblance to that given us of the Tartars, by the travellers and missionaries of the middle ages, which, says Huc, may be recognized feature for feature in the Mongols of the present day. John de Plano Carpini has described them as being of the middle size, with broad flat faces, prominent cheek-bones, short flat noses, little eyes placed obliquely, and separated by a great space, with the beard scanty, or entirely wanting. Friar Ricold says of them—"After leaving Turkey we entered Tartary, where we met with that wonderful and horrid people the Tartars, who differ so much in person, manners, and mode of life, from all the nations in the world. They differ in person, for they have great broad faces, and eyes so little and narrow that they look only like small slits in their faces; they are without beards, and many of them look exactly like upright old baboons."

In the reign of Arcadius, emperor of the East, a band of these adventurers ravaged the provinces of Asia Minor, from whence they brought away rich spoils and innumerable captives. They crossed the sea of Azof, penetrated by a secret path along the shores of the Caspian sea, traversed the mountains of Armenia, passed the Tigris and Euphrates, and occupied Cilicia and the Christian town of Antioch. Egypt trembled at the approach of the invaders, and the monks and numerous pilgrims of Jerusalem, prepared to escape their fury by a speedy embarkation from the Holy Land.* But, abandoning the direct road to Palestine, and advancing on the plains of Media, they were there encountered by a Persian army of superior discipline and strength, and, being forced to retire, effected a perilous retreat to their own country, with the loss of almost all their booty, but with their restless ambition unabated.

Attila, or Etzel, the son of Mundzuk, who received from his enemies and allies the title of the Scourge of God, and who boasted that the grass never grew where his horse's hoof had trod, succeeded his uncle Rugilas as joint king of the Huns, with his brother Bleda, whom he however, it is said, in imitation of the alleged murder of Remus by his brother the founder of Rome, soon deprived of his throne and life. His features, according to a Gothic historian, bore the stamp of his national origin, small, deep-seated eyes, a flat nose, swarthy complexion, and a few hairs in the place of a beard, broad shoulders, and a short, square, disproportioned body, though of great strength.† "His haughty step and demeanour," says Gibbon, "expressed the consciousness of his superiority over the rest of mankind; and he had a habit of fiercely rolling his eyes, as if he wished to enjoy the terror which he inspired. Yet this savage hero was not

---

* Gibbon's "Decline and Fall of the Roman Empire."
† Herbert, in his "Attila," has thus versified this description:—

"Terrific was his semblance, in no mould
Of beautiful proportion cast, his limbs,
Nothing exalted, but with sinews braced
Of Chalybæan temper, agile, lithe,
And swifter than the roe; his ample chest
Was overbrow'd by a gigantic head,
With eyes keen, deeply sunk, and small, that gleam'd
Strangely in wrath, as though some spirit unclean,
Within that corporal tenement install'd,
Look'd from its windows; but with temper'd fire
Beamed mildly on the unresisting; thin
His beard, and hoary; his flat nostrils crown'd
A cicatrised, swart visage; but, withal
That questionable shape, such glory wore,
That mortals quailed before him."

inaccessible to pity; his suppliant enemies might confide in the assurance of peace or pardon, and Attila was considered by his subjects as a just and indulgent master. He delighted in war; but, after he had ascended the throne at a mature age, his head rather than his hand achieved the conquest of the north, and the fame of an adventurous soldier was usefully changed for that of a prudent and successful general."

After having vanquished his enemies in Asia, subdued the kingdoms of the Persians and the Medes, and reduced to obedience every sovereign from the Danube to the Wall of China, an attempt to assassinate the king of the Huns, by the emissaries of the Emperor Theodosius, drew their army upon the empire of Constantinople. Attila ravaged the eastern provinces of Rome up to the suburbs of Byzantium, where fifty-eight towers fell before the storm of the invaders; and, compelling the Cæsar to make peace on most humiliating terms, Theodosius agreed from henceforward to pay tribute to the Huns,* who restored their innumerable captives for a sum that would have carried on a long and glorious war. Establishing his capital in a plain to the north of the Danube in Hungary, near the modern site of Tokay, the victorious prince, whom the Hungarians say founded Buda, encamped his court, harem, and followers in a village of wooden huts, where he surrounded himself with poets and minstrels, and received envoys from the various sovereigns of Europe and Asia, assuming the title of Attila, the descendant of Nimrod, king of kings, and lord of the Huns, Goths, Danes, and Persians.† Priscus, the Roman ambassador, has left a detailed account of his reception at the court of the Huns; the impatient gestures, though stern and inflexible gravity of their monarch, whose countenance never relaxed into any appearance of cheerfulness or mirth, either at the songs that his musicians were singing in his praise, or the absurd speeches and antics of a Moorish and Scythian jester, who acted before him, till the entrance of his youngest and favourite son, Eruac, whom he tenderly embraced, and for whom, predicting a fame and conquests superior even to his own, he betrayed an affection apparently

---

* Gibbon's "Decline and Fall of the Roman Empire."
† In the "Niebelungen Lied," the old poet, when describing the reception of the heroine Chrimhild by Attila (Etzel), says, that Attila's dominions were so vast, that among his subject warriors there were Russian, Greek, Wallachian, Polish, and even Danish knights. On a medal of the time, Attila is represented with a Teraphim or head on his breast.—CREASY's "*Fifteen Decisive Battles of the World.*"

incompatible with his usually fierce, unyielding, and rigid demeanour.* His own palace, which was surrounded by a wall and high towers, displayed some pretensions to architecture and ornament. It was supported by carved pillars of most curious and singular workmanship, and provided with a bath-house; and the whole encampment presented a remarkable mixture of luxury, rude magnificence, and barbarism. The most splendid carpets from Persia lined the tents, the most precious stones the trappings of the Huns, their clothes were made of silk and embroidery, and their tables were covered with dishes and goblets of gold. Attila alone preserved the simplicity of his ancestors, and dined like them on horseback off the roughest fare, presented to him on a wooden plate from a silver table by his courtiers, who held their banquets in the same hall with their chief. At the feast at which Priscus was present, a Gothic chief occupied the right, and the Roman ambassadors sat on the left hand of the monarch, which last, it is probable, was the place of honour, as among the Chinese and most of the Tartar nations at the present day.

In the year A.D. 447, the Huns again emerged from their Hungarian retreat, and turned their arms upon the Roman provinces in Western Europe. Leading his followers into the heart of Gaul, Attila drove before him the martial Franks, under their king Meroveus, and advanced as far as Orleans, which he surrounded and closely besieged. But the Roman governor Ætius, collecting an enormous army of Goths, Vandals, Franks, and almost every nation from the Vistula to the Atlantic, whose allegiance was claimed by Rome, or who forgot her oppression in their eagerness to join against the common enemy, Attila recrossed the Seine, and encountered the forces of his antagonist in the plains of Chalons.† Previous to commencing the engagement, the king of the Huns had consulted the priests and diviners with regard to the result, and they had predicted his defeat, though with the death of his principal opponent. But deter-

---

* Thierry's "Histoire des Huns."

† "About five miles from Chalons," says Creasy, "near the little hamlets of Chape and Cuperly, the ground is indented, and heaped up in ranges of grassy mounds and trenches, which attest the work of man's hand in ages past, and which, to the practised eye, demonstrate that this quiet spot has once been the fortified position of a huge military host. Local tradition gives to these ancient earthworks the name of Attila's camp, nor is there any reason to question the correctness of the title, or to doubt that behind these very ramparts it was that, years ago, the most powerful heathen king that ever ruled in Europe, mustered the remnants of his vast army which had striven on the plains against the Christian soldiers of Thoulouse and Rome."

mined to brave fate, or overcome it through the intrepidity of his followers, in a military oration he endeavoured to rouse their unusual despondency, and, reminding them of their former exploits and valour—"Warriors protected by Heaven," he exclaimed, " are safe and invulnerable amid the arrows of the foe! I, myself, will hurl the first javelin at the enemy, and the wretch who refuses to follow his master's example shall be devoted to instant death."* In front of the central column, Attila led his followers in person on to the attack, but after a most desperate battle, in which one hundred thousand Huns were left upon the field, and sixty thousand of their opponents, the former were forced to retreat, and, gaining their encampment, they prepared to destroy themselves, their wives, and treasure by fire, rather than yield or fall into the hands of the Romans.† Yet Ætius's victory had been too dearly purchased to enable him to pursue the fugitives or continue the war, and Attila finally abandoned Gaul without further molestation, and swept like a destructive torrent over all southern Germany and northern Italy. The Huns sacked and reduced to ashes the towns of Altinum, Concordia, Padua, Vicenza, Verona, and Bergamo, but spared the cities and all the inhabitants of Milan and Pavia, upon their submitting to their savage conquerors without resistance. Finding in the royal palace of Milan a picture representing one of the emperors of Rome on his throne, with the princes of Scythia prostrate at his feet, Attila commanded a painter to reverse the figures, and the emperors were delineated approaching in a suppliant attitude to empty their bags of tributary gold at the feet of the Scythian monarch.‡

After ravaging all the north of Italy, the Huns advanced towards Rome, under the pretence of releasing from imprisonment Honoria, the sister of the emperor Valentinian, who, prompted by ambition or jealousy of her brother, had sent to offer Attila her hand; and, upon her design being discovered by the Romans, was placed in close confinement.||

Marching almost to the gates of the eternal city, Attila was preparing to encamp within a short distance of its walls before commencing the siege, when his progress was arrested

---

* Gibbon's "Decline and Fall of the Roman Empire."
† Creasy's "Fifteen Decisive Battles."
‡ Gibbon's "Decline and Fall of the Roman Empire."
|| Creasy's "Battle of Chalons."

by the Pope Leo, who boldly advanced from the town, arrayed in his pontifical robes, and unattended but by a few unarmed priests. Proceeding towards the royal tent, the head and chief of the Christian world sternly confronted the barbarian monarch, and produced so powerful an effect upon the mind of Attila by his majestic appearance, and the courage and eloquence with which he courageously denounced the chief if he attempted to approach a step nearer, and dared to pollute by his atrocities the city which had been sanctified by the martyrdom of St. Peter and St. Paul, that the Hun consented to abandon his design, and, retracing his steps with his army, shortly afterwards evacuated Italy, and returned to his wooden capital.

Not long after this enterprise, Attila added a beautiful maid, called Idilco, to the already large number of his wives, and caused his espousals to be celebrated with great pomp in his palace beyond the Danube; but, on the night after his marriage, his attendants were roused by the shrieks and cries of his bride, and, entering his chamber, they discovered that their monarch had expired through the breaking of a bloodvessel; the effects, as some authors relate, of poison administered to him in his wine-goblet at the wedding-banquet, at the instigation of his young and reluctant wife; but his followers always persisted in denying this assertion, not being able to support the idea, that their hero, whom they looked upon almost as a divinity, should meet with his death from the hand of man. His remains were enclosed in three coffins of gold, silver, and iron, and the Huns bewailed his decease, according to their savage custom, by cutting off their hair, and gashing their faces with wounds; and having privately buried him in the night, they threw into his grave the most valuable portion of the plunder which he had wrested from prostrate cities and conquered nations; the captives who had opened the ground being inhumanly massacred over his tomb.* The power of the Huns did not long survive the decease of their great chief. Ellac, the eldest son of Attila, lost his life and crown in a battle fought against the Goths on the banks of the river Netad in Pannonia. His brother Dengisich maintained his ground against the oppression of those nations who had been his

* This practice prevailed among the Tartars of Central Asia so late as the seventeenth century, and they now occasionally sacrifice horses. Gibbon's "Decline and Fall of the Roman Empire."

father's slaves for about fifteen years longer on the banks of the Danube, when, invading the Eastern empire, he fell in battle, and his head, severed from the senseless corpse, was carried to Constantinople, and exposed in the Hippodrome to the idle gaze of the Greek populace. Ernac, the youngest and favourite son of Attila, retired subsequently with his own horde and his brother's followers into the heart of Lesser Scythia, where they were soon overwhelmed by a fresh torrent of invaders, the Igours, who, issuing from the icy regions of Siberia, finally extinguished the empire of the Huns.*

* Gibbon's ". Decline and Fall of the Roman Empire."

CHAPTER IV.

The Igours—Abars—Bulgarians—Slabonians—Chazars.

> Hardly the place of such antiquity,
> Or note of those great monarchies we find,
> Only a fading verbal memory,
> And empty name in writ is left behind.—FLETCHER.

THE country of the Igours or Ogars,* probably the Issedones of Herodotus, who, next to the Huns, were the most powerful nation among the Tartars of ancient Asia, comprised that territory on the borders of the Altai which is watered by the Selinga, Toula, and Orkhan rivers. Their earliest religion was probably Schamanism,† but they appear to have adopted later the faith of Buddha, since when the Buddhist pilgrim, Fo-Hian, visited their country, A.D. 399, it was prevalent there, as he found among them four thousand monks or lamas.‡ Their society was separated into three classes or castes, hunters, shepherds, and husbandmen, the two former being considered the most honourable ;|| and, according to Levesque, they had made great progress before their overthrow in the cultivation of the arts and sciences. "It was this people," says the French writer, "who communicated them, as well as the art of writing, to the other nations of the Tartar race, and probably to many others. Perhaps it is to them we are indebted for astronomical observations, which, made under a more northern climate than that of the ancient people who transmitted them, cannot be the result of their researches.§ These prove that,

---

* The word Ogre is derived from this name.
† "This religion, the same as that of the Samnæans and Gymnosophists, has been driven," says Levesque, "by the Brahmins, from India into the northern deserts; the naked philosophers were compelled to wrap themselves in fur, but they insensibly sank into wizards and physicians. It is formed on the idea of one Deity, his angels, and the rebellious spirits who oppose his government."—GIBBON.
‡ Pritchard's "Natural History of Man."
|| Gibbon's "Decline and Fall of the Roman Empire."
§ M. Bailly, in his "History of Ancient and Modern Astronomy," proves that the stellar observations collected by Ptolemy, must have been made in a climate where the longest day was sixteen hours in duration, which would agree with the latitude of the southern regions of Siberia.
"In the guiding arrow mentioned by Herodotus, which the Hyperborean magician Abaris carried in his hand, some commentators have supposed that they recognize the compass."—HUMBOLDT.

in very remote ages, the north contained a learned nation whose memory is lost to us, though we enjoy the benefit of its scientific intelligence."* It has been supposed that the third language of the arrow-headed inscriptions found in Assyria, is Ugrian or Igourian; and if so, they must have invaded, or had some communication with that country many centuries before Christ. While the empire of the Huns was predominant in Central Asia, the Igours became subject to their dominion; but on the decline of their power emancipated themselves from a foreign yoke, and maintained for some years their independence. In the beginning of the sixth century, the Emperor Justin sent an embassy to their Khan; and on reaching the royal encampment of tents and arabas, which was temporarily established near the source of the Irtish, the Roman envoys were forced to undergo purification, by passing between two fires, before they could obtain an audience of the Tartar prince.† After having driven the Huns from Siberia into Europe, the Igours were in their turn invaded during the fifth century by the Avars, another Tartar tribe; and having sustained a long and fierce warfare, at length, in one decisive and tremendous battle, the Khan with three hundred thousand of his subjects was slain, the flower of his chiefs, and every prince and warrior of his house. Upon this reverse, about twenty thousand of the Igour warriors,‡ abandoning their native country, settled down in the north-east of Russia, and in the territory on the Asiatic side of the Ural, where, in conjunction with the other Finnish tribes, they afterwards founded the remote commercial kingdom of Biarmaland, or Perm, who long kept up an intimate connection by their trade with Northern Asia and Europe. The rest of the nation, who remained in Tartary, partially recovered their power a few years after this event, and continued till 1125, when they fell beneath the yoke of the Keraites, then the predominating empire in Central Asia.

The descendants of the followers of Attila were known in the sixth century by the name of Bulgarians, at which time they divided with the Slavonians the territories of Russia and Poland.|| The country on the Volga was called from them Great Bulgaria, or by the inhabitants themselves Hun-

* Levesque's "Histoire de la Russie."   † Asiatic Researches.
‡ Gibbon's "Decline and Fall of the Roman Empire."
| Pritchard's "Natural History of Man."

garia; and the ruins of their capital, Bolgari,* situated on the shores of that river, and consisting of a few arches and tombs, still remain. They afterwards founded a kingdom on the banks of the Danube, and in the seventh and eighth centuries of the Christian era frequently harassed and invaded the Eastern Empire.

The name Sclavi appears in the works of the Armenian historian, Moses of Chorene, who flourished in the fifth century; but the Slavonians, now extending from the Pacific Ocean to the Adriatic Sea, are first described under that designation by the Gothic writer Jornandes, and his contemporary Procopius, the historian of Justinian's reign, who calls them Sclavini. The name is derived from their word *slava*, glory; and Pritchard, and other ethnologists, consider that they were undoubtedly the descendants of the Sarmatians. Gibbon says of them:—" The same race of Slavonians appears to have maintained in every age the possession of the same countries. Their numerous tribes, however distant or adverse, used one common language; it was harsh and irregular, and were known by the resemblance of their form, which deviated from the swarthy Tartar, and approached, without attaining, the lofty stature and fair complexion of the German. Four thousand six hundred villages were scattered over the provinces of Russia and Poland, and their huts were hastily built of rough timber, in a country deficient both in stone and iron. The sheep and horned cattle were large and numerous, and the fields, which they sowed with millet and grains, afforded a coarse and less nutritive food. They fought on foot almost naked, and, except an unwieldy shield, without any defensive armour; their weapons of offence were a bow, a quiver of small poisoned arrows, and a long rope, which they dexterously threw from a distance, and entangled their enemy in a running noose."† Like the ancient Scythians, they practised the rite of destroying the dead by fire, and widows were burned on the funeral pile of their husbands, with whom, if a man of wealth or consideration, a slave was buried alive, so that he might be immediately provided with an attendant in a future state. "The Sclaveni," says Procopius, "worship one God, the maker of lightning. They regard him as the sole governor of the universe, and sacrifice to him oxen, and victims of all

* See chapter 22.　　† Gibbon's "Decline and Fall of the Roman Empire."

descriptions. They likewise pay veneration to rivers and nymphs, and some other inferior divinities; to all of these they perform offerings and sacrifices, in the midst of which they make divinations."* They also worshipped the sun and moon, and the tempests, under the name of Pogoda, and represented the spirit of evil in their temples by the form of a lion sacrificing human victims, usually prisoners of war, in their sacred fire, which was kept perpetually burning, in honour of Peroun, the god of thunder, and, if the priests neglected it, they were punished with instant death. Like the Sarmatians, a plurality of wives was common among the Slavonians, and these were retained in the most abject submission to their husbands, while all their male children were dedicated to war; but, if female infants were considered too numerous, they were allowed to be destroyed, and aged and helpless people, as is common to this day among the Hindoos, were frequently left by their children to perish for want. Nevertheless, the opinion of the old was generally held in veneration and respect, and each tribe or village existed as a separate republic, over whom the elders of the community presided with almost absolute power. They were hospitable to excess, and a law existed among them permitting a poor man to steal from his rich neighbour the means of entertaining a guest. Their earliest records describe them as practising the arts of music and poetry; and, in the sixth century, a deputation sent from the northern Slavonians to the emperor of Constantinople, informed him that their highest pleasures were derived from music, and that in their journeys they seldom encumbered themselves with arms, but always carried lutes and harps of their own workmanship.† In their warlike expeditions they never appeared without music; and Procopius informs us that they were on one occasion, A.D. 592, so much engrossed by their amusements within sight of the enemy, as to have been surprised by a Greek general in the night, before they could arrange any adequate measures of defence. Many of the war odes and ballads of the Slavi are still in existence, and "exhibit," says a modern writer, "a wild and original spirit, are replete with mythological allusions, and those that are of a peaceful cast are particularly remarkable for the quiet sweetness of their character, of a kind quite distinct from the elaborate

* Pritchard's "Natural History of Man.'   † Karamsin's "History of Russia."

and artificial felicity of the Greek and Roman pastorals."* †
Jornandes distinguishes the whole Slavonic race by the
collective name of Winidæ.‡ After describing Dacia,
"surrounded by lofty Alps," he adds, "that on the left side
of these mountains, towards the source of the river Vistula,
lies an immense region which is inhabited by the populous
nation of the Winidæ. Different tribes of this race had,"
he says, "particular epithets; but the names by which they
were generally distinguished, were those of Sclavini and
Antes." Procopius, in describing them, observes, "their
complexions and hair are neither white nor yellow, nor
entirely inclined to black, but all of them are somewhat red-
haired. They dwell in miserable cabins, erected at considerable distances from each other, and not unfrequently
change the place of their abode." He describes them as
inhabiting the northern shore of the Danube, whence they
made frequent incursions into the provinces on the right
bank of that river;‖ but at the present day they spread over
Russia, Bohemia, Poland, Montenegro, and Croatia, and
for fifteen hundred years have inhabited nearly the same
countries. The figures of the Slavonians on the historical
pillar at Constantinople, are dressed similar to the Russian
peasants of the present time, who have made very little
alteration in their habits and manner of living from those of
their ancestors in the ninth century, and it is probable that
the Slavonic dialect, in which the church services are performed throughout Russia, and that commonly spoken in
the country, vary but slightly from the one used by the
Slavonians and Sarmatians. This language is interspersed
with many Chaldaic, Phœnician, and old Persian words, and
has a greater resemblance to Sanscrit, their common source,
than any other European language, with the exception of
the Lithuanian, which is also a Sarmatic tongue.§ During
the reign of the Emperor Justinian, the Slavonians and Bulgarians continually crossed the Danube, and invaded the
Eastern empire; and Procopius asserts, that in thirty-two
years ¶ their annual inroads had consumed two hundred

---

* According to Tooke, and other travellers in the last and present centuries, the Russians of the present day sing more than any other people in the world. The peasants
manufacture a kind of guitar, upon which they play; they have also another musical instrument, universal among the Tartar nations, a sort of horn; it is also to be found among
the peasants of Egypt and Syria.   † Bell's " History of Russia."
‡ From whence is derived the name of Wends, a Slavonic tribe, inhabiting a part of
Germany.   ‖ Pritchard's " Natural History of Man."
§ Art. " Phil. Enc. Brit."   ¶ Gibbon's " Decline and Fall of the Roman Empire."

thousand inhabitants of the Roman empire. In one invasion they penetrated the Balkans, and even crossed the Hellespont, returning to their own country laden with the riches and spoils of Asia; while another party advanced without opposition to the straits of Thermopylæ, and the isthmus of Corinth, the works that the emperor had raised to oppose them being deserted by his soldiers on the approach of the enemy, or the walls scaled by the enemy. Another year, three thousand Slavonians passed the Danube and Hebrus, defeated every Roman general who marched against them, and plundered without opposition the cities of Illyricum and Thrace, each of which had arms and numbers sufficient to repulse and overwhelm their rudely equipped assailants; and the invaders marched back beyond the Danube with innumerable captive Greeks. Procopius accuses them of committing the most horrid cruelties on their prisoners; but having been an eyewitness of the desolation and misery caused by their inroads upon the Byzantine empire, he was not likely to be lenient in his judgment of the perpetrators, and probably rather exaggerated their inhumanity. "For their mild and liberal treatment of their prisoners," says Gibbon, "we may appeal to the authority, somewhat more recent, of the Emperor Maurice; but in the siege of Topirus, a town near Philippi, whose obstinate defence had enraged them, they massacred fifteen thousand men, but spared the women and children; the most valuable captives were always reserved for labour or ransom, the servitude was not rigorous, and the terms of their deliverance speedy and moderate." *

The inroads of the Slavonians and Bulgarians upon the Eastern empire were checked in the following century, on the invasion of their own country by the Avars and Chazars.† The former, who by the writers of the time are said to have been a section of the Huns, after subjugating the south of Russia, penetrated into Hungary and Italy; and the latter, who were anciently known by the name of Akazirs, and in 212 A.D. made an irruption into Armenia, and of whom a horde had originally accompanied the Huns, and established a monarchy in Lithuania, spread themselves over the Crimea, and to the north of the Caucasus, where they afterwards

* Gibbon's "Decline and Fall of the Roman Empire."
† They were known even to the distant Chinese by the name of Cosa.

founded a kingdom at Astrakhan. Contemporary writers describe the Khazars of Lithuania as being of small stature, with black eyes, and rather resembling the Huns in feature, while the Chazars of Astrakhan, who were probably a very mixed people, were tall and handsome. In 740, the sovereign of the latter kingdom, Bula, was converted to Judaism by the Jews, who had been recently expelled from the Byzantine empire, and he introduced a law rendering that faith imperative on all future Chagans, or Khans (this title being borne by the Chazarian monarchs), the Hebrew religion being also at that time professed by most of the nobles and officers of state. Many of the Oriental Jews appear to have visited this kingdom, in the hope of obtaining some assistance in improving the condition of their countrymen in the East, though without success; but at that time there was one place where the Jews were still held in consideration and equality, for they formed a large and influential body at the court of the Moorish king of Cordova; and in a work anciently written in Arabic, but subsequently translated into the Hebrew tongue, called the Cusri or Cosar, there is a curious letter, which the learned Jews consider to be genuine, addressed in the year 860, by the Rabbi Hasdai, the son of Isaac, the son of Ezra, who retained a high office at the court of Abdorrahmen, the king of Cordova, designated by the title of Emiral Moumenin, "the chief of the faithful," to the Khan of the Chazars, in which he earnestly entreats that prince to send him information respecting his kingdom and people.*

* After a complimentary introduction he writes, "that Hasdai, the son of Isaac, the son of Ezra, of the Jewish community, presents his most humble respects to the mighty king of the Chazars, rejoices at his greatness, and prays for his welfare. That he feels himself too mean to address so glorious a monarch, but nevertheless presumes to write to him, as he (the writer) had the high honour of being near the person of the great, mighty, and glorious king of Cordova; and was most anxious to obtain certain information respecting the existence of a Jewish monarchy, which would greatly tend to the comfort of his brethren, and raise them in the public estimation. The great distance between the two nations was doubtless the reason why so little was known in Spain respecting the Chazarian monarchy; although a report was in circulation, that some learned Spanish Jews, particularly Rabbi Juda ben Meb, and Rabbi Joseph, had visited the court of the great Chagan, and been the happy and admiring witnesses of his might and splendour. That he greatly desires to enjoy the same happiness, although he serves a king who is the greatest of the caliphs, and whose alliance is courted by many other kings. That the office which he (Hasdai) held at the Moorish court, made it his duty to receive all the foreign ambassadors, who delivered to him the presents they brought to his master, and received from him those which were sent in return to their respective sovereigns. That he had availed himself of every opportunity to question the ambassadors from far distant lands respecting the Chazars, but without success; though some merchants from Chorasan had given him some information on the subject, but their statement appeared incredible, and made for a selfish purpose. The ambassadors of the emperor of Constantinople, however, had assured him that a Jewish monarchy actually did exist in Chazaria, and added, that though by land many nations intervened between their country and the Greek empire, a near connection subsisted between both by sea; that an active trade was carried on between the Chazars and Constantinople, and that their present Chagan was

The khan of the Chazars was assisted in his government by a council of nine, to which Jews, Christians, Mahometans, and Pagans were equally admissible. The highest veneration was paid to him; he rarely quitted his palace, and seldom received visitors, and an audience was only to be obtained on matters of the greatest importance. All who entered his presence were obliged to fall prostrate before him, and remain in that posture till they were commanded by their sovereign to rise; and the great officers of state, when condemned to death, were granted the privilege of self-destruction, and so spare themselves the ignominy of dying by the hand of an executioner.* No one ever passed a royal tomb on horseback, but always dismounted, bowed to the grave, and continued on foot till it was out of sight. Their principal towns were Belanshir, now Astrakhan, the seat of government, which was also called Itel or Nihirize; Sermend, or Serai Bauv, the palace of the lady, now Tarku; and old Chazar and Sarkel, which lay on the route to Archangel, with which port and Novogorod they carried on an extensive trade by caravans, till the Mongols subdued the plains of Kipzak, and numerous other fortified cities attest their advanced state of society, their wealth, and prosperous condition. They were particularly celebrated for their manufacture of carpets, and extended their dominions over all the south of Russia; the Caspian Sea being known in the middle ages as the lake or sea of the Chazars. But in the tenth century their power began to decline; they were deprived of a part of their dominions by the Russians, under their grand prince Sviatozlaf; and the conqueror destroyed their capital, which had been fortified by Greek engineers, and subverted the dynasty of Jewish

named Joseph." Hasdai goes on to state that he had despatched letters by a trusty Jew before, to the king of the Chazars; but that, after an absence of six months, the messenger had returned from Constantinople without reaching the place of his destination, because the sea was only navigable at certain seasons, and impassable at all other times of the year, through the great storms which prevailed, and that it was equally impossible to proceed by land, on account of the disturbed state of the intervening tribes. He had felt greatly grieved at this misfortune, but had requested some Palestine Jews to take charge of his letters, who would forward the same by way of Nisibis and Armenia, when the ambassadors of the king of Gubal had arrived, there being in his train two Jewish rabbis, who had faithfully sworn to forward the present letter to its destination. Hasdai also prays the king to answer his letter through his secretary, and to give him every information respecting certain legends of an emigration of Jews, a colony of whom are said to have settled in a far distant country, which he believes was Chazaria, and requests him to furnish him with every intelligence regarding his territories, the history of his nation, their language, and the wars he and his Jewish predecessors had carried on. He regretted that all his endeavours to find a certain Mar Amram, who about six years before had arrived in Spain, had been well received at court, and whom he had since heard was a native Chazar, had failed, and that therefore he and his brethren had no other hope of obtaining information respecting the kingdom of the Chazars, except his royal condescension would deign to answer this letter.—*Hebrew Review*, Vol. ii. No. 35.

* The same custom prevails at the present day in Japan.

kings, though the Jews themselves remained very numerous about Astrakhan till a much later time.* Their forces had previously been greatly weakened by the incursions of the Petchenegans and other Tartar tribes; and in 1016 they were again invaded by the Russians, who took their khan George Tzuda prisoner, a race of Christian sovereigns,† having succeeded the Jewish line. In 1140 they were again governed by a Jew, their chagan Cosro having been converted to Judaism by the Rabbi Isorah, a noted professor of that faith; but, shortly after, the monarchy of the Chazars sank under the successive attacks of the Polotzi and other wandering tribes, and was finally swept away by the Mongols under Ghengiz or Zingis Khan.

After the conversion of the Bulgarians on the Danube to Christianity, that nation settled down under a more regular and peaceable government, and, ceasing their invasions of Greece, they generally joined with the empire in their wars with the Slavonians, though they had long before adopted the language and manners of the latter people. They renounced their pagan faith about the middle of the ninth century; for, during a war they were carrying on against the Byzantine emperor Michael III., the sister of their king Bogaris was taken prisoner, and being a royal captive, she was conducted to Constantinople, and treated with great honour and courtesy, being also, at her own request, instructed in the doctrines of the Christian religion. Of the truth of this faith she became so convinced, that she desired to be baptized; and when, in 845, the Byzantine empire concluded a peace with Bulgaria, and she returned to her own country, being anxious for the conversion of her brother and his people, she wrote to Constantinople requesting that instructors might be sent to aid her in her endeavours to propagate Christianity.‡ Two distinguished bishops of the Greek Church, Cyrillus and Methodius, were accordingly despatched to Bulgaria; but for a long time the king refused even to listen to their arguments, and firmly adhered to idolatry. He, however, so

---

* Among the tribes of the Volga, particularly the Tchawashes, many Jewish customs still prevail.
"Benjamin of Tudela, in 1175, was informed in Persia, that on the high plains of Nishar, twenty-eight days' journey from Samarkand, in a territory covered with castles and towns, there dwelt an independent Jewish people, of the tribes of Dan, Zebulon, Asher, and Naphthali, under a prince Joseph Amarca, a Levite."—*Haxthausen, quoting Ritter.*

† The Emperor Constantine IV. of Constantinople married a daughter of one of the Chazarian khans.

‡ The "Works of James Montgomery." Finlay's "Byzantine Empire."

esteemed Methodius, for whom he formed a strong attachment; that he retained him as a friend and counsellor at his court, though he refused to become his proselyte, and, finding that he was a skilful painter, desired him to compose a picture which should exhibit, collected together, the most horrible devices his imagination could conceive. Methodius executed so terrific a representation of the day of judgment, and explained its scenes to the king so forcibly, that Bogaris was overpowered by his reasoning, and consented to receive baptism. To Cyrillus is attributed the translation of the Scriptures, which has remained in use for eight hundred years without alteration among those Slavonic nations, the Russians, Servians, and Montenegrins, who still adhere to the Greek church. It was first printed at Prague in 1519, and is probably the most ancient version of the Bible in a living tongue.

Bulgaria was at this period the most advanced and commercial kingdom of the north, and formed the chief medium for supplying Germany and Scandinavia with the manufactures, gold, and jewels, of Constantinople and Asia. Many treaties for regulating the trade, and fixing the amount of duty to be paid upon the Grecian frontier, had been concluded from time to time between the two powers, and their traffic was greatly augmented during the long peace that prevailed after the secession of Bogaris (who had taken the name of Michael on his baptism) and his people to the Eastern Church. This prince sent his second son Simeon to be educated at Constantinople, and in the year 885 resigned his throne to the heir-apparent, Vladimir, and retired into a monastery. But the misconduct of the new king, and the disorders into which he consequently plunged the state, compelled Bogaris, three years after, to emerge again from obscurity; and, consigning Vladimir to a cloister, having previously caused his eyes to be put out, the royal monk gave the crown to Simeon, and returned to his cell, where he expired in the year 907.*

At this time, though Constantinople was called the empire of the Greeks, the Greeks themselves occupied a very subordinate position in the state. The peasants and husbandmen in the provinces were chiefly Slavonians and foreign colonists; and the merchants and superior classes, Romans, and members of the Latin Church. The political

* Finlay's "Byzantine Empire."

administration was chiefly in the hands of Asiatics, and for a century and a half the Empress Irene was the only sovereign on the imperial throne whose origin was purely Greek. The emperors, who had generally been court favourites, successful generals, or mere adventurers, were seldom succeeded by more than two or three generations of their descendants, and most of these were Armenians, or other Asiatics, and one, Basil I., rose from a Slavonian groom. Greek, indeed, was the language of the government, yet even by the populace it was looked upon as a term of reproach.

CHAPTER V.

The Caucasus—Georgia.

> Ye ice falls; yet that from the mountain's brow,
> Adown enormous ravines slope amain,
> Torrents methinks, that heard a mighty voice,
> And stopp'd at once, amid their maddest plunge,
> Motionless torrents! silent cataracts.
>
> Ye living flowers, that skirt the eternal frost,
> Ye wild goats, sporting round the eagle's nest,
> Ye eagles, playmates of the mountain storm.
>
> Thou, too, hoar mount, with thy sky-pointing peaks,
> Oft from whose feet, the avalanche unheard,
> Shoots downwards. . . . COLERIDGE.
>
> The Hyrcanian cliffs
> Of Caucasus, and dark Iberian dales.—MILTON.

THE Caucasian* mountains, whose rugged rocks and narrow valleys form a boundary between Europe and Asia of seven hundred and fifty miles in length, are peopled by nearly seventy different tribes, and were considered by the ancients to mark the extreme limits of the civilized world, beyond which dwelt the unknown and barbarous nations of the north, whose country, according to the old religion of Persia, was the abode of all the followers of Ahriman, or the principle of evil, and clothed in perpetual night. The same traditions also relate, that after perpetual wars had been carried on between these inhabitants of Turan, or the Land of Darkness, and the nations of Iran, or Land of the Sun, a king called Dulkamein ascended the throne of Persia, and having defeated and driven back the Turanians, he built a wall along the Caucasus, extending from the Black Sea to the Caspian, to repel and shut out those savage and wandering tribes, whose dreary land, according to Herodotus, was guarded by dragons, and contained mines of gold.† So

---

* "The word Caucasus, according to Pliny, is derived from the Scythian words 'Grauka Sus,' or white from snow; others imagine it is from Kok Kaf, or Casp, which signifies white mountains. The Persians call it Elburz, a Persian word, which signifies ice mountains."—Dr. Wagner's "Caucasus."—Haxthausen's "Tribes of the Caucasus."

† Griffins or dragons are the symbols of all the Slavonic tribes. Many of the Siberian gold mines had apparently been worked by the former inhabitants, when the Russians conquered the country.

late as the eighteenth century, the traveller Reineggs found here the remains of a wall nearly ninety miles long, and in parts a hundred and twenty feet high,* and the ruins to this day may be traced at intervals, extending along the whole Caucasian frontier in one place for more than five miles, in tolerable preservation. The precise date of its erection is veiled in obscurity; but many writers are of opinion that it was constructed after the Scythians had penetrated through the mountains, in the seventh century before Christ, and subjugated Asia Minor, in order to secure the passes as closely as possible from all future invasions of the barbarous warriors from the north. The Caucasian ridge is formed by two ranges of hills, running parallel from east to west, of which the northern slopes, called the White Mountains, exposed to the harsh and rude blasts of Siberia, are rugged and barren, rising every where from 10,000 to 15,000 feet above the level of the sea—the most elevated, the Elburz, attaining the height of 18,000 feet. The southern range, or Black Mountains, do not rise to the limit of the snow-line; but all travellers unite in extolling the extreme beauty of the landscape and fertility of the soil, which produces spontaneously magnificent vines, mulberries, and fig-trees, interspersed with the southern laurel and northern birch, and on the mountains the most luxuriant pasture for cattle. The greatest diversity is also to be found among the animal kingdom, these rocks forming the most northerly limits of the jackal, and the extreme southern boundary of the reindeer; every variety of climate and temperature prevailing, and, while one district is scorched with heat, another is frozen in snow. The winter in the territory inhabited by the Suaves, round the foot of Mount Elburz, extends for nearly nine months in the year.†

The many tribes who, at the present day, inhabit the fertile valleys of the Caucasus, and who all speak a different language, appear in some instances to have resided there from the most remote times; in others, to have been compelled to seek a refuge among these mountains from the hostility of foreign nations, by whom they have been expelled from their

* Reinegg's "Researches in the Caucasus."
† "The eye, soaring over the hills and mountain capes, penetrates to the distant giants of the Caucasus. One sees their wonderful forms, peaks, stems, sunk in table-lands, cleft cupolas, &c., now right, now left, now forwards, now backwards. Grapes smiled upon us, and figs in plenty; and the country is enchanting and luxuriant."—Madame Pfeiffer's "Georgia and the Caucasus," in her "Voyage round the World."—Haxthausen's "Caucasus."

original, and in some instances distant, sites. Klaproth has discovered a great affinity in the languages of some of the Caucasians, particularly those spoken by the sixteen Circassian tribes, to the Finnish and Samoiede dialects of Northern Russia; the Ossetes are generally considered to be descendants of the Alans, a branch of the Slavonic race; and the posterity of the Avars, once so formidable to Europe, are supposed to exist in the inhabitants of Daghestan, on the eastern side of the Caucasus, who, fanatic Mahometans, are now the fiercest opponents of the Russian power, urged and commanded by Schamyl, their prophet. Among the Tchetechenzes, the many pieces of old European armour, swords, and other warlike equipments, adorned with Latin inscriptions that have been found, besides many of the habits and customs of the people, which bear more resemblance to those of Western Europe than to the slaveholding surrounding nations of Asia, appear to warrant the supposition, that a few of the vanquished crusaders may have taken refuge among these mountains, when escaping from the swords or dungeons of the Saracens, and settled down peaceably among the inhabitants. When the followers of Mahomet rendered themselves masters of Persia, the Ghebers or Fire-worshippers,* the ancient possessors of that kingdom, flying from their own land, scattered themselves over many countries of the east, and a colony joining their fellow religionists, of whom there were many in Georgia, established themselves in the Caucasus, where, about twelve miles from Bakù, they still preserve their sacred fire, in a temple dedicated to the glory, and consecrated to the worship, of the sun.†

Mingrelia, the ancient Colchis, was the scene of the almost fabulous expedition of the companions of the Greek Jason in search of the Golden Fleece, and, with the adjacent district of Abchasia, formed a province of the kingdom of Mithridates, the powerful and long-successful opponent of the Roman power in the east. Tigranes, king of Armenia, the ally of that ill-fated monarch, being vanquished by Pompey sixty-five years before the Christian era, fled to the Caucasus, and Athalus, the viceroy of Colchis, was carried prisoner to

---

* "They suppose the throne of the Almighty is seated in the sun, and hence their worship of that luminary."—Hanway's "Travels."
† The fire worship was exterminated in Georgia by Timur; but after his death a few of its votaries returned from the mountains of Hindustan and Persia, where they had fled to escape the fury of the Mahometans, to their old haunts at Bakù. The Ghebers have also erected a temple at Astrakhan, but their number is fast diminishing.

Rome, where in chains he adorned the haughty conqueror's triumph. The Abchasians were supposed by Herodotus to be descendants of the Egyptians of Sesostris, who carried his conquests over the peaks of the Caucasus, across the steppes of Southern Scythia, and to the shores of the Don, because in his time they had black complexions and woolly hair; and tradition affirms that the Egyptian king planted here a learned and polite colony, who manufactured linen, built navies, and invented geographical maps. They are among the most ancient inhabitants of the Caucasus, and some of their number served in the host of Xerxes, armed with daggers, wooden casques, and leathern bucklers;* and it was in this province, probably on the site of the little harbour of Souchum Kalè, that the celebrated town of Dioscurias was situated; where, according to Strabo, the representatives of seventy different nations met to traffic, and which was long resorted to by the merchant navies of Tyre, Carthage, and Greece. In Pliny's time, before the country was laid waste by the Romans, that writer affirms that a hundred and thirty languages were spoken in the market, for which as many interpreters were constantly employed; so extensive a trade and communication was carried on by the kingdom of Mithridates with all the rest of Asia Minor, and Georgia, India, Bactria, Egypt, Italy, and Greece.

The beautiful and fertile kingdom of Georgia,† stretching from the foot of the Caucasus to the borders of Armenia and Persia, is supposed to have been first peopled shortly after the deluge, probably by a branch of the Medes and Persians, of which empire it at one period formed a province; but the Georgians, who call themselves Kartli, according to their national traditions derive their origin from Kartles, a patriarch who flourished at the time of the confusion of tongues, and founded the town of Mtschekka, which was the seat of the Georgian government till A.D. 469. Before this, the earliest inhabitants had lived in caves and holes in the ground, of which traces are still to be seen in some of the southern districts. Several Chinese colonies appear to have early settled in Georgia, as well as in the countries on the eastern shore of the Caspian Sea; their existence is mentioned by Herodotus, and Xenophon speaks of Gymnias on

* Gibbon's " Decline and Fall of the Roman Empire."
† This name, by which it was not known till the time of the Crusades, is said by Gibbon to have been bestowed on this country in honour of St. George of Cappadocia.

the Araxes as an eastern colony, four hundred years before the Christian era. Ancient historians describe the Chinese colonists as a peaceable and civilized people, and skilful agriculturists, who constructed canals, and principally engaged in trading pursuits; and they appear to have been held in respect and esteem by the natives, the Caucasian tribes readily assisting them against the arms of Pompey when he invaded their land; where he set fire to their forests and villages, and laid waste all the country through which he passed.*

Georgia, which was known to the ancients by the name of Iberia (probably a native word, as it is still called Iveria by the inhabitants), was subdued by Alexander of Macedon on his passage to India, though at Mtschekka he met with an obstinate and heroic resistance. He levelled the fortifications to the ground, and treated the inhabitants with great rigour, leaving one of his officers, Ason, in command of the province; but this viceroy was subsequently expelled by the people under Pharnaces, or Pharnaz, a native chief, who, being a descendant of their ancient kings, was placed upon the throne B.C. 300.† One of his successors built the fortress of Dariel, but in the following century, B.C. 100, the Alans broke through the Caucasus and overran the country, which afterwards became tributary to Mithridates; but, upon his overthrow, it again emancipated itself from foreign dominion, and remained for many years independent. In the time of Strabo, the people are described by him as being divided into four distinct castes, besides the slaves; the princes, of whom the oldest member became king, soldiers, priests, and tillers of the ground, and a community of goods prevailed in families, under the stewardship of the eldest (who was always supreme) in a household.‡

Four narrow passes penetrate the mountains of the Caucasus, and Strabo describes the central one Pylæ Caucasiæ, or the Caucasian Gate, sometimes called the pass of Dariel, as being in his time closed by walls and gates, which Pliny

---

* The Chinese colonists were almost entirely extirpated by Tamerlane.

† Wagner's "Caucasus."

‡ "Charming hills, embracing cheerful valleys, while on the peaks of many o mountain stood the ruins of towns and fortresses. Here also there were times, as in the old German empire, when one nobleman waged feud with the other, and no man was sure of his life and property. Gentlemen lived in fortified castles on hills and mountains, went armed and harnessed like knights, and in case of impending hostilities the subjects fled to the castles. There are said yet to be people who, under or over their dresses, wear skirts of iron knitted wire, and helmets instead of caps, but I saw none of these."—PFEIFFER.

speaks of as a miracle of nature, and Ptolemy mentions by the name of the Sarmatian Gate; Procopius also describes it minutely, and observes that all the other passes of the Caucasus could only be crossed by pedestrians, but that this was passable by horsemen and carriages.* It was a frequent subject of dispute between Persia and the Byzantine empire, and in the sixth century this defile, together with the Caucasian provinces and Georgia, falling into the possession of the Persian Shah Cabades, he commenced the restoration of the entire wall of the Caucasus. But this vast undertaking was not completed till the reign of his son and successor, Chosroes Nushirvan, who erected iron gates and towers to strengthen the barrier and defend the passes,† and who, on concluding a peace with the emperor Justinian in 563, agreed that they should remain open to the eastern and western nations, both powers uniting to protect them from the incursions and depredations of the tribes of the north. Chosroes also founded the city of Derbend, or narrow gate, on the eastern or Caspian pass, where the Caucasian wall extends for some distance into the sea, adding to this a second rampart to protect the harbour against storms and hostile attacks, and constructing them with stones of such an enormous size that it required fifty men to move one. Derbend stands on a rock, and is guarded with two towers and seven iron gates, which, with a mosque, were erected during the Saracen sway by the caliph Haroun al Raschid, who made it a royal residence, and placed over each gate two lions or sphinxes, supposed to possess a magical power in alarming and frustrating the efforts of the infidels, that were constantly striving, as the Arabs affirmed, to undermine the walls, and penetrate into the country of the faithful followers of the prophet. According to Ritter, a prophecy still finds credit among the Mahometans of western Asia, that the empire of the faithful shall not meet with destruction till a nation of infidel enemies with yellow faces have forced their way through these walls; and this idea still arms the fanaticism of the Mussulman tribes of the Caucasus to resist to the last extremity every effort of the Russians ‡

* Haxthausen's "Tribes of the Caucasus."
† Edrisal, in 1151, states that the entire Caucasian wall had three hundred gates and towers, but this is probably exaggerated, though he mentions the names of a great many of them.—Haxthausen's "Tribes of the Caucasus."
‡ When the Caucasus in modern times was subject to the caliph of Damascus, a governor was placed there with the title of Viceroy of the Caliph, as a defence against Russia.

to establish their dominion over their mountainous retreats. Chosroes, to protect the passes from the northern nations, established several feudal principalities among the Caucasian districts, over which he placed viceroys, whom he intrusted with the defence of the gates. The chief of the territory of Serir, the principal of these states, and which lay to the north of Derbend, bore the title of "lord of the golden throne;" and the Arab traveller Abù Hawbal, describes the inhabitants in the year 960 as being entirely Christian, though they lived in close alliance with the Jewish kingdom of Chazaria, and the surrounding Mahometan tribes; but history is silent as to whether the Gheber chiefs who had been placed on the throne by Chosroes, who established the religion of Zoroaster throughout Georgia, had been converted to Christianity, or whether the crown had been usurped by a dynasty of princes from Byzantium.* This kingdom existed till the thirteenth century, when it was overthrown by Zingis Khan; and previously, in the middle of the tenth century, the Russians, under their grand prince Sviatozlaf, took possession of the western provinces of the Caucasus;† though a hundred and fifty years later they were expelled by the Polotzi, who were in their turn annihilated by the terrible invasion of the Monguls.

About two centuries after Christ, King Aspagur of Georgia passed a law, prohibiting the practice of sacrificing children to idols, which were finally abolished during the reign of his successor Micaus (who occupied the throne from 265 to 318), through the medium of a Christian slave, whom the Armenian chronicles call Nina, and who, having by her skill recovered the queen from a dangerous illness, succeeded in inducing her royal patrons to embrace Christianity. Tiflis, the modern capital, was built in 455, by king Vakhtang Gurgalatu, upon the site of an ancient village, called Iphilissi or Iphiliskalaki, or warm town, on account of the hot springs in its neighbourhood, to which he removed the seat of government from Mtschehka, fourteen years after its foundation in 469. In the course of the sixth century, the Persian Shah Cabades conquered Georgia and the Caucasus after a long war; and they remained subject to his empire till the throne of the Gaznevides, and the Gheber worship was overturned towards the latter end of the seventh century by the victorious arms

* Haxthausen's "Caucasus." † Wagner's "Caucasus."

of the Saracens, who had already embraced the faith and enthusiasm of Mahomet. These cruel and fanatical invaders having subdued Persia, sent an army into Georgia, under the command of Murhuireh, the brother of their caliph Valid, who took Derbend after a furious battle, in which the Saracen hero Kri Har was killed; he was buried near that fortress, and to this day the Lesghians, who. follow the doctrines of Islam, make pilgrimages to his tomb. From this time till the end of the ninth century,* the Arabs continually overran and wasted Georgia, compelliug those provinces which they conquered to profess the Mahometan religion, and mercilessly destroying with fire and sword all the towns, houses, and villages, where the inhabitants refused to submit to this decree. In 861 they seized upon the capital Tiflis, but shortly after, on the decline of their power in Asia, were finally expelled from Georgia, though they have left many traces of their dominion in their colonies, which still exist in the Caucasus. This deliverance from the rule of the Saracens was chiefly effected by the valour and military skill of the celebrated family of the Orpelians, who are said to have been the remnant of the royal family of China, or one of the counties bordering on Eastern Tartary, and who, having been driven from the throne by a great revolution in their native land, entered Georgia through the pass of Dariel, and offered their services to the dispirited and tributary king, to assist him in freeing his throne and country from the tyranny and oppression of the Mahometans. For their success in this undertaking, they received from the grateful monarch, the fortified castle of Orpeth, and have ever since proved the firmest supporters of the throne and kingdom of Georgia, and the bravest defenders of its people and government, to whom they have frequently rendered signal service.†
In A.D. 1049, during the reign of David I., the Seljuk Turks under Togrul Beg, their celebrated monarch, invaded and devastated Georgia, forcing the king with his court and treasures, and the principal families of the nobility, to fly to the mountains, and destroying the fields and villages, and wasting the country every where on their route; but Libarid Orpelian, the sbalassar or constable of the kingdom, assembled

* The Jewish family of Bagration ascended the throne of Georgia in the eighth century, and their descendants reigned till the Russian conquest; the present representative of the family being an officer in the Russian service.
† The oldest member of the Orpelian or Orbelian family is hereditary crown field-marshal of the kingdom.

a small band of devoted and valiant followers, and advancing against the enemy, whose force numbered twenty times more than his own few and brave adherents, encountered and engaged their whole army in the field, which he completely routed with great slaughter, carrying off all the standards and flags of the foe. But the victorious general met with a base return from his ungrateful though much indebted countrymen; for this success, and the popularity and influence he acquired in the government, excited against him the jealousy and animosity of the nobility, who caused him to be basely assassinated; and, depriving his son Ivane of his paternal estates, obliged him to flee for his life. But the death of Libarid was amply revenged by a second invasion of the Seljuks, under their fierce and merciless leader, the victorious Alp, who defeated and cut to pieces the entire force that the Georgians could muster against them, and, besieging Tiflis, they took the capital and reduced the whole country to their sway. Their dominion was, however, of short duration, for they were driven out in the succeeding reign by the valour and policy of David II., who, recalling Ivane Orpelian from exile, restored to him his father's domains, and also granted the reinstated chief the castle of Lorki, as some compensation for the unmerited severity with which his family had been treated and punished.* In 1160, on the death of David III., who had ruled with justice and moderation, and whose prudence had done much to repair the calamities caused by the Seljuk invasion, his only son Temna succeeded to the vacant throne; but the young prince being a minor, the king in his will had appointed his brother George regent of the kingdom, though he had intrusted the education and guardianship of his son to Ivane Orpelian III. When the prince attained his majority, the regent refused to give up the reins of government, but himself assumed the style and title of king; while his oppression and merciless exactions alienated the affection and esteem of the people, and rendered him odious to the nobles; and Ivane, having recourse to arms, was joined by numerous malecontents, and closely besieged the usurper and his adherents in Tiflis. But the army of Orpelian was repulsed from the walls of the capital, and forced to abandon the attack; and retreating with Temna to his fortress of Lorki, the king, George, marched

* Article "Georgia," *Encyclopædia Britannica*.

against and besieged him in his own castle among the mountains, where the garrison was soon reduced to the last extremity from famine. In the hope of obtaining mercy for himself and his soldiers, the young prince advanced from the gate, and, throwing himself at the feet of his uncle, implored his pity; but he was imprisoned and blinded by the hardhearted and inhuman monarch, who, on Ivane surrendering his castle, when unable any longer to resist the arrows and swords of the enemy, and the slower and more cruel ravages of famine, caused this noble to undergo the same rigorous fate. Although Orpelian had only yielded on the condition of being permitted to depart, with his few remaining followers, freely and unmolested to another land, George caused them all to be treacherously seized and imprisoned, and having commanded the execution of every other member of the vanquished house (with the exception of the brother and two sons of the unfortunate chief, who fled into Persia), and caused Ivane to be blinded in his dungeon, in order to obliterate all recollection of their deeds and name, he decreed that it should be effaced from the inscriptions on their tombs, and even struck off the pages of the histories and chronicles of Georgia. But on the death of George, who was succeeded by his only daughter Thamar, this princess, whose reign is the most glorious in the history of Georgia, recalled to her dominions the remaining members of the house of Orpelian, and, as Ivane had expired in prison, restored to them his forfeited estates.* She expelled the Persians who invaded her territories, and, extending the limits of her kingdom from the Black to the Caspian Sea, reduced several neighbouring princes to her sway. The arms of her son George IV., who made Ivane Orpelian IV. the commander of his forces, were also triumphant over the tribes lying to the south and west of Georgia, whom he compelled to embrace Christianity; but in 1220 his reign was marked by the dreadful ravages of the Mongul Tartars, who, entering the kingdom through the pass of Derbend, traversed it on their route to Persia, though in this, their first inroad, they gained no very decisive advantage over the inhabitants.† Two years after, on the death of George, who had intrusted the regency of the kingdom and the guardianship of her brother to the care of his

---

* Article "Georgia," *Encyclopædia Britannica*.
† Huc's "Christianity in China, Tartary," &c.

daughter Rhouzoudan, his son and successor, David, not being of age, they again invaded Georgia, and, presenting themselves as fellow-Christians and allies, prepared to assist the young queen against her enemies the Tartars. To carry out the deception, they placed in front of their army some priests whom they had taken prisoners, and carried before them the cross as a standard. The deceived Georgians were surprised and attacked unawares, losing six thousand men; but, discovering their fatal mistake, they rallied their forces, and, encountering the enemy, killed twenty thousand, besides capturing many prisoners, and putting their whole army to flight. The queen Rhouzoudan sent an ambassador to Honorius III. to warn him of the danger by which Europe was menaced if the Monguls were allowed to continue their victorious progress unopposed; and in her letter she states that she had been unable to send the assistance she had promised against the Saracens, because she had need of all her armies to resist a sudden invasion of barbarians. The death of Zingis Khan, which took place in 1227, for a moment arrested the arms of the Monguls, who hastened back to the imperial camp to assist in the election of a new chief; but, this accomplished, they again overran Georgia, and the queen, having in vain appealed for assistance to the Christian countries of Europe, saw her throne and people laid prostrate at the feet of the Tartar khan, under whose sway they remained till the year 1500.* She herself became a Mahometan, and the royal family, who have reigned since the eighth century, and assert that they are descended from Solomon, still retained their title and authority, though only at the pleasure of the Mongul chief, and so long as they obeyed his dictates and paid a sufficient tribute.

From the revolutions and almost continual wars with which Georgia has been distracted for so many hundreds of years, she has naturally made but little progress in literature, or in any abstruse science or art; but the Bible was translated by St. Euthymius into the native tongue as early as the eighth century, and there are some poetical romances still extant composed in the middle ages—particularly the poem of Tariel, by General Rusteval, a courtier of Queen Thamar, and another by the same author, recording her reign and exploits. The Georgians have also several other heroic songs,

* Huc's " Christianity in Tartary, Thibet," &c.

particularly the Baramiani and the Rostomiani, and hold in high estimation Visramiani and Dareganiani, two prose works by Serg of Thmogir, and Moses of Khoni; but these, with a collection of hymns by the patriarch Antoni, the Code of Vakhtang, by Vakhtang VI. in 1703, and the Chronicles of the same prince, make up almost the whole amount of the native writings of Georgia.*

Many traces of Christianity are still to be met with among the wild tribes of the Caucasus, and the ruins of churches and crosses are frequently seen in the mountains, which, according to some, are the relics of the attempt of Queen Thamar of Georgia to convert the natives to the Christian faith; according to others, they were planted there by the Genoese, who, in the thirteenth and fourteenth centuries, carried on an extensive trade with Georgia and Mingrelia, and formed many colonies in those countries, of which there are at the present day but few remains.†

* Article "Georgia," in the *Encyclopædia Britannica*.
† Wagner's "Caucasus."

CHAPTER VI.

The Finns—Russians—Nobogorod and Kiof—Rurik—Oleg—Igor—Olga.

> Fair spring supplies the favouring gale,
> The naval plunderer spreads his sail;
> And, ploughing wide the watery way,
> Explores with anxious eyes his prey.
> JOHN SCOTT.
>
> Equipp'd for deeds alike on land or see.
> BYRON.

THE Finns, or Tschudes (that is, barbarians, or nations alien to the Slavonic race), as they are called in Russia, formerly occupied all that part of the country which lies to the north of the Valdai Hills, between the Vistula and Ural Mountains,* and are commonly considered to have been the aboriginal inhabitants of Scandinavia, from whence they were expelled by the Goths. The Budini, described by Herodotus, appear to have been a Finnish tribe,† and Ptolemy in the second century mentions the Phinni, together with the Gythones and Venedæ, as nations of small extent and power, in the neighbourhood of the Vistula; while in the time of Pliny, the southern coast of the Baltic, to the eastward of that river, was vaguely termed Finningia. Pritchard and Latham are of opinion that the Finlanders, Laplanders, and most of the Siberian tribes belong to the same race, which appears to have borne a close affinity to the Huns and Igours, with whom they are by some writers identified, and collectively termed Ugrian. As the Slavonians became more powerful, they gradually reduced all the aboriginal hordes, and drove them further northward; for as we learn from Nestor, the ancient chronicler of Russia, the Finns in his time occupied all the territory from Lake Peipus eastward,‡ and traces of them are to be met with at the present day, more or less interspersed with the Slavonians, over all the northern part of Russia, particularly in the hilly district of Valdai and in the government of St. Petersburg, besides

---
* Pritchard's "Nat. Hist. of Man." † Herodotus. ‡ Chronicles of Nestor.

several tribes on the Volga, and the inhabitants of the province of Finland, by whom it is called Suonemma, or the country of lakes. The Magyars of Hungary also belong to the same race, which is remarkable for its love of music and poetry, and possesses many songs and heroic ballads, with long romances and legends in verse.* They worshipped the sun, moon, and stars, amongst which the constellation of the Great Bear received particular honours, besides the winds, lakes, rivers, fountains, and cataracts, and several goddesses; their principal deity was called Yomala,† and they believed in a future state. They were early acquainted with the art of smelting iron; Finnish swords are renowned in the Icelandic sagas,‡ and tradition ascribes to Finns the discovery of various mines in Sweden. They were also particularly attached to agriculture, and appear to have been well versed in all the implements of husbandry,‖ though, from the rigour of the climate, they were principally dependent for their subsistence upon the produce of their numerous lakes. The province of Finland was partly subject to Russia in the early period of her history; but in the twelfth century it was conquered by Sweden, who long endeavoured by force and tyranny to convert the natives to Christianity. An English priest called Henry, who had accompanied Eric, the Swedish general, in this expedition, was appointed bishop of the country, and zealously commenced the propagation of the Christian faith; but the violent measures which he used to compel the Finns to renounce their idols, produced an insurrection against the invaders, and Henry, falling a victim to the animosity of the inhabitants, was assassinated in a tumult, and, being after-

---

* One of the longest of their poems is the Kalevala, a composition half Christian, half heathen, relating the history of a mother (evidently intended for the Virgin) and her child, and of which the peculiar versification probably gave rise to Longfellow's poem of Hiawatha. The following, translated by Alexander Castren, from the Finnish into Russian, and by Herr Schriefen into English, is a specimen:—

"Wisely then the sun made answer,
Well I know thy child beloved,
It was he alone who made me—
Lets me rush in gold through heaven,
Lets me beam in silver splendour,
All the lovely days of summer—
Yes, I saw thy son beloved,
Him thy babe, O thou unhappy!
In the marsh, up to the girdle,
To his arms within the heather."

† The name for the Deity is Yuma with the tribes on the Volga.
‡ In the saga of St. Olaf, while relating the battle of Stiklestadt, the bard says—
"The king himself now proved the power
Of Finn-folk's craft in magic hour."

‖ Pritchard's "Nat. Hist. of Man."

wards canonized, has since been made the patron saint of Finland. Both before and after his death, great cruelties were inflicted upon the unfortunate people; all who refused baptism being mercilessly put to death by fire and sword; and, though they were ultimately compelled by persecution to profess the Christian faith, they still remain very superstitious.* In the middle ages, the word Finn was synonymous with that of sorcerer, and it was generally believed that this people had a particular intercourse with the devil;† and at all times they have been celebrated for their conjurers, who act precisely in the same manner as the Angekoks in Greenland, and the Shamans among the northern Tartars of Siberia.‡ Abo, the capital of Finland till 1827, when its destruction by fire caused the seat of government to be removed to the modern port of Helsingfors, a well-built city guarded by the strong fortress of Sveaborg, was founded about the twelfth century, and during the middle ages suffered severely five times from fire, besides in 1509 being sacked and almost totally destroyed by the Danes. It is built upon a promontory between the gulfs of Bothnia and Finland, and, before they were transferred to its rival, contained a university, museum, and library, besides several other public edifices. The greater part of Finland remained in the possession of Sweden till 1809, when she was finally subdued by Russia; and her loss was a serious blow to the former power, to whom she had always proved a valuable ally. Her soldiers distinguished themselves under the banners of Gustavus Adolphus in the Thirty Years' War; in the days of Tacitus she was celebrated for her archers; and a Finnish regiment fought valiantly in the army of William the Third at the Boyne.‖

The name of Russians§ is first mentioned in history in-

---

* Milner's "Shores of the Baltic."
† See "Paradise Lost," where these lines occur—
"Follow the night-hag when, call'd
In secret, riding through the air she comes,
Lured with the smell of infant blood; to dance
With Lapland witches, while the lab'ring moon
Eclipses nt their charms."—MILTON.
The Norwegian peasant even now thinks the Lapp and Finn can assume at pleasure the shape of animals.
‡ Pritchard's "Natural History of Man."
‖ Lord Macaulay's "History of England."—Milner's "Shores of the Baltic."
§ Harhertstein, in 1549, says that the people of Moscow assert that the ancient appellation of Russia was Rosseia, which in Russian means a dispersion.
Nestor, in his chronicles says, "This name of Russian was given us by the Varangians, and before that time we were known under the name of Slaves; and the Polanians, who were also among the Slaves, had no other language. The name of Polanians was given them from the fields they cultivated, and because they inhabited the plain, but they were of Slave origin, and had no other language than the Slavon."

the year 839, when a few who had visited Constantinople with their sovereign, whom the Byzantine chronicles call Chacanus (which was probably his title *chagan* or *khan*), accompanied the embassy sent by Theophilus, Emperor of the East, to Louis le Debonnaire, King of France, the son and successor of Charlemagne, in the train and under the protection of the pompous ambassador of the Greeks. Some historians suppose them to have been the descendants of the Roxolani, who invaded Mœsia A.D. 70, and defeated two Roman cohorts when Adrian made peace with their king, but who were subsequently driven to the north, where the geographer of Ravenna, A.D. 886, places them in the vicinity of Novogorod (the Russians having founded a kingdom there before that period), and consider them to have been a Slavonic or Sarmatic tribe; but the Russians are mentioned by Constantine Porphyrogenitus* as being a distinct people from the Slavonians, and in his time speaking a different language.† According to Levesque they are descended from the Huns,‡ but assumed the name and language of their Slavonic conquerors, who were undoubtedly the descendants of the Sarmatians; and the traditions of Sweden maintain, that the Huns anciently formed a powerful monarchy in Russia, which they relate was then very densely peopled, far more so than at the present day. It is certain that after the death of Attila, when his followers were driven back upon the plains of Scythia, the Slavonians were also expelled by the Goths from the shores of the Danube, having been forced by the Huns to the extreme north and south-west of Russia, and spreading over Sarmatia, or Western Scythia, they were scattered and divided into many tribes and nations, the principal of whom were the Poles, under their chief, Lech, from whose name they were anciently called Lechi; the Drevlians, who derived their appellation from the woods and forests among which they dwelt in Volhynia, and the Krivitches, who founded the city and fortress of Smolensko. According to some authors, the Russians were so designated

---

* In his map, he gives the *Russian* and *Slavonic* names for the cataracts on the Dnieper

† Some authors suppose that the Slavonians possessed a written language in these ancient times, prior to that now in use among them, but there appears to be very little ground for such an idea. In the year 1781, several manuscripts were found at Novogorod in a very perfect state; but although they were communicated to several academies, they have never been explained. They were written in the same characters as an inscription on a clock in the convent of St. Saba, at Svenigorod, near Moscow.—CAMPENHAUSEN.

‡ Levesque's "Histoire de la Russie."

from Rosseia, which in their language signifies a dispersion, or scattered people; others, among whom are Herberstein, and the Tartar historian, Aboulgasi Baiadour, Prince of Carizme, state from Russus, a brother of the Polish hero Lech, while it is also asserted that they received their name from the colour of their hair; and, according to Levesque, the common Oriental traditions affirm that they were at all times a distinct people, having a different origin from any other, and that from time immemorial their habits, manners, and language, bore no affinity to those of any race in Europe.*

Towards the early part of the fifth century, that portion of the Russian territory that was peopled by the Slavonians, became divided into several separate states, of which the largest and most important were Novogorod, Smolensko, Polotzk, and Kiof. The traditions of the latter city relate, that in the middle of the third century, three Sarmatian or Slavonian brothers, Kivi, Scieko, and Choranus, came from the east, with their sister Libeda, and divided all the south of Russia† among them, giving their names to their own states. Kivi founded the city of Kiof, and, heading an inroad of the Sarmatians upon the eastern empire, penetrated with his followers as far as Constantinople, and forced the Emperor Probus to cede a large treasure to the Barbarians, and propose terms of peace; but subsequently, leading another expedition into Bulgaria, he was killed in battle, and his kingdom, with those of his brothers, destroyed in the following century by the overwhelming and terrific invasion of the Huns. Some idea may be formed of what this invasion, of which we have comparatively so slight record, must have been, by the accounts which have descended to us of the more recent conquests of the Monguls, and how every vestige of civilization—had there been any to destroy—must have been annihilated, and utterly swept away, in their terrific and destructive course. They appear to have spread even as far as the marshy shores of the north; but about fifty years later, upon their descent into Hungary, and abandonment of the wasted steppes of Scythia, the Sarmatians or Slavonians wandered back to their old haunts, and a successor of Kivi,

* The Russians are mentioned twice in the Koran, and the Greek word 'Ρῶς, used to designate the Russians, occurs twice in the Septuagint, though not in our translation.—Finlay's "Byzantine Empire."—Levesque's "Histoire de la Russie."
† Herberstein's "Rerum Muscovitarum."

of the same name, rebuilt the city of Kiof, A.D. 430. It was subsequently conquered by Oleg, a warlike and victorious prince of Novogorod, in whose possession it remained till his death, after which the Chazars subdued the city and state, and ruled nearly all the south of Russia for more than two hundred years.

According to Nestor, the old historian and "Venerable Bede" of Russia, Novogorod was founded about the same time by the Slavonians as the second erection of Kiof. Advantageously situated near the confluence of the Volkhof with Lake Ilmen, and possessing by Lake Ladoga and the Neva a direct communication with the Baltic Sea, some writers have supposed that a large Finnish city existed on its present site, which idea appears rather to be supported by its name Novo Gordo, or New City, previous to the irruption of the Slavonians upon the north of Russia; and some ancient ruins, which till lately were to be seen in the neighbourhood of Novogorod, are considered to have been the remains of this old and unchronicled capital of the Finns, or what possibly may have been a city of the Huns.

The government was republican, under a chief magistrate chosen from among the boyards, and it early attained so much power and opulence, from the extensive trade carried on by its merchants and nobles, by means of caravans, among the Permians, Chazars, and Bulgarians of the Volga, and through them with Persia and India, that "who can resist the gods, and the great Novogorod?" was a common proverb among the surrounding nations,[*] and four hundred thousand inhabitants are said to have resided within its walls. But her territories were encircled by enemies, the adjoining Finnish or Tchudish tribes, and the Permians, continually invading the commonwealth, and the treasure which their temples were reputed to contain excited the avarice of the Scandinavian sea-kings—or Varangian corsairs as they are called in the Russian chronicles—who frequently devastated their coasts; and, possessing themselves of the provinces of Revel and Livonia, carried on for many years a perpetual war with the neighbouring Slavonic and Finnish nations. These pirates hired themselves as mercenary soldiers to the highest bidder, and their assistance was often purchased by

[*] Levesque's "Histoire de la Russie."

the Novogorodians against the plundering incursions of their other foes, who at length, strengthening themselves by union, so imperilled the existence of the republic, whose power had been weakened by constant warfare, that Gostromisla, the last male descendant of a long line of princes, advised his fellow-citizens on his deathbed to nominate his grandson Rurik, the prince of the Varangians, his successor as chief magistrate of Novogorod, and thus secure the alliance and protection of the Varangians. Rurik, who was the son of the Swedish monarch Ludbrat, and his queen Oumila, the daughter of Gostromisla, was born at Upsal, A.D. 830;* and in the year 861, responding to the invitation of the boyards of Novogorod, accompanied by his two brothers Truva and Sineus, and a motley crew of Finnish, Slavonic, and Norman adventurers, he sailed with a few ships up the Volkhof, and endeavoured to establish himself in the city. His claim was disputed, however, by a large majority of the inhabitants, who objected to the rule of a foreigner and a Varangian, whose followers they considered as mere uncivilized depredators, and, refusing them access into their town, they closed the gates against him. But, instead of returning to his ships, he resorted to arms, and building the town of Ladoga,† as head-quarters for his troops, he fortified it with a rampart of earth, his brothers also establishing themselves within a short distance of the city. The Novogorodians, assembling in large force, advanced from the town under their most able general Vadime, to expel the invaders from their intrenchments; but being defeated in a desperate engagement, their army completely destroyed, and their leader slain, Rurik, immediately quitting his stronghold, marched upon Novogorod, where the citizens, being without a general, and totally disorganized by their defeat, submitted to him without further resistance, and placed their government in his hands, A.D. 862. He appointed Sineus to the sovereignty of Bielo-Ozero, and Truva to that of Izborsk, chief towns in tributary territories, which, on their both dying without heirs, he again incorporated with his own dominions, and, abolishing the republican form of government, he took the title of Veliki Knez, or Grand Prince.

* Oustreloff's "History of Russia."
† The ruins of this castle still exist in the neighbourhood of Novogorod. The name is derived from the Slavonian word *lader*, a place of repose.—CAMPENHAUSEN.

He pacified and strengthened his dominions,* and appears to have ruled with justice and moderation, reconciling the people to his government by adopting the Slavonic language and manners, his followers taking wives from among that nation, and he himself espousing a descendant of the ancient ruling family of Novogorod, in order to procure an additional claim to the throne; and, at his death in 878, he was succeeded by his son Igor, who being only a year old, Oleg, the brother-in-law of Rurik, took upon himself the office of regent.

The Varangians were not long content with this northern extremity of the Slavonic dominions, and the territory of Kiof, whose capital is situated, like Rome and Constantinople, upon seven hills, with their summits overlooking the broad and rapid stream of the Dnieper, was too productive, thickly populated, and fertile, to be long overlooked by such daring and rapacious freebooters, ever in search of adventure and plunder; and who, though accustomed to the frozen and tideless waters of the Baltic, and its marshy and inhospitable shores, have, wherever the opportunity was afforded by the weakness, civil discords, or pusillanimity of those nations with whom they have come in contact, established themselves in the more favoured and genial atmosphere of the south, and in England, France, and the most sunny and fertile provinces of Italy, have made their power respected, and their vengeance feared, erecting kingdoms and noble houses whose descendants are now proud to trace their origin from the rude and warlike followers of the Varangian sea-kings. Shortly after they had occupied Novogorod, they turned their arms towards the rich and grassy plains upon which Kiof stands, and under the command of Oskold, the stepson of Rurik, and Dir, one of his chiefs, drove out the Chazars, who many years before had extended their sway over this city and province; and, having firmly established their power over the whole territory of Kiof, in 866 made the first warlike descent of the Russians upon Constantinople. Taking advantage of the temporary absence of the Emperor Michael from the city, they sailed with a naval armament of two hundred vessels through the Bosphorus, and even occupied the port of Byzantium, returning to their own country laden with the spoils

* According to Storch, the empire of Rurik extended over those territories now comprehending the governments of Revel, Riga, Polotzk, Pskof, Vyborg, St. Petersburg, Novogorod, Olonitz, Smolensko, Archangel, Vladimir, Jaroslaf, Kostroma, and Vologda; but Archangel certainly at that period belonged to the Permians, and Smolensko and Polotzk were independent states till subdued by Oleg and Vladimir.

of the Grecian cities; though a violent storm—according to the Greek legends, occasioned by the intercession of the Virgin Mary, a part of whose cloak was preserved by the Byzantines as a sacred relic, and carried out in procession, at the command of their emperor, on his hasty return—compelled them to evacuate prematurely the harbour and waters of Constantinople.*

About this time a regular communication was established between the Grecian empire and the coasts of the Baltic Sea, by the commercial enterprise of the merchants of Novogorod and Kiof. A lake and river in summer, and the ice in winter, connecting the former city with the Baltic, she received in her stores all the produce of the north, and transported it by canoes to Kiof, where it was accumulated in vast magazines till the annual departure of a fleet to Constantinople, which usually took place in June. The ships sailed down the Dnieper † as far as the thirteen cataracts,‡ whose rocks and rapid falls break the smooth and even course of that river, some of which they were enabled to cross by simply lightening the cargo, but avoiding the more precipitate and formidable by dragging the vessels past them overland; and then, resting on an island below the last fall, they held a festival in celebration of their escape from the perils of the river, and the attacks of the hostile tribes who roamed along its fir-lined shores, before proceeding to encounter the more formidable winds and breakers of the sea. But, preparatory to crossing the Euxine, the damages which their frail barks had sustained in their rough passage over land and water, were repaired on a second island near the mouth of the river, and with a fair wind a few favourable days would moor them in the harbour of Constantinople. The Russian canoes, which consisted of a single tree hollowed out, and this narrow foundation raised and extended on every side by planks, till it had attained the desired height and length, were laden with slaves of every age (the Russians

---

* A detailed account of the attack upon Constantinople by Oskold and Dir, is given by the Greek historians, Zonaras, Cedrenus, Constantine, Porphyrogenitus, and the patriarchs Photius and Ignatius, the two latter being eyewitnesses. Photius says, "Not only have the Bulgarians come over to the Christian faith, but also the nation of the Russians, who, proud of their success lately, even exalted themselves against the Greek empire, but are beginning to exchange the impurities of heathenism for the pure and orthodox doctrines of Christianity." The Russian chronicles also mention that the emperor, under whose reign the expedition was undertaken, persuaded them, after the conclusion of peace, to become Christians.—Blackmore's "Notes to Mouravieff's Church of Russia." Gibbon's "Decline and Fall of the Roman Empire."

† The Dnieper was anciently called Borysthenes, from the Scythian or Slavonic words, *bor*, a pine forest, and *stena*, a wall; the shores of that river being lined with vast forests of fir.—Levesque's "Histoire de la Russie."

‡ Thirteen are marked in the map of Constantine Porphyrogenitus, of which he gives the Slavonic and Russian names.

being in great demand as soldiers at Constantinople), hides, furs, amber from the Baltic shores, honey and bees' wax; and they returned at stated seasons with a rich cargo of corn, oil, wine, the manufactures of Greece, the embroidery of Persia, and the spices and ebony of the Indian Isles. A company of Russian merchants settled at Constantinople, and in the principal provincial cities and towns of the Greek Empire, for trading purposes, and the treaties formed between the two nations protected their persons, effects, and privileges. But the marvellous accounts which the merchants and sailors who accompanied the fleets in these commercial enterprises, carried home, of the wealth and magnificence of Constantinople, excited the desire of their countrymen for a larger supply than their comparatively scanty trade afforded, and, in the space of a hundred and ninety years, four naval expeditions were undertaken by the Russians to plunder the treasures of the Greek capital.*

The Christian religion appears to have been first transported to Kiof in the expedition of Oskold, who with many of his followers, on his return from his hostile enterprise against Constantinople, embraced Christianity; and Constantine Porphyrogenitus and other Greek historians relate, that during the lifetime of that prince a bishop was sent by the Emperor Basil the Macedonian, and St. Ignatius the patriarch of Byzantium, to Kiof, who made many converts, chiefly in consequence of the miraculous preservation of a volume of the Gospels, which remained unconsumed when thrown into the midst of flames by the unbelievers, and the Metropolitan of Russia appears in the catalogue of prelates subject to the Byzantine patriarchs as early as the year 891.† In the reign of Igor, a church of the prophet Elias

---

* Gibbon's "Decline and Fall of the Roman Empire."

† The Russians have a tradition that St. Andrew preached in their country. Herberstein, in his "Rerum Muscoviticarum Commentarii," says:—"The Russians openly boast in their annals, that before the times of Vladimir and Oleg, the land of Russia was baptized and blessed by Andrew, the apostle of Christ, who came, as they assert, from Greece to the mouth of the Dnieper, and sailed up the river against the stream, as far as the mountains where Kiof now stands, and there blessed and baptized all the country; that he planted his cross there, and preached the great grace of God, foretelling that the churches of the Christians would be numerous; that then he went to the sources of the Dnieper, to the great lake Volok, and descended by the river Lovat to lake Ilmen, and thence passed by the river Votcher, which flows out of the same lake to Novogorod; thence by the same river to lake Ladoga, and by the river Neva to the sea, which they call Varetsgkai, but which we call the German Sea (the Baltic), between Finland and Livonia, and so sailed to Rome. Finally, that he was crucified for Christ's sake in the Peloponnesus by Antipater."

Mouravieff, in his "History of the Russian Church," quotes the old chronicler, Nestor, who says—St. Andrew, penetrating up the Dnieper into the deserts of Scythia, planted the first cross on the hills of Kiof, and said to his followers, "See you these hills? On these hills shall shine the light of divine grace. There shall be here a great city, and God shall have in it many churches to his name."—Mouravieff's "Church of Russia."

is mentioned as existing at Kiof, where the Christian Varangians swore to the observance of the treaty, formed by the Russian prince and his people, with the ambassadors of Constantinople, and the catacombs and caves of the Pechersky monastery at Kiof are supposed to have been excavated by them.

In 879, the year following the death of Rurik, Oleg, the regent of Novogorod, assembling a large army from among all the numerous tribes who peopled his dominions, and accompanied by the infant prince Igor, marched against Smolensko, the capital of the Krivitches, a Slavonic tribe by whom it had been founded about the same time as Novogorod, having overrun and swept away all the smaller towns and villages that studded the plains between the two cities. He subjected Smolensko to his sway, and embarking his followers in a fleet of the small and precarious vessels used in the commerce of Novogorod, which he had compelled her merchants to supply, and caused to be transported with his army overland till he reached the shores of the Dnieper, a little to the north of Smolensko, he sailed down the river and arrived before Kiof. There, leaving his ships, he disguised himself as a Novogorod merchant, and, entering the town, professed to have arrived with a fleet of trading vessels, paying a visit alone and on foot to the palace of the grand prince, whom he induced to accompany him, with merely a few courtiers and attendants, to inspect his fleet and goods. As soon as the deluded Oskold had arrived on the banks of the river, the Novogorodians leaping from their barks seized upon the unfortunate prince, whom they instantly murdered, and Oleg, forcing his way into the city at their head, took possession of the whole province, and removed the seat of his government to Kiof, its nearer proximity to Constantinople, and the superiority of its climate and soil, with its central position, giving it a great advantage over his own capital. He subdued or won over to his authority many of the Slavonic and Lithuanian tribes, whose allegiance had hitherto been exacted by the Chazars, and commanded the Severians and Raditnitsches, two Caucasian nations,* to desist from paying their customary tribute to that people, and reconciled the Kiovians to his government by relaxing the severity of the laws, and reducing the taxes. After reigning some years

* Wagner's "Caucasus."

in Kiof, he resigned the government to Igor till his return, and, fitting out an expedition for the invasion of Constantinople, in the year 904 he sailed to the entrance of the Bosphorus, where the Greeks, who were prepared to resist him, had raised a strong barrier of arms and fortifications to defend the passage; but, avoiding this, he caused his ships to be dragged across the land, and arrived before Constantinople, where, hanging his shield as a trophy over the gates, he marched with his warriors into the capital. Completely taken by surprise, the Greeks, astonished and alarmed at the unexpected manner in which the savage chieftain had overcome the formidable obstruction they had erected to oppose him, fondly supposing that it would prove insurmountable to barbarians, with whom the art of engineering, as practised by them, was unknown, proposed to negotiate with the invaders, and concluded an immediate truce. While the strangers remained in the city, the Emperor Leo gave a banquet to the Russian prince and his soldiers, at which he attempted to rid himself of his troublesome enemies through the cowardly medium of poison; but the attempt failing, the Byzantine monarch was obliged to accept an ignominious peace, and ransom the city from destruction. The terms of the treaty bound Leo to pay a tribute to every vessel belonging to Oleg, and to remit all taxes and duties upon Russian merchants trading in the Greek empire. The grand prince returned with his fleet adorned with silken sails to Kiof, and after a few years formed a new treaty with Constantinople, for the security of the lives and fortunes of the Russian traders, in which it was agreed that the goods of a Russian dying without testament, in the dominions of the emperor of Constantinople, should be transmitted to his heirs in Russia, and, if bequeathed by will, should be forwarded to the legatees; that, if a Russian killed a Greek, or a Greek a Russian, the assassin should be put to death on the spot where the crime was committed; or, if the murderer had effected his escape, his fortune was to be adjudged to the nearest heir of the murdered, a provision being made for the wife of the criminal. It was also provided that, for striking another with a sword or any other weapon, a fine of three litres of gold should be exacted from the offender; and that a thief, Greek or Russian, caught in the fact, might be put to death with impunity; but, if he should be seized, the stolen goods were to be restored, and the criminal condemned to pay thrice their value.*

Although Oleg was only regent of the empire, yet he governed in his own person for thirty-four years, and Igor did not succeed to his father's throne till the death of his guardian, which took place in 913, from the effects of a serpent's bite, the reptile, according to the chronicles of Nestor, having crept into the skull of a favourite horse, which diviners had predicted, five years before, would be the cause of its master's death. On hearing that the animal was dead, which, since the fatal prophecy he had ceased to mount, Oleg visited the body, and placing his foot on the head, exclaimed, " So this is the dreaded animal!" when the serpent suddenly darting out, inflicted upon his foot a mortal wound.†

Igor, who was at this time thirty-eight years of age, spent the greater part of his reign in quelling the disturbances that arose in various parts of his dominions. He defeated and drove back the Petchenegans, a Tartar nation whose territory lay on the north of the Caspian sea, and who advanced against Kiof in great force; and subdued the Drevlians, who peopled the modern province of Volhynia, and were the last of the Slavonic tribes to abandon their wandering mode of life, having then but recently settled down in towns and villages. After encountering an obstinate resistance of three years, he also reduced to submission the Uglitches; a nation whose territory lay on the shores of the Dnieper, and had asserted its independence, and passed the first twenty-eight years of his reign in almost constant warfare. But having succeeded in restoring tranquillity to his states, the grand prince was urgently importuned by his chiefs and soldiers to follow the example of his predecessor, and endeavour to reimburse his country for the losses it had sustained in these civil wars, by plundering the riches and treasures of the wealthy Grecian cities. This advice agreed too well with his own ambition and avarice to be rejected or disregarded; and in 941 he equipped a fleet for the invasion of Constantinople, with which he advanced into the Black Sea, while the naval powers of the empire were employed in a war with the Saracens; and after devastating the provinces of Pontus, Paphlagonia, and Bithynia, entered the Bosphorus. But

* Karamsin's History of Russia."   † Chronicles of Nestor.

F

the Greeks, who were now aware of the real strength and pertinacity of their northern adversary, prepared energetically to resist this sudden inroad, and fitting out every remaining vessel and galley that was not employed on foreign service with an unusually abundant supply of the terrible fire,* that they always used in their warlike operations, and whose flames no water would allay, poured it from every side of their ships upon the enemy, sinking and destroying two-thirds of his canoes.† Many thousands of Russians, to avoid being burned, sprang into the sea, where the greater number perished in the waves; others, who were captured, were beheaded by order of the emperor, and the rest were inhumanly murdered by the Thracian peasants as they attempted to gain the shore. The remaining vessels escaping into shallow water, Igor returned with them to Kiof, where, recruiting his forces by alliance with the Petchenegans, his former foes, he prepared another expedition for the following spring, with which he hoped to retrieve his losses and accomplish his revenge. But the Greeks, anxious to avert the calamities of another Russian invasion, and not willing to encounter the chance of defeat from an infuriated and vindictive adversary, offered to revive the treaty that the Greek emperor had been forced by Oleg to accept, and pay to Igor the tribute which his more successful predecessor had exacted for each of his vessels; terms that, after some hesitation, were accepted by the Russian prince.‡ "In these naval hos-

---

* The composition of the Greek fire, which was so extensively used in the wars of Byzantium, being the most formidable implement of defence possessed by the Greeks, and occasionally lent by their emperors to their allies, was considered as a state secret of the utmost importance, and for nearly four centuries it was unknown to the Mahometans, but, being discovered by the Saracens, they used it in repelling the Crusaders and overpowering the Greeks. One of its principal ingredients is supposed to have been naphtha, or the bitumen which is collected on the shores of the Dead Sea, and when ignited it was scarcely possible to quench it, water having no effect. In sieges it was poured from the ramparts, or launched like our bombs in redhot balls of stone or iron, or was darted in flax twisted round arrows and javelins. It produced a thick smoke and loud explosion, and is thus described by the crusader Joinville—"It came flying through the air like a winged dragon, about the thickness of a hogshead, with the report of thunder and the speed of lightning, and the darkness of the night was dispelled by this horrible illumination."—*Count Robert of Paris.*

† Gibbon's "Decline and Fall of the Roman Empire."

‡ In this treaty, according to Nestor, it was stipulated that "the Russian princes are not in future to have any troops in the country of Kherson (the peninsula of Cherson in the Crimea), or in any of the towns that are dependent on it, still less to make war with this country, and to endeavour to conquer it. But if the Russian prince requires aid, we, the Cæsar, promise to furnish it, to replace under his authority those of the surrounding countries which have thrown it off. And if the Russians meet at the mouth of the Dnieper Khersonian fishermen, they shall not injure them, and they shall not have the right to winter at the mouth of the Dnieper, nor at Bielo Bejia (Berislaf), but at the approach of autumn they shall return to their own country, into Russia. If the Black Bulgarians attack the country of Kherson, we recommend the Russian prince to drive them back, and not to allow them to disturb the peace."—H. D. Seymour's "Russia on the Black Sea," &c.

This treaty proves that the Russians had been troublesome to the Greek towns of the Crimea, even at that early period.

tilities," says Gibbon, "every disadvantage was on the side of the Greeks; their savage enemy afforded no mercy, his poverty promised no spoil; his impenetrable retreat deprived the conquerors of the hopes of revenge; and the pride or weakness of empire, indulged an opinion that no honour could be gained or lost in the intercourse with barbarians. At first their demands were high and inadmissible, three pounds of gold for each soldier or mariner of the fleet; the Russian youth adhered to the design of conquest, but the counsels of moderation were recommended by the hoary sages. "Be content," they said, "with the liberal offers of Cæsar; is it not far better to obtain, without a combat, the possession of gold, silver, silks, and all the objects of our desires? Are we sure of victory? Can we conclude a treaty with the sea? We do not tread on the land; we float on the abyss of water, and a common death hangs over our heads." The memory of these arctic fleets that seemed to descend from the Polar circle left a deep impression of terror on the imperial city. By the vulgar of every rank it was asserted and believed, that an equestrian statue in the square of Taurus was secretly inscribed with a prophecy, how the Russians in the last days should become masters of Constantinople."[*]

Four years after his return to Kiof, Igor set out on a journey among the Drevlians, to enforce the payment of their tribute. He had already loaded them with heavy exactions, and provoked them at length to resistance by demanding double the ordinary amount. At a council they held among themselves, they decided no longer to submit to his tyranny and oppression. "This prince," said they, "is a mere wolf, who will steal the sheep one by one till he has destroyed the whole flock; he must be assassinated."[†] They stationed an ambuscade in a wood, through which he and his retinue would probably pass, near a town called Korosten, on the river Uscha, and there waylaid and murdered him. His death took place in 945, in the sixty-ninth year of his age, and he was buried near the spot where he fell; a kurgam or tumulus, according to the ancient Scythian and Slavonian custom, being raised over his tomb.[‡] He married Olga, or Precasna as she is called in the Russian chronicles, which

---

[*] Gibbon's "Decline and Fall of the Roman Empire."
[†] Karamsin's "History of Russia."
[‡] Tatischeff says, that in 1710 he himself saw the kurgam, or sepulchre of the grand prince, Igor.—Pinkerton's "Russia."

signifies very beautiful, and by whom he had one son, Sviatozlaf. She was born in a village called Sibout, about eight miles from Pleskof, and was originally the daughter of a ferryman, or, as some historians relate, of a reduced boyard, and descended from the ancient chagans of Russia. Igor met her first accidentally in a wood while hunting, and, being struck with her great beauty, elevated her to share his throne ; and in the year 903 their marriage was celebrated with great ceremony and feasting in the temple of Peroun at Pleskof.* On receiving the news of her husband's murder she assumed the reins of government in Kiof, and, resolving to avenge tenfold the assassination of the grand prince, an opportunity was not long in presenting itself; for, shortly after her accession, Male or Maldittus, the prince of the Drevlians, sent an embassy to her court to solicit her hand in marriage. She barbarously caused all the deputation to be buried alive, despatching messengers of her own to their country, saying, if the inhabitants wished her to be their princess and mistress, they must send her a larger number of wooers ; and then, ordering the new envoys to be scalded to death, immediately set out, accompanied by a large retinue, to the land of the Drevlians, before intelligence of the cruel fate of their countrymen could by any means have reached their province. Arrived there, she professed to comply with the proposals of the prince, whom she invited to a banquet with his principal nobles and chiefs ; and in the midst of the repast, when they were nearly all intoxicated with wine, they were suddenly massacred by the armed Russian attendants of Olga, who had previously given her servants instructions to that effect ; and her army pillaged and ravaged the country, reducing the town of Korosten,† the scene of the murder of Igor, to ashes, and, finally, subjugating the province and annexing it to her own kingdom.

On her return to Kiof, Olga devoted her energies and resources to the improvement of Russia, and the promotion of the welfare and prosperity of its people : she made a tour round her dominions, and, during her progress, caused bridges to be built, and roads to be constructed, encouraging commercial enterprise, and attempting to increase and facilitate the internal communication of the country. She founded

---

* Pinkerton's "Russia."
† Korosten occupied the site of the modern Isborosk, in Volhynia.

many towns and villages, and appears to have been deservedly loved by the nation, whom she governed with justice and moderation, and by whom she was long held in esteem and respect. In the year 955, during a period of profound peace in her dominions, she abdicated the throne; and, accompanied by numerous attendants, sailed from Kiof to visit the Emperor Constantine Porphyrogenitus at Constantinople, where she was received by the Byzantine sovereign with the greatest magnificence, and the polished and learned Cæsar himself appears to have been much impressed by the unusual intelligence and information possessed by his singular guest. The object of her journey appears to have been to obtain a more complete knowledge of the practice and doctrines of the Christian religion, whose votaries she had always protected in Kiof; for, shortly after her arrival in the Grecian capital, she embraced Christianity, and was baptized by the patriarch Polyceutes in the cathedral of St. Sophia in Constantinople— her example being followed by her uncle, thirty-four ladies, and twenty-two officers of her suite, two interpreters, and thirty-four Russian merchants, who composed her retinue, the emperor himself standing as her sponsor, and presenting her with many valuable and splendid gifts.* After her return to Kiof she firmly persisted in her new religion, and laboured assiduously to propagate it in her dominions, travelling to her native village of Sibout, and to Pleskof, for the purpose of instructing the inhabitants; but her exertions did not meet with much success, both her family and nation obstinately adhering to their ancient faith. She built several churches, and many Greek missionaries settled in the empire, no attempt being made by the people to destroy the Christian religion by persecution, it rather being treated with ridicule and contempt; but her example appears to have made some impression upon them, and many of the Russian traders from Constantinople, who had been struck with the magnificent churches of the Greeks, the splendour of their ceremonies, and the solemnity of their services, compared it, on their return home, with the idol worship and cruel religious rites of their own country, and in many instances professed the Christian faith. This was more especially the case in the city and province of Novogorod; where tradition asserts that,

* Some authors say that the Greek emperor made the Grand Princess an offer of marriage, but there appears to be no foundation for this story.

even during the life of Olga, the hermits Sergius and Germanus lived upon the desolate island of Balaam in Lake Ladoga, and that from thence St. Abramius went to preach to the wild and barbarous inhabitants of Rostoff.*

Olga, who ranks as a saint in the Russian calendar, and whom their chronicles compare to the sun, " for as the sun illuminates the world, so she illuminated Russia with the faith of Christ," died fourteen years after her conversion, in 967, at the advanced age of eighty-five; she had been succeeded, on her abdication, by her son Sviatozlaf, whom all her endeavours had failed to instruct in either the Christian religion or her own enlightened views of legislation and government. After her death she was buried in a spot which she had herself chosen, by a Greek priest named Gregory, who had accompanied her from Constantinople, though her bones were afterwards removed by her great grandson Jaroslaf, and interred in the Church of the Tithes at Kiof; and, in fulfilment of her last request, none of the pagan games and other ceremonies called Trezni, usually performed in Russia over the graves of persons of distinction, were permitted to be celebrated over her tomb.†

It is uncertain at what period coined money was first generally used in Russia, but some pieces which were cast about this period are still preserved in Novogorod, bearing the impression of a man on horseback.‡ The coin called grivna is mentioned for the first time in the Russian annals in 971, when, during a famine, a horse's head was sold for half a grivna; and the name appears to have been applied not only to the coin, which was worth a pound's weight of silver, but to the pound weight itself, and to the sum of fifty cunes, the latter being a coin of stamped skin or leather, of which the current value was a marten's skin, the taxes being usually paid in furs.

At this time, while the sovereigns principally resided at Kiof, Novogorod, their northern capital, was increasing, and

---

* Mouravieff's "Church of Russia." † Ibid.

‡ According to Sir Jerome Horsey, this stamp had its origin in an event which appears to be the same as that related by Herodotus with regard to the Scythian slaves. "The masters," says he, "were the only soldiers, as the discipline of those countries is; and in ancient times, having gone to fight against the Tartars, their slaves took possession of their houses, lands, and wealth. On their return, they perceived the self-emancipated bondsmen all assembled in battle array before the city walls; and, considering it beneath their dignity to use weapons of war in opposing so ignoble offenders, each raised his whip in a menacing attitude, and by thus recalling to their recollection their former servitude, so alarmed the slaves that they precipitately fled, and from that time, in remembrance of this easy victory, the coin of Novogorod bore a man on horseback raising his whip."

had again become an immense and important city. It was divided into five distinct towns, each of which was surrounded by a stone wall, defended by towers and ramparts, where a large body of archers and spearmen were continually mounted for its defence. The population amounted to about half a million of inhabitants.

CHAPTER VII.

Europe in the Ninth Century—Biarmaland—The Crimea.

> A hundred realms appear,
> Lakes, forests, cities, plains, extending wide,
> The pomp of kings, the shepherd's humbler pride.
> GOLDSMITH.

> The graves
> Of empires heave, but like some passing waves.
> BYRON.

THE period of the ninth century forms an important era in the historical annals of Europe;* for it witnessed the foundation of a settled monarchy and regular government in most of her kingdoms and states, and the popes first began to acquire that great ascendency which they afterwards exercised, not only as spiritual advisers, but as political arbiters of the continent. The Roman empire, weakened as it had become by the licentiousness and corruption of its rulers, the luxury and riches of its higher classes, and the absolute slavery of the lower, had been unable to repel the barbarian hordes who successively ravaged its territories and conquered its far-spread and unprotected provinces, and had

---

* CONTEMPORARY EUROPEAN SOVEREIGNS OF THE NINTH CENTURY.

EASTERN EMPIRE.
802. Nicephorus I.
811. Michael I.
813. Leo V. the Armenian.
820. Michael II.
829. Theophilus Logothetes.
842. Michael III.
867. Bazil I. the Macedonian.
886. Leo VI.

ENGLAND.
827. Egbert.
837. Ethelwolf.
857. Ethelbald.
860. Ethelbert.
865. Ethelred.
872. Alfred the Great.

DENMARK.
801. Godefried.
809. Olaf I.
811. Hemming.
812. Siward.
814. Harold.
840. Siward II.
856. Eric I.
854. Eric II.
878. Canute I.

FRANCE.
Charlemagne.
814. Louis I., le Debonnaire.

640. Charles the Bald.
877. Louis II., le Bègue.
879. Carloman.
884. Charles II. the Fat.
888. Eudes
898. Charles III. the Simple.

GERMAN EMPIRE.
800. Charlemagne.
814. Louis le Debonnaire.
840. Lothaire.
855. Louis II.
875. Charles the Bald.
878. Louis III.
879. Charles III.
887. Arnold.
899. Louis IV.

POLAND.
842. Plast, a country peasant.
861. Zemevitus.
892. Lescus IV.

RUSSIA.
Gostromlel.
862. Rurik.
878. Oleg.

SCOTLAND.
819. Congallus III.
824. Dougal.
831. Alpine.

834. Kenneth II.
854. Donald V.
859. Constantine II.
874. Ethus.
876. Gregory.
894. Donald VI.

SWEDEN.
825. Regnar Lodbrog.
Reigns uncertain.

SPAIN.
824. Ramirez I.
850. Ordogno.
862. Alfonso III.

POPES.
816. Stephen V.
817. Pascal I.
824. Eugenius II.
827. Valentinus.
828. Gregory IV.
844. Sergius II.
847. Leo IV.
855. Benedict III.
858. Nicholas I. the Great.
872. John VIII. Pope Joan.
882. Martin II.
884. Adrian III.
885. Stephen VI.
891. Fermosus.
896. Bouifucs VI.

been forced to recall its legions from the colonies which they held in subjection, to assist in defending the very walls of their own capital; so that, released from the thraldom of the Roman soldiers, the tributary nations one by one rendered themselves independent of the debased and degenerate Rome, who in 476 became the vassal, where once she had been the mistress, of the Greek empire, and remained for many years beneath her yoke. In 726 she released herself from the dominion of the Byzantine emperors, and became entirely subject to her Papal rulers, under whom for a time her ancient glory again revived; when kings trembled at the thunders of the Vatican, and princes and nobles made pilgrimages to her shrines.

In England, the stormy Heptarchy ceased to exist in 827, when the seven crowns were united on the head of Egbert; and the century was concluded by the memorable reign of Alfred, the greatest of its Saxon monarchs, who, delivering his country from its foreign oppressors, devoted his energies to the encouragement of learning, the promotion of commercial enterprise, and the formation of just and equitable laws; and whose grateful countrymen may reasonably consider as the founder of their nation's greatness, by the exertions which he made to establish that bulwark and chief strength of the British power, the navy; and, by turning their attention to discoveries on the ocean, first gave an impulse to that spirit which has since gained for them the empire of the sea.

The fair and long-haired Franks, who, issuing from the dense forests of Germany, crossed the Rhine under their leader Pharamond, giving to France its modern appellation, and, according to their historical traditions, the race of Merovingian kings, can hardly be said to have established that kingdom, or a settled government, till the reign of Charlemagne in 767, her sovereigns having, in the first instance, been mere military chiefs or leaders, whose power spread over a very small portion of the present country, and whose names were unknown beyond the narrow confines of their own domains. These were succeeded by a dynasty of *rois faineants*, whose mayors of the palace, the virtual rulers of the kingdom, first gained for it by their victories extent and fame, and extinguished for ever the hopes and endeavours of its Saracen invaders to establish their dominion and faith in north-western Europe, by the signal defeat inflicted upon the infidels by the most celebrated of the *maires du palais*, Charles Martel, who, assisted by his gallant army of Franks, gained the decisive and sanguinary field of Tours.

Norway, Sweden, and Denmark, furnished in their sea-kings that dreaded race of pirates, who, coveting the superior wealth of their more peaceful and settled neighbours, and preferring the adventurous lives of corsairs to the cultivation of the laborious arts of peace in their own inhospitable lands, harassed all the surrounding coasts by continual invasion in search of plunder; and who, under the name of Varangians, in 864, have been mentioned as overthrowing the republic, and founding the kingdom of Novogorod. A band of these warriors, leaving Russia, afterwards became the bulwark and most trusted guard of the later Byzantine Cæsars; while their Scandinavian kinsmen, in 905, wrested from France the extensive and fertile province of Normandy, and placed their chiefs upon the throne of England; and, in 1080, a colony of these Northmen took possession of Sicily and the southern part of Italy, establishing the kingdom of Naples, under their leader, Roger I.

Prussia, which was peopled by a branch of the Lithuanian race, who, following the course of the Vistula, had settled round its mouth on the borders of the Baltic, maintained till several centuries later its savage independence, idolatry, and primitive manners, though several attempts had been made to convert the inhabitants by the neighbouring states of Germany and Poland. It was conquered in 1230 by the Teutonic knights, who at length compelled them by force to embrace Christianity.

The German empire dates its commencement from the victorious Charlemagne, who, having annexed it to France in the year 800, caused himself to be crowned Emperor of the West at Rome, and added a second head to the eagle which represented the imperial power, to denote that the empires of Rome and Germany were united in him; but his successors inherited neither his political prudence nor military and legislative skill; his dominions were divided by his descendants; and, in 912, the princes and nobles of Germany asserting their independence, their country became separated from that of France under the first native emperor Conrad, whose successors were henceforth elected to fill the throne by a grand confederation of the princes, barons, and knights of the German empire.

The republic of Venice was founded in 803, the city having been built in the fifth century on seventy-two islands in the Adriatic Sea, by a colony of Italians, who, flying from the town of Aquila on the approach of the barbarous hosts of Attila, took refuge on those barren and desert rocks; where their industry and talent erected a rich and beautiful town, and their extensive and enterprising trade, subsequently established the greatest commercial state of the Middle Ages.

The history of Poland, which was peopled by the Sarmatian or Slavonic race, may be included in that of Russia, from the earliest ages to the fourth or fifth century of the Christian era, when it continues very obscure till the conversion of its duke, Mieczyslav I., in 965, on the occasion of his marriage with the daughter of the king of Hungary, a Christian prince; and at that time her sovereigns acknowledged—at least for a part of their lands—the suzerainty of the German empire, and took a part in its wars and diets. A daughter of Mieczyslav married Sweyn, king of Denmark, and was mother of Canute, the Danish conqueror of England; and his successor, Boleslaf, after a long war with the emperor, Henry II. of Germany, for the possession of Bohemia, added Silesia and Moravia to his kingdom, and absolved himself from his feudal obligations to the empire. He assumed the title of king of Poland, and died in 1025.*

At this period the Greek empire, though already a decaying power, was the chief seat of learning and science in Europe, and there the cultivation of the polite arts and literature was sustained, during a period that may well be termed the dark ages in the other nations of the continent; and "it should appear," says Gibbon, "that Russia might have derived an early and rapid improvement from her peculiar connection with the church and state of Constantinople, which in that age so justly despised the ignorance of the Latins. But the Byzantine empire was servile, solitary, and verging to a hasty decline; after the fall of Kiof, the navigation of the Borysthenes, was forgotten; the great princes of Vladimir and Moscow were separated from the sea, and Christendom and the divided monarchy was oppressed by the ignorance and blindness of Tartar servitude."†

* Krasinski's "History of Poland."   † Gibbon's "Decline and Fall of the Roman Empire."

The kingdom of Biarmaland, so celebrated in the sagas, and in all the traditions of the north, during the early middle ages of European history, comprehended the modern provinces of Permia and Archangel, from the banks of the Onega and Duna, to the borders of the gloomy peaks of the Ural chain. This was the country of the Biarmi, visited and described by Ottar, the old Danish captain, to King Alfred, and who, in his voyage along the coast of Scandinavia, examined the distant shores of the White Sea, and found there a peaceful and civilized people, living in well-built villages and cities, and cultivating the ground with industry and success. They appeared to him to speak the same language as the Finns,* who inhabited the north of Sweden, and were a very savage and primitive tribe. At that time, there existed on the Dwina a large commercial town called Sigtem or Birca,† frequented during the summer by traders from Scandinavia, where the Biarmi sold to the northmen, not only peltry, salt, and iron, the produce of their country, but likewise Indian wares, which came to them by caravans through the medium of the Chazars and Bulgarians, and across the Caspian Sea in the barks of the Persians. Tzordyn, or Great Perm, was, according to Strahlenberg, a great mart at that early period, and appears to have been frequented by merchants from Asia and all parts of Eastern Europe. In that region numerous ruins of fortresses and tombs still remain; "and," says Pritchard, "an unquestionable voucher for the real existence of an ancient trade with the east, are the great numbers of eastern coins which have been discovered in tombs, and in other places through the whole extent of this country, from the lakes Ladoga and Onega to the Dwina. These coins, which have been carefully examined by many antiquarians in Germany and in Russia, are pieces of silver money belonging to chaliffs and other eastern princes, who reigned before the year 1000 of the Christian era, and many of them are silver Persian coins of the kind used by the Arabs before the year 695, when the Arabian or Saracen money was first cast. From these facts, M. Frahn and other learned men have inferred that a great traffic was carried on during the middle ages through the eastern parts of Europe,

---

* The Lapps.
† Ad quam stationem (Bircam oppidum Gothorum in medio Sveoniæ positum), quæ tutissima est in maritimis Sveoniæ regionibus, solent Danorum, Slavorum, atque Sembrorum nerves aliique Scythiæ populi pro diversis commerciorum necessitatibus solleniter convenire.—ADAM OF BREMEN.

between the northern coast, then inhabited by Scandinavian and Finnish races, and the countries near the Euxine and the Caspian, which the arts and the refinement of Southern Asia had recently penetrated."*

The Arab writers also speak of a far distant kingdom to the west of the Upper Volga, and three months' journey from the land of the Bulgarians; where the summer had no night and the winter no day, and where the frost was so bitter, that those who came from that country brought with them, even in the summer, a cold severe enough to kill all trees and plants; "for which reason," an old historian observes, "many nations forbid them to enter their territories."†

The celebrated annual fair of Nisni Novogorod‡ is supposed to have been held at Makarief, in the neighbourhood of that town, from whence it has been removed only within the last few years from the most remote times; and it appears probable that merchants from every country of Asia, and even traders from Western Europe, occasionally resorted to barter their wares in its markets; coins of the Saxon kings of England have been found between lake Ladoga and Permia, and many fragments of English pottery have been excavated in the district and government of Orenburg.

In the Scandinavian saga of St. Olaf, there is an account of an expedition undertaken by two sea-kings, Karl and Gunstein, round the North Cape to Biarmaland, on the coast of the White Sea, where, after trading for skins at the mouth of the Dwina, in the town of Birca, near where Archangel now stands, they proceeded after the fair to plunder the temple and idol of Yomala,|| the principal deity of all the Finnish tribes; they took a cup of silver coins that rested on his knee, a gold ornament from round his neck, and then robbed the graves of the chiefs who were interred there of the treasures and jewels which their tombs contained; and, bearing away every article of value, they retired to the protection of their own ships.§ Many similar attempts appear to have been made by the avaricious Northmen to pillage the wealth and

---

* Pritchard's "Natural History of Man."
† Strinnham's "Wikingszüge Staatsverfassung und Sitten des alten Scandinavier."
‡ For an account of this fair, see Hill's "Siberia," Oliphant's "Shores of the Black Sea," Custine's "Histoire de la Russie" and many other works on Russia.
|| According to the annals of the Norsemen, the idol was so studded with jewels that it cast a radiance all around; upon its head was a golden crown set with twelve precious stones, and round its neck a collar which in value amounted to three hundred marks in gold, and a dress which outweighed the lading of three of the richest ships that ever navigated the Grecian seas.
§ Laing's "Sea-kings of Norway."

merchandise that the trade and industry of the Biarmi had accumulated in their towns; and, about the ninth century, the sea-kings formed a settlement on Kolmogri, an island near the mouth of the Dwina, where a monastery was afterwards erected in the thirteenth or fourteenth century by the Novogorodians, when under their general, Stephen, who was subsequently flayed alive by the inhabitants, they conquered and converted the flourishing kingdom of Biarmaland. In the tenth century Eric, the son of Harald Harfaager, king of Norway, sailed with a fleet into the White Sea, and landing on its shores, as the sagas relate, fought many a battle and won many a victory. His son, Harald Greyskin, several years later, also penetrated into the country, burning and destroying all the cultivated fields and villages that lay near his route; and totally defeating the Biarmi, with terrible slaughter, in a great battle on the banks of the Dwina, he withdrew from their land, after spreading waste and desolation far and wide.* A Scandinavian skald of the time, Glurn Giwsen, celebrates this foray in the following song:—

> "I saw the hero Harald chase,
> With bloody sword, Biarme's race;
> They fly before him, through the night,
> All by their burning city's light,
> On Dwina's banks, at Harald's word,
> Across the storm of spear and sword,
> In such a wild war-cruise as this,
> Great would he be who could bring peace." †

According to evidence collected by Muller, the province of Permia was conquered in the twelfth century by the beforementioned St. Stephen Permeki, a Russian of Novogorod, who invented the Permian alphabet, and founded a monastery at the mouth of the river Wym. The people of Permia are described by Everard Ysbrandt Ides,‡ in the account of his journey through Siberia in the year 1692, when he observes that they "speak a language resembling that of the Livonians|| near Germany, for some of his retinue, who understood that tongue, could comprehend a great part of what these people said." He mentions their capital as being a very great city, inhabited by merchants and artificers in silver, copper, and bone, and surrounded by salt-pits; but remarks that the natives of the province do not live in towns, but mostly in small villages built in the woods, and adds that the country terminates in a forest. "The stature and habits

---

* Laing's "Sea-kings of Norway." † Ibid.
‡ He was a Dane, sent by Peter the Great as ambassador to China.
|| The Liefi or Finns, who inhabit the province of Livonia.

of these people," says he, "are not different from those of the Russian peasantry. They all live by agriculture, except those employed in the manufacture of furs. They pay tribute to his czarish majesty, but are under no waywode, choosing judges among themselves. They are all Christians of the Greek Church."*

The most ancient inhabitants of the Crimea of whom we have any record, were the Cimmerians, a Celtic tribe, who, being driven from thence by the Scythians, retired to the Danube; and the latter having been expelled from the north of Persia by Ninus, king of Assyria, took possession of all the country which bears their name. A remnant of the Cimmerians, taking refuge in the mountainous regions of the Crimea, they were afterwards known by the name of Tauri, and to these people are attributed the excavation of the numerous caverns in the rock at Inkerman.† About seventeen hundred years before the Christian era, an Amazonian queen led her warriors beyond the Don, and established in Taurida the worship of Mars and Diana, at whose altars the savage Tauri sacrificed every stranger who landed on their shores, or fell into their hands;‡ and where Iphigenia had been appointed a priestess, when rescued by Orestes and Pylades.|| In the sixth century before Christ, the Greeks formed a colony in the Crimea,§ and built there Panticapœum or Bosphorus, where Kertch now stands, and Theodosia or Kaffa; and the Heracleots of the Euxine, with a colony from Asia Minor, about the same period founded Cherson, the name of the Heracleotic Chersonese, given by the Greeks to the peninsula on which that town was situated, being derived from them. The commerce of the Greek settlers soon became very flourishing; they built cities and temples, and

---

* Pritchard's "Natural History of Man."
† This name is derived from *In*, and *kerman*, a castle.—Renilly's "Travels in the Crimea."
‡ H. D. Seymour, in his "Russia on the Black Sea," &c., considers that the Euxine and the Crimea were the scene of the adventures of Ulysses in the Odyssey, from which he quotes a passage, which he supposes to be a description of the harbour of Balaklava, it being, as he states, a most exact picture:—

"Within a long recess, a bay there lies
Edged round with cliffs, high pointed to the skies.
The jutting shores, that swell on either side,
Contract its mouth, and break the rushing tide.

From thence we climb'd a point, whose airy brow
Commands the prospect of the plains below."
Pope's "Homer's Odyssey," 6. 10, v. 101.

|| See story of "Iphigenia," in the History of Greece.
§ The famous Miltiades, the hero of Marathon, was for some time governor of the Greek colonies in the Crimea, or "Tauric Chersonese."

introduced to the Crimea the arts and civilization of Greece; and at one time, as Demosthenes informs us in his oration against Leptines, Athens annually imported from the Crimea between three hundred thousand and four hundred thousand mediums or bushels of grain. In the year 480 B.C., the Thracians, driving the Scythians from the peninsula of Kertch, established at Bosphorus a monarchical state,* but three hundred years later, a tribe of Sarmatians or Sauremat æ, originally of Media, overran the Crimea, and, in conjunction with the Tauri of the mountains, invaded Bosphorus and Cherson, levying enormous contributions upon the inhabitants. From that time they continually harassed and ravaged these provinces till the year 81 B.C., when the whole of the Crimea was subdued by the arms of the king of Pontus, Mithridates the Great, who established at Panticapœum the capital of his kingdom, and drove the Sauremat æ into Scythia.† About sixteen years after, Mithridates having been defeated by Pompey, after a long war with the Romans, his son Pharnaces rebelled against him, and incited the army to revolt against their sovereign; and the king, finding himself besieged in his capital, put an end to his own life by poison; ‡ while the Romans ceded his territory to Pharnaces, except the town of Fanagoria, which they erected into a republic, as a reward to the citizens for having been the first to desert their unfortunate monarch.‖

About the year A.D. 62, the Alans, a Sarmatic tribe, penetrated into the Crimea, and forced the kings of the Bosphorus to pay them tribute. Their dominion lasted nearly a hundred and fifty years, when they in their turn were supplanted by the Goths, and it was under the rule of the latter people,

* The series of Greek kings of the Bosphorus, from B.C. 480 to B.C. 304, were Archæanactidæ, 480; Spartacus I., 438; Seleucus, 431; a reign of twenty years, but the name of the king unknown; Satyrus I., 407; Leucon, 393; Spartacus II., 353; Parysades, 348; Satyrus II., 310; Eumaius, 309; Spartacus III., 304. They were styled Archæantidæ from the founder of their dynasty, and claimed descent from Neoptolemus, who, on the death of his father Achilles in the Trojan war, is said to have emigrated to these coasts. Demosthenes, in one of his orations, alludes to Theodosia as being then one of the most famous cities in the world; and Leucon, during a scarcity in Greece, sent a hundred thousand mediums of corn as a present to the Athenians.

† Rouilly's "Crimea."

‡ A curious tradition prevails in Sweden, to the effect that Mithridates, instead of committing suicide, as the Roman historians relate, took refuge with his followers in Scandinavia, where, under the name of Odin, his exploits and valour procured for him the adoration of the primitive and savage people among whom he resided; and where, having been long regarded as the chief deity of their mythology, his fame has descended to posterity as their most ancient national hero.

‖ The ruins and tumuli of the Crimea, afford an ample field for the researches and speculations of the antiquarian, and several of the artificial mounds that abound in the vicinity of Kertch have been excavated by the Russian government, and have been found to contain the bodies, ornaments, and trappings, of what are supposed to have been the Scythian and Bosphorean kings, and some appear to have been constructed several hundred years before the Christian era.

during the reigns of Dioclesian and Constantine, that Christianity was introduced into the country, of which they remained in possession longer than any other people; and it retained its name of Gothia for more than a thousand years, almost to the end of the sixteenth century.* Several bishoprics were erected at Cherson, Bosphorus, and among the Goths on the borders of the Black Sea, whose Scythian shores were now crowned with neat and populous villages, surrounded with fertile and well-cultivated fields; but in the year 357, the peaceful and industrious Goths were forced to submit to the overwhelming hordes of the Huns, who burned and destroyed all their corn-fields, orchards, and habitations, and finally drove the whole nation from the steppes of Scythia. They, however, still held their dwellings among the mountains in the Crimea, and in the peninsula of Kertch, together with the remnants of the Alans and Tauri, where they maintained their dynasty of Christian kings; and, being again threatened by the Huns on the death of Attila, they implored the assistance of the Greek emperor, who built walls to protect their country against the nomades of the steppes, and two fortresses at Alouchta and Orsouf, on the southern coast. But in the early part of the fifth century, the kingdom of Bosphorus was entirely abolished, though the mountain Goths retained the fortress of Mangoup Kalé for another thousand years; and in 464 the Crimea was invaded by the Bulgarians, who remained masters of the country till 679, when they were conquered by the Avars and Chazars, who also subdued the Goths of Mangoup Kalé, the Tauri, and the well-fortified and defended Greek towns. The Chazars or Kazars, who were driven by the Huns to the north of the Caucasus, are first described by the Greek writers in 626, when one of their hordes transported their tents from the shores of the Volga to the mountains of Georgia, on the invitation of the Greek emperor Heraclius, to assist him in the war he was carrying on against Persia.† Their territory was frequently

---

* H. D. Seymour's " Russia on the Black Sea," &c.

† " Heraclius received them in the neighbourhood of Tiflis, and the khan and his nobles dismounted from their horses, if we may credit the Greeks, to adore the purple of the Cæsar. Such voluntary homage and important aid were entitled to the warmest acknowledgments; and the emperor, taking off his own diadem, placed it on the head of the Turkish prince, whom he saluted with a tender embrace, and the appellation of son. After a sumptuous banquet he presented Ziebel with the plate and ornaments, the gold, the gems, and the silk, which had been used at the imperial table, and with his own hand distributed rich jewels and earrings to his new allies. In a secret interview, he produced the portrait of his daughter Eudocia, condescended to flatter the barbarian with the promise of a fair and august bride, obtained an immediate succour of forty thousand horse, and negotiated a strong diversion of the Turkish arms on the side of the Oxus.

" Eudocia was afterwards sent to her Turkish husband, but the news of his death stopped her journey."—Gibbon's " Decline and Fall of the Roman Empire."

invaded by the Patzinaks or Petchenegans, another Tartar nation, who, towards the latter end of the ninth century, invaded the Crimea, and afterwards settled down near the mouth of the Dnieper; they carried on an extensive trade and correspondence with Constantinople, and their empire lasted about a hundred and fifty years, when they were attacked and vanquished by the Comans or Polotzi, another Tartar tribe, who took possession of the Crimea, made Soudak (Soldaya) their capital, and forced the Petchenegans to retire to their ancient homes, in the Asiatic deserts. In the southern and mountainous districts of the Crimea, upon an elevated limestone rock, with walls resting on the very edge of the precipice, and overlooking the rich and beautiful valley of Jehosaphat, stands the town or rather fortress of Tchoufut Kalé,* the central position and principal settlement of the Karaite sect of the Jews,† and which is probably the only town in the world which that people can call exclusively their own, and which is ruled and governed by their own municipal laws.‡ According to their own traditions, they entered the Crimea before the Christian era; and, coming from Assyria, where they had been carried in the captivity, all being descended, as they assert, from the tribe of Judah, they selected for their residence the summit of these steep and lofty crags, on account, so their legends affirm, of the resemblance of its situation to that of Jerusalem. They differ from the rest of their nation, by whom they are regarded as heretics and schismatics, in not receiving the doctrines of the Talmud, which was probably composed since their departure from Judæa; and their synagogue at Tchoufut Kalé is supposed to be at least a thousand years old, one of their tombs outside the town bearing the inscription A.D. 640. A few of the same sect still linger around the broken walls of Jerusalem, where they assemble every Friday, to mourn together the departed glory of the ancient city; and a considerable number are scattered among the towns and villages of Russia and Poland, having emigrated to the latter country when the Mongols invaded Taurida,

---

* Oliphant's "Russia and the Black Sea."
† The name is said, by Richter, to be derived from *Kara* and *ite*, words signifying in Arabic, black dog.—Oliphant's "Russian Shores of the Black Sea."
‡ "They enjoyed considerable privileges under the Tartar rule, and were exempted from some contributions that were imposed on the Greeks and Armenians, which, they assert, was on account of services formerly rendered to the Tartar khans; but, according to Peysonnel, a Jewish doctor obtained them for his countrymen as a reward, for curing a princess of the royal family."—H. D. Seymour's "Russia on the Black Sea," &c.

aud deprived them for a time of their rocky and mountainous retreat; but all in every land look to the Crimea, where they are respected even by their Russian masters for their extreme probity and upright dealing, as their proper home, and to the rabbi of Tchoufut Kalé as the highest ecclesiastical authority of their church; and all desire that their remains may lie with those of their forefathers, in the cemetery spreading over the valley beneath its hoary walls.*

In 840, the Emperor Theophilus of Constantinople erected the Crimea into a province under the name of Cherson, and united with it the Greek towns on the Kuban; and in the middle of the tenth century it still remained a part of the Greek empire, and was used as a place of banishment for the political offenders of the state. In the year 842 he built a fortress, and established a trading colony at Sarkel,† on the shores of the Don,‡ which brought Byzantium into connection with the Petchenegans and the kingdom of the Khazars, though the latter had already given an empress to the imperial throne.

* "All devout Karaītes, scattered through the Crimea, when increasing infirmities warn them of approaching dissolution, are brought hither to die."—Oliphant's "Russian Shores of the Black Sea."
† Now Bielaveja, near Tcherkask, the capital of the Don Cossacks.
‡ Finlay's "Byzantine Empire."

CHAPTER VIII.

Sviatozlaf—He subdues the Chazars—Invades the Greek Empire—The principalities—His death.

> To us 'tis equal, all we ask is war
> While yet we talk, or but an instant shun
> The fight, our glorious work remains undone,
> Let every Greek who sees my spear confound.
>
> Full on the Greeks, they drive in firm array.—POPE'S "Homer's Iliad."

In the year 955, before commencing her journey to Constantinople, the Grand Princess Olga formally resigned her throne and government into the hands of her son, Sviatozlaf Igorovitz,* who was at that time about thirty-five years old.

Upon her return to Kiof, after having received baptism at the hands of the Greek patriarch in the cathedral of St. Sophia at Constantinople, she endeavoured by argument and entreaty, assisted by the persuasive eloquence of the Greek priests who accompanied her, to induce her son to follow her example, and renounce the errors of the pagan faith; but though he forbore to persecute all the professors of Christianity, whom, throughout his reign, he allowed freely to practise all the rites and ceremonies of their religion, and confided to his mother the care and education of his children during his numerous military campaigns, all her efforts for his conversion were unavailing; for he remained a firm believer in the idolatry and cruel worship of his country, considering that the Christian religion, which he identified with the splendour and luxury of the Greeks, caused nations and men to become degenerate, cowardly, and effeminate. Contemning and despising all the arts of civilization, and even the common comforts of life, he discouraged and discontinued all the improvements of his mother, and attempted to revive in Russia the savage customs, primitive manners, and wandering, roving habits of his ancestors, the barbarous

---

* *Ovitz* or *ovitch* is the Russian for "son," and it is the custom in Russia for a son always to take his father's name added to his own; *ovna* or *evna* is "daughter," and is added to her father's name by a daughter, as Anna Ivanovna, Anna the daughter of John.

and unsettled Slavonians. Shortly after his accession he abandoned his palace at Kiof, and dismissing his body-guard and personal attendants, formed a large standing army, recruited from among the most savage tribes in his dominions, with whom he encamped upon an open plain outside the capital; and, abolishing all the distinctions of convenience, recognised no other rank than that afforded by superior military skill and valour. Neither huts, nor tents, nor any other covering than the open air, was permitted among his soldiers, who were devotedly attached to their prince, and whose privations and danger he equally shared; at night, wrapped in a bear-skin, with his head resting on his saddle, he always slept upon the bare ground, and never allowed his frugal meals to consist of any other food than a scanty supply of meat, which was often horseflesh broiled or roasted upon the coals, and the coarsest roots or grain. The simple and hardy life, and few requirements to which he accustomed his army, with the strict discipline which he maintained, enabled him to lead his troops to distant countries, and engage with an enemy in the field whose battalions were far more numerous, and whose arms and equipments were far superior to the wooden javelins, bows, and slings, which formed the sole implements of war in use among the Russians; and, unencumbered by baggage, his marches and impetuous attacks surprised the fancied security of his foes before they were aware of the neighbourhood of his troops, or had time to prepare any adequate means of defence.

The nation against which he first turned his arms was the kingdom of the Chazars, on the southern shores of the Volga, who had been lately compelled to relinquish their territory to the north of the Crimea, and at the mouth of the Dnieper, to the restless and unsettled Petchenegan tribes, and whose power was now very inferior to that which it had been when they subjugated Kiof, and threatened the independence of the Greek empire. About the year 963, Sviatozlaf penetrated into their provinces, and, advancing on the plains extending to the north of the Caucasian mountains, he defeated the Chazar armies in a pitched battle, marched upon their capital Belansher, which he took by storm, together with the fort of Belaia Vess, whose defences had been constructed by Greek engineers to form a protection to the wealthy and populous city; and, having besieged and carried Tamartargas, a Chazar town in the modern peninsula of Taman, on the Crimean Bosphorus, which he called Truntoracan, he ultimately compelled the whole kingdom to submit to his arms and acknowledge his authority. He then invaded the Caucasian province of Suania, and took possession of the western Caucasus, which the Russians retained from that time for a hundred and fifty years.

In the year 966, the European provinces of the Byzantine empire being threatened by an invasion of the Hungarians, Nicephorus, the Greek emperor, sent to solicit the assistance of Peter, king of Bulgaria, to prevent their passage of the Danube. Upon the refusal of this prince to agree with the demand, as he had himself lately concluded an alliance with Hungary, Nicephorus sent Kalohyres, the son of the governor of Cherson, as ambassador to Kiof, to propose to Sviatozlaf that the Russians should invade Bulgaria, and, at the same time, the Greek envoy presented the Grand Prince with fifteen hundred pounds of gold to defray the expenses of the expedition. "The high position," says Finlay, in his Byzantine empire, "occupied by the court of Kiof in the tenth century, is attested by the style with which it was addressed by the court of Constantinople. The golden bulls of the Roman emperor of the East, addressed to the Prince of Russia, were ornamented with a pendant seal equal in size to a double solidus, like those addressed to the kings of France."

But Kalohyres, on his arrival at Kiof, turned traitor to his sovereign, and, proclaiming himself emperor, negotiated for the support of the Russians in obtaining his own elevation to the throne of Byzantium. Sviatozlaf eagerly accepted the proposal, and, promptly availing himself of the opportunity thus offered of approaching a step nearer to Constantinople, the ultimate object of his ambition, led an army across the flat and marshy fields of Wallachia to the banks of the Danube, whose pestilential shores, nearly nine hundred years later, proved so fatal to the invading forces of Russia. He crossed the river in 968, and defeated the Bulgarians in a furious engagement; and the king dying shortly after, he possessed himself of Presthlava, the capital, and ultimately rendered himself master of the whole kingdom. But he was soon forced to abandon his new conquest, by the receipt of alarming intelligence from Kiof. The Petchenegans, taking advantage of the absence of the Grand Prince with nearly the whole army, to revenge themselves on the Russians for the losses they had formerly sustained from them, had advanced upon Kiof in great force after desolating the surrounding country; and, laying siege to the capital where the Grand Princess Olga and the sons of Sviatozlaf were residing, it was soon involved in all the miseries of famine. But their triumph was not of long duration; for Pritich, a Russian general, collecting a brave, though small and undisciplined band of his scattered countrymen, marched speedily to the succour of the city, and, arriving on the opposite bank of the Dnieper, crossed the river in the night. He then instructed his soldiers to fill the air with their shouts, and the sound of their trumpets; on hearing which the enemy was seized with alarm, and a rumour circulating in their camp, that Sviatozlaf with his victorious army had approached from the Danube, the invaders all fled precipitately from before the town, which was entered and relieved by Pritich. He shortly afterwards had an interview with Kour, the prince of the Petchenegans, when a mutual exchange of courtesies ensued; and, as proofs of their future peace and friendship, the Russian general presented the prince with a shield, cuirass, and sword, and received from him in return a horse, sabre, and a quiver of arrows; but the Petchenegans had hardly effected their retreat from the province of Kiof, before the arrival of Sviatozlaf with his whole army, who, on receiving intelligence of the dangers by which his capital was threatened, had immediately evacuated Bulgaria, and hastened to its relief. He followed the Petchenegans, and attacked and routed their army; after which he made a treaty with the remainder, and allowed them to return in safety to their own land.*

On the restoration of peace, Sviatozlaf remained for some time at Kiof. His mother urgently entreated him to abandon the Bulgarian war, and he consented to remain in his own empire during the rest of her life. "See," said he, "the extent of my power and dominions. This is my capital, to which from Hungary I bring iron and horses, from Constantinople silk and gold, from Asia swords and jewels, and from Russia honey and slaves. What more can I require?" "Then," said she, "I am content to die, bury me wherever thou wilt;" and, three days after, she expired. In the

* Karamsin's "History of Russia."

meanwhile, the Emperor Nicephorus had concluded an alliance with Bulgaria, and assisted Boris and Romanus, the sons of Peter, to recover their father's throne; but a few months later he was himself assassinated in his palace at Constantinople, by his nephew and general, John Zimisces, who immediately assumed the imperial crown.* The second, and most formidable invasion of Sviatozlaf took place soon after the accession of this prince. He divided his dominions between his three sons, Yaropolk, Oleg, and Vladimir,† and again marched southwards with an army of Russians, Chazars, and Croats, in all amounting to forty thousand men, and, entering Bulgaria about the year 970, advanced upon the city of Presthlava or Marcianopolis. He took it after a desperate siege, having been several times repulsed from its walls by the inhabitants, both sides engaging with the most reckless courage, and made the king of Bulgaria and his family prisoners, though Boris shortly after died in captivity.

Moldavia, Wallachia, and Bulgaria, "the principalities," of diplomatic language, have formed for ages the battle-field and theatre of contention for all the nations who have alternately ruled in Constantinople, and the restless and warlike tribes of the north. The Scythians and Macedonians, the Sarmatians and Romans, the Slavonians and Greeks, the Russians and Turks, have all at different times crossed the waters of the Danube, and fought for an empire upon its shores; for the rich city of the Bosphorus has formed the splendid goal to the ambition and victories of every conqueror in Western Asia during the last thousand years, and their inroads upon her territories and incessant wars, greatly contributed to the fall of the eastern throne of the Cæsars, when she succumbed at length before the persevering and untiring efforts of the Ottoman sultan, Mahomet. These provinces, which were known as Dacia to the Romans, and where they planted a colony, and jealously banished some of their most learned and virtuous men, originally formed a part of the kingdom of Macedonia, and coins have been excavated of as early a period as the reigns of the pre-

---

* Finlay's "Byzantine Empire."
† In Russian this name is commenced by a letter resembling our b, and taking the third place in their alphabet; but which is pronounced like our v, or the German w. The same occurs in Azov, Moscow, Oczahov, Rostov, words which in English are frequently but erroneously spelt with a w.—See Major's note to "Herberstein's *Rerum Muscovitorum.*"

decessors of Alexander the Great. Very little is known respecting Dacia till the time of its conquest by the Romans, whose invasion, according to Strabo, was opposed by the inhabitants with an army of two hundred thousand men. They at length yielded to the generals of Tiberius and Trajan; and constructed a stone bridge of more than five hundred fathoms over the Danube, though, on account of an inroad of the Sarmatians, it was destroyed by his successor, Hadrian. On the decline of the Roman power, Dacia was overrun by the Slavonians and Black Bulgarians, or Huns; and while the latter formed the kingdom to the south of the Danube, known by their name, and preserved till the Turkish conquest in the fifteenth century a nominal independence; Moldavia and Wallachia became united to Hungary, whose princes long took the title of Kings of Hungary, Wallachia, and Cumania, the latter name having been applied to Moldavia from the Polotzi or Cumans, who took refuge in this province when driven from Russia by the arms of the Mongul Zingis. These provinces at length solicited the assistance of the Ottoman Turks, who, expelling the Hungarians, have ever since ruled the country, though the inhabitants retained, till the beginning of the eighteenth century, the privilege of electing their own hospodars or chiefs. On being then deprived of this right, the office was held out for sale to the highest bidder, and has generally been filled by Greeks; and, during eighty years, from the middle of the last to the commencement of the present century, sixty of these princes have been deposed, and twenty-five suffered death by order of the * Porte. Such a government was not calculated to form either a great or civilized nation; and in consequence, while their country abounds in mineral wealth, and its soil produces in abundance, corn, fruits, and timber, with pasture, feeding thousands of cattle; these provinces have long been plunged in the lowest depths of degradation, the oppression of the foreign rulers and invaders upon the nobles has been reciprocated by the latter upon the unfortunate peasantry, who, holding their lives, liberties, and possessions at the mercy of an enslaved nobility, or of fierce and cruel intruders, have been long sunk in miserable poverty and the grossest ignorance and apathy. Contenting themselves with wretched underground hovels, rags, and almost the spontaneous produce

* Campenhausen's "Travels in Moldavia, Wallachia," &c.

of their fields, which they scarcely scratch with the same rude wooden plough that served their predecessors, the ancient Dacians; they care neither to plant nor labour merely to enrich their masters, or feed foreign soldiers; yet they still proudly claim their descent from the Roman colonists, and their uncultivated dialect still recalls the classic language of ancient Rome.

At the time of the invasion of Sviatozlaf, the new emperor, John Zimisces, was engaged in quelling some internal disturbances in the eastern provinces of his empire, and the Russians crossed the Balkan with little opposition, and besieged and captured Philopolis. There they received an embassy from Zimisces, offering terms of peace, and demanding their evacuation of Roumania; but the Grand Prince sent word in reply, that Constantinople might soon expect the presence of an enemy and a master. "We will never," said he, "quit so fine a country till you have ransomed your towns and your prisoners that are now in our power. Greeks! if you refuse these terms and will not pay, leave Europe and retire into Asia: you are women, we are men of blood."* At the same time he obtained the admiration of his enemies, by refusing all the gold, silver, and other gifts which were offered him by the nobles of the empire on his progress, who desired to conciliate the barbarians; and they declared that this was the kind of king they should wish to serve—one who preferred arms to gold, as he accepted no other present or ransom than arms or weapons of war, which, constructed of well-wrought iron by the skilful Greeks, were far more formidable than the wooden shafts and javelins, which, with a shirt of hemp chain, arrows, and leathern shields, were the sole equipments of his own soldiers and Asiatic allies.

On receiving the menace of the Russian chief, the emperor, in the following spring, 971, took the field at the head of an army of fifteen thousand infantry, and thirteen thousand cavalry, besides a body guard of chosen troops, called the Immortals, and a powerful battery of field and siege engines. He also despatched a fleet of three hundred galleys, with many smaller vessels, up the Danube, to cut off the communication of the Russians with their own country, and, marching from Adrianople, crossed the Balkan or Hæmus. In the meanwhile the Russian army had advanced to Arcadiepolis,

* Rabbe's "History of Russia."

where one of their divisions, being surprised and defeated by the Greek general, Bardas Shleros, the remainder again returned to Bulgaria, and, on the approach of the emperor, those troops who were stationed at Presthlava left the city, and encountered his forces in the open plain.* After a vigorous resistance, the Russians were completely defeated by Zimisces, and left eight thousand five hundred of their men among the dead; and a battalion which was intrenched in the neighbourhood of Silistria, perceiving that they were surrounded and hemmed in by the enemy's cavalry, slew themselves with their own swords rather than fall by the hands of their foes. "They believe," says Leo the deacon, "that he who is slain in battle will in the next world be the slave of the man who kills him; therefore they stab themselves when they have no hope of flight or victory, and die persuaded that they will at least preserve their freedom in a future state."† Two days after, Presthlava was stormed and taken by the Greeks, who, setting fire to the royal palace, which was fortified as a citadel, eight thousand Russians who defended it perished in the flames, and the remainder of the garrison, consisting of five hundred soldiers, were all put to the sword. The traitor, Kalohyres, had succeeded in escaping to Dorystolar, or Drissa, where Sviatozlaf had intrenched himself with the other half of his troops, and Zimisces, after celebrating Easter in Presthlava, and restoring the sons of Boris to the Bulgarian throne, followed the Grand Prince, and blockaded Drissa both by land and water, fortifying his own encampment with a strong rampart and ditch. Several desperate sallies were attempted by the garrison, headed by Sviatozlaf in person: their sufferings became extreme from famine, and at length, after a siege of sixty-five days, the Russian chief made one more attempt to cut a passage for himself and his soldiers through the enemy's troops. But his infantry, greatly reduced by privation, was no match for the steel armour-clad cavalry of the Greeks, who were greatly assisted by the numerous archers and slingers they had stationed under cover in every part of the camp, and who picked off the Russians whenever a missile could be discharged without danger to their own side. Nevertheless, the battle continued all the day, and the Russians fought so valiantly that contemporaries ascribe the victory of the emperor's army to

* Finlay's "Byzantine Empire." † Rabbe's "History of Russia."

the personal assistance of St. Theodore, who they affirm led the famous charge of the Greeks, that at length broke the Russian phalanx, and proved the superiority of the Christian soldiers over the forces of pagan barbarians.*

The morning after this defeat, Sviatozlaf sent an ambassador to the Grecian camp offering terms of peace. The liberal conditions that he obtained, prove that Zimisces considered it imprudent to drive him to extremity or despair, and was aware that, if he insisted upon the Russians laying down their arms, it would only lead to their destruction of Drissa, or a protracted siege and fresh bloodshed. The emperor was contented with the resignation of all their plunder, slaves, and prisoners, and the most solemn assurances on the part of the Grand Prince to relinquish for ever all hostile designs against the Grecian empire, or its colonies in Georgia and Cherson; and he agreed to allow the Russians to descend the Danube in their boats, renewing the treaty previously formed, for the regulation of the trade and naval communication between their respective empires.† At the same time he distributed a measure of corn to each of the Russian soldiers, whom the disasters of the campaign had reduced to less than one half of their original force; and this peace being concluded in July, 971, it was arranged that the following day an interview should take place between the two opponents.‡ Attended by a large body of guards on horseback, the emperor rode down to the banks of the Danube, clothed in glittering armour and on a splendid horse, and meeting Sviatozlaf, who arrived by water in a boat which he steered himself with an oar, they conversed for some time, while Zimisces remained mounted on the beach, and the Grand Prince, who had approached the shore, continued sitting in the stern of his bark. The Greeks all crowded round to view the Russian chief, and he is described by Leo the deacon, who was acquainted with many of those who were present, as being of the middle stature, well formed, with a broad chest. His eyes were small, and almost eclipsed by his thick and shaggy brows, his nose flat, and he had no beard, but long and thick mustaches. His hair was cut close to his head except two long locks in front; in his ears he wore gold ear-rings, ornamented with a ruby between two

---

* Finlay's "Byzantine Empire."
† Gibbon's "Decline and Fall of the Roman Empire."
‡ Finlay's "Byzantine Empire."

pearls, and his expression, says the imperial historian, was haughty, stern, and fierce.*

Immediately after this interview, the Grand Prince of Russia quitted Drissa with his diminished army, and Zimisces placed a strong garrison in the city, and ultimately reduced the whole of Bulgaria, which had revolted against the Greeks.

The Russians embarked upon their fragile barks, and set sail towards the mouth of the Dnieper; but, disappointed and frustrated of their once brilliant hopes of conquest, few among them were destined to see again the steppes of their native land. The weather was stormy, and the wind unfavourable to their progress; their vessels were tossed on the rough waves of the Euxine, and a passage which was usually made in a few days, now occupied many weeks. At length, after a long and perilous voyage, Sviatozlaf reached the mouth of the Dnieper with the remnant of his army; but the winter had set in with unusual rigour, and they were forced to pass several dreary months upon the ice. Their provisions being exhausted, they suffered the greatest misery from famine, and a considerable number of the Russians perished before they were enabled to proceed on their journey. But their misfortunes were not yet concluded; for, on the return of spring, the Grand Prince having embarked with his remaining followers upon the river, the Petchenegans with the neighbouring tribes, who maintained a constant correspondence with the Greeks, and by whom they were probably instigated to cut off his retreat, and prevent his return to Kiof, assembled in great numbers near the cataracts of the river, to dispute the progress of the Russians. The numbers and ferocious appearance of their assailants, for the first moment struck terror into the hearts of the dispirited and half-starved followers of Sviatozlaf; and their prince, seeing the panic which was spreading through his troops, mounted the prow of his vessel and thus addressed his little fleet, as their eyes wandered in vain along the banks, in search of some more secure spot to disembark :—" Since, O Russians! I see no place in which we can retreat with safety, and as at the same time it has never entered into my thoughts to surrender the soil of Russia to our enemies, I am resolved either to die or win renown, by fighting bravely against them; for, if we die fighting bravely, our names will be immortal,

* Finlay's "Byzantine Empire."

whereas, if we flee, we shall carry with us eternal disgrace. And since it is not possible for one who is surrounded by a host of enemies to escape, it is my intention to stand firmly, and at all risks to expose myself in the foremost rank for the sake of my country." The Russians, re-animated by the determination of their leader, replied to this speech—"Wherever thou leadest we will follow," and accompanying Sviatozlaf, as he leaped upon the shore, rushed with a furious onslaught through the ranks of the enemy; but, in an attempt to cut a passage for his army, the Grand Prince was struck down by a blow on the head with a javelin, and instantly killed, his body being seized and borne off in triumph by the foe. At the fall of their once dreaded and formidable opponent, all the Petchenegans uttered loud shouts of joy; and their prince caused the skull of the Russian chief to be formed into a drinking-cup, and encircled with gold, an inscription being placed upon it to this effect—"In the attempt to seize the property of others thou didst lose thine own."

CHAPTER IX.

Vladimir the Great*—The Russians are converted to Christianity.

> "A mighty king
> Of ancient days."—BRADSTREET.

A FEW of the followers of Sviatozlaf, under Svenald, an old and highly esteemed chief in the Grand Prince's army, escaping from the swords of the Petchenegans, made their way to Kiof, and entered into the service of Yarapolk, the eldest son of Sviatozlaf, who, at the time of his father's death, in 972, was twenty-seven years of age.

This preference, and the influence which he allowed his boyards,† and especially Svenald, to exercise over him, excited the jealousy and animosity of his brother Oleg, the second son of Sviatozlaf, and prince of the Drevlians; and this chief meeting Lutas, the son of Svenald, while engaged in hunting, suddenly attacked, and, without any further provocation, assassinated him. The indignant father, desiring to revenge himself upon the murderer, appealed for justice to Yarapolk, and entreated him to declare war against his brother and invade his territories; and the prince, yielding

---

* EUROPEAN SOVEREIGNS CONTEMPORARY WITH VLADIMIR THE GREAT.

EASTERN OR GREEK EMPIRE.	POLAND.	SPAIN.
976. Bazil II. and Constantine IX.	Nucislaf.	Ramiro III.
1025. Constantine alone.	999. Bulcslaf I.	982. Varemund II.
		999. Alphouse V.
GERMAN EMPIRE.	HUNGARY.	
973. Otho II.	997. Stephen.	POPES.
983. Otho III.		Boniface VII.
1002. Henry II.	SWEDEN.	984. John XIV.
	994. Olaf.	985. John XV.
ENGLAND.		986. John XVI.
974. Edward the Martyr.	DENMARK.	996. Gregory V.
979. Ethelred the Unready.	980. Sweyn.	999. Silvester II.
	1014. Canute the Great.	1003. John XVII.
FRANCE.		1004. John XVIII.
Lothaire III.	SCOTLAND.	1009. Sergius VI.
986. Louis de Fainéant.	Kenneth III.	1012. Benedict VIII.
987. Hugh Capet.	994. Constantine IV.	
996. Robert.	996. Grimus.	
	1004. Malcolm II.	

† Boyard is an old Slavonic word, still used when speaking of the Russian nobility; it is mentioned in the Byzantine annals as early as A.D. 764.

to the demand of his favourite, immediately marched an army from Kiof. Oleg advanced in person to meet the enemy; but, after a fierce battle, his forces were compelled to fly in confusion, and a bridge, across which he and his fugitive troops were retreating, breaking down, he was drowned in the river, borne under by the multitude of horses and soldiers who shared his fate. Yarapolk was overwhelmed with remorse upon hearing of this catastrophe, and, finding the body of his brother among the slain, gazed upon the ghastly countenance, exclaiming, "O Svenald, behold the accomplishment of thy desire!" and then with his own hands buried him. After the death of their prince, the whole of the province submitted to the army of Kiof without resistance; and shortly after, by the advice of his chiefs and courtiers, who completely ruled him, Yarapolk was induced to seize upon Novogorod, the possession of his youngest brother, Vladimir, and, during his temporary absence in Scandinavia, dividing the province among the boyards who had assisted him with their arms and followers.

As soon as he had assembled a small band of Varangians* to assist him in the recapture of his territories, Vladimir returned to Russia, and, entering Novogorod with his little army, was received with the greatest joy by the people, and immediately re-established by them upon his throne, without striking a blow. The usurping chiefs, having been surprised in their palaces before they were prepared with any resistance, were dismissed by the prince with a message to Yarapolk, informing him that, as he had crossed the frontiers of their dominions for hostile purposes, he might expect a visit in return from the troops of Novogorod. A fresh cause for contention soon arose between them; for Vladimir, demanding in marriage Rogueda, the daughter of the Prince of Polotzk, a small state on the Dwina, his brother at the same time became a suitor for the hand of the princess. Her father, Rogvoloda, fearful of giving offence to either of the two princes, desired his daughter to decide which of the two she would accept for a husband. She made choice of Yarapolk, objecting to Vladimir on account of his mother having been a slave, which so enraged him that he invaded Polotzk, defeated Rogvoloda in battle, and, taking him and his two sons prisoners, put them to death with his own hands, and

* Swedes or Northmen.

forced the princess to become his wife; then, turning his arms against Kiof, with a large force he marched against his brother's capital. In this emergency, Yarapolk appealed for advice and assistance to one of his chiefs, called Blude, in whose judgment and fidelity he placed great reliance, and on whom he had bestowed the highest honours; but this man, being secretly in alliance and correspondence with Vladimir, from whom he had received large bribes to bind him to his interests, advised his master to fly from the city, instead of attempting to hold it against the enemy, which its strong fortifications might have enabled him to do; and then sent information to Vladimir of the various places of refuge in which Yarapolk had vainly endeavoured to find a shelter. The miserable prince wandered from place to place, being continually traced and followed by his vindictive foe, till at length starvation, and the inclemency of the weather, induced him to determine to throw himself on his brother's mercy; but, as he was advancing with that intention, he was encountered at the entrance of Kiof by some of the Varangians who had been searching for him, with strict orders from Vladimir to allow him neither escape nor pardon; and these slew him with their battle-axes in the very sight of his brother, as he looked down upon the scene from a tower over the gate.

Vladimir Sviatozlafovitz was born in Kiof, A.D. 948, and, on the partition of his father's domains, received for his share, at the request of the inhabitants (his mother, Malusha, one of the ladies of Olga, having been a Novogorodian), the city and principality of Novogorod. According to one of the Russian chronicles, after having obtained possession of the whole empire by the murder of his brother, he took the title of Czar,* though it appears to have been not generally

---

* According to Karamsin, the title of Czar was used in Russia as early as the reign of Iziaslaf II. and Dmétri Dooskoi, (1363—1369.) "This word," says he, "is not a corruption of the Latin Cæsar, as some have supposed, but is an Eastern word which the Russians acquired through the Slavonic translation of the Bible, and was bestowed by them, first on the Greek emperors, and afterwards on the Tartar khans. In Persia it signifies 'a throne,' 'supreme authority,' and we find it in the termination of the names of the kings of Assyria and Babylon, as in Phalasaar, Nabonassar, &c. Ivan III. (1462—1472.) was the first grand prince who took the title of Czar, in writing to foreign powers, and in his public acts; he gave to his empire the name of White Russia, that is to say, great, or ancient, according to the acceptation of this word in Oriental languages."— KARAMSIN, vi. 438.

Von Hammer, in one of his notes, says, "The title Czar, or Tzar, is an ancient title of Asiatic sovereigns. We find an instance of it in the title 'the Schar' of Gurdistan, and in that of Tzarina of the Scythians." Some authors think it is the same as *chagan*, or *khan*, from which they also derive the word *kueg*, or *kniag*, the Russian for prince, and that the ancient Scythian kings and the early grand dukes of Russia, were known by that title.

"Sic unus (Vladimir) rerum Russiæ potitus auxit eo titulo Tzaris et magni ducis atque autocratoris Russorum, sedemque ducatûs Novogordiensis Kioviam transtulit."
MS. quoted in the Notes to French translation of Nestor.

assumed by his successors till the fifteenth century, and having adopted the infant son of Yarapolk, who was born after the death of his father, as his own child, he compelled his brother's widow to become his wife. She had belonged to a noble Grecian family in the Eastern empire, and, though celebrated equally for her beauty and accomplishments, had been early devoted to the cloister; but her convent having been desecrated and plundered by the army of Sviatozlaf, she was taken prisoner by that prince, and sent to Kiof, where she afterwards became the wife of his eldest son, for whom she now exchanged the fierce and cruel Vladimir. He shortly afterwards caused Blude, the noble who had acted so treacherously towards Yarapolk, to be put to death, after entertaining him for three days at his palace, and treating him with the greatest honour and magnificence, as a reward for his services to himself; though, as a judge, he affirmed that he was bound to punish the betrayer and deceiver of his prince.

Although, before the conversion of the Russians to Christianity, a plurality of wives was common among them, yet the second marriage of Vladimir roused the jealousy and indignation of Rogueda, the princess of Polotzk, more than even the murder of her father and two brothers appears to have done; and she so strongly expressed her resentment, that he expelled her from the palace, and obliged her to reside in a solitary dwelling, near the capital, where he occasionally visited her.

Here she brooded over her wrongs, till she came to the determination to revenge them, whenever a favourable opportunity should occur, by taking away her husband's life; and, entering his chamber one night while he was sleeping, she seized a dagger from his side, and was about to plunge it into his heart, when, suddenly awakening, he arrested her arm, and would have put her to instant death had not their child rushed in between them, and entreated Vladimir to spare his mother's life. His intercession was successful, for the prince, embracing his child, left the house, and afterwards bestowed upon Rogueda the principality over which her father had formerly ruled.*

The Varaugians, who had assisted Vladimir in recovering

* Karamsin's "History of Russia."

his throne and deposing his brother, and who now formed his guard and personal retinue, became clamorous in their demands for a large and sufficient recompense for the valuable services they had performed. They requested that the whole of the province of Kiof might be divided among them; and Vladimir, finding that his riches were quite insufficient to satisfy their avarice and silence their importunity, and being anxious to rid himself of these troublesome and overbearing allies, advised them to seek, not a more grateful, but a more wealthy master, and transfer their services to the emperor of Constantinople, where, instead of furs and skins, silk and gold would be the reward of their fidelity. "At the same time," says Gibbon, "the Russian prince admonished his Byzantine ally to disperse and employ, to recompense and restrain, these impetuous children of the north. Contemporary writers have recorded the introduction, name, and character of the Varangians; each day they rose in confidence and esteem; the whole body was assembled at Constantinople to perform the duty of guards, and they preserved till the last age of the empire the character of spotless loyalty, and the use of the Danish or English tongue. With their broad and double-edged battle-axes on their shoulders, they attended the Greek emperors to the temple, the senate, and the hippodrome; he slept and feasted under their trusty guard; and the keys of the palace, the treasury, and the capital, were held by the firm and faithful hands of the Varangians; their strength being recruited by a numerous band of their countrymen from England and the Scandinavian countries."*

During the early part of the reign of Vladimir, Eric, the son of Harald, king of Norway, fitted out a fleet and army, and, sailing up the Baltic and the Gulf of Finland, landed near the spot where St. Petersburg now stands, and advancing on the town of Aldeigiaburg,† on lake Ladoga, laid waste all the country on his route, plundering and slaying the inhabitants and burning their dwellings. He besieged and captured the town, which he destroyed with its castle by fire, spreading desolation over all the country round; and occupying

---

* Gibbon's "Decline and Fall of the Roman Empire."
† This town is supposed to be the same as Notaburg, now Schusselburg, which is on an island formed by the Neva and the lake.

altogether five years in this foray, which is thus mentioned in the Norwegian *Banda drapa.**

> " The generous Earl, brave and bold,
> Who scatters his bright shining gold,
> Eric, with fire-scattering hand,
> Wasted the Russian monarch's land.
> With arrow shower, and storm of war,
> Wasted the land of Waldemar;
> Aldeigia burns, and Eric's might
> Scours, through all Russia by its light."

In 982, the Bulgarians from the Volga invaded Russia, but were defeated, and forced to retreat; and, the following year, having also subdued the Yatvagers, a Finnish tribe, who up to this period had remained unconquered and independent of Russia, the Grand Prince upon his return to Kiof proclaimed a religious festival in honour of the gods, to show his gratitude for his various successes; and, according to the prevailing customs upon such occasions, lots were cast among the people for the choice of a human victim, to be offered up as a sacrifice to Peroun, the god of thunder, in the sacred fire that was kept perpetually burning before his decorated shrine.† The proclamation was received with enthusiasm by the people, and great preparations were made for the ceremony; but the lot falling upon a young Christian named Ivan, whose father Fedor had come from Constantinople and settled in Kiof, and the latter refusing to deliver up his son as the victim to their mistaken zeal, the people assembled in crowds round his house, which they attacked and destroyed, the two Varangians perishing amidst the ruins.‡ These, however, according to the Russian historians, were the only Christians who suffered persecution for their faith during the reign of Vladimir, though at this period he was zealous in erecting statues and altars to the pagan deities of his country, and exhausted the riches of his palace, and those which he had acquired in his foreign wars, by multiplying and adorning their temples and images. Rumours of his treasures and munificence, the strength of his army, the number of his guards, and his military exploits, spread among other nations beyond the borders of Russia; and several European and Asiatic sovereigns sent ambassadors to his court to obtain the security

---

* Laing's " Sea-kings of Norway."
† Peroun's body was of wood, his head of silver, and ears and mustaches of gold, his legs of iron, and in his hand he grasped a thunderbolt adorned with jaspers.
‡ MS. of the late Baron Rosenkampf, quoted by Blackmore.

and assistance of his alliance and friendship. But, about this time, misgivings began to fill the mind of Vladimir concerning the truth of the pagan worship of his country; and, on his making inquiries of the foreign envoys respecting the various religious creeds which they professed, the surrounding states became ambitious of the honour of converting so celebrated and powerful a heathen; and, anxious to propagate that religion which they considered the truth in the extensive empire of the Czar, they accordingly sent their most learned doctors to point out to Vladimir the excellence and superiority of their faith. The first ambassadors were from Great Bulgaria on the Volga, whose people had been lately converted to Mahometanism, but their arguments were without success; and he also rejected the Latin Church, which was represented by a deputation from Germany, as he did not choose to own the domination of the Roman pontiff. After listening to the reasoning of some Chazarian Jews, he inquired from them where their country lay, when the chief of the embassy replied—"At Jerusalem, but God in his anger has dispersed us through the earth." "What," said Vladimir, "do you, who are the cursed of God, pretend to teach others? away, we have no wish to be without a country, as you are." At length a Greek philosopher presented himself before the Czar, and endeavoured to explain the Old and New Testament, relating to him the principal events which they contain, and drawing a forcible picture of the last judgment, in which he attempted to represent, in glowing colours and striking language, the subsequent happiness of the blessed, and the punishment and extreme wretchedness of the wicked. Impressed with this description, the prince exclaimed—"What bliss for the good, and misery for the wicked!" "Be baptized," replied the Greek, "and heaven will be your inheritance." Vladimir dismissed him with valuable gifts, but he still hesitated before he made his final choice, and sent emissaries to Bulgaria, Germany, and Byzantium, to make observations on each religion, on the spot where it was professed. The wretched mosques of Bulgaria, and the rough and unadorned wooden churches of Germany, with their ignorant and unpolished people, appeared an unfavourable contrast to the splendour and magnificence of the Greeks,* whose lofty and decorated temples, and brilliant

---

* Karamsin's "History of Russia."

services, performed by richly clothed priests, and accompanied by the beautiful music of the choristers, dazzled and enchanted the commissioners from the north ; and, on their return to their own land, they made their report before the assembly of boyards and elders at Kiof. The assistance of this council had been required by Vladimir, to aid him in so important a selection, and they declared to the Czar, that "if the Greek religion had been a bad one, the Princess Olga, who was the wisest of mortals, would not have embraced it." This argument, and the reports and description which the Russian envoys brought him of Constantinople, entirely satisfied him, and he resolved that henceforward the faith of Byzantium should be the religion of his empire ;* but, too proud to receive baptism from the humble priests already established at Kiof, or any other than one of the highest dignitaries of the Christian Church, and not willing to solicit from the Greek emperors the favour of bishops or missionaries to convert his people ; in order to obtain a sufficient number of priests to spread over the whole country, in 987 he led an army into the Crimea, and laid siege to the wealthy and populous city of Cherson, on the small peninsula known to the Greeks as the Heracleotic Chersonesus, not far from the present site of Sebastopol. The territory upon which Cherson stood, was divided off from the rest of the Crimea by a wall five miles long, extending from the Tchernaya Retchka to Balaklava, and the whole of this enclosure was occupied by the gardens and villas of the inhabitants of the town, whose security was provided for on the land side by a wall nearly two miles in length, built of limestone, five or six feet thick, its massive strength being further increased by three towers, of which the largest, with a guard-house belonging to it, defended the principal gate.† The city was blockaded for twelve months by the Russian prince, who failed in several attempts to take it by storm, when a treacherous Greek, named Athanasius, shot an arrow into his camp with an inscription upon it bearing this advice :—" Thou canst stop or turn aside the source of the springs which are behind thee towards the east ; it is thence that the waters of the town are brought to us." He immediately took advantage of this

---

* Karamsin's " History of Russia."
† H. D. Seymour's " Russia on the Black Sea," &c.

information, and, by cutting off the aqueduct which supplied the town with water, in a few days compelled the citizens to surrender, and open their gates to his army.* He then proposed to treat of peace with the emperors Basil and Constantine, who reigned jointly at Constantinople, and offered to restore the town of Cherson, and also to assist the Greek monarchs in quelling a rebellion in their dominions, on the condition of receiving from the Byzantine princes the hand of their sister Anna in marriage; but threatening to carry his arms against the very walls of the Greek capital, if his terms were not immediately complied with. At the same time he caused the brazen gates and city bell of Cherson to be transported to Novogorod as a trophy of his victory, and erected before the first Christian church in that city, where the former, in the edifice of St. Sophia, still remain ;† though, according to some authors, the original brass was afterwards carried by Boleslaf II. of Poland to Grodno, and placed in that cathedral. It was not the first time that a Byzantine Cæsar had purchased a disgraceful peace by giving a sister or a daughter in marriage to a victorious chief, whom they disdainfully regarded as a mere ignorant barbarian; and, after some hesitation on the part of the Greek emperor, their fear of the vengeance of Vladimir prevailed over the prayers and entreaties of their sister, who was only induced to consent to become the wife of the Russian prince, through the influence of the artful and politic priests, who persuaded her that, by thus devoting herself to her country and religion, she would undoubtedly ensure the eternal salvation of her soul. Accordingly, the court of Byzantium agreed to the proposals of the Czar, and condemned the unhappy Anna to pass the remainder of her life in the rigorous climate of the north, far from the arts and refinements of her own gay and frivolous land; and the princess, bidding a mournful farewell to the pleasures and palaces of Constantinople, quitted for ever her native city, and, accompanied by a body of ecclesiastics, sailed to Cherson. In the cathedral of this place, on the same day that Vladimir was baptized, receiving the name of Bazil, with his twelve sons, and all the generals and boyards in his army, his marriage with the proud daughter of Constantinople

---

* "Chronicles of Nestor."
† Herbertstein's "Rerum Muscovitorum."

was celebrated by the Archbishop of Cherson,* and before the ceremony he formally repudiated the six wives and eight hundred concubines† he had till then possessed. He then returned to Kiof, having previously erected a church to St. Bazil ‡ in Cherson, in honour of his patron saint, and in remembrance of his conversion; bringing with him his wife, and all the priests of Cherson, including the archbishop of that city, and a priest called Michael, a Syrian by birth, whom, some authors relate, was the bishop of Kiof in the time of Oskold, and whom he had appointed metropolitan of Russia; and the six prelates who had accompanied the Greek princess from Constantinople. He caused also to be conveyed to his own capital the relics of St. Clement and St. Phira, with many images of saints, and books of religion that he had captured in the Crimea,‖ two images of brass, and four iron horses; and commanded the wooden statue of Peroun to be dragged by twelve soldiers through the streets of Kiof, and, after being battered by clubs, to be cast into the Dnieper; at the same time proclaiming, that all who should refuse to receive the rite of baptism should be treated as the enemies of God and their prince. §

It was unnecessary to compel the Russians to obedience by any more rigorous measures; for, supposing that that religion

---

* There remained till within the last few years extensive ruins of this city, but many of its stones were employed to construct the modern Sebastopol, and it suffered still further devastation in the late war, when the French converted them, with the fragments of a church, into batteries. They discovered the remains of a tower among the rubbish, upon which was an inscription, stating it to have been restored about the year A.D. 491. The traces of the ancient roads and gardens that covered the little territory of the colony, and the principal street, which was about twenty feet wide, with the great marketplace, are still distinctly traceable, and the remains of a large palace stand on one side of a small street leading to the market-place. Lieutenant Kruse was commissioned by the Russian government to make excavations among the ruins, and he uncovered the ancient cathedral of Cherson where Vladimir was baptized, in which a few columns of a fine white crystalline marble, striped with blue, were still uninjured; and a second church, which was larger than the cathedral, built in the form of a Greek cross, and fifty feet each way. The semicircolar seats for the clergy were found entire, and a coarse mosaic still existed as the pavement. It appears to have been a Greek temple transformed into a Christian Church, and was perhaps the ancient Parthenon of Cherson, dedicated to the famous divinity of the Tauri.—H. D. Seymour's "Russia on the Black Sea and Sea of Azof."

† Herbertstein says that he kept three hundred in a high tower in Kiof; three hundred in Bielograd, and two hundred at Berestof and Selvi.

‡ This church was also excavated by Lieutenant Kruse. Nestor, in his chronicles says, "that the Princess Anne was received by the Khersonians into their port," and that they conducted her to the palace. "The baptism of Vladimir took place in the church of the Holy Mother of God at Cherson, situated in the midst of the town, on the market-place. It is here near this church that is to be seen to this day, the palace of Vladimir, and that of the princess. Immediately after the baptism, the bishop conducted the princess for another ceremony, that of marriage. Vladimir ordered to be built a church in Kherson, which church may still be seen in our days."—Nestor's "French Translation," viii. 133.

‖ Mouravieff's "Church of Russia."

§ Clarke says that he obtained some copper coins of Vladimir, in the Chersonese, with a V upon them, probably marking the era of his baptism.—H. D. Seymour's "Russia on the Black Sea," &c., x. 159.

must be right which had been embraced by their Czar and his boyards, they sprang by hundreds into the Dnieper, and bathed in its waters while the priests read the prayers from the shores ; and the bones of Yaropolk and Oleg, the brothers of Vladimir, were taken from the grave that they might be sanctified by baptism, after which they were again consigned to the tomb. A mount adjoining the palace of Kiof, that had formerly been sacred to Peroun, was now surmounted by a Christian church, and a decree having been issued by the Czar, ordaining that every idol throughout the empire should be destroyed in the same manner as those of the capital, the metropolitan and bishops travelled through the whole of Russia to baptize and instruct the people, erect churches and schools, and appoint priests and bishops over the various provinces. In Novogorod,* where Dobrina, the uncle of Vladimir, had long ruled, and the Christian religion had already made some progress, no opposition was raised to the establishment of the new faith, and the destruction of the national idols, by the newly-appointed bishop Joachim, the former archbishop of Cherson, with the authority of the governor of the city ; but in Rostoff the five tribes who still retained their idols, notwithstanding the efforts of Abramius, obstinately resisted, and drove out of their province the first two prelates, Fedor and Hilarion, who were sent amongst them, though the zealous endeavours of their successors, Leontius and Isaiah, were at length crowned with success.† At first, five dioceses were formed in Russia, under the metropolitan; namely, Novogorod, Rostoff, Tchernigoff, Belgorod, and Vladimir ; the latter city having been founded on the Kliazma by the Czar, in 991, when he visited the province of Suzdal,‡ accompanied by Stephen, a native Russian, whom he appointed bishop over his newly-founded town, and where he built a church dedicated to the Virgin Mother, which still remains. Stephen, assisted by another prelate, at the same time baptized all the inhabitants of that extensive territory. Among the many churches and monas-

* A tradition that Peroun, after having been precipitated into the river at Novogorod, had risen out of the water and made a parting address to the people, was long commemorated by the citizens; who, on the anniversary of the event, were accustomed to arm themselves with sticks, and, running about the town, attempt to strike each other unawares.
† The practice of wearing crosses round the neck, originated in Russia at this time, for the bishops ordered all Christians to wear crosses as a distinguishing mark.—Mouravieff's "Church of Russia."
‡ Suzdal extended over the modern governments of Yaroslaf, Kostroma, Vladimir, Moscow, Tver, Nijni Novgorod, Tula, and Kaluga.

teries which Vladimir caused to be erected throughout his empire, was the Cathedral of the Tithes at Kiof, so called from a vow the prince made to endow it with the tenth part of his revenues, and which was constructed by Greek architects, brought for the purpose from Constantinople, who also founded stone buildings in the capital for the national assembly and halls of justice. Many of the Greek books of religion were translated into the Slavonic language by order of the Czar who introduced that version of the Bible into Russia which had been translated about a century before by Cyrillus; and he sent missionaries to preach to the Bulgarians on the Volga, who, however, did not meet with many converts.* But their representations induced four of the princes of that province to visit Kiof, where they all subsequently embraced the Christian faith. The Mahometan prince of the Petchenegans, who, with a large retinue, made a friendly journey to the Russian capital, was the most eminent proselyte of the Czar; for while he remained the guest of Vladimir, he carefully observed the rites and ceremonies of the Greek religion, and, obtaining a thorough knowledge of its doctrines, caused himself to be baptized, and, taking up his residence in the city, remained there till his death; and in the year 991 the Czar received an embassy from Rome, sent by the pope to assure him of his esteem and regard. The aversion with which his boyards regarded his innovations, and his efforts to spread the arts and scholastic learning of Byzantium among them, caused Vladimir to make a law obliging them to allow their sons to attend the schools he had founded; and he established a payment of tithes for the relief of the poor, aged, sick, strangers, and prisoners, as well as to provide for the funerals of those who died without leaving sufficient to defray the expenses of their burial. These tithes consisted of a fixed contribution of corn, cattle, and the profits of trade, besides a tax collected from every cause which was tried; the right of judging causes being granted to the bishops and metropolitan, who administered justice according to the ecclesiastical laws promulgated by the Emperor John the Scholar of Constantinople.†

* Mouravieff's "Church of Russia."
† The following is an exact and verbal copy of the edict in question, according to the text of the most ancient codex of the thirteenth century:—"In the name of the Father, and of the Son, and of the Holy Ghost, I, Prince Bazil, called also Vladimir, son of Sviatozlaf, grandson of Igor, and of the holy Princess Olga, having received the saving rite of baptism, from the Tsars of Greece, and from Photius, the patriarch of Constantinople, and have brought to Kiof the first metropolitan Leontius, who thereupon has baptized the

During the reign of Vladimir, Tryggve Olafssen, the king of one of the six provinces into which Norway was divided, and a grandson of Harald Harfager, falling a victim to the conspiracy of Gumilda, the wife of Eric, Harald's son, who wished to see her husband sole possessor of his father's kingdom;* and, leaving as his successor only an infant son, his inheritance was seized upon by the neighbouring princes, and Astrid, the widow of Tryggve, was compelled to fly from the country with her son Olaf, attended by Thoralf, a faithful adherent of her husband's, to the court of Haco, king of Sweden, who boldly refused to deliver her up to Norway. She remained two years with this generous prince; but, the usurping chiefs threatening him with signal vengeance if he resisted their demand, Astrid, fearing to endanger her protector, resolved to take refuge with her brother Sigurd, who had been long in the service of Vladimir, and filled a high office at his court. She therefore left Sweden, with the intention of joining her brother in Russia; but, while crossing the Baltic, her vessel was captured by some Esthonian

whole country of the Russians. Some years after that, I built to the Holy Mother of God, the church called the Church of the Tenths, and endowed this church as the cathedral, with the right of receiving tithe from the whole country of the Russians, so far as my dominion extends, with this proviso, that to this house of the Saviour, and of his holy mother, belongs the tenth mite (squirrel skin) of the judicial dues in the districts of the princedom, and from commercial imposts the produce of the tenth week; moreover, from every house and family, from cattle, and from reaped corn, the tenth must be paid. And since, upon reading the Greek Nomancon, I have discovered that, according to a precept therein contained, there are certain matters of dispute which it does not belong to the prince and his boyards and judges to take cognizance of, and to decide upon, therefore have I, after due deliberation with my consort the Princess Anna, and with my children, resolved to concede the administration of justice in certain fixed cases to the church, that is, to the metropolitan and collective bishops of the Russian territory. Accordingly, neither shall my children, nor grandchildren, nor my latest descendants, either cite before their tribunals ecclesiastical persons, or usurp that judicial power which has been conceded to the church, for this exclusively belongs to her according to my grant." He goes on to state all the various crimes upon which the church is to pass judgment, adding, "It is also among the ancient regulations, that the bishops should have the supervision of the measures, weights, scales, and balances of the town and of the market. Over these matters must the bishops watch, neither increasing nor diminishing them, and on the universal day of judgment they shall answer for this, and for the salvation of souls. Now, these are the persons which belong to the church: the stewards of their estates, the priests (popes), deacons, and their children, the wife of a priest, and the whole body of clerks; moreover, the monk, the nun, the woman who bakes the holy bread, the cloistered pilgrim, the physician, the man who by a holy miracle is restored to health, the slave whom his master releases for the good of his soul, the stranger, the blind, and the lame; especially the monasteries, the hospitals, and establishments for the care of guests and strangers. All these are the people who, for the sake of God, belong to the church. Between these parties, the metropolitan or the bishop is to act as judge, and to arrange the offences, disputes, and contentions which take place among them, as also the succession of property. Notwithstanding, when any judicial matter arises between a person belonging to the church and another man, the tribunal appointed to judge the cause shall be partly civil, and partly ecclesiastical.

"In case that any one, either of my children or descendants, shall act contrary to this decree, made in conformity with the regulations of the Holy Fathers and of the first Tsars, or shall any lieutenant, steward, or judge, or any other person infringe these privileges of the church, may the curse light upon him, both in this and the life to come, according to the judgment of the Holy fathers, and of the seven general councils."—From MS. of Baron Rosenkampf, quoted in Blackmore's "Notes to Mouravleff's Church of Russia."

* Laing's "Sea-kings of Norway."

corsairs, who, after putting some of the crew to death, divided the remainder among them; and Olaf and Thoralf were separated from Astrid, falling to the share of a pirate called Klerkon, who considering Thoralf too old to be of any service as a slave, killed him, but took Olaf to Esthonia, where he exchanged him for a ram with a peasant, by whom he was treated with much kindness, and with whom he continued nearly six years. At the end of that time, when he was nine years old, Sigurd, the brother of Astrid, came from Novogorod to Esthonia, accompanied by a splendid and numerous retinue, to collect the taxes of Vladimir; and, while passing through one of the towns, chanced to see Olaf, and, observing that he was a foreigner, sent for him, and inquired his name and country. Olaf related all his adventures, and Sigurd, discovering that he was his own nephew, bought him from the peasant to whom he belonged, and took him to Novogorod, though without making known his name and rank. It chanced that Olaf was one day in the market-place, when among many people assembled there, he recognised Klerkon, the corsair who had put Thoralf to death; and, having a small axe in his hand, he struck him on the head and instantly killed him, and then, hastening home to his lodging, informed Sigurd of what he had done. A law existed in Novogorod to the effect, that if any murder was committed in the city all the people should unite in seeking out and discovering the criminal, and according to the ancient Jewish law stone him to death in the streets; and, fearing lest Olaf should suffer this summary punishment from the hands of the citizens, who were making a strict search for the assassin, Sigurd conducted him to the palace* of the Grand Princess,† and informing her of what had happened, entreated her to protect his nephew. She was pleased with the appearance of the boy, whom she affirmed was far too handsome to be slain; and, interceding for him with Vladimir, obtained a commutation of his punishment to a fine, which she herself immediately paid, and expressed a desire to receive him into her household. As it was contrary to the laws of Russia for any foreign prince to reside in the country without the express permission of the Czar, Sigurd informed her of the real name and rank of Olaf, and

---

* It was the custom in Novogorod for the Grand Prince and Princess to reside in separate palaces, each being attended by an equally numerous retinue.
† She is called Allogia in the saga of Olaf Tryggveson, from which this account is taken.

entreated her to obtain that permission for the Norwegian prince from her husband; and Vladimir, pitying his misfortunes, entertained him at his court with all the honour due to the son of a king, and, after he had been several years in Russia, bestowed upon him a high command in his army. But the esteem in which he was held by the prince drew against him the hatred and animosity of the boyards, who, objecting to any foreigner holding rank, or exercising so high a power in their country, endeavoured to prejudice the mind of Vladimir against the exiled prince, and raise jealous suspicions in his mind; and at length Olaf, observing that he was treated with increasing coldness by the Czar, and fearing lest his safety should be compromised if he resided longer in Russia, requested to be allowed to leave Novogorod, as he longed to travel, and see the land where his family formerly reigned. Vladimir readily granted his request, and equipped a small fleet of ships for his escort; and the Norwegian prince leaving Russia, sailed to Denmark, Ireland, and England, where he a few years later became a convert to Christianity, and subsequently repossessing himself of his kingdom, about the year 995; he closed his adventurous career in 1000.*

In the latter period of his life, Vladimir is said to have felt great remorse for his former sins; and the tranquillity of his reign was much disturbed by the dissensions of his sons, among whom he had divided his empire, allowing each complete control in his own principality, and only exacting from them the payment of a small tribute. His favourite son, Vassili, died before him, and the rest, being discontented at the unequal size of the governments which their father had ceded to them, continually engaged in war with each other; and the turbulent Petchenegans, taking advantage of the divided and troubled condition of the empire, again invaded Russia. The Czar advanced against them, and the opposing armies were drawn up on each side of the river Sula, when the prince of the Petchenegans despatched a herald to the Russian camp, with proposals to spare the blood of their subjects, by deciding the fate of the war in a single combat between two soldiers chosen from the hostile armies—he possessing among his troops a man of extraordinary size and agility, on whose success he fully relied. The offer had been

* Laing's " Sea-kings of Norway."

accepted, when a young Russian stepped out of the ranks, and, falling on his knees before his prince, he requested that he might fill the honourable post of combatant for his nation in the approaching duel. He was ordered first to prove his valour in an encounter with an infuriated bull, and, having obtained a signal success, he was unanimously proclaimed the champion of Russia by the army and the Czar. The rival forces closed round the combatants, and waited with breathless anxiety the issue of the struggle between the gigantic Petchenegan and his smaller but more agile adversary. It lasted but a few moments, and terminating with the defeat and death of the former, the victor was elevated on the spot to the rank of a boyard, and an armistice of three years was agreed upon—the Petchenegans retiring to their own land. But, upon the conclusion of the truce, they again invaded Russia, and, laying siege to one of her frontier towns, Vladimir immediately marched to the assistance of the inhabitants. However, his early success had now abandoned him: the Russians were defeated in a fierce battle before the walls, their army was completely routed and dispersed, and the Czar only escaped death or captivity by concealing himself under a bridge, while the victorious troops passed on and plundered and devastated his territories.

Jaroslaf, the prince of Novogorod, taking advantage of this defeat of his father's army, as its almost complete annihilation would probably render it impossible for the Czar to enforce obedience upon his rebellious son; and being chiefly induced to take this step by the wishes of the citizens of Novogorod, who had always been jealous of the supremacy of Kiof, and desired to form an independent state, he refused to pay the accustomed tribute, and armed himself against his father. Vladimir, collecting his scanty number of followers, put himself at their head, and prepared to march against Novogorod; but the reverses his army had sustained, and the ingratitude of his son, so preyed upon his mind, that he died before he had advanced many miles on his route, on the 15th of July, 1015, at the age of seventy-seven. He left eleven sons, including his adopted nephew, among whom he had divided his empire; namely, Sviatopolk, prince of Tver; Soudeslaff, prince of Polotzk; Nicolas, prince of Tchernigoff; Vladimir, prince of Smolensko; Micislaf, prince of Tmuracatan or Taman; Boris, Gleb, Jaroslaf, prince of Novogorod;

Iziaslaf, Sviatoslaf, and Stanislaus; and one daughter, Mary, who married Mieczyslav II., king of Poland. Historians have bestowed upon Vladimir the title of Great; and he and his wife, the Greek princess Anna, who died before him in 1011, are enrolled among the saints of Russia. His remains were interred in a marble coffin, and buried in the Church of the Tithes, to which he had caused the relics of the Grand Princess Olga to be removed, and which was afterwards burned and destroyed by the Tartars when they gained possession of Russia; but, in 1636, Peter Mogila, archbishop of Kiof, discovered under its ruins the coffins of the Czar and the Greek princess, and, having removed the head of Vladimir to the Pechersky monastery, he left the remaining bones undisturbed.*

The introduction of Christianity forms a grand epoch in the history of every nation, from the complete revolution it produced in their manners and customs, by its creating a bond of union between them, which prevented their former perpetual and desultory wars. From that time they gradually settled to more peaceful and industrious occupations, living by agriculture or manual skill rather than by plundering their more wealthy or weaker neighbours, or following the restless and primitive pursuit of hunting; a precarious mode of life, which has ever allowed little scope for the moral and intellectual development of those nations whose harsh climate, or unproductive soil, have compelled them to adopt the chase as their only means of subsistence. It was hardly to be expected that in Russia, from the manner in which Christianity was forced upon the people, it should make as much alteration in their condition and habits as if their conversion had proceeded more slowly, and from conviction, and not merely from obedience to their sovereign's will and command. The figure of their household god, with which every Russian was accustomed to adorn the walls of his hut, was replaced by a picture of his patron saint, and the enthusiasm with which they performed the rites of their pagan creed, was transferred to the services of the Christian faith; but they assimilated these to many of their barbarous ceremonies, and retained many of their ancient superstitions, still regarding with awe and reverence the rivers and groves that they had formerly held as sacred to their gods, and keeping as holidays those days and seasons of the year which they had been

* Mouravieff's "Church of Russia."

accustomed to set apart for their heathen festivals.* To this day, in the more remote villages and provinces of Russia, many of their anniversary celebrations and customs rather resemble the idolatrous practices of their ancestors than those of a people who profess the Christian religion.† Little alteration appears to have been made in the clothing and manner of living of the peasantry; and even the form of their dwellings, from the days of Sviatozlaf and Vladimir to the present time; for the Russians have always been remarkable for the tenacity with which they have adhered to their habits and customs, and for their aversion to any change or innovation; and the same love of music and poetry, attachment to their place of birth, indolence, and respect to age, appears to have characterized their peasantry then, as it does now. The practice which still prevails among the latter, of forming themselves into village communities, and holding their lands in common, electing a chief from among themselves every three years, appears to have been in force from the period when they first abandoned their nomadic habits, and much resembles the ancient system of Hindostan. As in both Russia and China, at the present day, a father was supreme in his household, his authority being absolute over his wife and children, as that of masters over slaves, and on his death the eldest son succeeded to his position as arbiter and superior of the family.‡ Their women appear from the earliest

* The Russian peasantry at the present day, almost universally celebrate their marriages at the season of the year formerly dedicated to the Slavonic gods of love and marriage, a practice which prevailed amongst the heathen Slavonians.—Dr. Pinkerton's "Russia."

† "On Midsummer's eve a custom still exists in Russia, among the lower classes, that can only be derived from a very remote antiquity, and is perhaps a remnant of the worship of Baal. A party of peasant women and girls assemble in some retired and unfrequented spot, and light a large fire, over which they leap in succession. If by chance any one of the other sex should be found near the place, or should have seen them in the act of performing the heathenish rite, it is at the imminent risk of his life; for the woman would not scruple to sacrifice him for his temerity. I was assured that such instances had often been known."—"The Englishwoman in Russia."

For an account of the same ceremony, in which the men also joined, see Dr. Pinkerton's "Russia."

A feast resembling the heathen Saturnalia was celebrated as late as the present century, in the very streets of the capital, by the peasantry of Russia.

‡ Haxthausen mentions in his work, one or two instances of the extent to which even now the patriarchal system is carried in Russia. "It is the custom in Moscow for all the daughters, whether married or single, to pass the whole of their evenings in the apartments of their mother, which greatly deranges the domestic life of the husband. The Princess G—— was mentioned to me as the type of the wife of a boyard of ancient Russia: every evening till her death she was surrounded by her daughters. On one occasion, one of the daughters, the Princess A——, who held a high position at court, was prevented by her duty from visiting her mother, who, on the following morning, overwhelmed her with the bitterest reproaches. Her daughter excused herself by pleading her obligations to the etiquette of the palace; but the sole answer was, 'Every evening of a daughter belongs to the mother, that is the usage of Russia.' Her son, who had commanded a *corps d'armée* as general-in-chief, and who had been successively an ambassador, a governor-general, and had filled other high offices, was obliged, when at St. Petersburg, to wait on his mother every morning. He ventured one day to make a slight change in the stables of his mother, by substituting a good horse for one that he deemed bad; his mother resented this boldness, for the following morning she inflicted on him several severe blows, which he received with submission."

ages to have been retained in the seclusion common amongst the Asiatic nations; and, though this custom was somewhat relaxed during the short period that the Russians communicated so constantly and familiarly with the Greeks, it was renewed in full force when the Tartars conquered Russia. Till the time of Peter the Great, the wives of the nobility were seldom permitted to cross the threshold of their houses, and then always closely veiled; they were even forbidden to appear in church; and a custom existed in Russia, during the early years of her history, allowing no woman to put an animal to death, not even those that they required for food.* Although the nobles of this empire never encroached upon the prerogative of the crown, to the same extent as those in the other nations of Europe during the middle ages, yet they possessed some influence in the government of the state; and in the chronicles of Nestor he mentions the public assemblies which the Grand Princes occasionally convened to decide upon important affairs, and at which the clergy and even the simple citizens had a right to attend; the boyards were obliged to follow their sovereign to battle, with their guards and retinues ready furnished with horses, accoutrements, and provisions, recompensing themselves with the spoil and prisoners whom they captured. Though they possessed slaves, these were generally prisoners of war or their descendants, for the peasants were not at that period, as in the rest of Europe, feudal serfs bound to the soil; this regulation having only been introduced into Russia in the sixteenth century, but were termed *kabalnie*, because they hired themselves out in a written contract, which was called *kabala*, for a specified term of years, or till the death of their employer, who was bound to receive with them a character from the chief of their village, otherwise he could not punish the vassal who robbed or deserted him.† The succession to the throne, as in most other Slavonic nations at that time, and according to the custom that now prevails among the Mahometan nations of the East, devolved not upon the son of the former monarch, but upon the oldest member of his family, and it would have been well if this practice had always been adhered to; for the impolitic measure pursued

---

* Till the reign of Peter the Great, a husband could put his wife or children to death with impunity, and it was the custom, in the time of Vladimir, for a wife to take off her husband's boots on the day of her marriage, to show her complete subjection to him; and, till within the last few years, a bride always presented her husband on his wedding-day with a whip of her own construction.
† Babbe's "History of Russia."

by Sviatozlaf and Vladimir, of dividing the empire among their sons, produced great dissension in the state, and perpetual civil wars. Her strength and political importance being diminished, she thus became a prey to her foreign enemies, opening by her internal troubles a way for the entrance of the fierce and restless tribes of Asia, who, wandering in search of forage for their horses, and pasture for their herds, upon her borders, were ever ready to profit by her divisions or calamities to make inroads upon her territories; and their continual invasions retarded for years the advancement of commerce and letters, and the social progress of Russia; and ultimately, breaking off all communication with Constantinople and the West, replunged her people into the ignorance and barbarism from which, in the reigns of Olga and Vladimir, they appeared to be beginning to emerge.

From the introduction of Christianity into Russia till the time of Peter the Great, the Russians, like the Greeks, dated the current year, which began in September, though by an erroneous calculation, from the creation of the world. Thus, the year of Vladimir's death, A. D. 1015, was called with them A. M. 6523.

CHAPTER X.

Sviatopolk—The Poles invade Russia—Jaroslaf.

"In the delight of moral prudence school'd,
How feelingly at home the sovereign ruled,
Lo! he harangues his cohorts—there the storm
Of battle meets him in authentic form.
 . . . . .
 Yet high or low,
None bleed, and none lie prostrate but the foe."—WORDSWORTH.

From A.D. 1015 to 1053; or, according to the Russian dates, from A.M. 6523 to 6581.

SVIATOPOLK, the son of Yaropolk, the elder brother of Vladimir, having been born after the death of his father, had been adopted by the Czar as his own son, and had received the government of Tver as his share when that prince divided the empire among his sons; but the succession to the throne of Kiof had long been the object of his ambition, and he had chiefly resided there during the declining years of Vladimir, with the intention of seizing upon this important city of the empire, as soon as the grave should have closed upon the Czar. But a formidable rival existed in the person of Boris, another son of Vladimir, who was employed with the army against the Petchenegans at the time of his father's death, and who had rendered himself extremely popular with his soldiers and the nation at large. The former unanimously proposed to assist him in gaining the vacant throne, but he rejected their offer, declaring that it devolved rightfully upon the elder brother; this, however, did not preserve him from the cruelty of Sviatopolk, who, fearing that he might oppose his ambitious schemes, had already despatched assassins with orders to murder him. They entered his tent in the night, where he and his brother Gleb were engaged in prayer, and, having first struck down the sentinel who guarded it, put an end to their lives; and these two young princes, who possessed many virtues, and were much beloved by the people, whose sympathy they especially procured, from their falling victims to the ambition and cruelty of their brother while at their devotions, were, a few years after their death, canonized by the Russian Church, and their tomb is still shown in the ancient cathedral at Tchernigoff. Another brother, who attempted to fly into Hungary, was seized upon and brought back to Kiof, where he was put to death, and Sviatopolk, supposing that the remaining sons of Vladimir were established at too great a distance to give him any cause for fear, assumed the government of Kiof; but Jaroslaf, the prince of Novogorod, indignant at these cruelties, and resolved to avenge the murder of his brothers, advanced upon Kiof with an army, and, driving Sviatopolk from the capital, forced him to take refuge with his father-in-law, Boleslaf, king of Poland, whose assistance the deposed prince solicited for the recovery of his dominions. The Polish monarch with a powerful army entered Russia in the year 1018, and, having defeated the army of Jaroslaf, he compelled the city of Kiof to capitulate after a brave defence, and replaced Sviatopolk upon the throne; and Jaroslaf having formed a scheme to surprise and carry off the latter from his capital, and his design failing in the execution, retired to Novogorod, to which city he was pursued by the implacable Boleslaf, who defeated and destroyed his whole army at its very gates. Discouraged by his disasters, ashamed of his defeat, and fearing that his continued ill-success might alienate from him the affection of his people, Jaroslaf made preparations to cross the Baltic, and pass the remainder of his life as an adventurer in foreign lands, but, upon the entreaty of his subjects, he was induced to alter his determination and remain among them; they also levied contributions upon their own city to enable him to procure mercenary troops to assist him in the recovery of Kiof.

Meanwhile Boleslaf, with the Polish army, having re-established Sviatopolk in his dominions, though at the same time exacting from him a yearly tribute, refused to withdraw from Kiof, which was at that time the most wealthy and luxurious city of the north, till at length her citizens and soldiers, wearied by the oppressions and exactions of the Poles, formed a conspiracy against them, designing to destroy their whole army by a sudden massacre, or by the more secret and insidious means of poison. But Boleslaf, having discovered their intentions on the eve of its fulfilment, assembled all his followers who were in the town and surrounding country, and, after sacking and destroying the greater part of the capital, abandoned it with his subjects, every man loaded with the spoil and plunder of Kiof. This city had been so much increased and enriched by Vladimir, that, at the time of its occupation by the Poles, it contained three hundred churches and eight markets, and it had received from its people the boastful appellation of "the rival of Constantinople." Indeed, the historians of the time describe the splendid dresses worn by the inhabitants, their hot baths, and rich and sumptuous feasts, which their commerce with Greece provided with the wines of the Mediterranean, silver plate, and even the productions of the Indies; and they appear to have been entirely given up to luxury, dissipation, and idleness. Upon the retreat of Boleslaf, Sviatopolk immediately pursued him, but, encountering his army near the river Bog, was totally defeated, and forced to retire upon Kiof. At the same time, the Grand Prince received intelligence that Jaroslaf was advancing against him with the soldiers of Novogorod, their valour having been encouraged and revived by a successful campaign they had lately undertaken against the Chazars, who, during the latter years of the reign of Vladimir, had emancipated themselves from the yoke of the Russians, and whose khan, George Tzuda, Jaroslaf had taken prisoner; and in this distress Sviatopolk was forced to accept the assistance of the Petchenegans, who, tempted by the hope of plunder, flocked eagerly to his standard. The armies met near the spot where Boris and Gleb had formerly been assassinated; and Jaroslaf, before engaging with the enemy, harangued his troops, pointing out to them this circumstance, calling upon their valour to revenge the act, and concluding with a prayer to the Almighty to grant them success in the battle.* At the earliest dawn of day he attacked the foe, and continued in a fierce and desperate conflict till sunset, when the forces of Sviatopolk, though greatly superior in number to those of his adversary, having been routed with great slaughter, their leader was forced to quit the field, and, after being reduced to great misery, died upon the road, having wandered about from place to place after his defeat, which had dispersed his followers, disdaining to ask for mercy from his cousin, who, on the event of the battle,

* Bell's "History of Russia."

had taken possession of Kiof. But the King of Poland, unwilling to surrender entirely this principality into the hands of his former enemy, and elated by the victories he had lately gained over the Prussians, whose country he had invaded to avenge the murder of St. Adalbert,* again marched upon Kiof, and, surprising the army of Jaroslaf on the banks of the Dnieper, attacked the Russians before they had time to form, and, being seized with a panic, they fled in confusion, hurrying away their prince, who was almost trampled to death in their flight ; so that Boleslaf once more became master of the capital. It was not till after his death in 1025, that Jaroslaf succeeded in expelling his son and successor, Mieczyslaf II., and the Polish army, entirely from Russia, when a peace being concluded between them, it was confirmed by the marriage of the Polish king with Mary, the sister of Jaroslaf and daughter of Vladimir, and continued throughout the whole reign of Jaroslaf. As soon as this prince had re-established himself on the throne of Kiof, he invaded the principality of Polotzk, the territory of his elder brother Soudeslaff, who had taken part against him in the late wars, and, defeating and capturing the unfortunate chief, he threw him into prison, where he detained him in close confinement throughout the whole of his reign, though, on the death of Jaroslaf, Soudeslaff was released by his nephew Iziaslaf, the son and successor of the Grand Prince, and, embracing a monastic life, assumed the cowl in the cloisters of Pechersky at Kiof.

One of the sons of Vladimir, who had received the town and government of Smolensko from his father, appears to have taken no part in the wars of his brothers, but transmitted his principality to his descendants, which thus, for a time, became separated from the Russian empire.† The foundation of this city is supposed to have been coeval with that of Novogorod ; it was a flourishing town and state before the time of Rurik, and was annexed by Oleg to his dominions on his march to the conquest of Kiof.

On hearing of the successful result of the long war between the Poles and Russia, Micislaf, the seventh son of Vladimir, and prince of Tmutaracan, a town which had been captured

---

* St. Adalbert went to Prussia in 1010, to preach Christianity to the heathens of that country. According to Dr. Clarke, he preached in the tenth century in Russia, the Grand Princess Olga having requested the Emperor Otho to send missionaries to convert \erempire.
Ségur.

by Sviatozlaf from the Khazars, in the modern peninsula of Taman, on the sea of Azof, sent a letter to Jaroslaf, requesting from him the cession of a small portion of their father's vast dominions, of which the Grand Prince was now almost the sole possessor. Micislaf had proved himself a brave and successful general in many wars with the restless mountain tribes of the Caucasus, by whom his little kingdom had been frequently menaced; and, having terminated a hostility that had lasted for many years, by defeating in single combat the chief of the Circassians, he built the church of Taman in remembrance of his success; a memorial which exists at the present day. He also assisted the Greek Emperor in an expedition against the Khazars of the Crimea; but on receiving from Jaroslaf, in compliance to his demand, a small territory, which was insufficient to satisfy his ambition, he marched with an army into Russia, and, after carrying on for some time a successful war in his brother's dominions, agreed to conclude a peace. After this it was finally arranged that the two brothers should reign jointly and with equal power over the whole empire; and they continued to govern amicably together till the death of Micislaf, which took place seven years after the conclusion of the truce. By order of this prince, the cathedral of the Saviour at Tchernigoff was built.*

In 1030 the province of Esthonia revolted against Russia, and proclaimed itself an independent state. Jaroslaf marched against it, and, after re-establishing his authority, founded the town of Dorpat, called by the Russians Jourief,† where he placed a garrison to collect the tribute. Dorpat remained in the possession of the Russians till the year 1210, when it was captured by Volgum, Grand Master of the Knights of the Sword. To show his gratitude for the fidelity of Novogorod, and for its valuable assistance in his time of need, Jaroslaf granted to its citizens many privileges, and gave them a form of government which laid the foundation of the

---

* Mouravieff's "Church of Russia."
† Youri, or George, was the Christian name of Jaroslaf. Blackmore, in his notes to Mouravieff's "Church of Russia," quotes a short extract from a paper presented to the Society of Russian History and Antiquities, in which, with regard to the double names of these princes, he says, "The ancient Slavonians had only one name, to which was added their patronymic. The Russo-Slavonians had usually three names; one given by the father at their birth, another at their baptism, and the third, their patronymic, as for instance, Sviatopolk Michael Iayaslavich. The Christian names of many of the princes are not known, and it is imagined that they were purposely kept secret, that the bearers of them might not be subject to sorcery or incantation, which it was supposed could not effect unless done in the right name."

independence and prosperity they enjoyed during the middle ages. The governor of the province, who was always to be a prince of the royal family, on his installation was bound upon oath to observe the laws, and took no part in the deliberations of the people. The first magistrate in the city was the *posadnick*, or mayor, who was elected for a limited time, and under him was the senate, composed of the boyards, which was elective, and the *tisatski*,* or tribune, one of whose members was chosen by every hundred freemen, that class consisting of all who were neither nobles or slaves. The citizens sat in judgment upon their own order; none but Novogorodian magistrates could be appointed by the sovereign in the province, and those were to be approved of by the *posadnick;* and no citizen of Novogorod could be arrested for debt. They had also the right of imposing their own taxes, and framing their own commercial laws.†

Jaroslaf also promulgated a legislative code, called *Gramota Soudebuaia*, for the government of the whole empire, and they appear to have been the first written laws used in Russia. The judges travelled from place to place, and were supported and paid by the inhabitants of the district where they administered justice. The punishment of death was abolished; formerly, when a murder had been committed, the father, brother, son, or nephew, might avenge it, but no other; unless it had been inflicted upon a citizen of Novogorod, in which case the inhabitants of the town were bound to avenge him by stoning the offender to death; but this custom was no longer permitted, instead of it a fine being fixed as the penalty of the crime. For the assassination of a boyard eighty grivnas was exacted, a grivna being worth about a pound's weight of silver, for that of a free Russian forty grivnas, and for every woman half that sum; but for the murder of a female slave a larger fine was adjudged than for that of a man. For a blow with the fist, or the sheath or handle of a sword, for knocking out a tooth, or pulling a man by the beard, the fine was twelve grivnas; for a blow with a club three grivnas, and the punishment for stealing a horse was imprisonment for life. The only absolute slaves were prisoners of war, men or women bought of foreigners and their descendants; but a debtor who could not acquit himself of his obligations was sold to his creditors, whose

* Karamsin's "History of Russia." † Ibid.

servant he remained till he had ransomed himself by labour. A man could not put his slave to death, and freemen occasionally sold themselves to a boyard, some to obtain protection, others to procure subsistence; but they could only sell themselves or their children for a limited term of years. It was allowable to kill a robber, if caught in the fact, during the night, but if he were detained till morning, it was compulsory to bring him before the judge; and if proved by witnesses that he had been put to death when bound, and incapable of doing harm, it was considered as a murder, and punished accordingly. Usury was at that time so exorbitant, that a regulation was made permitting no lender to claim a higher rate of interest than fifty per cent. a year.*

The revenue of the sovereign consisted of the produce of his personal estates, voluntary contributions, and the fines that were exacted from criminals. Jaroslaf founded a college at Novogorod, where he maintained at his own cost three hundred noble youths; procuring for them instructors from Constantinople, and causing translations to be made of the works of the Greek fathers into the Slavonic tongue, in which labour he personally assisted the priests, he formed them into a small library, established by himself, at Kiof. In this reign psalms and hymns were first sung in the churches, the mode of choral singing, now prevalent in Russia, being introduced into the empire by three Greek singers, who were brought from Constantinople, with their families, for the purpose; and the Grand Prince engaged in his service the most skilful artists from Greece, who erected in Kiof the cathedral of St. Sophia, after the model of that of Byzantium, besides the monastery of St. George and the convent of St. Irene, in the same city. Novogorod Sieverski, and many other towns, owe also their foundation to Jaroslaf, who in 1044 built the Kremlin at Novogorod; and his court was the resort of exiled and unfortunate princes, his family having formed alliances with most of the royal houses of Europe.

About the year 1019, Jaroslaf sent an embassy to Olaf the Saint, king of Norway, demanding of him the hand of his daughter Ingigerd in marriage, who agreed to his proposals on the condition of receiving from her husband the town and principality of Ladoga; at the same time, she

* Karamsin's "History of Russia."

stipulated, that she should be accompanied to Novogorod by a Swede, who should hold the same rank in Russia* that he did in his own country; and, on her request being granted, she chose her brother-in-law, the Earl Rognvald, to conduct her there, bestowing upon him the government of Ladoga. Not long after the marriage of his daughter, Olaf was driven from his kingdom by Earl Hakon, a rebellious and turbulent vassal, and with his wife and son took refuge in Russia, where he was presented by Jaroslaf with a tract of land sufficient for the support of his followers; the Grand Prince, likewise, offering him the sovereignty of a province on the Volga, which he refused, as he purposed undertaking a pilgrimage to Jerusalem. But the death of Hakon taking place in 1030, and Olaf dreaming one night that an angel commanded him to return to Norway, he repaired to his own kingdom, leaving his son Magnus to receive his education at Novogorod, and endeavoured by force of arms to re-establish himself on his throne. The expedition, however, proved unfortunate, for the Norwegian king was defeated and killed in the fatal battle of Stiklestadt,† fought on the 29th of July of that year; and his half-brother, the celebrated Harald Hardrada,‡ having been severely wounded in the same engagement, escaped to Russia, where he was most hospitably and honourably received by the Grand Prince, who made him one of his generals. In the poem of "Bolverk the Skald," his residence in that country is thus mentioned:—

> "The king's sharp sword lies clean and bright,
> Prepared in foreign lands to fight;
> Our ravens croak to have their fill,
> The wolf howls from the distant hill.
> Our brave king is to Russia gone,
> Braver than he on earth there's none;
> His sharp sword will carve many a feast,
> For wolf and raven in the east.∥

After remaining several years in Russia, in 1034 he, with many of his followers, joined the Varangian guard, which was principally composed of his countrymen, at Constantinople; and accompanying the Greeks in many warlike expeditions to Sicily, and against the Saracens, both in Palestine

---

* Laing's "Sea-kings of Norway." "Saga of Olaf the Saint."
† Olaf was worshipped as a saint, and churches dedicated to his memory in Sweden, Norway, Denmark, England, Russia, and even in Constantinople, and his shrine was long resorted to by pilgrims.
‡ The Stern.
∥ Saga of "Harald Hardrada."

and Africa, he gradually amassed great wealth and treasure, both in gold and jewels. From time to time he sent this by Russian merchants to Novogorod, to be intrusted to the care of Jaroslaf until his return to his native land.*

During his residence at the Grand Prince's court, he had formed an attachment to Jellisaveta (Elizabeth), or Ellisof, as she is called in the Norwegian annals, the daughter of Jaroslaf; and while sailing across the Black Sea, on his return to her father's dominions, he composed sixteen songs in her praise, all ending in the same words, of which the following is a specimen:—

> "Past Sicily's wide plains we flew,
> A dauntless, never-wearied crew;
> Our viking steed rush'd through the sea,
> As viking-like fast, fast sail'd we.
> Never, I think, along this shore
> Did Norseman ever sail before;
> Yet to the Russian queen, I fear,
> My gold adorn'd, I am not dear."

On his return to Novogorod, in 1045, he took all the gold, silk, jewels, and precious stones, which he had accumulated while in the service of the Greek emperor into his own possession; and the Norwegian sagas relate that "they altogether made so vast a treasure, that no man in the northern lands had ever seen the like before belonging to one man;" for he had assisted the Greeks in the capture of eighty strongholds, and had been three times through the emperor's treasury, the soldiers and officers of the Varangian guard having the privilege of passing through the imperial treasury on the death of the emperor, and keeping whatever they could seize upon while marching across. The winter after Harald's return to Russia, he married the princess Jellisaveta, who had refused the hand of several princes during his absence, and the event is thus related by an ancient Norwegian bard, Stuff the Blind:—

> "Agder's chief now gain'd the queen,
> Who long his secret love had been;
> Of gold, no doubt a mighty store,
> The princess to her husband bore."†

Having remained two years longer in Russia, he embarked

---

* According to some authors, the princess Zoe, of Constantinople, wished to marry him, and on his refusal threw him into prison, from whence he escaped and returned to Russia.

† Laing's "Sea-kings of Norway." Saga of "Harald Hardrada."

for Norway, on the invitation of his nephew Magnus,* who had lived several years after the death of Olaf at the court of Novogorod, and only quitted it at the pressing solicitations of his subjects, with a small fleet of ships, for his native land. The voyage of Harald to Norway is commemorated in the verses of the Norse bard, Valgard of Valli :—

> "The fairest cargo ship e'er bore
> From Russia's distant eastern shore,
> The gallant Harald homeward brings,
> Gold, and a fame that Skald still sings."

He reigned jointly with Magnus till the death of the latter in 1047, when Harald became sole possessor of the kingdom; and subsequently assisting Tostig, Earl of Northumberland, the brother of Harold, king of England, in his invasion of that prince's dominions, they were both defeated and killed in a battle fought near York, on the 25th of September, 1066, and the Norwegian monarch was succeeded on his throne by his sons Olaf and Magnus.†

About the year 1040, Jaroslaf bestowed the government of Novogorod upon his eldest son, Vladimir, who was at that time twenty years of age; and had scarcely established himself on his throne before he again revived the project of a naval invasion of Constantinople—an expedition which had not been undertaken for hostile purposes since the unfortunate attempt of Igor, and which in this instance was not destined to meet with greater success. Under the pretence of obtaining satisfaction for the murder of a Russian in the Byzantine empire, he sailed to the entrance of the Bosphorus; but his fleet was repulsed in the attempt to force a passage by the Grecian ships, armed with their destructive artificial fire, and 15,000 men fell victims to the flames. But the fleet of Constantinople becoming dispersed in the pursuit, the

---

* Magnus reigned from about 1035 to 1047; after the defeat and death of his father, St. Olaf, he remained for several years in Russia. Sigvat the Skald says—

> "I ask the merchant oft, who drives
> His trade to Russia, 'How he thrives,
> Our noble prince? How lives he there?'
> And still good news, his praise I hear."

And Arwer, another bard, shortly before his return to Norway, says—

> "It is no loose report that he
> Who will command o'er land and sea,
> This generous youth who scatters gold,
> Norway's brave son, but ten years old,
> Is rigging ships in Russia's lake
> His crown, with friends' support, to take."

He was joined in Novogorod by many of his father's followers, whom he accompanied to Sweden, where they ultimately regained possession of Norway.
† Laing's "Sea-kings of Norway."

vanguard was surrounded by Russian ships, and their provision of fire being exhausted, twenty-four of their galleys were either captured or destroyed by the remaining vessels of Russia;* and the Emperor Constantine Monomachus, to revenge this partial defeat, caused the eyes to be put out of all those Russian prisoners who had fallen into the hands of the Greeks. Jaroslaf was very indignant at this cruelty to his subjects, and on the death of the metropolitan of Kiof, Theopemptus, after the conclusion of the war, he called together the Russian bishops, to elect a new primate from among themselves, without any reference or communication with the Byzantine patriarch.† A priest, Hilarion, was elected by the conclave; but not being satisfied at the irregular manner in which he had been chosen, and this infringement of the ecclesiastical rule, the new metropolitan sought, and obtained, from the patriarch, Michael Cerularius of Constantinople, a benedictory letter, and an order confirming him in his office.

In 1051, an embassy of bishops was sent by Henry I., king of France, to the court of Jaroslaf at Kiof, to ask the hand of his daughter Anna in marriage. She accompanied the ambassadors back to France, with many rich gifts from her father to her husband,‡ and the same year the death of Vladimir, Grand Prince of Novogorod, took place. He was succeeded in his government by his brother Sviatozlaf, and buried in the cathedral of St. Sophia at Novogorod, which had just been completed under his directions, and whose walls he had caused to be decorated by Greek artists, with paintings copied from those in the churches of Constantinople; it also contains the tombs of his wife Alexandra, his uncle Micislaf, the brother of Jaroslaf, and his mother Irene, the daughter of Olaf, king of Norway. ‖

The death of Jaroslaf occurred in 1053, about two years after that of his son. A short time before, he had divided his empire§ among his five surviving sons, making the younger ones tributary to the eldest, Iziaslaf, the prince of

---

* Gibbon's "Decline and Fall of the Roman Empire."
† Mouravieff's "Church of Russia."
‡ Anna Jaroslafovna was the mother of Philip I., king of France. She founded a convent in that country, and after her death was enrolled among the French saints.
‖ Coxe's "Travels in Poland, Russia," &c.
§ It is the custom at the present day in Russia for a father to leave his estate to be divided equally among his sons, so that a large property seldom descends to more than two or three generations; and, as in the case of Vladimir and Jaroslaf, it is not unusual, when a nobleman is growing old, for him to divide his property in his lifetime among his children, reserving to himself only a small portion, sufficient for his own maintenance, or residing with one of them till his death.

Kiof, and empowering the latter to put down any insubordination on the part of his brothers by force of arms; and on his deathbed, remembering the calamitous wars which had followed the decease of Sviatozlaf and Vladimir, and the dissensions which the partitioning of the empire had always occasioned, he entreated his sons to live at peace with one another, and not peril the safety and welfare of their country for their own selfish ambition. He was buried in the cathedral at Kiof, which he had founded, and whose walls have survived the storm of the Mongol invasion, and every fire, sack, and siege to which the unfortunate city has been since subjected; and the marble monument still stands that was erected over his tomb, and, being almost the only sarcophagus of the kind in Russia, it has been supposed that it was brought originally from Constantinople.*

For the period in which he lived, Jaroslaf was a learned and accomplished prince, and a diligent student at a time when reading was chiefly confined to the priests. He had restored to his empire the inestimable blessings of peace, which he generally preserved throughout his life, and his memory was long held in well-merited gratitude and esteem, for the justice and moderation with which he ruled, and the wisdom and equity of his laws; but the disastrous practice of the period to which he conformed, of dividing his dominions among his sons, produced at his death a repetition of the dissensions and revolutions which had ushered in the commencement of the former reigns; and the imperial princes, disregarding the dying injunctions of their father, and forgetting every other consideration in ambition for their own personal aggrandisement and desire for independent sovereign power, replunged Russia into all the horrors of a disastrous and desolating civil war.

In appearance, Jaroslaf was slightly made, with black eyes and hair, and rather below the middle stature. He married the princess Ingigerd of Norway, who, according to a custom that still prevails at the court of Russia,† took the name of Irene on embracing the Greek faith, and by whom he had six sons and four daughters; namely, Vladimir, who died before him; Iziaslaf, who married a daughter of the Emperor

---

* Pinkerton's "Russia."
† Every foreign princess, who marries a prince of the imperial family of Russia, is obliged to adopt the Greek religion, at the same time changing her name and taking that of a saint in the Russian calendar.

Henry III. of Germany, and succeeded to the throne of Kiof; Sviatozlaf, prince of Novogorod, who married the sister of Casimir, king of Poland; Vizislaf, prince of Polotzk; Vyzevold, who married a princess of the Greek empire, the daughter of Constantine Monomachus, and Halté the Bold; Jellisaveta, the wife of Harald Hardrada, king of Norway; Anna, the queen of Henry I., king of France; and two other daughters, of whom one became the wife of Boleslaf II., king of Poland, and the other espoused the king of Hungary.

The invasion of Constantinople by Vladimir Jaroslafovitz, was the last hostile attempt of the Russians upon the empire of the Greeks. From this time their friendly intercourse remained undisturbed for many years; but the civil wars that prevailed in Kiof during the reigns of the sons of Jaroslaf, greatly diminished their trade and commerce and as the Tartar tribes in Russia grew more powerful from the weakness of Kiof, their merchant vessels, unless strongly armed and attended, were frequently plundered in the Dnieper by these depredators, long before they had reached the shores of the Euxine Sea. But the Russians remained firmly attached to the religious faith of the Greeks, and were the only nation who responded with any assistance to the last appeal of the Byzantine emperor for support against the final invasion of the Turks; and as Constantinople became more deeply imbued with ecclesiastical prejudices, and more hostile to the Latin nations, "the Eastern Church," says Finlay, "became in their eyes the symbol of their nationality, and the bigoted attachment of the Russians to the same religious formalities, obtained for them from the Byzantine Greeks the appellation of the most Christian nation."*

* Finlay's "Byzantine Empire."

CHAPTER XI.

The Abars—The Turks—Mahmoud of Ghizni—He invades India—The Seljuks—Togrul Beg—Alp Arslan—Malek Shah—The Polotzi, &c.

> " 'Tis he of Gazna—fierce in wrath
> He comes, and India's diadems
> Lie scatter'd in his ruinous path,
> His blood-hounds he adorns with gems.
>
> Priests in the very fane he slaughters,
> And chokes up with the glittering wrecks
> Of golden shrines, the sacred waters."—MOORE.

HAVING seen the Russians settle down under a regular government, with a just and equal code of laws, and beginning to spread among themselves the polite arts and manners of the Greeks; before proceeding to the division of their provinces, and the decline of their power, which from this time gradually diminished till they had reached the comparatively insignificant position that they maintained in the middle ages, it is necessary to examine into the then existing condition of the Turanian or Tartar nations of Central Asia, by whom this change in their prospects was chiefly influenced, and their subsequent misfortunes introduced.

I have already mentioned the most powerful and anciently civilized of their race, the Huns or Hiongnus, their empire, their decline, their invasion of Europe, and ultimate fall. A few years after they had sunk into obscurity, the Avars first appeared on the confines of Europe; and, coming from Transoxiana, encamped near the foot of the Caucasus, entered into an alliance with the Slavonic tribe of the Alans, and, traversing the east of Russia, invaded Georgia, and besieged and captured the town of Bosphorus in the Crimea. They are stated, and it appears with probability, by the writers of the time, to have been a section of the Huns, whom they strongly resembled both in appearance and manners, with the exception that they wore their hair long; and Zeuss has observed, that one tribe among that people had formerly been distinguished in the works of a Byzantine writer, by their name.

In the reign of Justinian, the emperor of Constantinople, some ambassadors accompanied an Alan prince in a political mission he had undertaken to the capital of the Greeks. On obtaining an audience of the sovereign, Candish, the chief of the envoys, thus addressed him in the name of his own chagan or prince*—" You see before you, O mighty prince! the representatives of the strongest and most populous of nations, the invincible and irresistible Avars. We are willing to devote ourselves to your service; we are able to vanquish all the enemies who now disturb your repose; but we expect, as the price of alliance and reward of our valour, a yearly subsidy of that gold and those treasures with which you superfluously abound, and a rich and fruitful possession for our numerous people." But the emperor feared that these wild allies might prove as dangerous to their friends as to their foes; and, anxious to keep them at a safe distance from his own dominions, he recommended to their energies the subjection of the Slavonians and Bulgarians, who at this time perpetually harassed with their plundering inroads the border provinces of the Roman empire. Loaded with presents, the ambassadors returned to the encampment of their horde in Southern Russia, and informed their chiefs of the emperor's advice; and, precipitating themselves upon Poland and Germany, the Avars in ten years had obliterated every trace of many Bulgarian and Slavonic nations,† rendered the others tributary; and, though they sustained a signal defeat from the armies of the Austrasian prince, Sigebert, ended by founding a European kingdom, later known as that of the Magyars, in Hungary. The second in importance and extent to the Huns, among the Tartars, were the Turks, known to the Chinese as the Thu-kiu; and, according to Klaproth and Remusat, were themselves a tribe of those Hiong-nus who had entered the military service of China; and later, being driven from the province of Schensi by the dynasty of the Weï, had taken refuge under their leader Assena near the precipitous mountains of Altai. Here, dwelling under the foot of a helmet-shaped peak, termed from the circumstance by the Chinese Thu-kun, and from whence they derived their name, they became celebrated under their leader Thurnen,

* Gibbon's "Decline and Fall of the Roman Empire."   † Ibid.

who lived about A.D. 545; and a few years after, their khan, Dizabulus, was visited by ambassadors from Constantinople, whom he received with barbaric splendour and profusion, seated on a couch supported by two wheels.* Like the other Tartar nations, they supported large flocks, and lived in tents; a golden wolf on the top of a spear, formed the ensign of their tribe, and for years they carried on a desultory war with China, whom a Turkish prince once proposed that his people should rival and imitate, by founding cities and temples for themselves in their native deserts. But this advice was defeated by a stronger argument from another of the chiefs.† "The Turks," said he, "are not equal in number to one hundredth of the inhabitants of China. If we balance their power, and elude their armies, it is because we wander without any fixed habitation. When we are strong, we advance and conquer; and when weak, retire and are concealed. Should the Turks confine themselves within the walls of cities, the loss of a battle would be the destruction of their empire. The Bonzes of China preach only patience and humility. Such, O king! is not the religion of heroes."

The Turks, till they had invaded and adopted the faith of the various southern Asiatic states, believed in one Supreme Being, to whom alone they made sacrifices, though they had many religious songs in honour of the power and beneficence of the spirits of the elements; and, like all the Turanian nations, were extremely superstitious, consulting soothsayers, magicians, and witchcraft. Their laws were rigid and impartial as those of Sparta; the most serious crimes were punished with death; a robber was compelled to make restitution to the amount of ten times the value of the theft; and no punishment could be too horrible, or contempt and ignominy too severe, for any appearance of cowardice.‡ At the time of their emigration to the south, one of their tribes, separating from the rest of the horde, advanced northwards, and settled upon the barren and frozen plains of the Lena, where, under the name of Yakhutes, they still lead a wandering life, and speak a language which even now bears some resemblance to that of their more polished and luxurious brethren of Europe.

The Turks first became conspicuous about the middle of

* Pritchard's "Natural History of Man."
† Gibbon's "Decline and Fall of the Roman Empire."
‡ Ibid.

the sixth century, when they had already more than once invaded Persia and the districts of Mavarnalhar; and a few years later they possessed themselves of Khorassan, from whence they were shortly after expelled by the invasion of the Saracens, who had rendered themselves masters of Persia, and founded Bagdad. In the ninth century, the whole nation issued forth from the Mongolian steppes, and, following the path trodden by the more adventurous of their tribe, crossed the Jaxartes, and encamped in the plains of Transoxiana; then, turning towards the west, conquered and overran the kingdom of the White Huns at Carizme, who had maintained their existence on the eastern shores of the Caspian for several hundreds of years; and among whom, through the influence of Timothy the patriarch of the Nestorians,* who had sent thither several monks of his sect, Christianity was beginning to make some progress, though opposed by the votaries of the Mahometan faith. The latter had already made a considerable number of converts, and founded many mosques. The empire of the Turks, which now extended from the shores of the Caspian to the deserts around Cashgar and Samarcand, and from the banks of the Irtish and Permia to the borders of Iran or Persia, continued united in Asia till about the middle of the tenth century, when it fell to pieces and became separated into several states; and two of their hordes, again invading the northern unprotected provinces of Persia, wrested Khorassan and Ghizni, or Gazna, from the dominions of the caliphs. The position of this people with regard to Bagdad at that period, was very similar to the relations of the Slavonians and Bulgarians in respect to the city of Constantinople. Like her western neighbour, the wealthy Persian capital was looked upon with greedy eyes by all the wild and warlike tribes of the north. They continually invaded and plundered the frontier cities, and harassed her fertile territories; her gold was sufficient to attract their horsemen thousands of miles across sands and rocks; the science cultivated by the Saracens at Bagdad, has enlightened the whole civilized world; her merchants traversed Asia with their stores, and brought back fruits and tidings from the remotest East, yet she was unable to drive these warriors from her provinces, and often hardly prevented them from entering her own

* He was patriarch from A.D. 777 to 820.

well-guarded gates. Rising high on the banks of the mighty Tigris, on a plain where scarcely a hill intervenes between the Persian gulf and Mediterranean sea, and near the site of the ancient Nineveh and Babylon, she had been founded in A.D. 762 by Almanzor, the caliph of the Mahometan Arabians or Saracens, whose people about a century before, and in obedience to the decrees of Mahomet, had invaded simultaneously both the east and the west, and, conquering and overrunning Persia with fire and sword, had replaced the ancient creed of the fire-worshippers for the doctrines and faith of the Mecca prophet. Almanzor established the throne of the Saracen caliphs at Bagdad, which from this time rose in power and magnificence, till she became the most splendid and learned city of the east, and the virtues and wisdom of her sovereign, Haroun al Raschid, were acknowledged and respected throughout Europe. He sent ambassadors and presents to Charlemagne, who then swayed the sceptre of France, and at that period claimed the proud title of the Emperor of the West; but the subjects of the latter prince were, for the most part, still plunged in the savage ignorance which they shared with the rude Saxons of Britain and nearly all the other nations of the north, and exhibited a strong contrast to the polished and learned Saracens of the East, with whom later they were destined to come into so frequent and fierce a collision in the long and sanguinary wars of the Crusaders.

During the reigns of the second dynasty of the Mussulmen in Persia, the Sassanidæ, who sat on the throne of the caliphs for a hundred and twenty-five years,* the Turks subdued the province of Khorassan, from which they were expelled a few years after by a Saracen force. But in A.D. 964 they again advanced, and while a tribe under Seljuk established themselves in Khorassan, and, adopting the name of their leader, founded the kingdom of the Seljuk Turks, another division under Sebectagi, one of their chiefs, who, from a slave or common soldier, had raised himself to the sovereignty of Bactria, took possession of Ghizni, and embraced the faith of Mahomet. The humanity and probity of this prince is attested by many of the writers of the East, who, among other proofs, relate that, hunting one day in a forest, he captured a fawn, but, after tying it across his saddle, he chanced to look

* This family reigned over Persia from 874 to 999 A. D.

back, and saw the mother following apparently in great distress; his heart was melted at this sight, and he immediately released his prey. On another occasion, he rebuked his son Mahmoud, who had greatly interested himself in the erection of a splendid palace, informing him that he ought to study the welfare of the people and a good name, which would last for ever, rather than a perishable object for merely his own gratification.* Under Sebectagi, the Turks made two expeditions across the Indus, and invaded Moultan and Lahore, annexing Peshawur to their dominions; and this example was followed by the far-famed Mahmoud of Ghizni, the son and successor of Sebectagi, who, in no less than twelve hostile invasions, made the loud and fearful warcries of the Tartars resound on the plains of Hindoostan.†

This chief commenced his reign in 997, after deposing and condemning to perpetual imprisonment his brother Ismael, who had usurped their father's throne. His first campaign was against the ancient sovereign of his race, the emperor of Bokhara, who attacked his dominions, and whose family, the Samani, had maintained for a hundred years the chief authority in the regions of Mavar-ul-Nahar or Transoxiana,‡ and ruled all those provinces and Turkestan. After a long war, in which the Turks were repulsed in every engagement, Mahmoud utterly extirpated the whole family of their monarchs, and added all the provinces of Bokhara to his own empire; then, turning his arms to the East, in the year A.D. 1000, he ravaged the north of India. The unfortunate Jeipal, king of Lahore, opposed his progress with the united forces of fifteen other chiefs; but, being all defeated and taken prisoners, the splendid jewels with which their necks were encircled were formed by order of the conqueror into collars for his bloodhounds; and the captive monarch, to expiate the disgrace of his defeat, after the custom of his country ordered a funeral pile to be prepared, and threw himself into the flames. But his degenerate son, Annindpal, consented to acknowledge the supremacy of Ghizni, and received the crown from Mahmoud, though he only held it on condition of paying a heavy annual tribute. This expedition into Hindoostan was followed by three more on the part of the

* Murray's "History of British India."
† His history is written in the celebrated book called the "Yemini" by Abounair Otbi, who relates the numerous wars undertaken by Mahmoud and Sebectagi in Hindoostan.
‡ Literally translated, "Land beyond the river."

Tartars, of comparative insignificance, as they were merely to exact the punctual payment of the tax; but another campaign, which took place in 1009, and was provoked by the daring inroad of Annindpal, whose valour had been at length aroused by oppression, upon Affghanistan, carried desolation and bloodshed into the heart of India. The king of Lahore, having formed an alliance with the most powerful of the neighbouring monarchs, assembled under his banner the forces of Delhi, Carouge, Gwalior, Callinger, and Ajmere, and with an enormous army, passed the Indus, and entered the rocky districts of Cauhul. But a most terrible defeat awaited him on the borders of Peshawur Twenty thousand Hindoo soldiers were slain in the pursuit; and the conqueror, marching direct upon the fortress of Bheemgur, which had been considered as impregnable, and where an enormous amount of treasure had been deposited, chiefly the offerings of the idolaters and the wealth of the priests; he burst open the gates without opposition—the defenders, half dead with terror, falling flat on their faces at his approach—and, devoting every living thing to destruction, distributed the money and jewels it contained among his soldiers, his dervishes, and his poorer and aged subjects.*

The imprudent and unfortunate campaign of the Hindoos, having once revealed their weakness and riches to the eyes of the Turks, their country from henceforward, till the death of Mahmoud, was seldom free for above the short space of two years from his repeated and devastating attacks. Like an eagle, from his impregnable fortresses beyond the dark and stupendous peaks of the Indian Caucasus, or Hindoo Kosh, he perpetually and unexpectedly descended upon his prey; and, sweeping across the plains with his desolating force, returned to his own kingdom laden with plunder and spoil. At this time Carnouge was the chief and most magnificent of the capitals of Hindoostan; and the Eastern writers proudly boast of the sixty thousand musicians who formed but an insignificant portion of the populace; the thirty thousand shops for the sale of betel and opium; the pagodas with their towers rivalling the hills in elevation; the palaces of her princes, and her hundred idols of gold. Yet Carnouge yielded without a struggle to the first arrow of the archers of the north, and was rewarded by being exempted from de-

* Murray's "History of British India."

struction, while the Turks passed on, and ravaged all the districts to the south as far as Malwa and Guzerat; then returning, pillaged Delhi and Lahore. But upon their retreat the prince of Carnouge was attacked and defeated, and his city laid waste by the angry king of Callinger, who was indignant at the terms that the Indian monarch had concluded with the savage invader; when Mahmoud returning, engaged with his undaunted enemy, and forced him to fly before him, at the same time again besieging and capturing Lahore. Though in his early youth the conqueror of Ghizni had been chiefly inclined to scepticism, yet after his victories he became, or professed to be, a rigid follower and supporter of Mahomet; and, in his campaigns in India, his cruelties and destruction were chiefly perpetrated and directed against the Hindoo temples and pagodas, the idols and the Brahmins, and every order and rank among the priests. His last expedition was undertaken in the year 1024, when, for the first time, he saw himself threatened on the plains of Guzerat, with the probable chances of defeat. The native army was strong, and prepared to make a desperate resistance; his men wavered; he prostrated himself on the ground, imploring the aid of Heaven, then appealed to the religious zeal of his troops, and, placing himself in front of their ranks, besought them to obtain, if not the glory of conquerors, at least the no less honourable fame of martyrdom. His efforts were at length crowned with success; the Tartars charged repeatedly, and, after a fierce battle, drove back the armed elephants of the foe. Somnaut, the capital of Guzerat, opened her gates, and was entered by the victors in triumph; and advancing to the idol temple, which was supported by fifty-six columns, all of splendid workmanship, Mahmoud ordered the enormous figure of their chief deity, which was formed entirely of gold, to be immediately reduced to fragments. The Brahmins sank on their knees, and offered an enormous sum for its ransom; the Mussulman warrior was immoveable, and reiterated his commands, and the first tremendous blow was instantly given by the weighty sabre of an attendant Turk. This disclosed to the astonished view of the invaders innumerable diamonds, and other precious stones, of which the value is said to have exceeded all the rest of the booty that had been captured throughout India in any former campaign; and Mahmoud, who had contemplated at one time removing his seat of government to that province, resolved at least to unite it to his own empire, and on his departure placed over it, as viceroy, a native Brahmin, though after his death the people again became subject to the family of their former prince.*

At length, abandoning India, the Turks slowly returned towards the north, and Mahmoud received from his vassal or intimidated ally, the trembling caliph of Bagdad, the epithet of "Guardian of the faith and fortune of Mahomet," for his zeal in the propagation of the religion of the prophet. His capital of Ghizni, which had hitherto been little more than a rough military encampment, or horde of shepherds' huts, was enriched on his return with every decoration and ornament that his Indian expeditions could furnish, or Tartar ingenuity invent; many mosques and palaces were erected, and public institutions founded, and the city became celebrated throughout Asia by the name of the "Celestial Bride." He also invited several poets and philosophers to his court, who in their writings have applauded his government and recorded his fame; among others, the celebrated astronomer, Abdurrahman Sufi,† and they affirm that he caused justice to be so rigidly maintained, that in his reign, as they express it, "the wolf might drink with the lamb." On one occasion a woman, from a remote and lately conquered Persian province, appeared before him in the divan, and complained that she had been deprived of her son and property by a band of robbers. "It is impossible," said the monarch, "to preserve perfect order in so distant and inaccessible a district." "Why, then," exclaimed the woman, "do you conquer kingdoms which you cannot protect, and for which one day you will be called upon to answer at the last judgment?" Mahmoud saw the force of her argument, and issued prompt commands for the stricter enforcement of the laws in these parts. Another time, having contemplated the reduction of a neighbouring state—of which, the chief having lately died, his wife acted as regent during the minority of their infant son—he was induced to desist from his project by a message

---

* Murray's "History of British India." Gibbon's "Decline and Fall of the Roman Empire."
† A native Rai, in Irak, Persia. He observed and gave a name to the larger of the Magellanic clouds, which he calls the White Ox.
In his "Introduction to the Knowledge of the Starry Heavens," he says, "that below the feet of the Sukel, there is a white spot which is invisible both in Irak and in the more northern mountainous part of Arabia, but may be seen in the southern Tehama, between Mecca and the extremity of Yemen, along the coast of the Red Sea."—Humboldt's "Cosmos."

from the widowed queen, entreating him to wait till her child was of an age to oppose him. "During the life of my husband," said she, "I was ever apprehensive of your ambition; he was a prince and a soldier worthy of your arms. He is now no more; his sceptre has passed to a woman and a child, and you *dare* not attack their infancy and weakness. How inglorious would be your conquest, how shameful your defeat! and yet the event of war is in the hand of the Almighty."*

But her kingdom was shortly after extinguished, and her family, the Bowides, utterly destroyed, by the vigorous and rising power of the Seljuk Tartars or Turks, who, towards the latter years of the reign of Mahmoud, harassed and invaded his territories, and began rapidly to extend their dominions and influence over the more luxurious provinces in the south. From the mercenary soldiers of the caliph, they quickly became the masters of Bagdad; and after the death of Seljuk their leader, who, on being outlawed from Turkestan, had brought his followers into Khorassan, and founded this state, the Tartar generals held a council for the election of a new chief, at which it was agreed that the nomination should be decided by drawing lots, taken from a bundle of arrows held in the hand of a child. The prize was obtained by Togrul, the grandson of Seljuk; the latter, who lived to extreme old age, and long survived his son Michael, the father of Togrul, having adopted and educated the young prince, upon whom he had bestowed, some time back, the title and government of Neishabour, and who was forty-five years old when by chance he obtained the crown, which he was destined hereafter to embellish by new and more distant conquests. The old warrior of Ghizni saw their progress with uneasiness and mistrust. In the year 1030 he led an army into Khorassan, but the campaign was not accompanied with his former success; it was barren of any favourable or lasting result. The Seljuks retreated from before him, and then turned and routed the rearguard of his force; and, bewailing the instability of all human fortune and greatness, he died soon after his return at the age of sixty-three, a remorseful and broken-hearted old man. Avarice, which had always been a leading feature in his character, had greatly increased with advancing age, and his latter moments present

* Gibbon's "History of the Decline and Fall of the Roman Empire."

a melancholy picture of a struggle for the possession of earthly riches and power with approaching and inevitable death. A few days before this he caused all his jewels, ornaments, and riches, to be spread before him, and then enclosed in their former stronghold, determined to preserve them undiminished to the last; and commanding his whole army, which consisted of one hundred thousand foot, fifty-five thousand horse, and thirteen hundred elephants, to parade within his sight, he wept to think how soon his own possessions must pass from within his grasp, and how, like those of India, they might too soon become the prey and treasure of a foreign and hostile tyrant.*

His mournful predictions were speedily fulfilled; a few years after, the son of Mahmoud was driven by Togrul to the territory bordering on the Indus, where his descendants, confined to Ghizni and the stronghold of Caubul, reigned for above two hundred years, and until driven forth by the Monguls under Zingis.

In the mean time, Togrul had invaded and captured Bagdad; and, espousing the daughter of the Saracen prince, who united a sacred dignity with the duties of his regal office, assumed the title of Guardian of the Faith, and Protector of the throne of the Caliph. He also threatened the Asiatic provinces of the Byzantine empire, and burned Arzen, a large commercial city of Armenia, containing three hundred thousand inhabitants, and eight hundred churches, defeated the united armies of Georgia and Constantinople in Asia Minor, and laid siege to Manzikert. The Greeks who manned the walls showered fire, boiling pitch, arrows, and stones, upon the assailants, who were subsequently compelled to relinquish the attack, and return to Persia. But in 1052 the Turks again invaded the empire, though they retired without hazarding a battle, and Togrul their leader died in A.D. 1071, and, leaving no children, was succeeded by his nephew, Alp Arslan, or the valiant lion; while his cousin Koulturnish, a grandson of Seljuk, founded the dynasty of Sultans in Roum or Iconium, in Lesser Asia.† The great grandson of Koulturnish became later so celebrated in history as the valiant and generous Saladin.

As soon as their formidable opponent was dead, the Greeks,

* Gibbon's "Decline and Fall of the Roman Empire."
† Finlay's "Byzantine Empire."

unaware that he had bequeathed his dominions to a still fiercer and more terrible warrior, prepared to invade the territories of the Turks, but were defeated with immense slaughter, and their Emperor Romanus taken prisoner. The unhappy prince was forced to kiss the ground before the barbarian monarch, and pay a ransom of two hundred thousand pieces of gold for his deliverance,* while Alp subdued Georgia and Armenia, and forced the inhabitants of these kingdoms to profess the Mussulman faith; though, after his death, Georgia emancipated herself from the hated yoke of the Turks, and, through many ages of disasters and oppression, has firmly adhered to the Christian worship, retaining through every invasion of the Mahometans the succession of her native princes and bishops.

But Alp Arslan, preferring the conquest of Turkestan, the original seat of the house of Seljuk, to pursuing the fugitive Greeks, or continuing the Byzantine war, led an army so great across the Oxus, that it required twenty days to pass, and laid siege to the frontier fortress of Berzem, where he captured the governor, a Carizmian named Joseph. The conqueror reproached this officer with his folly, when brought before him, for having attempted to withstand his irresistible force; the prisoner replied angrily to the charge, and the barbarous Turk commanded that Joseph should die by the most painful and lingering death. On hearing this, the desperate captive drew a poniard concealed in his clothes, and plunged it into the victor's breast; he was immediately cut to pieces by the guards and attendants, but the event proved that he had inflicted a mortal wound, and Alp expired, after giving utterance to this dying reflection:—" In my youth," said he, " I was advised by a sage to humble myself before God, to distrust my own strength, and never to despise the most contemptible foe. I have neglected these lessons, and my neglect has been deservedly punished. Yesterday, as from an eminence, I beheld the numbers, the spirit, and the discipline of my armies; the earth seemed to tremble under my feet, and I said in my heart, Surely thou art the king of the world, the greatest and most invincible of warriors. These armies are no longer mine, and, in the confidence of my personal strength, I now fall by the hand of an assassin."†

---

* Gibbon's "Decline and Fall of the Roman Empire." Universal History.
† Ibid.

He desired that the inscription, "Ye who have seen the glory of Alp Arslan exalted to the heavens, come to Maru,* and see it buried under the dust," should be engraven upon his tomb.†

In the year 1080, and in the reign of Malek Shah, the son and successor of Alp, the Seljuk Turks consummated what may be considered as the most important of their conquests, as it was the one which first roused against them the anger and indignation of all Europe. This was the subjection of Jerusalem, where the most terrible outrages were committed by the infidels upon the defenceless pilgrims, who had resorted from every province throughout the Christian East, and the civilized nations of this continent, to worship on the steps of her sacred shrines. The Greek patriarch was dragged by the hair along the pavement, and thrown into a dungeon for the purpose of exacting a heavy ransom from his followers; and the priests of every sect were insulted and abused, wherever they ventured to appear in the streets. Many also who had passed through innumerable toils and dangers, to obtain pardon for their sins, and salvation for their souls, by offering up their prayers, or casting their wealth on the stones of the Holy Sepulchre, when they arrived at Jerusalem were not even permitted to enter her gates. But a zealous champion of their cause appeared, in an obscure hermit of Picardy, who heard and saw their wrongs with kindling eye; and, returning to Europe, he threw himself at the feet of the Pope, and conjured him to urge every Christian monarch to unite in expelling from Palestine the Mahometan Saracens and Turks.‡ The appeal spread like wild-fire through every country on the continent, and was responded to with equal enthusiasm by every prince and knight; and thus was commenced the first Crusade or Holy War, for the rescue of the Sepulchre and Palestine, by the followers and defenders of the Cross.

But, to return to the original hordes of the Turks or Avars who remained in Turkestan. Their subjection, which had been begun by Alp, was continued and completed by his son; Carizme, Bokhara, and Cashgar, received laws from Bagdad, and the name of her princes was inserted upon the coin as

---

* He was buried at Maru, 1079 A.D., in the forty-ninth year of his age, and tenth of his reign.
† Murray's "British India."
‡ Gibbon's "Decline and Fall of the Roman Empire."

far north as Siberia and Biarmaland. At this time the Polotzi first appeared in Europe, a people whose name signifies hunters, or people of the plain; and it is probable that they were a tribe of the Avars, driven out of Transoxiana, where the modern inhabitants, the Kirghiz Tartars, appear to belong to the same race. Driving the Petchenegans from the barren sands between the Don and the Ural, known at that time as the country of Kipzak, they afterwards followed and expelled them from the eastern districts of the Crimea, obliging them to retreat into Bulgaria, where, from the enemies, they subsequently became the valuable allies of the declining empire of Greece. The kingdom of the Polotzi or Cumans, continued on the Don for more than a hundred and fifty years, and the first settlements of the Genoese in the Crimea were held in dependence upon them. They were an extremely fierce and barbarous people, and when the extensive empire of Jaroslaf had become weakened by division, and exhausted by its long and frequent wars, carried their plundering incursions into the heart of Russia; they respected no treaties, and brought entire destruction and desolation on whichever side they turned their arms; and their invasions only ceased when the Monguls poured like a flood over their plains, and, having driven them out of Russia, forced them to take refuge in Moldavia, which was then a Hungarian province. There the king of that country, Bela IV., gave them lands and allowed them to settle, from which time they became quiet and peaceable subjects, and, amalgamating with the natives, their names have long ceased to be conspicuous, and were indeed ultimately blotted out from the political history of Europe.

The empire of the Keraites, or Kara-hitai, had succeeded to the power of the Turks on their descent from northern Asia. They quickly extended their dominions from the great wall of China to the Hindoo Koosh; and in the first year of the eleventh century, their prince, according to the Nestorian missionaries, was converted to Christianity through a miracle, and, with two hundred thousand of his subjects, consented to receive baptism. The ardent and adventurous missionaries of this church had traversed unknown districts from Bagdad to China, and braving every danger, and facing countless perils, had planted their doctrines and faith in the heart of the Chinese empire.* There, through hundreds of

---

* Huc's " Christianity in Tartary, Thibet, and China."

years, and innumerable revolutions and civil wars, the seeds which they sowed have survived, and they still maintain temples and convents in many districts; and the perverted germs of Christianity, now professed by the native rebels of China, who have long firmly opposed the influence and throne of the Mantchous, appear only to be the scattered remnants of the creed so earnestly propagated by these zealous priests. The royal convert of Kara-hitai erected a church on a plain to the north of the Gobi desert, which he dedicated to the martyr St. Sergius, and where he erected an altar and a cross. His successors, according to the usual custom in eastern nations, united in their person both a regal and priestly character, and a Keraite khan in the twelfth century invading Persia, ruining Ecbatana, and advancing to the Tigris, made his name known and celebrated in western Europe, and gave foundation for the story circulated in the middle ages, of the marvellous empire of Prester or Priest John, the word khan being mistaken for John. As this was his title, and of course borne by every monarch, the Europeans supposed that this Tartar prince was gifted with the virtue of immortality, or immense length of life, when travellers from time to time, returning from a journey into Asia, still brought tidings and reports of what they had seen or heard of the magnificent court of Prester John.

In the year 1046 the Keraites, who now ruled all central Asia, forty-five years after their conversion completed the subjugation of Cashgar. They are minutely described in a letter from the metropolitan of Samarcand to his superior the Nestorian patriarch, at Bagdad:—"A people," says he, "innumerable as grasshoppers, has opened for itself a passage across the mountains which separate Thibet from China, where, according to ancient historians, are to be found the gates constructed by Alexander the Great. Thence they have penetrated to Kaschgar. There are seven kings, each of whom is at the head of seven hundred thousand horsemen. The first of these is named Nazareth, that is to say, 'Chief, by order of God.' They have brown complexions like Indians. They do not wash their faces, nor cut their hair, but plait it, and tie it together at the top of their heads, in the form of a tiara, which serves them instead of a helmet. They are excellent archers. Their food is simple, and not very abundant. They practise, above all things, justice and humanity."*

In 1125 the Keraites conquered the Igours or Kalmucks, in the southern districts of Siberia, and they appeared to have continued Christians till they fell, in the thirteenth century, before the power of Zingis Khan.

* Huc's "Christianity in Tartary, Thibet, and China."

CHAPTER XII.

Iziaslaf—The Poles invade Russia—Sviatozlaf II.—Vyzebold—Novogorod—Increasing power of the Church.

> "The fairest cities of the land
> Are fired by an invader's hand;
> And famine follows in the car
> Of the fell demon, civil war."—ANON.

From A.D. 1053 to 1076, or from A.M. 6581 to 6604.

THE peace and prosperity which Russia enjoyed during the latter years of Jaroslaf, continued but a few years after his death. The army of Kiof having been very much reduced by its separation from those detachments who had accompanied the imperial princes as guards and retinues to their various sovereignties, Vizislaf, the prince of Polotzk, taking advantage of the diminished strength of the capital, to endeavour to throw off his allegiance to Iziaslaf, and increase his own dominions, marched an army into the territories of his brother, by whom he was defeated, and forced to retire upon Polotzk. To this town he was pursued by Iziaslaf, who, capturing him and his two sons, loaded them with chains and threw them into prison, threatening them with immediate death unless they renounced all claim to the principality, and acknowledged him as the lawful sovereign of Polotzk and Kiof. But the inhabitants, incensed at this treatment of their prince, rose up in arms against the usurper, and assisted by Sviatozlaf, the prince of Novogorod, and his brother Vyzevold, drove him from his kingdom, and compelled him to seek refuge in Poland, whose sovereign, Boleslaf II., was his cousin and brother-in-law, and in 1067 he was formally deposed from his throne by the National Assembly of Kiof. Upon this, Iziaslaf endeavoured to rouse the king of Poland in his behalf, who, urged by the hope of establishing for himself a claim to the empire, in right of his mother and wife, who were both Russian

princesses, advanced with a numerous army into Russia, and was encountered by the forces of Vizislaf within a few miles of Kiof. When Vizislaf perceived the Polish troops drawn up in order of battle, though in former wars he had shown himself by no means deficient in courage and intrepidity, he was seized with a fear and irresolution, which he vainly endeavoured to overcome. He escaped from his tent and fled from the field, and then ashamed of this pusillanimity, and attempting to recover his self-possession, returned; but at the sight of the enemy was again overcome with a panic, which all his efforts failed to conquer, and rendered him totally incapable of commanding his troops, till, finally abandoning the army, his soldiers, deprived of their chief, dispersed without engaging the enemy. The inhabitants of Kiof, finding themselves left to the mercy of the Poles, who were marching upon the city without opposition, solicited the assistance of Sviatozlaf and Vyzevold, who procuring a reconciliation between the citizens and their deposed monarch, Iziaslaf again ascended the throne. They also recovered for him the towns and provinces of which they had formerly deprived him. Polotzk and Minsk were the only cities that attempted to stand a siege; but the former was soon forced to capitulate, and in the latter, whose resistance had been more obstinate and protracted, all the men were cruelly massacred by the victors, and the women and children distributed for slaves among their warriors.* Vizislaf having escaped from his dominions, shortly afterwards died in obscurity, and the Polish king being recalled to Poland with his army by the prospect of a war with Hungary, Kiof was once more freed from foreign invaders.

But dissensions were continually arising among the princes, who perpetually encroached upon each others' territories. George, the metropolitan of Kiof, was so alarmed at these disturbances, that he abandoned his see and returned to Constantinople, his native place; and in 1072 Sviatozlaf again took up arms against his brother, and expelled him from his throne and country. Iziaslaf having vainly applied for the assistance of the emperor Henry IV. of Germany, accompanying his solicitations by rich and splendid presents, which dazzled and astonished the simple and unrefined court of the German kaiser, who, however, only remonstrated fruitlessly by an

* Pinkerton's "Russia."

ambassador with the usurper, sent his son to Rome to intreat the interference of the Pope in his behalf; while Sviatozlaf remained alike deaf to the bold reproof of Theodosius, a hermit, who dwelt in a cave near Kiof, where he founded a monastery, remarkable for the asceticism and severity of its rules, and the holy lives of its priests.* Gregory VII., the ambitious and zealous Hildebrand, who extended the power of the Church of Rome to a hitherto unknown extent, then filled the chair of St. Peter; and eagerly embracing the opportunity which appeared to present itself of including Russia within the bounds of the Papal see, and in the expectation that Iziaslaf would, on the recovery of his dominions, renounce the supremacy of the schismatical patriarchate of Constantinople, and acknowledge the authority of the tiara of Rome, he commanded the king of Poland to assist the Russian prince in regaining his throne, and addressed a long letter to Iziaslaf.† In this document he states, that, at the request of the son of the deposed monarch, he had administered to him the oath of fealty to St. Peter ‡ and his successors, not doubting that it would be approved by the king of Russia, and all the lords of his kingdom, since the apostle would henceforward regard their country as his own, and defend it accordingly. At the command of the Pope, Boleslaf once more entered Russia with a powerful army; and having ravaged the border provinces, and sacked and utterly destroyed the large town of Wolyn, he transported the plunder

---

* Mouravieff's "Church of Russia."
† Blackmore in his notes to Mouravieff's "Russian Church," gives the letter as printed in Baronius's Annals, tom. xl. 472.—
"Gregorius servus servorum Dei Demetrio," (this was Iziaslaf's baptismal name) "regi Russorum et reginæ, Apostolicem benedictionem. Filius vester limina Apostolorum visitans ad nos venit, et quod regnum illud dono Sancti Petri per manus nostras vellet obtinere, eidem beato Petro Apostolorum Principi debitâ fidelitate exhibitâ, devotis precibus postulavit, indubitanter asseverans illam suam petitionem vestro consensu ratam fore ac stabilem, si Apostolicæ auctoritatis gratiâ ac munimine donaretur. Cujus votis et petitionibus, quia justa videbantur tum ex consensu vestro tum ex devotione poscentis, tandem assensum præbuimus, et regni vestri gubernacula sibi ex parte beati Petri tradidimus, eâ videlicet intentione atque desiderio caritatis, ut beatus Petrus vos et regnum vestrum omnimodâque vestra bona suâ apud Deum intercessione custodiat, et cum omni pace, honore quoque et gloriâ, idem regnum usque in finem vitæ vestræ tenere vos faciat, et hujus militiæ finito cursu, impetret vobis apud supernum regem gloriam sempiternam. Quinetiam nos paratissimos esse noverit vestræ nobilitatis serenitas, ut ad quæcumque justa negotia hujus Sedis auctoritatem pro suâ necessitate petierit, procaldubio continuo petitionum suarum consequatur effectum. Præterea ut hæc, et alia multa quæ litteris non continentur, cordibus vestris arctius infigantur, misimus hos nuntios nostros, quorum unus vester notus est et fidus amicus; qui et ea, quæ in litteris sunt, diligenter vobis exponent, et quæ minus sunt vivâ voce explebunt. Quibus, pro reverentiâ beati Petri, cujus legati sunt, vos mites et affabiles præbeatis: et quicquid vobis dixerint ex parte nostrâ patienter audiatis, atque indubitanter credatis: et quæ illi ex auctoritate Apostolicæ sedis negotia tractare voluerint, et statuere, nullorum malo ingenio turbari permittatis, sed potius eos sinceræ caritate fovendo juvetis. Omnipotens Deus mentes vestras illuminet, atque per temporalia bona faciat vos transire ad gloriam sempiternam! Data Romæ XV. Kalendas Maii. Indictione decimatertiâ; hoc est anno 1075."
‡ Stephen's "Ecclesiastical Biographies."

which he had seized from the enemy's cities into Poland, and advanced upon Kiof. He was encountered near the city by Sviatozlaf, whom he defeated after a furious battle, in which the Grand Prince was killed; but the loss of the Poles was so great, that their monarch was forced to retire for a time, in order to recruit his forces, though the following spring he returned to Kiof and commenced the siege of that place. He remained for a long time before the walls, having failed in several desperate attacks to penetrate beyond, till the garrison was so weakened by famine and the plague, which broke out among them, that they were forced to capitulate, and Boleslaf entered the city, but treated it with a generosity too seldom practised in those days. He not only commended the valour of the citizens, but distributed an ample supply of provisions among them, and prohibited his troops from insulting them, or pillaging and destroying their houses. However, when Iziaslaf had been reinstated on his throne, the Polish soldiers, like their predecessors in the reign of Sviatopolk, refused to leave the country, which they found so much more opulent and luxurious than their own; and Boleslaf established himself as virtual sovereign, the Russian prince being little more than his vassal and dependant. Kiof, during the prosperous reign of Jaroslaf, had acquired riches and magnificence. Greek artists had been employed by him to build and decorate the churches, monasteries, and palaces; it had risen again from the desolation caused by the Polish army in the preceding reign with renewed lustre, and its extensive commerce had introduced the wealth and luxury of Byzantium; so that an ancient Polish historian remarks, "that Boleslaf, king of Poland, having remained during several years with his army in Russia, brought back his troops to their native country enervated by the seeds of corruption. That opulent country," says he, "steeped in pleasures, relaxed in energy, and destroyed by its commerce with the Greeks, proved no less fatal to the Polish army than did the voluptuous Capua to the soldiers of Hannibal."* Thus the Polish army with their monarch, who had become too indolent even to ride out on horseback, but passed his days engrossed in amusements and trifling pursuits in the interior of his palace, remained at Kiof, and appeared to have entirely forgotten their own country, till the reports of the serious disorders

* "Histoire de la Russie," par A. Rabbe.

that prevailed there at length obliged them to return, accompanied by an auxiliary Russian force to put down the insurrections that had broken out. But Boleslaf, though he had triumphed over all his foreign enemies at the time when he enjoyed the respect and confidence of his subjects, now having by his misconduct entirely lost their esteem, was unable to re-establish himself over his own people; and, being finally compelled to abandon his kingdom, he, according to most writers, ended his days in the humble capacity of a cook, in a monastery in Carinthia.*

No sooner had Russia been released from the oppression of the Poles than the Hungarians invaded her western provinces; and the two remaining years of the reign of Iziaslaf were continually disturbed by the invasions of the neighbouring Tartar tribes, particularly the Polotzi, who a few years before had driven the Petchenegans out of Kipzak,† and now extended their inroads and plundering excursions to all the countries round.

In 1078 they first extended their ravages into Russia, where they were met by the Grand Prince, with the Russian army, near the banks of the river Alta. He had previously visited with his suite the cave of a celebrated hermit, named Anthony, who, after visiting Greece and the Holy Land, had returned to his native country, where he lived in a secluded cell, excavated by his own hands, among the forests that surrounded Kiof, and who, it is said, foretold to Iziaslaf the disastrous result of the approaching battle.‡ On the 3rd of December, 1078, the Russians engaged with the enemy, but their army was completely defeated, in a furious engagement, by the overwhelming force of the Polotzi, and their Grand Prince was among the slain. His death took place in the fifty-fifth year of his age; and he was succeeded on the throne, according to the custom of Russia, by his brother Vyzevold, to the exclusion of his own sons.

From the death of Jaroslaf, Novogorod had become separated from Kiof, and continued so for about a hundred years; and, after the restoration of Iziaslaf, it joined but little in the wars, dissensions, and revolutions that at various times distracted the neighbouring states. Though itself a wealthy

---

* Article, Poland—*Encyclopædia Britannica*.
† Kipzak, or Kipshak, signifies the Hollow Tree; and these plains were known as Deshti Kipshak, or the Steppe of the Hollow Tree. It is the same word as Kamschatka.
‡ Mouravieff's "Church of Russia."

city, yet isolated as it was amidst the frozen and inhospitable marshes of the north, the country by which it was surrounded presented too barren an aspect to render it inviting to an invading army; and it was therefore comparatively free from the invasions of the unsettled and warlike tribes who surrounded Russia on every side, and who so frequently burned and plundered the less fortunate city of Kiof. A tumult was raised in the city in the year 1071, in the reign of Sviatozlaf, by an impostor who proclaimed himself a prophet, and instigated the people to rise up in arms, and endeavour to seize and murder their bishop, Fedor. The prelate made no attempt to conceal himself, but, taking the cross in his hand, he advanced in his pontifical robes, and called upon all true believers to resist the fury of the impostor, and the prince Gleb, the nephew of Sviatozlaf, having entered the street on hearing of the uproar, commanded the false prophet to appear before him. The wretched man, not daring to resist the summons, presented himself before the prince, who, producing an axe which he had previously concealed among his clothes, struck the impostor upon the head, and put an end to his life. The power and prosperity of Novogorod was increasing, while the other principalities of Russia were overrun and plundered by the neighbouring nations; and they extended their commerce far and wide, firmly resisting all the encroachments of their princes upon their liberty and privileges, and addressing remonstrances which, if not heeded, were speedily followed by deposition to those whom they deemed incapable of ruling them, or whose ambition of personal power appeared likely to endanger their freedom and privileges, so that a succession of no less than thirty-four princes alternately swayed the sceptre during the space of a hundred years.*

In 1071 a great famine occurred in Russia, and the idea arising that the women caused it by magic, great numbers fell victims to this absurd accusation; and, in 1129, Novogorod again suffered from the same calamity, the crops having been washed away in the spring by several furious storms; the people were reduced to the necessity of eating the bark off the trees in the place of bread; and the streets, being choked with the bodies of those who had fallen victims to starvation, a pestilence was induced, which destroyed

* Bell's "History of Russia."

thousands more of the inhabitants. This terrible scourge appears to have been very frequent in Russia during the early period of her history, and is even now of by no means an uncommon occurrence from the still undeveloped state of commerce, and the short summer season, and difficulty of internal communication; so that, if the harvest fails in a remote province, the inhabitants may be unable to repair their loss before the winter sets in, or if the winter happens to be of an unusual length, and their ordinary provision exhausted, though the other parts of the empire may be plentifully supplied, the obstructed state of the rivers and roads, during the breaking up of the ice, and the scattered and scanty population, has often precluded the arrival of any material assistance or relief before many have been carried off by this dreadful visitation.*

From the time when Christianity was first introduced into Russia, the priests had been gradually acquiring extensive power in the state, and over the minds of the rulers and people. Their revenues were continually increased by the gifts of the nobles and princes, who endowed churches with whole villages and forests; so that, when Peter the Great ascended the throne, one-third of the lands in Russia was the property of the Church. Vyzevold erected a chapel to St. Demetrius, on which he bestowed a grant of houses, woods, lakes, and rivers. It was the custom for the Grand Princes, when on their death-bed, to assume the habit and take the vows of a monk; and, if they unexpectedly recovered, the act was still binding upon them, and they retired into a monastery, to end their days in the devotions and seclusion of the cloister. The metropolitans of Kiof were always consecrated by the patriarch of Constantinople till the year 1147, when the Russians elected a monk of their own nation, named Clement, to the office, alleging, as a justification for this act of independence, that the patriarchal see was at that time vacant; but the nomination of this prelate, who was their fourteenth metropolitan, was nevertheless contested by Constantinople, and caused a division with that church which lasted several years. At this period, when literature was almost unknown in Scandinavia, Poland, and even Iceland, the Athens of the north in the middle ages, Russia produced an historian in the person of Nestor, a monk in the Pechersky

* See "Englishwoman in Russia," and other Travels.

monastery at Kiof. He was born at Bielozero in 1046, and entered the cloister at the early age of eighteen, where he composed his celebrated Chronicles, which form a history of Russia, extending from the year 858 to 1115, with an introduction containing a short history of the world; and this work was continued after his death, by the abbot Sylvester, till 1123, and by two other monks till 1203. He was acquainted with Greek, and many of the Byzantine authors, from whose writings he has inserted several passages in his history: and he was assisted in its compilation by the narrative of a fellow-monk, named Ivane, who, dying in 1106 at the age of ninety-one, had been born only a year after the death of Vladimir, and must have known many persons who were eye-witnesses of the establishment of Christianity in Russia. Nestor also wrote a geographical description of Russia, and a history of the Slavonians, and died about the year 1115.*

A curious monument of this period has been recently discovered on the Asiatic shore of the Straits of Kertch, in a marble slab, which appears to have been placed there in the year 1068, by one of the princes of Russia, and bears the following inscription:—"In the year (A.M.) 6576, Prince Gleb, the son of Vladimir, measured the Cimmerian Bosphorus on the ice, and found the distance from Tmutaracan to Kertch to be 30,053 fathoms."†

* Coxe's "Travels in Russia, Poland," &c.
† Spencer's Travels in Circassia, Krim Tartary, &c.

CHAPTER XIII.

Vyzebold Jaroslafobitz—Sbiatopolk Iziaslafobitz—Vladimir Monomachus.

FROM A.M. 6606 TO 6633, OR A.D. 1098 TO 1125.

> "The villain Arab, as he prowls for prey,
> Oft marks with blood, and wasting flames the way;
> Yet none so cruel as the Tartar foe,
> To death enured, and nursed in scenes of woe."—COLLINS.

THE reign of the Grand Prince Vyzevold Andrew is chiefly marked by the continual invasions of the surrounding tribes, particularly the Hungarians and Polotzi, or Cumans, who carried on a constant desultory warfare with the principalities of Russia; the contentions between his son and nephew; a dreadful plague that ravaged Russia; and the assistance he rendered to the emperor, Michael Ducas of Constantinople, that prince having requested his aid in suppressing the rebellion of the Chersonites, who had risen against the Greek Empire at a time when its forces were engaged in a war with the Bulgarians. Vyzevold sent a small detachment to the Crimea, under the command of his sons, Vladimir and Gleb, where the former received the surname of Monomachus,* or the Duellist, from his defeating in single combat, at the siege of Kaffa, the general who commanded the rebel town. Having unhorsed the Greek chieftain, Vladimir spared his life, but deprived him of his cap, enriched with diamonds, the gold chain he wore round his neck, and his girdle, as proofs of his victory. The Russians also compelled the citizens of Cherson to restore some of their merchant vessels that they had seized, and pay the expenses of the war, which was brought to a rapid conclusion by the death of the Emperor of Constantinople.

Vladimir also distinguished himself in numerous campaigns against the Polotzi, and caused his name to be dreaded by all

---
* Some writers suppose that he derived this surname from his maternal grandfather.

the Tartar tribes, whom he defeated in upwards of sixty battles and many petty skirmishes, and at length compelled them to respect those treaties for which his arms had forced them to entreat. Among other victories he made a successful expedition against Novogorod, and took the prince prisoner, whom he obliged to cede his possessions to his own son Harald, and content himself with a very small portion of his former territory. Monomachus had formerly received from his uncle, Sviatozlaf, the town and principality of Smolensko, as a reward for his services in the war between that prince and Iziaslaf; and his possessions were further augmented by Vyzevold, when he ascended the throne, who bestowed upon him the fertile province of Tchernigoff. This state lawfully belonged to Oleg, the son of Sviatozlaf, it having been bequeathed him by his cousin, the son and successor of Nicholas Vladimirovitz,* who, resigning his throne and embracing a monastic life, ended his days in the cloisters of Pechersky, and gave over his patrimony to this prince, who had already been deprived of his paternal rights. Oleg took up arms for the recovery of his domains, and, entering into alliance with the Polotzi, one of their tribes marched under his command against their former enemy; but a dispute arising between the prince and his barbarous allies, the latter, after murdering the unfortunate brother of Oleg, treacherously delivered their leader into the hands of Vladimir, who, sparing his life, subsequently permitted him to retire to Constantinople, where he remained during the life of Vyzevold, and from whence he only returned to raise another rebellion in the succeeding reign.

Vyzevold was born in Kiof, A.D. 1030, and married a daughter of the Emperor Constantine Monomachus of Byzantium. He left two sons, Vladimir and Gleb, prince of Volhynia, and two daughters, Anna and Eupraxia, the former of whom had made a journey to Constantinople, and founded a school and convent at Kiof; and both took the veil before their father's death, which took place on the 13th of April, 1094. He was buried in the cathedral of St. Sophia, in the capital, and on his deathbed declared his son Vladimir his successor, to the exclusion of his nephew, Sviatopolk, prince of Tver, the son of Iziaslaf, who, being the eldest member of the family, was the rightful heir to the

* A son of Vladimir the Great.

throne. But, upon being proclaimed as their sovereign by the people, Vladimir refused to accept the office, not wishing to violate the established order of succession which conferred the empire upon Sviatopolk. "His father," said he, "was my father's senior. I wish to preserve Russia from the horrors of a civil war." And, during the early part of the reign of Sviatopolk, he was the principal support and defence of his chief, whose guard, consisting of only eight hundred men, was inferior to the retinues of many of those princes who were nominally his vassals and tributaries, and with whom he was continually at enmity or engaged in a civil war.* At last, Oleg, taking advantage of the disturbed state of the empire to renew his claims, returned from Constantinople with his brother David, and, assisted by the neighbouring princes, regained Tchernigoff and Smolensko. In 1097, a congress, formed of all the chiefs who were descended from Vladimir the Great, was assembled at Kiof, over which Monomachus presided, and in which he is related to have displayed great diplomatic skill and sagacity, for the purpose of determining the limits of the territories, and satisfying the claims of the insurgent princes. The arbiters met in a tent pitched on the banks of the Dnieper, and after some deliberation it was agreed that Oleg and David should retain possession of the two provinces, and confirm their allegiance to Sviatopolk by an oath sworn on the cross. But the peace did not continue long; for David, having taken Volhynia, the territory of Basilko, the nephew of Monomachus, put out the eyes of its unhappy sovereign, whom he retained captive with the consent and support of Sviatopolk; and, indignant at this injustice and cruelty, Vladimir and the other chiefs of the empire immediately rose in arms against the two confederates. They marched against Kiof, and planted themselves before its walls, when there suddenly appeared as a peace-maker in their camp the metropolitan Nicholas, who, advancing towards Vladimir, exclaimed, "We beseech thee, O prince, be not so unnatural as to ruin your own country of Russia; for know that, if ye begin to fight among yourselves, the unbelievers will rejoice, and will take away from us our land, which your fathers won by great toil and valour, in all their wars in Russia; they sought even to conquer other countries, but ye now go about to ruin your

* Bell's "History of Russia."

own."* The soldiers all knelt as the venerable old man passed through their ranks, and a compromise was effected by his mediation, when the princes again assembling to consult on the restoration of peace and order in the empire, held their meeting as before, armed, and on horseback, in a tent near the capital, and summoning David to appear before them, deprived him of his title and dignity, and the province he had so savagely acquired; but in consideration of his near relationship to themselves, they presented him with the sum of four hundred grivnas before expelling him from their community, and agreed to allow him the tribute of four towns for his support. The death of Oleg, who retained possession of Smolensko and Tchernigoff, took place shortly after, and his descendants perseveringly contested for the throne with those of Monomachus, for a hundred and forty years, when Russia was crushed beneath the iron rule of her Mongul conquerors, and her princes only reigned, and were deposed or elected to the throne, by the will and caprice of the Tartar khans.

The weak and profligate Sviatopolk, whose name was also Michael, was born at Kiof 1051, and married Barbara, a daughter of the Greek emperor. He died on the 16th of April, 1113, and was buried with his wife in the church of the archangel Michael, at Kiof, which he had built and dedicated to his patron saint. A rumour having spread in the capital that he had been poisoned through the machinations of the Jews, a conspiracy was formed to massacre that unfortunate people, who at that period comprised a numerous body in Kiof, and a tumult arising, it was quelled, and the plot frustrated by the prompt interference of Vladimir, who also proposed to the boyards to nominate Vyzevold, the son of Oleg, to the vacant throne. But they, in conjunction with the people, unanimously elected Vladimir to the dignity of Grand Prince, being convinced that he was the only member of his family who had sufficient wisdom and influence over the other chiefs to preserve the empire from the anarchy and troubles with which they were threatened on every side; and he accordingly ascended the throne at the advanced age of sixty years. He so far yielded to the desire of his subjects as to publish an edict expelling the Jews from Russia; but he protected them from violence or ill-treatment during their

* Mouravieff's " Church of Russia."

emigration from the country, and allowed them to carry their property and wealth to another land. He received on his accession an embassy, with congratulations from the Emperor Alexius Comnenus, whom he had formerly aided in quelling an insurrection in Thrace, and who sent by his envoys presents, consisting of a golden sceptre, orb and imperial tiara, surmounted with a cross, and studded with precious stones. They were of the form employed in those of the Cæsars of Byzantium, and at the present day are preserved, with the imperial crowns and regalia, in the treasury of the Kremlin at Moscow, where they are still always used at the coronation of the Russian emperors. According to the poet and historian Lomonsoff, Vladimir assumed at this ceremony the appellation of Czar, a title only given in those times to the most powerful or most victorious among the princes of Kiof. His reign was a period of almost profound peace in Russia, and he greatly improved and modified the laws, at the same time enforcing their observance; for they had fallen much into disuse during the invasions and civil disturbances that had so long afflicted the empire, which, under his rule, enjoyed more prosperity than it had felt for many years. He built new towns, and improved those that had been burned and destroyed during the long and destructive wars; and his death was universally regretted by the nation, his reign having only extended over the short space of twelve years.

He was born in 1053, receiving at his baptism the Christian name of Fedor, and made his first campaign with Boleslaf, the king of Poland, in the expedition undertaken by that monarch against Bohemia. In 1070 he visited Denmark, where he married Gyda, the daughter of the unfortunate Harald, king of England, who, after her father's death in the fatal battle of Hastings, accompanied her grandmother, the Countess of Godwin, in her wanderings to Iceland and Norway, and at length took refuge with the other members of her family at the court of her kinsman, Svend, the Danish monarch. After engaging in all the wars between Iziaslaf and Sviatozlaf, Vladimir fought bravely under his father's standard in the battle in which that chief, with Sviatozlaf, was defeated, by Boleslaf and the Polish army, under the very walls of Kiof. By his first wife he had one son, Harald, whom he placed upon the throne of Novogorod, and who married Christina, the daughter of King Ingo Steinhelssen of Sweden, and, dying before his father, left two daughters, Malfrid and Ingeborg. The former married King Eric Egmund of Denmark, and the latter his brother, Duke Canute Lavard, and their son afterwards reigned as Waldemar the Great of Denmark. By a second marriage Vladimir left four sons, Micislaf, who married his cousin Eudosia, the daughter of Sviatopolk, Yarapolk, Viatcheslaff, and Yourii, who all reigned in succession, and to whom he bequeathed a written will or admonition, the oldest extant in Russia.*

His death took place on the 19th of May, 1125, in the seventy-third year of his age, and he was buried by the metropolitan Nicetas, in the cathedral of St. Sophia at Kiof.

During this reign literature appears to have made some progress in Russia; and Vladimir established libraries in

---

* "My children, praise God, and love men, for it is neither fasting, nor solitude, nor monastic vows that can give you eternal life; it is beneficence alone. Be fathers to the orphans; be yourselves judges for the widow; put to death neither the innocent nor the guilty, for nothing is more sacred than the life and soul of a Christian. Keep not the priests at a distance from you; do good to them, that they may offer up prayers to God for you. Violate not the oath which you have sworn on the cross. My brothers said to me—'Assist us to expel the sons of Rotislaff, and seize upon their provinces, or renounce our alliance.' But I answered—'I cannot forget that I have kissed the cross.' Bear in mind that a man ought always to be employed. Look carefully into your domestic affairs, and fly from drunkenness. Love your wives, but do not suffer them to have any power over you. Endeavour constantly to obtain knowledge. Without having quitted this palace, my father spoke five languages, a thing which wins for us the admiration of foreigners.† In war be vigilant; be an example to your boyards. Never retire to rest until you have posted your guards; never take off your arms while you are in reach of the enemy; and, to avoid being surprised, always be early on horseback. When you travel through your provinces, do not allow your attendants to do the least injury to the inhabitants. Entertain always, at your own expense, the master of the house where you take up your abode. If you find yourself afflicted by any illness, make three prostrations to the ground before the Lord; and never let the sun find you in bed. At the dawn of day, my father, and the virtuous men by whom he was surrounded, did thus; they glorified the Lord. They then seated themselves to deliberate or to administer justice to the people, or they went to the chase; and in the middle of the day they slept, which God permits to man as well as to the beasts and birds.‡ As to me, I accustomed myself to do every thing that I might have ordered my servants to do. Night and day, winter and summer, I was perpetually moving about. I wished to see every thing with my own eyes. Never did I abandon the poor or the widow to the oppression of the powerful. I made it my duty to inspect the churches, and the sacred ceremonies of religion, as well as the management of my property, my stables, and the vultures and hawks with which I hunted. I have made eighty-three campaigns and many expeditions. I concluded nineteen treaties with the Polotzi; I took captive one hundred of their princes, whom I set free again; and I put two hundred of them to death, by throwing them into rivers. No one has ever travelled more rapidly than I have done. Setting out in the morning from Tcheruigoff, I have arrived at Kiof before the hour of vespers. In my youth what falls from my horse did I not experience! wounding my feet and my hands, and breaking my head against trees; but the Lord watched over me. In hunting, amidst the thickest forests, how many times have I myself caught wild horses and bound them together! How many times have I been thrown down by wild oxen, wounded by the antlers of stags, and trodden under the feet of elks! A furious wild boar rent my sword from my baldrick; my saddle was torn to pieces by a bear. This terrible beast rushed upon my courser, whom he threw down upon me. But the Lord protected me. O, my children! fear neither death nor wild beasts. Trust in Providence; it far surpasses all human precautions."—See Karamsin's "History of Russia."—Laing's "Sea-kings of Norway."

---

† The Russians and Poles are still celebrated for the number of languages they are usually acquainted with.

‡ It is a common thing in Russia, and almost universal among the peasantry, to take a siesta in the middle of the day.

many of the monasteries, in which he collected numerous Greek and Latin manuscripts; and several theological works of this period still exist. Of these the most remarkable are the two epistles of Nicephorus, the metropolitan of Kiof, a Greek who had accompanied the princess Anna, the daughter of Vyzevold, from Constantinople; and there is also a description by a Russian abbot, named Daniel, of a journey undertaken to Jerusalem a few years after its conquest by the first Crusaders.

CHAPTER XIV.

The Poles invade Russia—Yourii Dolgoruki—Moscow founded—Kingdom of Halich.

"Massacre,
Treason and slavery, rapine, fear."—SHELLEY.

FROM the death of Vladimir Monomachus commences the most gloomy and disastrous period of Russian history; a period which is buried in darkness and obscurity, and of which few writings or authentic records remain. While the internal government of the country was given up to misrule and anarchy, the inhabitants suffered continually from the desolating inroads of the Tartars, who annually reduced many of the frontier towns to ashes, and carried off hundreds of the people to slavery or death. Riding their swift horses with the speed of the wind across the barren and trackless steppes between Asia and Europe, the wretched peasantry fled to the forests on their approach; while the invaders penetrated into the heart of the empire, sacked and pillaged the fields and villages to the very walls of the capital, and returned laden with spoil and plunder to their tents in the deserts, before the citizens had recovered from their consternation, or united for an attempt at self-defence. Micislaf or Peter, the eldest son of Vladimir, who, at the age of forty-nine, succeeded his father on the throne, had, before his accession, gained considerable renown in the numerous campaigns in which he had formerly engaged under the standard and command of Monomachus; but though his right to the crown was upheld by the citizens of Kiof, it was disputed by the sons of Oleg, and a fierce war ensued, which was carried on between the rival princes for many years. While his own character shines promiscuously in this age of lawlessness and vice, his reign was one long scene of terror; and, in the midst of the miseries that these dissensions produced, a terrible fire accidentally broke out in the capital, which destroyed, according to the Russian chronicles,* no less than four hundred chapels and churches, besides numerous houses. Micislaf was assassinated in 1132, when his brother Yaropolk succeeded in possessing himself of the throne, though violently opposed by the sons of Oleg, and Iziaslaf, the son of the deceased prince. At length, the latter finding himself without followers, succeeded in making his escape to Poland, where, appealing to the generosity of her king, Boleslaf III., he entreated that sovereign to lend him some assistance; which Boleslaf, rejoiced to find a pretext for humbling his ancient enemy, readily promised to do, and the following year the confederate princes marched with a large army into Russia. The Poles committed the most frightful ravages, and almost surpassed the Tartars in their waste with fire and sword; but the injured peasantry rose up at every step to oppose them. They united in bands, lay in ambush, or set fire to the woods through which the invaders advanced, and at length, defeating them in a furious battle, the scattered remnant of the Polish forces was compelled to make a hasty retreat; and their monarch, who, during a stormy reign of thirty-seven years, had preserved the fame and repute of a wise and ever-victorious prince, died broken-hearted at Cracow, a few months after his ignominious return. But, as soon as peace was restored, divisions again prevailed among the princes of Kiof. Yarapolk died at Tournoff † in the eighty-first year of his age, and was succeeded by his brother Viatcheslaff, and this prince only maintained his throne for twelve troubled days, being deposed ‡ by his cousin, Vyzevold of Tchernigoff, the son of Oleg; though, after the death of the latter chief, and that of his brother Igor, he again reigned, but was forced to accept as a colleague his turbulent nephew, Iziaslaf. He died in 1155, and in the short space of thirty-two years eleven princes swayed the sceptre of Kiof. One successively deposed the other, and in his turn suffered imprisonment or death; and, throughout the whole extent of Russia, the possession of influence, property, or wealth, was as uncertain and precarious as human life. Igor, the son of Oleg, was deprived of his throne by his cousin Iziaslaf, after a fortnight's exercise of sovereign power; and having been compelled by his rival to assume the habit and

---

* The "Chronicles of Nestor" say seven hundred; Mouravieff puts four hundred, and Tatischeff only thirty.
† In 1139. ‡ March 2nd, 1139.

take the vows of a monk, in 1148 ventured to emerge from his obscurity, and renew his claim to the princely crown; but, notwithstanding his priestly character, which it might have been supposed would have protected him from violence, was barbarously torn to pieces by the populace in the streets, during a riot which ensued on the deposition of Iziaslaf, by George Dolgoruki,* or the long-armed, the youngest son of Monomachus. This prince was born in 1091, and was one of the ablest and most powerful princes of the time, either in Russia or the other countries throughout Europe. He had reigned for many years in Suzdal, an extensive though thinly-peopled territory, bequeathed to him by his father, which he had greatly improved and strengthened, and where he had given lands to many foreign settlers, and planted several colonies of both Slavonians and Finns, successfully repelling three formidable invasions of the Novogorodians. A year before the event of his succession at Kiof, while hunting over the dense forests in the centre of his dominions, he passed through the demesne of Stephen Kutchko, a rich and powerful boyard, who possessed a large village on the confluence of the rivers Moskowa and Neglina, and concerning whom all his dependants spoke with extravagant raptures of the marvellous beauty of Eudosia his wife. Being desirous to see her, of whom fame reported so highly, the Grand Prince sent an order to Kutchko, desiring them both to come out to meet him, and present him with the honours due to a visitor and their prince; but the jealous and haughty nobleman suspecting treachery, refused to comply, for which he was soon punished by a dreadful fate. The fierce and imperious Dolgoruki, unaccustomed to disobedience or opposition, immediately commanded his followers to attack the castle of his uncourteous vassal: they fired it, and, as it was constructed of wood, it rapidly blazed to the ground; and, while its unfortunate master perished in the flames, Eudosia was rescued by her lover in person, who elevated her to share his throne. Admiring the situation of his victim's estate, crossed by two sparkling streams, and in an opening between thickly-planted woods, George established a royal residence on this spot, and so laid the foundations of the future city of Moscow, in this act of fraud and violence.

* "Dolgoruki," that is, "the long-armed." This appellation descended to another branch of the family, by whom it is still borne as a regular surname.—Blackmore's "Notes to Mouravieff's Church of Russia."

According to tradition, the picture of the Virgin of Ephesus, which the Russians consider the palladium of their city, and, their legends assert, was painted by St. John in Asia Minor, and from thence transported to Constantinople, was brought from the Byzantine capital by George, having been presented by the emperor Manuel Comnenus to his wife, the grand princess. It now adorns the Spassnaia Vorotu, or Holy Gate of the Kremlin at Moscow, under which, to this day, no faithful Muscovite passes with covered head; though from Moscow it was originally transferred in 1154 to Vladimir on the Kliazma, where a cathedral was built to receive it, and not restored to its old place in the capital till the year 1400, when Moscow saw herself threatened with destruction from the Tartar army of Tamerlane.*

In 1146 George entered Kiof with a small force, and after a brief struggle possessed himself of the throne; but, even he, was not able to retain long control over the restless and turbulent princes, and was twice expelled by his brother and nephew, though at last, bearing down all opposition, he resumed the government in 1155, and retained it till his death. It was during his reign that an illustrious stranger was received at the Russian court in the person of the Byzantine prince, Andronicus Comnenus; who, escaping from a dungeon in Constantinople, which his treason against the emperor Manuel his cousin had well merited, had proceeded as far as Halich, when he was intercepted by the emissaries of the emperor, and immediately placed under arrest. They were preparing to reconduct him to Constantinople, and had encamped near a wood to pass the night on their journey home, when, under cover of the darkness, he contrived to escape the vigilance of his captors, and freeing himself from his bonds fled to Kiof. He was there honourably received by the Dolgoruki, and soon rose high in the favour of the prince and his people, by the ardour with which he pursued falconry and hunting, and their other favourite sports; and he remained with a princely retinue and establishment at this court, till Manuel, having engaged in a war with Hungary, sent to offer his rebellious subject a pardon, on condition that he would procure the alliance of Russia against their enemies. George acceded to the request, and sent a detachment of Russian archers on horseback, under the command of Andronicus, to the shores of the Danube; and at the assault of Zemlin, which they stormed and captured with great slaughter, the assistance and personal valour of the exiled prince fully reinstated him in the favour and confidence of the emperor.* George or Yourii Dolgoruki died in 1157, and a struggle immediately commenced for the possession of the capital. The chief disputants were Iziaslaf, the son of Igor, who, undeterred by the remembrance of his father's horrible murder, clamorously preferred his claim to the throne, and Rotislaf the son of Micislaf, who had already once reigned, having been expelled by the predecessor of George; and, during this tumultuous period, many of the citizens abandoned the capital, and, retreating into distant parts of the empire, sought in other towns the peace and security to which they had long been strangers in their own. Meantime, all the contending princes, having each for a few months prevailed over his rival, and successively assumed the crown, were in their turn displaced, and succeeded by Micislaf, the son of Iziaslaf II., who in 1159 established himself in Kiof.

About this time, another large and powerful sovereignty began to rise in the western provinces of the empire, which comprehended a vast territory that has since formed a considerable part of Poland, being conquered by that monarchy in 1340. This was the kingdom of Halich; and spreading over the Ukraine, Podolia, and several of the surrounding states to the frontiers of Hungary, it was the most fertile and productive of all the numerous principalities of Russia, where it was commenced with the inheritance of Gleb, the brother of Vladimir Monomachus. His son Rotislaf, to whom he left Volhynia, the province of the ancient Drevlians, was succeeded by Volodar and Vladimirko, the latter of whom engaged in a long war with Poland; but, having received the Polish count Vlosezoviez at his court, who entreated his protection, pretending to have incurred the anger of his king, the treacherous refugee caused him to be seized while hunting in a wood, and carried through byroads into Poland, where he was put to death. His son Jaroslaf, to avenge his father, marched on Willisca, a town in the government of Cracow, and, having bribed the governor to surrender it, destroyed the place, and loaded the inhabitants with chains. A few months after, a Polish army which had invaded

* Gibbon's "Decline and Fall of the Roman Empire."

Halich was cut to pieces by the Russians, who had concealed themselves in ambush, and rushed out unexpectedly upon the foe; and Jaroslaf, during a long reign of thirty-five years, improved and extended his dominions, and, having concluded a favourable peace with Poland, was succeeded by his son Vladimir in the year 1188. After a reign of a few months, this prince was deposed and murdered by his cousin Roman, the son of Micislaf, prince of Novogorod, who obtained many victories over his surrounding enemies, twice sacked and burned Kief, compelling his father-in-law, the Grand Prince Rurik II., to retire into a monastery, and considerably extended the frontiers of his dominions, which in his reign attained some political importance and strength. He was a valuable ally to Alexius Comnenus of Constantinople in many sanguinary wars, but was subsequently defeated and killed in a battle fought with the Poles in the year 1200, when his country became a wretched prey to all the horrors and misery of civil war. As he had left only two infant sons as his successors, whose mother was unable to maintain them on the throne against the opposition of their ambitious kinsmen and the surrounding hostile states, Andrew II., king of Hungary, embraced this favourable opportunity to invade Halich, and, having subdued the principal cities and villages, proclaimed his son Koloman their king. The young prince made a triumphal entrance into his new kingdom, where he was crowned with much state by a Hungarian bishop; but their attempt to establish the Roman Catholic religion in the country irritated the people, who firmly adhered to the national faith, the Greek Church, and, rising up in arms against the invaders, the Russians of Halich, with the assistance of one of their princes, Micislaf the Brave, drove the foreign usurpers from their land in 1216, and Daniel, the son of Roman, succeeded to the throne. It was upon this temporary occupation of Halich, in defiance of any other right than that of conquest, that the Austrians asserted a claim, as lords of Hungary, to the province of Galicia, before the first dismemberment of Poland in 1772.* Peace was concluded upon the departure of the Hungarians, and continued for some years; till in 1224, the Monguls poured like locusts into Kipzak, and Daniel and Micislaf united their arms with those of the

* Krasinski's "History of Poland."

other princes of Russia, in a fruitless attempt to arrest the progress of their rapid and advancing conquests. The combined forces of the empire marched as far as the river Kalka, near the sea of Azof, but sustained a dreadful defeat on its banks; three of their princes were slain in the engagement, and the flying soldiers scattered and dispersed; and on their return to Halich, Micislaf buried his head in a monastery, and Daniel was compelled to pay homage for his throne to the Tartar conqueror, Batú Khan, who ravaged and laid waste the whole province on his passage to Hungary and Poland. At length, in the hope of emancipating himself from their merciless and intolerable oppression, Daniel appealed to the Pope for assistance; and, having consented to acknowledge him as his superior, and the true successor of St. Peter and vicar of Christ, he received a promise of aid and support from the Roman pontiff, and the title of Rex Russiæ, or king of Russia. He was solemnly crowned with this appellation by the Abbé de Messina, the Papal legate, who came to officiate at the ceremony as proxy for the pope; but, finding that Innocent was totally unable to render him any assistance, or even to secure his more ancient and nearer tributaries, Hungary and Poland, from ruin, Daniel soon broke off all connection with the see of Rome, and by his own efforts succeeded in ridding his country of her oppressors; while his energy and wise administration greatly contributed to raise her from her utter desolation and misery. His brother, Vassilko, who succeeded him in 1276, had already received from the pope the title of Rex Laudemariæ, or king of Vladimir, or Lodomeria, a district of Galicia; and on his death, in the year 1290, his nephew, Luo Danielovitz, ascended the throne, and established his capital at Luoff in Galicia, which he built, and which, under its modern name of Leopol, or Lemberg, now forms the chief town of that province. His decease created serious dissensions in the state, as the possession of Halich was long contended for by a prince of the royal house of Suzdal, and Bela, king of Hungary; but neither of the opponents being able to found any just claim, George, the son of Luo, succeeded in asserting his right, and established himself on the throne in 1301. On his death, fifteen years later, his two sons, Andrew and Luo, reigned jointly; and, on their successor George II. dying without heirs in 1336, his nephew, Boleslaf, Duke of Mazovia, took possession of the throne, but only lived to enjoy the dignity four years. As he left no sons, Cassimir the Great, king of Poland, under the pretext of relationship with the last sovereign, annexed it to his own kingdom, of which, from henceforward, it formed a considerable and important part; though the inhabitants long resisted the Polish domination, and appealed to the other Russian states for assistance, which the latter, who were themselves at that time suffering under the grievous oppression of their Mongol conquerors, were entirely unable to bestow.

It was during the early part of the reign of George Dolgoruki, that St. Anthony, a celebrated hermit, lived at Novogorod. He founded a convent on the river Volkhof, about a mile and a half below the city, in which his tomb is still shown, and where he died in 1147.

CHAPTER XV.

Continuation of the History of Russia—Invasion of the Poles—State of Society in Russia.

> "The wretched owner sees afar
> His all become the prey of war;
>
> Thy swains are famish'd on the rocks,
> Where once they fed their wanton flocks.
>
> Yet, when the rage of battle ceased,
> The victor's soul was not appeased;
> The naked and forlorn must feel
> Devouring flames and murd'ring steel."

WHILE the other nations of Europe were composing their civil discords, that they might unite the more strongly and efficiently in their wars with the infidels, and acquiring refinement and knowledge by their increased intercourse with foreign states, and by the science and improvements they brought from the East, the princes of Russia were exhausting their talents and strength in savage and unnatural discords with each other, so that their contemporaries of the west were fast forgetting their existence and name; and, despairing of effectually protecting their frontiers from the Tartars, the inhabitants deserted the country districts, and flocked to the towns, where the walls formed some shelter from the enemy, though the streets of the capital continually afforded a disgraceful scene of combat. Andrew, the son and successor of George Dolgoruki, wisely withdrew for a time from the struggle for the possession of Kiof; which was ultimately besieged by Miceslaf, a prince of the house of Tchernigoff, and making Vladimir on the river Kliazma his capital, he built the cathedral of the Assumption, for the reception of the picture of the Virgin of Ephesus, and caused it to be brought there from Moscow. In this church, his armour and princely vestments, comprising the purple mantle, helmet, and coat-of-mail, and his quiver, bow, and arrows, are still preserved. The position of the city of Vladimir was far preferable at that time to the site of the old metropolis; for though the climate of Kiof was so superior to the harsh air of her northern rival, and the land more productive and fertile, she so nearly approached the frontiers of Hungary and Poland, and the barbarous roving Tartars on the southern steppes, that she was always peculiarly exposed to the perils of a sudden invasion, and indeed her history from this time, during nearly five hundred years, is a mere dull record of civil wars and bloodshed. Andrew also enlarged and improved the still unknown and insignificant foundations of Moscow, where he occasionally resided for a few months, though chiefly for the amusement of hunting; and fearing lest Novogorod (which a century later was admitted into the Hanseatic * League, and had already formed commercial alliances with the principal mercantile towns of Germany and the Baltic provinces, as well as the extensive trade she had always carried on with the East) might prove a dangerous rival to the prosperity and traffic of his new capital, he marched against her at the head of his army, but was repulsed by the citizens from under her walls, and ignominiously forced to retreat. His pride refused to return to his own dominions, with, instead of the fame and trophies he had anticipated, a considerable loss of many of the bravest of his men, and the contumely that usually accompanies an aggressor's defeat; besides, his boyards clamoured for a higher recompence than his scanty funds could produce, or to be led to an easier victory, where they could repay themselves with the enemy's spoil. Accordingly he marched, with eleven princes of the royal family, against the unfortunate city of Kiof, which, having been deserted by the greater number of her inhabitants, and long abandoned to strife and anarchy, fell a ready prey to his arms; and, after an obstinate engagement outside the gates, he attacked and carried the town by storm, and, according to the Russian custom of a victor, hung his banner and ensign over the principal entrance. After condemning Micislaf to lose his eyesight, and to perpetual imprisonment in a monastic cell, Andrew carried the crown, with all the insignia of royalty, to Vladimir, and, reducing the ancient

* The Hanseatic League was a union of the principal towns in northern Europe, to defend their commerce and traders from the depredations of the Russian and Scandinavian corsairs of the Baltic. It was commenced in 1241, by the citizens of Lubeck, who connected themselves with Cologne, Brunswick, Dantzic, London, Bergen, Novogorod, and Burges, in the north; Augsburg and Nuremburg in central Germany, and the Italian republics in the south.

seat of government to a tributary province, intrusted the command to his brother Gleb, and returned to Suzdal. The following year he prepared another army for the subjugation of Novogorod, and placed it under the command of his son, Vyzevold, accompanied by seventy-one princes of the royal family, all of whom were descendants of Vladimir the Great; and many were the sovereigns of small principalities whom Andrew had compelled to renew their former allegiance and dependence on himself as Grand Prince, following him to battle, according to the ancient and established law of Russia. But his army was again repulsed by the valour of the citizens, and a long and desultory war ensued, till at length the Novogorodians, in the hope of securing for their country some prospect of peace, agreed to enter into negotiations with the ambitious monarch; and a truce was concluded, in which it was decided that, for mutual interest and defence, they should unite their city and its dominions to Suzdal, and acknowledge the supremacy of the Grand Prince, though retaining their former privileges, and their own code of laws, and mode of government.

But the order and tranquillity which Andrew had restored to the empire with an iron and heavy hand, was not of long continuance, for great discontent prevailed in his family, and among all the tributary princes of Russia; who returned to their private estates after the campaign against Novogorod, where they had obtained little honour or booty, and found themselves once more lords and masters among their own adherents and dependants. With these ranged beneath their banners they fancied themselves, with a fatal self-confidence, to be invincible; and, feeling no inclination to submit to the arbitrary will and pleasure of the Grand Prince, their exaggerated ideas of their own strength and influence induced them one by one to revolt against his authority. He sent bands of his guards and archers into their territories, burned their castles, and ravaged their lands, punishing all the offenders who fell into his hands with a cruel and vindictive severity. Many others, among whom were three of his brothers, accompanied by their mother, intimidated by the fate of those who had been captured, fled from Russia and took refuge in Constantinople; and they remained there till the year 1174, when Andrew was assassinated in his own palace, by a conspiracy of his guards and attendants, formed at the instigation of the exiled princes; and his subjects universally rejoiced at his premature death. His brothers received a pardon from Vladimir, his eldest son and successor, and shortly after returned to their native land; but the time they had passed as outlaws was not unattended with benefit, for the education which their children had received in the learned schools of Constantinople, proved of great advantage to their country, when later they rose to rank and influence in the state. On ascending the throne of Suzdal, the young prince Vladimir gave up the province of Kiof to his brother Michael, and by this act again divided the empire, whose scattered provinces had been united by their father at the expense of so much war and bloodshed. He also founded the town of Tver, where in 1182 he built a fortress to protect his dominions from the incursions of the Novogorodians, who had emancipated themselves from the yoke of the Grand Prince, and endeavoured by the subjection of their oppressor to ensure their own independence. About this time, two other republics * also arose in the empire: Viatka, which had been founded by colonists from Novogorod, and Pskof, formerly a dependency of the same city; and in 1217 the Novogorodians completed the subjugation of the whole kingdom of Biarmaland, or Permia, the marshy regions about the Onega and Ladoga lakes having been conquered as early as 1079, by the Russian prince Gleb, of Novogorod. The district on the shores of the White Sea had been subdued towards the end of the twelfth century by St. Stephen Permeki, who commanded the army of Novogorod, and founded a monastery at the mouth of the river Wym, or Dwina, invented the Permian alphabet, and endeavoured to convert the inhabitants to Christianity; and at this period all the north of Russia was under the dominion of Novogorod, whose throne was again occupied, in the early part of the thirteenth century, by Micislaf, a prince of the royal house of Suzdal, or Vladimir. Michael Androvitz of Kiof was succeeded in 1174 by his cousin Rurik II., who, after having been twice expelled from the throne, was forced by his son-in-law, Romanus of Halich, who twice besieged and sacked Kiof, to resign his crown, and, taking the vows of a monk,

---

* These republics, like those of Novogorod, were not presided over by an elected president, but the throne was occupied by a prince in whose family the office was hereditary, though his power was but nominal, the real government being vested in the elected magistrates and the assemblies of boyards and citizens.

retire to a cloister; but after the death of his enemy, he was enabled, by the troubles that succeeded in Halich, to expel the emissaries of his conqueror from Kiof, and, throwing off the cowl, again ascended the throne. He lived to be deposed for the fourth time by Vyzevold, the son of Sviatozlaf III., a former Grand Prince of the House of Tchernigoff, who had dethroned, and in his turn been expelled, by Michael Androvitz, and Rurik shortly afterwards died miserably in poverty and obscurity, unpitied and unaided by his subjects, whose religious feelings had been more shocked by his abnegation of his priestly office, than by the barbarities that had been committed by the rival chief. About this time, the Poles having driven their monarch, Mieczyslaf III., who had exasperated his subjects by his tyranny and oppression, from his kingdom, and established his brother, Casimir the Just, upon the vacant throne, the deposed monarch took refuge in Russia, where his death taking place suddenly, Casimir accused the Russians of having poisoned his brother, and entered Russia with an army, under the pretext of revenging his death. The Poles besieged and captured Kiof, which they held for several years; when Vyzevold, who had been driven out of his capital, having succeeded in collecting a small force from among his scattered subjects, expelled the invaders, and reinstated himself upon his throne, from which he was once more deposed in 1214, by Micislaf, a prince of the House of Monomachus. It was during the reign of the latter prince that the cloud which had long been gathering in Asia burst over the devoted country, and the terrible invasion of the Monguls threatened to efface every vestige of humanity or civilisation, and root out the very name of Christianity from Europe.

Since the death of Vladimir II., a space of less than a hundred years, no less than eighteen princes had successively worn the crown of Kiof. During that period the unhappy city had been twice captured and held for a few years by foreign invaders, several times consumed by fire, and frequently besieged, stormed, and given up to plunder. At the same time, the country around had been continually reduced to the greatest misery by the inroads and ravages of the Polotzi and other neighbouring tribes, who, as has been mentioned, often penetrated into the very heart of the empire, laying waste all the country on their route, and dragging off the prisoners, unless they saved themselves by suicide, into a captivity worse than death. The peasant sowed his field with the gloomy foreboding that his land might be trampled and destroyed by a hostile army before the wheat was in the ear; he piled up the log walls of his wooden cabin, from which he and his family might too soon be forced to flee, with no other refuge than the snow, or the smoking ashes of a neighbouring monastery or church; and the boyard stored his barn, with the prayer that its produce might not support the forces of his enemies, or himself be compelled to witness their revelling, while their horses were stabled, and themselves encamped in the rooms of his own palace. Driven from the innermost recesses of their forests, by the fires kindled by the Tartars on their forays, which often consumed in one vast funeral pile miles of grass and wood, the people flocked to the towns, in the hope that they might find safety in numbers, and to escape from the flames of their villages, and burning steppes; though, even there, they could not always find shelter from the invaders, but saw their churches and houses destroyed before their eyes, and their children with their wives, upon whom none before had been permitted to gaze, carried away into hopeless slavery. In the mean time, the perpetual contentions of their princes greatly increased the misery of the unhappy land; the accession of every monarch was the signal for a civil war, and, while some of these were expelled three or four times from the throne, others were blinded to incapacitate them for the regal dignity, or were forcibly constrained to adopt a monastic life; and one sovereign of Kiof, Roman Rotislafovitz, voluntarily abdicated in despair, at the disputes and dissensions he was unable to subdue, and a devastating expedition of the Tartars, which he had vainly endeavoured to repel. Few indeed of the Russian chiefs at this period descended by a natural death to the grave, or died in peaceful possession of the kingly power; and the efforts of those among them who endeavoured to introduce order and justice, a regular government, and a more general observance of the laws, were only partially successful; and their death plunged the state, where the uncertainty of life and fortune had given rise among all classes to the utmost recklessness and apathy, into its former troubles and anarchy. The metropolitans and priests occasionally endeavoured to mediate between the princes; several of the former, when newly elected by the patriarch of Constantinople, upon their first arrival in the Russian capital, terrified at the disorders and calamities that prevailed, returned in haste to their native city, or retreated to other provinces of the empire; and on one of these occasions the Grand Prince, in displeasure at the conduct of the prelate, appointed a native Russian to the office of metropolitan, without any reference to the patriarch, which created a division with the church of Constantinople that lasted several years. The laws and general customs at this period appear to have deviated very little from those which were in use in the days when Vladimir the Great and Jaroslaf sat upon the throne; but it is very improbable that in these turbulent times the former were much enforced or obeyed. The indolence of the Russians appears to have exceeded that of almost any other nation. They passed their lives in lounging about the public squares, or in their favourite amusements of music and dancing, and carousing in the wineshops; and a chronicle of the time bitterly laments over the luxury and indifference to religion, the empty churches, and general depravity and corruption of morals, that prevailed in those days among his countrymen. The houses of the lowest classes of the peasantry, who on St. George's day were annually accustomed to assemble and hire out their services for the year, were, as now in some parts of Russia, built, for the convenience of warmth, half under ground; while those of a higher rank were generally constructed with the same object in two stories, of which the upper, which was ascended by stairs outside, was alone inhabited, and round each apartment, benches or divans were fastened to the wall, serving in summer the purpose of seats and beds, in winter a couch of skins being spread upon the floor. The rooms near the entrance were occupied by the men; the interior, which was inaccessible to strangers, being set apart for the women, who were retained there in the closest imprisonment, never appearing in the churches or other public places, and seldom crossing the thresholds of their houses, where they had no authority or control; and the highest proof of confidence or esteem that a Russian could show to a friend was, to permit him to view his wife. A husband never saw his wife before she became his bride, and marriages were usually contracted by persons whose sole profession consisted in providing young men or women with wives or husbands. At their entertainments the nobles were accustomed to oblige their slaves to dance before them for the amusement of themselves and their guests, considering it derogatory to their rank and dignity to engage in such an occupation themselves; and music, performed with bagpipes and lutes, appears to have furnished them with an unfailing resource, especially the warlike songs which Russia always possessed. Of these some were of considerable length, but the most ancient have all unfortunately been lost, with the exception of the "Expedition of Igor," a poem of the twelfth century,* which celebrates the battle and captivity

---

* THE EXPEDITION OF IGOR, A PRINCE OF NOVOGOROD SEVERSKI.

"Igor, Prince of Novogorod Severski, is ambitious of glory; he beseeches his guard to march with him against the Polovtses. 'I will break my lance in distant deserts; there my ashes shall remain, if I cannot dip my helmet in the Don, and quench my thirst with its waters.'"
The author goes on to relate that many warriors assemble; the neighing of horses is heard beyond the Sula; the voice of glory resounds in Kiof; the blast of the trumpet rouses Novogorod, and at Pontiule the standards float in the wind. Igor is waiting for his beloved brother, Vyzevold, who soon arrives at the head of his troops, "like wolves eager for the carnage." Igor places his foot in the golden stirrup; he perceives the thick darkness before him; the heavens portend terrible storms; the wild beasts howl in their caverns; birds of prey soar above the soldiers, whose ruin is presaged by the eagles' cry; and the foxes raise their shrill voice on seeing the shining shields of the Russians. The battle commences; the barbarian legions are routed, their virgins now belong to the warriors of Igor, who acquire immense booty in gold and costly stuffs; the clothes and ornaments of the Polovtses fill up the marshes, and serve as a bridge to the victorious army. Igor is satisfied with a banner taken from the enemy. But a new army soon arrives from the south, and Igor again meets them in battle. It continues for two days, and on the third morning the Russian standards are lowered to the enemy, "because no blood remains to be shed." All is consternation when Igor is dragged away captive. "On the borders of the Blue Sea are heard the songs of the virgins (Polovtses), who strike together the pieces of gold taken from the Russians." The author then addresses the various Russian princes, whom he urges "to speedy vengeance on the Polovtses." To Vyzevold III., he says: "Thou canst dry up the Volga by the oars of thy numerous boats; or drain the Don with the helmets of thy warriors." To Rurik and David, "Your shining helmets have often been dyed with blood; your heroes are furious as wild bulls when wounded by red-hot iron." To Yaroslaf, whom he terms the wise: "From thy golden throne thou defendest the Krapack mountains by thine iron-clad legions; thou canst close the gates of the Danube, open the way of Kiof, and send thy arrows into the remotest regions." The poet then laments the death of a prince of Polotzk, who had been killed by the Lithuanians. "O prince, birds of prey have covered thy soldiers with their wings, and savage beasts drunk the blood of thy warriors. As for thee, thou hast suffered thy jewel, soul, to escape through thy golden collar from thy manly body." He then refers to the civil wars, and to the battle between Jaroslaf and the Prince of Polotzk: "The banks of the Meinon are covered with heads, as numerous as sheaves in autumn; and, like the descending flails, the swords separate warriors' souls from their mortal covering. O mournful times! why could not the great Vladimir remain on the mountains of Kiof? (that is, why was he not immortal?)" Meanwhile, the wife of Igor mourns her absent lord. From the ramparts of Pontivle, she casts her eyes over the plain and exclaims, "Cruel winds, why have you borne on your wings the light arrows of the Khan against the warriors of my love? Had ye not enough to do in swelling the waves of the Blue Sea to bear along the Russian ships? Great Dnieper! thou hast removed huge rocks to open thyself a passage into the country of the Polovtses; thou hast borne the vessels of Sviatozlaf to the camp of Koblah; bear back to me also the beloved of my heart, so that I may not every morning compel thy waters to carry him the tribute of my tears. Bright sun! thou favourest mortals with thy light and heat; but why have thy burning rays consumed in the wilderness the legions of my beloved?" But Igor is at liberty, he has eluded his guards, and on a flying courser he is approaching his country. For his subsistence he kills swans and geese. His horse at length falls down from fatigue; he embarks on the river Donetz, to which the poet gives speech: "Great Igor, what must now be the fury of Khan Koritschah, and the rejoicing of thy dear comrades!" "Donetz," replies the prince, "how proud thou must be to bear Igor on thy waters, and to prepare for him a grassy couch on thy silver banks! Thou surroundest me with thy refreshing vapours, when I repose under the shade of the trees on thy banks. The wild-fowl that swim on thy surface, are my protectors and guards." Igor soon rejoins his disconsolate wife.—Extracts of the Poem of Igor, from Karamsin's "History of Russia."

of Igor, a prince of Novogorod Severski, with the Polotzi; and in which the author mentions a still earlier poet, Bojané, none of whose works, however, are now extant.

In some instances, the boyards and people appear to have taken little or no part in the elevation and deposition of their princes, which were either entirely consummated among their own family or nearest relations, and by their courtiers or personal attendants, or occasioned no disturbance or feud beyond the palace walls. The law of succession, which devolved the crown upon the eldest member of the family, instead of the son of the preceding monarch, occasioned each prince to endeavour to provide for his sons, or protect them from the probable hostility of his successor, by portioning them in his lifetime with an independent principality from his own dominions, whose power might possibly be directed against the inheritance of his children, and which he therefore felt no great disinclination to weaken; thus Vyzevold, the son of George Dolgoruki, founded the province of Riazan, and a grandson of Andrew the sovereignty of Tver; while Polotzk and Smolensko had again become separated from Russia, which, in the middle of the thirteenth century, consisted of numerous small and unimportant states. These hardly owned a nominal allegiance to the Grand Prince, whose authority was then vested in the house of Suzdal or Vladimir, and scarcely able to resist the incursions of their neighbours, carried on neither communication nor trade with other countries, to whose progress, interests, and policy they were indifferent and unknown, though they still received their metropolitan from Constantinople, and professed the greatest devotion to the Greek Church. Their common religion was indeed their only bond of union'; for, with the rivalry that has usually existed between states of the same race and nation, they seldom united for the purpose of mutual defence, and thus greatly facilitated and encouraged their sudden and complete overthrow by the approaching invasion of the Monguls.

CHAPTER XVI.

Affairs of Poland — Esthonia — Livonia — Courland — The Teutonic Knights — Lithuania — The Ottoman Turks — The Origin of the Monguls.

> "Their limbs all iron, and their souls all flame,
> A countless host the red-cross warriors came;
> E'en hoary priests the sacred combat wage,
> And clothe in steel the palsied arm of age;
> While beardless youth, and tender maids assume
> The weighty morion, and the glancing plume."—HELIER.
>
> "The Turcoman hath left his herd,
> The sabre on his loins to gird."—BYRON.

WHILE the power of the princes of Russia declined, and their people became a prey to foreign hostility and civil anarchy, those provinces which, as now, had formerly made a part of this empire, gradually released themselves from her authority, or were incorporated into the dominions of the surrounding states. Of these Poland was fast rising to the chief place both in power and extent, though the same practice that had proved so fatal to Russia, of dividing the kingdom among the sons of the monarch, had prevailed there also in the early period of her history, and had been attended with the same disastrous results—internal dissensions, and almost perpetual civil war.

Vladislaf, the son of Boleslaf III., having been expelled from his duchy by his brothers in 1155, solicited the assistance of the German emperor, Frederick Barbarossa, and, aided by him, obtained possession of Silesia, which had formed a part of his confiscated principality; and his descendants, entirely separating themselves from Poland, and closely connecting their throne by family alliances with Germany, fell entirely under the influence of that country, of which Silesia has long been considered to form a part, though it was originally peopled by the same race as Poland, and the greater number of its inhabitants still speak that language.*

* Krasinski's "History of Poland."

GENEALOGY OF THE RUSSI

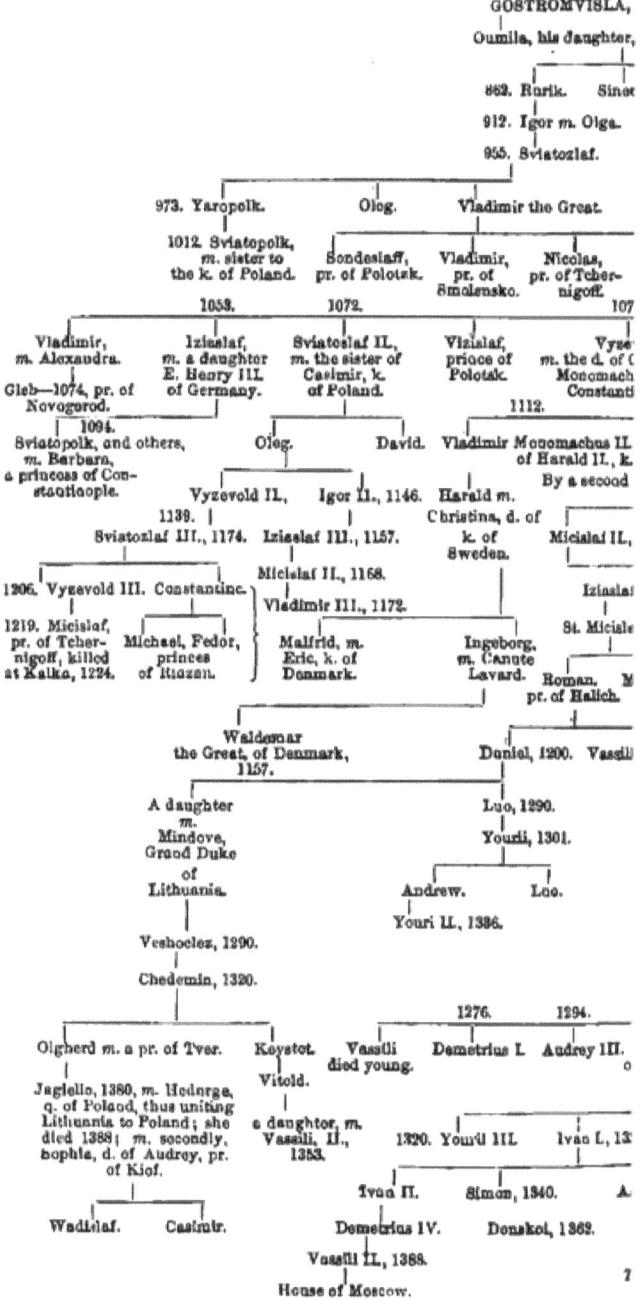

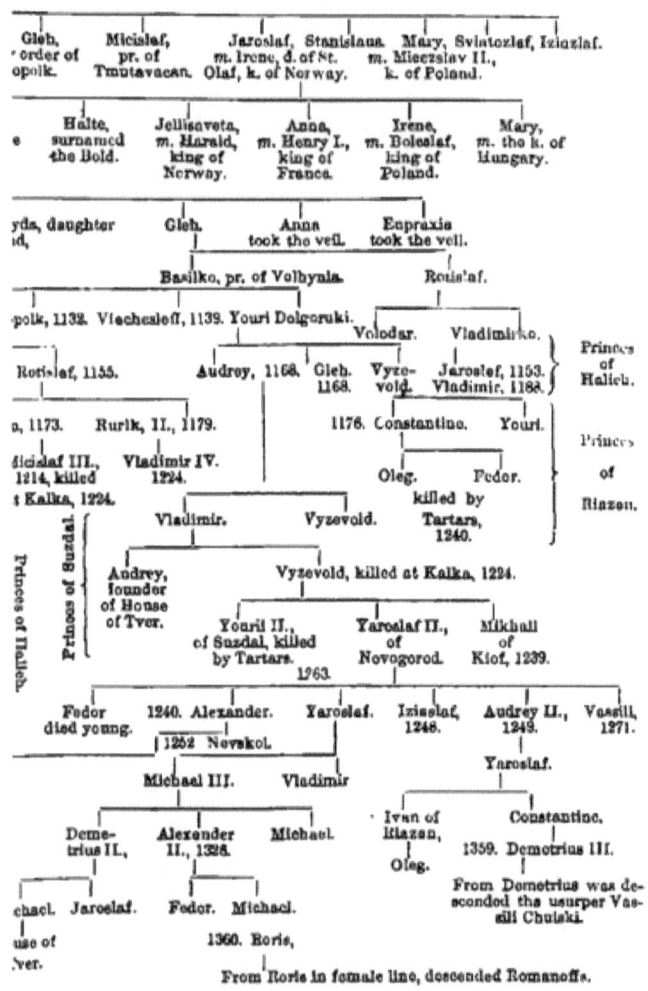

Literature was first introduced among the Poles by Christian missionaries and Benedictine monks; and their earliest chronicles are by Martinus Gallus, who flourished in 1110 and 1115, and is supposed to have been a Frenchman settled in Poland. Their language, being a branch of the Slavonian, differs less from the Russian than many of the provincial dialects of England do to one another; and at first they made use of the Slavonic alphabet* of Cyrillus, in common with the other nations of their race; but towards the end of the tenth century the Poles were obliged, by Pope John XIII., with the Bohemians and Latins of Moldavia, to adopt the Latin characters, which they henceforth employed. So late as the thirteenth century the same custom was still retained in Poland that prevailed among the ancient Slavonians, of putting to death all children who were born imperfect, and old men when incapacitated by age.

It has been previously stated that Esthonia, which is inhabited by a part of the Finnish race, under the early Grand Princes of Russia, formed a province of that empire; but, during the troubles and civil wars that ensued on the death of Jaroslaf, the Danish king, Eric, took possession of its northern coast. In 1093 he built a monastery on the Finnish gulf, dedicated to St. Michael, which was afterwards transformed into a convent of Cistercian nuns, of which the ruins still remain; and a fortress called Lindarnisse, or Danish town, the foundation of the modern Revel. The Russians shortly after this expelled the Danes from the country; though, towards the end of the twelfth century, the latter again took possession of the province under their king, Canute, who founded a settlement upon its shores, brought over a large body of priests to convert the inhabitants, and built several churches. Livonia, the adjoining province to Esthonia, appears also from the earliest times to have formed a part of Russia, and, according to Henry, the ancient Letton chronicler, the inhabitants had been converted by her to the Greek religion soon after its adoption by her own people; but in 1158, some Bremen merchants, landing near the mouth of the Dwina, traded with the natives, and terminated their

---

* It was composed, by Cyrillus, of the Greek alphabet, with the addition of certain other characters derived from other languages, chiefly Armenian or Hebrew, and originally consisted of forty letters. It is used still, with some alterations, in Russia, Wallachia, Moldavia, Bulgaria, and Servia. The characters now used in Russia for printing books not of an ecclesiastical nature, were introduced by Peter the First, who wished to make the Slavonic character approximate in appearance to the printing of the West.

negotiations by building a fortress and founding a settlement at Riga. Eighteen years after this first expedition, an Augustin monk, Meinhard of Holstein, established himself in the country, and obtained permission from the Russian prince, Vladimir of Pskof, to whom the province was tributary, to use his utmost endeavours to convert the inhabitants to Christianity.* In 1201 he instituted the order of Knights Sword-bearers by permission of the Pope, Innocent III., who gave them laws similar to those of the Knights Templars; and, granting to them the third part of the lands of Livonia and Esthonia, Meinhard, with the authority of the King of Denmark, placed the entire government of the provinces in their hands. In the year 1210, their grand master, Volgum, took Dorpat from the Russians by storm, and, having reduced it to ashes, ultimately caused it to be rebuilt. The possession of Revel formed a subject of long dispute in the thirteenth century between Denmark, Sweden, the Knights, and even the Pope, who, however, relinquishing his claim in favour of Denmark, in 1240 that nation took possession of the town, and erected it into a bishopric. During the regency of Margharetta Sambria, the queen-mother of Denmark, she selected Esthonia as her own dowry, and granted it an independent government, the right of coinage, and many other privileges; and, in 1284, Revel became one of the Hanseatic league, and monopolized with Novogorod the trade of the Baltic and the North. In the meanwhile Esthonia had fallen into the possession of the Margrave of Brandenburg, in right of his wife, a princess of Sweden, though towards the commencement of the 14th century she emancipated herself from his authority, and for a few years remained independent. But in 1347 she was sold, by Valdemar III., King of Denmark, to the Grand Master of the Teutonic Knights,† at Marienburg, for 18,000 marks of standard gold, and this governor presented the country to his ally, the Master of the Order of Sword-bearers, the latter having united themselves with the German knights. They remained a portion of this body till 1521, when the Herrmeister, Plattenburg of Esthonia, separating his esta-

* Tooke's "Russia Under Catherine II."
† This order was founded in Palestine, 1190, with the same object and rules as the Knights of St. John. It was called the Order of the Knights of the Blessed Virgin, and was recruited from the German nation; and, being expelled from Palestine in the 13th century by the Saracens, they settled in Prussia, where they subjugated, and forcibly converted the natives, and founded a powerful state.—Count V. Krasinski's "Poland."

blishment from the Teutonic, was admitted by the Emperor, Charles V., among the princes of the German empire. But the oppression of the nobles of this province was so great upon their unfortunate serfs, that a saying still exists among them—"Esthonia was an Elysium for the nobility, a heaven for the clergy, a mine of gold for the stranger, and a hell for the peasants;" and in 1560 the latter rose up in great numbers against their masters, attacked castles and monasteries, slew all the nobility, knights, and merchants, who fell into their hands, and prepared to attack Revel, where many of their lords had sought a refuge. The struggle continued for many months, till at length the citizens of Revel, and the other towns in the provinces, finding themselves threatened with destruction from an exasperated peasantry, and menaced by an invasion of the Russians—Esthonia being engaged at the time in a war with her powerful neighbour—agreed to throw off the domination of the feeble knights, who were no longer able to protect them from their enemies, and calling in the assistance of Eric XIV., King of Sweden, they took the oath of allegiance to that monarch, and Esthonia became a Swedish province.* The town of Narva was built on the river of the same name, in 1224, by order of Valdemar II. of Denmark.

In 1209, soon after the institution of the Knights Swordbearers, Albert, one of the order, was made Bishop of Livonia; and building a monastery at Riga, in the hopes of alluring the heathen Livonians to embrace Christianity, he established a theatre in its cloisters, and caused plays, of which the subjects were derived from the Old and New Testaments, to be performed. The natives flocked to it in crowds, and an interpreter informed them of the history of the various scenes which they saw represented, and this stratagem appears to have been attended with great success. At that time Livonia was still tributary to Vladimir of Pskof; and in a treaty entered into by Albert with this prince, the bishop gives security for the payment of the customary taxation and tribute. Like Esthonia, she was a frequent subject of dispute between the surrounding powers, but enjoyed for many years great prosperity under the Teutonic knights, who, after a long war with Russia, concluded in 1502 a peace of fifty years with that empire, during which the Reformation of Luther was introduced, and ultimately

* Lady Eastlake's " Letters from the Baltic."

adopted by the whole province.* She was subsequently invaded and devastated by the Muscovite armies, under their Czar, Ivan the Terrible, at the expiration of the fifty years' truce; and, in order to obtain protection against the Russians, the Livonians concluded, in 1561, a treaty with the Poles at Vilna, in which they submitted to the dominion of Poland, though retaining the free exercise of their religion, and their own laws and privileges. This occasioned a war with Russia; and Ivan, invading Livonia, placed on its throne Magnus, Duke of Holstein, the brother of the King of Denmark, and in 1570 married him to Maria Ivanovna, a princess of his own family. Magnus continued for several years the vassal of the Czar; and at length, having endured many insults and indignities at his hands, escaped with his wife into Poland, and Stephen Bathori, the king of that country, took possession of Livonia, which remained a province of Poland till 1660, when, at the peace of Oliva, it was ceded to Sweden.

In the eleventh century the people of Courland were noted for their extreme cruelty, and their auguries and magical arts. According to Adam of Bremen, they were consulted by all Europe for their divinations, more especially, notwithstanding the remote situation of their province, and their barbarous manners, by the comparatively polished and refined Spaniards and Greeks, whose vessels appear to have occasionally penetrated on trading expeditions to the distant waters of the Baltic. Courland afterwards became a province of Poland; and on the submission of the knights of Livonia to that power, the Grand Master of the Order, Gothard Ketler, received it as a hereditary fief of the crown of Poland, and it was not till the reign of Catherine II. that it finally became a part of the Russian empire.

During the progress of the thirteenth century, another powerful principality began to rise on the frontiers of Russia and Poland. This was Lithuania, who, strengthening herself by the conquest of the western provinces of the former state, after its overthrow and subjection by the Monguls, and successfully resisting the aggression of the Livonian knights, who harassed her northern frontier under the pretext of introducing among her heathen people the faith and doctrines of Christianity; extended her dominions to the

* Tooke's "Russian Empire."

shores of the Black Sea, the Dnieper, and the Danube. But the inhabitants long and obstinately retained the pagan worship of their ancestors, and adored the sacred fire which was kept continually burning on an altar in their capital at Vilna; and the last consecrated grove of the Lithuanians; one in the province of Samogitia, was not cut down till 1430. In 1252, their duke, Mindove, was baptized into the Latin Church by the legate of the Pope, who also crowned him with the title of king; but a similitude of faith was insufficient to protect him from the hostility of the German knights, and, on their again invading his states, he returned to his former idolatry, and became a most bitter enemy to the Latin Christians. They continued to harass his territories as long as their power endured, and in the year 1322 besieged and burned the town of Kovno, in Lithuania; three thousand of the inhabitants, who had bravely defended it, falling victims to the fury of the flames. Ghedemin, who succeeded to the throne in 1320, by the murder of his master, Veshoeleg, the last prince of the old dynasty, assumed the title of Grand Duke of Lithuania and Russia, and was one of the most celebrated monarchs of his country, or of the period in which he flourished. His *suzeraineté* was acknowledged by the republics of Pskof, or Pleskof, and Novogorod, and the Tartars of the Crimea, against whom he and his successor made many campaigns, and where he totally destroyed the ancient cities of Bosphorus and Cherson; and during his wars with the Russian principalities, he three times appeared in arms before the gates of Moscow.* His son, Olgherd, was baptized into the Greek Church on his marriage with a princess of Tver, and subdued Southern Russia, with the seaports of Kilia and Bialigorod. He established many churches and monasteries in his dominions, and when at Kiof always attended the services in the Christian cathedral; but on his death, in 1380, his body was burned on a funeral pile with all the heathen rites of his ancestors. His kingdom passed to his fourth son, Iaghellon, who, upon his union with Hedwige, the queen of Poland, in 1386, became a convert to the Latin Church, and Lithuania from henceforth remained in close connection with Poland. At this period the vast extent and alarming increase of the Mussulman power in Asia, and the reverses

* Krasluski's "History of Poland."

the crusaders had sustained on the plains of Palestine, having obliged the Christian knights to abandon their oft-repeated attempts to rescue the Holy Sepulchre from the hands of the sacrilegious infidels, they looked round for another opportunity of displaying their valour and their faith; and the forests of Lithuania offering a favourable field to the chivalrous achievements of the West, many English appear to have taken a part in the wars undertaken by the Livonian knights against the heathens of this province.* In 1390 a band of English nobles, under the Earl of Derby, afterwards Henry IV., embarked for Prussia, and advanced, in conjunction with the knights, to the walls of Vilna, but were unable to take the town; and on this occasion Henry killed, in single combat, Gleb, the Prince of Czartoriski, a direct ancestor of the celebrated Polish family of that distinguished name. Thirteen years before this the young duke, Albrecht, son of Albrecht II. of Austria, had penetrated with many German lords into Samogitia, and as far as Isborsk; and Suchemvirt,† an officer of his court who accompanied him, has left a poetical description of their journey, and of the various exploits of several of his countrymen who joined the banner of the Teutonic order in the same land.

In addition to the republics of Novogorod, Viatka, and

* Chaucer, in his "Canterbury Tales," when describing a knight, says:—
"At Alisandre he was, when it was won,
Full often time he hadde the borde begonne,
Aborren alle nations in Pruce (Prussia),
In Lethorve (Lithuania), hadde he reysed, and in Ruce," (Russia.)

† Suchemvirt relates:—
"Desdritten tages chom dazher
Vroleich in ein ander lant,
Dazwaz Russenia geunent,
Da sach man wuksten prennen,
Siahen, schiezzen und rennen
Ilaid ein, pusch ein, unverzagt."

Afterwards he informs us—
"Dazher wuchst drew gantzelant
Die ich mit namen tue bechaunt;
Sameyt Russein aragel
Wint regen und der hagel,
Begraif uns da mit grozzen vrost,
Da faultuns harnasch und die chost."

On the return of the expedition towards Memel, making their way through a trackless country, they passed through—
"Ein Wildung heist der granden,
Gen westen noch gen sanden.
So poz gevert ich nye gerayt,
Daz sprich ich wolanf meyn ayt."

They then reached Konigsberg, of which Suchemvirt says:—
"Tgu Chunigez perch sownz uns gach,
Do het wir rue und gut gemach."

—Von Herzog Albrecht's "Ritterschaft von Suchemvirt," quoted in Major's introduction to Herberstein's "Rerum Muscovitarum."

Pskof, the grand principalities of Vladimir or Suzdal, Kiof, Tchernigoff, Halich, Tver, Riazan, Polotzk, Kozolesk, and Lithuania, the kingdom of the Black Bulgarians still existed on the Volga, and the Polotzi retained possession of the Crimea and of Kipzak; and such was the position of Russia when the name of the Monguls was first heard in Europe.

Nearly a hundred and forty years had elapsed since the oppression of the Christian pilgrims at Jerusalem by the fierce and merciless followers of Mahomet, who, towards the middle of the eleventh century, rendered themselves masters of the sacred hills of Judea, had first roused the religious ardour of the nations of the west; and Peter the Hermit called upon all Europe to arm and join in the deliverance of the Holy Sepulchre from the hands of the Saracens. Multitudes of nobles, knights, and soldiers, of every age and degree, had flocked to the shores of Palestine from almost every country in Europe; even the remote Iceland had sent forth its warriors to join in the expeditions that were again and again fitted out by the chivalry of the West, and destined to perish on the sandy plains or among the deserted hills of the Holy Land. But now, in the middle of the thirteenth century, the repeated reverses that the Crusaders had encountered from the swords of the Infidels, and the shipwrecks, pestilence, and other disasters that had overtaken and almost annihilated their armaments, before they had crossed the intervening seas, or engaged with a single Mussulman, had diminished the ardour and cooled the courage of the rulers and nobles of Europe; and the religion of Mahomet was spreading far and wide, unopposed, except by the feeble efforts of those nations whose territories were overrun by its followers; and the Ottoman Turks had already appeared on the south-eastern frontiers of Europe, and wrested from the tottering empire of Byzantium some of its richest and most fertile provinces in Asia.

This people, once so celebrated and so formidable in the annals of the world, derive their name from Othman, or Osman, one of their sultans, who began to reign in 1299, and is generally considered as the founder of their empire, whose limits he first extended from the region about Mount Taurus, to which country they had emigrated under his grandfather Solyman. The followers of this chief appear to have been a mixed horde from all the different Tartar or

Turkish nations who, within the last three hundred years, had established themselves among the provinces of Western Asia; particularly by the Avars, who, overthrowing the kingdom of the White Huns at Carizme, and the empire of the Saracen caliphs at Bagdad, occupied for many years the thrones of Transoxiana and Persia, till they fell in their turn before the still more formidable power of Zingis Khan. When the hordes of this conqueror invaded Persia, and destroyed the kingdoms of the Turks or Turkomans at Khorassan and Ghizni, Solyman assembled a few of the scattered tribes, and prepared with three of his sons to lead them across the deserts of Mesopotamia to the more secure provinces of Asia Minor. But, as he was fording the Euphrates on horseback, his charger stumbled, and the sultan perished in the waves, and his two elder sons, alarmed at this calamity, and dismayed at so unfortunate an omen at the commencement of their enterprise, abandoned their fugitive countrymen, and returned to their former habitations; while the youngest, Ortogrul or Togrul, who had previously crossed the river with his three sons, Conda, Sambani, and Othman, remained for some time with his followers encamped on the western bank. At length he obtained permission from Aladdin, the sultan of Iconium, to settle with four hundred Turks in the mountains of Armenia, where he died in 1288; and, eleven years after, on the death of Sambani and Conda, the crown devolved upon Othman, his youngest son, under whom commenced the powerful and dreaded empire of the Othman or Ottoman Turks, who in less than two hundred years had established a firm footing in Europe, and subdued its most civilized people, the refined, though artificial and effeminate Greeks.

But, in the beginning of the thirteenth century, the Monguls * first rose into power, and rendered themselves, by their extensive conquests and horrible ravages and massacres, the most formidable of all the Tartars or Turanian nations; though, till the time of their celebrated leader, Zingis Khan, their name was unknown to the civilized world; and the future conquerors of Asia and half Europe were a few obscure tribes, wandering with their flocks on the dreary shores of Lake Baikal, and the rivers Angara and Selinga, in Siberia.

* From this time the whole race of Turkish or Turanian people is often very improperly termed Mongul.

A slight notice of two tribes called Mokho and Thatha occurs in the early Chinese annals; and, from the position of the regions where they are said to have resided about the year A.D. 860, these nations appear to coincide with the later Monguls and Tartars, while all historians agree that they were of but comparatively recent appearance on the political theatre of Asia; and, according to Sanang Setseu, a prince of the tribe of Ordos, who wrote a history of the Mongolian people, they originally came from India, though this assertion has been proved to be entirely destitute of foundation. It is evident, however, that they derive their descent from the same source as the Turks, and formed one of that great horde of nations who, under the several denominations of Huns, Avars, Chazars, Polotzi, and Scythians, had already preceded them in the conquest of the East; and, according to their national traditions, twenty generations before the time of Zingis Khan, and at a period subsequent to the age of Mahomet, they made their escape, under their leader, Bourte-chino, or the Blue Wolf, from the straitly guarded valley of Irguene-koun, among the Altai mountains, where for four hundred and fifty years had been confined the descendants of two warriors, Tchouzan and Kayan, who had taken refuge there with their wives, on the general defeat or massacre of their tribe, of which they were the only survivors. There they had been compelled to forge, for their Turkish masters and conquerors, the iron and other metals which the surrounding mountains plentifully contained, till the tribe, becoming too numerous to find subsistence within these narrow limits, they accumulated an enormous quantity of fuel in an iron mine, and with seventy bellows melted an aperture in the side of the mountain, through which the whole tribe issued, and, asserting their independence, proclaimed Bourte-chino their chief. This prince, upon the refusal of the Khan, his former sovereign, to grant him his daughter in marriage, demanded, and obtained a higher honour in the hand of a Chinese imperial princess;[*] and his successors subsequently disputing with the Mantchous the dominion of Mangi, or the northern provinces of China, were defeated, and expelled by their rivals to the frozen deserts and steppes of Siberia. From Bourte-chino were descended

[*] Gibbon's "Decline and Fall of the Roman Empire."

all the princes of the Mongolian hordes, and from Tartar and Mongul, the two sons of Alancova, the widow of Donyuk Bayan, his tenth descendant, and whose birth was affirmed to have been occasioned by a miracle, the two nations received their name, and from the posterity of the eldest son of Mongul, whose name in their language signifies melancholy, the celebrated chieftain and conqueror Temudschin, or Zingis Khan. According to Raschid, Alancova must have flourished about the time of the dynasty of the Abasside caliphs in Bagdad.

A ceremony, in commemoration of their escape from the valley of Irguene-koun, was annually celebrated by the Monguls, so late as the end of the thirteenth century, when the princes and nobles forged a bar of iron in remembrance of their former occupation ; and this legend is common to all the Turanian nations, many of the other Turkish tribes * also professing to derive their origin from the same source. Upon the irruption of the Mongul hosts into Europe, their brethren, the Tartars, the first tribe whom they had subdued, led the van ; and this was the cause of the name Tatar or Tartar being bestowed by the nations of Europe upon the whole race, a designation which is generally retained at the present time, and which was then considered the more appropriate as it was a common opinion that they were demons, and had issued from the depths of Tartarus.

In the twelfth century, the empire of the Keraites, or Kara-hitai, was still the most powerful state in Central Asia. Their sovereign took the title of Ung Khan, or the Great Monarch, and appears, as before mentioned, with many of his subjects, to have been converted about this time to Christianity, by the adventurous missionaries of the Nestorian church, who had already acquired great influence among the Igours ; and who, penetrating through wide deserts and thick forests to spread their faith among the tents of this distant kingdom, carried home marvellous accounts of its power, magnificence, and wealth. All the historians of the Middle Ages unite in ascribing to the Monguls the same physiognomy peculiar to the Huns of Attila † and the Tartar nations of the present day ; and their wandering habits and ode of living, as described by the Franciscan monk Rulru-

---

* Pritchard's "Natural History of Man."   † See Chapter II. the Huns—Attila.

quis,* who was sent by St. Louis of France on a mission to the Grand Khan, when they had settled down after the conquest of Russia, were very similar to those of their descendants, who still roam over the grassy steppes of Central Asia and Southern Russia.† "The Tartars," says he, "have no permanent abode, and never know where they may be the next day, though every chief of a horde knows the bounds of his pasture-ground, and whereabouts he ought to be, according to the season of the year. When winter comes they ascend towards the south, and in summer go up again towards the cold regions of the north. The houses they inhabit are placed upon wheels, and constructed of a kind of wooden lattice-work, with an opening at the top that serves for a chimney. This wooden frame is generally covered with white felt plastered with lime or powdered bones, but sometimes these houses are black. Before the entrance there is suspended a piece of felt enriched with paintings, representing flowers, trees, birds, and fantastic animals. These dwellings are sometimes thirty feet long, and there were as many as twenty-two oxen harnessed to one of them." The idea that the Monguls were demons, or at least in league with infernal spirits, which, it may be remembered, was formerly reported of the Huns, was strengthened by their acquaintance with the composition of a kind of inflammable powder, which they generally discharged in the midst of their battles, and which exploding, raised clouds of smoke and flame, and this was incomprehensible to the Europeans, with whom gun-

* Ruiruquis accompanied Bartholomew of Cremona on a mission from St. Louis to the Grand Khan, and, proceeding first to Constantinople, they embarked from thence for Soldaya, then in the possession of the Genoese, and after three days' journey first met with the Tartars. In the account of his journey to the king of France, he says among other details—"In the tents of the Tartars, above the place of the head of the family, there is always a small image, a kind of doll made of felt . . . Their ordinary drink is kumys, a spirit made of mare's milk . . . They live chiefly on their flocks and the produce of the chase . . . The beginning of winter is the season for the grand imperial hunts, which are conducted like great military expeditions . . . The cotton and silk stuffs, embroidered in gold or silver, which the wealthy Tartars wear in summer, come from China and Persia; the costly furs that they wrap themselves in, in winter, chiefly from Russia and Bulgaria. Their usual plan in winter is to wear two pelisses, the one with the hair inwards, the other with it turned out . . . of sheep or goatskin for the poor, and of fox or wolf's skin for the rich, or sometimes the latter line them with silk, or cotton wadding, or fine wool . . . The Tartar dress is in the form of a tuoic, and that of the women does not differ greatly from that of the men; so, when you see a company of these women on horseback, you might take them for men at arms, with helmet and lance —as they wear a lofty headdress—especially as they ride astride. They never wash their clothes, saying that God is angry if they do, and sends thunder while they are hanging up to dry. The sound of thunder terrifies them so much that, when they hear it, they hide themselves under their felt carpets, and remain buried thus till it is over . . . Their mode of washing their faces and hands is, by filling their mouths with water, and squirting it out over them. They never clean any of their domestic utensils, unless indeed when they are boiling meat; they then sometimes dip into the pot the bowls they eat from, wash them with the liquor, and pour it back into the caldron."—Bergeron's "Relation des Voyages en Tartarie," quoted by l' Abbé Huc.

† Bergeron's "Relation des Voyages en Tartarie," quoted by M. l' Abbé Huc.

powder was yet unknown, and in these days of ignorance and superstition was naturally considered by them as the work of fiendish agency or magic. They originally made war equally on the Mahometans and Christians, and professed a belief in one God; but their descendants subsequently adopted the religion of the different nations whose government they had overthrown, and among whom they settled and dispersed. These hordes, with those of the other Tartar tribes in conjunction with whom they accomplished the subjugation of Asia, are still as numerous, though scattered and divided, in Western Tartary, and upon the elevated and extensive plains of Thibet, or Land of Grass, as it is termed by the Chinese; some tribes acknowledging the Russian sway, others that of the Celestial empire; as in the days when they united for conquest under the banners of Attila, Zingis Khan, and Tamerlane; but though still connected by their faith in the Grand Lama of Thibet, they appear little likely again to prove dangerous to the liberties of Europe, even if there arose among them a leader or chief of sufficient skill, ambition, and enterprise to unite their scattered clans, and direct their forces; for at present the strongly guarded frontiers of Russia oppose a powerful barrier to so undisciplined and roughly armed a foe, and her influence and policy, while it seeks to overawe and conciliate them, is gradually inducing those families on her borders to settle down in villages as traders, or peaceful and indolent agriculturists; though they remember with mournful regret their former glory and exploits, and look with longing eyes upon their nominal mistress, the ancient Chinese empire, which they once conquered, and now affirm is still theirs by right. They follow the roving lives and most of the customs of their ancestors, and though many engage as merchants in the extensive commerce carried on by them with Russia and China proper, their principal employment is still tending their flocks and herds; "and these formidable shepherds," says the Abbé Huc, "after having invaded and ravaged the world, have resumed, in the midst of their immeasurable steppes, the wandering lives of their forefathers."*

---

* "The Mongul," says the Abbé Huc (speaking from his experience of the Monguls of the present day), "passes suddenly from extravagant gaiety to a state of melancholy; his disposition is full of gentleness and good-nature. Timid to excess in his ordinary habits, when fanaticism or the desire of vengeance arouses him, he displays in his courage an impetuosity which nothing can stay; very hospitable, indolent, honest to each other, but given to pilfer."

BOOK II.

FROM THE CONQUESTS OF THE MONGULS TO THE RISE OF TIMUR.

FROM A.D 1201 TO A.D. 1336; OR, A.M. 6709 TO A.D. 6844.

" A boisterous race, by frosty Caurus pierced,
   Drove martial horde on horde, with dreadful sweep,
   Resistless rushing o'er the enfeebled south,
   And gave the vanquish'd earth another form."
                                              THOMSON.

BOOK II.—CHAPTER I.

Zingis Khan*—The conquests of the Monguls.†

On nomme ce tyran, du nom de roi des rois,
C'est ce fier Gengis Khan, dont les affreux exploits,
Font un vaste tombeau de la superbe Asie.
VOLTAIRE'S " GHENGIS KHAN."

TOWARDS the end of the twelfth century, the Mogul or Mongul horde, was divided into thirteen tribes, all governed by one khan, and comprised about thirty or forty thousand families and tents, who pastured their flocks on the plains of south-eastern Siberia. But in the year 1175, Jehangir Bahadar, their chief, expired while his subjects were encamped on the shores of the river Selinga, and more than two-thirds of the nations refused to acknowledge the claims of his son Temudschin, a boy of eleven years of age, whose mother was the daughter of a neighbouring prince, the khan of their kindred tribe, the Tartars. Violent contentions broke out in the horde, which were increased by an invasion

---

* EUROPEAN SOVEREIGNS CONTEMPORARY WITH ZINGIS KHAN.

EASTERN EMPIRE.		
Alexius Angelus.		
1203. Isaac Angelus rest.		
1204. Alexius Mourzonflens.		
1204. Baldwin of Flaoders.		
1206. Henry.		
1217. Peter de Courtenal.		
1219. Robert de Courtenai.		

GERMAN EMPIRE.
Philip.
1208. Otho V.
1211. Frederick II.

ENGLAND.
John.
1216. Henry III.

FRANCE.
Philip II.

1223.	Louis VIII.

POLAND.	
1200.	Miscislaf IV.
1203.	Vladislaf III.
1206.	Lescus V.

HUNGARY.	
1200.	Ladislaf II.
1201.	Andrew II.

SWEDEN.	
	Suercher III.
1211.	Eric XI.
1220.	John I.
1223.	Eric XII.

DENMARK.	
1182.	Canute V.
1202.	Waldemar II.

SCOTLAND.	
	William the Lion.
1214.	Alexander II.

SPAIN.	
	Alfonso IX. of Castille.
1214.	Henry I.

PORTUGAL.	
	Sancho I.
1212.	Alfonso II.

POPES.	
	Innocent III.
1216.	Honorius III.
1227.	Gregory IX.

† In the year 1204, by the command of Kazan, khan of Persia, the great-grandson of Zingis, a collection of traditions was transcribed in the Persian language, by the vizier Fadlallah, and this work has been the chief foundation of the history of Zingis, by M. Petit de la Croix.—GIBBON.

of the Tartars, till at length Temudschin and his adherents, being defeated in a desperate engagement, were forced to take refuge in the dominions of the emperor of the Keraites, who kindly received the fugitive prince at his court, bestowed upon him a high office, and subsequently gave him the hand of his daughter in marriage. But a few years later he incurred the suspicions and distrust of the friendly monarch, who issued a decree for his immediate arrest; and Temudschin collecting those Monguls who had hitherto remained steadfast in their allegiance, and escaping by night from Karahtai, returned to his own dominions, where he utterly routed his rebel subjects in a furious battle, and causing seventy caldrons of boiling water to be placed over a fire, ordered the most forward of the insurgents to be plunged into them alive. He then turned his arms against the Tartars, and vanquished and subjugated their tribe, and the following year, 1202, totally defeated the army of the Keraites, under their emperor, who had marched in person against his son-in-law, and was slain in the fight; and, according to the barbarous custom of the Scythian conquerors, the victor caused the skull of the vanquished monarch to be encased in silver and converted into a goblet for wine. Alarmed at the overthrow of the powerful Keraites, the other kingdoms of central Asia united to offer a resistance to the further progress of the victorious prince; but, recruiting his forces with the warriors of the conquered tribes, he overran and subdued them in succession, and before the year A.D. 1205 had rendered himself master of every province in the north-eastern districts of Asiatic Scythia.*

In 1206, a general assembly was held on a wide plain in Mongolia, near the stupendous range of the Altai, which was attended by the Mongul nobles and warriors, and many of the chiefs and princes of the dependent and tributary hordes. Seated on a high throne formed of bucklers, and covered with foxes' and wolves' skin, surmounted by a simple piece of felt, Temudschin presided over the meeting, which had been convened for the election of the provincial governors, and the promulgation of a new code of laws; when suddenly an old hermit, mounted on a white horse, appeared in the midst of

* "Histoire du Grand Ghenghizcan," par M. Petit de la Croix.
A report at this period gained credence in Europe, that the first invasion of the Monguls had been occasioned by the preaching of one of their prophets, who foretold the near approach of the destruction of all things; whereupon they fled to the south, in hopes of finding some land to shelter in that was exempt from this curse.

the conclave, and addressing the spectators, exclaimed, "My brethren, the Great God of Heaven has appeared to me in a vision, seated on a throne of fire, surrounded by celestial beings, and judging all the nations of the earth. I heard him give the empire of the world to Temudschin, and proclaim him King of kings."* This extraordinary intelligence was received with acclamations by the people, who solemnly and unanimously bestowed upon their sovereign the title of Zingis Khan, or Great Khan of the Strong, and Emperor of all the Monguls and Tartars, crying out with one voice, "Ten thousand years of life to Zingis;" and thus prophecy strengthened Temudschin in his determination of acquiring the empire of the world, and threw a divine authority round his most barbarous acts, in the eyes of his superstitious and impressible subjects. Like Attila, and supported by the alleged vision of the hermit, he endeavoured to clothe himself in the eyes of his followers and foes with a more than mortal character, and making war alike on every sect and faith, fought under the pretext of establishing a belief in one supreme God; and to the humbled and conquered inhabitants of a vanquished city, he declared himself to be the instrument of the divine wrath and retribution upon sinners, thus attempting to justify the almost unparalleled devastation, and atrocities, committed by the forces of the Monguls, on whichever side they turned their arms. In after days, when his armies had stormed and entered a city, his generals were accustomed to drive all the inhabitants into a square in the midst of their ranks; and after drawing off the younger men to serve in their forces, and a certain number of the women and children to make use of as slaves, a few, who generally consisted of the aged, and those incapable of bearing arms, were allowed to remain among the ruins of their homes, while the remainder, with all who attempted to resist the former decrees, were massacred on the spot by their enemies, who, with pointed spears and bended bows, were ranged around the captive multitude.†

But though so barbarous and unscrupulous as invaders, and terrible and unmerciful to their foes, yet the Monguls maintained justice and order most rigidly among themselves, and received from their monarch a code of laws still used by

* Huc's "Tartary, Thibet, and China."
† Gibbon's "Decline and Fall of the Roman Empire."

every Tartar chief in Asia, who claims his descent from Temudschin, and still known there under the name of "Isa Gengis Khane,"* or "the laws of Zingis." His immense hosts were divided into companies, presided over by officers who were responsible for the lives and liberties of their men; and the punishment of death was inflicted for perjury, murder, and the robbery of a horse or an ox. At the same time, in support of the idea of his divine mission, he bestowed upon his followers the appellation of "the Celestial people," which was the origin of the application of this term to the Chinese empire, whose sovereign, upon the successors of Zingis possessing themselves of the throne of Pekin, became the supreme head and chief over the rest of the Mongul race, investing every khan with his regal office, and sending forth his decrees to be obeyed on the borders of Poland and Greece. Thus, China having adopted, still retains the proud name of her former conquerors, though she has long driven them back from her gardens and crowded cities to the solitary wastes and heaths of their desert steppes. But the northern provinces of China, where the Monguls first commenced their conquests, had been subdued some years before by the Mandshus, a fierce, eastern Tartarian race, who, rivalling and repelling the Monguls, had broken through the strong barrier of the great wall, and, forcing the imperial dynasty of the Soug to retreat to the district around Canton, had called the half of the empire which they held Mangi, and established their chief and his throne in Yenking,† near the modern site of Pekin, instead of the old capital of China, Nankin, which was situated much further to the south. After subduing all the nations of Central Asia, Zingis turned his eyes towards the territory of the ancient enemies of his race, who, being firmly established in their new conquest, had laid aside their weapons, which had won for them an empire, and in for-

* They seem to have been a collection of the old usages of the Moghul (Mongul) tribes, comprehending some rules of state and ceremony, and some injunctions for the punishment of particular crimes. The punishments were only two, death and the bastinado, the number of blows extending from seven to seven hundred. There is something very Chinese in the whole of the Moghul system of punishment; even princes advanced in years, and in command of large armies, being punished by bastinado with a stick, by their father's orders. Whether they receive their usage in this respect from the Chinese, or communicated it to them, is not very certain, as the whole body of their laws or customs was formed before the introduction of the Mussulman religion, and was probably in many respects inconsistent with the Koran, as, for instance, in allowing the use of the blood of animals, and in the extent of toleration granted to other religions, it gradually fell into decay."—Erskine's "Translation of Memoirs of Zehir-eddin Baber, Emperor of Hindostan."

† Yenking stood a few miles from the site of Pekin, the modern capital; its ruins are still to be seen.

mer days been their only ornaments and pride; and, adopting the luxurious habits of the native Chinese, were fast sinking down in sloth and apathy. The Mongul conqueror had fixed his capital, in a district about six hundred miles to the north-west of Pekin, in an old city of the Keraites, called Karacorum, or the Camp of the Golden Horde, where his guards and followers lived around him in their felt huts and tents, and from whence he issued forth his commands and laws, his sons, all eminent for their talents and valour, holding under their father the principal offices of state. Toushi, the eldest, was his grand huntsman; Octai the prime minister of his empire; Zagatai his judge; and Touloui the commander-in-chief of his troops. Here an extraordinary mixture of simplicity and barbaric magnificence distinguished every ceremony at the court; the greatest splendour and solemnity were observed in the receptions, halls of justice, and banquets; while the latter were solely composed of roasted sheep and mare's milk, with a kind of spirit distilled from it, and Zingis distributed among his soldiers in one day five hundred wagon loads of jewels, silver, and gold. From this spot he prepared his expeditions for the conquest of half Asia and Europe, and led his forces in the year 1206 upon the neighbouring empire of Mangi, where the Chinese historians have described in moving language the dreadful desolation committed by his arms, and where the progress of the Monguls was marked at every step by universal slaughter, and perfect seas of blood. Among other atrocities, taking unworthy advantage of the proverbial Chinese reverence for age, they placed all the old men whom they had taken prisoners in front of their ranks as they advanced; so that every son in the native army feared to commence the attack lest he should inadvertently incur the guilt of parricide.* The unmartial Chinese, and the Mandshus, their masters, were swept away like chaff before the Tartar force, who converted the land in a few short months into one vast mass of ruins, and covered the wastes and deserted fields with unburied corpses and mouldering bones. Ninety-six cities, besides numerous villages, were pillaged and utterly destroyed; throughout the whole country ten towns only escaped; but the cruelty of the foe had urged the vanquished to a desperate resistance, and at the siege of Yenking the inhabitants

* Gibbon's " Decline and Fall of the Roman Empire." Gutzlaff's " History of China ".

held out after famine had reduced them to devour their fellow-men, and after they had been compelled, by the exhaustion of their ammunition, to discharge from their war-engines their money, silver, and even gold. But, if the Chinese have been unable to fight, they have always known how to die; and they would not yield till after the Monguls had fired a mine in the centre of the palace, which blew up with a tremendous explosion, and, burning for thirty days, left the palace a heap of blackened stones. At the same time China was distracted by a domestic revolt, and the inhabitants eagerly embraced an offer of peace, which was bought from the victors, satiated with plunder and murder, for a heavy tribute of gold and silk, three thousand horses, one thousand of their children for slaves, and an imperial princess, destined to become the bride of Zingis. The Monguls then retreated, leaving behind them one continued scene of desolation; but a few years later they had spread themselves again over the land, and, after driving the Chinese monarch beyond the shores of the Hoang-ho, united the five northern provinces of China to their own empire. Owing to the difficulty they experienced in procuring forage for the immense number of horses that accompanied them, and their droves of cattle; in a deliberative assembly held by the chiefs of the army, they actually debated upon the expediency of exterminating every inhabitant throughout its wide and populous extent, and converting the land into a pasture and hunting ground; but Yebutchoucai, a Chinese mandarin, adroitly averted this horrible proposition by appealing to the avarice of the khan, and representing the enormous amount of revenue, food, and manufactures, which his country was capable of producing for their conquerors under a just and wise government; and, his argument availing, the idea was abandoned, and Mangi given up to the legislation of native magistrates, presided over by a Mongul chief.

In 1218, the unprovoked arrest and massacre of a caravan of three Mongul ambassadors, and a hundred merchants at Otrar, by command of Mahommed, the sultan of Carizme, or Turkestan, and his refusal to grant any reparation or acknowledge his injustice, first drew the forces of Zingis to the regions of the west. The treacherous descendant of Togrul and Arslan, ruled the vast territory extending over Khorassan and Persia, and his laws were obeyed from the mouth of the Euphrates and the borders of Georgia, to the frontiers of Ghizni and Hindostan, and the stupendous rocks of the Hindoo Kosh. After fasting and praying for three days and nights on a mountain, the Mongul emperor declared his intention of appealing to the judgment of Heaven and the sword; and, accompanied by his four sons and seven hundred thousand men, marched upon the plains of Turkestan. "Our European battles," says Gibbon, quoting Voltaire, "are petty skirmishes if compared to the numbers that have fought and fallen in the plains of Asia;" and in the first battle in which the Monguls encountered the Carizmians, and which was only terminated by the darkness of night, the latter, who numbered four hundred thousand soldiers, left a hundred and sixty thousand among the slain. The Turks retreated to their cities, and armed each for an obstinate defence; the Monguls, aided by captive Chinese engineers, sapped and mined the walls, and brought up their war machines against every fortification with irresistible force; slowly, and after long and weary sieges, each town fell before them, and their triumphs were marked by the most awful atrocities and terrific massacres.* Protracted by the energy and courage of Jellaladin, the son of Mahommed, who several times inflicted upon the Monguls a signal defeat, the war continued for some years under the conduct of Touloui, occasionally assisted by Zingis, who passed between his capital and the camp; and during this time the cities of Otrar, Cojende, Bokhara, Samarcand, Carizme, Herat, Maru, Neisabour, Balkh, and Candahar, were successively reduced; while all Transoxiana, Khorassan, and Persia, were traversed and laid waste; so that, according to Gibbon, five centuries have been unable to repair the ravages caused by the Monguls in four years of terror and conquest. As in China, so then in Western Asia, and later in Russia and the Eastern countries of Europe, wherever they met with the slightest opposition to their arms, they massacred, without mercy and without restraint, men, women, and children of every age and degree, not sparing even the brute creation, and razing every temple or habitation to the ground; so that long after, travellers, while crossing the districts traversed by these savage conquerors, were horror-struck by encountering, in regions now totally deserted

* Gibbon's "Decline and Fall of the Roman Empire." Universal History.

and waste, innumerable pyramids of human bones, the sole remains to be traced upon the spots where flourishing and wealthy cities once stood. In Maru, Neisabour, and Herat, the three great capitals of the province of Khorassan, the number of the slain, according to both the Mongul and Persian authorities, amounted to four millions, three hundred and forty seven thousand persons; and at Neisabour, Touloui having discovered that a few had saved themselves from the general massacre by feigning death, commanded the heads to be cut off the bodies of the slain, and piled in heaps around the ruined city.*

In the meanwhile Mahommed had taken refuge on a desert island in the Caspian, where he died dethroned and alone; and the gallant Jellaladin, retreating as he fought, was driven gradually to the banks of the Indus by the Monguls, under the personal conduct of Zingis; and, sustaining a last defeat on its banks, and perceiving that all was lost, he leaped his horse into the midst of its rapid waters, and sought a shelter on the plains of Hindostan. Gladly would the Graud Khan have followed the fugitive, and carried his arms among the groves and temples of Brahma,† but his troops clamoured for a speedy return to their native land; and, loaded with half the wealth of Asia, he slowly commenced his march towards the north.‡ While passing over the forlorn scenes of his sanguinary success, he appears to have felt a slight remorse for this useless destruction and prodigal waste of life, and announced his intention of rebuilding the cities he had laid waste; and beyond the Oxus and Jaxartes, the Monguls being joined by two generals and thirty thousand horse, who had made the whole circuit of the Caspian, subduing all the nations on their route, the united armies returned to their homes in Central Asia, and again prepared to issue forth on a new career of conquests.

These two Mongul generals, Chin Nojan and Souda

* Huc's " Christianity in China, Tartary," &c.

† " As when a vulture on Imaus bred,
Whose snowy ridge the roving Tartar bounds,
Dislodging from a region scarce of prey,
To gorge the flesh of lambs, or yeanling kids;
On hills where flocks are fed, flies towards the south
Of Ganges, or Hydaspes, Indian streams,
But in his way lights on the barren plains
Of Sericana, where the Chinese drive
With sails and wind, their cany waggons light."
                                    MILTON's "Paradise Lost."

‡ Gibbon's "Decline and Fall of the Roman Empire."—Sherrefeddin Ali's "History of Timur Bek."

Bahadar, had separated from their countrymen when engaged in Transoxiana, to accomplish the subjugation of the Polotzi, and the last feeble remains of the empire of the Chazars. Proceeding with incessant victories, they crossed the Caucasus, destroyed the principality of the Golden Throne, and routed and dispersed the other nations who dwelt among the Hyrcanian cliffs; and, having penetrated the narrow pass of Derbend, traversed Georgia. In the hope of deceiving the inhabitants with the idea that they were Christians and allies, they placed in their van some priests whom they had taken prisoners, and carried the cross as their standard; then, suddenly attacking the Georgians, they defeated and killed 60,000 men. But on discovering their fatal mistake the Georgians rose in arms against the intruders, killed 20,000 of the Monguls, took many prisoners, and put their army to flight. The Georgian queen, Rhouzondan, in a letter which she sent at this time by ambassadors to Pope Honorius III., warning him of the danger with which Europe was menaced by a desolating invasion of the Tartars, states that she had been unable to fulfil her promise to the Roman pontiff, of assisting him in a crusade against the Saracens, as she required the aid of her whole army to repulse a sudden invasion of the barbarians. But the Monguls marched straight through the country without pausing, except to fight, on their progress; and, returning through the north of Persia, joined the army of Zingis near Tashkand.*

Towards the close of the year 1223, Toushi, the eldest son of Zingis, was despatched with an army of 600,000 men for the invasion and conquest of Europe. On the confines of this continent the Polotzi and Circassians had united to oppose the common enemy; but each listened to the treacherous words of the ambassadors of the Mongul, who dissolved their alliance by offering to each his friendship and support, and then attacked and defeated both nations separately, driving the Polotzi from Kipzak. Toushi himself died soon after this event, but his chiefs and generals continued the war; and the expelled tribes having retreated upon Russia, some of the fugitives were pursued by the Tartars as far as to the gates of Novogorod, while another division of the horde spread over the south of Russia to the Crimea. The rumours of the horrible devastations of the Monguls in

* Huc's "Christianity in China, Tartary, and Thibet."

Asia had filled the neighbouring nations with terror and dismay, and their almost uninterrupted success had completely disheartened the inhabitants, who considered that it was vain to oppose them, and believed themselves to be abandoned by Heaven, when they saw the rapid progress and conquests of those whom they believed to be the arch-enemies of God. More especially they shuddered when they thought of the terrible retribution that had been inflicted by the Monguls upon every city whose courage or self-confidence had urged her to stem the torrent which threatened to engulf every civilized nation on the earth, and attempt a brave though fruitless resistance. But in Novogorod the citizens, who were left without a leader, their prince having marched against the enemy in the south, and unable to assemble any competent force to withstand, if they had been so inclined, the enormous number of their savage assailants, rested their hopes on the justice of their cause, and the aid of Heaven in support of Christianity; and, advancing from the city, came to meet the invaders, each warrior bearing in his hand a cross, fondly trusting that their enemies would respect their lives when protected by the sacred emblem of their faith. Vain, indeed, was this hope, for they were promptly received by the loud and piercing war-cries of the Monguls, who, in the fierce battle that immediately ensued, killed ten thousand men; but the march of the barbarians was arrested, and the north of Russia for a time spared by the death of Zingis, at the camp of the Golden Horde; and his generals, who commanded the Mongol army, hastened back to Asia with their followers to assist in the election and inauguration of a new Grand Khan. In the meanwhile the other division of Toushi's tribe had driven the Polotzi from the Crimea, and capturing Soudak, or Soldaya, where the Genoese had formed a trading settlement tributary to these people, made it the capital of the peninsula, and razed the flourishing town of Theodosia to the ground. They had been preceded into Russia by their ambassadors, whom they sent to the princes of Halich and Kiof, declaring their peaceful intentions and friendly inclinations towards the Russian states; but these princes remembering the deceitful manner in which they had acted with regard to the Polotzi and Circassians, and that it was their usual custom to send envoys into these countries upon which they meditated an invasion, to survey the land,

and observe its strength, capabilities of defence, its peculiar aspects, fords, rivers, and land tracts, superseded the Monguls in the act of treachery, and inhumanly caused the ambassadors to be put to death. They then called upon all the princes of Russia to lend their aid to the general defence; and all justly estimating the danger responded to the appeal. From the northern province of Vladimir, the grand prince Vyzevold brought every efficient warrior of his fur-clad troops, armed with hempen shirts of mail, wooden shields, and long spears, the soldiers of Tver and Novogorod marched each beneath the banner of his respective chief; the bowmen of Moscow, under Michael the Brave, hastened with all speed to the south, and with gallant detachments from Riazan and Tchernigoff, joined the ranks of the gorgeously-attired horsemen of Halich and Kiof. The united armies, joined by the fugitive Polotzi, advanced as far as Mariopol, on the Sea of Azof, and encountering the Tartars on the banks of the Kalka, were soon engaged in a fierce and long-contested combat. The Polotzi, who were the first attacked by the enemy, were unable to withstand the furious onslaught with which the Monguls always commenced an engagement, and fled through the battalions of Halich, commanded by its young prince, Daniel, and his uncle, the veteran Micislaf, causing disorder and confusion among the troops. Micislaf attempted to rally his forces, and rushed to the front, but was overpowered by the number of his opponents, and his battalions almost entirely dispersed; and the victorious Tartars cut to pieces in succession the armies of the other Russian chiefs, who had become scattered and separated during the attack, while the Grand Prince, Vyzevold of Vladimir, and the princes of Moscow and Kiof, were left upon the field among the dead. The other commanders fled; and Micislaf of Halich, on reaching his own country, unable to overcome the haunting sense of his disgrace and defeat, retired to hide his head in a monastery, a prey to melancholy and remorse. So ended the fatal battle of the Kalka, fought on the 1st of May, 1224; but though seldom has been witnessed a more sanguinary and terrific defeat, its event was not followed by any important result. The Monguls, indeed, two years after, having subjugated and possessed themselves of the Crimea, pursued the retreating Russians to the walls of Kiof, and had prepared to commence the siege or attack, but the same event—the death of their sovereign—that had recalled their countrymen in the north back to Asia, had a like effect on the forces who surrounded the walls of Kiof; and the Monguls, abandoning Russia for a time, and summoning their troops from Georgia, which they had again invaded with a few squadrons of horse, all collected at Karacorum to make choice of a new chief.

Since the close of the campaign in Transoxiana, and the subsequent conquest of Cashgar, which, held by a Keraite tribe called the Naymans, after the conquest of their countrymen, long successfully resisted the Monguls,* Zingis Khan, though more than sixty years of age, had undertaken, in the year 1225, another campaign against the kingdom of Tangout, whose prince had afforded shelter to two of his enemies, and now obstinately refused to deliver them up. The emperor marched against the rash potentate in person, and, encountering his army in the midst of a wide frozen lake, a tremendous battle was fought upon the ice, in which the Tangoutians were totally defeated, with the loss of 300,000 men. But so many of the Monguls had also fallen in the fight, that they were forced to return for a time to Karacorum to recruit their exhausted force; and it was not till the middle of the following year that Zingis again prepared to set forth. But Death had stretched out her hand to lay hold on the mighty monarch, and from his approach there was no retreat; and while encamped for a few days on their march near the borders of China, the emperor expired, after a week's illness, on the 18th of August, 1227, in the sixty-seventh year of his age. While on his death-bed he earnestly recommended his sons to finish the conquest of the world. "My children," said he, "I have raised an empire so vast, that from the centre to one of its extremities is a year's journey. If you wish to preserve it, remain united." His body was secretly transported to Mongolia; and, accord-

---

* A curious record of this conquest by Zingis has been found in an inscription at Nertschink, near the borders of China, and brought from thence to St. Petersburg. It is eograven upon a grey granite block, five feet high, and more than one foot broad, in four perpendicular rows of Ingour characters, which, when read from left to right, has been translated by Schmidt into the following beginning of a formula of oath to the Ellyas or winged demons:—

"Zingis Khan, after his return from the subjection of Sartagol, after the annihilation of all hatred between all tribes of Monguls to all the 335 Ellyas."

Sartagol is Khara; Khital (the empire of the Keraites), the capital of which, Cashgar, held by the Nayman chief, Gushluk khan, was conquered in the years 1219 and 1220. The stone is therefore a talisman against the return of the hatred of the Ellyas, to whom vows or offerings, it is probable, had been made here.—Pritchard's "Natural History of Man."

ing to a practice generally followed at the burials of the khans, to prevent the intelligence of his death from spreading, the troops who accompanied his coffin killed all whom they met on their route, at the same time exclaiming, " Go, serve our master in another world." He was buried among the Borkan Caldoun mountains, though the precise locality is unknown; and, according to a barbarous custom long prevalent in Tartary, an immense number of horses and men were sacrificed over his grave.*

Zingis Khan, who, with the exception of the fierce and cruel Timur, subdued more kingdoms, and occasioned the destruction of a greater number of human lives† than any other conqueror of whom we have record in ancient or modern times, was in religion a deist, consulting soothsayers and magicians—in appearance broadly made, and rather above the middle stature, and of immense strength, with a large head, and loud and thundering voice. His harem contained at least five hundred wives, by the chief of whom, the Keraite princess, he had his four eldest sons and successors—Toushi, who died before him, and to whose horde and posterity he bequeathed the region in Western Asia, extending to the extreme north, and from the lake of Aral towards the west, as far as, in the words of a Mongul historian, "a Tartar horse had trod;" Octai, who inherited the Chinese empire,* and was elected to the throne after his father's death; Zagatai, whose horde possessed the country of the Igours, all Transoxiana, Carizme, and extended to the borders of Hindoostan; and Touloui, who, as the youngest son, retained, according to the ancient custom of the Tartars, the home and immediate sovereignty of his father in the East. All these princes were, however, only viceroys to the Grand Khan, to whom they referred before undertaking any important expedition, and joined when he required their aid in any distant war; and, for several years after the death of

---

* A French missionary of the time remarks, that the Tartars were so superstitious that they imagined that all the slaves who were slain at their master's funeral immediately joined him as his attendants in another world. This superstition appears to have been shared by the Scythians, Sarmatians, Huns, Slavonians, and all the Tartar tribes.—Huc's " Christianity in Tartary, China, and Thibet."

† It is said that on one occasion Zingis Khan asked one of his generals what was, in his opinion, the greatest pleasure of men. " To go hunting," was the reply, "on a spring day, mounted on a fine horse, and holding a falcon on your fist, to see him bring down his prey." "No," said Zingis: "the greatest enjoyment of man is to conquer his enemies, to drive them before him, to snatch from them all that they possess, to see the persons dear to them with their faces bathed in tears, to mount their horses, and carry away captive their daughters and their wives.—Huc's " Christianity in Tartary," &c.

‡ Pritchard's " Natural History of Man."

Zingis, they remained at his camp in central Asia and China to complete these important conquests. The whole empire was ruled more like an army than a state, and the limits of the authority of each governor was defined rather by the localities of the families of his horde, than the natural or political divisions of the provinces. No Mongul could change his place of abode, or transfer his allegiance to another chief, without the express permission of the Imperial court; and the power of the Grand Khan extended over every other viceroy and ruler from the borders of his own patrimony to the most remote and distant Mongul tent. "Since the commencement of the world," says the Chinese historian, Toung-kien-kammou, "no nation has been so powerful as the Monguls are now; why does Heaven permit that?" Their conquests in Western Asia spread terror through all Europe, and caused the emperor, John Ducas of Byzantium, to reinforce all his garrison and fortify his cities; while the story found credence among his subjects, that the Tartars had the heads of dogs and eat the flesh of men; yet no effort was made by the nations of the West to stem the coming torrent by strengthening the kingdom on the frontiers of Europe. Russia, indeed, was almost too inaccessible, shut out as she then was from the Euxine, to receive any efficient assistance; but the queen, Rhouzoudan of Georgia, appealed again and again for the aid of her fellow-religionists, and was only answered by cold refusals, or perfect indifference and neglect.*

The Polotzi, after their defeat at Kalka, and expulsion from Kipzak and the Crimea, had wandered for some years in the southern steppes of Russia, ravaging the borders of Halich and Kiof; and, at length retreating into Hungary, the king, Bela IV., allowed several of their families, under their chief, to form a colony in Moldavia, then a part of his territory, and from that time they settled down to a peaceful and agricultural life.

It was not until the spring of the year 1229, that all the Tartar nobles and generals had reached the distant tents of Karacorum, to deliberate on the choice of a new khan. Touloui had been invested with the office of regent till the election should have taken place; and, after three days of feasting, the grand council was held, in which many voices

* Huc's "Christianity in China, Tartary, and Thibet."

declared in favour of this prince, who had led them so often to battle and to victory. But Touloui himself proclaimed that Octai had been appointed his successor by the last words and directions of Zingis, and that the will of their father must be obeyed; and, though his brother refused at first to accept the crown, wishing to place it on the head of Touloui, the latter declined the generous offer, and was the first to take the oath of allegiance. Then all the princes bent the knee nine times before Octai, and he was saluted with the title of Khakan or Grand Khan, and acknowledged as their lawful and imperial chief.

Toushi had left three sons, Batù, Bereka, and Shebiani, who divided between them the command of their father's horde. The two former remained for a time at Karacorum, till they marched forth on new conquests in the west; while Shebiani, taking up his abode to the north of the Aral, invaded Siberia with fifteen thousand families and tents, and with these he founded an empire, and erected a wooden capital near the present site of Tobolsk. Here his descendants reigned for above three hundred years, till the conquest of these wilds by the band of a Cossack outlaw, who purchased, by more than a third of Asia, a pardon for his political offences from the Czar; and the sultans and leaders of the Tartar tribes, who still roam in comparative independence over the wide Siberian steppes, wear an eagle's feather in their caps, as the proud mark of their descent from Zingis. The Monguls appear to have penetrated as far as the frozen shores of the Arctic Ocean; for only fifteen years after the death of their great chief, we find that they were acquainted with the names and manners of the Samoyedes, whose fur and ivory, their only riches, were not secure from the depredations of the Tartars, even in their subterranean huts on the borders of the Polar Sea.*

In the year 1240, Turmechirin, the son of Zagatai, crossed the Indus, and subdued the principal towns of Hindostan, and his descendants ruled in Transoxiana and Samarcand till the last khan of their race was slain in a battle with the Kalmucks, when the empire, after a long civil war, became subject to the sway of Tamerlane.

* Gibbon's "Decline and Fall of the Roman Empire."

CHAPTER II.

The Princes of Kiof—Batu Khan—He conquers Russia, and ravages Poland and Hungary—Embassy sent by the Pope to the Grand Khan—Election of Cougach—Karacorum—Camp of Batu at Serai.

> "The populous cities blacken in the sun,
> And in the general wreck, proud palaces
> Lie undistinguish'd, save by the dun smoke
> Of recent conflagration."—H. MORE.

UPON the sudden and unexpected departure of the Monguls from before Kiof—though their country was utterly laid waste, their prince Micislaf fallen at Kalka, and a severe famine and pestilence were already making their presence felt throughout the land—the Russians at Kiof gave themselves up to the most extravagant joy: the sounds of war were exchanged for perpetual feasting and amusement, and the clash of swords and dust of battle for hunting and dancing, and other national sports. But these amusements were succeeded too soon by other and graver cares: the scattered Polotzi tribes, who roved on the southern borders of the empire after their expulsion from Kipzak, kept up a perpetual desultory war with the inhabitants, and, a few years after the death of Micislaf, took prisoner his successor, Vladimir IV., a prince of the house of Monomachus, and caused him to be cruelly put to death. Nature and man appeared alike to have leagued against the unhappy Kiof; and, during the few years that elapsed between the first and second invasion of the Monguls, many houses were overthrown, and many persons killed or injured, by several shocks of earthquake that were felt throughout southern Russia; while, during the whole of one summer, the country was enveloped in a thick fog, which, destroying the crops, was productive of a dreadful famine, only succeeded by a still more terrible plague. The depopulation and national discouragement of which these misfortunes were the cause, still further incapacitated the Russians from offering any adequate resistance to the approaching storm of Tartars; and, added to this, the people appeared utterly indifferent to their danger, and the utmost recklessness of defence and life every where prevailed.

After the death of Vladimir, the princely sceptre again became the subject of controversy and civil wars; it was held by several chiefs in succession, each of whom was compelled in turn to yield it to a more powerful competitor, and each of whom, if he escaped with life, was only destined to suffer loss of sight by the cruelty of a successful rival, or linger out a few miserable years in a dungeon or monastic cell. At length Mikkail, a prince of Suzdal, succeeded in establishing himself at Kiof; but, abandoning the city, he fled into Hungary on the second approach of the Tartars, leaving his dominions to be defended by his eldest son, Demetrius, the worthiest and bravest of his race. The father of Mikkail, the Grand Prince of Vladimir, had been succeeded by his sons Jaroslaf in Novogorod, and George in Vladimir, the latter of whom gained considerable success and fame in his wars with the Bulgarians on the Volga, who had frequently harassed his territories, though the invasion of their kingdom by the Monguls shortly after, induced them to intreat the Russian princes for assistance; which, being refused, Bulgaria was unable to contend alone against her powerful enemy, and her kingdom was finally swept away in 1236 by the overwhelming force of Batù Khan.

In 1235, Ogotai, or Octai, the son and successor of Zingis Khan, having completed the subversion of all Central Asia, first prepared to establish his dominion over the eastern countries of Europe. His entire army consisted of fifteen hundred thousand men—for every Mongul who had attained to the vigour of manhood was a soldier—and the forces of the Khan were further increased by captives from the many nations whom his own and his father's conquests had reduced to a state of servitude. He divided these forces under different generals, for the subjection of India, Corea, and the more distant nations of the west, and intrusted 500,000 warriors of the tributary Finnish, Turkish, and Slavonic nations, with 160,000 Monguls, to the command of his nephew, Batù Khan, the viceroy of Kipzak, who, after celebrating a grand festival for forty days at the Tartar camp at

Karacorum, set forward on this stupendous expedition, and, overrunning the kingdom of Bulgaria, entered Russia.* Well skilled in the art of forging metals, which their own country plentifully afforded, the Tartars, armed with pikes hooked at the end, weighty bows, from which they let fly iron shafts, and tremendous battering-rams, that in one day overthrew the fortifications of Kiof, had little difficulty in contending against the wooden swords and slings of the Russians, and committed the most frightful ravages every where on their route. The tortures and barbarities which they inflicted on the natives, of all ages and degrees, are too hideous and shocking for description, and can scarcely even find a parallel in the horrible executions of China, or among the wild Indian tribes of North America. In many parts of the empire, they spared scarcely one out of fifty men, and the province of Kiof alone lost 60,000, besides women and children. Riazan, whose princes, Oleg and Fedor, had solicited and obtained the assistance of George, the Grand Prince, was taken and razed to the ground—all her chiefs, priests, and inhabitants, perishing in the carnage that ensued, and her army with its allies entirely destroyed; while Periazlaf —though bravely defended by its youthful prince—Rostoff, Moscow, Tver, and all the district of Suzdal, shared the same fate. At length the Tartar army marched upon Vladimir and closely besieged it, while the Grand Princess and her sons attempted to defend the town in the absence of Yourii, its sovereign, who was engaged in the celebration of a marriage feast at a short distance from his capital. But their courage, inspired by despair, was unavailing against the furious onslaught of the Tartars; who, destroying the walls and bastions, massacred the two princes with every inhabitant whom they encountered in the streets, and the princess, having taken refuge with her daughters and the ladies and officers of her court in a church, which she refused to open to the invaders, disregarding all their promises of security and offers of quarter, calmly received the sacrament from the hands of the archbishop, and perished

---

* "A Russian fugitive," says Gibbon, "carried the alarm to Sweden; and, in the year 1238, the inhabitants of Gothia (Sweden) and Frise, were prevented, by their fear of the Tartars, from sending as usual their ships to the herring fishery on the coast of England, and, as there was no exportation, forty or fifty of these fish were sold for a shilling.(?) It is whimsical enough, that the orders of a Mongul Khan, who reigned on the borders of China, should have lowered the price of herrings in the English market!"—Gibbon's "Decline and Fall of the Roman Empire."

in the flames of the edifice, which the Monguls had fired in order to induce her to abandon the protection of its walls.* The unfortunate George tore his hair and became almost desperate when he learned his family's fate; and, collecting a small army, he marched to oppose the strongly armed hosts of the enemy, but was defeated and killed in a battle fought on the banks of the Siti, on the 4th of March, 1238, and his forces destroyed to a man—the wounded and prisoners, among whom was his nephew Vassilko, being all put to death with horrible tortures by their barbarous conquerors. To ascertain the number of dead left upon the field, the Monguls were accustomed after an engagement to cut off an ear from each of the slain; and in the year 1239 they gathered 270,000 of these ghastly trophies from the desolated plains of Russia;† and, after the battle of Leignitz, where they defeated the united forces of the Poles, Silesians, and the order of the Teutonic knights, they filled nine sacks with the right ears collected from the field.‡

Having completed the total destruction of Vladimir and its dependencies, Batù Khan led his forces to within a short distance of Novogorod, but did not pursue his conquests further north; and on Yaroslaf, the brother of George, and Prince of Novogorod, tendering to him his submission, with offers of allegiance, he granted that chief the province of Vladimir, with the title of Grand Prince, to be held tributary to the khan; and, withdrawing his army from the north of Russia, marched towards the more fruitful and populous principalities of the south, where, sacking all the towns and villages, and burning and laying waste every forest and field through which his forces passed, he advanced upon the old and so frequently captured city of Kiof. No bridge in those days spanned the breadth of the Dnieper, and the Monguls were unprovided with boats; but they speedily surmounted this obstacle by crossing the river, after the fashion of the ancient Scythians, upon boughs of trees covered with hides, to which they fastened their baggage, and tying it to the tails of their horses, and seating themselves upon it, using their bows for oars, were thus conveyed safely across. Arrived at the other side, they established themselves before the town, where its prince had abandoned the defence of his

---

* Mouravieff's "Church of Russia."
† Huc's "Christianity in China," &c.
‡ Gibbon's "Decline and Fall of the Roman Empire."

P

own dominions to the skill and courage of his eldest son Demetrius, with the energetic assistance of his boyards, by whom the enemy was long bravely withstood. But the formidable storming machines of the Tartars, and the inflammable powder, whose composition was a secret to the rest of the world, and with which they raised smoke and flames in the midst of their engagements, confounding and baffling their enemies, and inspiring them with the belief that they were opposed by demons rather than by mortal men,* soon effected for them an entrance into the city, and, according to their usual custom, they destroyed the inhabitants, among whom was Joseph, the Greek metropolitan of Russia, without distinction or mercy, and fired every house. But the commander still refused to yield, and after every church and monastery, all of which had been fortified by the citizens, had successively fallen before the enemy, he intrenched himself with the rest of the people in the cathedral of St. Sophia, prepared to resist to the last extremity every effort of the Monguls to dislodge them from this, their last stronghold and retreat. But their efforts were of no avail; for the roof breaking in, owing to the weight of the crowds who had sought safety and shelter in the upper rooms and every part of the building, many perished among the ruins, and their chief was taken alive and dragged a prisoner before the fierce and savage Batù Khan. When brought, however, into the presence of the Mongul prince, the calmness and fearlessness of his demeanour inspired even the Tartar with some respect for his courage and misfortunes; and, sparing his life, Batù allowed him to plead successfully for the protection of his few remaining followers, who, with a large sum of money that they had concealed in the ground from the avaricious eyes of their enemies, ransomed the cathedral of St. Sophia from destruction, though all the rest of the city was reduced to ashes; at the same time, the conqueror listened to the arguments of his captive, when he attempted to divert him from pursuing his desolating course any further in Russia. Demetrius represented to Batù that his country had long been weakened by the dissensions of her princes, and the continual invasions of her foreign enemies, who had encroached upon and appropriated her provinces, plundered her cities, and reduced her to so barren and enfeebled a con-

* Huc's "Christianity in China," &c.

dition, that she was totally unable to resist the arms of the Tartars, who, now that they had captured and destroyed her chief cities, and rendered barren and waste all her fields and cultivated lands, could obtain neither advantage nor booty by pursuing the war any further, but would suffer severely from want of forage and provisions; and that, owing to the prostrate condition of Russia, the Monguls need fear no outbreak or reprisals, if they abandoned her to seek wealth and further fame among the more favoured nations of the West. Poland and Hungary, he urged, contained iron mines, whose produce would be valuable in renewing the bent and rusty weapons of the Tartars; and they had for many years enjoyed the blessings of peace, during which they had greatly prospered, accumulated riches, and cultivated their land; their fields would afford ample forage for the horses of the Monguls, and they were already making formidable preparations to resist the arms of the invaders. Batû dismissed the Russian with many presents and marks of his esteem; and, proceeding to act upon his advice, invaded and overran Halich, Silesia, and Poland, where he encountered the united armies of these kingdoms, who had joined the banners and martial array of the Teutonic knights, in a desperate fight at Leignitz, and were commanded by the Duke of Silesia and the Polish king, Henry the First. Before the engagement, the mother of Henry, St. Hedwige, had abandoned the convent in which she had been long self-immurred, and, rushing through the ranks of the soldiers, urged them to fight heroically in the cause of their country and of Christianity. They indeed made a desperate resistance, and inflicted a severe loss upon the enemy; but the Crusaders, who had demanded the honour of commencing the battle, which was fought on the 9th of April, 1241, were deceived by a feint of the Mongul cavalry, who first retreated and then charged, and, having separated from the main body in pursuit, the enemy rallied, and overthrew the divided forces in succession, leaving the king and duke among the countless dead. The barbarians struck off the head from the corpse of the unfortunate monarch, and mounting it on a pike, presented it before the town of Leignitz, calling upon the inhabitants to surrender; but before the Poles had decided upon their answer to the imperious summons, the Monguls furiously burst open the gates, and gave up the town to utter destruction, with all the ravages of fire and sword. Laying waste the whole country, they drove the wretched captives, who were chained together, and of all ranks and ages, in crowds before their hosts; and despatched an outlawed Englishman as their ambassador, to the neighbouring Hungarian king, demanding the submission of that prince. But upon his positive refusal to listen to their proposals, they devastated Hungary for three years, and retreated to their camp on the Volga, having left in that kingdom * only three cities standing, and driven her unfortunate monarch to seek refuge in the dreary retreat of a solitary isle on the Adriatic. They had previously ravaged both shores of the Danube, which they crossed on the ice, and inducing the fugitives, who had fled to the woods from their burning towns, to abandon their hiding-places, under solemn engagements of protection and pardon, they massacred them all without mercy; and three hundred women, who had escaped from the indiscriminate carnage, and belonged to the highest families of the nobility, were coolly executed in the presence

---

* The monk, Roger of Varadin, an eyewitness of the Tartar invasion of Hungary, in a book, entitled "Miserabile Carmen," thus relates his own adventures:—"Whilst the Tartars were sacking Varadin, I escaped by night into a fortified island, but not thinking myself safe there, I took refuge in a neighbouring forest. In the morning, the island was occupied by the Tartars, who killed all the people in it; my very hair stood up on hearing of these massacres, and a cold sweat, as of death, burst from me, when I thought of that army of murderers. I continued to wander about the woods, but I was starving with hunger, and was obliged to venture at night into the island, in order to search among the bodies for morsels of food or flour, which I secretly carried away. I lived thus for twenty days, hiding myself in caverns and ditches, and in the hollow trunks of trees. The Tartars then promised that they would do no harm to the inhabitants who would come out of their concealment. I did not myself depend much on this promise, and my suspicions were but too just; but I thought it better to go at once to their camp, than to await my fate in a village, and I therefore gave myself up to a Hungarian who had gone into the service of the Tartars, and who deigned, as a great favour, to place me among the number of his servants. I was almost naked, but my business was to mind the waggons; and I had the fear of death continually before me, for I knew that in one night the Tartars had murdered the inhabitants of all the surrounding villages. Nevertheless, as the princes had received orders to return to Tartary, we began to move away with the herds of cattle, and horses, and waggons, laden with booty. The army retired slowly, and when it had quitted Hungary to enter Coumania, it was no longer allowed that any cattle should be killed for the use of the captives. The Tartars gave us only the intestines, heads, and hoofs, of the animals they had eaten, and we heard from the interpreters that it was intended to kill us very soon." He goes on to relate, how, having with his servant contrived to make his escape, they hide for several days in a forest, and, having reached the outside, mounted a tree to look about them. "Oh, what a sorrow! the country was entirely desolated, and it was a desert that we should have to cross, with nothing but the steeples of the churches to direct our steps; and happy did we think ourselves, if we could find now and then some peas, onions, or garlic, in the ruins of the villages, otherwise, we had to support ourselves on roots. In about a week after leaving the forest, we arrived at Alba, where we found nothing but human bones, and the walls of the churches and palaces still stained with Christian blood. Ten miles off there was, near a wood, a country-house commonly called Frata; and four miles from this forest, a high mountain, where many individuals of both sexes had taken refuge. When we reached it, the fugitives congratulated us with tears in their eyes, and questioned us concerning the perils we had encountered. They offered us black bread, made of a mixture of flour with oak bark, and we thought it the most delicious thing we had ever eaten."—(Quoted by Huc, in his "Christianity in China," &c.)

of the Tartar chief.* As Batù advanced with his followers to the borders of Austria and Bohemia, Vinceslas, the king of the latter country, in alarm for its safety, wrote to all the neighbouring princes, urging them to unite in arms against the common enemy. In his letter to the Duke of Brabant, he says—"A body of ferocious savages, in countless numbers, are occupying our frontiers. The misfortunes predicted for the sins of men in the Holy Scriptures, are overwhelming us on every side;" and, in conclusion, he remarks, that "the people of both north and south, are so oppressed by calamity, that never since the beginning of the world were they so cruelly scourged."† But in 1246, before entering Bohemia, the Mongul general was suddenly recalled to Asia by the death of Ogotai or Octai Khan, whose son, Couyuk or Gayuk, succeeded him as chief of the Golden Horde; and this event probably saved Europe, whose armies had been defeated, and her kingdoms overthrown, wherever they had been opposed, on every side; as, while it caused the Tartars for a time to return to Karacorum, their ambition and enterprise were subsequently diverted to another quarter of the globe.

At the same time that Batù invaded Russia, another army of Tartars entered Georgia, which they burned and pillaged with Albania, and Great Armenia, where the princes, finding it impossible to oppose them effectually, submitted to the Mongul general Tcharmagan, and consented to serve in his armies, though the Georgian queen again urgently wrote for assistance from the powers of the West; and, in a letter addressed to the Pope, Gregory IX., she professes entire submission to the Church of Rome, and promises to unite Georgia to the Holy See. But she received for her only answer, that the pope mourned deeply the evils suffered by Georgia, but was unable to send her any help, since the Emperor Frederick II. had just raised a tempest within the Church; still he greatly approved of her design of bringing Georgia within the pale of the Romish faith, and would send her some monks of the order of St. Dominic to assist her in the pious work. But the priests, if they ever reached her country, could not aid her against the enemies, who were pouring across her frontiers; and Rhouzoudon, finding her-

---

* Gibbon's "Decline and Fall of the Roman Empire."
† Huc's "Christianity in China, Tartary," &c.

self deserted by all the Christian princes, ultimately renounced Christianity altogether, and became a Mahometan.*

All the sovereigns of Europe participated, with just cause, in the alarm, and felt their thrones insecure, when they heard of the conquests of the Tartars. The brave and virtuous Louis IX., at that time, wore the crown of France; and Matthew Paris relates, that his mother, queen Blanche, on receiving intelligence of Batù's invasion of Europe, burst into tears, and sending for the king, exclaimed—"My dear son, what fearful rumours are these? Surely the irruption of these Tartars threatens our total ruin, and that of our Holy Church." "Let us look to Heaven for support and consolation, my mother," replied he; "and, if they come, these Tartars, we will drive them back into Tartarus, whence they have issued; or, it may be, that they will send us to Heaven to enjoy the bliss that has been promised to the elect." †

The Emperor Frederick Barbarossa, whose long feud with the papal see caused his enemies to accuse him of having favoured and encouraged the Tartar invasion, and whom the pope reproached with behaving more like an idle, pompous orator making speeches, than a Christian sovereign at the head of his troops, was invited, in the name of the Grand Khan, to do homage for his states, and offered in recompence to hold some office or dignity, like the conquered kings of Asia, at his court. He observed in jest, that being well acquainted with birds of prey, he had better take the office of falconer, but appears nevertheless to have been well aware of the danger with which his states were menaced; and in a letter addressed to Edward I. of England, draws the following picture of their enemies:—"A people issuing from the utmost confines of the world, where they had long been hidden under a frightful climate, has suddenly and violently seized on the countries of the north, and multiplied there

---

* "The letters," says Huc, "which Gregory IX. addressed to the people, to animate them to the Holy War, paint in lively colours his grief and alarm. Many affairs of grave importance," he writes, "are, at this time, incessantly occupying our thoughts; the melancholy state of the Holy Land, the tribulations of the Church, the deplorable condition of the Roman Empire. But we confess, we forget all these causes of affliction, and even what most particularly concerns us, when we think of the evils caused by the Tartars; for the bare thought that the Christian name might be destroyed by them in our days, is enough to break our bones," &c.

† "This play upon words," says Huc, "attributed here to St. Louis, is perhaps the real cause of the alteration which the Westerns have made in the name of the Tartars. They are frequently designated Tartares, from the first moment of their appearance; and *Tartari imo Tartarei*, as the Emperor Frederick calls them, was an expression that found much favour," from the idea that the Monguls were demons sent to chastise mankind.

like grasshoppers. One knows not whence this savage race derives the name of Tartar, but it is not without a manifest judgment of God that they have been reserved for these latter times, as a chastisement for the sins of men, and perhaps for the destruction of Christendom. This ferocious and barbarous nation knows nothing of the laws of humanity. They have, however, a chief whom they venerate, and whose orders they blindly obey, calling him the God of the Earth. These men are short and thick-set, but strong, hardy, of immovable firmness, and at the least sign from their chief, rushing with impetuous valour into the midst of perils of every kind. They have broad faces, eyes set obliquely, and they utter the most frightful cries and yells, which correspond but too well with the feelings of their hearts. They have no other clothing than the hides of oxen, asses, and horses, and up to the present time they have had no other armour than rough and ill-joined plates of iron. But already —and one cannot utter it without a groan—they are beginning to equip themselves better from the spoils of Christians, and soon the wrath of God will perhaps permit us to be shamefully massacred with our own weapons. The Tartars are mounted on the finest horses, and they now feed on the most dainty viands, and dress richly and with care. They are incomparable archers. They carry with them leathern bags, skilfully fashioned, with which they cross lakes and rapid rivers; and it is said that their horses, when they have no other forage, will feed on the leaves, bark, and roots of trees; and notwithstanding these privations, are full of spirit, strength, and agility."*

Upon the first entry of the Tartars into Europe, under Toushi, the son of Zingis Khan, Gregory IX. published a crusade against the invaders and their allies, the Russians, so designating the latter, from the many prisoners of their nation who had been forced into the service of the Grand Khan, and compelled to fight under his banner against their own countrymen and fellow-Christians; and the same pardons and indulgences were offered by the pope to all those who should bear arms against the Monguls, as to him who had made a pilgrimage to the Holy Land. Upon the retreat of Batù into Asia, the successor of Gregory, Innocent IV., attempted, by the more peaceful mode of negotiation,

* Huc's "Christianity in Tartary," &c.

to ward off the threatened invasion of the western countries of Europe, and despatched an embassy to the court of the Grand Khan, composed of Franciscan monks, who, like the Roman ambassadors at the camp of the Scythian king, on the shores of the Irtish, were forced to walk between two fires, to purify themselves, before they could enter the presence of the Tartar chief. On leaving Poland, they entered the dominions of the Russian prince, Vassilko of Vladimir, or Lodomeria, who entertained them some time at his capital; and on their departure, gave them one of his own attendants to conduct them safely through the country of the Lithuanians, and as far as Kiof, which was then in the hands of the Monguls. They were charged with letters from the Roman pontiff, addressed to the king and nation of Tartars, in which Innocent IV. exhorted that people to embrace Christianity, and honour him in the persons of his ambassadors, whom he desired the khan to respect and protect; and having accomplished their perilous mission, and obtained an audience of the chief, in 1247 they returned to Europe, bearing a reply* to the message of the pope, from the successor of Octai, the Emperor Couyuk, who then reigned as Grand Khan. Carpin,† one of the envoys, has left us the following interesting account of the interview of his fellow-travellers and himself with the Tartars. "The first place," said he, "where I met the Monguls, was at a short distance from Kiof, named, 'the khan's bourg.' They immediately surrounded us, inquiring

---

* Letter of Couyuk Khan to the Pope.

"Couyuk, by the power of God, Khan, and Emperor of all men, to the Great Pope.

"You, and all the Christians who inhabit the West, have sent me, by an ambassador, certain authentic letters, with the design of forming with me a treaty of peace. According to the words of your envoys, and the tenor of your letters, you desire to have peace with us. If then you wish to have peace—you, pope, and your emperors, kings, chiefs of towns, and governors of countries, do not delay to come to me, and settle this peace. You shall hear our answers and our pleasure. The tenor of these letters declares that we ought to be baptized, and to become Christians; to that we briefly reply, that we do not understand why we should do any thing of the kind. It was said in your letter also, that you were astonished at our slaughter of men, especially of Christians, and in particular of the Hungarians, Poles, and Moravians. We reply that we do not understand this either. Nevertheless, that it may not appear that we pass over this point in silence, we have thought proper to give you this answer: It was, because they did not obey the command of God and of Tchinguiz Khan, and because, yielding to bad counsels, they put to death our ambassadors. In consequence of that, God has commanded me to annihilate them, and has delivered them entirely into my hands. And if it were not the work of God, what could one man do against another man? But you, inhabitants of the west, you adore God you say; you believe that you are the only Christians, and you despise others. But how do you know on whom He will deign to confer his grace? We adore God, and it is in his strength and power that we shall destroy all nations. If man had not the strength of God, what could man do?"—Huc's "Christianity in China," &c.

† John de Plano Carpin, or Carpini, was a native of Perouse, and had been the companion of St. Francis d'Assis, in many of his journeys. He founded convents, and monasteries, in Hungary, Bohemia, Norway, Dacia, Lorraine, and Spain.—Huc—Carpin's "Travels."

our motives for travelling, and where we were going. I replied, that we were sent by the father and sovereign of all the Christians, who, never having offended the Tartars, had learned, with the greatest astonishment, that Hungary and Poland, inhabited by his subjects, were ravaged by the armies of the khan, and that desirous of peace, the pope, by his letter, exhorted him to embrace the Christian religion. The Monguls, who were contented with some presents, furnished us with guides, to conduct us to the horde of Bati (Batù) Khan, the second in command, who had placed his camp on the banks of the Volga, with six hundred thousand men. We were conducted to his tent on Friday, in the Holy Week, when we found Batù established on his throne, with one of his wives, his brothers, his children, and several Tartar warriors, seated on benches, the rest of the assembly being on the ground, the men on the right, and the women on the left. This tent, made up of fine linen, had formerly belonged to the king of Hungary, and no one dared to penetrate into the interior, except the family of the khan, without special permission. Batù read with much attention the pope's letters, which were translated in the Arab, Tartar, and Slavonic languages, and he received us with much affability, though he generally inspires awe and terror. He is renowned for his cruelty in war, and for his cunning, deceitfulness, and experience; and he ordered us to the presence of the Grand Khan Couyuk, where, before we could gain an audience, we were kept a whole month in front of a tumultuous camp. This chief was encamped in a magnificent tent,* called the Golden Horde, ornamented within and without with the richest stuffs, and the columns which sustained it were decorated with figures of pure gold. We were at length admitted to an audience, with some other ambassadors, of whom the secretary pronounced the names, but very few persons were admitted into the khan's tent. The presents which were made him consisted of stuffs of gold, girdles, furs, saddles, camels, and mules, richly harnessed; with an immense number of presents, ornamented with precious stones, and at some distance from the tents, were fifty chariots, all laden with these precious offerings, to the vanity and power of Couyuk, the Great Tartar khan. We were the only ones who had nothing to offer, and found that Couyuk was deter-

* A present from the Emperor of China to Zingis Khan.

mined on making war. He, therefore, would not enter into any negotiation, and we remained at his camp nearly a month, idle, and overwhelmed with *ennui*, without provisions sufficient to sustain us, and should have perished of want, had we not happily been supplied by a Russian jeweller, who, having made a throne of ivory for the khan, was in high favour with his master, and the court. We were at length charged with letters from the khan, composed by his secretary in Arabic, which I translated into Latin, and he proposed to send a Mongul ambassador with us to the pope, but this I declined, lest they should witness the dissensions which exist among the Christian princes. Before our departure, we took leave of the emperor and his mother, who presented us with a pelisse of fox-skin and red cloth, and after a weary journey we arrived at the camp of Batù, who furnished us with the passports, by which we finally happily reached Kiof. The two Russian princes, Daniel and Vassili (of Halich), gave us a very gracious reception in their dominions. They convoked the abbots, the bishops, and the most illustrious men, and declared publicly that they were resolved to acknowledge the holy father, as the head of their church." The Tartar khan took the title of Prince of the Universe, to which he added, " God reigns in heaven, and I on earth." When the Emperor Mangou dismissed the ambassadors of France from his court, he sent a letter to their sovereign, concluding in the following defying terms :—" In the name of the all-powerful God, I order you, King Louis, to obey me, and to declare to me solemnly your choice, for a truce or war. What Heaven decrees shall be accomplished. When the universe has recognized me for her sovereign, all the earth shall enjoy a happy tranquillity and peace. Then the happy people will see what we can do for them ; whereas, if you dare to despise the Divine orders, and to say that your country is distant, that your mountains are inaccessible, that your seas are deep, and that you fear not my power—the Most High rendering easy what might appear impossible, will prove to you what we are in a condition to do."*

Upon the death of Ogotai, who had been poisoned by one of his concubines, his widow Tourakina was invested with the office of regent, till the election of a new khan ; but she left no stone unturned to procure this dignity for her son ; and

* Carpin's " Travels."

to assist at the ceremony of installation, all the lieutenants and governors of the provinces were recalled from Europe and Southern Asia. Among other eyewitnesses of the gorgeous ceremonial, were the humble Franciscan monks, who have left us a minute description of the deliberation, the election, and the imperial feasts. The Kouriltai, or General Assembly, had been convoked to meet at a spot in a district near Karacorum, called the Seventy Hills, and the roads from all parts of Asia to the centre of Tartary were covered with travellers and horsemen. The princes of the blood came attended by a numerous military escort, and among them were the widow of Touloui, with her children; the sons of Ogotai, Toushi, and Zagatai, followed by the chiefs of the tribes over whom they exercised sovereign power; the governors of the Mongul possessions in China, Argoun, and Massend; the governor-generals of Persia, Turkestan, and Transoxiana, with the native princes and nobles of those countries in their train; the Sultan of Roum-Rok-ud-din, Yaroslaf, the Grand Duke of Russia, two princes named David, who disputed between them the crown of Georgia, the brother of the sovereign of Aleppo, and ambassadors from the Caliph of Bagdad, and from the princes of Ismail, Mossoul, Kars, and Karman, who were all richly attired, and all brought magnificent gifts for the future khan.* The Tartar princes, with their generals, assembled in an immense tent, capable of containing two thousand persons, which was also surrounded by two thousand of a smaller size, where the merchants of India, China, and Persia, had flocked in immense numbers, with the most precious productions of the East; and garments of silk and gold were daily distributed by the sovereign to the members of the convocation, who, after spending several mornings in deliberation, and evenings in drinking and music, agreed to elect Couyuk, and unanimously gave him their votes. According to custom, he at first refused to accept the throne, but, after a long resistance, agreed to the wishes of his subjects, and received their oaths of allegiance, the immense multitude that covered the plain, falling prostrate on the ground before him, and afterwards accompanying him to another Tartar encampment, a few leagues distant, where the ceremony of enthronization was to take place. This was accomplished by the princes and nobles

* Huc's "Christianity in China," &c.

placing him on a golden throne, at the same time exclaiming, "We will, we pray, and we command, that you have power and dominion over us all." He replied, "If you wish that I should be your king, are you resolved, and disposed, each one of you, to do all that I command? To come when I shall call you, to go where I shall send you, and to kill those whom I command you?" To this they all answered, "Yes;" upon which he said, "From henceforward my simple word shall serve me as a sword." Then rising from his throne, he seated himself on a piece of felt they laid on the ground, the same which had covered the imperial seat of Zingis, and received this exhortation from the principal nobles and chiefs: "Look up, and acknowledge God, and consider well the piece of felt upon which thou art. If thou governest thy state well, if thou art liberal and beneficent, if thou causest justice to reign, if thou honourest thy princes and officers, each according to his rank and dignity—thou shalt reign in all splendour and magnificence, and all the earth shall be subjected to thy sway; but if thou dost the contrary of all this, thou shalt become miserable, vile, and contemptible, and so poor that thy possessions shall not even amount to as much as this piece of felt." After this speech, the chiefs caused the wife of Couyuk to seat herself beside him, and raising them both on the felt, in the air, proclaimed them with loud cries, emperor and empress of all the Tartars.* This was followed by an enormous banquet, attended by all the princes, princesses, and dignitaries of the empire, and which consisted of nothing but meat, with a profusion of rice wine and kumys, their national spirit, an intoxicating liquor, that the Russian slaves and captives superstitiously believed if a Christian once tasted his soul was for ever lost.

   The guests drank long and deeply till past midnight, to the sound of musical instruments and martial songs, and renewed their feast every evening for seven days in succession; and at the end of this period, the emperor marched forth from his tent, and raising a great banner towards the west, waved it, threatening at the same time to carry fire and sword over every one of those countries that should not, along with all the rest of the earth, submit to his authority and government. He was at that time about forty years of age, and is described by the missionaries as being of small figure, and very grave

* Huc's "Christianity in China," &c.

deportment, never listening or replying to any thing, but through his prime minister; and his first act was to command the execution of the Mongul lady who had caused his father's death. Every one addressed him kneeling.

The mission that was sent by Innocent IV. to the Tartar general, Baidjow in Persia, met with no better success than the embassy which set out the same year to Karacorum, but its members were treated with far more abuse and contempt, an officer even proposing to flay one of the friars alive, and send his skin, stuffed with straw, back by his companions to the pope. When the monks confidently requested the Monguls to become Christians, and informed them that the pope, the dictator of the world, and vicegerent of heaven, was above all other men, Baidjou inquired,—" Who ever heard that the name of the pope was spread every where, and respected, and feared by the whole earth, as that of the khan is?" and sent back a letter by the priestly envoys to their master, in which he says,—" Know, O pope, that thy messengers, have come, and brought us letters. They bore, amongst others, these words,—' You kill many people; you massacre, and you lay waste.' The immutable command of God, and the order of him who rules the whole earth, is this,—' Whosoever will obey us, let him remain in possession of his land, his water, his patrimony, and let him give up his forces to the master of the universe. Whosoever shall resist this order and command, let him be annihilated and destroyed.' " †

The superior wealth and luxury that the Monguls observed among the nations whom they conquered and overran, introduced great changes in their simple, though barbarous, mode of life, and the immediate successors of Zingis Khan, with their principal officers and lieutenants, removed from a tent to a house or palace, which affording all the luxuries and conveniences that art could furnish, was surrounded by an ample and well enclosed park, instead of the pathless forest and boundless plain, where wild animals of all kinds were preserved to provide the Grand Khan and princes with the amusement of hunting, without having to seek for game at considerable distances from their camp. At the beginning of winter, a grand imperial chase, conducted with the importance and regularity of a great military expedition, was annually held on a convenient spot near Karacorum, when

† Huc's " Christianity in China," &c.

parties of hunters, despatched from all the tribes within a month's journey of the place of rendezvous, drove every wolf and elk they encountered into a circle of about two or three leagues, remaining in a close line outside the enclosure to prevent any from escaping the Imperial bow. The Grand Khan having first entered with his wives, and shot as many as he desired, retired to an elevated spot, from whence he witnessed the performances of the princes and generals; who in their turn made way for the officers of a lower rank, who were finally replaced by all the common men. The hunt lasted several days; and so late as the year 1824, when the practice was abolished, owing to the indolence of the then reigning sovereign, who could not bring himself to abandon his luxurious palace at Pekin, for the labour and fatigue of the chase, the emperors of China annually resorted to the wilds of Tartary, to follow the same pursuit, and according to the same arrangement, as the expeditions conducted under Octai and Couyuk Khan. The French missionary, Rubruquis, saw at Karacorum, among other captive foreigners, his countryman, Guillaume Boucher, a goldsmith of Paris, who had been carried off with a Norman bishop, and a woman of Metz, in Lorraine, from Belgrade, when the Tartars invaded Hungary, a Flemish cordelier, a singer named Robert, and numerous Russian artificers and mechanics. These decorated the palace of the khan with paintings and sculpture, and executed statues and ornaments for his use, in gold, silver, and precious stones; with salvers, goblets, and basins, to enrich his tables and equipage, while his feasts were supplied with the products and luxuries of all Asia, the wines of southern Europe, and even the fruits and spices of the distant Indian isles. A silver fountain, in the form of a tree, supported by four massive lions, who each spouted forth a different liquor from its metal throat, graced the centre of the festal board of the khan, where frequently more than a thousand guests were entertained in one night. All forms and sects of religion were alike tolerated at Karacorum; a Nestorian church, two mosques, and twelve temples, dedicated to various idols, being supported and attended by the many foreign traders, who had been induced by commercial enterprise, or compelled by the hard chances of war, to take up their residence in the camp of the Golden Horde. Indeed, till the time of Kublai, the third in descent from Zingis, who adopted the religion of Buddha,* and Bartù, the brother of Batù, who succeeded him in his lieutenancy, in the kingdom of Kipchak, and embraced Mahometanism, the khans professed no other creed than the belief in one Supreme Being, treating with equal ridicule or condescension, every sect of religion and faith; and Mangou, the successor of Conyuk, who frequently assembled priests of the Buddhist, Christian, Nestorian, Chinese, and Mahometan faith, and listened to their discourses respecting their different creeds, and their theological disputations, and controversies, said one day to Rubruquis, that all the men at his court who adored the one Eternal Deity, ought to be free to do so each in his own way.† To this city resorted also suppliant princes and captive monarchs, who only held their thrones and liberties at the capricious will of the Mongul chief, and came to solicit his favour, or pour their tribute at his feet. On the banks of the Volga, Batù, the viceroy of the west, established his camp, which, like the wooden capital of Attila, occupied as much ground as a large city, on the site of the ancient Serai, once a flourishing town under the Chazars, and placed his own log palace, whose interior was decorated with jewelled goblets and ornaments, and where the throne, furniture, and dresses of the attendants were loaded with gold, with the tents of his sixteen wives in the midst. Here he received the embassy of the pope, on its road to Karacorum, and the Franciscans who were sent by Louis IX. of France, when a report had spread in Europe, that Prince Sartak, the son of Batù, and governor of a district on the Volga, had renounced the errors of paganism, and consented to receive baptism. But the monks discovered on their arrival at Serai, that the Tartar prince had embraced the Nestorian, not the Latin faith, and they looked upon this as little better than idolatry; and, at an audience which Batù granted the friars in his tent, and at which they were compelled to kneel before him, their attempts to induce the khan to conform to Christianity, and their representations of the eternal misery reserved for the wicked and unbelievers, were received by the chief with smiles of derision, and by his courtiers with

---

* "The earliest introduction of Buddhism among the Mongolians took place in the year 1247, when in the east at Langtschen, in the Chinese province of Schensi, the sick Mongolian prince, Godan, sent for the Gahya paradita, a Thibotian archbishop, in order to cure and convert him."—Humboldt's "Cosmos."
† Huc's "Christianity in China, Tartary," &c.

clapping of hands and ironical cheers.* From this camp, Batù gave laws to the Russian princes, and frequently required their personal attendance at the steps of his throne, as humble petitioners for their lives or sceptres; and here, during the two hundred years of the Tartar power in Russia, two hundred and fifty of her princes prostrated themselves before the Mongul khan, and twelve suffered death by his order at different times, besides many of the boyards and inferior officers from the Russian court.

The Tartar capital in Mongolia is described by travellers of the time† as being surrounded with an earthen rampart, entered by four strong iron gates, lying exactly according to the points of the compass, and enclosing several public offices and markets. It was traversed by two streets, called the bazaars of the Chinese and of the Saracens, and fairs were occasionally held there, which attracted numerous merchants and traders from all parts of Asia, and Russians and Bulgarians from Eastern Europe.

* Huc's "Christianity in China, Tartary," &c.
† Travels of Rubruk in Hakluyt's "Voyages."

CHAPTER III.

Yaroslaf of Nobogorod—Mangou Khan—Kublai conquers China—Holagou conquers Persia—The Monguls of China—Khans of Kipzak.

> Such the gay splendour, the luxurious state,
> Of caliphs old, who on the Tygris' shore,
> In mighty Bagdad, populous and great,
> Held their bright court.—THOMSON.

WHILE the greater part of Russia was ravaged and overrun by the Monguls, who even consumed the grass on the steppes as they passed, and invaded by the Lithuanians, Poles, Swedes, and Teutonic knights, who, all at the command of the pope, united against her as an ally of the infidel Tartar khan, with his horde of those whom they believed to be inhuman and fiendish followers, Novogorod and Pskof, or Pleskof, which was justly renowned for the peaceful disposition of her inhabitants, appear to have been almost the only towns that escaped the general destruction, which had plunged the whole people into misery and mourning, and covered the empire, from north to south, with ashes, ruin, and blood. The monk Carpin in his travels relates, that while passing through Russia he encountered, in many places, heaps of unburied skulls and human bones; and thousands of the inhabitants, who had been driven by the Tartars into Mongolia, were there made drovers and herdsmen to their masters' flocks, or placed in colonies on the shores of the rivers, to keep the bridges and fords. But the citizens of these states, through the prudence and caution of Yaroslaf, their prince, experienced a milder fate. Upon the overthrow of Vladimir, and the death of her sovereign upon the field of battle, finding his own territories menaced at the same time by the

Christians in the west, and the wild and undisciplined armies of the Mongul emperor in the east, he offered peaceable terms to the invader; and, visiting in person the camp of Batù, tendered his allegiance to the viceroy of the khan, receiving as a recompense the domains of his deceased brother, George, to be held as a fief of the Golden Horde, and with them the title and authority of Grand Prince. From this period till the reign of Ivan the Great, when they finally emancipated their country from the Tartar rule, the Russian princes were obliged, as a mark of their degradation and complete servitude to the Grand Khan, to offer his ambassadors and lieutenants, whenever they received one at their courts, with a glass of milk, which they presented bareheaded and on foot, while the Mongul remained seated and on horseback; and if a drop fell while the delegate of the khan was raising it to his lips, the Russian princes were compelled to lick it up, and also to feed the horse of the envoy of their tyrant with corn from their caps of state. At the same time the heavy tribute and fines that they were continually called upon to pay to the Monguls, ruined their overtaxed people, without satisfying the extortionate demands of the Tartar prince, who further exhausted the country by carrying off the young men to recruit his restless armies, and the most skilful artificers and mechanics to construct his newly-founded cities and decorate his palaces. Yaroslaf in the south, and Daniel of Halich in the west, by their wise government, and the exertions they made to collect the scattered people together, and rebuild the towns and villages that the Monguls had destroyed, greatly contributed to restore some order and tranquillity in their dominions, and encourage their disheartened and dispirited countrymen, who groaned under the weight of taxation and Tartar oppression; for the revenues of Russia were totally exhausted, and her princes were even unable to maintain the court and retinue usually supported by their richer and more fortunate predecessors.

On the death of Octai, in 1246, Yaroslaf was summoned to attend the election of a new emperor at Karacorum, and renew his former oath of allegiance. He accordingly departed for Mongolia with many followers and horsemen; but after witnessing the ceremony of the installation of Couyuk, and joining in the banquets and hunts, he was unable for many days to obtain permission to return to Russia; and the Franciscan missionary, Carpin, who was then at the Mongul court, and an eyewitness of the event, relates, that the Grand Prince, having been invited to dine with the empress-mother, Tourakina, and her attendants, was immediately after the ceremony seized with a sudden illness (which the friar affirms was the result of poison), and turning blue from head to foot, died in a few days, on the 30th of September, 1246.* The common supposition, that his death was compassed through the machinations of his enemies, receives further support from the fact that his son Alexander, on the banks of the Volga, afterwards experienced the same fate, when returning from a similar expedition among the notoriously crafty and treacherous Tartars. Yaroslaf was in the fifty-fourth year of his age, and had reigned altogether in Novogorod and Vladimir more than twenty-two years. He was buried in Mongolia, near Karacorum, and left five sons, who all subsequently reigned—Alexander, prince of Novogorod, Iziaslaf, Yaroslaf, Andrea, and Vassili, and of whom the third, Iziaslaf, was the immediate successor to his father's precarious inheritance.

In the year 1250, the grand khan, Couyuk, having been murdered by an emissary of the Assassins, a famous heretical sect of Mahometans, who, in 1090, established themselves in Persia, and possessed a large tract of land among the mountains of Lebanon, he was succeeded by his cousin, Mangou, the son of Touloni, at Karacorum; and the new chief, shortly after his accession, fitted out two formidable expeditions, under his brothers and lieutenants, Kublai and Holagou—the one for the subjection of the southern provinces of China, which till this time had escaped the ravages of the Monguls; the other, accompanied by a body of Chinese artillery, for the complete reduction of Persia and Mesopotamia, who, since the death of the Great Tartar conqueror, had been partially abandoned by his followers, and were gradually emancipating their provinces from the less vigorous grasp of his successors. In China, previous to its conquest by Zingis, the empire had been divided into two separate states, Mangi and Cathay; the former, and most northerly of which, as I have said, was subdued and cut off from the southern district many years

* Carpin's "Travels."

before by the Mantchous,* a nation of Tartars, who for ages had opposed the arms and progress of the then weak and insignificant Mouguls, and who now, enervated by the superior luxury and civilization, and milder climate of the Celestial empire, were in their turn trodden under foot by their former foes; while the sceptre of the southern provinces was still held by the ancient and native dynasty of the Soug, who preserved in the neighbourhood of Canton their throne and authority, and, till the expedition of Kublai, had remained undisturbed and secure from the arms of the Tartars. Upon the reduction of Mangi by the forces of Zingis, the Mantchou emperor had been compelled to flee from Yenking; and escaping with only seven horsemen from Kaisong, where he had also attempted to make a stand, he took refuge in a third city, which was still held by his adherents.† But finding his cause desperate, and hopeless of victory or succour, he ascended a funeral pile, which he ordered his attendants to light, and, drawing a dagger from his vest, put a speedy end to his life. Forty-five years later, Kublai, who, as an easy mode of conveying his vessels and his troops, projected and completed the grand canal, which, passing through a district of a thousand miles, traverses forty-one cities on its course, and extends from Pekin to Nankin, the ancient capital, marched against the still unsubdued and fertile territories in the south, where the cities and strongholds were obstinately, though fruitlessly, defended by the Chinese, with not only Greek fire, but all the appliances of the modern artillery of the West; for bombs and gunpowder ‡ appears to have been long known to the skilful

---

* It was first under the Huns, then under the Mandshus, or Mantchous, and lastly, when it became a permanent custom, under the Mouguls, that the Chinese were compelled to follow the Tartar fashion, and shave their heads, leaving only one long lock of hair on the crown. Before these invasions they had been celebrated for their long locks, and were often called the black-haired people. Under the Mantchous, China first became closed to commerce and intercourse with other nations. "Accustomed," says Huc, "as we have been in our own time, to see the Chinese shutting themselves up jealously within their own empire, we have been too ready to believe that it was always so—that they have always cherished an inveterate antipathy to foreigners, and done their utmost to keep them off their frontiers. This is, however, quite a mistake; this jealously exclusive spirit characterizes especially the Mantchou Tartars, and the empire has only been thus hermetically closed since their accession to power."
† Gibbon's "Decline and Fall of the Roman Empire."
‡ Père Gaubil affirmed that gunpowder had been known to the Chinese sixteen centuries. The Tartars conquered China before they entered Europe, and it is probable that they may have learned there some of the uses of gunpowder, and that the inflammable material, with which they so much alarmed the nations of the West, was only a peculiar kind. Roger Bacon, who first introduced it into Europe, and in 1216 wrote a treatise upon its composition and effects, having been acquainted with two travellers from Tartary, from whose plans and descriptions he made a map of that country, the first seen in England, might, it appears not unlikely, have received from them some information of the manufacture of gunpowder, and the formidable purposes to which it might be applied.

inhabitants of China, whose passive courage caused every step of their enemies to be only gained by fire and death. At the same time, the Monguls had brought with their army, from their conquered and tributary provinces, the most skilful engineers and artificers of Western Asia and Eastern Europe, for they well knew how to avail themselves of the arts and abilities of their captive enemies, to supply their own deficiencies in the science and knowledge belonging to more civilized life; and while in China, Russians, Persians, Arabs, and Georgians filled the ranks of their armies; in Europe they were assisted by the genius or valour of the inhabitants of China, Hindostan, and Tonquin, and the most remote nations of the Asiatic East. But, finally driven from the land, the Chinese had recourse to their ships; and on their fleet being surrounded by the powerful armament of the enemy, an officer, taking the infant emperor in his arms, leaped into the sea, exclaiming that it was more glorious to die a prince than to live a slave; and his example being followed by a hundred thousand of his countrymen, their empire became the undisputed possession of the Monguls.* In the meanwhile, Holagou had spread the terror of his name, not only over all Western Asia, but also in Europe; where he threatened to march on Constantinople; and so great was the fear he inspired, even to the borders of France and Western Italy, that the inhabitants added this sentence to their litany, "From the fury of the Tartars, good Lord, deliver us." After completing the conquest of Khorassan and Persia, he marched on the expiring hierarchy of Bagdad, and on the 22nd of January, 1258, appeared with his army before its sacred gates. Mostassim, the last and degenerate successor to the throne of the caliphs, who, since the fall of their oppressors, the Seljuk Turks, had recovered their former inheritance and independence, had long rendered himself despicable in the eyes of his subjects and enemies, by his absurd vanity, frivolous amusements, and puerile occupations, which chiefly consisted in visiting his aviaries and ape-shows, watching the performances of his conjurers, and listening to their anecdotes and jests. When he rode to the mosques, he caused the streets that he must traverse to be covered with magnificent cloth of gold, and continually wore

---

† Gibbon's "Decline and Fall of the Roman Empire." "Histoire des deux Conquérans Tartars, qui out Subjugué Tartars." Par le R. P. Pièrre Joseph d'Orleans.

a veil over his face, that it might not be defiled, as he affirmed, by the looks of a vile populace. All who came to his palace were required to kiss its threshold before they entered; and he demanded the same honour and respect for a piece of black velvet hung over his door, as that paid to the famous black stone, which is worshipped by the Moslems, in the temple of Mecca, and dedicated to their sacred prophet. After defeating the Saracen army in several engagements before the city, which he had straitly blockaded with his troops, Holagou summoned the caliph to surrender, informing him that, if he razed the walls of his capital, filled up the ditches, and presented himself in person to the conqueror, he should retain his life; but that, if his obstinacy compelled the Tartars to attack and storm Bagdad, he should surely not escape, even were he to hide in the innermost recesses of the earth. "Young man, who, seduced by ten days' good fortune, imagine yourself master of the world," was the caliph's reply, "and dream that your commands are irresistible like those of fate; what audacity is this to ask of me what you will never obtain? Follow, then, the way of peace and prudence, and return to Khorassan." The Tartar envoys who received this answer were assailed with stones, on their return to their master, by the Mussulman populace, who treated them with every indignity as they passed through the streets, and would have torn them to pieces had they not been rescued by the vizier with a portion of the guard, who preserved them from outrage till they had departed in safety from the city gates. On their informing Holagou of this ill-treatment, he exclaimed, "The behaviour of the caliph is more crooked than a bow, but, with the aid of the Almighty, I will make it as straight as this arrow." And he indeed took a terrible revenge;[*] for on the 1st of February, having taken Bagdad by scaling the walls with his soldiers, he delivered it up to pillage and slaughter, and 800,000 persons are said to have perished; the caliph, as some writers state, having been killed by molten gold being poured down his throat, in mockery of his ostentation and avarice; according to others, having been imprisoned in an iron cage, where, by the command of the Mongul general, he received no other food than the gold and jewels he had so fondly prized when on the throne, and for the accumulation of which he had heavily

---

[*] Huc's "Christianity in China," &c.

taxed his subjects, and starved and defrauded his troops. From Bagdad, Holagou passed on to Syria with 70,000 men, where he extirpated the odious sect of the Assassins, with their chief, the Old Man or Ancient of the Mountain, before whom, when on a march, one of his followers, armed with a hatchet, surrounded by swords and knives, would proceed, crying, "Back, back; fly from before the face of him who holds in his hands the life and death of kings;" and the Monguls laid siege to Aleppo, calling upon its sultan, Nassir, to surrender unconditionally to their chief. But on his refusal, and expressed determination to resist the arms of the Tartar to the last extremity, Holagou commanded the city to be attacked; and for five days the Monguls hurled fire and missiles from catapults against its walls, and captured it by assault on the sixth. The massacre which then commenced was, if any thing, still more horrible than that at Bagdad; and 100,000 of the women and children, who were taken prisoners, were sold for slaves throughout the cities of Western Asia, and even in the markets of Eastern Europe. But owing to the circumstances of his wife, Dhozoig Katoun, being a Christian, Holagou treated all of that religion with a lenity and respect before unknown to his race; their lives and churches were spared in the destruction of Aleppo and Bagdad; Armenia and Georgia were untouched by his desolating course, and given over to the government of their native princes; and he protected the Nestorians, and every denomination of Christians in the East, treating them with great favour, and granting them many privileges, even causing a chapel to be fitted up in his camp, where they all freely celebrated religious worship. Having advanced as far as Egypt, where his further progress was arrested by a defeat he sustained from the corps of Mamelukes, the lords and masters of that ancient kingdom, Holagou marched against Jerusalem, with the intention of extricating the city from the hands of the Saracens, and delivering it up to the care and defence of the Christians; but his purpose was changed by the intelligence of the death of Mangou, who had been killed by a bomb while conducting the siege of Hochew, in China, in 1259, and his own election to the dignity of Grand Khan; though, owing to the great distance he was then from the Golden Horde—which caused him to receive the news a full year after the event—by the time he had accomplished the journey to Karacorum, he found that the Tartars had raised his brother Kublai to the throne in his place, and he shortly afterwards returned to Persia. During the transportation of the body of Mangou to the burial-place of the khans among the mountains, the soldiers, according to the savage custom followed at the funeral of Zingis, killed 20,000 persons on their route.*

Five years before this, the Franciscan priest Rubruquis and his companions, charged with letters from Louis IX., had made their way through the Crimea, Kipzak, Bulgaria, and Mongolia, to ask for permission at the court of the khan to propagate their doctrines throughout his states. They have accurately described the Volga, the Ural, and the bleak and desolate country beyond, where they encountered wild oxen and horses, and where, to use Rubruquis's words in his narrative, "the frost was so terrible that it split trees and stones." Dressed in clothes of sheepskin, which they had been forced to adopt, like the inhabitants, to protect them from the intense cold, they wended their dreary path across wide plains of snow, till at length, after six months' journey from the time that they departed from Serai, they saw before them the towers and gilded minarets of Karacorum. The first building they entered was an Armenian church, surmounted, according to custom, by a cross, where they found a monk standing before a splendid altar engaged in meditation and prayer, and round the walls paintings were displayed, representing figures of the Saviour, the Virgin, and St. John, embroidered in gold and jewels; and a large silver cross studded with rubies and pearls. The monk informed the missionaries that he had long lived as a hermit in the Holy Land, and, guided by divine inspiration, had undertaken a journey into Tartary to convert the Grand Khan, whom he had assured that, if he embraced Christianity, the whole world should obey him, and even the pope and the king of France acknowledge his sway.† Buddhism was at this time gaining many converts in Mongolia, though principally among the common soldiers and people; for all the Tartar nobles had confided the education of their children to the Nestorians, who, in order to obtain favour and disciples in the land, would ordain mere infants priests, so that there

---

* Huc's "Christianity in China, Tartary," &c.
† "Travels of Rubruquis," Edition of Bergeron.

were few Monguls of consideration and wealth who did not lay claim to the office.* Shortly after their arrival, the Franciscans obtained an audience of Mangou; but, before entering his palace, their clothes were strictly searched, lest they should have brought any poison or weapon concealed, and a knife carried by their interpreter was retained outside, before they could be admitted into the presence of the Tartar prince. He was seated on a divan, dressed in a rich furred robe, in the midst of a room hung round with cloth of gold; a chafing-dish, filled with burning wormwood, stood beside him, and he was apparently about forty-five years of age, broadly made, and of the middle stature. His wife, who was young and handsome, was seated near him, with their daughter Cyrina, and several little children playing around; and he ordered kumys, rice wine, and mead to be set before his guests, whom he seemed to take a pleasure in regaling, and after they had partaken, he began a conversation with their Tartar interpreter. "But for my part," says the plain-spoken Rubruquis, "I understood nothing from what our interpreter said, except that he was very drunk, and the emperor, in my opinion, not much better."

The Grand Khan and his family attended equally the religious services and ceremonies at the Mussulman, Buddhist, and Christian churches; and on one occasion, when Mangou was seated with the empress on a gilded divan opposite the altar, in the Nestorian church, he sent for Rubruquis and his companion, and desired them to sing him a Latin hymn, in the meanwhile examining their bibles and breviaries with much apparent interest. But still he showed no decided preference for any particular faith, treating equally the professors of each, "and," says Rubruquis, "they all flutter round him like bees about flowers; for, as the emperor gives to all, they each wish him all sorts of prosperity." At the same time he was exceedingly superstitious, consulting magicians and soothsayers; and it is curious that one of their modes of invoking spirits was by rapping on a table, when they feigned to receive answers to their inquiries, and proclaimed them as oracles, and certain truth.† On Easter-day he issued a proclamation, commanding that the priests of every sect and denomination throughout his capital, should assemble at a stated time at the palace, and each in turn deliver his

* Huc's "Christianity in Tartary, Thibet, and China." † Ibid.

arguments in favour of his particular faith; that beforehand they were to send him a statement in writing of the various articles of their creed, and that three of his secretaries, a Mussulman, a Buddhist, and a Christian, should act as umpires in the theological contest. Before commencing the discussion, a minister of the khan's read an order from their master, forbidding any, under pain of death, to say any thing abusive of his adversaries; and the assembly was opened by a Bonze from China, who challenged the Franciscans to prove the existence of only one Supreme Being. A sharp controversy then ensued, in which the judges declared in favour of Rubruquis, and the Mahometans, refusing to enter into a dispute with the Nestorians, alleging that they considered the Christian law a true one, and believed the gospel, the orators dispersed; and the following day the emperor desired an interview with Rubruquis. "We Monguls," said he, when the missionary entered, "believe that there is one God, by whom we live and die, and towards whom our hearts are wholly turned; but, as He has given the hand several fingers, so has He given men various paths to heaven. He has given the gospel to the Christians, but they do not obey it; he has given soothsayers to the Monguls, and the Monguls do what their soothsayers command, and therefore they live in peace." He then declared that the missionaries had resided long enough in his empire, and that it was quite time for them to think of returning home; and this was the last audience that the missionaries were able to obtain of the Mongul prince. "I took my leave," says Rubruquis, "thinking that if the Almighty had been pleased to let me perform such miracles as Moses did, perhaps I should have converted him." *

Some writers have reported that Mangou was subsequently baptized through the pursuasions of Hayton, a king of Armenia, who, in the year 1256, made a peaceful visit to the Mongul court; but it is uncertain if he ever seriously professed the Christian faith, and three years after this event, accompanied by the sons of Batù, he joined his army in China, where his brother Kublai had already entered upon his long career of conquest. A few months later the emperor received his death-wound at Hochew; and Holagou, being the elder of his brothers, was elected by a large majority among the nobles to the dignity of khan. But the great distance the Persian general was then from the seat of govern-

* "Travels of Rubruquis," Edition of Bergeron.

ment in Mongolia, and the immediate necessity for a leader to continue the prosecution of the Chinese war, caused the officers and princes, after a few months had elapsed, unanimously to declare in favour of Kublai for their chief, and he was accordingly, after the usual ceremonies, duly invested with the imperial crown.

On leaving his army for Mongolia, Holagou had appointed one of his generals, Kitou-baga, to the chief command, and deputed to him the consummation of his project for the conquest of Palestine; but the sultan of Egypt, uniting his forces with those of the queen of Aleppo and the Christians at Acre, marched upon the Tartar encampment in the plains of Tiberias,* and, taking them by surprise, defeated their army in several engagements, when Kitou-baga and many thousands of his warriors were put to the sword, and his children taken prisoners. This victory created the greatest sensation all over the East, where the Monguls were thought to be invincible, and, as soon as it was proclaimed at Damascus, the Mahometans, again raising their heads, committed the most horrible atrocities upon all the defenceless Christians in their city, burning their churches and dwellings, and massacring those who had been unable to retreat; and this overthrow was the forerunner of the decline of the Mongul power in Western Asia, which soon divided into separate states; large and formidable indeed, but not so great as to make Europe and Asia tremble, as in the days when they were united and unbroken, and all bowed to one khan. This collision with the Mussulmen in Syria, caused the alliance of the Monguls to be courted by the Christians as a defence against the Saracens and Turks; and on the demand of Holagou, who is supposed to have meditated embracing Christianity, the emperor Michael Paleologus granted him his daughter Maria in marriage, and agreed on a permanent peace. But on arriving at Cesarea, under the conduct of the Greek patriarch of Antioch, who was charged with her attendance to her husband in Persia, she received news of Holagou's death, though she nevertheless continued her journey; and reaching the court of his son and successor, Abaga, in place of his father she espoused this young Tartar prince, and thus, for the first time, a European princess became a katoun, or queen of the Monguls.

* The Grand Master of the order of St. John of Rhodes, with many of his knights, were killed in this engagement. See Major Porter's "Knights of Malta."

Holagou died in his camp, at the age of forty-eight, in the year 1265, and was buried in an island in the midst of the lake of Ormia, his chief wife Dhozoig Katoun, a Keraite princess, following him a few months after to the grave.* His rule is celebrated for the encouragement he offered to literature, mechanics, and science; and he established an observatory and gymnasium at Tabriz, after the manner of the ancient museum at Alexandria. In the meanwhile, the arms of Kublai were extending the career of the Mongul conquests in the furthest provinces of the East and the South. His forces, and the terror of his name, spread his sway over Corea, Tonquin, Cochin China, Pegu, Thibet, and Bengal, and his ambition even aspired to the subjection of the far-famed islands of Japan; but the fleet † which he fitted out for the purpose, twice suffered shipwreck in the stormy seas that wash her shores, and one hundred thousand Monguls and Chinese fell victims in this unfortunate expedition. ‡ The voyages which his navy, consisting of a thousand ships, undertook in the Indian Ocean, were attended with more success; they traversed the equinoctial line, and filled their vessels with plunder and fruits from Borneo and the adjacent fertile and fragrant isles; || and the court of the khan at Pekin, which he founded, was maintained in the greatest magnificence and splendour, while he attached the people to his throne and government, by restoring their ancient constitution and laws, which had all been subverted and destroyed by the usurping dynasty of the Mantchous, and respecting and adopting their customs and prejudices.§ He introduced the practice now usual with the Chinese emperors, of resorting once a year to pray at the tombs of their ancestors, and offered the highest honours and rewards for proficiency in learning or science. The first set of Chinese mathematical instruments were collected by his orders, and their holidays and anniversaries were first arranged on fixed days in the year; and he caused an alphabet to be composed for the Monguls,¶ who hitherto had promiscuously used those of con-

* Huc's "Christianity in China, Tartary, and Thibet."
† Ranking, in his historical researches on the conquest of Peru and Mexico, endeavours to prove that his fleet was driven on the shores of America; and were the invaders known in Peruvian history, as the founders of the religion and dynasty of the Incas; and he asserts that the Manco Capac, of the Mexican annals, was the commander of this expedition, and a son of Kublai Khan.—Wiseman's "Science of Revealed Religion."
‡ Gibbon's "Decline and Fall of the Roman Empire."
|| Ibid. "Universal History." Gutzlaf's "History of China."
§ Kublai is described by Marco Polo as having rather fair hair, and, unlike the generality of Tartars, a large prominent nose.
¶ Article China, "*Encyclopædia Britannica.*"

quered nations. His reign, which extended over a period of thirty-three years, is one of the most celebrated in the annals of China; and on his death in 1292, leaving twenty sons, most of whom he had installed as governors over the various provinces of his empire, he was succeeded by his grandson Timur, whose father Zingis, the eldest son of Kublai, had been destined by the khan as his successor, but greatly to his grief, died before him. Under Timur the Monguls of China became almost separated from the khans of the west, who, after veering between Christianity, Judaism, and Mahometanism, finally proclaimed the latter as their national faith; while the rulers of China, to the dissatisfaction of their subjects, the followers of the philosophy of Confucius, adhered to the worship of the Lamas of Thibet, though they still occasionally issued laws and decrees to the Mongul khans, even as far as Russia and Kipzak.* But this branch of the Tartar race did not long maintain their rule over the Chinese; a hundred and forty years after the death of Zingis, the grand khan, his family, which is known in the Chinese annals as the dynasty of Yueu, and amidst the pleasures and riches of Pekin and the fertile regions of China, had lost their warlike inclinations, and, like the Mantchous, become soft, indolent, and effeminate, were expelled from the celestial empire by a revolt of the natives under their leader Hongou, or Chu, who, from a servant in a monastery of Bonzes, raised himself and his family to the throne. In 1636 the Chinese were again subdued by the Mantchous, their ancient enemies, who having recovered new vigour in the harsh air of the north, poured, as before, across the great wall upon Pekin; and the last emperor of the native dynasty, Whaztsong, having hanged himself on a tree in the garden of his palace, to escape falling into the hands of the invaders, was succeeded on the throne by Schunchi, the commander-in-chief of the enemy, whose family have worn since that time the imperial crown of China.

But the princes of the house of Yueu, or Zingis, are the most renowned of any in the history of the Chinese race. It is still called the holy by the Chinese, and, notwithstanding its foreign origin, still regarded with fond remembrance and regret.

While his countrymen were extending their conquests and consolidating their power in Asia, Batù had firmly established

* Huc's "Christianity in China, Tartary," &c.

his empire over Russia and the Crimea, where he founded many towns and villages, particularly New Kazan and Bakchi Serai (the city of Batù), now the capital, and almost the only town exclusively possessed by the Crimean Tartars, the descendents of his followers, and which, while Taurida formed an independent state, was the residence of the court of her khans. In 1255 he equipped a powerful force which he commanded in person, and prepared to march upon the dominions of the Greek emperor, with the intention of attacking the city of Constantinople itself; but before he had proceeded many miles on his route, he was seized with an illness, of which he died, near the banks of the Volga, or, as some writers of the time affirmed, from the effects of poison, leaving many sons, of whom two, Sartak the eldest and Ullaghzi the youngest, successively ascended the throne. As both died after only a few months' reign, their uncle Bartù, or Bereka, deposed the second and third sons of his brother, and driving these princes from the land, in 1257 he succeeded to the throne of Kipzak.

The new khan, who was the first of his family to adopt the faith of Mahomet, upon his accession commanded that all those among his subjects who should refuse to conform with the creed of the prophet, should suffer immediate death, and travelled through all Russia, even as far as Novogorod, to enforce his intolerant edict; but the firmness of the people in resisting this decree, caused him at length to ameliorate the punishment; and after deposing two of her princes, Romanus of Riazan and Michael of Tchernigoff, and commanding their execution with several of their nobles, at his camp, he ordered a general census to be made of the lands and population of Russia, for the purpose of imposing a capitation tax; and decreed that the amount should be doubled to all those of the peasantry who persevered in the faith of their ancestors. These were enrolled under the name of Christians, which, to this day, is the most common term by which the Russian peasant is designated; but all the priests were exempted from the impost, for, in order to unite this powerful body to their interests, the khans were accustomed to court their favour by granting them many privileges, and always supported the influence which they exercised over the people and state. The Tartars also introduced the punishment of the knout, the postal regulations for travelling, which have always been commodiously and methodically arranged in Russia, field jaegers or couriers, and the postage of letters by payments according to the weight. The calculating machine, in universal use throughout Poland and Russia, and which is similar to the one known in China, was also brought by the Monguls from Asia, where it was known as early as four hundred years before Christ.

In 1260, Bereka assembled his forces for another invasion of the West, and for the second time wasting Poland with fire and sword; he wrote to Bela, the king of Hungary, with offers of alliance and peace. His ambassadors proposed to that prince, on behalf of the khan, the union of their families and interests, by the marriage of two of their children; and in that case, the Monguls would respect the frontiers of Hungary, and exempt her from invasion and tribute, provided that the son of the king brought a company of Hungarian troops, who should receive in recompence a fifth portion of the booty, as auxiliaries of the Tartars. In case of a refusal of his terms, Bereka threatened Hungary with total destruction, her towns with flames, and her people with massacre and slavery. In this emergency the Hungarian monarch appealed to the pope, Alexander IV., for advice and assistance, reminding him that Gregory IX. had abandoned his kingdom to the mercy of the Monguls, and that the cardinals, when they elected a new pontiff, had engaged that he should drive the barbarians from the confines of Europe.* In reply, Alexander expressed astonishment that any Christian sovereign should entertain for a moment the idea of accepting such conditions as those offered to Bela by Bereka. "Turn with horror, my son," said he, " from the thought of clouding the splendour of your titles with shame, and staining with perpetual ignominy the beauty of your reign." But counsel appeared to be the only aid that the pope was able to offer to the distressed prince, and Bela would probably have been compelled to resign his throne, or submit unconditionally and unhesitatingly, to the terms of the arrogant Tartar, if Bereka had not found Bohemia a more convenient ally; and after sacking Sandomir, and covering Poland with ashes and ruins, he was recalled with his army to Kipzak, by disastrous news from the East. The Monguls of Russia had been engaged for some years in a contest with Holagou, who ruled in Khorassan, and had lately allied himself with the Christians of Asia and the Grecian monarch; and in 1250, Nogai,

* Huc's "Christianity in China and Tartary."

an able general and a near relation of Bereka, had been despatched by his sovereign with an army against the Persian prince. The hostile forces encountered each other on the banks of the Terek, near the foot of the Caucasus, on the 19th of January, 1263; and after a furious battle, which terminated at length in the total defeat of the Mongul army of Kipzak, the fugitives were almost entirely lost, by the breaking of the ice on the river, which they had crossed in their flight; and the intelligence of this calamity reaching Bereka while engaged in pursuing his victorious career in the West, caused him to return in haste, and march with his army towards Persia, to avenge his soldiers' and general's defeat; and for this reason he abandoned for the time his design of conquering and desolating Europe.*

* THE GREEK AND RUSSIAN CHURCH.

The Greek and Roman Churches finally separated, after ages of hatred and controversy, in 1055, during the pontificate of Leo IX. The patriarch of Constantinople had been only nominally subservient to the pope, since the time of Photius in the ninth century; and the synod of Constantinople, held in the year 869, is the last recognised by the Church of the West. The Greeks boasted of the superiority of their knowledge both secular and religious, and that the decrees of the seven general councils had been promulgated by them, and they refused to admit the innovations continually introduced by the Latins, condemning the alteration of the Nicene creed by the synods of France and Spain as heresy, and prostration before the images of the saints as idolatry. Among other innumerable points of dispute, was the use of leavened or unleavened bread in the Sacrament, the administration of both kinds to the laity, which was permitted among the Greeks, the marriage of priests, and the too lax observance of Lent by the Latins, who allowed the use of cheese and milk, and exempted those enfeebled by age or disease. The Greeks, also, like the Jews, abstained from things strangled and from blood, a practice not followed in the Romish Church. At length the legates sent by Leo IX., to remonstrate with the Greek patriarch, Michael Cerularius, pronounced against him the sentence of excommunication, and laying their anathema on the altar of St. Sophia, condemning the whole people and their priests to eternal punishment, they shook the dust of the city from their feet, and departed for Rome. The patriarchs of Alexandria, Antioch, and Jerusalem, though they condemned the creed of the Latins, at the same time attempted to separate from the Greeks; but the latter obtained the cordial support of the Russians and Bulgarians, their proselytes, and the Bohemians also, for some years, adhered to the Eastern faith. The Russian Church, therefore, closely following the doctrines of Constantinople, divide their clergy into two orders, the Black or Monastic, and the Secular or White. The latter are allowed to marry once, though it must be to a virgin, and previous to ordination. They compose the parish papas or priests, while the bishops and higher dignitaries of the ecclesiastics are universally chosen from among the monks. The office of priest was hereditary till within the last few years; but established usage now generally follows what formerly a law enforced, and hermits, whose devotion is now condemned by the Latin Church, are still often to be met with in the remote districts of Russia. There are many dissenters from the Greek Church, some of which allow polygamy, and follow many of the precepts of Moses and Mahomet. The Greek Church does not admit purgatory, but believes that the soul may occasionally haunt its former abodes on earth, and therefore allows the efficacy of prayers for the dead. Her adherents practise auricular confession, adopt the Athanasian creed, and conform to the established liturgy of St. Bazil; but, though they condemn images, sacred pictures are extensively used in their worship. Their churches, which are gorgeously decorated, are built with the sanctuary turned towards the east, and in the midst stands the high altar, separated from the congregation by a screen, and called the "Holy of Holies." They have neither side-chapels nor side-aisles, and those who are destined for priests never cut their hair or beard from birth. They observe four great fasts in the year, besides every Wednesday and Friday, during which they abstain from every species of animal food—even sugar was prohibited, on account of its refinement by bullocks' blood, till the introduction of that extracted from the beet-root. They have also numerous festivals, of which the Carnival and Easter are the chief; and with them predestination is as universally recognized a dogma as among the disciples of Mahomet. Monastic establishments of all kinds are very numerous in Russia, belonging to both the established church and the schismatical sects; and many of the latter practise the most rigorous penances, frequently even suicide by starvation or fire, supporting their doctrines by the verse in the Gospel—"He that findeth his life shall lose it; and he that loseth his life for my sake, shall find it."

CHAPTER IV.

Reign of Alexander Nebshoi in Russia—Noghai's rebellion—The Monguls of Persia—Abaga—Argun—Voyage of the Chinese Princess to Persia—Kazan.

> They fight for freedom who were never free.—BYRON.

ON the death of Yaroslaf of Russia, all his sons were commanded by Coujuk, the Grand Khan, to appear within a year at his court in the Golden Horde, that the Tartar monarch might select from among them a successor to their father's throne. The young princes immediately repaired to Karacorum, with the most splendid retinues that the exhausted treasury of Russia could command, and each loaded with presents to propitiate the khan in his favour, except Alexander, the eldest son of Yaroslaf, who had reigned for some years in Novogorod, and was hardly even a nominal vassal of the Tartars. After an interregnum of nearly two years, caused partly by the length of time they occupied with their journey to Mongolia, and partly by the delay of the emperor in making his choice, Iziaslaf, the third son of Yaroslaf, was appointed to the throne of Vladimir, with the title of Grand Prince of Russia, he being at that time nineteen years of age; but his reign was speedily terminated at the end of a few short months, by his death on the field of battle, while engaged with the Lithuanians, who had invaded and plundered his dominions. Previous to this event, Batù Khan, jealous of the independent position of Novogorod, had caused this message to be conveyed to Alexander:—"Prince of Novogorod, is it not known to thee that God has subjected to me a multitude of nations? Shalt thou alone be independent? If thou wishest to remain in peace, repair instantly to my tent, and there thou shalt see the power and glory of the Monguls;" and Alexander, complying with the imperious demand, set off with his brother Andrea to Serai. There, receiving intelligence of the defeat and death of Iziaslaf, they both proceeded to Karacorum, where the khan greeted them most honourably and courteously, and declared to the Prince of Novogorod, that though " he had heard a great deal in his praise, rumour had fallen far short of the truth," at the same time bestowing upon him the additional and important province of Kiof, and conferring on Andrea the princedom of Suzdal and dignity of Grand Prince. They both returned to their respective dominions; but in 1215, Andrea impatient of his own servitude, and that of his country and people, rose up in arms against their Tartar masters, and attempted to expel them from the empire. A fierce and sanguinary battle ensued, which was lost by the Russians; and their prince, being refused by his brother an asylum at Novogorod, fled to Sweden, where he died in the year 1276, at the age of fifty-four; and Alexander, having made a second journey to Karacorum in 1252, received from the khan a formal appointment in writing to the throne of Russia.

This prince was born in Novogorod, May 30, 1221, and, on the death of his elder brother Fedor, in 1232, became heir-apparent to the throne. Upon the invasion of Russia by Batù Khan, and after the plunder and destruction of Vladimir, his father Yaroslaf, resigning the government of the principality into the hands of his son, appeared at the camp of Batù, furnished with large bribes and magnificent presents, as a ransom for his life and throne, and presenting them to the Tartar chief, with promises of submission and fealty, received in exchange for his freedom, as before stated, the province of Vladimir as a Tartar fief. But all Europe had been called to arms by the declarations and admonitions of the Pope Gregory IX.; and while the Monguls in the south were ravaging Kiof and Poland with fire and sword, the Teutonic knights, who were established in Esthonia and Livonia, under their Grand Master Hermann von Balk, marched upon Pskof, almost the only city in the empire that had been spared by the Tartars, and, after a brief siege, took the place by storm. At the same time Eric XII., king of Sweden, had despatched a large fleet manned by Swedes, Norwegians, and Finlanders, to the mouth of the Neva, where, on the 15th of July, 1240, among the marshes upon which St. Petersburgh now stands, but where then roamed, unmolested and undisturbed, the bear and the wolf, their sole inhabitants, it was attacked, and totally defeated by Alexander, who obtained from this victory the title of Nevskoi, or of the Neva,* and immediately repaired to the relief of Pskof. He succeeded in driving the Teutonic knights from the town, but during the winter was forced to disperse his army, on account of the difficulty of procuring forage, and the bad state of the roads, which prevented him from bringing provisions from any distance; and in the spring the enemy again appeared in the field, with their forces renewed and invigorated, and marched to within twenty miles of Novogorod. Hastily assembling a small body of troops, the prince led them against the foe, whom he encountered while crossing Lake Peipus, and completely defeated them, in a battle fought upon the ice, on the 5th of April, 1241, when four hundred of the knights were slain, and fifty taken prisoners. He pardoned all the Germans captured in the engagement; but considering the natives of Esthonia, which was tributary to Novogorod, as his subjects, and therefore rebels, he caused all who belonged to that country, whether knights or private soldiers, to be hanged, and built several forts on the Neva, to repel any future attacks of the Swedes. But his rule was too arbitrary and despotic to please the independent citizens of Novogorod, who, rising up against him, drove him from the throne, and forced him to retire to Vladimir, where he endeavoured to procure from his father a guard sufficient to control his rebellious subjects. But Yaroslaf, refusing to comply with his request, conferred upon him the inferior province of Periazlaf, and sending his second son Andrea to rule over the discontented people of Novogorod, they for a time submitted to his milder yoke. They were, however, shortly after, harrassed by another invasion of the Danes, whom their new prince was quite unable to repel; and at length driven to despair, they sent an embassy to Alexander, humbly and earnestly requesting his return. But haughtily reminding them of the ungrateful manner in which he had been treated, he indignantly refused; and the distressed citizens, having no efficient general to lead them against the enemy, sent another deputation, with the archbishop at its head, entreating him to alter his

* An account of this victory, professing to be by an eyewitness, is inserted in several of the Russian chronicles.

determination, and come to their assistance. The remonstrances of the archbishop, and his account of the dangerous state of the province, had their effect; and returning, Alexander placed himself at the head of the army of Novogorod, with which he entered Livonia, and defeated the combined armies of the knights, Danes, and Lithuanians, compelling them to sue for peace. In 1247, by the order of the khan, he visited the Golden Horde at Karacorum; but on his brother being appointed to the dignity of Grand Prince, he returned to Novogorod, where he received at his court the embassy of cardinals, who in the Russian chronicles are called Gald and Gemont, and were sent by Innocent IV. with a letter dated January 23, 1248, exhorting Alexander to unite the Church of Russia to the Roman Catholicism of the West. If he consented to this proposal, the message went on to state, and would acknowledge the supremacy of the See of Rome, he would be permitted to unite his forces with those of the other nations of Europe, in the general and holy crusade against the Tartars. At this time the patriarchs of Constantinople were in exile at Nice, and the office of metropolitan of Russia had not been filled since the destruction of Kiof; but, nevertheless, Alexander refused to comply with the demands of the pope, and the envoys who had previously visited the princes of Halich and Lodomeria, on the same errand, departed from Novogorod for Lithuania, where the Grand Duke of Mindove was induced, by their representations, to discard his idols and embrace the Christian Faith. He consented to this in the hope of obtaining the Christians' assistance; but finding ultimately that a unity of creed was not sufficient to protect him against the hostility and incursions of the Teutonic knights, he finally abandoned his new religion, and became a most bitter enemy to Christianity.

Shortly after these ambassadors had left his court, Alexander invaded Finland, and, having defeated the Swedes in several engagements, laid the country under tribute. The war-cry in this and every other battle fought by the warriors of Novogorod, Kiof, or Polotzk, was "St. Sophia," the cathedrals in those cities being all dedicated to that saint; while the troops of Vladimir, Rostoff, Smolensko, and Moscow, fought in the name of the Virgin, or "for the House of the Most Holy Trinity." The ancient princes of Russia, after their conversion to the Greek religion, took for their arms three circles in a triangle, in one of which was an inscription upon the Trinity, in the second the name of the reigning prince, and in the third their titles and appellations.*

The acknowledgment by Daniel of Halich of the pope's supremacy, was only a temporary expedient; for, finding that Innocent was totally unable to assist him against the Monguls, while, under pretence of expelling these invaders, his dominions were continually wasted and overrun by the Poles, Hungarians, and Bohemians, whose depredations were little better than those of the Tartars, he determined to become reconciled to the Church of Constantinople and the other princes of Russia; and sending Cyril, a native priest, to the exiled patriarch at Nice, requested him to nominate his envoy the metropolitan of the empire at Kiof. The patriarch gladly received his renewed allegiance; and, acceding to his wish, Cyril returned to Russia, and travelled all over the empire, rebuilding the ruined churches, and appointing bishops to the many sees which had for so long been vacant.† One of his nominees, Theognostes, whom he created bishop of Serai, was afterwards sent upon a secret embassy to Rome, by Mangou Timur, the successor of Bereka.

In 1252, on the return of Alexander from his second visit to Karacorum, he was met, at a short distance from his new territory of Vladimir, by a procession of priests and citizens, with Cyril at their head, to congratulate the prince upon his recent elevation; and, removing his throne to that capital, he appointed his son Vassili, the governor of Novogorod. But upon all Russia being taxed by Bereka, the Monguls of China, that same year, having laid a similar impost upon the Celestial empire, the people of Novogorod rose up in arms against their merciless oppressors, and having driven out all the tax-gatherers and garrison soldiers of the khan, Alexander marched against them in person with an army from Vladimir, and put down the revolt. His son fled to Sweden, and the Grand Prince, fearing lest he should compromise his own character for loyalty, by mercy to the insurgents, caused all the rebellious citizens to be punished with the greatest severity, the principal among them having their eyes put out and their noses cut off; and by his cruelty and subservience reinstated his family in the favour of the khan, who, if

---

* H. D. Seymour's "Russia on the Black Sea," &c.
‡ Mouravieff's "Church of Russia."

Alexander had appeared for a moment to waver in his allegiance, was prepared to invade Russia with his hordes, and again render it a forlorn and barren waste. At the same time, Mangou issued a decree that every Russian who could not pay the heavy taxes he had enforced, should be sold for a slave. As this regulation was rigorously carried out, it caused the greatest misery throughout the empire; and in 1260 another rebellion against the Tartar authority broke out, in which the Russians massacred almost every Mongul collector of tribute. The insurrection was again quelled by the Grand Prince; but it had so much irritated the Mongul emperor, that, in order to clear himself from any suspicion of having connived at or encouraged these repeated revolts of his disaffected subjects, Alexander again visited the Golden Horde, and took a fresh oath of allegiance to Kublai, who had lately succeeded his brother, the emperor Mangou, upon the throne. But, as he was returning, he was seized with an illness, like his father, supposed to be the result of poison, and, according to a frequent practice of the time in Russia, while on his deathbed caused his head to be shaved, and received the habit and took the vows of a monk. He had married a daughter of Wratislau, the prince of Polotzk, by whom he had four sons—Vassili or Bazil, who died before him, Demetrius, Andrea, and Danilo; and his death took place on the 10th of November, 1263, his remains being interred in the monastery of the Nativity of the Virgin at Vladimir, where, after his canonization, several years later, many pilgrims annually resorted to worship at his tomb. Nearly four hundred and fifty years after his decease, Peter the Great, in order to reconcile the Russians to his newly-founded capital of St. Petersburgh, caused the bones of Alexander to be transferred from the shores of the Kliazma to those of the Neva, and enclosed in a magnificent sepulchre, in the monastery of St. Alexander Nevskoi, where they still remain, and also created an order of knighthood in his honour. Alexander was succeeded by his brother, Yaroslaf III., the Prince of Tver.

Owing to the mischief which was caused to the trade and prosperity of Novogorod, by the law condemning all her citizens who could not pay their taxes into slavery or death, a deputation was sent to Mangou Timur, who, in 1266, succeeded Bereka in Kipzak, by the German merchants of

Lubeck and the other Hanseatic towns, who had long been allied with Novogorod for the purposes of commerce. They reached the Mongul camp in 1269; but their representations appear to have been attended with little result, and Mangou Timur dying in 1283, was succeeded by Tuday Menghu, who, after reigning a few months, was deposed by Talakowka, and this prince, following the example of Batù and Bereka, again invaded Europe. Ravaging Hungary and Poland, he threatened Germany with the terror of his arms, but kept up friendly diplomatic relations with France; and upon his death, about the year 1290, Toktai was raised to the throne of Kipzak, through the influence of his cousin, the general Noghai, and married a daughter of the emperor Andronicus of Constantinople. For a time Noghai completely ruled the kingdom, and the khan was a mere tool in his hands; till at length a dispute arising among his sons, who all filled high and important offices in the state, it created a complete revolution in Kipzak, and Noghai, abandoning the capital of his ungrateful prince, and accompanied by several tribes of Monguls, whose descendants still perpetuate in their name the appellation of their leader, formed an empire of tents and encampments, extending from the Don to the Danube, in the steppes to the north of the Crimea, and there, in these sandy wastes, enjoyed the independent authority of a sovereign despot. The rule of Toktai was more tolerant and beneficent than that of his predecessors, and he introduced into Russia the circulation of paper-money, an old invention, which was afterwards revived by the Monguls in Persia many years before it was known or used in Europe. Abandoning the Mahomedan religion, he adopted the ancient worship of fire, and adored the sun and stars, but granted toleration and freedom of thought to all; and on his death, in 1313, he was universally regretted by his subjects, as a good and wise prince. His son and successor, Uzbek, being only thirteen years of age, for a time had some difficulty in establishing his authority; the Russian princes refusing to take the oath of obedience, till, by some terrible instances of severity, he had enforced a due submission to his rule. In the meanwhile, Noghai had expired, in 1295, from a wound received in a lost engagement with the forces of Kipzak. Subsequent to his rebellion he had invaded the Greek empire, where, surrounding with an army of twenty thousand Tartars a Thracian castle,

in which the emperor himself was located, with but few
guards and attendants, he obtained as the price of a peace
the deliverance from captivity of his ally, the Turkish prince,
Azzadin, then a prisoner in the territories of Constantinople,
a large amount of treasure, and an imperial princess for a
wife; and from henceforth he became a valuable friend and
defender of the Byzantine States.* The simultaneous attack
by the Sultan of Egypt upon the King of Armenia, a vassal
of the Monguls of Persia, and upon Antioch, the most powerful principality of the crusaders in the East, united in a common war with the Mahometans, Abaga, the Tartar khan of
Persia, and the Christians of Europe; while the sovereigns of
Kipzak allied themselves with the Mamelukes, against their
own brethren and countrymen, and sent a body of three
hundred thousand horse through the gates of Derbend to their
assistance. Concluding a treaty with the Egyptian prince,
they bound themselves to invade the dominions of Abaga
every time that he should trespass upon the territories of
Egypt. But the unfortunate expedition of Louis of France,
in 1270, and his death, with the flower of his army, from the
plague which broke out in his camp, upon the sandy shores
of Tunis, had deprived the crusaders, whose enthusiasm had
long been dissolving, of their most ardent and powerful
leader; and the return of Edward, the eldest son of the King
of England, to his native land, whose throne he shortly after
ascended, broke up the coalition of the Monguls and princes
of Europe, which had never existed but in theory; though
Abaga made one more attempt to induce the latter to enter
into a confederation, to root out the followers of Mahomet
from the face of the earth. With this design, he, in concert
with his father-in-law, the Greek emperor Michael Paleologus, sent Tartar ambassadors to Clement X., Valentia Iago,
King of Arragon, Thibant, King of Navarre, the King of
Castile, Philip III., King of France, and Edward I. of England; but though all advised him by every means to destroy the
power, religion, and even the name of the Saracens, assuring
him that it would be a work well pleasing to Heaven, and
obtain for him eternal salvation,† yet each refused to join in
the expedition, or risk any more ships or men in the cause
of the Holy Land. So terminated the last of the crusades,

---

* Gibbon's "Decline and Fall of the Roman Empire."
† Huc's "Tartary."

a national fever that had prevailed in Europe for more than two hundred years.

In 1282, as Abaga was preparing to commence another war with the Saracens, he perished by poison, administered to him at a banquet by a Mahometan, and was succeeded by his brother Tagoudar, who had become a Christian a few years before, and received the name of Nicholas. On his first accession he built many churches throughout Assyria and Mesopotamia, and exempted all bishops, priests, and monasteries from taxation or tribute; but subsequently adopting the faith of Islam, he took the name of Ahmed, and commenced a violent persecution of the Christians, punishing all who refused to renounce their belief with exile, tortures, or death, and, destroying all their sacred edifices, threatened to extirpate their very name. Abandoning the alliance with Constantinople, he endeavoured to form one with the Sultan of Egypt; but the latter, mistrusting his sincerity, repelled his advances; the Kings of Georgia and Armenia threw off their allegiance to Persia; the Grand Khan menaced him with his displeasure for acceding to the religion of their most bitter enemies; and Argoun, his nephew, the son of Abaga, rebelling against his authority, defeated him in a fierce battle, in which Ahmed was taken prisoner, and, causing him to be beheaded in front of his army, in 1284 ascended the vacant throne. The forces of Argoun had been principally composed of Christians, who were then very numerous in the armies of the Monguls; and it is related that he decorated his standards and arms with the sign of the cross, and caused a coin to be struck in remembrance of his victory, upon one side of which was represented the Holy Sepulchre, and upon the other this inscription, "in the name of the Holy Trinity." On his accession he issued a manifesto, stating that the princes of the blood had expelled Ahmed for abandoning the ancient laws of the Monguls, and adopting the faith of the Arabs, a faith unknown to their forefathers; and, having demanded justice from the Grand Khan upon the guilty monarch, Kublai had permitted his deposition, and allowed the princes to place him (Argoun) on the throne, to govern the countries between Dijihoun and the land of the Franks. Shortly after this event, having extended the power of the Persian Monguls over Armenia, and over King David of Georgia, who married a sister of Argoun's, and both of whom had rendered themselves independent of his predecessor, the young prince attempted to renew diplomatic negotiations with the pope and other sovereigns of Europe.* Not discouraged by the vague and uncertain replies he received to his proposals of alliance with the Christians, in 1288 he sent a fresh envoy in the person of Barsuma, an Igour Tartar monk, to Nicholas IV., who informed the Roman pontiff that Touhtan, the wife of Argoun, was a Christian, and that the latter only waited to become one, till, in conjunction with the armies of the Franks, he should enter the city of Jerusalem in triumph. The letter of Argoun was written in the Mongul language and Igour characters, and sealed with a similar inscription to that on the imperial seal of China. It was sent by the pope to the French king, Philip the Fair, and has since been found, where it still remains, in the historical archives of France.† But the khan was unable to induce any of the European princes, who were at that time engaged in war with each other, to join in another crusade; and being of an undecisive and irresolute disposition, and standing much in awe of the numerous Mussulmans who thronged his court and dominions, he never made an open profession of Christianity, though, like his father, he practised and joined in many of its forms and ceremonies; and his two principal wives, Touhtan and Eruhkhatoune, with one of his sons, Kharhendé or Nicholas, and many of the Tartar princesses and nobles at his capital, Tauris, were baptized by the Keraite Tartar and Franciscan monks.‡

Upon the death of Touhtan and Eruhkhatoune, Argoun sent an embassy to Pekin, to demand in marriage one of the

---

* Huc's "Christianity in China, Tartary," &c.
† This curious letter has been translated by M. Schmidt, a learned Oriental scholar, of St. Petersburgh, who has also preserved the original Mongul manner in which it was inscribed, the words of God and Khakan, whenever they occur, being placed in a line above.—"Letter of Argoun to the Pope. ''Thou has sent to me. When the troops of the Khakan shall march against Egypt, we will set out from here to join him. Having received this message on thy part, I tell thee that we purpose, trusting in GOD, to set off in the last month of the winter of the year of the Panther (1291), and to encamp before Damascus towards the 15th of the first month of spring. If you keep your word, and send your troops at the appointed moment, and if GOD should prosper us, when we have taken Jerusalem from that nation we will give it to you. But to fail us at the rendezvous, would be causing the troops to march in vain. Ought it to be so? and if afterwards we know not what to do, of what use is it? I shall send Mouskeria, who will tell you, that if you send us ambassadors who can speak several languages, and who bring us presents, rarities, coloured pictures of the country of the Franks, we shall thank you, by the power of GOD, and the fortune of the Khakan. Our letter is written at Coundoulen, on the sixth day of the first month of summer, in the year of the Ox.'" The Mongule divided their time into cycles of twelve years, to each of which they gave the following names:—*The Mouse, the Ox, the Leopard, the Hare, the Crocodile, the Serpent, the Horse, the Sheep, the Monkey, the Hen, the Dog, and the Hog.*
‡ Huc's "Christianity in China, Tartary," &c.

numerous princesses of China; and Kublai Khan, who was great uncle to the Persian monarch, assenting to his proposals, selected one of his grand-daughters, a beautiful girl of seventeen, who set out with the ambassadors and a splendid retinue for Persia. But owing to a fierce war having broken out between two of the intervening countries, she was after a few months compelled to return to Pekin, when the celebrated Venetian traveller, Marco Polo, who held the command of the Chinese fleet, with which he had just returned from a voyage in the Indian Ocean, proposed to the emperor that the princess should proceed to Persia by sea.* This advice was urgently seconded by the envoys of Argoun, who had now been three years on their mission, and were anxious to return to their native land; and their representations being acceded to by Kublai, he caused a squadron to be fitted out to accompany them of fourteen magnificently furnished ships, each with four masts† and nine sails, and each manned with between two and three hundred men, appointing the two Venetian merchants, Niccolo and Matteo, with Marco the son of the former, to the command of the whole expedition. The emperor furnished the admirals with a golden tablet or royal passport, permitting them to proceed freely and safely throughout his dominions, which extended over a larger portion of the globe than those of any other potentate of ancient or modern times; and procuring for them, from any of his officers or lieutenants, the supplies necessary for their men. The fleet set sail from the mouth of the Peiho, the river of Pekin, in the year 1291, and after a voyage of three months reached a small and remote port on the northern shores of Sumatra, where it was forced to remain for another five months, till the monsoon had set in which was to carry it across the passive Bay of Bengal. Having erected fortifications round the harbour to protect their lives and properties, from the, at first, hostile attacks of the natives, a race of most fierce and cruel savages; before their departure they had so far conciliated them as to procure regular supplies of water, fruits, and provisions, which were daily brought to the Chinese encampment; and Marco Polo made a tour round the island, visiting six of the eight provinces into which it was divided, and over which eight independent sovereigns reigned. On

* Travels of Marco Polo.
† According to Mr. Barrow, in his "Travels in China," this is still the usual number of masts on the Chinese vessels.

the fleet sailing from Sumatra it proceeded to the Andamans, from whence the travellers steered to the rich and fragrant isle of Ceylon, and also visited the neighbouring shores of India, where they heard of the diamond mines of Golconda; for the timid Chinese and Mongul sailors appear to have seldom ventured out of sight of land, and to have entered every port that they passed, and their commander has left us a minute and accurate* account of the natives and productions of these islands and countries where they landed, or at which they touched on their route. From the coast of Coromandel they diverged towards the south, and visiting Madagascar and the African shores of Zanzibar and Adel, finally reached Ormuz in the Persian Gulf, the place of their destination, after navigating the Indian seas for eighteen months. From the day that they had departed from the Chinese capital, they had lost by death six hundred of the crews and passengers, two of the Persian ambassadors, and one lady of the suite of the princess. But on landing, the first intelligence that they heard was, that Argoun himself had long since been dead, having expired before the fleet set sail from Pekin, and that the reins of government were held by his brother Kiahato, who, like Ahmed, the predecessor of Argoun, was a professed Mussulman; while Kazan, the son of the late monarch, was engaged with an army of 60,000 men at the pass of Derbend or the Caspian Gates, in repelling an inroad of the forces of his relative, Toktai, the khan of Kipzak.† To this prince whom she espoused on her arrival at his camp, the Chinese princess was conveyed by the surviving ambassador and her conductors,‡ the three Venetians, who had intended to proceed to China by this route; but as they heard there of the death of their patron, Kublai, they resolved in-

---

* He describes the persons of the inhabitants of Andaman and their customs, as the same which the accounts of modern travellers verify; the fisheries of Ceylon, the mines of Golconda, the camelopard, and other animals on the coast of Africa; though at Madagascar he draws a little on his own imagination, and the fabulous stories of the East, introducing the ponderous roc, celebrated in the "Tales in the Arabian Nights."
† "Travels of Marco Polo."
‡ Marco Polo carried back with him great wealth from China, and in the chapter of his work, denominated "Della Provincia di Russia," he says, "La Provincia di Russia è grandissima, et divisa in molte parti, et guarda verso la parte di Tramontana, dove si dice essere la regione delle tenebre. Li popoli di quella sono Christiani, et osservano l'usanza de' Greci nell' officio della chiesa. Sono bellissimi huomini, bianchi et grandi, et similmente le loro femine bianche et grandi, con li capelli biondi et lunghi et rendono tributo al Rè di Tartari detti di Ponente, con il qual confinano nella parte di loro regione che guarda il Levante. In questa provincia si trovano abondanza grande di pelli di Armelini, Ascolini, Tebellini, Vari, Volpi, et cera molta; vi sono anchora molte minere dove si cava argento in gran quantità. La Russia è region molto fredda et mi fu affermato che la si estende fino sopra il Mare Oceano, nel qual (come abbiamo detto di sopra) si prendono di Girifalchi Falconi pellegrini in gran copia che vengono portati da di verse regioni et provincie."—Marco Polo's "Voyages," collected by Ramusis.

stead to revisit their native city, which they reached in the year 1295, after an absence of more than twenty years. The same year Kiahato, the reigning khan of Persia, after a disgraceful reign of five years, stained by every vice and infamy, was assassinated by some of the nobles of his palace, and succeeded by his brother Baidou, a humane and well-intentioned, though impolitic and imprudent, prince. By forbidding the preaching of the Mahometan religion to the Tartars, and rebuilding the churches and monasteries, he raised against himself the enmity of the Mussulmans, who expelled him after a reign of a few months, and elevated his nephew Kazan to the throne, with the condition that he would adhere to their faith ; a condition with which he readily complied, and, renouncing the Christianity that he had formerly professed, a fierce persecution of the Christians immediately ensued. Their houses and churches were given up to destruction and pillage, and their enemies, the Mahometans, with whom, since the Tartars first obtained possession of Persia, owing to the indifference and religious vacillation of the khans, they had vied in monopolizing the conversion of the Monguls and chief offices of state, now ruled supreme, and the Christians were insulted or massacred, by order of their rivals, wherever they dared to appear in the public places. The bodies of their priests and patriarchs were taken out of the cemeteries and buryinggrounds in which they had been interred, and thrown into the streets ; and, from 1296 to 1298, dreadful atrocities were committed against them throughout all Persia, especially in the cities of Arbela, Tauris, Mosoul, and Bagdad, when the persecution was suddenly stopped by the second apostasy and conversion of the khan. This has generally been attributed to the influence of one of his wives, the daughter of the king of Armenia, the only province in the Persian dominions where the Christians were allowed to remain in peace; and who, being distinguished by great piety and extraordinary beauty, is said to have induced her husband to again profess her own religion, though the ecclesiastical chronicles of the time* allege that her representations were assisted by an extraordinary miracle, the transformation by baptism of one of his sons from a hideous infant to a most beautiful child.† An alliance was now formed by Kazan with his father-in-law, the

---

* The Chronicles of Saint Denis.
† Huc's "Christianity in China, Tartary," &c.

king of Armenia, against Malek-Nassir, the sultan of Egypt, and having checked, and for the present subdued, the fast rising power of the Ottoman Turks, he marched against Damascus, which his forces took after a short siege by storm and sack, and, ravaging all Syria, attacked the united armies of the Mamelukes and Saracens in the sandy plains of Judea; where, according to a contemporary historian, 100,000 Saracens were left dead upon the field. This victory of the Persian khan placed Jerusalem itself at the mercy of the Tartars, who entered it in conjunction with the Christian king of Armenia, and for the first time for many years the feast of Easter was openly celebrated by the Christians in the Holy City. The war continued for some years longer between the Monguls and Mahometans, and his success caused Kazan to renew the proposal of a universal crusade with the nobles and princes of Europe; but before the ambassadors, whom he had despatched to Edward of England and Philip of France, had returned to his court with any reply, his armies had been overtaken by defeat and loss; and a victory gained by the Mussulmans, which forced his troops to retreat beyond the Euphrates, so preyed upon his mind as to bring on the illness which caused his death in 1302. His successor attempted with some success to restrain the encroachments of the Turks in Bithynia, but the descendants of Zingis Khan became extinct in Persia in 1335; and the empire was divided among numerous Mahometan chiefs, who maintained their sway for only a few years, all being ultimately conquered and dethroned by the victorious armies of Tamerlane.

The Mongul emperors and khans sent twenty ambassadors altogether, at different times, to France, England, Germany, Italy, and Spain, to attempt to rouse the flagging zeal of their princes in the cause of the expiring crusades, and urge them to join their forces with the armies of the Tartars, in expelling the Mussulmans from Palestine. But all were without effect, though the communication thus carried on between them was not altogether bare of fruit; for it occasioned a more intimate acquaintance of the east with the west, and caused several arts and inventions, then only known to the nations of Asia, to be introduced by the Mongul envoys into Europe. Among these may be mentioned woodengraving and playing cards, which had originally been invented in China, and a Tartar artisan was employed as a helmet-maker in the armies of Philip the Fair.

In the year 1294, by command of the Khan Kazan, all the existing histories and traditions, respecting his great-grandfather Zingis, were collected by several Mongul and Persian writers, and transcribed by the Vizier Fadlallah into the Persian tongue.*

* Gibbon's "Decline and Fall of the Roman Empire."

CHAPTER V.

Continuation of the History of Russia—Reigns of Yaroslaf, Demetrius, and Andrey—Lithuania—The Genoese Colonies—Uzbek Khan—Executions of Michael, Demetrius, and Alexander—Ivan I.

> What mighty shocks
> Have buffeted mankind, whole nations razed,
> Cities made desolate, the polish'd sunk
> To barbarism, and once barbaric states
> Swaying the wand of science and of art.—KIRKE WHITE.

A FEW years after the death of Alexander, fresh dissensions arose between the people of Novogorod and their prince; and, refusing to acknowledge the supremacy of his brother, Yaroslaf, a man of a harsh disposition, and very unpopular with his subjects, the citizens obliged him to fly from their city, and he long remained in exile. At length a reconciliation was obtained through the persevering efforts of the metropolitan Cyril, who threatened Novogorod with an interdict, and her people with excommunication from the church, unless they received back their sovereign. Cyril was the last primate of Russia who was interred amid the cloisters of the old capital Kiof, which had now for some time been annexed to the kingdom of Halich.

Yaroslaf died shortly after his restoration in 1271, leaving two sons, Michael, prince of Tver, and Vladimir, who subsequently competed with the grandsons of Daniel for the crown of Halich; and his youngest brother Vassili, or Basil, was appointed to succeed him by the Khan. The reign of this prince lasted but a few years, and was unmarked by any important event; but at his death those scenes ensued, so often repeated here, of which the details only weary and disgust; when princes, caring for nothing else than their own selfish dignity and elevation, recklessly bring upon their country and people the scourge of a civil war. Vassili was succeeded in 1276 by his nephew Dmitri, or Demetrius, the son of Alexander, who was thirteen years old at the time of his father's death; and a savage feud immediately commenced between the new sovereign and his brother Andrea, by whom he was twice expelled from his dominions, and who called to his assistance a large army of Monguls. Upon this, the Poles, Hungarians, and the forces of the princes of Halich, all entered Russia to oppose their inroad, and ensure the safety and tranquillity of their own states, which would greatly have been endangered by another Tartar inroad upon Muscovy, and reinstated Demetrius in his principality. But in 1294 the unfortunate chief was again deposed by his brother, and died the same year in Volokampsk, at the age of forty-four, and Andrea retained undisputed possession of the throne till 1304; when, feeling the approach of death, he assumed the habit and took the vows of a monk, and died a few days after in the monastery to which he had caused himself to be borne, and where he had previously enrolled himself as a priest. He was succeeded by his brother Danilo, the prince of Moscow. At this period, owing to the privileges granted to the monks by the Tartars, and the protection which the monasteries afforded from the oppression and discord that reigned throughout the empire, numbers of the weak, timid, or helpless among the boyards, citizens, and women, of all ages and degrees, annually entered the cloister, and assumed the veil; for the priests, and religious communities, usually received peculiar favour from the Monguls; and in 1313 the khan, when on a tour through Russia, not only treated the metropolitan with the greatest respect, but even solicited his prayers.

Mindove, the Grand Duke of Lithuania, who, in the expectation of assistance from the pope against the Tartars, and immunity from the incursions of the Livonian knights, had embraced Christianity, and married a daughter of Danilo, the prince of Halich, and finding his hopes disappointed, had resumed his former idolatry, was succeeded by his son Voesheleg, who after a short reign retired into a monastery, and bequeathed his dominions to his cousin Yourii, or George, the prince of Halich. But Ghedemin, a Lithuanian chieftain, established himself in Vilna in the early part of the thirteenth century, and wresting Kiof, and the surrounding provinces from the hands of Andrew and Lvo, the sons of

s

Yourii, established his sway as far as the western district of the Crimea, where he razed Cherson to the ground, and destroyed in that peninsula the last possessions of the Greeks; while in 1340, the king of Poland also seized upon the western provinces of Halich, and, annexing it to his own states, the Greek Church was gradually replaced among the inhabitants by the Roman Catholic, the national faith of Poland. The Lithuanians remained heathens for some years longer; they worshipped fire, the sun, moon, stars, and serpents, and their last sacred grove was not cut down in Samogitia till the year 1430.

While the khan of Kipzak, from his capital Serai, ruled all Russia by his emissaries, and caused her to be governed by his laws, in the northern part of the empire, owing to the severity of the climate and thicker population, the Monguls had settled down in no great numbers or strength; but in the south, where the steppes and grassy plains resembled their native deserts in Central Asia, they overspread the whole face of the country, and, overrunning the Crimea, disputed, on the shores of the Euxine, with the adventurous merchants of Genoa, for the possession of the seaport towns. These traders, during the middle ages, and till, their wars with the powerful queen of the Adriatic having materially weakened the strength of both republics, they were eclipsed by the superior science and enterprise of the sailors of Portugal and Spain, had long contended with Venice for the empire of the sea, and the monopoly of the commerce of the world; and, before the invasion of Europe by the Monguls, possessed the harbour of Soldaya, for which they paid tribute to the Polotzi. The suburb Galatea of Constantinople had been given up to them by the Greeks as an emporium for their commerce, and formed a communication between the mother country and this remote port, with several on the coast of Circassia, from whence they traded with Russia and Persia, and even to the distant Indies and remoter countries of the East. Upon the invasion of the Tartars in 1226, when they forced the Polotzi to retreat into Moldavia, the Genoese were expelled from the Crimea; but, in 1280, they attacked and captured Kaffa or Theodosia, where they planted a colony, and ultimately recovered Soldaya, the peninsula of Kertch being held at the same time by the Circassians. The produce of the same corn-fields of Taurida, that had stored the granaries of Athens in the days of Miltiades and Solon, was now distributed over the Mediterranean by a fleet of four hundred mercantile vessels, and supplied the cities of Greece, the republics of Italy and Tunis, and a regular communication with caravans was carried on by the Genoese colonists with Carizme, from whence they obtained overland from China, and by way of the Oxus and Caspian, from India gold and the diamonds of Golconda, ivory and spices from Ceylon, with the silk, camphor, and rice, of the Celestial empire. Their commerce in Russian and Circassian captives supplied the sultans of Egypt with the formidable corps of Mamelukes, and, a few years later, the Egyptian sovereign Bibaus, who had been himself a Tartar slave, obtained from the successors of Zingis permission to build a splendid mosque in Bakchi-serai, the capital of the Crimea.*

The Tartars finding Kaffa a commodious market for the innumerable slaves they had procured in Poland and Russia, left Genoa in peaceful possession of this port, and by a treaty of August 7, 1333, the first formed for mercantile interests between any of the Mongul nations with those of Europe, considerable commercial advantages were granted by Usbeg or Bek, the khan of Kipzak, to the Venetians, who had founded a small settlement in the peninsula of Taman and Azof. More than a hundred years after this, when Russia had long emancipated herself from Kipzak, the khan of the Crimea made a sudden inroad upon Moscow, which he sacked and burned; and, carrying off three hundred thousand Russian prisoners, he sold them all for slaves at Kaffa to the Turks.

At this time Lithuania was one of the most powerful Russian states; Poland was also increasing her influence in the west; Novogorod and Pskof had again emancipated themselves from the sway of the Grand Dukes of Vladimir, but were compelled by the arms of Ghedemin to acknowledge the supremacy of Lithuania † during his lifetime; and the capital of the Grand Dukes of Russia was removed by Danilo Alexandrovitz from Vladimir to his original patrimony Moscow, which from henceforward became the capital of his estates, at this time beginning to be known as the king-

---

* Gibbon's "Decline and Fall of the Roman Empire."
† Krasinski's "History of Poland."

dom, or grand principality of Moscow or Muscovy. He built the Kremlin, and surrounded the whole city with wooden fortifications, and also erected the monastery of St. Daniel,* which, in 1307, he entered himself as a monk, and died shortly after, being succeeded by his son George, or Yourii, who was at that time twenty-six years of age.

Mahmoud Uzbek, who had succeeded his father Toktai upon the viceregal throne of Kipzak, shortly after his accession abandoned the Gheber faith of the late khan, and, adopting the Mahometan religion, it became from henceforth the established faith of all the Tartar and Mongul tribes in Western and Southern Asia, as it had already previously, under Bereka and Mengu Timur, been that of Kipzak. His reign forms a brilliant epoch in the annals of his horde; the success he obtained in a war with the Greek empire, obliged the emperor to conclude a humiliating peace, and cede to him his daughter for a bride; and, on the event of these victories, he assumed the additional title of "Conqueror of the enemies of God, the inhabitants of Constantinople the Great." Persevering and indefatigable in conducting the business of his empire, he was at the same time remarkable for his splendour and the magnificence of his court, and is called by the Mahometan writers of the time, one of the seven great sovereigns of the earth. The Moorish traveller, Ibn Batutah, who visited his capital Astrakhan, has described that city as being of great wealth and extent; it was called by the Tartars Haj Tarkham, from a devout pilgrim, or Haj, by whom it was founded, and the Khan made it his residence during the summer, and till the Volga became covered with ice, when he repaired to Serai in sledges with his family and court. His four wives, who, with his daughters, were permitted to remain unveiled, travelled from place to place in state waggons, surmounted with domes of silver, and drawn by horses attired with gold and silk equipments; and in both Serai and Astrakhan, each khatoun was accommodated with a separate palace, and several hundreds of Greek, Turkish, and Nubian slaves, a band of musicians and dancers, jugglers and magicians, besides numerous other attendants.† For the sake of procuring companions on his return, Ibn Batutah accompanied the escort of the Christian khatoun, or Greek wife of the Khan, on a visit

* Mouravieff's "Church of Russia."   † Travels of "Ibn Batutah."

which she paid to her father, Andronicus the Third, at Constantinople. Her retinue was guarded to the Grecian frontiers by a corps of five thousand Mongul soldiers, when she was met by her brother with a battalion of Greeks, who conducted her from the shores of the Danube to the imperial palace at Byzantium. But on finding herself once more with her family and home in a Christian land, and among civilized people, she refused to return to her Tartar husband, but, sending back her Mongul attendants to Astrakhan, passed the remainder of her days at her father's court.

The same Arab traveller also describes Kaffa, which was then possessed by the Genoese, and where, never before having seen a Christian town, he heard with surprise the bells of their churches, but saw with satisfaction that the Mahometans were allowed to support a mosque. He traversed the flat and desolate plains of Kipzak, in the same wicker waggons, drawn by camels and oxen, formerly used by the Scythians, and to this day by the modern Tartars of the steppes. At every stage, and when halting by their watch-fires for the night, he was lulled to sleep by the martial songs of the Monguls who, he observes, eat no bread, nor any other solid food, but lived on a kind of porridge made of millet, in which they boiled pieces of meat; a mode of preparation which was customary with their predecessors in those parts, the Scythians, Sarmatians, and Slavonians. He was desirous of visiting the Land of Darkness (Siberia), where his guides informed him that the natives were drawn by dogs, whom their masters prized so highly that they fed them before themselves, and where the trade of the country consisted of fur, chiefly ermine, which was exported to all parts of Asia, even India and Persia; but he was discouraged from attempting the journey, by the reported distance and difficulties of the route. He also observes that the laws of the Tartars were very severe against theft; the criminal was forced to restore goods or money to the value of nine times the worth of what he had stolen, and, if unable to pay this fine, his children were seized and condemned to slavery, while, in case he had no children, he suffered death.*

One of the daughters of Uzbek married the Sultan Kusum of Egypt, who had himself been a Mameluke, and originally a Tartar slave from Kipzak.

* Travels of " Ibn Batutah."

The revolt of the Tartar chief, Noghai, and the wars which his successors henceforth carried on with the khans, increased the miseries by which unhappy Russia was now almost overwhelmed. Each empire claimed her fealty and allegiance, each regarded her princes and people as their lawful prey, and her territories became the battle-field for their armies, her sovereigns usually allying themselves with the strongest, or her whose forces were nearest, or who was most prompt to revenge their defalcation upon their unhappy subjects with slavery and death. George the prince of Moscow, the ambitious son of Danilo, allied himself with the khan of Kipzak, and obtained his protection by espousing the daughter of Uzbek. In a revolt against his cousin Michael, who, in virtue of his seniority, had been raised to the throne of Russia in 1305 by the nomination of the khan, he procured the assistance of a Mongul army from his father-in-law, under the command of a Tartar general, Kavadgi; but was repulsed from the walls of Tver with great slaughter, and his wife taken prisoner. The Tartar princess soon pined and died in captivity; and, without any evidence to justify the suspicion which the previously virtuous life of Michael would appear to refute, he was accused by George of having basely caused the death of his bride by poison, and was summoned by Uzbek to appear at the Golden Horde. His sons earnestly entreated the Grand Prince to allow them to undertake the journey in his place, and answer the foul accusation; but aware of the peril, and fearful for their safety, and knowing the miseries that disobedience to the command of the khan would entail on his country, he refused to comply with their request, and resolved to obey the summons. After making his will, and delivering his last charges to his children, he set off to Serai, and there, confronting his accusers, the princes of Moscow and Kavadgi, in presence of the khan, earnestly protested his innocence. A judicial tribunal was assembled, before which Michael was formally heard and condemned, and after twenty-five days' close imprisonment, during which he was so loaded with chains that he was unable to move either his head or arms, his head was struck off by a Tartar executioner in the year 1319, in the forty-eighth year of his age. He had been permitted to see his sons before his death, and his confessor, the metropolitan Peter, who had accompanied him to the horde; and it was after an interview of this priest with the khan, that the latter issued the following curious manifesto : *—" Let no man injure the Church, the metropolitan Peter, the archimandrites, or the popes in Russia ; let their lands be free from all tax and tribute ; for all this belongs to God, and these people by their prayers preserve us ; let them be under the sole jurisdiction of Peter, the metropolitan, agreeably to their ancient laws ; let the metropolitan lead his life in quiet and meekness, and let him pray with a true heart, and without fear, for us and for our children ; whosoever shall take any thing from the clergy, let him restore it threefold ; whosoever shall dare to speak evil of the Russian faith ; whosoever shall injure any church, monastery, or chapel, let him be put to death."

The satisfaction which George expressed upon the death of Michael, excited the reprobation even of his ally Kavadgi the Tartar, who, upon entering the tent where the execution had taken place, and beholding the body of Michael, turned to the Grand Prince, who had accompanied him, exclaiming, " How canst thou gaze so unfeelingly upon the corpse of thy injured kinsman ! " Immediately dissembling his pleasure, George professed to lament the deed, and ordered the remains of Michael to be conveyed in state to Russia, and interred with the customary honours in his capital ; but this hypocrisy only increased the indignation felt against him by the sons of the murdered prince, and Demetrius the eldest never rested from that day till he had revenged upon the head of the perpetrator his father's untimely death. In 1322, he procured by various accusations the deposition of George from the throne of Suzdal, which he had ascended after the execution of Michael, and was himself raised to the dignity of Grand Prince in his cousin's place ; and upon being summoned to appear at the Golden Horde, where George had urged the khan to allow him to make his defence, no sooner had Demetrius found himself face to face with the destroyer of his father, than, regardless of the presence of Uzbek, he ran his enemy through the heart with his sword, and was in his turn immediately condemned to death by the khan for the offence. He was executed in the year 1326, and was succeeded by his brother Alexander as Grand Prince.

A few months after Alexander's accession, a conspiracy was formed by the Tartar garrison of Tver, with Shefkhal,

* Mouravieff's " Church of Russia."

a near relative of the khan, at their head, to assassinate the Grand Prince, and compel the Russians, by persuasion or force, to embrace the Mussulman faith; but their design was frustrated by a general revolt of the Russian inhabitants, led on by Alexander, who surprised and cut to pieces every Tartar soldier in the city, and asserted their independence. But no sooner had the intelligence of this short triumph reached the horde, than Russia was invaded by a Mongul army, commanded by Uzbek in person, who caused the inhabitants to be massacred without mercy or distinction, and, defeating Alexander in battle, obliged him to take refuge with his family in the forests and remote provinces of the empire. There the unhappy prince wandered about for years in disguise, and in the greatest misery and destitution, while the khan caused Ivan of Riazan, the cousin and ally of the Grand Prince, and who had been taken prisoner, to be beheaded, and placed Ivan I., the prince of Moscow, upon the throne, March 26, 1327, at the same time directing him to pursue and capture Alexander, and deliver him up to the Tartars for punishment. For nine years the outlawed chief eluded the vigilance of his enemies, till in 1336 he was induced by the offer of pardon to abandon his hiding-place, and was reinstated in his kingdom by the caprice or mercy of the khan; but two years later, through the intrigues of Ivan of Moscow, his inveterate enemy, he was summoned to appear at the horde; and the old accusation of having instigated the murder of Shefkhal being revived against him, he was executed there, with his two youthful sons, Fedor and Michael, in 1338.

The title of Grand Prince of Russia, with authority over all the other princes of Russia, was at length definitely settled by the khan upon the family of Ivan of Moscow and his heirs for ever, upon the payment by this prince of a large sum of money to the sovereign of Kipzak. Ivan I., the son of Danilo, and brother of George, was born in 1300, and received the surname of Kalita or purse, from the wealth he had amassed, and from his causing himself to be constantly accompanied by an attendant bearing his purse, out of which he continually distributed alms to the poor. By his protection and encouragement of trade, he greatly increased the revenues and prosperity of Russia; the ancient fairs and markets, that were annually celebrated before the Tartar invasion, were now revived, and the old chronicler Kamenevitch informs us, that at Makarief on the Volga, the traders of Europe and Asia met every year in the seventy inns of the suburb that the Russians inhabited, and the duties the prince received from their wares amounted to seven thousand two hundred pounds' weight of silver, as Ivan had imposed a heavy tax upon all articles of sale. The dissensions of the princes of the Golden Horde also gave the empire some relief from the thraldom under which she had hitherto groaned, and allowed her time to arouse her prostrate energies, and develop her resources and strength. Uzbek had died in 1340, and his descendants, being driven from their kingdom to the east of the Caspian, became chiefs of the wandering tribes in Turcomania, of Uzbek Tartars, who ultimately expelled the descendants of Timur from the throne of Samarcand. His successor, Khanibeg, was deposed and murdered in his old age, by his ferocious and unnatural son Berdibeg, who, clearing for himself a path to the throne by strangling his twelve brothers, assumed the title, on his accession in 1359, of "king of the just, the sublime support of the world and of religion." But, endeavouring to conciliate the Russian princes, he interfered little with their government, and confirmed them in many privileges which they had formerly received from Khanibeg, on the recovery of his wife, Taidoula Khatoun, from a dangerous illness, through the medical assistance of the Russian ambassador at Serai, who had made use of the gratitude and favour he had thus obtained from the monarch, in ameliorating the condition of his country, and furthering her interests. Novogorod, also, during the reign of Ivan, was again brought under the rule of the Grand Prince, who received an embassy from Magnus the king of Sweden, requesting the archbishop of Novogorod to hold a conference with his envoys, being desirous to convert the people of that city to the Latin faith ; and on the conquest of the last provinces of Halich, by Ghedemin, the prince of Lithuania, and the flight of the metropolitan from Kiof, notwithstanding the liberal offers of this chief, in whose territory the old capital was now included, and who wished to retain in his own hands one whose influence was so great in the empire, Ivan induced the fugitive prelate to establish his see at Moscow, which from henceforward became the principal city for the ecclesiastical as well as the secular affairs of

Russia. He also impressed upon his sons the necessity for living at peace, if they wished to secure the prosperity of their country; and on his death, which took place on the 31st of March, 1340, after having assumed the habit of a monk, they both took an oath upon the sepulchre of their ancestors to live in harmony, and make an equal partition of their inheritance. Simeon the eldest, surnamed the Proud, took the title of Grand Prince with one half of the revenues of their dominions, and reigned in Moscow; while his brother Ivan, with the other half, ruled over some of the inferior provinces of the empire; and Russia enjoyed a period of greater tranquillity than she had experienced for several hundreds of years.

In the year 1293, during the civil war between the princes of Novogorod, Demetrius and Andrew, the sons of Alexander, the Swedes wrested the Finnish provinces of Carelia and Kexholm from the Russians; and, though a part was restored to its ancient masters in 1338, yet the greater portion remained in the possession of Sweden till the reign of Peter the Great.*

* The traveller, Erman, in his "Travels through Russia and Siberia in 1848," remarks of the French invasion in 1812, that it "has left but a faint impression upon the popular mind in Russia, even in Moscow itself, which suffered so much at their hands" (though Napoleon declared, and perhaps truly, that the empire could not recover it for fifty years). "Conflagrations," says he, "have been common occurrences in that city, and the inhabitants are accustomed to be burned out. We read of seven such events from the thirteenth to the beginning of the nineteenth century, in all of which the destruction was complete, or very nearly so. The fire of 1812 spared many of the stone churches," (which from religious scruples were not lighted by the Russians) "and on whose towers the Mahometan crescent rises above the cross, a monument of earlier revolutions. The yoke of the Tartars was so lasting and oppressive, that later events of a similar kind seem comparatively unimportant; and even the French invasion is here thought little of, being usually compared with the irruption of the Pechenegues and that of the Poles in later times, but never set on a level with the Tartar domination."

CHAPTER VI.

Character of the Russians.—The Black Death.

> The demon of the plague had cast,
> From his hot wing, a deadlier blast,
> More mortal far, than ever came,
> From the red desert's sands of flame.—MOORE.

THE effects of the devastation created by the invasion of the Monguls was beginning, towards the middle of the fourteenth century, to disappear from the external face of Russia. The wasted lands were in most places again brought into cultivation, the towns were rebuilt, though it was long before the principal cities regained their former magnitude, and now, under the sway of Simeon, comparative peace appeared to reign at last. But the people, though they remained in dress and manner of life the same as in the days of Rurik and Vladimir, were altered in character and in many of their laws. In place of the enlightened code of Yaroslaf, they had been compelled to adopt the stern edicts and military regulations of the Monguls; their princes and nobles, though they despised and abhorred, still followed the Tartar chieftain's mode of life, and so many of the Russians had been carried into slavery, their conquerors leaving Monguls to fill their places throughout the land, that the very population, especially among the peasantry, was changed. Their national historian, Karamsin, in lamenting the ill effects that the invasion of the Monguls produced upon the character of his countrymen, observes, that "national pride being extinguished among them, they had recourse to those artifices which supply the want of strength, among men condemned to a servile obedience. Skilful," says he, "in deceiving the Tartars, they became adepts in the art of deceiving one another. Buying from the barbarians their personal safety, they became more greedy of money, and less sensible to insult or to shame, exposed, as they were, incessantly to the insolence of foreign tyrants. Force took the place of law; pillage, authorized by impunity, was exercised by the Russians as well as by the Tartars. There was no safety on the roads nor within the houses; till after the time of stupor, when the law awoke from its dream, it was necessary to have recourse to a severity unknown to ancient Russia." And the social condition of Russia remained in this wretched state till the memorable accession of Ivan the Third. But during the temporary calm, maintained by Simeon with a strong hand throughout his territories, that terrible scourge, known in the middle ages as the Black Death, appeared in Russia, and carried off more than a fourth part of the whole population of the empire. The nobles, wealthy citizens, and merchants, endeavoured to propitiate the wrath of Heaven, and atone for their sins, on account of which they supposed this calamity had befallen them, by erecting churches, and giving their villages, estates, and treasures, for the benefit of the clergy and monasteries; and the priests carried relics in procession, and made pilgrimages to the shrines of celebrated saints, to ask their intercession in allaying the fury of the plague. The sick were deserted in the hour of death by their friends and nearest relatives, or abandoned to the care of any attendant whom money or compulsion could procure; the streets of the capital were blocked up by the dead and dying; and the plains of Kipzak, where it especially raged, were strewn with the bodies of those Tartars who had fallen victims to its ravages, the wretched survivors being scarcely enough to bury them. Yet many noble instances of self-devotion are on record, and few, as in other countries, abandoned their native towns, in the forlorn hope of escaping, when distant from the abode of man, the scourge that was spreading desolation around. Every rank and age fell victims alike to the universal contagion that pervaded the tainted air; in April, 1352, it proved fatal to the Grand Prince, his wife, and every member of his family, and shortly after to the metropolitan Theognostes, the Archbishop Bazil of Novogorod, and multitudes of the priests and monks, who, in obedience to their vows, had been throughout the whole course of the pestilence the assiduous attendants of the dying, from whom all the rest of humanity had fled, and by them the dead were borne in haste and silence to the grave, unaccompanied by mourners or the customary funeral ceremonies and feasts.

Simeon the Proud, from the commencement had used his utmost exertions to prevent the spread of the infection, to reanimate the courage of his people, and provide all who were attacked or left desolate with proper means of relief. Charms and incantations were indeed the chief means resorted to by the superstitious populace, and celebrated magicians were brought from all parts of the empire to invoke and exorcise the evil spirits, whom they supposed had possessed those who were seized, and had originally occasioned the Black Death. When dying, the Grand Prince at first steadfastly refused to adopt the shaven crown and monastic gown of the cloister; but his confessor, and the priests who surrounded him, by their earnest entreaties succeeded in inducing him to conform to this practice of his fathers, by which they had been accustomed, when dying, to manifest their repentance and humility, and a few moments after he expired, and was buried the same day with his children in the cathedral of the Kremlin, at Moscow. But Russia was not alone in her sufferings from this awful visitation, for it attacked every other nation on the globe of whom our records ascend to those times; and commencing in China, in 1347, it was preceded, according to the writers of that period, by the most singular appearances in the heavens, and the most terrible convulsions of the earth.* Floods and draughts, famine and heavy mists, volcanic eruptions, and winds of poisonous odour, were alternately experienced throughout Africa, Asia, and Europe, and the pestilence appears to have quitted each country through which it had spread, before it proceeded on to the next. From Central Asia it was brought by caravans to the camps of the Turks in Asia Minor, and the Genoese colonies in the East; and, depopulating the Tartar tribes on the northern shores of the Euxine, it advanced to the city of Constantinople, where, amongst thousands of the inhabitants, a son of the Emperor perished; while, in Caramania and Cesarea, none who remained in their homes were left alive, and entering Egypt, having already been introduced into Persia and India by caravans and traders from Thibet, it destroyed daily in Cairo, during the height of its rage, from ten to fifteen thousand persons. In these countries, and throughout the continent and islands of Europe, frightful earthquakes had preceded its appearance, rendering the fruitful Cyprus

* Hecker's " Epidemics of the Middle Ages."

a desert, and ruining thirty villages in Cariuthia alone, from whose remains were excavated more than a thousand corpses. The ships of Genoa communicated the Black Death to the shores of Italy and France; even animals were not free from its effects. Vessels wandered unguided along the Mediterranean, all on board having perished; and in Spain, where it prevailed till 1350, it carried off the King Alfonso XI., and in France the Queen Consort and the Queen of Navarre, while the churchyards, no longer being able to contain the heaps of dead, the Pope, at Avignon, found it necessary to consecrate the waters of the Rhone, that the bodies might be thrown into the river without delay. A solitary bark floated into the port of Bergen with no sign or appearance of life; it was boarded by some hardy Norwegians, who discovered that its crew consisted only of corpses; and these communicated the plague to the whole of Scandinavia, where, in Norway, a third of the people perished, so that many ancient towns being left desolate, were allowed to fall into decay, till their names have disappeared from the records of history, and their very sites are now hardly known. In Sweden, the Princes Hako and Knute, two brothers of the king, died, and in the province of Westgothland alone, 466 priests. The snows of Iceland and Greenland, and their distance from the continent, were no protection against the fury of the Black Death; and in the latter country it so decimated the Norwegian colonists on the western coast, that in many of the settlements none survived; and as the ships of Norway were no longer able, for want of men, to supply the rest during many years with the usual provisions and assistance, they were unable to defend themselves from the attacks of the American Esquimaux, by whom, it is supposed, the few who had lived were either captured or prematurely cut off.* The huge blocks of ice that shortly after accumulated round that part of the coast, long prevented any vessel of Europe from ascertaining their too probable fate. In 1349, Poland was first visited by the universal pestilence; while in Russia, contrary to the usual course of these visitations, it did not appear till the end of 1351, after it had died out in all the rest of Europe. A terrible cry against the Jews, as the authors of these misfortunes, in 1348 rang throughout all the western nations of the con-

* Hecker's "Epidemics of the Middle Ages."

tinent; and while, in Hungary, the order of Flagellants *

* The ancient song of the Flagellants —(Translated from manuscript by Masson.)

1 Whoe'er to save his soul is fain,
Must pay and render back again,
His safety so shall he consult:
Help us good Lord to this result!
5 Ye that repent your sins draw nigh;
From the burning hell we fly,
From Satan's wicked company:
Whom he leads,
With pitch he feeds.
10 If we be wise, we this shall flee,
Maria! Queen! we trust in thee,
To move thy son for sympathy:
Jesus Christ was captive led
And to the cross was riveted.
15 The cross was redden'd with his gore,
And we his martyrdom deplore;
Sinner, canst thou to me atone?
Three pointed nails, a thorny crown,
The holy cross, a spear, a wound.
20 We through thy death to thee have sued,
For God in heaven, we shed our blood;
This for our sins will work for good,
Blessed Maria, mother, queen,
Through thy loved Son's redeeming mean.
25 Be all our wants to thee portray'd;
Aid us mother, spotless maid!
Tremble the earth, the rocks are rent,
Fond heart of mine, thou must relent,
Tears from our sorrowing eyes we weep.
35 Therefore so firm our faith we heap,
With all our hearts, with all our senses,
Christ bore his pangs for our offences:
Ply well the scourge for Jesus' sake,
And God, through Christ, your sins shall take.
40 For love of God abandon sin,
To mend your vicious lives begin,
So shall we his mercy win.
Direful was Maria's pain,
When she beheld her dear One slain.
45 Pierced was her soul as with a dart,
Sinner, let this affect your heart!
The time draws near,
When God in anger shall appear,
Jesus was refresh'd with gall.
50 Prostrate crosswise let us fall,
Then with uplifted arms arise,
That God may with us sympathize!
Jesus, by thy titles free,
From our bondage set us free.
55 By this warning man abide,
God shall surely punish pride.
Christ in heaven, where he commands,
Thus address'd his angel hands:
Christendom dishonours me,
60 Therefore her ruin I decree.
Then Mary thus implored her son,
Penance to Thee, loved Child, be done,
That she repent, be mine the care,
Stay then thy wrath, and hear my prayer.
65 Woe, usurer! though thy wealth abound,
For every ounce thou makest, a pound
Shall sink thee to the hell profound.
Ye murderers, and ye robbers all,
The wrath of God on you shall fall;
70 Mercy ye ne'er to others show,
None shall ye find, but endless woe!
Had it not been for our contrition,
All Christendom had met perdition.
Satan hath bound her in his chain,
75 Mary hath loosed her bonds again.
Benignant Michael, blessed saint,
Guardian of souls, receive our plaint,
Through thy Almighty Maker's death,
Preserve us from the hell beneath.
—(Hecker's "Epidemics of the Middle Ages.")

arose, professing to take upon themselves the sins of the people, which they endeavoured to expiate, and to appease the wrath of the Almighty by processions, self-scourging, and abasement; the unhappy Israelites were accused of poisoning the springs, and tainting by their spells and sorcery the heavy and foggy air; and in Germany, Spain, Switzerland, Italy, and France, they were dragged, with any Christian who might have harboured them, before ignorant and bigoted tribunals, and condemned, without mercy or discrimination, to imprisonment, exile, tortures, and the stake. The only countries in which they could safely seek a refuge were Poland, whose enlightened monarch, Boleslaf V. had, in 1278, granted them liberty of conscience, and where now the king, Casimir the Great, allowed them to shelter their heads; Russia; the duchy of Lithuania, under its heathen prince, Olgherd, where they are still more numerous than in any other part of Europe; and in the tottering empire of the East.

The plague had raged less fiercely in Germany than in any other country on the continent; but in Italy* it made frightful ravages, and it is supposed to have carried off 25,000,000 of the inhabitants of Europe, a fourth part of the whole people. In the south and west of Asia, according to the report made to Pope Clement, at Avignon, it destroyed 23,000,000 inhabitants, in China 14,000,000; besides multitudes, whose exact numbers are unknown, throughout Mongolia and the north of the continent, and the more remote and less visited provinces in India, and the extremities of the East.†

---

* During this terrible visitation, "the hearts of all the inhabitants," says Boccaccio, speaking of Florence, "were closed to feelings of humanity. They fled from the sick and all that belonged to them, hoping by these means to save themselves. Others shut themselves up in their houses, with their wives, their children, and households, living on the most costly food, but carefully avoiding all excess. None were allowed access to them; no intelligence of death or sickness was permitted to reach their ears; and they spent their time in singing and music, and other pastimes. Others carried their precaution still further, and thought the surest way to escape death was by flight. One citizen fled from another, a neighbour from his neighbours, a relation from his relations; and in the end, so completely had terror extinguished every kindlier feeling, that the brother forsook the brother, the sister the sister, the wife her husband, and at last even the parent his own offspring, and abandoned them unvisited and unsoothed to their fate. Many breathed their last without a friend to soothe their dying pillow; instead of sorrow and mourning appeared indifference, frivolity, and mirth, this being considered, especially by the females, as conducive to health." The Pope Clement VI., though he caused great relief to be afforded to the sick, shut himself up while the plague lasted at Avignon, and forbade all who had been in reach of the contagion to approach him. In Germany, the merchants and other rich inhabitants of her cities gave their treasures to churches and monasteries, though it was frequently refused by the monks, who feared lest they should receive the dreaded infection with the gold; but, on their closing their gates against these penitents, it was often cast to them over the convent walls.—See Hecker's "Epidemics of the Middle Ages."

† Hecker's "Epidemics of the Middle Ages."

CHAPTER VII.

Reign of Demetrius Donskoi—Kipzak—Lithuania—Battle of the Don—Moscow burned—Monasteries—Literature—Poland—The Teutonic Knights.

> As when the Tartar from his Russian foe,
> By Astracan, over the snowy plains
> Retires.—MILTON's "Paradise Lost."

ON the death of Simeon the Proud, his brother Ivan, surnamed the Handsome, succeeded him in Moscow, while the princes of Tver, Suzdal or Vladimir, and Riazan, each assumed the style and title of Grand Prince; though Ivan alone had received it from their common chief, the Mongul khan. During his short and feeble reign, in which the affairs of the state were entirely conducted by the metropolitan Alexis, the empire again became the prey of internal dissensions and civil war; and on his death, in 1358, Demetrius Constantinovitz of Vladimir received from Urus, the Khan of Kipzak, the supreme authority, and Alexis became regent of Moscow, and guardian of its young prince, Demetrius Ivanovitz. His throne was assailed by the Lithuanians in the west, and the princes of Tver in the north, between whom and their uncle a fierce war was long waged, until the latter, by the marriage of his daughter with Olgherd of Lithuania, obtained the support of this powerful ally; and, by his assistance, not only possessed himself of the crown of Tver, but three times, in 1368, in 1370, and in 1373, appeared in arms with his son-in-law, and their united forces, before the gates of Moscow. The walls of this city were now separated by only a very few miles from the territories of the Lithuanian chief, who had lately extended his frontiers as far as the border town of Mojaisk. But the small and endangered provinces of Muscovy were ably defended during the troubled minority of Demetrius, by Alexis, who resisted all the solicitations of the Grand Prince to remove his episcopal see again to Vladimir; and while he assiduously laboured by his policy and arms to reduce the other princes of Russia under the sway of Moscow, was frequently called upon to act as mediator between these same princes and their domestic adversaries; particularly in the case of Constantine, the brother of Demetrius of Vladimir, who, rebelling against his sovereign, had seized upon Nijni Novogorod. This city was laid under an interdict by Alexis; but shortly after, Demetrius, having rebelled against the khan, and released from a long captivity among the Tartars, a prince of the house of Tver, whom the regent of Moscow subsequently seized, and retained as a hostage, to ensure the peace of his father's principality, the Grand Prince was defeated, and deposed by the Tartar monarch; and in 1362, the young prince Dmitri, or Demetrius, having secured by his conquests and treaties the fealty of all the other Russian dukes, took upon himself the title of Grand Prince without any appointment from the Tartar sovereign. This was the first time that a Russian chief had ascended the throne, independently of the interference of the Monguls, since the conquest of the empire by the armies of Batû Khan.

But the power of Kipzak was now declining, and her princes were too much occupied in preserving their own crowns, to interest themselves, as they had hitherto done, in the succession and civil wars of the Russian chiefs. Rival claimants of the sceptre divided the land, and the people, and the kingdom had long been a prey to their fierce contentions and endless feuds. In 1361, the Khan Berdibeg was assassinated in Serai, by a conspiracy of his nobles and courtiers, and Naurus, or Urus, a scion of the house of Zingis, ascended the throne; and from this time till the extinction of the descendants of the great Mongul conqueror in Kipzak, by the arms of the still more formidable and victorious Tamerlane, their empire was rent asunder by domestic feuds, and distracted by civil war. The reigns of the succeeding princes were short and bloody, and unmarked by any political occurrence or event of any interest beyond the borders of their own sandy plains, and for a few years their territories were divided into several khanates; the most powerful of which were Kazan, Astrakhan, the Crimea, and Yaik, or the district on the Ural, until they were all again united by Mamai, a powerful Tartar chief. Some years before the accession of this prince, Demetrius had refused to pay the customary tribute to Kipzak, and a barbarous desultory war was carried on for nearly twenty years between the Tartar and Russian states.

In 1380, Olgherd of Lithuania died, and though, since his marriage with a princess of Tver, he had professed the Greek religion, and caused his sons to be baptized and educated in that faith, himself attending the service in the Christian churches when residing at Kiof, or the other cities which he had wrested from the Russian empire; he had still been accustomed, when in his native provinces, to sacrifice to the national idols, and his body was burned on a funeral pile, with all the ceremonies and pagan rites of his ancestors.* He left several sons, of whom the fourth, Jagellio, who had relapsed into idolatry, succeeded him as Grand Duke, and immediately allied himself with Mamai against the Russian states. These had all united their armies to the black flag of Demetrius of Moscow, whom they had appointed commander-in-chief; and, receiving intelligence of the intended junction of the forces of the Tartar khan with those of his new ally, preparatory to overwhelming the intervening provinces, with the idea of totally extirpating the Christian religion, and rendering the country a barren desert; they anticipated this manœuvre, by marching to intercept the Monguls before they should have crossed the Don. On his route, Demetrius was joined by every Russian capable of bearing arms; boys and aged men seized the javelin or bow, and hastened to join the gallant army, which they fondly hoped was destined to free their country for ever from the odious yoke of the Tartars; while the women bore their armour, and urged them to maintain their ground to the last; nor rest till the Christian banners floated over those of the Moslem, that had so long waved supreme throughout the land; and four hundred thousand Russians assembled on the banks of the Don, anxiously watching for some sign or appearance of the enemy. But after a few days had passed without obtaining any intelligence of the foe, Demetrius gave his soldiers the option of remaining where they were, and awaiting the probable attack of the Tartars, or advancing at once, crossing the river, and encountering them first on their own fields. Not a man dissented from the general wish to adopt the latter alternative;

* Krasinski's "Poland."

and, having received a blessing and absolution from the priests and metropolitans who had accompanied them, and who promised the crown of martyrdom to all who should fall in the war—a war which they affirmed was sacred, as it had been undertaken in the cause of their country and faith—the whole army passed over a bridge of boats to the opposite shores of Kipzak, and immediately after, their prince caused the bridge to be destroyed, to cut off all hope of escape in case of defeat. On the 8th of September, 1380, the Russians met Mamai, with an army of seven hundred thousand Tartars, upon the plains of Koulikoff, and both sides immediately engaged with the utmost fury; the fight commencing early in the morning, and continuing far into the night. Fresh battalions came on, and relieved those exhausted in the front; now the advantage appeared to be with the Russians, now with the Tartars. Wherever the arrows flew thickest, or the contest appeared to be urged most desperately, there was Demetrius leading on his men, and inspiring them with confidence by his own courage, self-possession, and commands. At length, when the overwhelming number of the Tartars appeared to have almost broken the Russian force, of whom few, and those scattered and at distances, were left alive upon the field, Demetrius, who was severely wounded, heading a detachment, consisting principally of aged and enfeebled men, whom he had left hitherto in charge of the baggage, and to guard his army from an attack in the rear, fell upon the Tartars at an unexpected moment, when they considered their triumph almost complete; and, causing them to waver, the other battalions rallied, and united in making one grand charge, which drove the enemy in haste from the field, and gave the Russians a decided victory. More than two hundred thousand Tartars were left dead upon the plain, and the rest of their army dispersing over the country, Mamai escaped almost alone, and under cover of the darkness of night. He subsequently again rallied his forces, but was attacked and sustained a dreadful defeat near Mariopol, from an army of Tartars commanded by an exiled Toushi prince. Flying to Kaffa, he perished a few months later by an assassin's hand, and was succeeded on the throne of Kipzak by the young Toktamish, the rightful heir to the kingdom, who was a son of the deposed and assassinated Khan Urus, and only reigned to complete his country's fall. So enormous was the loss of the Russians in the battle of the Don, that it took the survivors eight days to bury the dead; but the Tartars who fell never received the rites of sepulture, their bodies being left to decay upon the field, as a prey to the vulture and the wolf. As soon as the news of this victory had spread throughout the empire, the whole people indulged in the most extravagant joy. The retribution of Kalka; it was the first time that they had ever signally defeated their tyrants in an engagement of any note; and they celebrated it as the commencement of their independence, and the fall of the Mongul power, giving the Prince of Moscow the title of Donskoi, or of the Don, in commemoration of his victory, a name by which he is always distinguished in history.

But in 1382, the khanates of the Volga and Don having again united under Toktamish, they once more prepared to invade the territories of Russia; and whilst Demetrius was absent from his capital, which he had left under the command of his nephew, and was endeavouring to assemble a sufficient force to oppose them in the field, as his army had been almost completely destroyed at Koulikoff, the Tartars made a sudden and unexpected descent upon the frontier provinces of the empire, and proceeded as far as Moscow, which had been strongly fortified with ramparts and iron gates. But the absence of their prince, and the terrific accounts which they received of the massacres and devastation perpetrated by the foe on their route, so discouraged and alarmed the inhabitants, that many of them, with the metropolitan Cyprian, abandoned their native city; and the small garrison that remained having been induced by their faithless enemies to capitulate under solemn assurances of pardon, had no sooner opened their gates and admitted the Tartars, than every house was delivered up by Toktamish to the flames, and every living person whom they encountered was murdered by his followers in the streets, few having been able to effect a hasty escape. After this destruction of Moscow, the khan obtained from the Grand Prince the repayment of the tribute, from which Demetrius had exonerated his country at the expense of so much blood; and he also exacted a ransom for the bodies of those Russians who had fallen, that their friends might bestow upon them Christian burial. Toktamish returned to Kipzak, and the impoverished boyards and citizens commenced rebuilding Moscow; but they received many important privileges from Demetrius, as a recompence for the loss they had sustained from the enemy, and as some acknowledgment for their patriotic endeavours to avert and sustain the war. It was a part of the policy of this prince to create a powerful nobility, to counteract the influence of the merchants and commoners in the state; so that on his deathbed, when addressing them, and requesting their services and support for his young and inexperienced son, he observed— "Under my reign you were not subjects and boyards, but really Russian princes." He also abolished the office of mayor or tysiatsky of Moscow—a dignitary elected by the common people—upon some dispute that arose between him and the boyards, and placed the municipal government of the city entirely in the hands of the nobles and priests. The metropolitan Alexis being dead, and his successor Cyprian having abandoned Moscow on the approach of the Tartars, for the court of the allies of the invaders, and the deadly enemies of Demetrius, the treacherous princes of Tver, the Grand Prince appointed another priest to fill his place, and in consequence various disputes arose amongst the highest dignitaries of the Russian Church. Three priests at one time assumed the title of primate, and, though they all pleaded their rights at Constantinople before the Byzantine patriarch, the matter was not peaceably arranged till one of the claimants having died, and another being detained a prisoner by Vladimir the son of Olgherd, and Prince of Kiof; the third, who was Cyprian, remained undisputed possessor of the office, and in 1390 was honourably received upon his entrance into Moscow by its Grand Prince. But Demetrius himself had been unable to overcome the disasters and humiliation with which he had seen his country and throne overwhelmed during the last few years of his reign; and, a prey to melancholy and despair, he expired on the 19th of May, 1388, at the age of thirty-eight, and was buried in the Church of the Archangel in Moscow. He was succeeded by his son Vassili or Bazil, who was subsequently confirmed on his throne by a decree of the khan Toktamish, and assumed on his coronation the title of Czar; and to whom, on his deathbed, Demetrius gave many injunctions to govern with justice and mildness, and allow a moderate freedom to his people.

LINE OF MONGUL KHANS.

1175. ZINGIS MARRIED A PRINCESS OF CHINA, AND NUMEROUS OTHERS.

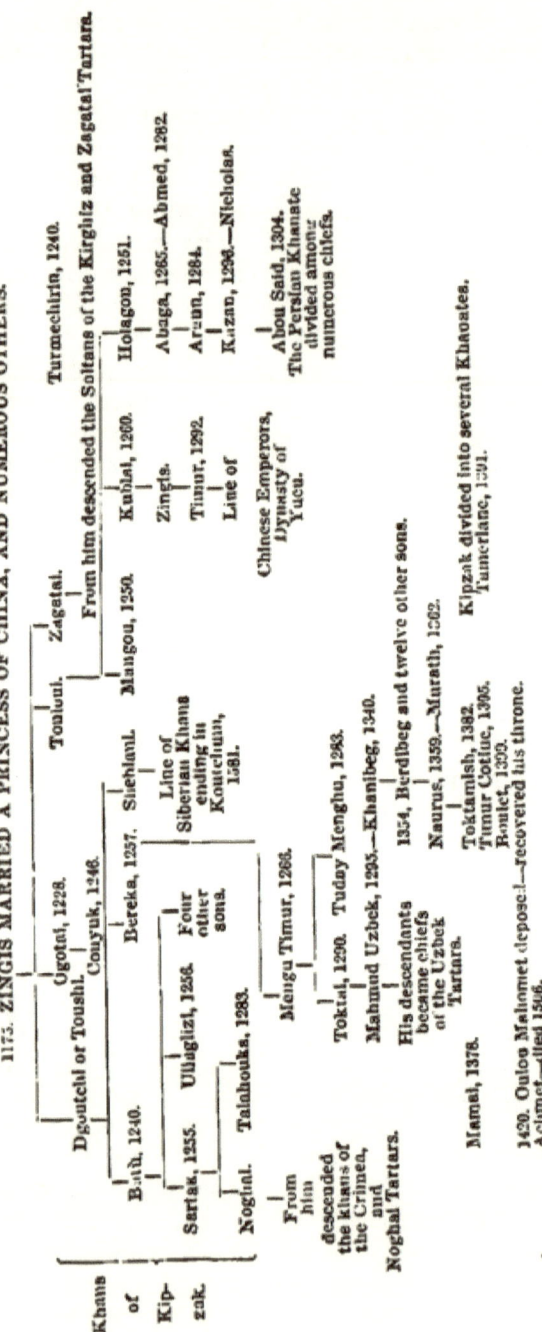

In 1392 Roris, the son of Demetrius III., and the last prince of Vladimir or Suzdal, gave up his kingdom to Bazil, upon the urgent representations of his nobles, who wished to unite all the Russian states in one firm and powerful empire, and entered a monastery where he ended his days in peace. About the same time his example was followed by Oleg, Prince of Riazan, who, after the invasion of Toktamish, had become reconciled to Demetrius, and had for some years lived in close alliance with Moscow. Michael, Prince of Tver, so long the rival and deadly foe of Demetrius, also died a few months after in a monastery; and with him closed the power of his province, though it retained for some years longer a nominal independence.

During the reigns of Demetrius and Bazil. many celebrated monasteries were erected throughout the north of the empire, and under the direction of the primate; and several missions were undertaken by the zealous priests and monks, for converting the Laplanders and more remote tribes of Russia. The cloisters of Solovetskoi were erected by St. Zosimus on an island, near the mouth of the Dwina, in the White Sea; those of the Assumption by a monk, Lazarus, on the shores of the Onega Lake; while in Moscow, Eudocia, the widow of Demetrius, founded the convent of the Ascension in the Kremlin, and became its first abbess. In 1398,* the Greek emperor, Manuel, sent to request some assistance from the Russian princes, either in forces or treasure, against the invasion of the Turks, who had long threatened the empire, and even the very city of Constantinople. Twenty thousand roubles, (£17,000)† were collected by the priests from the monasteries and ecclesiastical revenues, and forwarded to Byzantium, to whom they owed all the support they could furnish, as from her Russia first received the Christian faith. It was accepted with gratitude, and acknowledged by a present in return, from the emperor, of many miraculous images, ecclesiastical books, and sacred bones and other relics of saints. During the Mongul domination, literature appears to have been but little pursued, and to have made small progress in Russia, though many heroic songs and poems of that period now exist; for the people solaced themselves under their slavery and oppression, with recounting the ancient deeds of their heroes in more favourable times, and the ex-

---

* Mouravleff's " Church of Russia." † Platon.

ploits of Vladimir and other national warriors always formed a fertile topic for their poets.* The deacon Ignatius, who in 1389 had accompanied Pimen, one of the claimants for the dignity of primate, on his journey to Constantinople to plead his cause before the patriarch, has left a detailed description of his visit; and Sophronius, a priest of Riazan, towards the end of the fourteenth century wrote a poetical history of the invasion and defeat of the Tartars at the battle of the Don; but these appear to be the only works of any note that were written during the course of the fourteenth century. In the meanwhile, Poland, under its able and successful monarch, Casimir the Great, had been rapidly increasing in power and political importance. According to the expression of an old Polish chronicle, he found his kingdom, at his accession, built of wood, and left it converted into stone. He attracted settlers from abroad, particularly the oppressed and persecuted Jews, and greatly increased by this means the population of Poland; and, by promoting industry and commerce, left his finances in so flourishing a state, that he and his successor were justly considered the most wealthy and opulent monarchs of their time. At the marriage of his granddaughter, Elizabeth of Pomerania, with the emperor Charles IV. at Cracow, he entertained the three foreign potentates of Hungary, Denmark, and Cyprus, with the greatest wealth and magnificence; and in 1347 proclaimed a code of laws, of which the chief object was the protection of the peasantry against the growing oppression of the nobles, who bestowed upon him, among themselves, for that reason, the contemptuous appellation of the peasants' king.† Leaving no sons, he had secured the succession of the throne, before his death in 1370, to his nephew, Louis of Hungary; but this choice proved disastrous to Poland, as the new king was entirely occupied with the affairs of Hungary and Naples,

* "At the present day," says a modern writer, "Russian songs are innumerable. It is said that in one government alone, as many as eight thousand have been collected. The deacons of the Russian church are said to be the chief popular editors. Russian songs are either rhymed or unrhymed, or, in what seems to me the most common form, with rhymes introduced here and there. Generally the metres are trochaic; and, though the subjects are various, love and melancholy seem to be the prevailing features. A song on one of Kutusoff's battles begins:—'It is by no hailstorm, or shower, that the harvest hath been laid low on the broad plain; there hath been a cutting down, there hath been a grapple with sharp swords, with the points of daggers.' There are camp songs sung about the fires, or songs of sentries on watch, or those which celebrate battles, the storm of towns, and death on the field of honour: 'Go, my horse, my trusty steed,' is the first line of one of them; and some are stories from the old times of Russia. Generally I have been struck, in the lyrics of so devout a people, by the absence of allusions to religion."—Russia by a recent Traveller.
† Krasinski's "History of Poland."

where his younger brother, Andrew, had been married to its celebrated queen, Joanna, and was afterwards murdered at her instigation; and he only visited Poland twice during a reign of twelve years. But on his death, in 1382, he left the crown of the latter kingdom to his youngest daughter Hedwige, or Iadwiga; who in 1386 married Jagiello, prince of Lithuania, and thus united this powerful duchy to Poland. Casimir was the last of the dynasty of the Piast and absolute kings of Poland, which had sat on the throne since 882, when the Poles had elected a Piast, or common peasant, for their prince; but under Hedwige, the government assumed a more constitutional form, and the crown was rendered entirely dependent for its supplies upon an assembly of nobles convoked for this purpose, who now first began to acquire that unbalanced power which in later times became the principal cause of the final destruction of the state. At the time of his marriage, Jagiello adopted the Roman Catholic faith, which from henceforth gradually replaced the Greek church and mode of worship throughout Lithuania; and the united kingdoms were still further strengthened by the destruction of the power and influence of their warlike and inveterate enemies, the Teutonic knights, who never recovered from the serious defeats they sustained at the hands of this prince. They had long been more dangerous and hostile to their Christian neighbours than to the idolaters among whom they had settled, with the intention to convert them to their own religion, or to exterminate all who resisted from the face of the earth; but in 1331 they had suffered a terrible loss in the battle of Polowce, gained over them by Vladislaf Lokietck, or the Short, king of Poland, and since that time had been only supported by the continual reinforcements of adventurous warriors, fitted out and commanded by the chivalrous nobles of Western Europe. These, in 1348, penetrated into White Russia, and stormed and captured the strong town of Isborosk; and in 1377 the knights, accompanied by Duke Albert of Austria, laid waste the provinces of Aragellen and Grodno, and returned after a successful foray to their capital, Konigsberg. Again, in the year 1390, the Earl of Derby, afterwards Henry IV., with a band of English nobles, attacked Vilna, but was repulsed with great slaughter from before the town; and in 1410 the Teutonic order received a death-blow to its power and influence in the Polish territories on the field of Grunwald, from the forces of Lithuania and Poland, their grand master, Uric von Jungingen, being left among the slain, with the flower of his nobility and knights.* After this defeat they retired into Prussia, and sank into political insignificance, being deprived of all their fortresses and possessions in the Russian and Polish dominions by the treaty of Thorn, in 1466; and in 1524, when the Reformation spread over the north of Prussia, the form of their establishment became changed from an ecclesiastical proselyting order, to a Protestant temporal state. They had been separated since the treaty of Thorn from their brethren, the Livonian Knights of the Sword, who still ruled the Baltic provinces, and these remained, till their extinction in the same century, a separate community and province.†

* Krasinski's "History of Poland."
† The following is an ode to Kiof, or Kieff, by the Russian poet, Ivan Kozlaff, (translated by T. B. Shaw, B.A.)—

"O Kieff! where religion ever seemeth
 To light existence in our native land,
Where, o'er Petcherskoi's dome, the bright cross gleameth
 Like some fair star that still in heaven doth stand;
Where, like a golden sheet around thee streameth
 Thy plain and meads, that far away expand;
And by thy hoary wall, with ceaseless motion,
Old Dnieper's foaming swell sweeps on to ocean.

How oft to thee in spirit have I panted,
 O, holy city! country of my heart;
How oft in visions have I gazed enchanted
 On thy fair towers—a sainted thing thou art;
By Lavra's walls, or Dnieper's waves, nor wanted
 A spell to draw me from the life apart.
In thee my country I behold victorious,
Holy and beautiful, and great and glorious.

The moon her soft ray on Petcherskoi poureth,
 Its domes are shining in the river's wave,
The soul the spirit of the past adoreth,
 Where sleeps beneath thee many a holy grave.
Vladimir's shade above thee calmly soareth,
 Thy towers speak of the sainted and the brave;
Afar I gaze, and all in dreamy splendour,
Breathes of the past a spell sublime and tender.

There fought the warriors in the field of glory,
 Strong in the faith, against their country's foe;
And many a royal flower, yon palace hoary,
 In virgin loveliness hath seen to blow.
And Bayan sang to them the story,
 And secret rapture in their breast did glow.
Hark! midnight sounds: that brazen voice is dying,
A day to meet the vanish'd days is dying;

Where are the valiant, the resistless lances,
 The bands, that were as lightning when they waved
Where are the beautiful, whose sunny glances
 Our fathers with such potency enslaved?
Where is the bard whose song no more entrances?
 Ah! that deep bell hath answer'd what I craved;
And thou alone by these grave walls, O river!
Murmurest the Dnieper still, and flows for ever.

BOOK III.

THE HISTORY OF TIMUR AND HIS SUCCESSORS.

From A.D. 1336 to A.D. 1530.—A.M. 6844 to A.M. 7038.—A.H. 755 to A.H. 955.

> Chiefs of the Uzbek race,
> Waving their heron crests with martial grace,
> Turkomans countless as their flocks led forth,
> Wild warriors of the purple hills, and those
> Who dwell beyond the everlasting snows
> Of Hindoo Kosh, in stormy freedom bred,
> Their fort the rock, their camp the torrent's bed.
>
> MOORE.

BOOK III.—CHAPTER I.

Timur Bek or Tamerlane—His conquests—Toktamish—Vitold—Bulgaria—Muscovy.

> By one man's crime; by one man's lust of power,
> Unpeopled: naked plains and ravaged fields
> Succeed to smiling cities, and the fruits
> Of peaceful olive, luscious fig, and vine.—MORE.

So great an ignorance prevailed in England, Germany, and France, during the middle ages with regard to the Eastern nations of Europe, that a canon of Bremen, writing in the year 1010, describes Sweden and Norway as being two vast realms unknown to the civilized world, and gravely asserts that in Russia the natives possessed only one eye and one leg! Towards the end of the fourteenth century, his countrymen appear to have made comparatively but little advance in their knowledge of the latter empire; and, while the tribes of the Toushi Monguls, who had settled in Kipzak,

* EUROPEAN SOVEREIGNS CONTEMPORARY WITH TIMUR.

EASTERN EMPIRE.
1341. John Cantacuzene.
1355. John Paleologus.
1391. Manuel Paleologus.

ENGLAND.
1327. Edward III.
1377. Richard II.
1399. Henry IV.

FRANCE.
1328. Philip le Bel of Valois.
1350. John.
1364. Charles V.
1380. Charles VI.

GERMAN EMPIRE.
1347. Charles IV.
1378. Wenzel of Bohemia.
1399. Frederick of Brunswick.
1400. Robert, Palatine of the Rhine.

HUNGARY.
1342. Louis I.
1383. Mary.
1389. Mary and Sigismund.

POLAND.
1333. Casimir the Great.

1370. Louis of Hungary.
1383. Hedwige and Jughellon.
1385. Jaghellon.

RUSSIA.
1340. Simon the Proud.
1353. Ivan II.
1362. Demetrius Donskoi.
1389. Vassili Dmitrovitz.

SCOTLAND.
1341. David II. rest.
1371. Robert II.
1390. Robert III.

SPAIN.
1350. Pedro the Cruel.
1368. Henry Trastamare.
1379. John I.
1390. Henry III.

PORTUGAL.
1357. Pedro the Cruel.
1367. Ferdinand I.
1385. John I.

SWEDEN.
1318. Magnus III.
1365. Albert.
1397. Margaret.

DENMARK.
1340. Waldemar III.
1375. Olaf III.
1375. Margaret I.

POPES.
1342. Clement VI.
1352. Innocent VI.
1362. Urban V.
1370. Gregory XI.
1378. Urban VI.
1389. Boniface IX.

KIPZAK.
1340. Khanibeg.
1354. Berdibeg.
1359. Aculpa.
1359. Naurus.
1360. Chidir.
1361. Timur Oscha.
1362. Murath.
1376. Mamai.
1378. Toktamish.
1380. Urus.
1381. Toktamish restored.
1385. Timur Cotlue or Melik.
1396. Toktamish restored.
1398. Timur Cotlue restored.
1401. Schatibeg, or Boulet.

were chiefly prevented from overwhelming the whole continent of Europe by the rigour of the Muscovite climate, and the extent of her snowy and barren wastes which they must have crossed, as well as by the defensive strength of Poland, and the constant resistance of that warlike and restless state, the plains beyond the Vistula were tracts utterly unknown to the geographers and statesmen of the west. Shut out by the Tartars of the Ukraine and the Crimea, as Kiof and Novogorod were then, from their former trade and communication with Greece, that empire appears to have remained totally indifferent to the unhappy Russia's fortunes and fate; besides, Constantinople was herself now distracted by barbarous invaders from Asia and civil war, and the last successors of Cæsar were too much occupied in preserving their own throne from the Turks, to heed the policy or revolutions of a nation which they considered too insignificant and remote to possess at any time either influence or interest in the events of Southern Europe.

But, towards the middle of the fourteenth century, a terrible shock and revolution was preparing in the East—one of those mighty conquerors that at various times have appeared in Asia, and before whose tremendous exploits the victories of Cæsar, of Charlemagne, and of Napoleon, sink into comparative insignificance and obscurity, was about to enter upon the scene and play an important part in the world's history. An obscure scion of the imperial house of Zingis Khan, triumphing over the machinations of his enemies, the faithlessness of his friends, and the jealousy and treachery of his competitors and allies, and profiting by the anarchy which then prevailed among the thrones of Western Asia, from the son of a petty chieftain became the arbiter of that great continent; and carried his arms over regions more extensive than any other general or prince who has yet appeared upon the earth*—the area of his empire exceeding even that of his celebrated predecessor Zingis. This was Timur Bek,† or Tamerlane, as he is usually designated: the ingratitude of Toktamish, the khan of Kipzak, who, by the influence and forces of Timur had been reseated upon his father's throne, brought him first into Europe; and, by his victories over Bajazet and the Ottoman Turks in Asia

* Creasy's "Ottoman Turks."
† Beg, or Bek, is the Tartar for prince, and Timur means Iron.

Minor, he probably, says Gibbon, retarded the impending fall of Constantinople for at least fifty years.*

The throne which Zagatai, the son of Zingis, had founded in Transoxiana, where he ruled over part of Southern Siberia, including the country of the Igours, to Cashgar and Balkh, on the borders of Persia and Thibet, had become vacant in 1346, through the death of the last of his descendants, the khan Kazan,† on the field of battle, while warring against Mir Cazagan, the sultan of a Turcomanian horde; and the latter after crowning and deposing in succession several native chiefs, was himself assassinated in 1357. The troubles that arose in the kingdom, through the misgovernment of his son Abdallah, and the contentions that prevailed among the numerous princes, and tomans,‡ who boasted a relationship or connection, however distant, with the imperial dynasty of the Monguls, afforded occasion and space, for want of which in another country, or at another time, his name might for ever have remained in obscurity, to the elevation of Timur, who at the age of twenty-four, came forward as the deliverer of his country, when threatened with destruction by the invasion of the khan of a powerful tribe of Kalmucks, and endeavoured to restore peace and unity among his distracted countrymen.||

The fourth ancestor of Zingis, and ninth of Tamerlane, were brothers; and, according to a tradition of the Tartars, it had been agreed between them, that while the descendants of the elder should always fill the office of khan, those of the younger should be their ministers and generals; and one of these, Carashar Nevian, had been the first vizier of Zagatai, whose posterity being now extinct, the country was reduced to subjection by the khans of Turcomania, a former dependency of Zagatai; and these opposed in their turn by their rivals, the Getæ or Kalmucks in the northern districts, both nations cruelly taxed and oppressed their new subjects.§

Timur was born on the 9th of April, 1336, in the village of Sebzuar, about forty miles south of Samarcand, and where his father, the Emir Tragai, was the hereditary chief, and

---

* Gibbon's "Decline and Fall of the Roman Empire."
† This Kazan must not be confounded with the Mongal khan Kazan of Persia.
‡ Tomans were chiefs of small districts, which they were bound to govern according to the laws of Zingis, and furnish their sovereign, when required, with a troop of 10,000 horse.
|| De La Croix's Translation of Shorefeddin Ali's "Hist. of Timur Bek."
§ Gibbon's "Decline and Fall of the Roman Empire."

commanded a regiment of horse.* At twelve years old he served as a soldier in many desperate engagements, and subsequently passed nine years as a traveller in foreign lands, where he minutely observed the character and laws, and various modes of government, obtaining all the information and instruction within his reach; and at every period of his life he was a diligent reader of history, poetry, philosophy, and works on science and art. Educated as a Mahometan, he became ultimately an intolerant and fanatical supporter of the doctrines of the prophet; but his disposition appears to have been originally neither unfeeling nor cruel, till it was hardened by a military life, long engagement in a barbarous warfare, and the most unrestrained and unscrupulous ambition. According to the historian Arabshah,† at the middle time of life, in appearance he was tall and rather corpulent, with long legs, a large head, high forehead, and great strength: his eyes full of fire, his complexion fair, with an agreeable countenance, and his voice loud and piercing. He had lost the use of his right hand from a severe wound he had received as early as 1360, in a skirmish with the Turcomanian troops; or, according to some authors, by a fall from a battery upon which he had headed an assault, and this causing an attack of paralysis, rendered him lame all his life in his right leg; and, as one of his historians has informed us, blind on the same side, which procured him from his enemies the nickname of Timur Lenc, or the Lame Timur, since corrupted by the Europeans into Tamerlane.‡ He was passionately fond of chess, which he played with unusual skill ||—of a grave and rigid deportment, he permitted neither jesters nor fools to appear before him, and no crime enraged him so much as deception, insincerity, or the least appearance of an untruth. After he had obtained the imperial crown, his signet-ring bore merely this inscription—" Safety consists in fair dealing," and his palace was known by the lofty appellation of the abode of science and virtue.

In 1359, his uncle Hadgi Berlas, who had succeeded to the emirship of Sebzuar or Kech, the paternal inheritance of

---

* Sherefeddin Ali's "Hist. of Timur Bek."
† Arabshah's "Hist. of Timur."
‡ Kezarien.
|| He invented a new system, multiplying the pieces from thirty-one to fifty-six, and the squares from a hundred and ten to a hundred and thirty; " but, except in his own court, the old game has been considered sufficiently elaborate."—Gibbon's "Decline and Fall of the Roman Empire."

Timur, on hearing of the approach of the army of the khan of the Kalmucks, who threatened his defenceless little district with total desolation, had determined to abandon his native province; and, with the few warriors who still rallied round him, to take refuge in the country of Khorassan, under the protection and in the dominions of the Persian khan. With this intent he had proceeded with his nephew and their troops as far as the river Gihon; but the heart of young Timur smote him for leaving their unhappy subjects to the merciless fury of their enemies, and, perceiving that his country was beset, and overrun on all sides by foes from without, torn to pieces by contending factions within, and menaced with almost inevitable destruction and slavery, he resolved to attempt its rescue by himself joining the forces of one of the hostile tribes, and by their assistance succeed in emancipating the nation from the rest, for he considered that it would be better to submit to one powerful master than to be trampled under foot by a thousand minor chiefs. While encamped on the banks of the Gihon and preparing to cross, Timur entered his uncle's tent, and, communicating to him his design, informed him that he should yield to the khan of the Kalmucks, and join his troops. "As a kingdom without a leader," said he, "resembles a body without a soul, I think it right, since you intend to go into Khorassan, that I should return to Kech, and, after encouraging the inhabitants of that country, go from thence to throw myself at the feet of the grand khan and offer him my service; I will gain acquaintance with the princes and lords of his court, and strive in every way to avert the tempest with which our country is threatened, and save from ruin the unfortunate people whom God hath put under our care, and of whom one day he will assuredly require of us a strict account." His idea being approved by Hadgi Berlas, who, says the Persian historian, believed his nephew to be inspired, and predestined to some glorious work, Timur immediately departed for the Kalmuck camp, and being subsequently confirmed by the khan in his title of Prince of Kech, he served for some time with their army, and cleared Transoxiana and Turkestan of every other hostile force.* Meanwhile, another chief had succeeded to his ally among the Kalmucks, and Timur, taking advantage of a dispute that arose between himself and the new

* Sherefeddin Ali's "History of Timur Bek."

potentate, to break off all connection with his troops, joined a confederacy of native princes, whom he had urged to unite in a general war for independence, and placed himself at their head. Frequently reduced to the greatest state of distress, he was at one time attacked in the desert by the enemy when accompanied by only three horsemen, the rest, who were Carizmians, having deserted their leader; and, concealing his wife in a cave, rushed alone and unsupported upon the foe. On another occasion he was taken prisoner with his constant companion and brother-in-law, the Emir Hussein, by Ali Bey, a treacherous and jealous ally, and confined for sixty-one days in a loathsome dungeon; and again he was forced to swim for his life across the Gihon, and wander for months as a fugitive in the wilds of the desert. But, persevering in the pursuit of his design, he allowed no danger or wounds to deter him, and, reassembling his scattered followers, reanimated them by his own example and courage, and finally succeeded in expelling the Kalmucks from the provinces around Samarcand, and driving them back to their own barren districts. But finding that the poorest chief who had assisted him, now that their country was freed from enemies, expected to become an independent sovereign, and reign alone and supreme in his own village and state; and well aware that such a system would only provoke a renewal of the civil war, and another torrent of invaders, the victorious young general called a congress of princes and nobles, and proposed to elect Kabulshah Aglen, a dervish of the family of Zingis, to the dignity of khan. At the coronation of the new emperor, Timur received the title of "Saheb Caran," the Hero of the Age, and released from confinement all the princes and officers of the enemy who had been taken prisoners in the war.

But Transoxiana was not destined to remain long in peace; the Kalmucks again invaded the land; again Timur came forward with his faithful bands and defeated them, yet was afterwards compelled with his lieutenant, Hussein, to retreat; the enemy besieged Samarcand, but he drove them with frightful slaughter from before its walls, and ultimately expelled their whole army from the province. But when these foes had been reduced to take refuge in flight, a still more formidable opponent appeared in the field, in the person of Hussein, the hitherto constant companion of his dangers and

triumphs, who, jealous of the increasing power and fame of his brother-in-law, took up arms against Timur, and induced many to join in the revolt. A coolness had been long growing between the two chiefs, but they had remained at peace with each other till the death of Olajai Turcan Aga, Timur's wife, who, combining the most fearless disposition with gentleness and amiability, had accompanied her husband and brother in most of their expeditions, and was the only bond of union that for some time had connected them, as by the former she had been tenderly loved. Hussein possessing himself of the province of Balkh, with several strongly fortified cities and fortresses, appointed an insurgent chief to the dignity of khan, and marched towards Samarcand with a formidable and well-disciplined force. He was encountered half-way by Timur, who, before engaging with the enemy, assembled his army and delivered to them the following short and singular speech :—" This day, brave soldiers, is a day of dancing for warriors, the dancing-room of heroes is the field of battle, the cries of war are the songs sung and danced, and the wine that is drunk is the blood of the enemy." They then attacked and completely routed the followers of Hussein, compelling them to flee to the deserts; but, nevertheless, a few months after the insurgent chief had so efficiently reinforced his scattered troops as to renew the contest, and the war was continued on each side with redoubled rage and violence. At length, having been defeated in many battles, his fortresses besieged, and his forces totally dispersed, Hussein was taken prisoner, and led trembling before his injured conqueror; but Timur received his captive most courteously, granting him his release on condition that he should proceed on a pilgrimage to Mecca, and replying to a neighbouring sheik, whose brother Hussein had slain, and who sent to request Timur to avenge the murder by taking his captive's life :—" Leave him who hath offended you in the hands of time, for time and fortune will avenge you." *
According to his Persian historian, Timur shed tears after the interview, in which he had parted from his formerly dearest friend; and the sheik, fearing that the remembrance of their ancient affection had overcome his prudence and anger, and that he had suffered the wretched man to escape only to raise another revolt, caused Hussein to be waylaid

* A quotation from a Persian poet.

and assassinated in a lonely spot, before he had proceeded many miles on his route. But though the conqueror had dealt so leniently with the emir, yet he punished the other insurgents with the greatest severity; two of Hussein's sons who had fallen into his hands were burned, and their ashes cast into the air; two more fled to India, where they perished; the rebel khan was put to death; his palace, with that of the emir, razed to the ground, and every recollection of the rebellion and its chief obliterated and crushed.

In 1369, immediately after the suppression of the revolt, Timur was unanimously elected to the imperial throne of Samarcand by his officers and chiefs; he being at that time thirty-three years of age.

From this period his life, as it had indeed been before, was one continued scene of war and bloodshed. It would require too much space to enumerate all the events of the thirty-five campaigns in which he swept through Asia in his desolating course; of these, written it is believed from his dictation by the hand of his secretary, he has left us a full account in the "commentaries of his life" and the "institutions of his government." Here, though he manifests some correct ideas of the duties of a sovereign, which he tries to prove that he had signally fulfilled, he numbers among them the enforcement and propagation by arms of the Mussulman faith, and extensive conquests; and approves the axiom, that when a prince has issued a command, though he becomes sensible it is wrong, he ought nevertheless to require its execution, lest his authority should be compromised or disregarded. He studied in his empire to promote justice and the prosperity of his subjects, and nominally employed a council in his government, which he conducted, according to the code of laws bequeathed by Zingis Khan, in tradition, not writing, to his descendants; and he established officers independent of each other, and subject to his will alone, over the various provinces of his empire, in the same manner that has usually been pursued by powerful sovereigns in the East, and after the same system that Napoleon attempted, in later times, to introduce into Europe. Though he generally permitted criminals to stand a fair trial, his anger occasionally overcame his sense of justice, and he would cause those who had offended him, abused their trust, or ruled tyrannically, to be beheaded without a moment's delay: less guilty political offenders were punished by exile to the deserts of Mongolia, near the mountains of Altai, or by degradation from their rank; and he never permitted the interest of any private individuals to interfere with a public work. Most of the eastern writers, dazzled by his victories and fame, and regarding him as the champion of their faith, and the zealous follower and defender of the precepts and creed of the prophet, extol the liberality with which he distributed among his followers the treasures and spoil he had acquired in war, the hospitals and charitable institutions that were built by his command, the piety with which he rigidly performed all the penances and offices of his religion, the lenity of his rule over those of his subjects, who peacefully submitted to the rule of his sway, his virtues as a relation and friend, and his unfailing and indomitable courage; but the historians of the time in Europe shuddered at his very name, and reproach him with every infamy and vice, from the basest cowardice * and pusillanimity, to the most savage and wanton cruelty. Indeed the destruction he created, and the horrible massacres committed by his order upon the defenceless prisoners whom the fate of war had thrown into his power, though his eulogists have attempted to excuse them, by alleging political necessity and self-preservation, his most bitter enemy could hardly exaggerate; and if the story, so often repeated and believed, of his condemning his captive Bajazet to the confinement of an iron cage, where the unhappy prince, by dashing out his brains against the bars, shortly terminated his miserable life, has been long since exploded and proved to be a mere fable; yet in Persia, India, Georgia, and Kipzak, the atrocities of Timur have been seldom equalled in history, and, considering that the Monguls then possessed a comparative degree of civilization, certainly never surpassed.

While Zingis fought ostensibly to establish the doctrine of one God, and to root alike from the earth every nation of Mahometans, Jews, Christians, and idolaters, and all who attempted to exalt any prophet, saint, or lawgiver, to an equality or approximation to the one Supreme Being, Timur professed to make war alone for the glory and propagation of the Mussulman faith, and to spread to the uttermost parts of the earth the creed and doctrines of the prophet. His

---

* Arabshah accuses him of concealing himself in women's clothes, during the engagement before Fars, though Shereleddin Ali gives a very different account.

army was governed by the same regulations that had kept in unity and discipline the enormous forces of the first Mongul conqueror, whose laws and military directions had been rigidly obeyed by his successors, and from whom there is not a Tartar chief, between Russia and the walls of Pekin, who does not claim his authority and descent. Every officer and soldier was made responsible, under pain of death, for the life and honour of his companions; courtesy, honesty, and justice was required in their intercourse with each other, and capital punishment was inflicted for murder, perjury, and the robbery of an ox or a horse. It had also been enjoined by Zingis Khan to his successors and descendants, that, when once having undertaken a war, the Monguls should neither give quarter nor peace unless at the humble and earnest prayer of a conquered and suppliant enemy; but Timur, on his first accession to the imperial throne, showed neither selfish nor immoderate ambition, and only undertook his first foreign war when urged by the necessity of self-defence.

About the year 1370, the troubles that arose in Kipzak, which had rent that kingdom into several independent sovereignties, which each owned a separate khan, compelled Toktamish, a prince of the royal house, and the son of the assassinated Urus, to yield his father's throne to another Urus, and fly from his country; and, entreating the protection of Timur, he was received by the emperor with the greatest kindness, and obtained the command of a province.* No sooner was he established in Otrar and Sabran,† his new government, which, bordering on the shores of the Aral,‡ approached the confines of Kipzak, than Cotluc Bonga, a son of the khan of Yaik, or Astrakhan, from which place the exiled prince had fled, brought a large army against him; but though he defeated Toktamish, who was left stripped and wounded upon the field, he was himself killed in the fight. His brother, Touka Kaya, made a vow to revenge his death; and his father sent ambassadors to Timur with a letter, of which the following was the purport :—" Toktamish has killed my son, and has fled for refuge to you; you ought to deliver up

* Sherefeddin Ali's "History of Timur Bek."
† Otrar and Sabran are two cities on the Gihon.
‡ It is generally supposed that the Aral Sea formed a bay of the Caspian; for it is not mentioned by any geographer or historian, either of ancient or modern times, till a very recent period, and the isthmus between them is now a mere sandy marsh, intersected with lakes.

this prince, who is my enemy; if you refuse, I declare war against you, and there remains nothing more for us to do than to meet in the field of battle." To this demand the emperor replied—" Toktamish has put himself under my protection, and I will defend him. Return to Urus Khan and inform him, that I not only accept his challenge, but that my preparations are already begun, and my valiant soldiers have no other duty than the trade of war. They are lions, who, instead of living in forests, have their residence in camps and armies."

The ambassadors of Astrakhan having returned to their master, Timur marched to encounter the troops of Kipzak; but the two armies were overtaken by the winter in the barren steppes between the Caspian and Samarcand, and remained for several months within a few leagues of each other's quarters, both incapacitated for action by the deep snow and excessive cold. But on the approach of spring the emperor advanced; and, having inflicted a signal defeat on the enemy's troops, forced him to retire across his borders; after which, Timur, placing his vanguard under the command of Toktamish, who acted as a guide, led his forces into Kipzak. He captured and pillaged several towns on the frontiers, and slew all the inhabitants; when, the death of Urus taking place, and his eldest son, Touka Kaya, a few months after following him to the grave, Toktamish was placed on the throne with little opposition, and the emperor returned to Samarcand. Again the restored prince was forced to fly before the arms of Timur Melik, another son of Urus; but, owing to the depravity and misconduct of this chief, when he had recovered his crown, was again reinstated by the Zagataians, and the following year Mamai, the khan of Serai, having sustained the terrible defeat at Koulikoff, from Demetrius of Moscow, on the shores of the Don, where, after the battle, thirteen miles were strewn with the bodies of the slain, Toktamish marched an army along its banks and possessed himself of the capital, and so again united in one empire the divided tribe of Toushi in Kipzak. It was a year after this event that he invaded Russia, and burned and sacked Moscow, which was defended by a prince of the royal family; and, having demanded from the Muscovites a rouble for every eighty of their slaughtered countrymen, upon whom they wished to bestow the last solemn funeral rites, the boyards ransomed with a sum of three thousand silver roubles two hundred and forty thousand of their dead.*

Persia which, since the death of Abou Said, the last successor of Holagon, had been a prey to dissension and misrule, and divided among various minor chiefs, by the unprovoked inroad of one of her princes upon Bokhara, and a short and fruitless siege of Samarcand, drew upon herself a fearful retribution from the Monguls, and Timur descended upon her plains with an overwhelming force. Instead of uniting for the purpose of mutual defence, each province rashly attempted to oppose him separately and alone, and the army of each was swept like dust from before his troops on their advance. Shah Mansour, prince of Fars, whose character is stained with the grossest cruelty, and who had caused † the eyes of several Persian princes to be put out when, flying from before the invaders, they had taken refuge in his state, though one of the least powerful, was almost the sole Iranian chief who opposed the Monguls with ability and energy, and firmly resisted their progress. Before Shiraz, with only three or four thousand soldiers, he penetrated a battalion of thirty thousand Mongul horse, and, bearing down all before him, advanced to within a yard of the emperor, who fought in the midst. Fourteen guards alone remained around Timur's standard, but he fought with the courage of a common soldier, and kept his ground with a desperation worthy of a struggle for life. Two blows of a scymitar from the hand of Mansour fell upon his helmet, but he remained firm as a rock; his followers, reanimated, closed around him, and in a few seconds the head of the Shah fell before the stroke of Charoc, a youth of seventeen, the youngest son of Timur, who presented it on his knees at his father's feet. Every prince among the Muzaffers, the family of Mansour, was sentenced by the emperor to suffer death, though all the imprisoned chiefs whom he found in the dungeons of Fars he treated with great kindness; and after reinstating those in their dignity who had been blinded or otherwise maltreated by the Shah, he garnished the city of Ispahan with towers of seventy thousand human heads.‡ Then, marching to the shores of the Persian Gulf, he threatened the rich island of Ormuz with

---

* Herberstein "Rerum Muscovitorum."
† Sherefeddin Ali's "History of Timur Bek."
‡ Sherefeddin Ali says that many of the Mongul soldiers, objecting to slaughter Mussulmans in cold blood, brought heads from other executioners, and carried them about as if they themselves had assisted in the savage butchery.

destruction, but spared it upon its immediate submission, and the assent of the peaceful inhabitants to an annual tribute of six hundred thousand dinars of gold.* While he was engaged in this campaign, the inhabitants of Sebzuar were incited by their chief, who had been lately appointed by the emperor, to raise the standard of revolt. Timur marched against them, and, having crushed the rebellion, caused two thousand of the unhappy people who had been taken prisoners to be piled alive, one upon the other, and built up within a lofty brick wall, where they were all left to perish.†

In 1388 Timur invaded Georgia, which, since its conquest by the Monguls under Zingis, had suffered every indignity and degradation ; and, though it still nominally owned the sway of the Tartars, it had incurred their displeasure by refusing to embrace the Mussulman faith, and its people had already prepared for a bold and energetic resistance. The emperor, according to his custom before entering a new country with his army, had previously sent spies to survey the land, who had brought him a faithful report of the strength of its towns and their garrisons, the fords across its rivers, the passes through its mountains, and the roads and tracks over its plains. He almost utterly extirpated the peaceful Chinese colonists in its northern districts, replacing them by Monguls, and drove out the Genoese, who had planted many trading settlements on its coasts, and worked several of the mines in Mingrelia, slaying every inhabitant who refused to declare himself a Mahometan. It was professedly a holy war, and solely for the glory and propagation of the faith of the prophet ; and, surrounding Tiflis with their forces, each soldier shouting "Allah Akbar," "God is great," the Monguls took the city after a furious assault, and led its prince, Isocrates, bound in chains, before their monarch, who granted the captive king his life and freedom upon his consenting to renounce his religion, and afterwards bestowed upon him a high office at his court. The coat of armour which the Georgian had worn during the engagement, and which on his submission he presented to the conqueror, was believed by his credulous people to have belonged to the Jewish king, David, and to have been forged by him in a blacksmith's shop in Judea, and was accordingly held in great reverence both by Chris-

* Gibbon's "Decline and fall of the Roman Empire."
† Sherefeddin Ali's "History of Timur Bek."

tians and Mussulmans, the former of whom bitterly regretted its loss. The prince of Shirvan, to propitiate Timur, brought him presents to the amount of nine times nine, a sacred number among the Tartars; and, having entirely subdued the whole country, the emperor held a grand hunt with his princes and nobles among the hills not far from Tiflis. But many of the inhabitants who had fled for refuge to the wilds of the Caucasus, were pursued even there by the relentless foe, and, having concealed themselves in caves in the most secret recesses in the rocks, were discovered, and expelled from their hiding-places by soldiers let down with ropes from the summits of the crags, who either put them to instant death, or drove them chained together from the mountains, and afterwards sold them for slaves. The province of Daghestan was invaded by an emir of Samarcand, all the natives who were Christians slain, and the worship of the prophet rigorously enforced throughout that district, where it still prevails, the churches and castles of the nobility, and the fortresses and villages of the Caucasus, being all pillaged and sacked. The nations of the Caucasus had long been considered by the Toushi khans as a part of the kingdom of Kipzak, though they had latterly paid her no tribute, and were virtually free and independent; and the invasion of that country gave the pretext to Toktamish which he had long earnestly desired, to throw off his obligations to Timur, and, greatly against the advice and entreaties of his wisest counsellors, to declare war with the Mongul prince. An emir was sent with a large force against him, but sustained a total defeat near Derbend; and the troops of the emperor being required in Persia, where an insurrection had broken out, Timur shortly afterwards quitted Georgia, and desisted for a time from revenging this repulse upon Kipzak. But Toktamish seemed bent upon hastening his own ruin; and, accusing his benefactor of being a base usurper, unlawfully wearing a crown that only belonged as a sacred and indefeasible right to the direct descendants of the emperor Zingis, he penetrated the pass of the Caspian with a force of ninety thousand horse, traversed the desolated Georgia, and advanced on the plains of Persia. While Timur was occupied in quelling a revolt in that kingdom, and not a prince of the imperial house remained in Transoxiana, Toktamish passed the Gihon, and marched towards Samarcand with an army of Russians, Black Bulgarians, and

Tartar and Cossack troops; altogether so numerous, says the Persian historian,* "that poets have compared it to the leaves on the thickest trees, or the drops of rain in the most violent storms." He burned the splendid palace at Zendgi Serai, built by the khan Kazan of Zagatai, and pillaged many towns on his route; and at this moment the death of a favourite daughter of Timur, plunged the emperor into so deep a grief that he appeared totally incapable of action, and indifferent to his throne and empire's fate. But the entreaties and representations of his family and officers at length roused him to exertion, and induced him to make head against the enemy; and, encountering Toktamish in the midst of the wide wastes beyond Bokhara, where the snow was so deep that it reached the horses' girths, he inflicted upon the army of the rebel a fearful and decisive defeat. Passing on, the khan of Kipzak again rallied his force and besieged Sabran, but on the approach of the emperor with the Zagataians, fled, and returned to his own dominions across the Ural or Yaik.

Again Timur for a short period desisted in his pursuit of the fugitive prince, and despatched an army into Mongolia against the Kalmucks, whom his generals followed to their most northern and frozen deserts. The campaign was conducted for five months in the southern regions of Siberia: the Monguls passed over barren plains, and found the rafts and the bridges that the enemy had used in crossing on the dreary shores of the Irtish, and engraved their name and the object of their enterprise upon the trees that sheltered its banks, but no trace of a human being appeared; animal and vegetable life alike faded from before them, and the army subsisted on roots, or the scanty productions of a daily chase. At length, having justified the relinquishment of the pursuit by having reached, as they averred, the dwelling of the sable and the ermine, the land of perpetual daylight, where no true Mahometan could dwell, as he would be forced to dispense with the sunset and midnight prayer enjoined by the laws of the prophet, they retraced their steps and returned to Samarcand, and Timur set out the same year in person, to

* Timur's historian, Sherefeddin Ali, a native of Yezd, was a contemporary. Before his work was translated into French, by M. Petit de Croix, the Eastern traveller, very erroneous ideas regarding the origin and descent of Timur were prevalent in Europe. He was generally represented as an obscure adventurer of mean birth, and one story related that his father was a sort of robber or bandit, and that his lameness was caused by an arrow shot after him by a shepherd, one of whose flock he was attempting to carry off. But Arabshah, his bitter enemy, acknowledges that he was related to the family of Zingis.

revenge the ingratitude of Toktamish. His enormous force stretched over an area of thirteen miles in breadth, and he was accompanied by several exiled princes of the tribe of Toushi, from Kipzak. At a short distance from his capital, the emperor received ambassadors from Toktamish, who brought a submissive and repentant letter* from their master, entreating his pardon and forgiveness; but he refused all the offers of the khan, and marched on.

For six months the Zagataians trod the formidable steppes that extend towards the north to Kipzak, till they reached, says the Persian historian, "a country so near the pole, that in the evening, before the sun had finally disappeared in the west, the first brilliant rays of the morning were beginning to shine in the east." They halted at the foot of the Uralian mountains, denominated by the Muscovites the Girdle of the Earth, near where the troops of Toktamish were encamped; daily skirmishes took place between the scouts and foragers of either army, and each side anxiously awaited the combat. All the sons of the emperor commanded detachments of his forces, which, when ranged in order of battle,

---

* TOKTAMISH'S LETTER TO TIMUR.

"Your Majesty has always performed the part of a father to me; you have always treated me as your son, and the favours I have received from you are innumerable. If my wicked proceedings, and the war I have carried on by the instigation of malicious persons, who are the authors of my evil, of which I repent and am ashamed, can once more find pardon from the clemency of my lord, this will be an addition to the obligations I owe to him; this goodness will make me think of what I am, and hereafter, far from acting against your majesty, I will only consult your pleasure in token of my respect and thankfulness."

TIMUR'S REPLY TO THE AMBASSADORS.

"When your master Toktamish was wounded and ill-used by his enemies, and came for refuge to us, every one knows that I ranked him among my children, and treating him with kindness, looking upon his interest as my own, I made war on Urus Khau, and marched my troops against him; in which march I lost great part of my cavalry, with an infinite number of riches and equipments through the cold, which that winter was extremely violent. Notwithstanding this misfortune, I endeavoured to maintain and defend him against every one. I separated his country and subjects from those of Urus Khan and put them into his hands; at length I rendered him so powerful that he was crowned emperor of Kipzak, and ascended the throne of Toushi. I confess, indeed, that this good fortune came from God; but, at the same time, I know that I have been the instrument of it, and the friendship I felt for him induced me to call him son, while he called me father. When he saw himself powerful, and fortune had become favourable to him, he forgot the obligations he owed to me, and, without thinking in what manner a son ought to behave towards a father, took the opportunity, while I had marched into Persia, and was subduing the land of the Medes and Persians, to betray me, and commit acts of hostility against me. He had sent his troops to ruin the borders of my kingdom; I did not notice it that he might consider with himself, be ashamed, and for the future abstain from such extravagance. But, too drunk with ambition to distinguish good from evil, he has sent another army to invade my dominions. It is true that, as soon as we began to march against the vanguard, they fled before they could perceive the dust our horses made; and now Toktamish asks for pardon, because no other way appears able to save him from his well-merited punishment. But, since he has so frequently violated his oaths and treaties, it would be imprudent to rely on his promises. We will execute, with the assistance of God, the resolution we have taken, that all the world may see that God punishes ingratitude. Yet whatever reason we have for making war and exterminating him, if he will but tell the truth, and sincerely desire peace, he must send Ali Bey (his first minister) to meet us, and to negotiate with our emirs, and we will do whatever is consistent with our dignity and the present conjuncture."—Sherefeddin Ali's "History of Timur Bek."

were divided into seven parts, seven being a sacred number with the Tartars; while the army of Toktamish, whose generals and captains were all princes of the royal house, were placed in the form of a crescent. Before engaging with the enemy, every Zagataian soldier knelt in prayer, and the dervishes paraded their ranks reciting passages and texts from the Alcoran, accompanied by the beating of kettle-drums and music; and the soothsayers, throwing dust in the direction of the foe, exclaimed with loud piercing shouts, "Your faces shall be blackened with the shame of your defeat!" On the 6th of July, 1391, the two armies commenced the attack, and even their enemies have recorded how well that day the followers of Toktamish fought. They drove back and defeated the whole horde of Selduz, and for a moment caused the enemy to waver; then Timur in person routed their main body, but his rival again brought up the flank; and the fate of the day was at length only decided by the treachery of a standard-bearer, who, reversing the flag of his countrymen, raised that of Zagatai in the midst of the squadrons of Kipzak, causing their general to suppose that the enemy had penetrated his ranks. This producing a confusion, it was increased by a cavalry shock, and, to use Timur's own words in his "Institutions," "Toktamish gave the horde of Toushi to the wind of desolation." He fled, his whole army was tumultuously dispersed, and for the space of eighty miles, where they were pursued by the enemy, nothing was to be seen but broken bows, scattered standards, the plains strewn with the bodies of the dead, and lakes and pools of blood. Immediately after the battle, Timur dismounted from his horse, and, according to his usual custom, kneeling down on the field, first returned thanks to the Almighty for his success, and then deputed seven out of every ten horsemen in his army to go in pursuit of the fugitives. But few of the unfortunate tribe of Toushi succeeded in making their escape; before them was the Volga, behind them enemies on every side; all their women, children, and baggage, became the prey of the conquerors, who returned loaded with plunder and slaves to Samarcand, and the emperor chose Coudge Aglen of the royal family of Zingis to ascend the throne of Kipzak.*

Yet even this terrible defeat could not utterly destroy the fortunes and influence of the Toushi prince, and within less

* Sherefeddin Ali's "History of Timur Bek."

than five years after the battle, Toktamish had not only reestablished himself on his throne, and driven out the new khan from Serai, but had invaded the territories of Timur, to retrieve the losses of his chiefs, who persuaded him to undertake this campaign, and repair his own disgrace. The emperor received this intelligence while engaged in quieting a disturbance in Georgia, and immediately marching towards Kipzak, encountered the army of Toktamish on the 18th of June, 1395, on the banks of the Terek in the Caucasus, and after a long and for some time doubtful combat, put the enemy's forces to flight. The cousin of Jaghellon, the Grand Duke Vitold, then ruled Lithuania, and he gave the fugitive Toktamish shelter at his court; while his followers, being scattered over the steppes, Timur pursued his victorious career with four hundred thousand men into Europe. He burned and pillaged every Russian village and town on his route, and advanced as far as Kolomna, on the Oka, within a short distance of Moscow; where the inhabitants, on hearing of his approach, had sent to Vladimir for their famous image of the virgin of Ephesus, and, advancing from the capital, carried it before their ranks. The retreat which Timur made towards Serai they attributed to her influence, which, they say, caused him to be visited with a troubled dream; and, placing the image over a gate at Moscow, where it still remains,* the Russians have ever considered it as the palladium of that city, and its most powerful guardian and defence; but "the Muscovites," says the Persian historian, "never saw their empire in so terrible a state as this; for while their fields were covered with the slain, the army loaded themselves with the most precious spoil of their cities, and every soldier obtained so large a share of gold ingots, silver blades, Antioch flax, armed skins of Condoz, cloth woven in Russia with great skill, black sables, and ermines, furs unknown to the Zagataians, and horses, and young unshod colts, that it was sufficient to furnish both himself and his children to the end of their lives. From Little Russia or the Ukraine they also took enormous droves of cattle, and multitudes of women and girls of all ages, of wonderful shape and beauty."

At Riazan, Timur took the prince captive amidst the ashes of his capital, and, diverging towards the south, swept the banks of the Don, and, encamping on its shores, received a

* It was left untouched by the French, when they sacked Moscow.

terrified deputation from the consuls and merchants of Egypt, Venice, Genoa, Catalonia, and Biscay, who were established at the rich and extensive trading city of Azof; and brought him presents to propitiate his avarice, entreating him to spare and protect their warehouses and ships.* He received them graciously, and despatched an emir to inspect their harbour and magazines; but the undefended wealth they displayed, was too great to be resisted by his soldiers or their chief, and the inhabitants mourned among the ruins of their citadel, the credulity that had made them trust for a moment to the mercy or forbearance of a Mongul conqueror. The Mahometans of Azof were merely pillaged and then dismissed; but every Christian who had not fled to the vessels outside the port, was condemned either to death or slavery; and even the Noghai Tartars of the desert were compelled by the victors to fly to the extremity of their inhospitable steppes. Ravaging the country of the Cossacks to the north of the Caucasus, the Zagataians put all whom they had captured to the sword; and crossing the ice, which was three feet in thickness, robbed even the huts of the humble fishermen who lived on the islands in the Don, carrying all the inhabitants away for slaves to the imperial camp. Serai, the capital of Kipzak, was razed to the ground, and suspecting Mahmoudi, the governor of Astrakhan, of treason, Timur sent an emir to that city to reduce it. It was in the middle of the winter, which was that year unusually severe, and at this season the inhabitants were accustomed to build a wall of ice round their town to defend it, through which they placed an archway and a gate.† The Mongul general besieged it, but without succeeding in obtaining an entrance till the arrival of the emperor in person, when the inhabitants tendered their submission, and were permitted to remove their cattle and goods from Astrakhan. Immediately afterwards, Timur caused the city to be razed to the ground, and the governor Mahmoudi to be drowned in the Volga; and he was accordingly thrust under the ice. All the plunder that had been seized throughout Kipzak was then divided among the Mongul soldiers and chiefs, to reward them for the sufferings they had undergone from the excessive cold: multitudes of both

* Gibbon's "Decline and Fall of the Roman Empire."
† Sherefeddin Ali says, "and as the river is frozen in the winter, they usually build a wall of ice as strong as one of brick, upon which they fling water in the night that the whole may congeal and become one piece, to which wall they make a gate."

X

horses and men had perished, and famine was at one time so great in their camp, that a pound of millet sold for seventy dinars, a sheep's head for a hundred, and that of an ox for three hundred and fifty. They then slowly abandoned the country, after ravaging the southern provinces of Russia to the borders of Lithuania and Hungary, and returned with their emperor to Georgia, where he carried his arms to the most remote valleys and recesses of the Caucasus.*

While Timur was overrunning Russia in the east, Vitold of Lithuania had attacked her in the west; and courteously receiving the unfortunate Toktamish at his court, he agreed to assist that prince in the recovery of his dominions, on condition that he would relinquish to Lithuania all claim and suzerainety over the Russian states. This proposal being accepted, the dauntless Tartar once more found himself the commander of a numerous military force, and with Vitold he assembled at Kiof a powerful army, composed of Lithuanians,† Russians, Poles, and Wallachians, a small body of his own followers, and five hundred well-equipped and armed horsemen, sent to his assistance by the grand master of the order of Teutonic knights. They marched to the river Vorskla, on whose shores, in later times, Charles of Sweden met his first and most fatal defeat at Pultowa; and their armament appeared so formidable to Timur Cotluc, the new khan of Kipzak, that he proposed terms of peace, and even offered to pay an annual tribute. But this compromise was refused by the allied princes, whom nothing less would satisfy than his kingdom and crown; and he was fearfully awaiting their attack, when the arrival of Edigée, a general of Timur's, with a large reinforcement, at his camp, revived the courage and hopes of his soldiers, and decided the fate of the war. On the 12th of August, 1399, the rival forces met, and a fiercely contested battle took place; the victory was long fought for and undecided, but finally Vitold and Toktamish were driven from the field, leaving more than twothirds of their army among the dead, with seventy-five Lithuanian and Russian princes, and many nobles and knights. The Grand Prince Vitold returned to Lithuania, where the Tartars pursued him as far as Volhynia; while Toktamish took refuge in Great Bulgaria, on the Volga, and a few years

* Sherefeddin Ali's " History of Timur Bek."
† Krasinski's " History of Poland."

after closed his checkered career among the pine forests and marshes of the north. His unfortunate Mongul followers, on being deserted by their prince, had accompanied the rest of the army in its retreat to Lithuania; and, too few to attempt to penetrate through the intermediate hostile states to their own native steppes, they wandered about as vagrants and outlaws, supporting themselves by hunting in the forests, till Vitold granted them permission to settle on the waste lands in Lithuania, where they founded a colony; and their officers and mirzas were enrolled among the Polish nobility, adopting Polish coats-of-arms and crests. There, the descendants of these fugitives still adhere to the creed of the Koran, and in Grodno, Minsk, Vilna, and several other towns, erected mosques, where they still worship the prophet; and, repaying their adopted country for the protection she afforded them by an unshaken fidelity to her interests, have ably supported her in all her troubles and wars, even those against their co-religionists the Turks; and all classes of this community are proverbial among the natives of Poland for their peaceful industry, integrity, and honesty, in every branch or transaction of life.*

Immediately after the defeat of Toktamish, and while Timur was engaged in a distant Indian campaign, the khan of Kipzak renounced his allegiance to the throne of Samarcand, and attempted to drive from the country the Zagatai generals who had so successfully assisted him in the war. He died in the beginning of the year 1400, and his successor, Boulet Sultan, succeeded in expelling the emirs from the district about Serai, one of whom, Kostlogh, established a kingdom at Kazan; and another proclaimed himself lord of Astrakhan and of all the contiguous districts on the Yaik. At the same time, the Muscovites possessed themselves of Great Bulgaria, which for years had been much harassed by the armies of the republic of Novogorod; and driving out the khan, who had made himself independent of Kipzak, and forcing him to fly to Kazan, they utterly ruined the town of Bulgari,† where the wall, an archway, and a few other curious monuments, are the sole vestiges now to be seen of this

---

* Krasinski's "History of Poland."
† "The site of Bulgari is sixty miles from Kazan. It stood in a rich and fertile plain, and still boasts some interesting monuments of antiquity. The wall which encompassed the city is still traceable, and is four miles in circumference. At present, a small village and church occupy a part of the site, the gardens being actually spread over a bed of human bones."—Cochrane's "Journey to Siberia."

capital of the last remaining province of the enormous empire of the once powerful and victorious Huns.*

In the year 1399, the Grand Prince of Lithuania made peace with Basil, or Vassili of Muscovy, and a treaty of alliance being formed between them, it was further cemented by the marriage of Basil with Anastasia, the daughter of Vitold, who took the name of Sophia, when, according to custom, she embraced the Greek faith. The reign of Basil is one of the most disastrous that occurs in the annals of Russia, and for a third time within twenty years, Moscow was fated to tremble before the armies of an invader. Boulet Sultan, wishing to establish himself more firmly than his predecessors on the throne, and gain the esteem and affection of his subjects, by leading them to victory and plunder, under the pretext of espousing the cause of several malecontents among the native Russian princes and chiefs, marched against their capital, from which Vassili fled; and, burning and sacking the city, inflicted the most horrible cruelties upon the unhappy people, returning laden with the spoil of the whole province to his camp on the shores of the Don. As this foray took place in the winter, and thousands in the surrounding districts and villages had been rendered houseless and destitute by the invaders, multitudes perished from want and cold; the following year many more were swept away by famine; an earthquake destroyed two-thirds of the houses in Novogorod; and the plague, which had been introduced by the Tartars, raged violently for many months throughout the land. The assembly of the citizens in Moscow had been abolished in the preceding reign, and the indolence of the Grand Prince threw all the government of the empire into the hands of his boyards, who rendered his name odious to his subjects by their exactions and oppression; they only had access to his person, and through their intervention was obtained every audience, privilege, or pardon from the Czar. The forms and ceremonies in vogue at this period at the Muscovite court, presented an almost exaggerated reflection of the servile prostrations before the Emperor Timur at Samarcand, and in the palaces of the other sovereigns of the East. The prince reclined nearly all the day on a divan, with his courtiers and favourites ranged on cushions around, while a

* Rubruquis, who passed through Bulgaria on his way to Karacorum, mentions that it was still called Hungary by the inhabitants.

juggler entertained them with his feats; Polish, Greek, or Wallachian slaves danced before them, or the musicians sang their songs in praise of Vladimir and the ancient heroes of Russia, or played on their bagpipes and lutes. The place of honour was on the left hand side of the monarch,* as being nearest the heart, and was usually occupied by the fool or jester, retained at every palace of the princes or of the nobility, to banish melancholy or despondency with his jests, anecdotes, and wit. A hunt occasionally relieved the monotony of existence at the court; for the sports of falconry, hawking, and chase, were followed with the greatest ardour by both Russians and Tartars of every rank. But the whole empire groaned under the heavy taxation which was exacted by the prince, to enable him to pay the annual tribute to the Monguls, and support his own retinue and numerous dependants; and though the Tartar garrisons had long been removed from many of the towns, as they had been recalled by the troubles in Kipzak; yet levies of recruits for their armies were constantly drawn by the khans, and the silver coin in Russia, which was first cast in Moscow and Tver at the end of the fourteenth century, bore an inscription in the language of the Monguls. About this time, in the year 1404, the first striking clock seen in Russia was erected in the capital by a Servian of the name of Lazarus, and many other improvements in manufactures and arts appear to have taken place. The ancient arms of Moscow, when it was an independent principality, had been the figure of St. George mounted on a white horse, on a red field; and when this city became the capital of the empire, its banner was adopted by the Grand Princes, instead of the three triangles, which had formerly been borne by the sovereigns of Kiof. In 1380, after the victory over the Tartars at Koulikoff, a slight change was effected by Demetrius Donskoi, who added the vanquished dragon to St. George, a dragon being symbolical of the Tartar nations as well as those of the Slavonic race. Upon the flag of Novogorod was represented two bears, supporting an altar on the ice; with, over it, two crucifixes crossed before a picture of the Virgin, and a candelabrum with a triple lustre, emblematical of the Trinity.†

---

* This is still the case among the Chinese and Tartar nations.
† Clarke's "Travels in Russia."

In 1388, upon the death of Hedwige the queen of Poland, without children, her husband, Jagiello, still retained possession of the Polish crown; and shortly after espousing Sophia, the daughter of his subject, the Prince Andrea Ivanovitz of Kiof, he had by her two sons, both of whom ultimately succeeded him as kings of Poland.*

* Sir Jerome Horsey's "Travels in Russia."

CHAPTER II.

Timur invades India—The Gipsies.

> Land of the Sun! what foot invades
> Thy pagods and thy pillar'd shades?
> Thy cavern shrines and idol stones,
> Thy monarchs and their thousand thrones?
> Moore's "Lallah Rookh."

WHILE Toktamish was encountering his last overthrow on the banks of the Vorskla in Russia, Timur had contemplated and undertaken a still more hazardous and stupendous expedition than any which his ambition had yet formed, or his generals even conceived. This was the subjugation of India; and when he first proposed it in his council to the emirs,* he was responded to with murmurs of disapprobation and discontent, and exaggerated reports of the real and fabulous dangers that lurked among its distant woods and rocks. They predicted that, beneath its sultry sky, the children of Zingis would degenerate into effeminate Hindoos; and the mighty rivers, the unknown beasts, armed elephants, and steel-clad troops, presented a frightful picture to their imaginations, and struck terror into their hearts. But the emperor's determination was immoveable, and his commands were more potent than their fears, and, in 1398, the army and its sovereign set forth.

Since its conquest, nearly four centuries before, by the Seljuk Tartars, under Mahmoud of Ghizni, India had been ruled by several successive dynasties, all of princes of the Mahometan faith. They had twice repulsed the descendants

---

* He proposed it in these words—"Fortune, my children, furnishes us with such happy opportunities, that it appears as if she offered herself to us, and called upon us to profit by them. For, as we have already seen the empires of Iran and Turan, and almost all Asia under our command, she now shows us India, through the disorders of the princes who govern her, opening her gates to receive us. My name has spread terror throughout the universe, and the least movement I make is capable of shaking the earth. It is therefore time to invade Hindoostan, where, having overcome what opposes our designs, we shall oblige this kingdom to acknowledge no other sovereign but me. What think ye, my children—companions of my victories—of this great and glorious undertaking? Speak all, and each one alone, and let me know your opinion of this proposal, which appears to me reasonable, since fortune has not yet withdrawn her protection from us."

of Zingis in Transoxiana, called by the Hindoos Mavar-ul-Nahar, who had poured with a mighty force upon their plains; in the first instance, defeating the Monguls from before the strongly fortified city of Lahore, and the second time driving back their army when they had advanced as far as Delhi with two hundred thousand men. But the country had been debased and degraded by the tyranny and atrocities of her princes ; and now in the days of Timur, and since the death of its sultan Firouz in 1389, while far before the northern nations in the arts, sciences, and learning of refined and civilized life, it had been a prey to civil war, misrule, and a barbarous and destructive anarchy. Mahmoud, the nominal sultan of Delhi, was a mere boy and of inferior capacity, and the administration of public affairs was in the hands of his uncles, one of whom ruled at Moultan, the other at the capital; while the crown being disputed by Nuserit, the grandson of Firouz, the soubahs of the provinces had raised the standard of revolt, and all the cities of northern India were asserting and fighting for their independence.

Pir Mahomet, the grandson of Timur, had been invested by the emperor with the government of Cabul and Candahar, and, availing himself of the disturbed state of Hindoostan, the Mongul khan sent directions to this prince to proceed across the Indus into the Punjab, and besiege the city of Moultan ; while he himself, after appointing his grandson Omar Sheik as regent, marched with ninety-two squadrons, each consisting of a thousand horse, from Samarcand. Crossing the Oxus by a bridge of boats, which his army constructed of reeds in two days, Timur advanced to the foot of that extensive branch of the Himalayas known as the Hindoo Kosh, and exterminating several tribes of mountain robbers, who dwelt in its valleys and defiles, and among whom were the Siapouches, who increased the terror which their depredations inspired among the surrounding people, by always clothing in black ; he caused his army, which consisted entirely of cavalry, to be transported with ropes and pulleys over the more stupendous rocks, he himself being carried down five precipices on a platform, each of which required cords of one hundred and fifty cubits in length. But his ingenuity was unable to triumph over the rigorous atmosphere of so lofty an elevation, and multitudes of men and horses perished from the cold, or were smothered and lost in the snow.

He then encamped on the plains of Cabul, where he spent some time in regulating the affairs of this lately conquered province, and caused an aqueduct of five miles long to be constructed in a district where water had formerly been very scarce. He also received ambassadors here from various parts of Asia, and his lieutenant, the Emir Noureddin from Persia, who brought so immense a treasure of jewels, birds, rare animals, silk, and velvet from Ispahan, that the secretaries and comptrollers of the divan were employed three days in merely numbering the amount. The emperor distributed them among his generals and principal officers, and sent back the foreign envoys with magnificent presents to the sovereigns of their respective courts.*

After putting down several insurrections that had broken out in various parts of Cabul, and having repaired the strong fortress of Jellabad, where an attempt was treacherously made upon his life, Timur marched towards the frontiers of Hindoostan after giving audience to a fresh embassy from Mecca and Medina, who, in the name of all the princes and sheriffs of Arabia, prayed the conqueror to favour them some day with a visit, and take them under his mighty protection, at the same time offering him the title of caliph, though it was then held by the Ottoman sultan Bajazet. Timur thanked the envoys, and dismissed them with presents, and crossing the Indus at Attok, near the point to which Zingis Khan with his wild hordes had advanced, entered upon the desert of Jerow or Tchal Jelali, so called from the brave Jellaladdin of Carizme, who had forded the river and penetrated these wilds at this spot, when escaping from the fury and sword of the first ruthless and merciless Mongul khan. Following the footsteps of the hero of Macedon, who, more than seventeen hundred years before, had pursued that same route, Timur, after subduing the princes of Lahore and the chief of the isle of Chenaub, united his forces with those of his grandson on the plains of the Punjab, or Seven Rivers, and proceeded to the fortress of Batnir, where all the fugitives from the armies he had already defeated had fled. It was reported to be impregnable, yet he led only ten thousand of his warriors against its walls; and the garrison, who were principally Ghebers, encouraged by so apparently insignificant a foe, adopted the fatal determination of descending from the

* Sherefeddin Ali's "History of Timur Bek."

protection of their ramparts, and offering him battle in the field. At the first tremendous shock of the Monguls the Hindoo troops were entirely dispersed, and the Zagataians soon rendered themselves masters of the whole place except the citadel, which was still held for many hours by the inhabitants with the courage and frenzy of despair.* But the barbarous massacre of all their countrymen who had been captured in the engagement by Timur's army, and which they witnessed from their retreat, extinguishing their last hope of succour, they killed their wives and children, set fire to the fort, and rushing from the flames, waving their sabres, fell fighting to a man among the foe. Thousands of the Monguls perished, and this loss, joined to that which they had sustained in the mountains, and from the attacks of the Kalmucks and other hostile tribes on his route, greatly reduced the strength of his squadrons before Timur had reached Delhi, a distance of six hundred miles from Attok. This city was then divided into three distinctly fortified towns, entered altogether by thirty gates, and here the sultan with his uncles had intrenched themselves with forty thousand foot and ten thousand horse, and might probably, as they were well furnished with provisions, have protracted the siege for many months; while Timur encamped at Gehanumai, a splendid palace, formerly erected by Firouz Shah, and denominated from its beauty "The Mirror of the Universe." But, deceived with a false idea of the enemy's strength, Mahmoud, after a stormy council with his ministers, resolved to meet the Monguls in the field without awaiting their attack, and advanced from the walls with his vizier and whole army, supported by a hundred and twenty elephants, whose sides and trunks bristled with a formidable array of arrows, poisoned daggers, and darts. Before meeting them, the astrologers and soothsayers in the Tartar army consulted the disposition of the heavens; and, imagining that their aspect was unfavourable to the success of the Monguls, endeavoured to dissuade their master from hazarding an engagement, as they were persuaded that during this month it would be assuredly lost. But the emperor told them, that neither joy nor sorrow, adversity nor prosperity, depended upon the planets, but upon the will of the Almighty Creator, the maker of the stars themselves, of the

* Murray's "History of British India."

Universe, and of man. "I confide," said Timur, "in the assistance of God, who has never abandoned me; what avail the conjunctions or movements of the stars! I will never for a moment delay the execution of my projects, when I have taken sufficient measures and precautions to bring them to perfection!" The next morning, in presence of all his forces, the emperor raised a public prayer, and ordering a Koran to be brought to him, from whence he might judge of his enterprise, he opened the book at what he imagined was a favourable answer to his prayer, as it was a passage describing the destruction of a people by the wonderful effect of an Almighty providence. He explained the event in his own favour, and thus re-animated the courage of his men, who, on first sight of the elephants, had been seized with a panic, from the prevalent idea that their skins were invulnerable to either fire or steel; but hearing that the Hindoo prisoners in his camp, who amounted to the enormous number of a hundred thousand, besides women and children, had been seen to smile, when they heard of their countrymen's approach, Timur feared lest the slaves should turn upon their captors in the event of a defeat, and therefore issued the horrible order that every male prisoner should be put to death by his owner before the fight commenced. Such a decree as this appears even to have produced consternation in the iron hearts of the Moguls, so that the emperor was obliged to threaten every warrior with death who refused instantly to carry his order into effect; and he desired, at the same time, that one soldier out of every ten should be appointed to keep watch over the Hindoo women and children who were left in the tents. He also caused a rampart of bucklers to be placed before his camp, and strengthened it with a ditch filled with buffaloes tied fast to the sides; and, brambles being attached to their heads, he commanded that these should be lighted, and the animals let loose, in order to frighten the elephants if the battle went hard with his men. But they afterwards found that there was no occasion to bring this contrivance into use.*

On the 3rd of January, 1401, the Mogul and Hindoo armies first met, and the emperor proceeding to the summit of a neighbouring hill, from whence he could view the combat, spent the whole of the time that it lasted in reciting

* Sherefeddin Ali's "History of Timur Bek."

passages from the Koran and in prayer. "This battle," says Sherefeddin Ali, "was the hottest in which the Monguls had ever yet encountered the foe;" and, upon the total defeat of the Hindoos, the sultan and his vizier fled to Delhi, and, as soon as they themselves had passed into the city, ordered all the gates to be shut. As their unfortunate followers were now deprived of their only hope of escape, they were easily made prisoners by the enemy, and every elephant fell into the hands of Timur, who sent them as presents to his mirzas in Persia and Samarcand; one being led into the camp by his grandson Calil, a boy of fifteen, who, after slaying its bearer in single combat, brought it fastened by a bridle, like a horse, to the tents. That night the Indian sultan with his uncle, the Prince of Moultan, and a few other officers and attendants, secretly abandoned Delhi and fled to Guzerat, and, the intelligence reaching the emperor in the morning, he sent a flying troop in their pursuit, who succeeded in capturing all their baggage, several officers, and a son of the prince; and the same day, the 4th of January, the flag of Zagatai waved over the towers of the capital, and Timur entered the city in triumph. Admiring the magnificent buildings, and profusely decorated temples and palaces, the emperor commanded that they should all be spared by his soldiers, and the masons and architects transported to Samarcand, to adorn his own capital in the same manner, and render it equal in beauty to the extensive and far-famed Delhi, upon which had been lavished every erection and ornament that could be achieved by Hindoo art. Then, entering the palace of the Hindoo sultans, he seated himself upon their gilded throne, and gave an audience to the cadis and principal inhabitants, to whom he promised his protection upon the payment of a ransom, which he desired the council of his divan to appoint. The banner of the Monguls, a horse's tail and two kettle-drums, were fastened over the principal gate, and the musical band of their army performed the tune Rihavi, an air of triumph only played after the greatest achievements.

But, though the emperor had commanded that only a select body of his troops should be permitted to remain in the city, a large crowd followed in the train of the sultanas, the wives of his grandsons Pir Mahomet and Hussein, who had accompanied their husbands during the campaign, and never rested till they had been allowed to visit the interior of this famous capital with their numerous court; and particularly the celebrated palace of a thousand columns, built by an ancient king of Hindoostan. Accordingly, the following night a tumult arose between these intruders and the Gheber inhabitants, and several Mongul soldiers being killed, their comrades revenged them on the citizens, a serious affray commenced, and Delhi was sacked and pillaged by the Tartar army, almost unrestrained by their chief, who left it with a portion of his forces on the 18th of January, and proceeded to exterminate the settlements of the Ghebers* or fire-worshippers, on the Ganges. After fighting many battles, both by land and water, he completely destroyed all the Indian votaries of that faith, causing their chief to be thrown, when dead, into the fire he adored, and his followers barbarously flayed alive; and penetrating into the valleys of the Himalayas, where he extirpated many ancient tribes, and drove others to seek shelter in distant lands, he proceeded to the banks of the Indus, which on the 28th of March he crossed; his conquests in Hindoostan, from the time that he quitted Samarcand, having only occupied the short period of nine months.†

On his return, the emperor caused a large hospital to be built for his fatigued and wounded men in the chief town of Cabul, and joined here the empress, and the princes his sons, who had departed from Transoxiana to meet him, and congratulate him upon his glorious campaign. But, as he was taken seriously ill on his march homeward, the result of over-anxiety and fatigue, he was forced to descend from horseback and proceed in a litter, in which, after a little more than a year's absence, he finally arrived in Samarcand.‡

After the emperor's departure from Hindoostan, his officers and successors exercised very little authority over the regions to the east of the Indus; money indeed was coined in his name, and its princes owned his rule and authority, but each province assumed a temporary independence, till, in the year 1413, the viceroy of Moultan seized the throne of Delhi as the representative of the Mongul khan, and during his reign, which was conducted with ability and vigour, the empire began to recover its former union and strength. Upon his

---

* The Ghebers had fled to this spot from Persia and Georgia, when they were overrun by the conquering Saracens, and, after the destruction of their settlement on the Ganges, many returned to Bakh.
† Sherefeddin Ali's "History of Timur Bek."
‡ Murray's "History of British India."

death, the three sultans who successively governed Hindoostan gradually released themselves from their nominal allegiance to Samarcand; the last of these, Bheloli, ruling with firmness and energy for a period of thirty-eight years, and leaving his crown to his son, Secunder I. But in the year 1526, and during the reign of Ibrahim, the son of Secunder, the throne was again seized by a Tartar prince; and the khan Baber of Kokan, a great-grandson of Timur,* with an army of 13,000 horsemen, establishing the dynasty of the Monguls or Moguls, his posterity ruled India till they fell before the British power, and the only children of the great Emperor of Zagatai, who still retained a kingly crown and state, became from henceforward her imperial pensioners, and humiliated though still haughty dependants.

A remarkable and yet lingering result of the conquest of India by Timur, was the emigration of the gipsies into Europe, where they first appeared on the borders of Bohemia, in the year 1414. This singular people, who, like the Jews of old, have for more than four centuries so tenaciously retained their identity among foreign nations, and the customs, language, and laws, that they brought from their homes in the East, were long generally supposed to have been Egyptians (hence the word *gipsy* in England, and *gitano* in Spain), from the circumstance that many families travelled first to the banks of the Nile before entering Europe. But it is a strong proof of the fallacy of this belief, that those who are now found there, where, as in other lands, they lead a wandering life, are looked upon as aliens by the inhabitants, and their manners and dialect are perfectly different to those of either the Saracens or Copts. Others have affirmed them to be of Mongul origin, and descendants of the conquered followers of Toktamish, and they are still called Tartars by the Swedes, Norwegians, and Danes; while to the Germans they are only known as Zigeuner or wanderers, and to the Russians and Turks as Zigani and Zingarri, words supposed to be derived from Zincali, the name by which they are sometimes self-designated, and which signifies the "Black Men of Zend or Ind."† But from the latest researches there appears to be little doubt that they originally belonged to one of the

---

* He was a grandson of the Mirza Miran Shah, and has left commentaries, written by himself, of his life, which was most eventful and romantic.
† Porthon.

inferior tribes in Hindoostan,* from whence it is conjectured that they were expelled by the terrible irruption of the Monguls, and this supposition is strengthened by the resemblance, in their appearance and language, to the Sudra or lowest Hindoo caste, and to the Bazegues, who like themselves are a wandering race. It is remarkable that, while they are known in India by a name which means thieves, the same word, with the same signification, is applied to them by the Finns.

The gipsies extend to the number of about 800,000, throughout almost every country in Europe, and are found in the Russian empire as far north as Tobolsk.† They first appeared in Paris in the year 1427, and are mentioned by the chronicles of the time as all riding on horseback, with silver ornaments in their ears, and with hair and complexions perfectly black; and the same propensity to fortune-telling and thieving appears to have characterized them then as it does at the present day.

* The following table shows the resemblance of the gipsy dialects throughout Europe to the Hindoostanee:—

English.	German Gipsy.	English Gipsy.	Hungarian Gipsy.	Spanish Gipsy.	Hindoostanee
Gold	Sonnikey	Sonnekar	Sonkay	Sonacal	Suna
Water	Panj	Parnee	Pani	Pani	Panj
House	Ker	Karo	Ker	Quer	Ger
Eye	Aok	Yock	Jakh	Aquia	Awk
Nose	Nah	Nack	Nakh	Naqui	Nakh
One	Ek	Yake	Jek	Yeque	Ek
Two	Duj	Duea	Dui	Dui	Dw
Three	Trin	Trin	Trau	Trin	Trin
Four	Schtar	Stor	Schtar	Estar	Ischar
Five	Pautsch	Pau	Punsch	Pansche	Pausch

† Gullmin.

CHAPTER III.

Timur marches against Georgia, Syria, and the Ottomans.— Captures Bajazet.

> Ecbatana is thine; the Euphrates, Persia,
> And glorious Egypt, with the Indian shores,
> Shall fall beneath thy yoke.—VOLTAIRE'S "Les Scythes."

THOUGH Timur was now more than sixty years of age, and his hair, we are informed by his contemporaries, was as white as snow, his ambition had remained uncooled, and his vigilance and energy unabated, and every fresh conquest he had achieved appeared only to increase his insatiable love of war. It was his favourite saying, that "as there was only one God in heaven, so should there be only one monarch upon earth;" and, as soon as he had returned to Samarcand, he began to prepare troops and resources for another and a seven years' campaign. His presence indeed was immediately required by the troubles in Georgia and Persia, where the Mirza Miran Shah had become insane, owing to a blow he had received in a fall from his horse. The Mirza Pir Mehemed, who was skilled in chemistry and medicines, had been accused of attempting to poison his brother, and affairs were in the utmost confusion, the government having been left entirely in the hands of officers and court dependants, who wasted and exhausted the revenues of the state in banquets and fêtes, while the princes increased the expenditure by enormous presents to their unworthy favourites; yet Timur already contemplated a more distant enterprise when he should have quelled the disturbances in the provinces. He had long seen with impatience the rapid growth of the Ottoman empire, which now approached his own borders, and the progress she had made, under her sultan Bajazet I., began to make him fear that, now he was growing old, a rival would supplant his family in the dominion of the world, and the vicinity of this powerful nation filled his mind with misgivings and mistrust.

Having employed the architects whom he had transported from Delhi in building a palace at Samarcand, and deputed to the most famous of his emirs the conduct of a military expedition in the northern districts of Asia; the emperor left his capital on the 11th of October, 1399, and proceeded first to Persia, where he condemned his grandson Mirza Mehemed to the bastinado, caused his son to be placed in confinement, and punished his attendants and the officers of his household, who, availing themselves of the insanity of the shah, had encouraged his extravagance, and turned it to their own advantage and profit. From Persia he entered Georgia, where a more serious difficulty awaited him. Her prince, Isocrates Bagration, whom he had formerly taken prisoner, and induced, by the fear of a cruel death, to become a Mahometan, after residing for some years in Transoxiana, had requested to be allowed to return to his native land, to convert to Islamism, as he affirmed, his Christian subjects. Timur fell into the snare, and, advising the deposed king to employ compulsion, granted him the assistance of a body of Mongul cavalry for that purpose; but no sooner had Bagration arrived in his own dominions, and the emperor engaged in a distant war in Hindoostan, than the prince threw off his assumed creed, and exhorted his subjects to assist him in recovering their independence. But his treachery, which cost him his life, was terribly revenged upon his devoted people: wherever the Monguls had passed the most total desolation and misery remained, the villages and corn-fields were sacked and burned by the enemy, the fruit-trees and vines were uprooted, and every living creature fled from before the fanatical Mahometan troops, who, fired with an intolerant religion, and as they deemed patriotic revenge, massacred or enslaved every Christian whom they encountered on their route. In the first battle in which the Georgians ventured to oppose the Monguls in the open field, and in which the former sustained a dreadful defeat, Isocrates was left dead upon the plain, his son George fled to the mountains, where he was pursued by the army of the emperor, and the war was carried on for many months amongst the hills and rocks. The barren and frozen district of Suania was pillaged for the protection it had afforded to the fugitive prince; Abchasia and Imeritia were trodden down by the squadrons of the foe, till at length, in 1404, having rendered Georgia a desert, and ruined and decimated the inhabitants, Timur finally abandoned the country, where he had destroyed seven hundred villages, and all the monasteries, gardens, and cultivated land; and its prince, George, descending from his hiding-place in the Caucasus, having previously tendered his submission to Timur, reigned for several years over his prostrate and exhausted dominions in comparative rest and peace.

While the army of the emperor was still encamped upon the Georgian plains, ambassadors were received from the court of Manuel Paleologus of Constantinople, who humbly requested the assistance of Timur for their master, to aid him in opposing the increasing power and conquests of the Ottoman Turks. As early as 1321, a body of these warriors had crossed the Euxine, and harassed the defenceless shores of Macedonia and Thrace; and Urkhan, the first of their sultans who set foot on the opposite shores of the Hellespont, obtained permanent possession of Gallipoli, and established the celebrated corps of Janissaries, recruited from among his Christian slaves, whose blood-red* flag in later years was so dreaded and well known by their enemies, from the shores of the Danube to the sands of Egypt, and from the banks of the Tigris and Euphrates to the heart of the Numidian deserts. Since then, province after province had been gradually wrested from the feeble and dismembered successor of the Roman empire: Wallachia and Servia now owned the Mahometan sway—Amurath the conqueror had established his capital at Adrianople, and Bajazet his son, surnamed Ildurum or the Thunderer, had laid a seven years' siege to Byzantium, defeated the united armies of France, Hungary, Bavaria, and Constantinople, in a tremendous engagement at Nikopoli,† and conquered, laid waste, and overrun the whole peninsula of Greece. He now threatened the possessions of the Christians and Greeks in Palestine, and demanded tribute from Taharten, the prince of Eastern Anatolia, a province which had long been under the protection of the Mongul emperor, whom he stigmatized and

---

* They carried a blood-red flag before them in all their military expeditions.
† In this battle, a German knight born at Munich named Schildberger, was taken prisoner while fighting on the side of Sigismund of Hungary, and by order of Bajazet sent to Asia. There, on the last and total defeat of the Ottoman army by Timur, he fell into the hands of the Mongul emperor, whom he accompanied in all his expeditions, till his death in 1405. He ultimately returned to Munich in 1427, by way of Constantinople, Lemberg, and Cracow, after an absence of thirty-seven years, and dictated an account of his travels from memory to a transcriber, from whom they have descended to the present time.

proclaimed as the thief and rebel of the desert. On receiving intelligence of this encroachment upon his authority, Timur despatched a letter* to Bajazet, in which he informed him that hitherto he had permitted no insult or offence to be offered to any town or province subject to the Turcomanian empire, from the consideration that for so long she had waged a successful war with the infidels, and might be looked upon as the bulwark of the Mussulman faith;† but that, while the greater part of Asia was ruled by his (Timur's) officers, and his armies extended from sea to sea, he advised the Ottoman prince not to stir up hostilities between them, nor peril the safety of his own domains by incurring the anger of the Moguls, for none had ever prospered who ventured to oppose them, and fate protected their empire. "The dove," said he, "which rises up against the eagle, only seeks its own destruction." To this admonition, the sultan returned the following haughty reply—"It is long since we have desired to make war upon you. Thanks be to God and the prophet, our desire is about to be fulfilled, for we have resolved to march against you at the head of a formidable force. If you

---

* LETTER OF TIMUR'S TO BAJAZET.

"To the Emperor of Roum, Bajazet the Thunderer.

"After the usual greetings, we inform you that by the infinite grace of God, the greatest part of Asia has been conquered by our power and the terror of our arms, and is now subject to the authority of our officers. Know also, that the most mighty sultans of the earth obey our mandates, and that fate protects our empire; our armies extend from one sea to the other, and our guard is composed of sovereign princes, who form a hedge before our gate. Where is the monarch who dares resist us? who is the potentate that does not glory in forming one of our courtiers? But as for thee, whose true origin commences in a Turcoman sailor, it would be well, since the vessel of thy unfathomable ambition has suffered shipwreck in the whirlpool of self-love, if thou wouldst lower the sails of thy rashness, and cast the anchor of repentance in the port of sincerity, the only haven of safety and security; lest, by the tempest of our vengeance thou shouldst perish in the sea of our well-founded chastisement. But as we have learned that in obedience to the precepts of the Koran, which commands us to wage war with the enemies of the Mussulman faith, you have undertaken a vigorous war with the Europeans, we have refrained from insulting any nation or province subject to you; and, reflecting that your country is the bulwark of the Mahometans, we have allowed it to remain prosperous and unharmed, for fear an invasion from our empire should raise a division among the inhabitants, and cause the faithful to be disquieted, and the infidels to rejoice. Therefore be on your guard, and seek by your good conduct to preserve the dominions of your ancestors, nor suffer for the future your ambitious feet to wander beyond the limits of your power, which is but small. Cease your proud extravagance, lest the cold wind of hatred should extinguish the torch of peace. Remember the command of Mahomet, to let the Turks (Tartars) remain in peace while they are tranquil. Seek not to make war on us, for none has ever prospered who opposed us. The evil one inspires you to compass your own ruin. You have gained considerable battles in the woods of Natolia, and many advantages over the Europeans; but these are not to be attributed to your own valour so much as to the will of the Most High, and the prayers and intercession of the prophet. You indeed are but a pismire, and seek to fight against elephants, who will crush you beneath their feet. The dove which rises up against the eagle only accomplishes its own destruction. Shall an insignificant prince like you contend with us? But your boasting is not extraordinary, for a Turcoman never spake with judgment. If you follow not our counsels, you will assuredly repent. This is the advice we have to give. Act as you think fit."—Sherefeddin Ali's "History of Timur Bek."

Timur calls the Ottomans, Turcomans; and the Moguls, Turks.

† Sherefeddin Ali's "Hist. of Timur Bek."

refuse to march against us, we shall seek you and pursue you as far as Tauris and Sultana. Then shall we see in whose favour Heaven will declare, and who shall be exalted by victory, and who abased by a shameful defeat."

War was immediately declared between the two empires; but, during the first year of combat, the Ottoman sultan never appeared in the field, and Timur having captured the strongly fortified city of Sebaste, where he spared only the lowest of the inhabitants, causing four thousand of the garrison, who were Armenian Christians, to be buried alive in a manner so as to aggravate their sufferings by a prolonged death from starvation, commanded the Mahometans of high rank, among whom was Ortogrul, the favourite son of Bajazet, to be put to death. He then turned aside from the prosecution of the Turcomanian campaign, to revenge himself on the dynasty of the Egyptian Mamelukes, whose sultan, Barkok, while Timur was engaged in Kipzak, had occasioned two Mongul ambassadors, sent to him from the emperor, to be assassinated upon their arrival at his court. A Circassian by birth, this prince, commencing with the murder of an indulgent master, had raised himself from a slave and a prisoner to the perilous throne of Cairo. He had died, but his son Farradge, who succeeded him, had still further exasperated Timur, by causing one of his officers to be seized, when in command of a fortress on the frontiers of Syria, and closely confined, where he still remained in chains, in a dungeon in Egypt. The terrible defeat of the sultan's emirs with an enormous army of Syrians before Aleppo, was the retribution for this treachery inflicted by the emperor's troops; and a few Monguls, forcing their way with the flying soldiers in a mingled mass into the city, raised a panic, and caused the fortress to be surrendered, and a ransom was exacted, by the barbarous order of Timur, of several hundreds of pyramids of human heads. He released the cadis and learned men, of whom there were many in Aleppo, and even entered into a dispute with them upon many controversial points; and, inquiring the age of one, the Syrian replied, "Fifty years." "Fifty years," said the emperor, "would have been the age of my eldest son: you see me here a poor, lame, decrepit mortal, yet by my arm has the Almighty been pleased to subdue the kingdoms of Iran, Turan, and the Indies. I am not a man of blood; and God is my witness, that in all my wars I have never been the aggressor, and that my enemies have always been the authors of their own calamity."* On this occasion he caused several of his own soldiers to be put to death, for having, after the publication of quarter, continued to plunder the inhabitants.

It was Timur's ordinary custom, on the first day of a siege, to hoist a white flag over his pavilion, to signify that, if the place surrendered immediately, the lives of all the garrison should be spared: on the second day it was replaced by one of red, to show that the governor and leading inhabitants would be executed, but the rest receive quarter; and on the third day, if the city had not yielded, a black ensign surmounted the imperial tent, which all his enemies were aware was a proof that every soldier and citizen had nothing to expect but death.†

From Aleppo the emperor marched to Damascus, where he met with a considerable repulse from the Egyptian troops. The Mirza Sultan Hussein, his grandson, deserted after a banquet in his pavilion, and went over to the enemy; but Timur, subsequently obtaining entrance into the city under cover of a truce, basely violated the treaty, and exacted a heavy tribute from the inhabitants, who were afterwards compelled to see their houses reduced to ashes by his army at the instigation of their leader, who in an animated discourse excited them to revenge, as he alleged, the crime of the ancestors of the Damascenes, for permitting, in the precincts of their capital, the murder of a grandson of the prophet. Towards the borders of Egypt, and beyond the walls of Jerusalem, Timur extended his triumphant march; and in that city, where the Holy Sepulchre was hired to the Christians by the Mamelukes, and the entire place reduced to a most desolate and ruinous state, he treated the inhabitants with an indulgence and lenity equally unusual either from him or to them; and, distributing many presents among the priests and devotees of the different sects, freed the citizens from all subsidies and taxes, and the presence of any garrison or troops. After quitting Jerusalem, the Monguls abandoned Palestine, and crossed the Euphrates under their chief; and after the capture of Bagdad, where the emperor commanded that not a building should be spared

---

* Gibbon's "Decline and Fall of the Roman Empire."
† Porter's "Knights of Malta."

with the exception of the colleges, hospitals, and mosques, he caused the ruins to be crowned with the ghastly and horrible trophy of a pyramid of ninety thousand heads. A hunt in Mesopotamia terminated this successful campaign, and money was coined and circulated in Palestine in his name till many years after his death; and, finally returning to Samarcand by way of Georgia, he immediately prepared for a renewal of the Ottoman war. The Sultan Bajazet for two years had been collecting and increasing his strength, and his army amounted to 400,000 men, while that of Timur has been computed at not less than 800,000; and, having distributed their arrears of pay for the last seven years, the emperor marched upon Asia Minor with this enormous force.

And now the two great Mahometan empires of the east and of the west were about to encounter each other in mortal combat. Superiority in numbers was indeed greatly upon the side of the Monguls, who had drawn soldiers and slaves from all Asia to assist in swelling their tremendous host; but the Ottomans had measured swords with, and proved victorious over, the most valiant knights and warriors of the chivalrous nations of Europe; and the sultan's squadrons were increased by fugitives from the vanquished hordes of Toktamish, who had settled near Adrianople, upon being driven by Timur out of Kipzak. Yet the difference either in force or discipline was not so great in the armies as in the habits and conduct of their chiefs; and while Bajazet for a long period had abandoned himself to indolence and excess, the sixty-six years that had passed over Timur's head appeared only to have increased his activity, and strengthened his arm. While the sultan was idly awaiting his rival in his camp, near the ruins of Suvas in Anatolia, Timur passed him in a rapid march from the Araxes, and surrounded Angora, to which place he was pursued by his antagonist, and each army, equally eager to meet the other in the field, drew up their forces in battle array upon the memorable plains outside the town.* A line of elephants from Hindoostan was arranged, to intimidate the enemy, in front of the Mongul ranks, whose main body was commanded by the eldest grandson of Timur, the Mirza Mehemed; and their right and left wings by the Mirzas Miran Shah and Charoc, while before them was borne the military banner of the Tartars,

* Sherefeddin Ali's "History of Timur Bek."

a red horse-tail, surmounted by a crescent. A Servian, the brother-in-law of Bajazet, led the right wing of the Ottomans, their other battalions being commanded by his five sons, and both Monguls and Turkomans made use of the artificial fire of the Greeks; but, on the eve of battle, the sultan's forces were thrown into confusion and dismay, by a mutiny, provoked by his avarice, breaking out among their ranks, and his Tartar allies deserted to the enemy, having been tempted by the secret emissaries of the emperor, with the hope of their re-establishment in Kipzak, and shamed by the reproach that they were about to serve against their brethren on the side of their forefathers' slaves.* Their defection was a serious loss to the Ottomans, who, so unequally matched, engaged their opponents on the 1st of July, 1402; and, though Bajazet himself fought and commanded with his accustomed valour and ability, his son Solyman prematurely abandoned the field, and, carrying off the baggage and treasury, crossed the Hellespont † and took refuge in Europe. After a vain attempt to rally the scattered Turkomans, and make head against the foe, the sultan was himself compelled to fly, but was pursued and captured by the Monguls, and while one of their detachments, under the Mirza Mehemed, proceeded to Brusa, and burned and pillaged the Ottoman metropolis, he was led a prisoner before the stern and haughty conqueror. Yet Timur appears to have received the unfortunate prince with much consideration and kindness; having assured him that neither he nor his friends should receive any injury at their captor's hands—" All misfortunes," said he, " occur through the will of the Most High; and no man, however powerful he may be, can conduct them as he may wish." But the victor went on to represent to the captive monarch, " that he owed his calamities entirely to his own obstinacy and ambition, and that if he would only have consented to remain at peace, and restore the emperor's subjects whom he had imprisoned, and the fortresses that he had seized upon in the Mongul territories, to Timur; that he (the emperor) had contemplated uniting his forces with the Ottomans, and carrying on the war for their religion with greater vigour, not resting till they had totally exterminated the enemies of

---

* Gibbon's " Decline and Fall of the Roman Empire."
† At this time the straits of the Bosphorus were in the hands of the Greeks, and those of the Hellespont in the possession of the Turks.

Mahomet."* He also observed that he was not ignorant of the fate that Bajazet had reserved, in the event of success, for himself and his troops; but that he scorned to retaliate, and would show his gratitude to the Almighty by clemency to man. The sultan's chief concern was with regard to the fate of his two youngest sons, whom he had missed in the flight; but one of them being subsequently brought to the emperor's camp, he was honourably treated by Timur, who caused a handsome pavilion to be prepared for the residence of father and son adjoining his own, but insisted upon the Christian brother-in-law of Bajazet embracing the faith of Mahomet. He also commanded that the sultaness should be restored with her daughters to her husband; but an attempt to escape upon the part of the royal prisoners, by digging a mine beneath their tent, appears to have provoked from the victor a harsher treatment, and the ex-monarch, during the frequent marches of the Monguls, was carried in a litter upon the back of a camel or in a waggon, which probably gave rise to the story circulated by Arabshah, that Timur confined his illustrious victim within an iron cage, a punishment that the latter had formerly designed for himself. Bajazet expired of apoplexy on the 23rd of March, 1403, and his body was conveyed with regal magnificence to his capital, and interred in the mausoleum that he had erected at Brusa, and the emperor conferred the government of Anatolia upon his son Mousa, while his sultana with the rest of his family were released from captivity.

After the battle of Angora, Timur repaired with his army to Smyrna, which was strongly fortified, and defended by a garrison from Rhodes of the Knights of the Order of St. John, and had held out seven years against Bajazet with a strong Ottoman force. Burning naphtha, boiling oil, Greek fire, and stones, were poured by the Christians from the walls upon their assailants with unwearying perseverance, and all the resources which their desperate condition could prompt; while the rain poured down every day in ceaseless torrents, so as greatly to incommode the besiegers, whose arms were rusted and blunted by the moisture, which, from their camp being completely under water, penetrated all their tents. The blockade continued for three weeks, until the Monguls forced the breaches in the ramparts, and stormed and carried the

* Sherefeddin Ali's "History of Timur Bek."

place, when the emperor caused every knight and soldier to be put to death. In the mean time, the Grand Master of Rhodes had despatched reinforcements and supplies, to assist his comrades in Smyrna to maintain their heroic resistance, as he considered the possession of this city by the Christians of the utmost importance, for, so long as they retained it, Smyrna formed for them a gate into Asia, through which they easily passed to the Holy Land. The vessels carrying this relief appeared off the coast a few days after the Monguls had entered the place, and Timur commanded that the fate of their countrymen should be made known to them, by casting the heads of the knights from his machines upon their decks. Upon receiving this horrible confirmation of the fears that they had entertained for the safety of their countrymen, from the moment they had appeared within sight of the ruined fortress, the ships of Rhodes weighed anchor, and returned with their cargoes to the island, from whence they spread the intelligence of the Mongul conquests in Anatolia throughout all Europe.*

The fear in which Bajazet had been held by the nations of the West was replaced, on his defeat, by a dread lest Timur should extend his conquests across the sea to the Christian shores of the Grecian Hellespont; and an ambassador was sent from even the distant kingdom of Castille, to negotiate a treaty and alliance with the Eastern monarch, to whom he brought from his master, Henry III., several pieces of Spanish tapestry, and other splendid gifts.† At the same time, there appears to have been some correspondence between the Mongul emperor and the court of Charles VI. of France; and the Byzantine Cæsar, Manuel, consented to pay the same tribute to Timur that had formerly been wrested from his coffers by the arms of the victorious Ottomans. Solyman, the son of Bajazet, accepted from his father's conqueror the investiture of the kingdom of Roumania, which was already virtually his own, and the Sultan of Egypt averted a second invasion of his dominions by proposing terms of peace, and sending an envoy, with a present of nine ostriches and a giraffe to Samarcand, he agreed that in future all the Egyptian money and coin should bear the inscription and name of the Zagataian khans. But though the Ottoman empire

* Sherefeddin Ali.—Porter's "Knights of Malta."
† Gibbon's "Decline and Fall of the Roman Empire."

was compelled for a few years to bow before the horsemen of Transoxiana and the archers of the north, she was doomed subsequently to arise in replenished lustre and glory, far outstripping her then declining rival in the race of conquest and fame ; and in less than half a century after the death of Timur, while his dominions were divided and in confusion, and fast separating from beneath the sway of his successors, the grandson of Bajazet had captured and subdued the most ancient and polished sovereignty of Europe ; and, driving her princes into exile, had seen the last of the Cæsars perish in the storm of his capital, and had led the fierce soldiers of Asia to victory, in the centre of the Christian continent.*

* When Timur undertook a distant campaign, he was accustomed to sow seeds along his line of march, that the crops might supply his army on its return. " When I clothed myself in the bed of empire," says he, in his Institutions, " I cast from myself the down of safety and repose."

CHAPTER IV.

Timur returns to Samarcand—Sets out for China—His death—Troubles in the Empire—His successors—The Emperor Baber.

> Weigh'd in the balance, hero dust
> Is vile as vulgar clay;
> Thy scales, Mortality, are just
> To all that pass away.—LORD BYRON.

AT length, having laid at his feet all Syria, Mesopotamia, and Asia Minor, and after an absence of nearly five years, the Emperor Timur, towards the middle of the year 1403, began to retrace his steps towards his native land. Pausing on his route to complete the reduction of Georgia, and the turbulent provinces of the Caucasus, he occupied himself entirely, upon his arrival at his capital in Transoxiana, in the administration of justice, and the reform of abuses in the government. His return to Samarcand was hailed with a clamorous joy by all ranks among the people, and for many weeks the court and city was one long scene of riotous feasting and mirth; the Zagataians abandoned themselves to amusement and revelling, and the marriages of six of the grandsons of Timur were celebrated in one day in the royal palace. After this ceremony, the emperor gave a banquet to his family and subjects, at which the Spanish ambassadors from Castille were permitted to be present; "for the smallest fish," says the haughty Persian historian, "has its place in the ocean;" and he subsequently gave a reception to the envoys of Egypt, Arabia, and Hindoostan, and several princes of the family of Toktamish, the exiled khan of Kipzak. To these he pledged his word to assist, at some future time, their unfortunate sovereign in the recovery of his forfeited dominions; but at present the Mongul armies would have sufficient occupation in the project that he was about to undertake, which was no less an enterprise than the conquest and conversion to Islamism of the whole Celestial empire.

He appears at this time to have felt some remorse for the terrible slaughter that he had caused in his numerous campaigns; and, in a proclamation to his soldiers, he justified this war by conjuring these veterans to cleanse their swords from the blood of their fellow Mussulmen, the Ottomans, by washing them in that of the infidels and rebels of China. "As our vast conquests," said he, "have not been accomplished without great violence, and the destruction of many creatures of the Almighty,* I have resolved to perform some good action, which may atone for the sins of my past life; and by what better means can we obtain the pardon of our offences, than in demolishing the temples of the idols in this holy war, and erecting on their sites mosques and buildings for the worship of the prophet."†

Nearly forty years before this period, a native chief of that empire had risen against the imperial and degenerate Mongul who occupied the throne of Pekin; and after a long and fierce warfare, and the mutual slaughter of a million of the people, had succeeded in expelling the last Chinese emperor of the family of Zingis beyond the walls of China, to the Tartar deserts. To revenge this insult to the Mongul race, who had accompanied their deposed chief to Mongolia—to drive the successor of Hong-vu,‡ the usurper, from China, and increase the followers of Mahomet—was the ostensible cause for which Timur undertook this campaign; and on the 8th of January, 1405, he departed from Samarcand to join his army and emirs, who had already preceded him on their route. Notwithstanding his age, and the severity of the season, he marched three hundred miles on horseback, crossed the frozen Sihon, and arrived at the Mongul camp near Otrar, where his troops, the conquerors of Syria, had assembled to the number of two hundred thousand, with five hundred large waggons of baggage and provision, and multitudes of loaded horses and camels. But a mightier conqueror than himself was awaiting the emperor; and on the 25th of March he was seized with a violent fever, and believed that he heard the houris calling, and saying to him, "Repent, for thou must appear before God!" He then ordered his family and officers to assemble round him, and having requested them to make

---

* It is computed that Timur, during his career, caused the death of 18,000,000 human beings.
† Sherefeddin Ali's "History of Timur Bek."
‡ Chu assumed the name of Hong-vu on attaining the imperial power.

no useless lamentation upon his decease, but to pray for his soul, he observed—That since he had been so highly favoured as to be enabled to give laws to the earth, so that throughout all Iran and Turan no man dare encroach upon his neighbour, nor during his reign had any poor suffered from the oppression of the rich, he hoped that his sins might be forgiven him, though they were so many and so great. "I have cleansed this empire," said he, "from the enemies and disturbers of its people; but if you, my sons, allow discord to enter among you, misfortune will attend all that you attempt, irreparable mischief will arise both in the government and in religion, and be assured that, at the day of judgment, a strict account will be required from those to whom I have intrusted this nation's safety and peace." He then named his grandson, Pir Mehemed Gehangir, as his successor, that prince being the oldest member of the family* of the emperor, whose two elder sons had been long dead, and commanded all the emirs and generals to obey him, "that the world might rest in equity and tranquillity, and that the fruit of so many years of labour and bloodshed might not be lost." A few days after, Timur expired in his military tent, on the night of the 31st of March, 1405, in the sixty-ninth year of his age, and thirty-sixth of his eventful reign; and his body was transported to a mausoleum he had erected at Canicah in Samarcand, being laid beside that of his distinguished grandson, the Mirza Mehemed, and the coffin of a renowned Mussulman prophet. He left thirty-six sons and grandsons, of

MODERN MONGUL SONG IN PRAISE OF TIMUR.

"When the divine Timur dwelt within our tents, the Mongul nation was formidable and warlike. Its least movement made the earth bend. Its mere look froze with fear the ten thousand tribes upon whom the earth shines.
O, divine Timur! will thy great soul soon revive?
Return, return, we await thee, O Timur!

"We live in our vast plains, tranquil and peaceful as sheep; yet our hearts are fervent and full of life. The memory of the glorious age of Timur is ever present to our minds. Where is the chief who is to place himself at our head, and make us once more great warriors?
O, divine Timur! will thy great soul soon revive?
Return, return, we await thee, O Timur!

"The young Mongul has arms wherewith to quell the wild horse; eyes wherewith he sees, afar off in the desert, the traces of the last camel. Alas! his arms can no longer bend the bow of his ancestors, his eye cannot see the wiles of the enemy.
O, divine Timur! will thy great soul soon revive?
Return, return, we await thee, O Timur!

"We have burned the sweet-smelling wood at the feet of the divine Timur; our foreheads bend to the earth: we have offered him the green leaf of tea, and the milk of our herds. We are ready; the Monguls are on foot, O Timur! And do thou, O Lama! send down good fortune upon our arrows and our lances.
O, divine Timur! will thy great soul soon revive!
Return, return, we await thee, O Timur."
—Huc's "Travels in Tartary, Thibet, and China."

* See Descendants of Timur, next page.

* DESCENDANTS OF TIMUR.

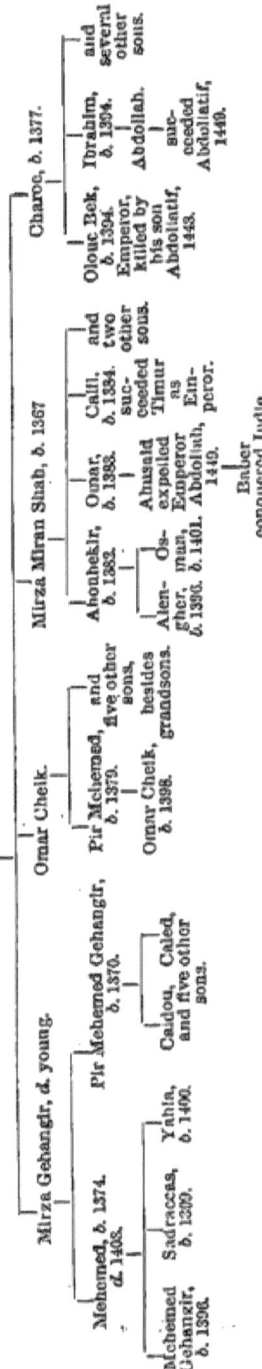

whom the most famous were his third son, the Mirza Miran, Shah of Persia, and his son Calil, who was elected emperor by a faction among the princes, in opposition to the Mirza Pir Mehemed; Charoc, his youngest and favourite child, who, renowned alike for his courage and humanity, subsequently united for a few years under his sway the contending factions that were consuming his father's empire; and Hussein, the son of Ahia, a daughter of the emperor, who in Syria had deserted to the Egyptians, and by opposing the council of generals after his grandfather's death, and disbanding his division of the troops, caused the Mongul army to return to their homes, and abandon the Chinese war.* The eldest son of Timur, the Mirza Gehangir had died shortly after his father had ascended the Transoxianian throne, and his son Mehemed, who was bastinadoed for misgovernment in Persia, and subsequently made generalissimo under the emperor in Asia Minor, where he greatly distinguished himself in the Ottoman campaign, had been seized with a severe illness when returning in 1403 from the borders of the Turkish empire in Anatolia, and expired at the age of twenty-nine, before he had accomplished the march to Samarcand. The Mirza Pir Mehemed was the next brother of this prince; but though chosen by Timur as his successor, he was soon forced to relinquish his pretensions to the disputed throne, which was seized and held for a few years by Calil, during whose reign the whole empire was a prey to civil war. He had been elected by several of the emirs immediately after the emperor's death, who had met together to decide upon the expediency of carrying out or abandoning the projected expedition into China, and had finally decided that it should be continued under his command, as he had been a brave and able officer in his grandfather's army, and was considered the most capable among the princes of conducting it to a glorious termination, and he was finally and unanimously chosen by the soldiers to fill the imperial throne. But his right was disputed by many of the officers and mirzas, and the nearest relations of the deceased monarch, who supported the claims of Mehemed, as having been nominated his heir by Timur himself. At the same time Hussein raised a revolt among the forces, and disbanded his own squadrons upon their refusal to acknowledge him as

* Sherefoddin Ali's "Hist. of Timur Bek."

chief; and with a small body of followers marching upon Samarcand, he was intercepted by the partisans of Calil, and forced to retire into Persia, while Mehemed, who until then had held the capital, abandoned it with the empresses and viziers, and established himself at Bokhara, where he was proclaimed khan. The rebellion of Hussein threw the army into confusion, and caused Calil to assemble his adherents and repair with them to Samarcand, where he was crowned emperor; and the ice on the Sihon giving way while the waggons and baggage-camels were crossing, several were lost in the river, being heavily loaded with gold. Thus the campaign was entirely abandoned, and the empire of Zagatai given up to dissension and misrule, when Calil, having reigned for several years, and squandered all the treasures that had been accumulated by his grandfather in so many wars, while Syria, Georgia, and Asia Minor had been reclaimed by their ancient masters, was deposed in 1411 by his subjects, and Charoc mounted the throne.

But the empire of the Monguls was setting, and after Timur's death began surely and rapidly to decline. On being driven out of China, and expelled into the deserts by the arms of Hong-vu, all the principal cities and fortresses throughout Mongolia had been burned or razed by the Chinese to the ground, and these having never been rebuilt by the inhabitants, their ruins still lie scattered over the steppes. The people returned to their former patriarchal mode of life, and again dwelt in tents and among their flocks. In Persia the conquering race shortly met with the same fate. After the death of Charoc, his descendants were massacred or carried into slavery by the Turkomans, and the land becoming divided among numerous local chiefs, the natives alternately groaned under their tyranny, or were oppressed by the inroads of surrounding invaders. At length these provinces were re-united in the year 1510 by the powerful arm of a Persian nobleman, the Shah Ismael Safi, and his family continued to rule over the kingdom till 1716, when they were forced to give way to the Afghans, whose dynasty was shortly after overthrown in turn by the conquests of the celebrated Nadir Shah. But the Emperor Charoc preserved peace and prosperity in his dominious during his own life, and, cementing with a firm hand the scattered khanates of the empire, ruled over

Transoxiana and Persia, Kandahar, Khorassan and a part of India. He is celebrated for his accomplishments and the equity of his government, and less honourably for his avarice, which accumulated vast stores of riches; and in 1419 he sent a friendly embassy to Pekin, and formed an offensive and defensive alliance with the ancient enemy of his race, the Celestial empire. His eldest son Ulugh, who has acquired lasting renown by the astronomical tables composed from his directions, succeeded him in 1425, while the second, Ibrahim, swayed the sceptre of Farsistan in Persia; but Ulugh was assassinated in 1448 by his own son Abdollatif,* who six months later was put to death by the soldiers, after inflicting the same fate upon his brother; upon which his cousin Abdollah, the son of Ibrahim, seized the perilous crown. After a year of contention and misgovernment, this prince, the last descendant of Charoc, was expelled by the Mirza Abusaid, the Prince of Ferghana, and a grandson of Miran Shah. The new emperor kept his throne till 1468, when he was taken prisoner and put to death by his rebel subject Hassan Bey; and his son Zehireddin Muhammed or Baber, who succeeded him, being driven out by the Uzbek Tartars from Samarcand, retired to Ghizni, from whence he subsequently issued forth as a conqueror, and rendered himself master of the rich and extensive empire of Hindoostan.

This prince, who was an excellent poet and accomplished scholar, notwithstanding his chequered career, and the countless military expeditions in which he took a prominent part, was born in 1482, when his father's dominions had been reduced to the insignificant province of Kokan, or Ferghana, and the magnificent city of Samarcand. He was early deprived of his capital by his northern enemies, and at one time was nominal sovereign of a large though turbulent empire, at another period owned scarcely a tent, for he was

---

* "At the period of the Mongul supremacy, when, in the fifteenth century, astronomy flourished at Samarcand under Ulugh Beg, photometric determinations were facilitated by the subdivision of each of the six classes of Hipparchus, and Ptolemy, into three subordinate groups, distinctions for example being drawn between the *small*, *intermediate*, and *large* stars of the second magnitude, an attempt which reminds us of the decimal gradations of Struve and Argelander. This advance in photometry by a more exact determination of degrees of intensity, is ascribed in Ulugh Beg's tables to Abdurrahman Sufi, who wrote a work 'on the knowledge of the fixed stars,' and was the first who mentions one of the Magellanic clouds under the name of the White Ox."—Humboldt's "Cosmos."

"The name, Abdurrahman Sufi, was contracted by Ulugh Beg from Abdurrahman Ebn Omar, Ebn Mahommed, Ebn Sahl, Abroll Hassan el Sufi et Ragl. Ulugh Beg who, like Nassireddin, amended the Ptolemaic star positions from his own observations (1437), admits that he borrowed from Sufi's work the position of twenty-seven southern stars not visible at Samarcand."—*Ibid.*

defeated almost as frequently as he was victorious, and appears, till he had attained a mature age and experience, to have been deficient in the talents of a great military commander, though his valour was undaunted, and his energy and daring unsurpassed. Like his great ancestor Timur, he has left most interesting commentaries* of the extraordinary events of his varied and romantic life; and in these he has given descriptions of the aspect and productions of those countries which he traversed, with a truth and exactitude that all modern travellers can vouch. In speaking of the state of Transoxiana at this period, his translator, Mr. Erskine, observes—" It is evident that, in consequence of the protection which had been afforded to the people of Maveralnahar by their regular governments, a considerable degree of comfort, and perhaps still more of elegance and civility, prevailed in the towns. The whole age of Baber, however, was one of great confusion. Nothing contributed so much to produce the constant wars, and eventual devastation of the country, as the want of some fixed rule of succession to the throne; for the ideas of regal descent, according to primogeniture, were very indistinct, as is the case in all Oriental, and in general all despotic kingdoms. The death of the ablest sovereign was only the signal for a general war. The different parties at court or in the harem of the prince, espoused the cause of different competitors; and every neighbouring potentate believed himself to be perfectly justified in marching to seize his portion of the spoil. The grandees of the court, while they took their place by the side of the candidate of their choice, do not appear to have believed that fidelity to him was any necessary virtue; and the nobility, unable to predict the events of one twelvemonth, degenerated into a set of selfish, calculating, though perhaps brave, partisans. Rank, and wealth, and present enjoyment became their idols; and the prince felt the influence of the general want of stability, and was himself educated in the loose principles of an adventurer." Such was the state of Transoxiana at the time when the descendants of Timur were driven beyond the waters of the Oxus; and Baber, chased even from Kokan by his adversaries, and his followers reduced to only two hundred and forty men, formed the bold

---

* These have been most ably translated and annotated by Dr. Leyden and Mr. Erskine.

resolution of attacking the strongly defended Samarcand, which was then held by a large army of Uzbeks, headed by Sheibâni their khan. Aided by his friends within the walls, he stormed and entered the place, and the hostile sovereign fled; but a short time after, it was again surrounded and besieged by the enemy, when Baber finding himself without hope of succour, and his brave little force suffering severely from famine, evacuated the stronghold by night, and retreated to Cabul,* where, after encountering considerable opposition, and challenging and slaying successively five chiefs in single combat, he established himself at Ghizni, from whence in the year 1526, to quote his own words, "placing his footstep in the stirrup of resolution," he marched forth from his rocky kingdom beyond the Indus, for the conquest and subjection of Hindoostan. He thus describes in his commentaries the blockade by the Uzbeks of Samarcand.

"During the continuance of the siege, the rounds of the rampart were regularly gone once every night, sometimes by Kasim Beg, and sometimes by the other Begs and captains. From the Firozeh gate to that of Sheikh Zadeh we were able to go along the ramparts on horseback, every where else we were obliged to go on foot. Setting out in the beginning of the night, it was morning before we had completed our rounds.

"One day Sheibâni Khan made an attack between the iron gate and that of the Sheikh Zadeh. As I was with the reserve, I immediately led them to the quarter that was attacked, without attending to the Washing-green gate, or

---

* Baber thus describes Cabul in his commentaries :—

"This country lies between Hindoostan and Khorassan. It is an excellent and profitable market for commodities. Were the merchants to carry their goods as far as Khita (Northern China) or Rum (Turkey), they would scarcely get the same profit on them. Every year seven, eight, or ten thousand horses arrive in Cabul. From Hindoostan every year fifteen or twenty thousand pieces of cloth are brought by caravans, with slaves, white cloths, and sugar candy. The productions of Khorassan, Rum, Irak, and Chira, may all be found in Cabul, which is the very emporium of Hindustan. Its warm and cold districts are close by each other. From Cabul you may in a single day go to a place where snow never falls, and in two hours you may reach a spot where snow lies always, except now and then when the summer happens to be peculiarly hot. In the districts dependent on Cabul there is great abundance of the fruits both of hot and cold climates, and they are found in its immediate vicinity. Grapes, pomegranates, apricots, peaches, pears, apples, quinces, jujubes, damsons, almonds, walnuts, orange, and citron, grow in abundance there, and I caused the sugar-cane, and sour cherry to be transplanted here, which continue thriving. Cabul is not fertile in grain, a return of four or five to one is considered favourable; the melons too are not good, but the climate is extremely delightful, there is no such place in the known world. In the nights of summer, you cannot sleep without a lambskin cloak. Though the snow falls very deep in the winter, yet the cold is never excessively intense. Samerkand and Tabriz are celebrated for their fine climates, but the cold there is extreme beyond measure. (He then describes a garden he caused to be made near the Cabul river.) Apes are found near the mountains, towards Hindustan. The inhabitants used formerly to keep hogs, but in my time they have renounced the practice."

the Needlemakers' gate. That same day, from the top of the Sheikh Zadeh's gateway I struck a white horse, an excellent shot, with my crossbow; it fell dead the moment my arrow touched it; but, in the meanwhile, they had made such a vigorous attack near the Camel's-neck, that they effected a lodgment close under the rampart. Being hotly engaged in repelling the enemy where I was, I had entertained no apprehension of danger on the other side, where they had prepared, and brought with them five or six and twenty scaling-ladders, each of which was so broad that two or three men could mount abreast. He had placed in ambush, opposite to the city wall, seven or eight hundred chosen men, with these ladders, between the Ironsmiths' and Needlemakers' gates, while he himself moved to the other side, and made a false attack. Our attention was entirely drawn off to this attack; and the men in ambush no sooner saw the works opposite to them empty of defenders, by the watch having left them, than they rose from the place where they had been in ambush, advanced with extreme speed, and applied their scaling-ladders all at once between the two gates that have been mentioned, exactly opposite to Muhammed Mâzid Terphan's house. The Begs who were on guard had only two or three of their servants and attendants about them. Nevertheless Kuch Beg, Muhammed Kûli Kochin Shah Sûfi, and another brave cavalier, boldly assailed them and displayed signal heroism. Some of the enemy had already mounted on the wall, and several others were in the act of scaling it, when these four arrived on the spot, fell upon them sword in hand, and drove the assailants back over the ramparts, putting them all to flight.

"It was now the season of the ripening of the grain, and none had ventured to bring in any new corn. As the siege had been greatly protracted, the inhabitants were reduced to extreme distress, and our affairs came to such a pass, that the poor and meaner sort were forced to feed on dogs' and asses' flesh. Grain for the horses becoming scarce, they were obliged to eat the leaves of trees; and it was ascertained from experience that the foliage of the mulberry and blackwood answered best. Many used the shavings of wood, which they soaked in water, and gave to their steeds; and for three or four months Sheibâni Khan did not approach the fortress, but blockaded it at some distance on all sides, changing his ground from time to time. I looked for aid and assistance from the princes my neighbours; but each of them had his attention fixed on some other object; as, for example, the Sultan Hússain Mirza, who was undoubtedly a brave and experienced monarch, but neither did he give me succour, or even send an ambassador to encourage me."

At length, having abandoned Samarcand with his followers, Baber describes how they lost their way among the many streams of the district; but at length, regaining the desired road, their spirits rose with the brightness of the morning, and they urged their horses to a race, which had nearly cost the emperor his life. His saddle turned, and he fell on his head to the ground. "I did not recover full possession of my senses," says he, "till the evening, and the world, and all that occurred round me, passed before my eyes and understanding like a fantasy or dream. At dawn the following day, we arrived at the friendly town of Dizah, where we found abundance of bread, melons, and grapes; thus passing from the extremity of famine to plenty, and from an estate of danger and calamity to ease and peace." At a spring, near which they halted on their route, Baber inscribed these words in Persian upon a stone—

> "Many a man like us has rested by this fountain,
> And disappeared in the twinkling of an eye;
> Should we conquer the whole world by our manhood and strength,
> Yet could we not carry it with us to the grave."

The adventurers subsequently united their arms to those of a friendly chief, who assisted the emperor in his campaign against Cabul, where he established himself about the year 1506, and from whence, twenty years later, he marched against the Sultan Ibrahim of Delhi. The Mongul army amounted to only thirteen thousand horse, and were opposed by a hundred thousand cavalry and a thousand elephants; but the brave and hardy archers of Ghizni, notwithstanding the disparity of numbers, were invincible to the effeminate Hindoo, whose forces were swept away or fled in legions, leaving the two chiefs to decide the battle by an almost single combat. This was terminated by the death of Ibrahim after displaying signal courage; and the few remaining followers, who still rallied round him, immediately took to flight, so that Baber in the year 1526 proclaimed himself Emperor of Delhi.*

But the war was still sustained in the western provinces of Hindoostan by the energy and valour of the deceased sultan's brother, Mahmoud, who, refusing to acknowledge the usurper, mustered an army of one hundred thousand men to support his own rights. A panic seized the Mongul horsemen, who tried to induce their prince to return to Cabul. "Never!" exclaimed he; "for since death is inevitable, it is glorious to meet him with courage, face to face, rather than to shrink back, to gain a few years of a miserable and ignominious existence, since we inherit but fame beyond the grave." He then appealed to the religious zeal of his terror-stricken troops, from whom he exacted an oath on the Koran, that they would either conquer or die; and having himself made a vow to the prophet, to renounce for ever the use of wine, in which hitherto he had too freely indulged, he caused all his golden goblets and other drinking-vessels to be broken up and distributed among the poor. He then advanced with his small army against the tremendous force of Mahmoud, over whom, however, he possessed a great advantage in the superiority and number of his musketeers and artillery, a mode of warfare then almost unknown in Hindoostan; and after a long and sanguinary engagement, in which the greater part of the adverse princes and officers were left dead upon the field, he compelled the entire forces of the enemy to take refuge in flight, and became master of the Indian throne, though his possession was long disputed by insurrections both round Delhi and in Cabul. But in less

* He thus speaks of Hindoostan—"Hindoostan is a remarkably fine country, but its hills, rivers, forests, and plains, animals, plants, inhabitants, and languages, its winds, and rains, are all entirely different from ours. This disparity commences immediately you cross the river Sind, where we came upon several countries in the range of the northern mountains, such as Pekheli and Shemeng, most of which, though formerly included in the territories of Kashmir, are now independent. About these hills are other tribes of mon. All the towns and lands of Hindoostan have a uniform look, its gardens have no walls, and the greater part is a level plain, which in many places is covered by a thorny brushwood, to such a degree that the people of the Pergamas, relying on these forests, take shelter in them, and trusting to their inaccessible situation, often continue in a state of revolt, refusing to pay the taxes. In Hindoostan, if you except the rivers, there is little running water; all the cities are supplied by wells or tanks, in which it is collected during the rainy season. Here the populousness, and decay or total destruction of villages, nay, of cities, is almost instantaneous. Large cities that have been inhabited for a series of years (if on an alarm the inhabitants take to flight), in a single day, or a day and a half, are so completely abandoned, that you can scarcely discover a trace or mark of population. This is a country that has few pleasures to recommend it. The people are not handsome. They have no idea of the charm of friendly society, of frankly mixing together, or of friendly intercourse. They have no genius, no comprehension of mind, no politeness of manner, no fellow feeling, no good horses, no good flesh, no grapes or musk-melons, no good fruits, no ice or cold water, no good food or bread in their bazaars, no baths or colleges, no candles, no torches, not a candlestick. The chief excellence of Hindoostan, is its abundance of gold and silver."

than five years he was overtaken by death, in 1530, and in the forty-ninth year of his age, when he bequeathed a name which, though occasionally stained by great cruelty to his enemies, was, on the whole, of singular clemency and mercy for an Asiatic conqueror : through his greatest troubles, he was always a gay and cheerful companion, in some instances a generous warrior, and ever a sincere and faithful friend. Intemperance appears to have been the chief blot upon his character, and indeed eventually shortened his life ; and in his commentaries he frequently mourns this propensity, which he acquired during a visit he paid in 1506 to the court of the Sultan of Khorassan. "Till that time," says he, "I had never been guilty of drinking wine, and was ignorant of the sensations it produced ; yet I had a strong longing to wander in this desert, and my heart was much disposed to pass the stream. I was a guest at Mezeffer Mirza's house, who had placed me above himself, and, having filled up a glass of welcome, the cupbearers in waiting began to supply all who were of the party with pure wine, which they quaffed as if it had been the water of life. They tried to make me drink too, and bring me into the same circle with themselves ; and it came into my head that, as they urged me so much, and as besides I had come into a refined city like Herat, in which every means of heightening pleasure and gaiety was possessed in perfection, I might never have another opportunity of gratifying the desire with which my youthful imagination had possessed me, if I did not seize the present." After this first relapse he appears to have given perpetual banquets, though he never allowed them to interfere with the affairs of state ; but one of these being attended by the tragical consequence of the death of a friend from a fall over a precipice—for whom the emperor wept ten whole days—he made a resolution to give up wine when he should have attained the age of forty ; and in one part of his memoirs he informs us that, as he only wanted one year of that period, he now drank copiously. However, in the year 1527, when threatened by the arms of Mahmoud, he made a vow of temperance, which he appears to have kept, and issuing a firman, announcing his reformation, he advised all his subjects to imitate it. "But," says he, "I had much difficulty in reconciling myself to the desert of penitence ; my desire and longing for wine and social parties was at one time so great, that I have found myself shedding tears from vexation and disappointment; though now, thanks be to God, these troubles are over, and I ascribe it chiefly to the occupation afforded to my mind by a poetical translation on which I have employed myself. Last year I wrote to Abdallah,

> 'I am distress'd since I renounced wine,
> I am confounded, and unfit for business;
> Regret leads me to penitence,
> Penitence leads me to regret.'"

Muhammed Baber* left, as his successor to his troubled throne, his eldest son Humaioon; whose son, the celebrated Akbar, in a long reign of fifty-one years firmly established his family in the imperial power; and Hindoostan, merely exchanging one race of foreign despots for another, reluctantly accepted the dynasty of the Monguls.†

---

* His tomb is still to be seen on the top of a hill overhanging the town of Cabul.
† The historian Ahmed ben Arabshah, makes the spirit of winter thus address Timur on his death-bed—"Stop thy career, thou unjust tyrant! How long dost thou mean to carry flames over an unhappy world? If thou art a spirit of hell, so am I. We are both old, and our occupation is the same, that of subjugating slaves. But proceed to extirpate mankind, and make the earth cold, yet thou wilt find at last that my blasts are colder. If thou canst boast of countless bands, who faithful to thy orders, harass, and destroy, know that my wintry days are, with God's aid, destroyers also; and, by the Almighty that liveth, I will abate thee nothing! Thou shalt be overwhelmed with my vengeance, and all thy fire shall not save thee from the cold death of the icy tempest."

BOOK IV.

CONTINUATION OF THE HISTORY OF RUSSIA

TO THE

FINAL EXTINCTION OF THE MONGUL POWER IN EUROPE.

FROM A.D. 1404 TO A.D. 1506; OR, A.M. 6912 TO A.M. 7014.

So perish all
Who would man by man enthral.—BYRON.

BOOK IV.—CHAPTER I.

The Fifteenth Century*—Fall of Constantinople—The Monguls—Their Conquerors and Descendants—The Cossacks.

> Raised oft and long their wild hurrah,
> The children of the Don.—SCOTT.

THE fourteenth century had passed away, and the career of the fifteenth had commenced; that century so important and so celebrated in the history of the world. Besides innumerable minor events, it added a new hemisphere to the known regions of our earth; it gave to Europe a Luther and a Copernicus, whose doctrines were destined to be dispersed far and wide by its prior discovery of lithography and printing; it

* CONTEMPORARY SOVEREIGNS.

MUSCOVY.	SPAIN.	HUNGARY.
. Vassili Dmitrovitz.	. Henry III.	. Mary.
1425. Vassili Vassilovitz.	1406. John II.	1437. Albert.
1462. Ivan Vassilovitz the Great.	1454. Henry IV.	1440. Ladislaf IV.
	1474. Ferdinand and Isabella.	1444. Ladislaf V.
		1458. Mathias I.
GREEK EMPIRE.	ENGLAND.	1490. Ladislaf VI.
. Manuel Paleologus.	. Henry IV.	
1425. John Paleologus II.	1413. Henry V.	PORTUGAL.
1448. Constantine Paleologus.	1422. Henry VI.	1433. Edward.
	1461. Edward IV.	1438. Alphonso V.
OTTOMAN TURKS.	1483. Edward V.	1481. John II.
. Isa Belis.	1483. Richard III.	1495. Emanuel.
1403. Solyman.	1485. Henry VII.	
1410. Musa.		POPES.
1413. Mahomet I.	POLAND.	1404. Innocent VII.
1421. Amurath II.	. Vladislaf V.	1406. Gregory XII.
1451. Mahomet II.	1434. Vladislaf VI.	1409. Alexander V.
1481. Cortacus.	1444. Boleslaf.	1410. John XXIII.
1481. Xemin.	1447. Casimir IV.	1417. Martin V.
1481. Bajazet.	1492. John Albert.	1431. Eugenius IV.
		1447. Nicholas V.
GERMAN EMPIRE.	SWEDEN.	1455. Calixtus VI.
1400. Robert, Rhenish Palatine.	1411. Eric XIII.	1458. Pius II.
	1441. Christopher.	1464. Paul II.
1410. Sigismund of Hungary.	1448. Charles VIII.	1476. Sixtus IV.
1437. Albert of Austria.	1458. Christian I.	1484. Innocent VIII.
1440. Frederick III. of Austria.	1497. John II.	1492. Alexander VI.
1493. Maximilian I.		
	SCOTLAND.	KIPZAK.
	. Robert III.	. Condge Aglen.
FRANCE.	1406. James I.	1401. Boulet.
. Charles VI.	1437. James II.	1420. Oulon Mahomet.
1422. Charles VII.	1460. James III.	. Wars and Divisions in the Khaoate.
1461. Louis XI.	1488. James IV.	
1483. Charles VIII.		1465. Achmet.
1498. Louis XII.		

witnessed the final division of the Mongul empire of Timur in Asia; and it saw the sun set for ever upon the throne of the Cæsars in Constantinople.*

All the enthusiasm that had once been excited by the Crusades had now long since expired; but, notwithstanding the disasters of famine, shipwreck, and plague, that had so scattered and decimated the Christian armies on the Syrian and African shores; nor the anarchy and misrule to which their people became a prey, while the sovereigns were engaged in a distant and fruitless campaign—these wars for the rescue of Palestine had not entirely been unproductive of benefit to the nations and countries of 'Europe. Instead of shutting themselves up in their castles, and spending their days and the lives of their vassals in fierce conflicts with each other, or rebellion against their monarchs, till strangers dare only travel strongly guarded, or through by-ways, and beyond the gates of the walled cities—no man's property or life was secure from the robber baron's or marauding soldier's hand; the minds of the nobles were raised to a higher and more worthy aim. If their object had been mistaken, and their zeal spent on empty air, the motives of the first warriors, who abandoned their former pleasures to meet unknown toils and dangers on a barren and far off shore, though perhaps tinged with a love of adventure, had in many instances been disinterested and pure, and they were thus brought into contact with other nations, and with the science and literature of the East.

If the spirit which had then actuated every soldier and knight, to respond so readily and eagerly to the call of the hermit who first roused their ardour in the cause of the Holy Land, had existed at this time among the princes and people of the West; the Greek empire, in spite of their jealousy of her creed, might perhaps have been saved from her impending fate, and rescued from the sword of the common enemy, the barbarous and infidel Turk. But, though many French and English adventurers were enrolled beneath the flag of Constantine, who was still guarded by the weighty axes of the Varangians, the emperors appealed in vain to their fellow-Christian monarchs for assistance, and the other nations of Europe looked coldly and in-

---

* Invention of Printing, 1452—Copernicus born, 1473—Luther born, 1483—Constantinople taken, 1453—Discovery of America, 1492—Monguls driven from Samarcand, 1468.

differently upon her fall. Surely and steadily had the Turks been long gaining upon her frontiers, and had gradually wrested city after city from her feeble and expiring grasp; yet though the Greeks were divided into hostile factions, servile, profligate, and degraded, and dependent on their once formidable fire bombs and catapults, which the artillery and mining skill of their enemies now far surpassed; though the Mahometans, elated by their conquests, and the dazzling prospect of her wealth, and urged to victory by the precepts and commands of the prophet, had long meditated and prepared her destruction, the Christian empire still maintained a protracted and heroic resistance; and the death and defence of the last Constantine was worthy of the greatness of the first.

It was now many years since the sultans had placed their throne in Adrianople, and erected castles and fortifications within the very sight of Byzantium, on the opposite shore of the Bosphorus; but the glory of the conquest of the capital was reserved for the skill and valour of the second Mahomet, before whom—after a siege of forty-five days, in which, following the precedent of the Russian Oleg, he caused his ships to be transported overland, and a most obstinate defence on the part of the desperate Greeks—it fell on the 29th of May, 1453, after a tremendous bombardment and terrific assault; the young emperor, Constantine Paleologus, falling fighting to the last in the sack, and being scarcely distinguished amidst the ruins, where he lay under heaps of dead. But the same event which extinguished the progress of civilization in Eastern Europe, had a most beneficial effect on the advance and refinement of the West: the capture of Constantinople drove the fugitive Greeks to all parts of the western countries of Europe, where they spread the taste for letters and the arts to a hitherto unknown extent. A more regular government throughout the continent, untrammelled by a turbulent nobility, and enslaved people, gave a peace and security that allowed scope for the encouragement of learning, in a manner that had never been afforded before; and the brilliant names that, a few years after, grace the historic page—of authors, poets, painters, astronomers, navigators, musicians, and sculptors—are a proof that its advantages were not lost.

But far different has been the progress of Asia, the ancient continent; Asia, the first peopled and once most civilized quarter of the globe, yet whose heroes, sages, and philosophers, are now all of the past. Whilst the rest of the world was enveloped in a savage darkness and barbarism, she shone clearly and vividly in the earlier ages of mankind; but her nations, as they advanced in power and knowledge, have sunk between despotism and slavery; and while in Europe the march of progress, and refinement of manners, has been marked by relaxing the bonds of serfdom, and extending liberal institutions among the people, in Asia a settled government and civilization has only given to tyranny a more iron hold; there liberty has ever been unknown: with the harshest despotism of Europe she would have been comparatively free. For many centuries, also, the minds of the Asiatics of the south and west have been confined to the narrow and unyielding doctrines of the Koran, which limits all the researches of its votaries to its own long-exploded ideas of the order of the universe and of man; and content to reflect on their former conquests, and the stupendous monuments that still exist of their ancient grandeur and fame, they appear generally to have sunk into indifference, and to a hopeless state of indolence and apathy; and, while all their princes are despots and oppressors, the people are the most absolute slaves.

I have already related how the successor of Hong-vu drove the Monguls from China, and destroyed the castles and cities that they had erected on their deserts and steppes, and how these conquerors resumed their former pastoral and nomade life, and again lived among their flocks and in tents. From this time their country formed a nominal dependence upon Pekin, and long paid her a humiliating tribute; but towards the middle of the seventeenth century, one of their tribes, the Kalmucks, rose to considerable power and influence in the south, and in a few years had made themselves masters of all central Tartary and Thibet. This supremacy was, however, of very short duration; they were attacked and defeated by the other Monguls, united with the Chinese; and while some settled in the country around the Lake Kokonor, many thousands crossed the Ural and the sandy steppes of Astrakhan, and took refuge beyond the Volga, where a few tribes of the horde of Toushi still remained, after the extinction of the kingdom of Kipzak in Europe. The emperors of China now pay a tax to the Mongul chiefs in their dominions, to restrain them from plundering the wealthier provinces of their empire; and though, if a horde becomes too powerful, it is checked by an army of Chinese, they frequently propitiate these unruly subjects with the hand of an imperial princess. The Kalmucks, including those of both Russia and China, are at the present day probably the most numerous of this race. Their favourite food is still horse-flesh and kumys, and in religion, like all the Monguls, they are Buddhists; and, leading a careless and idle life in their felt huts and tents, spend their lives in hunting and dancing, or the more sedentary pursuits of chess* and music. They have a literature of their own, and ornament their walls with grotesque figures and paintings, and are often clothed in the most filthy rags, while their feet and arms are adorned with jewelled bracelets of gold. As early as towards the end of the fifteenth century, the Monguls in Russia appear to have been commonly known by this name of Kalmuck, which they obtained from the custom of wearing the hair long; while all the other Tartar tribes and Muscovites at that period wore the head shaven, or left merely one lock on the crown, like the Chinese.

The first in power, and the second in number and extent, of the descendants of the former masters of Asia, are probably the Uzbeks, another of their hordes, who are stated by the historian Abulghazi to have been originally a tribe of Toushi from Kipzak. During the troubles that ensued after the defeat of Toktamish in that distracted khanate, they fled from Russia into the regions of Eastern Tartary, from whence, towards the end of the fifteenth century, they descended upon Mavarnalhar or Turkestan, and, driving the descendants of Timur from Samarcand to the province of Ghizni and Hindostan, the white heron-plumed chiefs† now govern all the district of Transoxiana, whose chief kingdoms at the present day are Bokhara and Kokan. The former city, which covers a great extent of ground, contains one hundred and twenty thousand houses and eighty colleges, handsomely built of stone, each attended by from forty to

* It is curious that there is scarcely a tribe throughout Tartary or Siberia who are not acquainted with chess; and this fact would appear to lend some support to the theory, that it was invented by the ancient Scythians.
† The Uzbek chiefs wear a white heron's plume in their turbans.
"Chiefs of the Uzbek race,
Waving their heron plume with martial grace."—MOORE.

three hundred students; and about two hundred miles to the east of its site lies the once famous city of Samarcand, known formerly to its people as the " Glory of Asia, and the flower and star of the earth ;" but which now is little better than a mass of ruins, and falling rapidly still further into decay. The observatory of Ulugh still stands, and the tomb of Timur, paved with green stone and jewels, is still watched by a few dervishes, long supported by his descendants at Delhi; but, since the overthrow of the empire of the Monguls in Hindostan, these protectors of the mausoleum of their great prince have been deprived of their former liberal emolument, and have sunk into a state of great poverty. Khiva stands on the place of the ancient kingdom of Carizme, and is separated by a vast desert from Bokhara; her capital is the great slave mart of Central Asia, and is inhabited by a low and brutalized people; and the few travellers who have visited her in the present century, have estimated that, within the space of a very few years, she has supplied Turcomania and Bokhara with fifteen thousand Russian captives, and from one hundred and fifty thousand to two hundred thousand Persians for slaves.

On the steppes extending from the north of Khiva and the Sea of Aral,* or the Lake of Eagles, to the swamps and marshy regions of Western Siberia, and where in summer the long waving grass, as it is undulated by the wind, resembles the green waters of a troubled sea, the Kirghiz Tartars, justly called the robbers of the deserts, feed their flocks and half-wild cattle, and rob the loaded caravans of the Russian merchants, that are despatched at certain periods of the year from the frontier city and fortress of Orenburg to trade with Khiva and Bokhara. They are generally considered to be the descendants of a division of the Polotzi, called the Kazaks,† whom Constantine Porphyrogenitus describes as inhabiting the district to the north of the Caucasus, and from whom the modern Cossacks probably derive their name. The Kirghiz Tartars, and the wandering tribes of Turcomania, chiefly supply by their prisoners the markets of Khiva with slaves.

The Cossacks, who form so considerable and important a portion of the Russian forces, and were called the eye of his army by General Suvaroff, are divided into two distinct

---
* Aral is a Tartar word, meaning island. The lake is so called from the number of islands in it.
† Kazak is a Tartar or Turkish word for a light-armed horseman or robber.

communities, the Zaporaghians, or Cossacks of the Ukraine,* and those of the Don. The Ukraine is the general name for the fruitful provinces of Kiof, Pultowa, and Tchernigoff; its fields are well watered, and its soil unsurpassed in fertility, producing abundance of fruit and grain, and feeding large droves of cattle; it in former years supplied the storehouses of Athens and Macedonia, and now distributes its corn over half Europe. The inhabitants, who were long subject to Poland, are among the finest and most intellectual in the Russian empire, which has derived many of her greatest men from this district, and are generally considered to be the most unmixed descendants of the ancient Slavonians of Novogorod and Kiof, though their principal nobility derive their origin from their conquerors, the Petchenegan Tartars.† Their dress is a mixture of the Polish and Tartar costumes, particularly that of the rich; and the cottages of the peasantry, according to a modern traveller,‡ strongly resemble the Swiss châlets in their structure and exterior, and the Welsh in the well-kept garden with which they are generally surrounded. Their language is replete with songs ‖ and ballads,

* From the Russian word Ukrayu, "frontier." † Campenhuusen's "Travels in the Ukraine." ‡ Dr. Clarke's "Travels in Little Tartary."

‖ The following is an extract from a Cossack ballad, translated by Bodenstedt in his "Poetische Ukraine," and quoted by Count Krasinski in his "History of Poland."

It begins with the description of a storm raging in the Black Sea, and then says:—"The fleet of the Cossacks is separated into three parts; one of them is stranded on the distant coasts of Anatolia, the second wrecked near the Danube, but the third still floats above the waters. Alas! where can it steer? Will it founder in the Black Sea? On that fleet is the Lord Zbororwshi, the valiant atteman of the Zaporaghues. He walks along his vessel in sadness, hot calm, and speaks these words to the Cossacks:—'The waves rise so high, the wind roars so loud, because a crime must have been committed by one of us. Come all together, and confess your sins before the merciful God, the Black Sea, and me your chief, and let the guilty die in the foaming waves. The whole fleet of the Cossacks must not perish because one has committed a crime.' And the Cossacks stood wondering in silence, and none knew who was the guilty man.

"Then stepped forward Alexis, the son of the priest of Piriatine, and said to his companions—'Take and sacrifice me, O brothers! for your safety. Bind a red band before my eyes, tie a white stone round my neck, and throw me into the dashing waters, and the fleet of the Cossacks shall not perish for my sin.' And the Cossacks wondered when they heard it, and said, 'O Alexis! we are no better than thou; thou canst read the sacred writings, and thy example has oft kept us from evil. How, then, can a grievous sin weigh upon thy soul?'

"'It is true, my brothers, that I am more learned than you; I read and explain the holy writings; I counsel you to reject evil, and seek the paths of righteousness, and yet a grievous sin presses upon my soul.

"'I left my home at Pirintine, and asked not the blessing of my father; I parted in anger from my brother; I took from my neighbour his last morsel of bread; I proudly rode about the streets, and insulted the women and little children; I passed the churches without uncovering my head or making the sign of the cross. I ought now, O my brothers! to perish, and my name be extinguished for ever on the earth. Behold the sea, how it rages and foams; it awaits and expects its prey.'

"But Alexis, the son of the priest, had hardly finished his confession when the storm abated, and the surface of the waves became calm; and the fleet, thus saved by the Almighty's hand, safely landed on the island of Tentra. Not a vessel of their fleet foundered, and the Black Sea had not engulfed a man. And Alexis, the priest's son, abandoned the vessel, and passed the rest of his life in reading the scriptures, and expounding them to the Cossacks, who attentively listened round. To these he spoke words of wisdom—'Walk righteously, O my brothers! before the Lord. Those who follow his commands, shall not perish by the hand of the assassin; the prayers of their father shall safely lead them through every danger; it will keep their souls clean from every mortal sin, and be their protection on land and sea.'"—The original is in verse.

2 A

of which many, with their musical accompaniments, have been composed by the unlettered serfs;* and they have always been impatient of their servitude, from which they have frequently attempted to release themselves, though hitherto their efforts for independence have not been attended with success.

In the year 1240, these provinces were overrun and depopulated by the army of the conqueror Batù Khan; but at the beginning of the fourteenth century the greater part of the Tartar garrison was recalled from Kiof, and in the year 1320, after the city had been captured, and its Russian governor, the Grand Prince Stanislaus, defeated by the Lithuanians under Ghedemin, a body of Russians, flying from the cruelty of the savage conqueror, took refuge among the marshes near the mouth of the Borysthenes, which had been deserted and laid waste since the prior invasion of the Monguls. In the year 1415, the Tartars once more sacked and pillaged Kiof, and many of the citizens sought a shelter among the tents of the Cossacks, who began to build houses and villages, in which they resided during the severity of the winter, while in the summer they carried on plundering excursions in the territories of the Tartars and Turks. In their rough unstable vessels, sailing down the Dnieper, they frequently, like their ancestors, braved the storms of the Black Sea, and, entering the Golden Horn, menaced the city of Constantinople. Their standard of a horse's tail, as it waved from the mast's head of their barks, was well known and dreaded by all the Turkish towns near the sea-coasts; and an Ottoman sultan bitterly lamented, that while his name was known and feared by all Europe, "his rest was disturbed by the perpetual inroads of a few insignificant Cossacks." They extended their colony from the shores of the Black Sea to the banks of the Bog and Dniester, and formed too powerful a bulwark to Poland to be unnoticed or unprotected by her; and Sigismund, in the year 1566, on the occasion of a signal service that their community had rendered to his arms in a war with the Muscovites, induced them to unite with him for mutual defence against the Tartars, and, taking them into his pay and service, appointed them a prince, who took the title of Hetman of the Cossacks. But from these had arisen the singular community called the Zaporaghues, or people "behind the cataracts," a name which

* Krasinski's "Poland."

they obtained from the settlement they formed on the uninhabited islands that lie below the falls of the Dnieper, and to which they had retreated before their countrymen had united themselves with Poland. Their organization was entirely republican, and they were divided into kurens or hearths, each of which contained a certain number of warriors who lived together, holding their wealth and goods in common, and were presided over by a chief elected from among themselves; yet all were ruled alike by the "koshovy attaman" or commander of the camp, who in war had absolute control over every Cossack, but at home could not decide upon any affair of importance without the consent of a select body of officers, comprising the sudia or judge, the pisar or secretary, the assaul or adjutant, the pushkar or chief of the artillery, and the debosh or drummer, who convoked the assembly by beating a drum through the camp.*

Celibacy was as strictly enforced as in the most rigid monastic establishment; no woman was allowed to appear in the settlement, and the Zaporaghues augmented their number by kidnapping children from the neighbouring states, though they were constantly increased by fugitives from Polish oppression, or captives escaping from the neighbouring Tartars, and all firmly adhered to the Greek Church. Their general assembly was held on the 1st of January, when they elected their hetman, who at the end of the year became a simple Cossack, and they could often bring as many as 400,000 fighting men into the field. Perfect equality was preserved among them, and justice rigidly maintained; a murder in their camp was punished by the assassin being interred alive with the corpse; and a thief, after being exposed for three days in a pillory, was beaten to death. No stranger could be enrolled among the Zaporaghians till he had submitted to the severest ordeal, and proved his skill in riding and hunting; and a long and rigorous penance was required from all who aspired to the dignity of chief. This colony had been formed originally during a war between the Cossacks and Poles, in which several of the former had fortified themselves on the Dnieper, and, building forts to the north of Oczakof and Kilburn, had declared themselves independent of Poland, and united for the purpose of opposing the infidel Turks. They wore their hair long, and fought on land with bows and

* Krasinski's "Poland."

long spears; and they continued in their island settlement till the reign of Peter the First, who caused their camp to be destroyed after the battle of Pultowa, as a punishment for their rebellion under their attaman Mazeppa, a Polish fugitive, who had united his followers with the Swedish forces under Charles XII. The Zaporaghues then joined the Tartars in the Crimea, with whom they remained till the Russian conquest; and, by a ukase of the 30th of June, 1792, the Empress Catharine transferred them to the peninsula of Taman, and to the territory at the north of the Caucasus, where their community received a district of about a thousand square miles, between the Black and Caspian Seas, and where they are now known as the Tchenomerskii, or Black Sea Cossacks. In the year 1664, the oppression of the Poles drove the Cossacks of the Ukraine to throw off their allegiance to Poland, and under their hetman, Bogdan Kelminikski, to seek the protection of Russia. Kiof, and all the towns on the eastern bank of the Dnieper, which they almost exclusively inhabited, followed their example, and acknowledged the sway of the Czar;* and thus, after a separation of 334 years, her ancient capital again formed part of the Russian empire.

A Frenchman,† who, during the seventeenth century, served long in the service of Poland, has left an accurate description of the camp and habits of the Cossacks, whom he relates were often extremely rich; and, when they visited the towns in the Ukraine, would perambulate the streets, entertaining every passenger whom they met at the houses of amusement or the beer-shops. Those of the Ukraine frequently joined the Zaporaghues in their expeditions to the Turkish shores of the Euxine, when they repaired to the islands in the Dnieper, and constructed about a hundred boats in the short space of three weeks. Their vessels had no keel, but consisted of a flat bottom of willow, about forty-five feet in length, with the sides built up of reeds thickly bound together, and the whole covered with a coating of pitch; and, having only one small mast, they rowed each bark with ten or fifteen oars, carrying a store of boiled millet and dough, which served them for both meat and drink. Sobriety was a prominent virtue with the Zaporaghues; a drunkard was

* Alexis, father to Peter the Great.
† "Description de l'Ukraine, par le Sieur de Beauplan."

expelled from their community, and no Cossack was permitted to carry brandy or kumys on a voyage.

"Between fifty and seventy Cossacks man each vessel," says the French narrative, "every man bearing a firelock and a scymitar; and this flying army of the Cossacks in the Black Sea, are able to terrify the richest towns in Anatolia. The commander of the expedition leads the van, and carries his standard (a horse's tail) upon the mast of his ship. The Turks have generally obtained warning of their coming, and keep several galleys prepared near the mouth of the Dnieper to oppose them; but the Cossacks, who are cunning, slip out in a dark night, having watched till the moon has set, lying hid among the reeds that are three or four leagues up the river, and where the Ottoman ships dare not venture; since formerly, when in pursuit of the pirates, they were assailed by a concealed armament, and their retreat cut off. The Turks think it sufficient to wait at the entrance of the Dnieper till the Cossacks shall issue forth; but they are always surprised, and then the alarm spreads over the whole country as far as Constantinople, where the sultan sends expresses to all his officers on the coasts of Anatolia, bidding them to be upon their guard, for the Cossacks are at sea. But all this is to no purpose, for the Cossacks are before them, and in less than forty hours land in Asia Minor, where, leaving only two of their men and two boys in charge of each boat, they advance a league up the country, pillaging and burning the towns; and, immediately returning on board with their booty, sail away to try their fortune in some other port. If they meet with a Turkish vessel on the sea, they capture it in this manner:—Their boats are not more than two feet and a half above the water, so that they discover other ships long before they can be perceived themselves; and, striking their masts, they keep within a certain distance of the enemy till midnight, when a signal being given, all simultaneously close round the Turks, who are astonished to be attacked by eighty or a hundred barks, which soon fill their vessel with men, and in a moment bear all down. The Cossacks, after taking all that they can bear away from the Ottoman ship, sink it with the whole of its crew. But when these pirates are encountered by the enemy's galleys in broad day, their boats are often scattered and dispersed; and though, lashing their oars to the side with withes, they make a desperate resistance with their muskets, so that they are never boarded by the Turks, the cannon of the Ottomans makes fearful havoc among their ranks, and they seldom come off with more than one-half of their men.

"When the Turks hear that the Cossacks are returning to their camp loaded with Spanish dollars, Arab sequins, carpets, gold cloth, and silks, they double their guards at the mouth of the Dnieper; but, though weak, the Cossacks laugh at this care, and, landing in a creek about three or four miles east of Oczakof, take their vessels over land to the river's banks. Besides this, they have another refuge; they return by the mouth of the Don through a strait that lies between Taman and Kertch, and run up the mouth to the river Mius, and as far as they can navigate this river, from whence to Yaczavoda is but a league, and Yaczavoda falling into the Samara, a branch of the Dnieper, they make their way by this means to their river settlements. But they seldom return by this route on account of its length, though they often use it when they go out to sea and the mouth of the Dnieper is obstructed by a large force of Turks, or their fleet, as sometimes happens, consists of only about twenty boats." The two forts at Kilburn * and Oczakof were erected to defend the entrance of the river by the Turks, who supported a large garrison with an ample store of artillery in these parts, and hoped by this means to protect the cities of their empire from the harassing and perpetual attacks of the Cossacks.

The settlements of the Cossacks on the Don, arose a few years before the final extinction of the Tartar power in Kipzak, and appears to have been principally composed of Muscovite outlaws, and captives escaping from the servitude of their Mongul masters; but these were, from time to time, increased by fugitives from the neighbouring Tartar, Circassian, and Armenian nations, many of the latter having fled into Russia after the destruction of their city Anni, in the pashalic of Kars, by the terrible earthquake of 1319; and the Cossacks of the Ural and Siberia are only colonists from this camp. Herberstein mentions them under the name of Cosatski in the early part of the sixteenth century, and, a few years later, their courage and enterprise solely completed the

---

* The narrow spit of land on which Kilburn lies, was known to the ancient Greeks as the course of Achilles, who was worshipped here as Lord of the Pontus.

discovery and subjugation of Siberia. They call themselves Donskoi, or of the Don, considering the appellation Cossack as a term of reproach; and all, when they leave their homes, either for battle or to perform their six years of service in guarding the frontiers of Russia, carry a bag of earth from the banks of the Don, to be buried with them if they die at a distance from their native land.

The word "hurrah," the war-cry of the Cossacks, is derived from the Slavonian *hurraj* (to Paradise), and was adopted from the idea entertained by their warriors, that the souls of all who fell in battle were carried straight to the abode of the blest.

Herberstein, writing at the beginning of the sixteenth century, describes the habits and settlement of the Cossacks of the Don, but confounds them with the neighbouring Circassians.* He says, "the Russians assert that they are Christians, that they live under their own independent laws, conform to the Greek ceremonials and ritual, and perform their sacred service in the Slavonic language, which, indeed, they use in general. They are most audacious pirates, and sail down to the sea by the rivers which flow from their mountains, and plunder whomsoever they can, especially those merchants who take the route from Caffa to Constantinople."† "Few of their number," says Beauplan, "die of sickness or old age, but all lie upon the bed of honour, and perish in war or victory."

---

* He even calls the Ukraine Cossacks Circassians, though he says they derive their origin from the Muscovites.
† Herberstein's "*Rerum Muscovitarum.*"

CHAPTER II.

The Horde of Toushi—Reign of Vassili or Bazil Jernuoi, or the Blind—Manners and Customs of the Russians.

<small>New empires rising on the wreck of old.—COLLINS.</small>

OF the three great divisions of the Mongul empire, the horde of Toushi was the last to fall; and her former subjects, the Uzbeks, whom the cruelty of Timur had caused to fly from Kipzak, and take up their abode in desert regions, nearer and more accessible to Samarcand, had no sooner seen his dominions melting away beneath the sceptre of his more feeble successors, than they poured like a flood upon the capital he had so fondly enriched by his conquests, and drove his descendants to seek a throne among the wild mountain fastnesses of Ghizni. But Kipzak never recovered the repeated defeat of her forces under Toktamish; her power from this time gradually weakened, and her dominions were divided and given up to anarchy and civil war. While her Russian tributaries were asserting their independence in the centre, the Muscovites were extending their eastern frontiers, and bringing the other principalities of the empire beneath their sway; and the Grand Prince Bazil, the son and successor of the hero of the Don, frequently threatened and invaded her northern provinces, in the year 1396 capturing and utterly wasting the city of Kazan. Vassili died in 1425, after a long reign of thirty-six years; but having previously confined his wife Anastasia, the daughter of Vitold of Lithuania, in a monastery, he refused to acknowledge their only son Bazil, a boy of ten years old, as his successor, and on his deathbed left the throne to his brother George. But the boyards, relying on a prophecy of a blind monk of Moscow, who had foretold, the day of the young prince's birth, that this grandson of Donskoi should become sovereign of all Russia, supported his claims against his uncle, and procuring his formal appointment from Oulou Mahomet, who had succeeded Boulet Kipzak, placed him upon the Muscovite throne. George immediately took up arms against his nephew, and the war was carried on for some years, till at length both agreed to refer the matter to the decision of the Golden Horde. The two princes departed, each with a strong body of archers, to Serai, and fell down on their knees before the Tartar monarch; and Oulou Mahomet, by the advice of his ministers, who had been previously bribed by George, declared that the succession to the throne ought to go by seniority, according to the ancient law of Russia; and that, as the late sovereign had left the kingdom to his brother, that prince undoubtedly had the greatest right. "Alas! most mighty khan," exclaimed the disinherited Bazil, prostrating himself at the feet of the Mongul chief, "permit me for one instant to speak. Thou hast announced thy decision upon lifeless words, but I trust that the living documents which I possess, and which distinctly express, under the authority of thy golden seal, thy former wish to invest me with the grand duchy, may be held by thee to be of far greater weight and importance;" and he earnestly besought the khan to hold his own words in remembrance, and adhere to his former promise. After listening to his arguments, Oulou Mahomet observed—"That it would be more consistent with justice to keep the promises contained in living documents, than to admit the lawfulness of dead ones;" and he not only decided the contest in favour of Bazil, but also exempted him from tribute, and decreed that George should hold the horse of his successful opponent upon his entrance into his capital. The elder prince was greatly enraged by the result of his appeal, and, raising a large army, marched against Bazil, whom he drove out of Moscow, and forced to retreat to the north, where he intrenched himself in the town of Kostroma, and reigned during the remainder of his enemy's life. But when George was on his deathbed, and the archbishop of Moscow had come, according to custom, to invest him with the priestly garments, and perform the last offices of religion, the latter boldly addressed the dying prince, and told him that, before he could make his peace with Heaven, he must repair his former injustice, and acknowledge his nephew as his successor; and, yielding to his directions, the Grand Duke dictated a will in favour of the injured Bazil, excluding his own sons, Andrea and Demetrius, from the throne. He expired a few moments after, and his testament being proclaimed, gave occasion to another war between Bazil and the two disinherited princes, who considered that they had been unjustly deprived of their father's dominions; but their cause was upheld by very few adherents, and at length, falling into the hands of their cousin, he commanded them to be thrown into prison, where their eyes were barbarously put out.

The city of Kazan, after being ruined by Bazil Dmitrovitz, had been rebuilt by its inhabitants in 1438, and had remained since the days of Toktamish independent of Kipzak. Its fortunes, since its first erection, had been most varied and unhappy; originally a flourishing town of the Khazars, its caravanserais had then been the resort of Arabs, Persians, Georgians, Khazars, and other strangers from all Asia, even the distant southern Hindoo; while, by the White Sea and Dwina, Norwegians, Novogorodians, and occasionally adventurous merchants of Western Europe, had come from the north, and met to traffic and barter the wares of three continents in its markets. Then came the invasion of the Monguls, who rebuilt it after the city had been reduced to stones and ashes by order of Batù Khan, and it was united to the possessions of the horde of Toushi in Kipzak, but never regained its former influence and commerce. In the year 1363 it was captured and burned by the Novogorodians; but these were driven back to the north in 1390 by Toktamish, who destroyed the republic of Viatka, which, with Nijni-Novogorod, he wrested from the invaders, giving the latter to a Russian prince, Demetrius.* Simon, the prince of Suzdal, who claimed this province, united with Katieha, whom Toktamish had appointed viceroy of Kazan, in endeavouring to wrest it from Demetrius, but was defeated by the Russians with great slaughter; and, shortly after, the Muscovites under Bazil advancing upon the town, it was stormed by them, and again totally destroyed. After it had only been rebuilt three years, Oulou Mahomet, surnamed the Great, invaded the eastern provinces of Russia, and captured Nijni-Novogorod. He then attacked the old and strongly fortified castle of Murom, but was repulsed from its walls by Bazil with a large army, when two of his sons, reassembling their scattered forces, marched upon Suzdal, and

* Cochrane's "Siberia."

plundered the whole country up to Moscow, where, after several hard fought engagements, they stormed and sacked the capital, and took the Grand Prince captive. In the mean time, their father had besieged and pillaged Kazan, and executed her khan Ali Bey, placing one of his sons, Mametak, upon the throne; and, shortly after, Mahomet consented to release Bazil in October 1446, upon the payment of a moderate ransom, which, with some difficulty, was collected by his nobles among his oppressed subjects. They at length brought it and laid it at the feet of the khan, and conducted their prince to Moscow; but Schemiaka, the only surviving son of George, had assembled many adherents, with promises and bribery, throughout the empire, during the prince's captivity, and, advancing with a considerable force, closely besieged him in the capital. Bazil fortified himself in the monastery of St. Sergius; but his enemy, having contrived to effect an entrance into the city under cover of the night, with some of his soldiers concealed in waggons loaded with merchandise, he was surprised and taken prisoner in his stronghold, and his eyes being put out by command of his adversary, in revenge for his cruel treatment of the brothers of Schemiaka, he was subsequently sent in chains with his wife to Uglitz.

But the cause of their unfortunate prince was unanimously espoused by the Russian boyards* and people, who, led on by the powerful voice of the Church, a few months after drove Schemiaka from Moscow, and brought back the blind prince. Ivan, the son of the usurper, who, being an infant, had been left behind by his father when he fled from the palace in the capital, was condemned to close imprisonment for the rest of his life, and he remained in captivity throughout the few remaining years of the reign of Bazil, and during the lives of his son and grandson, and at length expired in his dungeon at a very advanced age.

Demetrius was poisoned soon after his flight to Novogorod by some of his own followers, and a heavy fine was exacted from the republic by the Muscovites, as a penalty for harbouring a rebel. The last few years of Bazil's eventful life passed away in comparative peace; and at his death, in 1462, his sceptre devolved upon his eldest son Ivan, whose long and

* This word is derived from Boi, a battle, and was originally given to the chiefs who surrounded the prince in the field.

glorious reign obtained for him from posterity the title of Veliki or the Great, and who may justly be considered as the founder of the present empire of Russia. But when he commenced his reign, his territories comprised only Moscow and Vladimir, and the inferior principalities that had been subdued by his great-grandfather, Demetrius; and Novogorod and Pleskof were hardly even nominally dependent on Muscovy, as they only paid a tribute to its princes when urged by fear of a hostile attack. The Grand Princes assumed the pompous titles of the "Great Lord Vassili, by the grace of God Lord of all Russia, and Grand Duke of Vladimir, Moscow, Novogorod, Smolensko, Tchernigoff, Riazan, Tver, Jugaria, Permia, and Bulgaria, and key-bearer and chamberlain of the Most High;" yet they knelt before the Mussulman envoy of the Monguls, and every letter from the khan was read by the Tartar ambassador, seated on a carpet of the rarest furs, while the Muscovite sovereign and his nobles all remained prostrate around. Surrounded as they were by enemies, and debarred from all intercourse with foreign nations, pride, exclusive reserve, and contempt for all other creeds and countries, marked the character of the Russians; no Jew had been permitted to reside in their territories since the days of Monomachus, no subject could leave them, and no foreigner could enter them, without the special permission of the prince; a member of the Church of Rome was esteemed as more unholy than a Pagan or Mahometan, and the Russians rigidly purified themselves if they touched even the clothes of an alien to their customs or belief; they might not eat with a heretic or unbeliever, and at all times abstained from many species of food as unclean, among others, hares, rabbits, and strangled animals, or those that had been violently killed by another of its kind, and they never permitted a pigeon or dove to be put to death, as they considered them to be emblems of the Holy Ghost. No daughter of a prince or noble might espouse a husband of a different faith.

The national councils, that had occasionally been convened by the Russian princes even in the most troubled times, before the invasion of the Monguls, had now long since been discontinued, the last having been dissolved in Moscow by the great-grandfather of Ivan, Demetrius. Despotism pervaded every ordinance and institution throughout the state; the Tartars tyrannized over and oppressed the Grand Princes and all the people; the princes, the nobles; the nobles and soldiers, the peasantry and slaves; and the lot of these last, who were generally prisoners of war or their descendants, was scarcely more severe than that of the wretched free labourers, who were exposed to perpetual pillage from the military marauders and outlaws; and when they had hired themselves for a year to their masters, as was the custom on St. George's day, for the small wages of a silver coin, worth something less than a halfpenny a day, were usually driven regularly to their work by blows. The Mongul law, condemning all who could not pay their tribute into slavery, drove thousands of the poorer Russians to seek a refuge in the remote forests, and desert districts, and marshes of the empire; where, some becoming hermits,* subsisted on roots and grass, and spent their lives in religious meditations, while others turned robbers and plunderers, and supported themselves by pillaging travellers or the nearest towns in the summer, and in the winter often perished from the cold, or were destroyed by the numerous wild beasts. It was a band of outlaws such as these that first gave rise to the tribe of the Don Cossacks.

Although the law was in most respects a dead letter, yet the wise code and regulations of Jaroslaf still remained; no capital punishment or torture could legally be inflicted, even upon a slave, without an express order from the Grand Prince, but the authority of a husband was supreme to life, liberty, and death, over his wife and children; and the poor had no access to their sovereign, who, except when on a military expedition, was seldom seen by any but his ministers, the nobles of his court, and attendants. When he declared war, or was forced to take up arms in self-defence, his standard was joined by all the princes and boyards, with their dependants; all who could afford it equipping themselves and fighting without pay, and, if victory attended their arms, these gratuitous warriors were recompensed with the enemy's spoil. The Muscovite forces were entirely composed of cavalry, who rode without spurs, and stirrups so short that they could seldom sustain a severe shock from a javelin or spear; their saddles were constructed to turn round in any direction when they used their chief weapon, the bow; and they also carried a long pike, a hatchet, a sabre, and a stick with a leather thong, from which depended an iron ball covered with

---

* Anchorites are still not uncommon in Russia.—See "Englishwoman in Russia."

spikes. A long knife or poniard was suspended from the arm of the soldier, to use if driven to extremity, and he held the rein on the little finger of the left hand, and the whip on that of the right, these completing his ordinary outfit. But many of the boyards wore coats of mail, highly ornamented with devices and mottoes in silver, on the breast, and a helmet of a peaked form, like the common fur cap; while others clothed themselves in silk habits stuffed with wool, to resist the blow of a sabre, and used a round target or shield like those of the Tartars. On the banner of the Grand Prince, which was borne, surmounted by a crescent and horse's tail, in token of his subjection to the Mahometans, was depicted a figure of Joshua at the head of the Israelites, in the act of commanding the sun to stand still. The Russian horses were small and unshod, but strong and swift; and on their military expeditions the soldiers carried no other food but salt and millet-seed, and occasionally a little pork, with fuel, a hatchet, and copper kettle; and, collecting the herbs that grew about their encampment, they lighted a fire, and boiled these together while halting for the night, though, when passing over a barren or waste country, they would often fast for two or three days during a march. At these times they were forced to depend for subsistence on the uncertain fruits of the chase, or cook for their only provision, leaves, sticks, and grass; but the princes and nobility, who were generally more amply furnished, would frequently invite the poorer officers to share their board, and, after they had dined, leave the rest to be finished by the men. The sons of the boyards were early exercised in those sports and amusements that would fit them for soldiers in after life; hunting, running at the tilt, archery, and races, both on horseback and on foot, were their favourite occupations, and prizes were offered by the government to the most skilful and accomplished in these arts. But the Russians of all classes, from the poorest peasant to the Grand Prince, were most passionately addicted to games of chance, particularly cards and gambling with dice; it was no uncommon spectacle to see labourers, resting from their work, seated in the centre of the field, deliberating over chess or draughts; and, among the higher classes, houses, lands, and slaves, were frequently lost or gained in a night. Usury was most exorbitant, as it had always been in Russia, and the common interest of money was twenty per cent. In counting they reckoned by forties and nineties, called *sorogs* and *dewenosts*, instead of hundreds, and always used the calculating machines of the Tartars. The money of Moscow was oblong instead of round, and, till the reign of Ivan, inscribed with Mongul characters; the lowest silver coin was a dina, with the impression of a rose on one side and an inscription on the other; and six of these made an altin, twenty a grivna, a hundred a poltin, and two hundred a rouble, the last having been introduced and first coined, in bars of silver, in the reign of Vladimir Monomachus. In Novogorod, the dina bore the figure of a prince seated on his throne, while a man was prostrating himself before him, and was worth twice as much as that of Moscow; and, in Pleskof, the head of an ox crowned was depicted on the coin, while all of these had inscriptions on the reverse. The goldsmiths of Muscovy also cast money for themselves, and practised the most flagrant adulteration and clipping of the current coin; and every merchant bringing wares into Moscow was compelled, before entering the city, to exhibit them, at a fixed time and place, to the magistrate or officer of the gates, who placed a price upon them to prevent extortion, which the owner could not vary, and they could not be sold to a subject till they had been offered and displayed to the prince. Post stations had been established by the Monguls in all parts of the empire, each supplying a regular number of horses; so that, when the royal couriers rode from place to place, they were furnished with a steed without delay. But all travellers were equally at liberty to avail themselves of this convenience, on payment of a charge of about six dinas for every ten or fifteen versts,[*] and a passport from the Grand Prince; and, if the horse fell exhausted on the road, they were expected to restore it, or give an adequate price to the postmaster or yamstchink for the owner. Indeed, the regulations for travelling, and the caravanserais provided freely in the different villages on the way, appear to have been conducted throughout Russia, at the end of the fifteenth century, in a manner very similar to those of the present day.

The houses of the nobility were generally large, and the rooms lofty, with windows glazed with thin sheets of talc [†] instead of glass, and fitted round with divans, which served

---

[*] A verst is equal to three-quarters of an English mile.
[†] It is still in almost universal use for windows throughout Siberia.

both for seats and beds; and in every dwelling was placed the image of a saint, before which each guest prostrated himself on entering, previous to addressing his host. The greatest ceremony was observed in all social intercourse; and no boyard would walk on foot five yards from his door without causing his horse to be led in attendance. When he rode out he was attended by several slaves, who ran along by the sides of his horse, and of whom many were possessed by every man of consideration or wealth; often they were his own countrymen, who had sold themselves to obtain protection and security. The dress of all the Russians consisted of a long caftan with a girdle or sash, and surmounted by a jacket of fur; and only differed in quality and material according to the rank of the wearer. The caftan was generally worked in various coloured silks on the sleeves and down the front, and was ornamented among the higher classes by a collar set with pearls; their caps were of black fur, and of a high peaked form, worn equally when in their houses or abroad, as they commonly shaved their heads; and long hair was only displayed as a sign of mourning, or that the wearer had fallen into disgrace with the Grand Prince. Full trousers, gloves, and scarlet slippers or high boots, peaked at the toes, and among the peasantry a knife or hatchet at the girdle, completed the ordinary dress of the Russians, which very much resembled that of the modern Persians.

Marriages were always arranged between the parents, for no husband beforehand ever saw the face of his bride; and it was contrary to the laws to marry more than twice, or a relation within cousins of the fourth degree. Following to the letter the precepts of the apostle, "that a priest should be the husband of one wife," no man could be ordained a parish or secular priest till he was married; the office was hereditary, and, as the church revenues were generally devoted to the support of the monasteries, he maintained himself by the cultivation of a piece of land set apart in every village for the use of the priest; but if he became a widower he was forbidden to contract a second alliance, and was forced to enter a monastery, where he became one of the black clergy, or monks. From these last the bishops and archbishops were selected, whose chief, the metropolitan, since the fall of Constantinople, had been appointed by the Russians and their prince; and under his authority were the archbishoprics of Tver,

Riazan, Permia, Suzdal, Colonna, Tchernigoff, and Serai, and the monasteries, which were numerous throughout the empire, and presided over by abbots or archimandrites. The ecclesiastical regulations and ordinances were remarkably severe; a hundred and ninety-five ordinary fasts had been appointed throughout the year by the church, and perpetual abstinence from meat, fish, milk, and eggs, was exacted from the higher dignitaries, while no priest might join in any species of amusement, or touch any kind of food on a fast-day or before performing divine service.* Service was performed in all the churches three times a week, and then once in the day; and while the priests chanted the prayers or read the accustomed portions of the Holy Scriptures, the people would accompany them with ejaculations of, "O Lord, have mercy upon us!" or by weeping and striking their foreheads on the ground. The principal monastery in Moscow was that of St. Sergius, or the Holy Trinity, where the bones of the saint had been interred, and where the monks freely entertained every visitor, from the Grand Prince to the meanest peasant, who came there to dine, with the contents of a large copper caldron kept continually filled with soup and herbs. But many priests and monks frequently resorted to the thick forests and wild districts of Russia, where they lived as hermits, in caves excavated by their own hands, or in narrow huts raised high upon a column, called a Stolpa (from which they obtained the name of Stolpniki), and subsisted on roots and grass; while others travelled to the remote tribes of the Lapps and Samoyedes, on the borders of the Icy Sea, or among the other distant provinces of the empire, to preach against the oppression and exaction that everywhere prevailed, and endeavour to convert and reform the people. The dress of the common clergy, whose office was hereditary, was very similar to the laity, with the addition of a large broad-brimmed hat, and they all carried a staff to lean upon, called a possack; but the archbishops and bishops wore black mitres and robes of silk, and their staffs were surmounted by a cross, while the monks were always clothed in black. They wore their hair shaven at the crown, which was covered with a skull-cap, but at the sides, with the beard, grew long and flowing, as among all the priests of the Greek church at the present day; and for many years the Russian bishops collected tithes in

* Nearly all these ordinances are still in force in the Greek and Russian church.

Lithuania, till they were at length compelled to desist from this practice by its heathen prince, Vitold, who feared that his country would be impoverished only to enrich the revenues of his enemies the Muscovites.

When a Russian Grand Prince wished to marry, it was the custom to send a summons to all the nobles throughout the empire, commanding them to bring their daughters on a stated day to his palace. All who came were ushered into a state apartment, from which every male attendant was carefully excluded, and, the doors being closed and guarded, the ladies were compelled to unveil while the Prince walked before them and selected the most beautiful for his bride.* No women, except the old, were permitted to walk in the streets, or attend the churches or public places of amusement; a sort of gallery or terrace is still shown, near the Cathedral in the Kremlin, where the Czarina and her ladies remained closely screened from public view during the performance of the usual church service. They had no influence or authority in their household, and, among the higher classes, passed their days in chess-playing and music, or any frivolous amusement, while she who attempted to escape from her husband was punished by being buried alive. Among the lower classes the wife of a peasant usually occupied herself in lace-making, sewing, or spinning, and was occasionally permitted on special holidays to amuse herself by swinging with her daughters in a field, but was not permitted to take the life of any fowl or other animal as all that had been killed by her hands was considered to be defiled and unclean. The dress of a Russian woman much resembled that of the men; but, except when quite alone, she was always closely veiled. She also wore ear-rings and bracelets set with brilliant jewels, and painted her face red and white, and her teeth black.

Such was the state of Russia and the habits of its people, at the time when Ivan III. ascended his father's throne. He had been educated in strict seclusion till the age of fifteen, and then presented to the boyards as their future sovereign, according to the custom usually pursued with regard to the Russian princes at this period; but his heart

---

* Vassili, the son of Ivan the Great, chose his empress out of fifteen hundred.
The first time a Russian Czarina appeared in public, was in a pilgrimage to the monastery of St. Sergius, in which the wife of Alexis (the father of Peter the Great) accompanied her husband veiled, in an open carriage, but most of the spectators turned their faces from her, and looked on the ground as she passed.

had long in secret revolted against the servitude and degraded position of his countrymen: he saw the mischievous influence of this degradation on their character, and the lawlessness and depravity that existed throughout the state. The clergy, whose power, next to the Tartars, was predominant in the empire, too often brought scandal upon their profession by their tyranny, usurious exactions, and vices; and occasionally, when brought to justice by their infidel masters, presented the disgraceful spectacle of a priest receiving the just reward of his crimes from the hand of the common executioner. Many of the monasteries in the provinces distant from Moscow, and far from the supervision of the metropolitan, were little better than a den of outlaws and robbers; and the monks would even venture forth in the night, and pillage the caravans of passing merchants or traders, and the equipages of lonely and unguarded travellers. Bands of soldiers, who had been hastily assembled in time of war, and then dispersed without money or homes over the country, pillaged the oppressed peasantry and villages; and every where anarchy and disorder prevailed. But, with the reign of Ivan, a tragic page is passed in the history of Russia, and a new and more brilliant era commenced. Ascending the throne at the age of twenty-two, of a handsome person and almost gigantic stature, his appearance prepossessed his subjects in his favour, and, from the first year of his reign, they regarded him as destined to be their deliverer. After refusing to pay tribute to the khan, and freeing the nation from their foreign tyrants, which was, however, accomplished more by the valour of his subjects than his own courage or military skill, he turned his efforts to the re-establishment of justice and order, and, reviving the code of Jaroslaf, gave them other and new laws more suitable to the age and state, and attempted to raise the poorer classes of the people by putting a check upon the unbearable oppression of the nobility. He abolished the temporary militias, and organized a standing army, which, with the assistance of the gunpowder and artillery he introduced, ably supported him in his numerous wars; but his character is stained with a merciless and unscrupulous cruelty, which is but too commonly seen in the reforms and acts of victorious despotic sovereigns, however wise or great. "Founders of empires," says the Russian historian Karamsin, "are rarely distinguished for their gentleness; and the firmness requisite for great political actions is nearly allied to harshness and severity. As history is no eulogium, but should be entirely impartial and true, it is impossible to disregard many errors in the lives of the greatest heroes and monarchs. In regarding Ivan only as a man, he had not the amiable qualities of Monomachus, or of Dmitri Donskoi; but, as a sovereign, he may certainly be placed in the highest rank. Ever guided by foresight, he sometimes appeared timid or indecisive; but this irresolution arose always from an excessive prudence, a virtue which does not please us like a generous temerity, but is nevertheless more fitted to consolidate a new and slender foundation, though its progress may be slow, and at first appear incomplete. How many illustrious princes and warriors have merely bequeathed to posterity the bare remembrance of their glory! But Ivan has formed and left to us an empire of immense extent and strength; powerful, indeed, from the number and energy of its people, but still more so from the policy and spirit of its government."

In 1430, in the early part of the reign of Bazil, his grandfather, the renowned Vitold of Lithuania, expired in Vilna at the advanced age of eighty, having been baptized some time before into the Greek faith, when he took the name of Alexander. The year previous to his death, he had assembled a peaceful congress of sovereigns, very rare in those times, at the town of Troki in Lithuania, where he entertained them for seven weeks with extraordinary splendour, and every species of hunting, feasting, and amusement; so that, as the Polish chronicler informs us, there was "much drinking and but little work." On this occasion, there were present Bazil III. of Moscow, then a boy of fifteen, the Russian princes of Tver, Riazan, and Odoyeff, the Duke of Mazovia, the Grand Master of the Order of Teutonic knights, the Khan of the Crimea, the Prince of Wallachia, and the ambassador of the Greek emperor, John Paleologus.*

No foreign merchant at this period was permitted to trade with Moscow; and, though all Europeans might carry on free commerce at Novogorod, Turks and Tartars were compelled to confine their traffic to a town called Chlopigrod, about twelve miles distant from the latter city, but of which neither trace nor stone remain at the present day. The inhabitants

* Krasinski's "History of Poland."

of Novogorod, unlike most of the Slavonic race, were bold and ready sailors, and manned many of the ships frequenting her port; and, as late as the middle of the sixteenth century, Russian corsairs from Novogorod were known and dreaded on the shores, and among the fishing villages, of the Baltic.

In the reign of Ivan the Great, the first watch seen in Russia was sent as a present from the king of Denmark to his eldest son; but the Muscovites imagined that it was enchanted, or an evil spirit sent to work some mischief in their empire, and it was hastily returned to the donor, though with many thanks and expressions of gratitude.

CHAPTER III.

The reign of Ivan Vassilovitz—His conquests—Marriage with Sophia of Byzantium—The church—A new code of laws—War with Kipzak—Embassies to Moscow.*

> Who would be free, themselves must strike the blow.
> By their own arms the conquest must be wrought.—BYRON.

AT the period when Ivan ascended the throne of Muscovy, the population of his empire amounted to six millions; and, notwithstanding the great increase of his territories during a long reign of forty-four years, it had only augmented at his death to ten, owing to his numerous and sanguinary wars. The old writer, Eden, in the sixteenth century, observes, that "the Muscovites appear to be the only nation who have never

* LINE OF PRINCES OF MOSCOW.

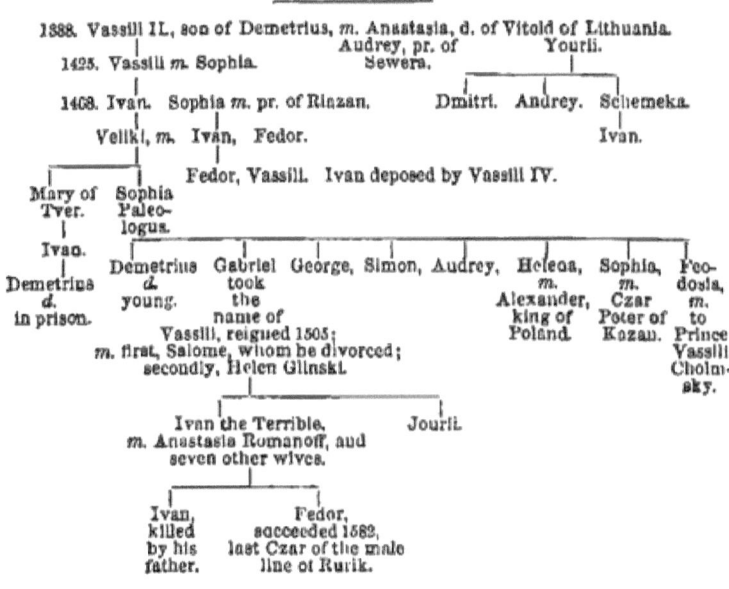

enjoyed the blessings of peace; for if nature had not so strongly defended their territories as to render them almost impregnable, they had often before now been completely obliterated from the face of the earth." Ivan had espoused at an early age Mary, the daughter of Boris, Grand Prince of Tver; and, upon the death of this prince, he seized upon the principality of his son and successor, Michael, ostensibly to revenge an attack upon Muscovy by the army of Tver, in the preceding reign. The prince fled to Lithuania, where he died an exile; some years after, Ivan possessed himself with the same pretext of the duchy of Riazan, whose chief, Fedor, had married his sister Sophia; and brought his two nephews, Ivan and Fedor, prisoners to Moscow.

The introduction of gunpowder and cannon into Russia, by Ivan—who caused many pieces to be cast in his capital by an Italian, Aristotle of Bologna,* whom he sent for from Venice for the purpose—greatly aided him in his numerous campaigns, and placed him on an equality with the Tartars, to whom it appears originally to have been known, though they strictly kept the secret of its composition, and allowed it latterly to fall into disuse. The same artist recast the coin of Muscovy, still disfigured by Tartar characters, and impressed upon it an inscription in Russian, and also rebuilt several churches in Moscow, particularly that of the Virgin, in the Kremlin.

Upon his coronation Ivan assumed the title of Czar, a practice always followed henceforth by his successors; and from this period it was generally used by the European sovereigns in addressing the Grand Princes of Russia; and in a letter from King Philip of Castile, in the year 1504, it was not only applied to Ivan, but also to his eldest son. The word "czar," which was always used in Russia when speaking of the Mongul khans, was, besides, occasionally translated into emperor † by the foreign courts, when mentioning the Grand Prince; but this was always energetically opposed by the Poles, who were extremely jealous of the slightest increase of power or consideration on the part of their hostile neighbours of Russia. But, before his death, Ivan had increased his titles to "Emperor and lord of all the Russias, and Grand

---

* Ivan sent Dmitri Ivanovitz, and Mitrofan Kuratscharoff, in March 1499, to Italy, for the purpose of engaging architects, cannon-founders, and a few other workmen, for Russia.
† Herberstein says, "All now call him emperor."

Prince of Vladimir, Moscow, Novogorod, Pleskof, Bulgaria, Viatka, Smolensko, Tver, Jugaria, Permia, Nijni Novogorod, and Tchernigoff; Riazan, Vologda, Rostoff, Belaia, Rjer Vladimiroff, Yaroslaf, Bielozeria, Udoria, Obdoria, and Condinia the White* (or Great) czar, and keybearer, and chamberlain of God." In return, he used the title of king to the German emperor, king of Sweden, the princes of Prussia and Livonia, and the sultan of Turkey, but merely conceded the appellation of doctor to the pope.

No sooner had Ivan succeeded to the crown of Muscovy, and, defying the power of the Golden Horde, refused to take an oath of allegiance, than the khan, assembling a numerous force, marched into Russia to punish his rebellious vassal with the sword. But the Czar, foreseeing this conjuncture, had hastily raised a levy of soldiers from among every rank in the population, and succeeded in collecting a more numerous native army than had ever before trod the steppes on the Don; "so that the Russians shone over the plains," says the Muscovite historian, "like the waves of the sea when illuminated by the beams of the sun." Their number and formidable appearance struck terror into the heart of the Tartar monarch, who withdrew his troops without hazarding a battle or striking a blow; and Ivan, to satisfy and employ his men, who were eager for war and plunder, sent them under the most experienced of his generals against Kazan, while he himself returned to Moscow. This kingdom was still held by the Toushi prince Mametak, the son of Oulou Mahomet, who had been succeeded in Kipzak by his nephew Achmet, with whom and Mametak had long existed a deadly strife; and Ivan, availing himself of these divisions among the Monguls, concluded for the time a peace with Kipzak, who, blind to the certain fact that the ruin of Kazan would only herald her own destruction, anxiously watched and expected the sister kingdom's fall. In the year 1469, or 6847 of the Russian calendar, the Muscovites appeared before the walls of the fortified city, and soon effected a breach with cannon and ball. A few days after, it was stormed and carried by a vigorous assault; and the khan falling in the attack, the Russians placed a garrison in the city, and appointed Alega, the son

* All the Tartars, Calmucks, Chinese, and other Asiatics, still call the Czar, Tzagan Zar, or White Czar. White was formerly the Khan of Tartary's royal colour, and is still worn by the Chinese Emperor when he visits Tartary, for in China he wears pale yellow. The Tartars called all royal residences white cities, and the crown lands are still so called in Russia.

of a former sovereign, to the throne. From this time, for many years, Kazan was little more than a Russian dependent province. Ivan nominated all her khans, and upon Alega appearing impatient of this servitude, sent secret orders to the Muscovite officers who commanded the garrison in the city, to procure his immediate deposition, and cause him to be conveyed to Russia. In order to accomplish this, without the danger of a rescue or outbreak, the Russian governor invited the khan to a banquet, and, having spared no persuasion or temptation to induce him to drink to excess, caused him to be placed in a carriage while in this state, under the pretext of conveying him back to his palace, and privately directed the postilion to drive over the frontier towards Moscow. They were met near the borders of the Muscovite territories by a body of armed horsemen, who, binding the unfortunate prince, conducted him to the capital, where, after a long imprisonment, he was sent a captive to Vologda, and remained there till released by death. His mother and two brothers were also removed from Kazan to the monastery of Bielozero; but the former was restored to freedom upon the khan of the Crimea demanding her in marriage, though she afterwards returned to Russia, to share the captivity of her sons. Of these, the elder, Codaicula, consenting to receive baptism, went to Moscow, where he espoused Sophia, second daughter of Ivan, and resided during the remainder of his life, being known by the name of the Czar Peter; and the family of the younger, Meniktair, subsequently embracing Christianity, ultimately settled in Muscovy.

In the meanwhile, after the dethronement of Alega, Ivan had appointed, first the prince Strelecherai to the throne of Kazan, and upon his death Machnedin, the youngest brother of Alega; but this khan, though he revolted against the Russians, and reigned for several years independent, rendered himself most unpopular with his subjects by his attempts to prevent their inroads upon Siberia, Kipzak, and the other surrounding states, and in the year 1519 he was chased from the kingdom by the Tartars. During the war with Kazan, the neighbouring republic of Viatka, a colony of Novogorod, at first declared herself neutral between the two belligerents; but the mother city, perceiving that the eyes of Ivan were now turned upon her, more boldly called upon this province to unite with Pleskof and its twelve tributary cities, and join her in a general war against Muscovy, to forestall the designs of the ambitious prince, and accordingly commenced by expelling the officers of the Czar from her territories. The chief instrument in this movement was Marfa, the rich widow of a former posadnick, or chief magistrate; and who, being seized with a romantic passion for Alexander Vitold, the waywode of Lithuania, was desirous of bestowing her country as her marriage-dower upon the possessor of her heart. This anxiety was further strengthened by a prophecy of a former archbishop, Euthemius, who had foretold at the birth of Ivan that he would be the author of their country's fall. Her unlimited hospitality and liberality had gained for her unbounded influence among all classes of the citizens; her palace* was always open to the wayfarer of every rank; and the great bell of Novogorod, at whose sound all the judges and deputies of the republic were accustomed to assemble in the Hall of Justice, and deliberate in solemn council upon the most important affairs of state, was now rung merely to summon guests to her sumptuous banquets.

The Novogorodians, acceding to the proposals of Marfa, who argued that, in placing their country under the protection of Lithuania, they would ensure for her the support of this powerful duchy and of Poland, proclaimed that they renounced for ever the dominion and *suzeraineté* of the Czar; and in 1470 formally submitted themselves and the republic, by treaty, to Alexander of Lithuania. He appointed the archbishop of the city to the chief direction of affairs, and exacted annually, as the price of his protection, the enormous tribute of one hundred thousand roubles, a protection which ultimately entirely failed them at the time of their greatest distress.

Upon receiving intelligence of this act of defiance, Ivan immediately declared war against Novogorod, and for seven years carried on a desultory strife with the inhabitants. But, during this time, his forces overran Permia and the north, where he exacted tribute from the Laplanders, as far to the west in Norway as Trondheim; and, forbidding the commercial intercourse that had hitherto existed between the former state and Novogorod, and through her with the cities of the Hanseatic League, he thus cut off from the republic one of

* Marfa's house is still shown in Novogorod.

the chief sources of her wealth. In 1476 he caused the city and fortress of Ivanogrod to be constructed in one year upon the river Nerva; the river which forms the boundary between Novogorod and Livonia, and a year after, defeating the forces of the citzens in a long and sanguinary engagement upon the river Scholona, he obtained their submission at discretion, and appointed a Russian governor over the province.

But this officer, in obedience to the commands of his imperial master, required that the republic should receive within their gates the Muscovite boyards, with privileges equal to its own citizens; that they should surrender up the palace of Jaroslaf for his residence, and abolish the national assemblies. The citizens, indignant at these demands, assembled in tumultuous crowds in the market-place, attacked the houses of those nobility whom they suspected of being traitors to their country and devoted to the Russian interest, tore the unfortunate owners to pieces in the streets, and expelled the oppressive envoy of the Czar. But this revolt was most promptly and severely punished; Ivan marched upon Novogorod, and, entering the Hall of Justice, expressed his determination to the magistrates to reign as supreme there as he did in Moscow. He caused Marfa and the richest inhabitants of the city to be seized and conveyed prisoners to his capital, at the same time confiscating their wealth: on the 15th of January, 1478, the national councils were for ever dissolved, and a few days after he despatched three hundred carriages, laden with gold, silver, and precious stones, besides many other wagons containing furniture and merchandise, with all the most powerful and influential of the citizens to Moscow, replacing them, that Novogorod might not utterly be deserted, by Muscovite artificers and colonists.* He imprisoned forty-nine German merchants, whom he found in Novogorod, and seized upon all the goods belonging to the Hanseatic league; though, afterwards liberating these prisoners, they embarked in a vessel for Hamburg. But the ship foundering on its passage, the unhappy traders were almost all lost, and terminated their sorrows and misfortunes in the dark and tideless waters of the Baltic.

Among other trophies of his victory, Ivan conveyed to Muscovy the great bell of the Hall of Justice in Novogorod,

* Herberstein's "Rerum Muscovitarum."

which he placed in the tower of St. Ivan in Moscow, and where (weighing 127,835 lbs.) its size is still only exceeded by that cast later by order of the Czar Alexis, which now stands in the centre of the Kremlin.*

But Novogorod never recovered this terrible and decisive blow, though, towards the end of the sixteenth century, she still numbered four hundred thousand inhabitants. At this period, in the hopes of releasing herself from Ivan the Terrible's tyrannical sway, she entered into a secret treaty with Poland, with whom he was then at war; and the plot being discovered in the year 1570, he marched against the devoted city, and committed some of the most horrible massacres and atrocities that have yet stained the pages of history with a frightful and sickening record of human barbarity and crime. The tribunal of blood, as it was but too justly called, that he erected there, executed daily in the presence of the sovereign, and often with horrible tortures, five hundred of the miserable inhabitants; the surrounding country was laid waste, and sixty thousand of the dead and dying blocked the streets, and the ghastly scene was only concluded, when the waters of the Volkhof had been rendered so corrupt by corpses that the plague began to appear in the Russian camp. As might be expected, these two sieges completely alarmed the foreign merchants who had hitherto traded so largely with Novogorod, and prevented them from residing or carrying on any further intercourse with this province. Some of their commerce was transferred to Revel when she placed herself beneath the yoke of Sweden, and the foundation of St. Petersburg gave the final stroke to the mercantile superiority of the ancient city, which now presents a melancholy picture of departed grandeur, extensive ruins, and every appearance of dilapidation, poverty, and decay. Ivan the Third even deprived her of the dignity of an archbishopric, and left the see for some time vacant; but on the urgent request of the citizens, several years after, appointed a bishop of Novogorod, though he received a very small portion of the revenues and tithes that had formerly been paid to his predecessors; and which had all been confiscated and appropriated by the avaricious Czar. The former archbishop, Theodosius, who had pleaded successfully with Ivan for the lives of many of the inhabitants, had been sent in 1478 to

---

* The great bell of the Kremlin, the largest in the world, weighs 443,772 lbs.

the monastery of Choudoff, where he closed, in the peace and calm of the cloister, a most troubled and eventful life.

The siege and submission of Pleskof followed shortly upon that of Novogorod; Viatka was also united to the dominions of the Czar, after her three chief magistrates had been hung over the gates; and, in the year 1496, the Russian troops stationed at Kazan having repelled an attack of the khan of Siberia upon that town, they followed the invaders across the Ural mountains to the marshy and desolate regions of Obdorski, where they exacted from the Samoyedes and Ostiacks an annual tribute of oil and fur. A few of these Polar chiefs, whom they brought to Moscow, were so struck with the splendour of the houses as compared with their own mud huts, the carriages and horses, and the magnificently dressed citizens whom they saw around, that they immediately proffered the submission of their remote district to Ivan, and returned loaded with presents, to spread on the shores of the Obi the marvellous report of his empire's power and wealth. A viceroy was appointed over Permia and all the provinces of the north, whose residence was established first at Kholmogori, and afterwards at St. Nicholas, a little town on the White Sea, now known as the port and city of Archangel.

Poland saw with alarm the conquests of her powerful neighbour, and, after the fall of Novogorod, formed an alliance with the Tartars of Kipzak, and declared war with Russia. Ivan sent an army into Lithuania, and seized upon several of the frontier towns; but the Muscovites had lost the important fortress of Smolensko in the year 1413, and this, considered as the bulwark of their empire, they did not regain till the year 1514, when it was captured by Bazil, the son of Ivan, and from henceforth belonged to Russia. A truce was, however, soon concluded with the Poles after their king, Casimir, had appealed in vain for the assistance of Hungary; but the Tartars and Russians still continued at enmity, and for many years carried on a frightful war. In 1490, the Servians, who had hitherto been under the protection of Poland, took offence at an insult offered to their envoys at Vilna, and transferred their allegiance to the Czar of Russia.*
At this time, though Wallachia was in the possession of the Turks, Moldavia was alternately claimed by Hungary and Poland, and the expulsion of her prince, Alexander, by a

* "Universal History."

usurper called Bogdan, was the occasion of a long war with the latter power, and caused the Ottomans to invade Poland in the year 1498, where, though they gained no decisive advantage, they spread the usual desolation and ruin.*

While the troops of Ivan were triumphant abroad, and he had united beneath his rule the last independent principalities of Russia, he was not indifferent to the internal affairs of his empire at home, which he laboured energetically to reform, though he crushed all abuses under an iron despotism, instead of investigating and eradicating their root, and thus they survived, only concealed, to spring up with increased vigour in another reign, and bear riper and more abundant fruit. Above all, the greatest corruption had pervaded every branch of the church; their copy of the Scriptures was inaccurate, and read by ignorant and superstitious priests; and since the fall of Constantinople, where the Greek faith had become very degenerate, and where the Latin had long been spreading, and prevailed over the greater part of the state; the metropolitan and bishops of Russia had been generally Muscovites, and elected by a Russian synod, while in the church services many changes had been gradually and almost unconsciously introduced. A peculiar sect of dissenters, the Strigolniks, had already appeared in the empire, where their doctrines had extended far and wide, and to this day maintains many monasteries in the state; and, in the beginning of the reign of Ivan, a Jewish heresy, founded by Zacharias, a Lithuanian Hebrew, had been propagated in Moscow, which, denying the divinity of Christ, and establishing many extraordinary rites, had gained converts, not only in every rank among the people, but of several of the highest dignitaries of the ecclesiastics. The followers of this creed were punished with great severity, and among them was Ivan Kuritzin, a secretary of the Czar's, who in 1505 was publicly burned. In the reign of Vassili, the father of Ivan, a great commotion had been raised in Russia by the defection of Isidore, the metropolitan of the empire, to the doctrines and supremacy of the church of Rome. He had been appointed in 1432 by the patriarch of Constantinople to fill the vacant office of primate; and Russian writers have not hesitated to allege that his nomination had been effected through the intrigues of the secret emissaries of the pope, who were

* Krasinski's " History of Poland."

then engaged at Byzantium in a fruitless endeavour to unite, in a bond of union with the Latins, the schismatic and discordant church of the East. Shortly after the elevation of Isidore, he was invited by the pontiff to join a conference at Ferrara, at which the pope, the German emperor, the cardinals, and many prelates, were to be present; and he was conducted in great state to the Russian frontiers by the archbishop of Novogorod, and a large body of Muscovite ecclesiastics.* Arrived in Italy, he not only declared the entire adhesion of Moscow to the papal see, but received the dignity of cardinal from the pope, and returned to Russia clothed in the purple gown and scarlet cowl of his new office in the Latin church, and invested with the authority of a papal legate. But an unforeseen reception awaited him at Moscow; he was met on his entry in the capital by a gloomy and ominous silence, and when he repaired to the Cathedral of the Annunciation to return thanks for his safe return, and mentioned the name of Eugene in his prayers immediately after that of the Czar, a furious tumult was raised around the church; he was seized and with difficulty rescued from the angry populace, and Bazil indignantly reproaching him as "a traitor to his country and his faith," caused his goods to be confiscated, and himself strictly imprisoned in a cell of the monastery of Choudoff. But, through the assistance of a friendly priest, Isidore ultimately effected his escape, and fled to Rome, where he was most honourably received by the pope, and afterwards sent to Constantinople to make further attempts to conciliate the discordant factions in the church, and induce her to proffer obedience to the Latin pontiff. These machinations, which in time might probably have succeeded, owing to the then religious indifference and frivolity of the Greeks, were, however, cut short by the last invasion and conquest of the Turks; and Isidore, retreating to Rome before the infidels, remained there for the rest of his life, receiving the title and dignity of patriarch of Constantinople.†

A Russian priest named Jonah, who succeeded him as Muscovite primate, afterwards addressed a long letter to the pope, pointing out the objections of Russia to the doctrines of Rome,‡ and on his death was enrolled by his countrymen

---

* Mouravieff's "Church of Russia."—† Ibid.
‡ LETTER OF JONAH TO THE ARCHBISHOP (POPE) OF ROME.
"I have loved thy glory, O blessed father! most worthy of the Apostolic see and vocation, who from afar hast looked down upon our humility and poverty, and cherishest us with the wings of love, and salutest us as thine own in thy charity, and inquirest spe-

among their long list of saints. During the rule of his successor, Theodosius, who was elected to the office in 1462, Joseph, the patriarch of Jerusalem, flying from the oppression of the sultan of Egypt, embarked from Palestine with the intention of seeking shelter in Russia, but before he had proceeded further than Kaffa, in the Crimea, was overtaken by death. His brother, however, arrived at Moscow with commendatory letters to the metropolitan, and was ordained to the archbishopric of Cesarea by a synod of Russian bishops; and this is the first instance on record of the intervention of

cially concerning our true and orthodox faith, and when thou heardest, admired, for so the bishop related to us, of your blessedness. And since thou art such and so great a priest, I therefore in my poverty salute thee, honouring thy head, and kissing thy hands and arms. Mayst thou be joyful, and protected by the supreme hand of God; and may He grant good order to thee, thy spirituals, and us! I know not whence heresies have arisen respecting the true way of salvation and redemption, and I cannot sufficiently wonder what devil was so malignant and envious, so hostile to the truth, as to alienate our brotherly love from the whole Christian congregation by saying that we are not Christians; we, for our parts, have from the beginning acknowledged that, by the grace of God, ye are Christians although ye do not keep the faith of Christ in all things, and are in many things divided—a fact which I will shew from the seven great synods, by which the orthodox Christian faith has been established and definitely confirmed, in which also the wisdom of God has built herself a house, as it were, upon seven pillars. Moreover, all the popes who sat in these seven synods were held worthy of the chair of St. Peter because they agreed with us. In the first synod was Pope Silvester, in the second Damasus, in the third Celestinus, in the fourth the most blessed Leo, in the fifth Vigil, in the sixth Oaphinus, a venerable man, and learned in the Holy Scriptures, in the seventh the holy Pope Adrian, who first sent Peter as bishop and abbot of the monastery of St. Sabas, whence have subsequently arisen dissensions between us and you, which have principally prevailed in ancient Rana. Truly, there are many evil things done by you, contrary to the divine laws and statutes, of which we will briefly write to thy charity. First, concerning the unlawful observance of fasting on the Sabbath, secondly, concerning the great fast from which ye cut off a week, and eat meats, and allure men to you by the gluttony of feasting. You reject also those priests who lawfully marry wives; ye also anoint a second time those who have been anointed in baptism by the presbytors, and say that baptisms may not be performed by simple priests, but by bishops only. So likewise with respect to unwholesome, unleavened bread, which manifestly indicates Jewish service or worship. And, which is the chief of all evils, ye have begun to alter and pervert those things which were ratified by the Holy Synods, and say that the Holy Ghost proceeds not only from the Father, but from the Son, with many more things, concerning which your Blessedness ought to refer to your spiritual brother, the patriarch of Constantinople, and to use all diligence that such errors should be removed, and that we should be united in spiritual harmony, as St. Paul says in his instructive words:—"I beseech you therefore, brethren, by the name of our Lord Jesus Christ, that ye think and speak the same thing, and that there be no division among you, and that ye be joined together in the same mind and in the same judgment." We have written to you as much as we could of these six excesses; we will hereafter write to thy charity of other things also. For if it be true, as we have heard, thou thyself wilt acknowledge with me, that the canons of the holy apostles are transgressed by you, as well as the institutes of the seven great councils, at which all your first patriarchs were present, and united in pronouncing your doctrines to be vain. And that you are manifestly wrong, I will now plainly prove. In the first place, with reference to fasting on the Sabbath, you see what the holy apostle, whose doctrines ye hold, taught respecting it, as well as the most blessed pope Clement, the first after the Apostle St. Peter, who thus writes concerning the Sabbath from the statutes of the Apostles, as it is given in the 64th canon:—'If an ecclesiastic be found to fast on the Lord's day, or the Sabbath, except the great Sabbath, let him be degraded; but if a layman do so, let him be excommunicated and separated from the church.' Secondly, with reference to general fasting, which ye corrupt. It is a heresy of the Jacobites and Armenians, who use sheep's milk even on the great holy fast, for what true Christian dares so to do or to think? Read the canons of the sixth great synod in which your Pope Oaphinus forbids these things. We indeed, when we learned that, in Armenia and some other places, they ate cheese made from sheep's milk at the great fast, ordered our people who were there to abstain from such food, and from every sacrifice to devils; from which, if a man abstain not, he should be suspended from performing the sacred offices. Moreover, the third error and sin is very great concerning the marriage of priests, for ye forbid those who have wives to receive the Lord's body; whereas the holy council, which was held at Gangra, writes in the fourth canon—'He who despises a priest who has a wife according to law, and says that it is not lawful to

Russia with regard to the churches in the East. Five years after his election, Theodosius voluntarily abdicated his high title, and retired into the monastery of Choudoff; where, bringing a poor and feeble old man into his cell, he waited upon him as his servant, and, in humble imitation of his divine Master, daily tended his sores and washed his feet. He was succeeded in the dignity of metropolitan by a priest named Philip.* In the year 1587, nearly a century and a half after the fall of Constantinople, the Greek patriarch

* Mouravieff's "Church of Russia."

receive the sacrament at his hand, let him be accursed.' The council also says, 'Every deacon or priest putting away his own wife, shall be deprived of his priesthood.' The fourth sin is the anointment or confirmation. Is it not said every where in the councils, 'I acknowledge one baptism for the remission of sins?' If, therefore, there is one baptism there will be also one anointing, and the virtue of the bishop will be the same as that of the priest. The fifth error is with reference to unleavened bread, which error indeed is the beginning and root of all heresy, as I will prove and, although it might be necessary to bring to the proof many Scriptures, yet I will do otherwise, and for the present will merely say—That the Jews make unleavened bread in memory of their deliverance and flight from Egypt; but we are Christians, we never were in Egyptian bondage, and we have been commanded to omit this kind of Jewish observance with respect to the Sabbath, unleavened bread, and circumcision. And, as St. Paul says, whosoever follows one of them, is bound to keep the whole law; for the same apostle says, 'Brethren, I have received from the Lord that which also I have delivered unto you; how that the Lord, on the night he was betrayed, took bread, blessed and sanctified it, broke it, and gave it to the holy disciples, saying, Take and eat,' &c. Consider what I say: He did not say 'unleavened bread,' but 'bread.' On that occasion no unleavened bread was used, and that it was not the Passover is probable from the fact, that the Jews' Passover was eaten standing, which was not the case at Christ's supper, as the Scripture says, 'While they were lying down with the twelve,' and 'the disciple lay upon His bosom at supper.' For when he himself says, 'With desire I have desired to eat this Passover with you before I suffer,' He does not mean the Jews' Passover, which he had often before eaten with them. Nor when He says, 'This do in remembrance of me,' did He impose the necessity of doing as at the Jews' Passover. Nor does he give them unleavened bread, but bread, when he says, 'Behold the bread which I give you;' and likewise to Judas, 'To whomsoever I shall give the bread, when I have dipped it in the salt, he shall betray me.' But if ye argue, 'We use unleavened bread in the sacraments because in divine things there is no admixture of the earthly, why then have ye forgotten divinity, and follow the rites of the Jews, walking in the heresy of Julian himself, of Mahomet, of Apollinarius and Paul the Syrian, of Samosata, and Eutychius, and Diastertos, and others who were pronounced at the sixth council to be most depraved heretics, and filled with the spirit of the devil? For why do you say, 'I believe in God the Father, and in the Son, and in the Holy Ghost, who proceeds from the Father and the Son?' Truly, it is marvellous and horrible to speak of, that ye thus dare pervert the faith; while from the beginning it has been constantly sung in all churches throughout the world, 'I believe in the Holy Ghost, the Lord and Giver of Life, who proceedeth from the Father, who, together with the Father and the Son is worshipped and glorified.' Why then do you not say, as all other Christians do, instead of making additions, and introducing a new doctrine? while on the other hand the Apostle declares, 'If any man preach to you more than those things which we have declared to you, let him be anathema.' I hope ye may not fall under that curse, for it is a dangerous and a fearful thing to alter and pervert the scriptures of God, composed by the saints. Do ye not perceive how very great is your error? For ye introduce two virtues, two principles, and two wills, with reference to the Holy Spirit, taking away and making of small account his honour, and ye conform to the Macedonian heresy, from which God preserve us. I bow myself at thy sacred feet, and beseech thee to cease from errors of this kind which are amongst you, and, above all, abstain from unleavened bread. I wished also to write something concerning strangled and unclean animals, and of monks eating meat, but, if it please God, I will write of theee hereafter. Excuse me, of thy extreme charity, that I have written to thee of these things. Examine the Scriptures, and you will find whether the things which are done by you ought to be done. I pray thee, my lord, write to my Lord the Patriarch of Constantinople, and to the holy metropolitans, who have in themselves the word of life, and shine as lights in the world; for it may be that, by their means, God may inquire concerning errors of this sort, and correct and settle them. Afterwards, if it shall seem good to thee, write to me who am the least among all others. I, Metropolitan of Russia, salute thee and all thy subjects, both clergy and laity. The holy bishops, monks, kings, and great men, salute thee also. The love of the Holy Spirit be with thee and all thine. Amen.'—(Herberstein's "Rerum Muscovitarum.")

Jeremiah came to Russia to beg for money and assistance in rebuilding the desecrated churches of Byzantium, and, grateful for the honourable reception he received at Moscow, he conferred upon her primate the title of patriarch. But in 1475, during the pontificate of Paul II., another opportunity appeared to present itself of bringing the extensive empire of Russia beneath the paternal sway of the head of the Latin church. Upon the fall of Byzantium, Thomas Paleologus, the brother of the last Constantine, and despot of the Morea, held out in that peninsula for six years against the Turks; but the Grecian cities succumbing one by one to the invaders, he abandoned the vain defence of his provinces, and removed to Rome with his daughter Sophia, the sole heiress of his house; where, in their religion professing the catholicism of the West, they lived under the protection of, and with a pension of five thousand livres from, the pope. Upon the death of the Czarina Mary, leaving only one son, Ivan her husband sent to demand in marriage for himself the hand of the Greek princess, and Paul, hoping that Sophia might convert the Czar, eagerly recommended her father to accede to the proposition, and sent her to Russia, accompanied by the Cardinal Antonia and a large and brilliant retinue. In order to create an impression upon an always susceptible populace, Antonia declared his intention of making a public entry into Moscow with the cross borne on high before him, and attended by a body of Latin ecclesiastics. But this was prevented by the indignant remonstrance of Philip, the metropolitan, with the Czar. "Whoever praises and honours a foreign faith," said he, "that man degrades his own. If the legate enters with his cross at one gate of the city, I shall abandon it at the other."* The hopes of the Romans were further doomed to disappointment by the fickle conduct of Sophia herself, who, far from trying to induce her husband to acknowledge the holy see, as soon as she had arrived in Moscow consented to conform to the practice required from the Czarinas, and professed the Russian faith. It was a general impression throughout the empire, that the world would come to an end in the year 7000 (1491), and consequently, as that time drew near, the greatest gloom prevailed over Russia. The boyards built churches in the hopes of atoning for their sins; highway robbers delivered them-

* Mouravieff's "Church of Russia."

selves up to justice, or attempted to gain an entrance into the monasteries; and the country was threatened by a famine, from agriculture being entirely neglected, as they fancied that, by the time the following summer should set in, there would be none living to reap the fruits of their work. Robbers and banditti at this period infested every corner of the state; the severest laws were enacted against them, and a horrible torture inflicted on every thief caught in the fact, who was not considered worthy of death; and Ivan caused the secular law to be also carried out against the priests, who had hitherto been only tried by their own order, so that on one occasion, when a magistrate caused a priest to be strangled for theft, and the metropolitan expostulated and laid the matter before the prince, he briefly observed— "According to the ancient custom of Russia, a thief who was not a priest was hanged," and sent the magistrate away unblamed. Capital punishment was always inflicted by strangling or hanging; and, if a man discovered a robber when committing a theft, he might slay him with impunity, provided that he afterwards brought the corpse to a court of justice, and explained how the occurrence had taken place. No subject dare put another to the torture, not even a slave, and malefactors were brought to Moscow, or to one of the other principal cities, to be tried; but this ceremony seldom took place except during the winter, as in the summer military expeditions generally drew off all attention from other affairs in the government. Ivan was accustomed to bring into the field a hundred and fifty thousand men, all cavalry; as, till the reign of his son, infantry appears to have never formed a part of the Muscovite regular force. These were generally encamped during the fine months of summer at a short distance from Moscow; and as many as twenty thousand were annually employed in garrisoning the numerous fortresses, or guarding the unprotected shore of the Don.

In the year 1497, or 7006, the Czar promulgated a new code of laws, which ordained that, when a culprit was fined one rouble, he should also pay two altins to the judge, and eight dinas to the notary; and, if two contending parties came to terms before the cause was decided, they should nevertheless be charged to the same amount. When a cause had been decided according to the established rule, by a duel between the plaintiff and defendant, the conquered, and consequently by law the guilty man, was forced to render up his weapons and a poltin to the judge, besides paying the established fine to the state, with fifty dinas to the notary, and four altins to the constable. But if the injured party had suffered any loss by the culprit, whether from incendiarism, the death of a friend, plunder, or theft, he received a suitable compensation procured from the property of the criminal, who was besides forced to pay the accustomed fine to the judge and constable, and was often also condemned, according to the magnitude of the offence, to undergo corporal punishment. Murderers of their masters, church robbers, kidnappers, and those who secretly introduced their goods into another man's house, and then pretended that they had been stolen from themselves, incendiaries, and traitors, were liable to capital punishment. He who was convicted for the first time of theft, was sentenced to be fined and flogged; but if detected in a second crime of the same nature, was doomed to suffer death. And, if a convicted thief had not sufficient property to recompense his accuser, he was condemned before his punishment to serve him for a time as a slave. The provincial governors, whose authority was not sufficient to decide a verdict, might condemn either party to pay a small fine, and then send the case for judgment to the ordinary judges; and whoever accused another of murder, plunder, or theft, was obliged to go to Moscow, and procure a constable, who arrested the culprit, and brought him to the capital on an appointed day to meet his accuser. If the defendant denied the crime, even when the plaintiff was supported by witnesses, he was at liberty to appeal to a decision by single combat, in which case he would say, "I commit myself to the justice of God and the sword, and desire a fair field and a duel." Either of the disputants was at liberty to procure a substitute, or make use of any weapon except a gun or a bow, though they generally fought with a dagger and a lance; and each was supported and encouraged by spectators and friends, who stood around to ensure fairness and equity. But bribes were given and received on all sides with the most shameless frequency, both by the magistrates and judges; so that few poor men had any chance in maintaining a cause against the rich, more especially as they were never permitted to obtain a personal interview with the prince.*

* Herberstein's "Rerum Muscovitarum."

Upon his marriage with the princess Sophia, Ivan adopted the double-headed eagle, the arms of the Greek empire, for his banner, and placed in the centre upon a shield the figure of the dragon and St. George, which had formerly been depicted on the flag of Moscow; and this, replacing the three triangles, the ancient arms of the Grand Princes of Kiof, became from henceforth the established ensign of the Russian empire.

Since the close of his first war in 1469, Ivan had regularly for six years paid the tribute to Kipzak; but when Sophia discovered that Mongul officers resided by agreement within the very palace of the Czar, where they narrowly watched his every action and ordinance; when she saw her husband stand uncovered before these dignitaries, and heard of the degrading ceremonies and humiliating position he was compelled to assume when receiving the ambassadors of the khan, who, shortly after her marriage, came to collect the tribute, she indignantly informed him that she discovered she had married a slave of the Tartars. Stung by this reproach, at a time when the empire was filled with the disaffected and malecontents, who, disappointed at the failure of the hopes they had formed of him when he first ascended the throne, and condemning the apathy and cautious policy of their monarch, loudly murmured at his neglecting to seize the present favourable moment, and follow up his victories at Kazan by freeing them from this galling and disgraceful yoke; Ivan promised her that at least the Kremlin should be freed from the presence of their tyrants; and accordingly sent a formal embassy to Serai, informing Achmet that the Czarina had been favoured by a vision from above, desiring her to destroy that part of the palace which happened to be the abode of the Mongul envoys, and erect a temple to the glory of the Most High in its place. He added that, if the khan would graciously permit Sophia to fulfil the Divine command, a suitable dwelling should be provided for his officers in another quarter; but, on Achmet's consenting to the change, the building was demolished, and no other residence for the Tartars supplied, so that they angrily quitted Moscow. A difference having arisen with his allies of Poland, the khan was unable for the present to revenge this breach of faith; and the following year, when his envoys came to Moscow for the tribute, the Czar caused them all to be executed, and sent word to their master that the time of servitude was now past. Immediately this answer became public, the Muscovites gave themselves up to the most extravagant delight; a picture of Achmet was dragged at a horse's tail through the streets, and cast into the waters of the Mosqua; the crosses on the summit of the churches, which had been surmounted by the Monguls, on their conquest of the empire, by a gilded crescent, were now placed above the emblem of the Mussulman faith; but their rejoicings were cut short by the intelligence that the Tartars were collecting all their forces for one last and desperate effort to maintain their power in Europe, and, uniting with the formidable army of the Poles, had prepared to march on Russia.

Novogorod had just fallen after a war of seven years, and her spoil had enriched the coffers of the Czar: the army, well equipped and provided, and elated by its triumphs in the north, was now left free to oppose their enemies; the khan of the Crimea, in alliance with Moscow, had marched to her assistance in Lithuania; but Ivan, though he had joined in the late conflict, appears to have been at all times deficient in common nerve and courage; and, fearful of losing all by too precipitate a shock, was seized with a sudden fear and indecision, when he saw the storm that he had raised around, about to burst, as he imagined, over his head. He had sent the Czarina, for greater safety, to the monastery of Bielozero, and would gladly have fortified himself in his capital, and come to terms with the foe, but it was too late to recede. All Russia appeared to have armed herself to join the deadly contest; the peasant with his hatchet, the noble with his bow, alike flocked to meet the squadrons of the enemy; and the Czarovitz, who commanded the advanced force of the Muscovites on the Oka, from whence Ivan had retreated in haste to Moscow, and was prepared to encounter with a resolute defence any attempt of the Monguls to cross, refused to obey his father's positive command to return, and abandon his post. The excited people accused their sovereign of base cowardice, and a tumult would inevitably have been the result, had not Ivan listened in time to the friendly voice and warning of the church. "Would you," exclaimed the primate at an interview with his sovereign, who had anxiously inquired if it were still possible to come to any arrangement, "give up Russia to fire and sword, and the churches to plunder and sacrilege? Where would you fly? Can you soar upward like the eagle, or seek a nest amidst the sparkling stars of heaven? The Lord will cast you down from even that retreat! You cannot, you dare not desert your people; you would blush at the name of fugitive and traitor to your country." The venerable Bassian, bishop of Rostoff, boldly addressed a written remonstrance to his prince, in which he says among other arguments: "Dost thou dread death? thou, too, must die like the least of thy subjects; death is the lot of man, beast, and bird, and none, however great, can escape it. Let me command these warriors, and, old as I am, *I* will not turn my back upon the Tartars."*

Ashamed of the hesitation which had called forth so humiliating a reproof, Ivan returned to the camp on the Oka, upon which the Tartars were advancing under Achmet, with a well-armed and well-disciplined force; but the vanguard, which was several miles in front of his army, was destined to retrieve his dishonour and slower movements by their success, and turn the course and fortunes of the campaign in favour of Muscovy and the Czar. By a rapid march across the steppes, the squadrons, headed by the governor of Svenigorod and the Czarovitz, with a band of Tartars under their ally of the Crimea, eluding the vigilance of the enemy, penetrated into the heart of Kipzak, sacked the city of Serai, which they razed to the ground, and returned in haste to their own frontiers, before the Monguls could effect a precipitate and disorderly retreat. But the march of the Mussulmen, who had immediately turned on receiving intelligence of this sudden attack, was intercepted by the hetman of the Don Cossacks, who, in a terrible battle fought near the Volga, left more than two-thirds of their army for dead, put the rest to flight, and a few of the scattered fugitives, faint and bleeding, at length gaining the smoking ashes of their homes, proclaimed to their terrified and ruined countrymen, who, with wild looks and anxious gestures came forth to meet them, the total defeat of their khan, and that their power, which had endured for so many ages over Russia, was now and for ever lost.

The war having been brought to so fortunate a termination—though for many years the Monguls continued to

* Mouravioff's "Church of Russia."

harass the Muscovite territories—Ivan returned with his army in triumph to his capital, where the victories of his generals had obliterated all recollection of the accusations of cowardice and indecision, which the Muscovites had, so short a time before, brought against their monarch, whose wavering they now attributed to a humane and prophetic policy, which, anxious to spare the blood of his subjects, was unwilling to bring the whole army of Russia to oppose a foe, which, the event had proved, might be subdued by so inferior and insignificant a force. About this time, the Czar reinstated his nephew Ivan in his father's principality, though dependent upon Moscow; but this young prince died a few years after, leaving three sons, Bazil, Fedor, and Ivan, and the two eldest long contending for the province, it became a wretched prey, for several months, to a disastrous and desolating civil war. At the end of that time, Fedor was killed in a battle fought at Riazan against his brother, who was, however, so severely wounded, that he only survived his victory a few days, and, being buried with the rest of the slain amid the plains near the city, an oaken cross which long existed was erected to their memory on the ghastly field of combat. Their mother seized the government upon the death of the two claimants, but her right was disputed by Ivan her youngest son, who, forming an alliance with the Tartars, threw her into a monastery, and appealed for assistance to Bazil IV., who then reigned in Moscow. But the Czar, hearing that Ivan had formed a matrimonial alliance with the daughter of the khan of the Crimea, with whom he was then at war, caused him to be arrested by his officers, and kept under strict surveillance; and, to prevent an insurrection in Riazan, dispersed its people in colonies over different parts of his empire. In 1521, when the Tartars of Kazan invaded and besieged Moscow, Ivan escaped from prison in the tumult, and fled to Lithuania, where he died in obscurity, and his patrimony was henceforth comprised within the wide domains of Muscovy.

A similar fate awaited the province of Severa, the inheritance of the children of Andrea, the youngest son of Demetrius of the Don, and which, during the war with Poland, fell into the hands of Ivan III. Its prince was brought in chains to Moscow, where he shortly after expired in his dungeon, and the Czar, on his deathbed, bequeathed it to his second son George, whose successor, Bazil Severski, subsequently lost his liberty and principality by his own treachery and inordinate ambition. Two of his cousins, another Bazil and Demetrius, owned castles not far from his own of Novogorod Severski, and, seizing upon the possession of the former, he drove the unfortunate chief into exile, while he falsely accused the latter to the Czar, Bazil IV., of treason, and received orders to take him prisoner by any contrivance, and send him forthwith to Moscow. Severski accordingly caused Demetrius, who was advanced in years, to be waylaid, and captured in a wood while hunting, and sent to Moscow, and his son, flying to the Crimean Tartars, entreated their aid in the rescue of his father from the grasp of Muscovy; and, in order to enlist them more readily in his cause, renounced his religion and became a Mahometan. But unhappily he became possessed with a violent and hopeless attachment for a young Tartar girl of Batchi-Serai, and in an attempt to carry her privately by night from the harem of her father, who had refused to grant him an interview, they were both shot by a servant who guarded the stern old Mussulman's gate. On hearing of this young prince's flight to his enemies, the Czar had caused Demetrius to be placed in most rigorous confinement; but in the year 1519, when the unhappy old man received intelligence of his son's untimely death, he abandoned himself to grief and despair, and, refusing all food and nourishment, died in a few days. The ruin of Severski, however, soon followed his wretched victim's decease: he was accused to Bazil of having charged Demetrius with treason to conceal his own rebellious machinations, which he feared that chief might reveal, and he proved in a long and hopeless imprisonment, which only ended with his death, the danger and insecurity of the friendship of a suspicious and despotic tyrant, and the instability of all alliances when utterly destitute of fidelity or truth. He had refused to repair to Moscow on the first summons, unless he should previously receive letters of safe-conduct, ratified by the solemn oaths of the metropolitan and the prince: these were forwarded to him without hesitation, and he incautiously confided in the word of a monarch whose treachery and insincerity were equal even to his own. It was rumoured at the time, that some of his letters had been intercepted to the king of Poland, which expressed a wish to desert to the Poles; but it appears more probable, that as Severa was now the only province in the empire which, containing fortified towns and castles, was still independent of Moscow, Bazil had invented and circulated this account, as a plausible pretext for taking possession of his government. When Severski, relying on the Czar's promise of security, was about to enter the capital, the court jester, taking a broom, began to sweep the streets, and on being asked what he meant, exclaimed—"The Czar's dominions are not yet thoroughly cleansed; but now is the time for sweeping all briars from the empire." *

Rostoff and Yaroslaf, the inheritance of George and Bazil, the two brothers of Ivan III., were also conquered, and added by that prince to his own extensive territories: George escaped to Livonia, but Bazil, less fortunate, was seized and placed in irons, though unable to endure this harsh treatment: he shortly after died in Moscow. The Czar is said to have shown much remorse on this event, as he had hardly expected his cruelty would have been so soon attended by fatal results; and he might indeed well feel, if not thoroughly insensible, that he had morally incurred the guilt of fratricide; but he easily obtained an absolution from the subservient metropolitan on professing sincere repentance; and the dungeons and monasteries of his capital, during his own reign and that of his successor, were filled with his unhappy kinsmen, generally rebels, whom for years he relentlessly maintained in the strictest and severest captivity.

In the year 1492, an illegal duty, exacted from some Russian merchants in Kaffa, coupled with various slights and insults from the Turks, provoked an angry remonstrance from Ivan with the Ottoman sultan Bajazet, to whom he proposed a diplomatic intercourse between the Russian and Turkish empires. "Whence do these acts of violence arise?" says he in his letter; "are you aware of them, or are you not? One word before I close: Mahomet, your father, was a great prince; he intended to have sent ambassadors to pay me a due respect, but God prevented the execution of his project. Why should it not now be accomplished?" Three years afterwards, Michael Pleschief, the first Russian ambassador to Turkey, arrived at Constantinople as plenipotentiary of the Czar. Before leaving Moscow, he had received the strictest injunctions from Ivan, not to bow the knee to the

* Herberstein's "Rerum Muscovitarum."

sultan, or address him through any minister or attendant, and not to allow precedence to any other foreign diplomatic agent, on any occasion, at the Ottoman court.*

Nine years previously to this, the first German ambassador to Muscovy had been sent by the emperor Frederick III. to Ivan. But it appears that the letters brought by Nicolaus Poppel the envoy, from his imperial master, were written in too condescending a spirit to suit the haughty Muscovite, who at first affirmed that he believed them to be forged, or written by Poppel himself, and that he had in reality been sent by the king of Poland to negotiate for the advantage of the latter with the Russian monarch; and when at length he had accepted them as genuine, he sent word in reply to a proposition of Frederick's, who offered to bestow upon him the title of king, that he would not degrade himself by accepting titles from any prince on earth, for that he held his crown from God alone. The same ambassador was again despatched by the German emperor to the court of Moscow, in 1489, when Poppel appears to have made great exertion to gain the favour of the Czar and the boyards, and whom he informed on his first audience, that, when returning from his former embassy, "he had been questioned by his sovereign, and all the princes, concerning the kingdom of Russia, of which little was then known in Germany; and that he had described to them the almost boundless extent of the countries and nations subject to its monarch, on whose power, riches, and wisdom, he had been able to speak as an eyewitness." The proposals he now brought from Frederick, were chiefly that a close union should be formed between the two courts by the marriage, "if the Grand Prince were not indisposed, of one of his princesses, to the margrave Albert of Baden, the emperor's sister's son, in which case the emperor would forward the matter, and enter into an alliance of love and friendship with the Grand Prince."† The Czar replied that such a desire required consideration; and on Poppel, at a second interview, expressing a wish to see the princess, he answered "that it was not the custom in Russia to let the daughter be seen before the befitting time." When the German ambassador again referred to Ivan's title, and said, that if it was the wish of the Muscovite prince, he would interest himself with the

---

Creasy's "Ottoman Turks."
Major's Introduction to Herberstein's "Rerum Muscovitarum."

emperor to confer upon him the dignity of king, though the matter must be kept very secret lest the king of Poland should hear of it; the Czar proudly answered—" Through God's grace, I am sovereign of my own countries, and have been so from the beginning, by right of my ancestors. I hold my station alone from God, and pray to Him that it may be so preserved to me and my children; for as, in times past, I have never desired the nomination of any other power, so neither do I now." The negotiations were ultimately entirely broken off by the reiterated refusal of Ivan to allow his daughter to be seen, by even her future husband, before her marriage; and Poppel quitted Moscow in 1489, and returned through Livonia and Sweden to Austria. A third attempt was made by Vienna, to form an alliance with Russia, in the year 1490, when Georg von Thurn was sent by Maximilian, the king of the Romans, to Moscow, where he was far more courteously received than his predecessor, and admitted not only to an audience with the Czar, but to the more unusual honour of an interview with the Czarina Sophia. He stated the desire of his master to enter into a defensive alliance with Ivan, and also to marry a Muscovite princess; in which case Maximilian engaged to allow the free and undisturbed exercise of her religion to his bride, and promised that she should also maintain in Vienna a Greek church, and suitable attendance of priests. Thurn however required, in case the Czar thought favourably of this request, that he should be allowed to see the princess, and be enabled to send to his sovereign a faithful report of her beauty; and also that he should know the amount of her dowry. But the presumptuous envoy was informed, that it was not the custom in Russia to set out the princesses for show, and that it was an unheard of practice among great monarchs to mention the dowry before the marriage ceremony had been completed; after that, the Czar would certainly bestow upon his daughter a sum proportionate to her high rank. He was further requested to give a letter of assurance that she should be permitted to have a Greek church and priests, but Thurn did not think that his instructions had been sufficiently positive to authorize him to do this; he succeeded, however, in concluding a treaty of alliance between the Russian and Austrian courts, and conveyed a letter from Ivan to Maximilian, of which the former had confirmed the sincerity by kissing the cross. Before his departure, the Czar presented him with a gold chain and cross, an ermine mantle lined with satin worked in gold, and a pair of gold spurs;* and he was accompanied to Vienna by two boyards, Bazil Kuleschin and Trachoniata,† who carried with them a duplicate of the treaty of alliance drawn up by Ivan, and ready for the signature of the Austrian emperor. But the ambassadors were so long upon the road, as they left Moscow on the 20th of August and did not reach Germany till the following 23rd of April, that a report gained credence in Europe, that the ship in which Thurn had sailed from Konisberg to Livonia had been lost; and Maximilian supposing that his proposals had not been mentioned, by the advice of the emperor and the lords of the empire betrothed himself to Anne of Brittany,‡ and gave up the idea of marriage with a Muscovite princess. To explain this to Ivan, Thurn was again sent that same year to Moscow, and he also requested the Czar, as Maximilian had ratified the treaty by a solemn vow, in presence of the Russian deputies, to perform the same ceremony on his side; and this was immediately carried out by Ivan, who took an oath to observe it, sworn on St. Andrew's cross. The same year another Austrian, Michael Snups, came to Moscow, with instructions from the archduke Sigismund to obtain permission to make a scientific tour through Russia, as far as the banks of the Obi, and the shores of the Icy Sea; but the desire was refused by the Russian government, owing to the distrust with which they regarded all foreigners, though they alleged as a pretext, that the difficulties of so hazardous a journey were too great for a stranger, when even the officers who were sent to collect tribute in those parts, frequently encountered the greatest dangers on their route. Twelve years after this, another ambassador was sent by Maximilian to the Czar, to condole with him upon the disastrous defeat that he had lately sustained from the Livonians at Pleskof, and requesting a present of some white falcons, which he heard were especially fine in Russia. Five were immediately sent to Vienna under the care of a Muscovite officer named Mikhail Jeropkin. A few months after, the German emperor and his son, king Philip of Castile,

---

* Major's Introduction to Herberstein's "Rerum Muscovitarum."
† He was a Greek who had accompanied Sophia to Moscow.
‡ He ultimately espoused Mary, the heiress of Burgundy.

the son-in-law of Ferdinand and Isabella, sent letters by an Austrian named Julius Kantinger, though this envoy only procceded as far as Narva, to the Czar and his son Gabriel Ivanovitz; and addressing them both by the former title, he requested the liberation of several distinguished Livonian prisoners of war, who, as German knights, were under the protection of the empire.

During the reign of Bazil IV., surnamed the Courageous or the Handsome, several other ambassadors arrived at Moscow. The most noted of these was the Baron Herberstein, sent by Maximilian of Austria to negotiate both with Sigismund king of Poland, and the Czar, and he has left us a full and graphic description of the countries and their people through which he passed. A Milanese envoy by whom he was accompanied, parted with him at Vilna and returned to Germany, being unable to endure the severity of the climate; and he crossed the Dwina on a strip of ice, where six hundred Russians had been drowned not many days before in attempting to pass. At Moscow he was lodged at the house of prince Peter Repolouski, which had been hastily fitted up for his reception; and there received a daily allowance for himself and suite, of a large piece of beef, a live sheep, one live and one dead hare, six live fowls, vegetables, oats, dried sturgeon, a bottle of brandy, three different sorts of mead, and two of beer, and once a week as much pepper, salt, and saffron as he required; but he was kept under the strictest surveillance, an officer being deputed by the Grand Prince to watch narrowly that none entered or left the house without his knowledge. At length he received a message brought by the boyard Vassili Jaroslovski, a near relative of Bazil's, informing him that the Czar would grant him an audience on the morrow; and the following day he repaired to the court, under the escort of several noblemen and courtiers on horseback. Crowds assembled on all sides to gaze at the rare sight of a German, as the Muscovites called all Europeans, and as they drew nearer to the Kremlin, in front of which soldiers were marching to and fro, it was necessary to repel the people by force. Herberstein was compelled to dismount before approaching the castle, as none were permitted to pass the abode of their sovereign on horseback, though he informs us that, in order to claim peculiar honour for his master, he spurred as closely as his conductors would allow him to the palace steps. He was received at the outer gate by the Czar's counsellors, who saluted him, and on the stairs many courtiers joined his suite; but though in the anteroom several noblemen, richly dressed, were sitting and standing, none took any notice of him. In the first state-room he saw some boyards clothed in silk and brocade, and in the second were the princes wearing caps adorned with pearls and jewels, and those gentlemen who held offices about the court. From this apartment he passed into the reception-room of the Czar, who was seated on a raised chair with a footstool, one of his brothers on either side; and next to the prince, on the right hand, was Bazil's brother-in-law, the converted Tartar khan, who, since his baptism, had been called the Czar Peter, and resided at the palace. On the wall, over the head of the sovereign, was a picture of an angel or saint, and by his side his staff, with two jugs, a towel, and a basin of water, that he might, after the departure of the foreigners, purify his hands from the defilement they had sustained by contact with those of a heretic. All rose, except the Czar and his family, as Herberstein entered, and when he mentioned his master, the German emperor, Bazil inquired—"How is our brother Maximilian, elected Roman emperor, and high and noble king?" The ambassador replied that he had left him in good health, and, on his presenting his credentials, the Czar again inquired, through the interpreter, if Herberstein had made a fair journey. The latter was instructed to reply—"God grant that thou mayst live many years in health; through the mercy of God and your grace, I have;" and then, after delivering his messages, he was informed that it was customary for foreigners to dine with the Czar the day of their presentation. Bazil invited him by saying—"Sigismund, thou wilt eat thy bread and salt with us." He had first been introduced by one of the chief councillors of the empire, who approaching Bazil, and bowing so low that his forehead almost touched the ground, said, "My great lord and sovereign of all the Russias, Baron Sigismund strikes his forehead before thee for thy great favour."* The ambassador then retired to prepare for the feast. His description of the entertainment is worth quoting, from the curious pic-

---

* Herberstein's "Rerum Muscovitarum."

ture it gives of the manners and customs of the Muscovite court.

When they returned to the palace in the evening, they were ushered into the banqueting-room, where the princes and ministers had already assembled. Tables were arranged all down the hall, and covered with a profusion of gold and silver plate; the princes, and oldest courtiers and councillors, sat with the Czar, while the ambassadors and their suites were placed opposite; and the attendants, wearing magnificent robes studded with jewels, walked after the guests, round a stand in the centre which held the wine, and goblets filled with malmsey and mead, and stood before Bazil awaiting his commands. The higher the rank of the nobles and officers of the court, the nearer were their tables placed to that of the Czar; who, immediately they were all seated, called to a servant, and, giving him two pieces of bread, desired him to take them to the ambassadors. They were delivered with this speech, "Oh, Baron Herberstein, the Grand Duke Bazil, by the grace of God czar and lord of all Russia, extends his favour to thee, and sends thee bread from his own table." The same ceremony was repeated with regard to the princes and several of the boyards, who all expressed their acknowledgments, by rising with the rest of the party and bowing all round; and brandy was handed to each person before the feast commenced. All down the tables were rows of golden dishes, containing salt, vinegar, and pepper, and upon each was placed almonds, sugar, and confectionery, nuts, plums, and other fruits, with pickled cucumbers, and sour milk to eat with the meat; the latter alone being removed from the board during the whole of the banquet. At length the attendants all left the hall, and brought in the dinner, which chiefly consisted of roasted swans, cut up and handed round, while two or three were placed before the Czar, who had four cupbearers standing behind him, one of whom first tasted every thing that he eat or drank. To all those of the guests whom he particularly wished to honour, he sent meat on golden dishes from his own table; but it was considered a mark of more especial favour to send bread; and to a very few, as a proof of his affection and friendship, he sent salt. On receiving either, it was the custom for every guest to rise and bow, so that the court banquets often occupied an immense length of time, and the prince seldom rose till past midnight, when he gave the signal that all might depart. When foreign envoys were present, he was accustomed to order his goblet to be filled, and then, having tasted it, caused the wine to be handed round in succession to the ambassadors, saying at the same time, "Sigismund," or whatever the Christian name might be of the dignitary whom he addressed, "thou art come from a great sovereign to a great sovereign, and hast made a long journey; it is well for thee to have experienced my favour, and to have beheld the lustre of my eyes; drink, and drink well, and eat well, even to thy heart's content, and then take thy rest, that thou mayest return in health to thy master." At the close of the feast, the Czar himself stood up, and taking his cup said, "Sigismund, I wish to drink this wine to the affection that I bear to our brother Maximilian, emperor and king of the Romans, and to his health; and thou also shalt drink this toast, and all who are present in their turn, that thou mayest witness our love towards our brother Maximilian, and report to him what thou seest." He then gave the goblet to his cupbearer, who handed it to each of the guests.*

"The proposing of toasts in Russia," says Herberstein, "is done with great grace; the person who wishes to honour another stands in the middle of the room, and pronounces the sentiment, such as fortune, or victory, or health, with the wish that not so much blood may remain in his enemies as he means to leave of wine in his goblet. Having said this with uncovered head, and finished the draught, he turns the goblet over upon his head."

The chief amusements of the Czar and his boyards were hunting, hawking, and bear-baiting, and a heavy fine was the penalty for cutting the woods, or killing a hare in the neighbourhood of Moscow. A hunt was conducted in a very similar manner to those formerly ardently pursued by the Grand Khans on the plains of Tartary. An immense number of hares, or other game, were driven into an enclosure surrounded by nets, and the boyards and officers were summoned to attend it, with this message from the Czar—"We have come out for our amusement; we have commanded you to take part in it, hoping that you may derive pleasure therefrom; mount your horses, therefore, and follow us." The prince's hunting-dress was a white peaked cap, bordered with

* Herberstein's "Rerum Muscovitarum."

precious stones, and adorned in front with golden feathers, which waved with every movement of his head;* his coat was cloth of gold, and from his girdle hung two knives and a dagger, while he was attended by about three hundred horsemen, and mastiffs, greyhounds, and all species of dogs. The enclosure was guarded by other horsemen and soldiers, to prevent any of the game from making its escape; and every person of rank held one or more hounds, whom he let loose directly the Czar had given orders to the huntsmen to begin the chase. But all of those who joined in the sport were carefully gloved, as the Muscovites considered a dog unclean, and that it was defilement to touch one with the bare hand. After the hunt was over, they collected and counted over the game that had been killed, and he whose hound had destroyed the greatest amount was considered to have spent the most successful day. Hawks and falcons were then often produced, which the Russians used for taking even swans and cranes; and when both hunting and falconry were concluded, the court repaired to some tents which had been pitched temporarily in the neighbourhood, where the prince, first changing his dress, received the nobility and ambassadors on an ivory throne. After making their obeisance, the guests all seated themselves, and the attendants brought in preserved fruits, sugar, and other refreshments, which they presented to the Czar on their knees; and as soon as the repast was finished, all mounted their horses and returned to Moscow. When Herberstein left Russia, he received a present in money from Bazil, besides many sables and ermines, a few Russian hounds, and several rare specimens of the productions and natural curiosities of the empire.†

Bazil IV. sent ambassadors to the German emperor, the king of Poland, and to the pope; and from this time Russia appears to have maintained a constant diplomatic intercourse with the Porte. The Muscovites began occasionally at this time to wander forth from their own territories, though chiefly in the direction of Asia. In the year 1468, a Tver merchant called Nikitin travelled into Hindoostan and Ceylon, and has left an account of his journey; and, even during the sway of the Monguls, numerous votaries and penitents appear to have resorted as pilgrims and as hermits to the holy

---
* Major's Preface to "Herberstein."
† Herberstein's "Rerum Muscovitarum."

shrines of Palestine, and to the birthplaces and tombs of various celebrated saints.

Ivan the Terrible, in the year 1583, sent two merchants, Korobeinskoff and Grekoff, with a present of 77,000 florins to the patriarchs of Constantinople and Alexandria, and to the monks who guarded the Holy Sepulchre, desiring them to pray without ceasing for the soul of his murdered son;* and it has been computed at the present day, that no less than ten thousand Greek Christians annually flock from Russia alone to the churches and sanctuaries of the East.†

* Ivan IV. struck his son on the head with an iron bar in a fit of passion. A favourite seized his arm, and prevented him from giving a second blow; but the prince expired a few days after, and his father from that time became a prey to the most terrible remorse, and is generally supposed to have lost his mind.

† In Russia, a man who has made a pilgrimage to Jerusalem is looked on in much the same light as a hadji among the Mussulmen.

NOTE TO CHAPTER III.

Athanasius Nikitin, a merchant of Tver, appears to have visited the East Indies, principally for the purposes of commerce. He accompanied Vassili Papin, who was sent by the Czar, Ivan III., with a present of falcons to the Shah of Shirvan (the son of Achmet, the last khan of Serai), and, before setting out, offered up prayers for a safe journey at the Convent of the Trinity, on the shrines of the martyrs Boris and Gleb. At Astrakhan he was robbed and imprisoned by the Tartars, but was subsequently released at the intercession of Hassan Beg, the ambassador of Shirvan, and proceeded to Bakh, where he says the fire burns inextinguishable (the springs of naphtha). He then crossed the Caspian Sea and travelled on to Bokhara; and, afterwards traversing the provinces of Persia, went to Ormuz, and from thence sailed to Choul, a town a little to the south of Bombay. He particularly laments the loss of all his books of devotion, of which he had been robbed at Astrakhan; but, notwithstanding, he diligently observed all the fasts and festivals of the Russian Church, when he could discover on what day they fell. "But I pray," says he, "to the one only God, that he will preserve me from destruction; God is one, King of glory, and Creator of heaven and earth." He commences his book thus:—

"By the prayer of our holy fathers, O Lord Jesus Christ, have mercy on me, thy sinful servant Athanasius, son of Nikita.

"This is, as I wrote it, my sinful wandering beyond the three seas; the first the Sea of Derbend, Doria Khvalitskaia; the second, the India Sea, Doria Hindustanskaia; the third, the Sea of Stamboul (Black Sea), Doria Steinbolskaia.

"I started from the Church of our Holy Saviour of Zlatoverkh, with the kind permission of the Grand Duke Michael Borissovitz, and the bishop Gennadius of Tver, went down the Volga, came to the Convent of the holy life-giving Trinity, and the holy shrines of Boris and Gleb, the martyrs, and received the blessing of the hegumen Macarius, and his brethren. From Koliazin I went to Uglitz, thence to Kostroma, to the knez Alexander with an epistle. And the Grand Duke of all Russia allowed me to leave the country unhindered; and I went on by Plesso to Nijni Novogorod, to the namestrick Michael Kisseleff, and to Ivan Saraeff, the collector of duties, both of whom let me pass freely."

He took a horse with him through all his travels, and when in India he says:—

"At Jooneer the khan took away my horse, and having heard that I was no Mahometan, but a Russian, said—'I will give thee the horse, and a thousand pieces of gold, if thou wilt embrace our faith, the Mahometan faith; and, if thou dost refuse, I shall keep thy horse, and take a thousand pieces of gold upon thy head.' He gave me four days to consider, and all this occurred during the Fast of the Assumption of our Lady, on the eve of Our Saviour's Day (Aug. 18th). And the Lord took pity on me, because of his holy festival, and did not withdraw his mercy from me, his sinful servant, and allowed me not to perish at Jooneer among the infidels. On the eve of Our Saviour's Day, there came a man from Khorassan, Khoznlecha Mahmet, and I implored him to pity me. He repaired to the khan in the town, and praying him, delivered me from being converted, and took from him my horse. Such was the Lord's wonderful mercy on the Saviour's Day.

"Now, Christian brethren of Russia, whoever of you wishes to go to the Indian country may leave his faith in Russia, confess Mahomet, and then proceed to the land of Hindoustan. Those Mussulman dogs have lied to me, saying, I shall find here plenty of our goods; but there is nothing for our country. The sea is infested with pirates, all of whom are Kofirs, neither Christians nor Mussulmen. They pray to stone idols, and know not Christ.

"In Beda there is a trade in horses, stuffs, goods, silks, and all sorts of other merchandise, and also in black slaves; but no other article is sold but Indian goods, and every kind of eatable; no goods, however, that will do for Russia."

Speaking of the Isle of Ormuz, he says, "The heat is not great in Hindoosten, but it is great at Ormuz. Ormuz is a vast emporium of all the world; you find there people and goods of every description, and, whatever thing is produced on earth, you find it in Ormuz. But the duties are high, one tenth of every thing."

After travelling to many places in India, and describing the state and attendants of her sovereigns, he proceeds to Calicut and Dabul. At this place he says, "And there it was, that I, Athanasius, the sinful servant of God, bethought myself of the Christian religion, of the Lent fastings ordained by the holy fathers, of the baptism of Christ, and of the precepts of the apostles, and I made up my mind to go to Russia. May God preserve the Russian land, God preserve this world, and more especially from hell; may he bestow his blessing on the dominions of Russia and the Russian nobility, and may the Russian dominion increase."

At Dabul he took his passage for two golden coins to Ormuz, and from thence, passing through Shiraz, Ispahan, and Tabriz, he again entered the territory of Shirvan. He then embarked at Trebizond, and after a stormy passage arrived at Kaffa, but died before he had reached Smolensko; and the record of his voyage was brought the same year (1475) to Moscow, and delivered over to the secretary of the Grand Duke. He gives this table of the time that it required to go from various places in the east.

By sea from Ormuz to Kalat ....10 days.	From Chaoul to Dabul .... 6 days.
From Kalat to Degh .... 6 days.	From Dabul to Calicut ....25 days.
From Degh to Muscat .... 6 days.	From Calicut to Ceylon ....15 days.
From Muscat to Guzerat ....10 days.	From Ceylon to Shibait .... 1 month.
From Guzerat to Cambay .... 4 days.	From Shibait to Pegu ....20 days.
From Cambay to Chaoul.............12 days.	From Pegu to China and Macheon. 1 month.

Travels of Athanasius Nikitin, translated by Count Wielhorsky, and edited by R. Major, in "India in the Fifteenth Century." Published by the Hakluyt Society.

CHAPTER IV.

Embassy to Vienna and to Copenhagen—War with Finland.

> Hard by these shores, where scarce his freezing stream
> Rolls the wild Oby, live the last of men,
> And half-enliven'd by the distant sun.—THOMSON.

WHEN the ambassador from Vienna to Bazil IV. returned to his master's dominions, he was accompanied by Gregory Istoma, an envoy from the Czar, with his secretary, Vladimir Semenoff Plemannikoff, who brought a reply from their sovereign. They were received with great honour by the emperor Maximilian, who was desirous that they should attend a service in the Latin church; and upon objections being raised by the clergy of Innspruck, where they were staying, to the admission of heretics within the sacred walls, high mass was performed for them in a smothered tone by the private choir of the emperor, which Herberstein observes pleased the Russians, who said that "it was far better to perform the service of God in a low or soft voice." While at Innspruck, Istoma engaged the services of several gunners for his country, and five of these subsequently returned with him to Moscow.* In 1492, several years previously, Istoma had repaired with about twenty other Muscovites on a mission from his sovereign to Copenhagen, and there concluded a treaty between John of Denmark and Ivan, in which the former promised the Czar to aid him in the reduction of Lithuania, but required assistance against his rebel subject Swanton, who had lately usurped the government of Sweden. It was also agreed that, when either of them attacked Swanton in Stockholm, or Captain Eric Struve at Viborg, or any of the other insurgents in the Swedish dominions, notice should be given to the other party to the

* Hamel's "England and Russia."

treaty.* Two years before this a declaration had been published by the inhabitants of Kemi, in Finland, to justify the execution of several Russians, and to raise a crusade against their empire. In their manifesto, they described the repeated inroads of the Russians during many years, into north and east Bothnia; where, treacherously availing themselves of a profound peace, and under pretence of commercial motives, they had effected an entrance, and robbed and murdered the defenceless inhabitants; besides claiming the whole of the salmon fishery, and exacting a tribute of three white furs from the Finns and Lapps. On one occasion, when a large band crossed the Ulea, the boundary between Russia and Sweden, Hans Anderson, the governor of Orta, a town and island on this river, came out against them with a body of the inhabitants, and slew twenty-one of the intruders, while the rest fled towards their settlements on the White Sea. Near the chapel of Mukos, on the banks of the Ulea, was a stone three ells high, marking the extreme limits of the two powers, and inscribed with a lion for Sweden, a cross for Russia, and a hammer for Lapland. The year following these disturbances, the Russians declared war against Finland, and their army marching on Viborg, remained some time before it, but were unable to take the place. In 1495, a Swedish fleet sailed from Stockholm, and destroyed the recently erected fort of Ivangorod on the Narva, and the Muscovites to avenge it crossed the gulf of Finland on the ice, and, notwithstanding the great severity of the season, committed frightful ravages on the opposite shore. In March 1496, the two Muscovite princes Uschatoi recruited a fresh and powerful body of troops in the district about Onega and the Dwina, and, arming and equipping them from the magazine in the fortress of Orekhof on the Neva, they led them as far as Kemi and Tornea, on the northern extremity of the gulf of Bothnia, and to the Swedish town of Kaliksef, which they pillaged; and a few months later burned the more southern strongholds of Jokhas and Nyslott.† The same year Istoma, with a suitable retinue, was despatched by Ivan to Norway and Denmark, to renew a treaty with regard to their com-

* "Contra suos inimicos et hostem Swantonem regni Suecie occupatorem gubernatorem. Et quum aliquis nostrûm incipiet lites adversus Swantonem, qui nunc gerit se pro gubernatore regni Suecie, Ericum Struve capitaneum in Wiburg, aliosque occupatores regni nostri Suetli infideles, subditos atque rebelles, tunc primus inter nos alterutri significabimus."—Hamel's " England and Russia."
† Hamel's " England and Russia."

merce; and as the envoys were prevented from travelling by the ordinary route, owing to the war then raging between Russia and Sweden, or from passing through the provinces on the Baltic, as hostilities were still continued with Lithuania, they embarked at Archangel on the bay of St. Nicholas, or, as it is now always called, the White Sea, and rounded the North cape in vessels so small, that they were with ease hauled over narrow tongues of land. At length, reaching Trondheim, they proceeded from thence to Copenhagen. Another embassy was sent by Ivan to king John in the year 1500, to demand the hand of the Danish princess Elizabeth in marriage for his son Bazil; but the envoys were informed that it had been already bestowed upon the Margrave Joaquim of Brandenburg, though John, irritated by another Swedish rebellion, engaged that a portion of Finland should be given over to the Czar. As John Jacobson, the Danish ambassador who returned with Ivan's boyards to Moscow, afterwards came in the same capacity to London, it is probable that he gave some account of the Russians to England; for, about this time, the English court first began to take notice of Muscovy, and at a masked ball held in the Parliament hall at Westminster by Henry the Eighth, in 1510, the Earl of Wiltshire and Lord Fitzwalter appeared in Russian costumes, " in two long gowns of yellow satin, traversed with white satin, and in every bend of white was a bend of crimson satin, after the fashion of Russia or Russland, with furred hats of grey on their heads, either of them having a hatchet in their hands, and boots with pikes turned up." Friendly communications were continued between Moscow and Copenhagen during the remaining years of the life of Ivan, and also during the reign of Bazil his successor,* whom John

---

* BAZIL'S LETTER TO JOHN OF DENMARK, IN ANSWER TO ONE RECEIVED AT MOSCOW TO THE CZAR IVAN, AFTER THAT PRINCE'S DEATH.

"Most serene and dear brother, we send you many and friendly greetings. We write to your highness, innsmuch as your highness sent your spokesman and herald, Master David Kocker (a Scotchman), to our father Ivan, Emperor, Grand Prince, and Lord of all Russia. By the will of God, our father has departed in the Lord. Subsequently, your messenger, John Plagh, came to us with your credentials and letters; for whereas your Master David brought a message from you after the death of our father, your messenger John Plagh has acquainted us again with your wish, that, as divine Providence has willed that our father should depart in the Lord, we should be united with you, as our father was, in fraternity and friendship, against all enemies; and that we should also send a messenger to you, our brother John the king, together with your messengers. Truly, we desire to have the same friendship and fraternity with you our brother John, king of Dacia, Sweden, and Norway, as you had with our father, and we now send you our ambassador Yschonia, together with your ambassadors. We desire, moreover, that your letters to us be conceived in the same strong terms of friendship as those you wrote to our father, and that you order your seal to be affixed to these letters in the same manner; and we request that, in the presence of our ambassador Yschonia, you kiss the cross on

of Denmark sent to congratulate on his accession to the throne.*

As the year 1491 approached, the year 7000 according to the Russian calendar, a gloomy presentiment and dread pervaded the empire, that the career of this world would then come to a final close; and its passing without the event so much feared having taken place, gave occasion to several arguments in writing among the dignitaries of the Russian church. Among these the "Triple Hallelujah," and the "Seven Thousand Years," by Demetrius Mannilovitz Trachaniot, in answer to the Archbishop of Novogorod, are still extant.

those your letters to us (Russian form of taking an oath), and that you send them to us, so confirmed, by your ambassador together with our ambassador, sealing up your said letters in the same manner; and God willing, when our aforesaid ambassador returns to us with your ambassadors, bearing your letters so ratified, and when the same have been seen by us, we shall write to you letters in return, the same word for word as yours, and shall also order our seal to be affixed thereto. On the same letters we shall kiss the cross in the presence of your ambassadors, and then send you our letters so ratified. Therefore we request that, with God's assistance, you will sign and send us back our ambassador Yachonia without delay." Dated at Moscow on the 7th day of July, in the year 7015.

THE KING OF DENMARK'S REPLY.

"John and king, to the Emperor of all the Russias, health, and sincere and fraternal love in the Lord. Dearly beloved brother and confederate, your majesty's ambassador Ysconia applied and came to us with David our herald, exhibiting and presenting your letters; from which letters we have clearly understood that you wish in all things to follow the footsteps of the lord Ivan Vassili of pious memory, and especially to enter into brotherly friendship and confederacy with us, and so to frame our letters with reference to such friendship and confederacy, and send them to you by our aforesaid ambassador and Ysconia. We therefore, by these presents, address and transmit them to you, greatly desiring and requesting that you will send us letters from you, containing the assurance of the same friendship and confederacy, O prince, our brother, father-in-law, and parent."
—Hamel's "England and Russia."

* Hamel's "England and Russia."

CHAPTER V.

Survey of Russia—Siberia—Its Conquest—The Crimea—Her Khan submits to the Turks.

Les glaçons
Dont l'éternel rempart protége la Russie.—CASIMIR DELAVIGNE.

UPON the return of Baron Herberstein* from his embassy to the court of Bazil, at Moscow, he received from his sovereign, the emperor Maximilian, the title of Discoverer of Russia, so little known had that country remained to the rest of Europe since the glorious days of Vladimir the Great. But a few years after, when the Czar of Muscovy sent an ambassador, prince Demetrius, described by the writers of the time as a venerable white-bearded old man, to the Roman pontiff, Clement VII., the bishop of Nuceria, in Italy. Paulus Jovius, interrogated the strangers regarding their northern land, and from the information he received from the Muscovites, and his own observation in a subsequent journey to Moscow, wrote a description or survey of Russia.

"The journey from Vilna," says he, "the head city of Lithuania, to Moscow, is travelled in winter with speedy sledges, and incredible celerity over the snows, hardened with long frost, and compact like ice. But in summer the plains cannot be overpassed but by much difficulty and danger. For when the snows, by the continual heat of the sun, begin to melt and dissolve, they cause great marshes and quagmires, able to entangle both horse and man, were it not that ways are made through them with bridges, and causeways of wood, after almost infinite labour.

"The name of Muscovites is now new, although the poet Lucan makes mention of the Moscos dwelling near the Sarmatians, and Pliny also places the Moscos at the springs of the great river Phasis, in the region of Colchis, above the

* Herberstein's "Survey of Russia," is chiefly derived from a native itinerary published in Moscow.

Euxine Sea, towards the East. Their region hath very large bounds, and extends from the altars of Alexander the Great, about the springs of Tenais, to the extreme lands and North Ocean, in a manner under the north stars called Charles's Wain, or the Great Bear, being for the most part plains and fruitful pastures, but in summer in many places full of marshes. For, whereas all that land is replenished with many and great rivers, which are much increased by the winter snow and ice, when it has been resolved by the heat of the sun, the plains and fields are thereby overflowed with marshes, and all journeys encumbered with continual waters, till another winter again freezes the rivers and swamps, and gives a safe passage to the sledges that are accustomed to travel by them.

"The wood or forest of Hercynia occupies a great part of Muscovy, and is here and there inhabited with houses built therein, and has been made so much thinner by the long labour of man, that it does not now show that horror of thick and impenetrable woods as many think it to have. But it is so filled with wild beasts, and extends so far through Muscovy, with a continued tract between the east and north, towards the Scythian Ocean, that its infinite greatness has deluded the hopes of those who have curiously searched for its limits.

"On the east side of Muscovy are the Scythians, now called Tartars, a wandering nation, and famous in all ages for war. Instead of houses they have waggons covered with animals' hides; and for cities and towns they use great tents and pavilions, not defended with trenches, or walls of timber or stone, but enclosed with an innumerable multitude of archers on horseback. The Tartars are divided into companies, which they call hordes, a word signifying in their language a company of people gathered together in the form of a city. Every horde is governed by an emperor, whom either his parentage or warlike prowess hath promoted to that dignity; for often they carry on a war with their borderers, and contend ambitiously and fiercely for dominion. So it appears that they consist of innumerable hordes, as the Tartars possess the greatest deserts, even to the famous city of Cathay, in the furthest ocean in the east. Beyond the Kazanites, towards the north, are the Shebiâni, rich in herds of cattle; and the passage to the Ugrians and Ugolicans is by certain rough mountains, which, perhaps, are they that in old times were called Hyperborei, and where on the tops are found the best kind of falcons. Somewhat towards the south and the Caspian Sea, dwell the noblest nation of the Tartars, called the Zagatai, who inhabit towns built of stone, and have an exceedingly great and fair city called Samarcand. From their regions are brought great plenty of silk apparel to the Muscovites, from whom they receive in return coats of cloth and silver money, with other bodily ornaments and household furniture. Although they generally fight with arrows, which they shoot as well backwards flying, as when they assail their enemy face to face; yet on their invasion of Europe, under Timur, their princes and captains had helmets, coats of armour, and hooked swords, which they bought of the Persians."

The city of Moscow* is described by Herberstein and other travellers, who visited it during the reigns of Ivan Veliki and his son, as spreading over an immense space of ground; for it was confined by no settled boundary, and undefended by any bastion or wall round the outskirts, which gradually melted into villas, smaller houses, and the poorest peasants' cottages and huts. It was traversed, and the central part almost surrounded, by the three rivers of the Moskwa, Jausa, and Neglina, and contained forty-one thousand, five hundred houses, which extended for five miles along the Moskwa's banks. The town was principally built of wood, though there were a few stone houses, churches, and monasteries; and most of the streets, which were very broad and spacious, and carried by many bridges over the streams, were guarded at early nightfall by watchmen, who after a certain hour permitted none to pass. There were several mills on the Jausa for the use of the city, and at one end a row of numerous refiners' and blacksmiths' shops and furnaces; for the mechanics and other artisans had separate quarters for their trades, and every quarter of Moscow was provided with its own church. The houses were generally large and lofty, and built apart in the midst of a private garden and spacious courtyard,† and in the centre of the city stood the castle or Kremlin, which was surrounded by a stone

---

* Sir Jerome Horsey, in the reign of Ivan IV., says, "The Tartars, when they last burned Moscow, in 1571, destroyed so many houses, that it is now not much bigger than London."
† Paulus Jovius.

wall, fortified with towers, and a moat.* It enclosed an extensive and magnificently built stone palace of the Czar, the cathedral of the Assumption, and several churches, the houses of the princes, the metropolitan, and many of the nobles, and the huts of their retainers and dependants, and from its size might itself have been taken for a large city.† "The fortress was at first surrounded only by oaks," says Herberstein,‡ "and up to the time of the Grand Duke Ivan Danielovitz, was small and mean in appearance. It was he who, by the persuasion of Peter the metropolitan, first transferred the imperial residence to this place. Peter had originally selected that place from love of one Alexis, who was buried there, and who is said to have been famous for miracles, and after his death, being buried in this place, miracles were likewise done at his tomb; so that the spot itself acquired so great a celebrity from the idea of its sacred and religious character, that all the princes who succeeded Ivan thought that the seat of the empire ought to be held there." Moscow was surrounded by forests, containing numerous herds of deer and other game, which were all preserved for the hunting of the Czar and his court; and, during the extreme severity of the winter, the bears and wolves were occasionally known to leave the woods, stimulated by hunger, and rush through the streets and into the houses; while in the summer of 1525, the heat was so intense, that the woods and corn-fields around the city took fire, and burned for several days, filling the whole district with clouds of smoke and flame.‖

At a short distance from Moscow was the enormous

* In 1801, Dr. Clarke says of Moscow—"One might imagine that all the states of Europe and Asia had sent a building by way of representative to Moscow; timber huts from regions beyond the Arctic, plastered palaces from Sweden and Denmark, painted walls from the Tyrol, mosques from Constantinople, Tartar temples from Bucharia; pagodas, pavilions, and verandas, from China; cabarets from Spain; dungeons, prisons, and public offices from France; architectural ruins from Rome; terraces and trellises from Naples; and warehouses from Wapping. Some parts have the appearance of a sequestered desert, and the traveller is tempted to ask, Where is Moscow? Here are seen wide and scattered suburbs, huts, gardens, pigsties, brick walls, churches, dunghills, palaces, timber-yards, warehouses, and a refuse, as it were, of materials sufficient to stock an empire. In other quarters the throng is so immense that the traveller asks what cause has convened such a multitude, and hears that it is the same every day. At some points, and particularly from the Kremlin, where all its deformed features are hidden, and the eye roves over the towers, domes, and spires of its gorgeous temples and palaces, Moscow presents an aspect of rude and varied magnificence, which scarcely any other capital can equal."
† Herberstein's "Rerum Muscovitarum."
‡ Herberstein speaks of a kind of plague that often prevailed in Moscow, and indeed throughout Russia, which carried off one of his servants while he was there, and appears to have been the cholera.
‖ "The smoke of this so filled the country, that the eyes of those who walked out were severely injured by it, and, besides the smoke, a certain darkness supervened, which blinded many."—Herberstein's "Rerum Muscovitarum."

monastery of St. Sergius, having the appearance of a little city, which contained above three hundred monks.

Staraia Russia, which was almost the oldest town in the empire, was about twelve miles from Novogorod, and contained an artificial river, or reservoir, from whence water was brought by channels to every house. Novogorod itself, situated in the midst of a marshy and barren country, never entirely recovered the terrible devastation of the Muscovites, and a few years later its ruin was completed by the arms of Ivan the Terrible, who, as before stated, on the discovery of a secret alliance between this city and his enemies in Poland, wasted it with fire and sword, caused thousands of the inhabitants to be cast into the river Volkhof, and others massacred with horrible tortures, and disgusted even his own unscrupulous soldiers and princes, by his dreadful cruelties and barbarities, and lavish waste of human life.

The province of Ingria, now called St. Petersburgh, was said in former times to have been an independent kingdom, but in the early ages of its history belonged to Novogorod. It was converted by the Russians to the Greek Church, but subsequently fell into the hands of Sweden, who forced the inhabitants to adopt the Protestant faith; and from this time till its reconquest by Peter the Great, the Neva formed the boundary of the Russian and Swedish territories, and the fortress of Orekhof, the modern Schusselburg, was built by the Novogorodians on that river, and garrisoned by Russian soldiers, for the defence of the frontier.

Kiof, which had long formed a part of Poland, was still at this period, and for two centuries later, in a very desolate and ruined state. "Its former magnificence and ancient regal splendour are still shown," says Herberstein, "by its extensive remains, and the monuments which are lying in heaps. To this day may be traced over the hills in the neighbourhood, the fragments of churches and deserted monasteries, as well as numerous caverns, in which are now seen very ancient tombs, with the bodies in them not yet decayed." This city was chiefly inhabited by the Ukraine Cossacks.

The provinces between the Petchora and Oby were first accurately explored during the reign of Ivan III., by two of his generals, the princes Simeon Fedorovitz Kurbski, and Peter Uschatoi, and the inhabitants, like those of Lapland and all the north of Siberia, appear to have followed then the same customs and mode of living as their descendants in the same regions in the present day. These early travellers describe the reindeer and magicians, the Lapland Samoyede witches, who boast their empire over the winds, with their magic drums and enchanted chains, the stony and barren aspect of the country, and the perpetual summer day and winter night. About Olonetz and Archangel the land is flat and marshy, and produces plentiful crops of rye and flax, and in the more southern districts even barley and oats; but in Lapland, where the vegetable earth is shallow and scanty, and the sandy ground overspread with stones and rocks, it brings forth merely plains of lichen, the common food of the reindeer, and a spare and insufficient supply of grass; while forests of stunted pine, birch, and larch, stud the silent shores of the White Sea and Arctic. Kola,* the capital of Lapland, was founded early by the Novogorodians or Permians, and is now chiefly inhabited by fishermen; its church, built in the year 1506 by a Russian priest named Elias, who came here to preach Christianity, was destroyed with many of the houses in the late war; and the Laplanders, though they are some of them still heathens, and all exceedingly superstitious, have generally been converted, according as they are claimed by Sweden and Russia, to the Greek and Lutheran Church. In the fifteenth century, when the districts of the Petchora and Obdorski were first subdued by the Muscovites, many Greek priests from time to time traversed their country, and, by presents of silver crosses and images, induced crowds to receive Christian baptism; but it appears that the people soon relapsed into their former idolatry, as even now there are among them many Schamanists. Near the mouth of the river Oby, on its discovery by the soldiers of Ivan, stood a wooden temple, containing a golden statue of a woman and child, apparently a relic of Christianity, and which was worshipped by the heathen of those parts; and all along the banks of the river were wooden fortresses, or mud castles, for the Tartar collectors of tribute; probably erected by their Mongul conquerors under Shebiâni, the grandson of Zingis. The governors of these forts were at this time all made tributary to the Czar, who used this district as a place of banishment for his subjects, and several salt and

* Kola was visited in 1597 by two Dutch ships, who describe it with a large Inn situated at a short distance, of which the sign was a huge pair of scales. Its first vaivode was Averki Ivanovitz in the year 1582; the second, Maxaka Fedorovitz Sudimontoff, in 1583.

iron mines were now first opened on the Ural, some of which were worked by the boyard Strogonoff, and other private noblemen; others for the benefit of the state. Siberia, or Tumen as it was occasionally called, was then hardly known to even the contiguous Muscovites. Vague reports, exaggerated by fable, of an immense plain extending a limitless distance north and east, a land clothed in darkness and ice, and where the people, who were hideous objects, with the heads of beasts, travelled in sledges drawn by dogs, or rode on reindeer like horses, occasionally found credence in Europe. From the days of Herodotus, who peopled it with griffins and gold, the north of Asia had been involved in an apparently impenetrable obscurity; though the western districts, the sole part unprotected by mountains, or a stormy and annually frozen sea, were early subdued by an army of Monguls under Shebiâni, who carried on some intercourse with his brethren in Kipzak, erected a wooden capital called Sibir, on the banks of the Irtisch, and several fortresses, particularly Jerom and Tumen, near the frontiers of Europe. Sir John Mandeville, in his journey to the Golden Horde, mentions a sea surrounded by mountains, which accurately corresponds to the site and appearance of Lake Baikal, now known to the Russians as the Charmed or Holy Sea; and Tartar writers of those times have described the shape and position of Kamschatka, so that it seems probable so errant a people may have penetrated to the neighbourhood of even this distant and remote province, either in search of further conquests, or on the more peaceful mission of traders; or they may merely have heard a description of the extreme east of Asia, from natives who had made their way from these regions to the more favoured and genial provinces of the south.

But though none have been found to record them, yet Siberia cannot have been destitute in the wars and vicissitudes of history, and may still be destined to play an important part in the pages and annals of a future age. Numerous remains of a more advanced civilisation than that presented by the modern inhabitants have been excavated, and traces that her gold-mines have been formerly worked, have been discovered upon her silent rivers' banks; while hostile nations have contended for dominion in her valleys, which in summer are bright with vegetation, though in winter deeply imbedded in snow, and even the timid inhabitants of Kamschatka have fought with desperation for their native rocks. In the provinces of Omsk, Kolyvan, and Tobolsk, and also further north among the Ostiaks, a vast number of tombs have been opened, containing gold and silver ornaments, golden idols, metallic mirrors, coins, arms, and the bones of both men and horses, and which were all unscrupulously robbed of their contents by the early Cossack invaders and traders; while many ruins of splendid edifices, though inferior in grandeur to the sepulchral monuments, have been discovered, particularly the Semipaltnoi, or Seven Palaces, and the dilapidated walls of Ablaikit. The latter is a temple which, according to tradition, was erected by a Kalmuck prince named Abloie, and is filled with more than forty statues of deities, of the most horrible and grotesque shape and appearance; some having seven arms and ten faces, the claws of dragons and the tails of fishes or snakes, and it is supposed to have been consecrated to the prevalent creed of the country, viz., the Schaman worship. The walls were originally covered with inscriptions, but these are now illegible from the injuries they have sustained from the ignorant peasantry, and from the regiments quartered in the neighbourhood of the Cossack and Kirghiz troops.*

Siberia—which slopes gradually from the mountain range of the Altai, that skirts her southern frontiers for two thousand miles in length, to the desolate shores of the Arctic, rich in the fossil remains of the elephant and the buffalo, and many varieties of animals that now no longer exist—is, like Russia, flat and marshy in the north and western districts; where the rivers, among the longest in Asia, overflowing every spring, flood the country, and form fresh swamps and lakes for miles around. But, in the south, the productive soil is peculiarly rich and fertile, and colonies of banished Poles and Muscovites are gradually bringing the barren wastes into cultivation; and thus the cruel policy of Peter the Great, who banished to Tobolsk eight thousand Swedish officers and privates captured at Pultowa, has proved, as he intended, of great benefit to that province; where the unfortunate exiles, to gain a livelihood, employed themselves as watchmakers and mechanics, and a few years later opened a school for their children, and built a Lutheran church. At the end of the last century, Kotzebue saw one of his own tragedies,

* Pallas's "Travels."

"The Stranger," ably performed in the theatre of Tobolsk; and travellers agree in stating, that the villages and peasantry of Siberia are more advanced and better educated than the same class in the interior of Russia.

On the subjection of Obdorski by the Muscovites, that place, as I have said before, was used with Archangel, by Ivan III., for a place of banishment for his disaffected or criminal subjects; and an adventurous merchant, Anika Strogonoff, crossing the Ural in search of furs, of which he had seen that the most valued species were used for shoes by the Siberians, who frequently repaired to his mines for salt, revealed to Russia the unknown treasures, in this respect, of their country; and, after the conquest of Kazan, a tribute was exacted from the Siberian khan, Judiger, by the Czar. A few years later, a tribe of Cossacks, consisting of six thousand men, were dispersed under their attaman Yermak, by the army and fleet of Ivan IV., who attempted to extirpate these pirates, and drove them from their homes on the Don; and the fugitives, penetrating through the Ural Mountains, from whence they looked down on vast and immeasurable plains, and spreading towards the shores of the Obi, attempted to form a settlement in Siberia. They found that a civil war had lately expelled the khan Judiger from Sibir, and placed Kuchum, his successful rival, on the throne; and this prince, hating the Muscovites, and arming against the new colonists, marched upon their village with a considerable force, which was defeated by the bold Cossacks with immense slaughter, and in retaliation for his unprovoked attack, they besieged and obtained possession of his capital. The khan fled to the wild Kalmucks of the steppes, and his sons were subsequently conveyed prisoners to Moscow. But still pressed by the army of Muscovy, Yermak found himself compelled to tender his submission to the Czar, and for a pardon offer to his sovereign his new conquest, far greater than those he had lost, on the condition that he should still rule it as viceroy; and Ivan, accepting the rich gift from his submissive subject, engaged in future to leave the Cossacks unmolested on the Don, and presented Yermak with a complete suit of armour, manufactured of the purest gold. But, shortly after this, the attaman was waylaid near his capital by a Tartar ambuscade, and his attendants cut down almost to a man; and, escaping alone under cover of the darkness, in an attempt to swim across the Irtisch, he perished in its gloomy waters, borne under, it is supposed, by the weight of his equipments, the splendid gift of the Czar. At his death the Tartars again possessed themselves of Sibir, but were driven out by a fresh band of the undaunted Cossacks, who, marching through the barren steppe of Barabinski, reached the fine pastoral regions of the Yenesei, and easily induced the mild and scattered Ostiaks to pay to Muscovy a moderate tribute of fur. The Yakutes, a Turkish race, made more defence, but were propitiated by presents, and offers of friendship and alliance, and are now completely amalgamated with their conquerors; though the Buriats, a tribe of Mantchous in the south, made a fiercer and more determined resistance, and for some years compelled the Russians to stay their victorious progress, and halt on the borders of those districts, most rich and most productive in jewels and gold. Undeterred by snow and ice, the Cossacks pushed on towards the desolate marshes of the north, and in 1639, fifty years after their first conquest, one of their number, Demetrius Kopilof, had gazed with his followers across the waves of the Ochotzk Sea, while reinforcements to the first adventurers had subdued the tribes around Lake Baikal and Nertschinsk, and fought with the Chinese on the banks of the Amour for the possession of her fertile and fruitful shores. As they advanced on their career of conquest, the Cossacks wisely built fortresses and villages in the deserts through which they passed; these were garrisoned and peopled by adventurers and outlaws from all parts of Muscovy and Russia; princes and boyards were frequently exiled thither by the Czar, who from this time sent prisoners of war to colonize the wilder parts of his empire, instead of condemning them, as formerly, to pass the rest of their lives as hopeless slaves;* and thus Tobolsk rose in 1587; Pelym, Berezof, and Surgut, in 1592; Tara, in 1594; Narym, in 1596; Wercheturie, in 1598; Tarinsk and Mangasea, in 1600; Torusk, in 1604; Turchansk, in 1609; Kusneyk, in 1618; Krasnojarski, in 1627; Yakutsk, in 1632; Irbit, 1633; Ochotzk, in 1639; Nertschinsk, in 1658; and Irkutsk, in 1669. In the year 1637, fleets manned by hardy Cossacks

* Boris Gudunoff, who attempted to destroy the power of his rivals, the Romanoffs, the ancestors of the reigning dynasty in Russia, sent nearly all of them to Siberia. Sir Jerome Horsey, who wrote in the time of Ivan IV., says that six thousand Russian soldiers were generally employed in Siberia.

sailed down the Lena, Alaska, and Kolyma, to ascertain the termination of these rivers, and the distance from their settlements of the Frozen Ocean, into which they fell; nine years after, Ankudinof and Deschnef sailed round the peninsula of the Tchutchi, on the north-eastern extremity of Asia; but though the former was drowned in the Kolyma, and the latter, after many vicissitudes, suffered shipwreck in his fragile bark, near the Anadyr, they led the way to another enterprising band, who, a few years later, crossed the straits of Behring, and explored the skirts of the opposite country on the American coast. But from this period their energy abated, and the Cossack spirit of adventure in Siberia appears to have declined; and other attempts to explore the bounds of the ocean that washes, on the north and east, the rugged Siberian shores, have been generally undertaken and fitted out by Russian officers, or at the cost and instigation of the Russian government.

But while the Monguls were yielding cities and fortresses to Russia, in Siberia, Kazan, Astrakhan, and Kipzak, the Tartars of the Crimea had for the time escaped the yoke of Moscow, by placing themselves beneath the protection of Constantinople, and acknowledging the supremacy of the Turks. This peninsula, two-thirds of which consists of steppe, was stated by Pliny to have been an island, and is now only connected with the continent by a strip of land five miles in width, defended by an irregular fortress of freestone erected on the south side of a deep ditch, and strengthened by a high and massive wall, said to have been formed in ancient times by the inhabitants, to protect their homes from the incursions of the nomades of the steppes. The ruins of a still older fosse and embankment, mentioned by Ptolemy, lie about a mile and a half to the south of Perekop, and are described by one writer as having been destroyed in the tenth century, when a thick wood was planted from sea to sea, through which ran two roads, leading to the east towards the kingdom of Bosphorus, and to Cherson, the principal city of the colony of the Greeks. The ditch was again cleared by the Tartar khans of the Crimea about the end of the fourteenth century, and they built another fortified wall across the isthmus; but this was destroyed by the Russians in their conquest when they overran the peninsula, and burnt above eight hundred palaces, two thousand private houses, and the rich libraries of the Jesuits and the khans. Perekop is now only protected by a fosse, across which runs a bridge with a stone archway and a gate.*

Though the northern part of the Crimea is chiefly a flat and barren steppe, the southern coast is beautifully diversified with luxuriant vegetation, hills, and rock. The valleys of Baidar, Jehosaphat, and Djurouk Su, with vineyards, orchards, and corn-fields, interspersed by the conical Tepekermen, the fort-crowned height of Tchoufut Kalé, the caverns of the monastery of Uspenskoi and Inkerman, and the mountains and crags round the still more elevated Tchatir Dagh, present an agreeable picture to the traveller after a weary journey across the plains of the north; while the whole peninsula contains innumerable monuments of the turbulent and creative ages of the past, from the site of the ancient temple of Diana, now covered by the monastery of St. George, and the ruins of the rock fortress of Kermentchik, the abode of the Taurian king Skilouros,† to the castles and fortresses of the Genoese, the mosques and palaces of the later Mongul khans, the gardens and baths of Batchi-Serai, and the Tartar and Jewish cemeteries and tombs.

The rock of Mangoup, which rises to upwards of a thousand feet, and was surmounted on the very summit by a fortress, was for a period of no less than eleven hundred years in the exclusive possession of the Goths. The valley beneath still bears the remains of a Greek church adorned with frescoes, and surrounded by tombs marked with a cross, and the castle shows the traces of an anciently fine palace of two stories high, resting on a spacious terrace, and approached by a handsome flight of steps. While their countrymen were expelled from the plains, the Goths of Mangoup maintained their position in this stronghold of the hills, which was defended by two walls across the entrance, while another guarded the valley on the side of Inkerman; and they lived here under Christian princes till the latter part of the fifteenth century, when in the year 1475 it was taken and sacked by the Turks. Eighteen years after this event, the ruin was completed by an accidental fire which broke out in the town, then garrisoned by a small Mussulman force, and destroyed every thing but the Acropolis and a few buildings in stone. The last settlements of the Greeks in

* Seymour's "Russia on the Black Sea and Sea of Azof."
† He was the energetic opponent of Mithridates.

the Crimea was at Theodori, a fortress on the promontory of Inkerman, and below which they excavated a regularly constructed and complete Byzantine church; Alexis, one of their princes (who were all dependent on Constantinople), took Balaklava in the fifteenth century from the Genoese, but, a few years after, was again driven forth; and in 1475 the Greek colony was completely exterminated by the Turks, who placed a garrison at Theodori, and allowed the castle to go to ruin, though, a hundred years later, Greek inscriptions and heraldic bearings were still legible over the buildings and public gates.* At the same time Balaklava fell into the hands of the Mahometans, with whom it remained till they were expelled, in 1780, by its present people the Arnaout Greeks: it was called Cembalo by the Genoese, who, in 1365, took it from its former inhabitants the Chersonites, and after its capture by the prince of Theodori, it was retaken by a Genoese captain, Carlo Somellin, who was sent from Italy with a fleet of twenty vessels for the purpose, and arrived before the harbour with an army of 6000 men. The modern fortress owes its foundation to Genoa, as also the two castles whose ruins surmount the rocks on either side of the narrow entrance to the port. The adventurous citizens of this once powerful and haughty republic—who have been mentioned as forming settlements in the Crimea as early as the latter part of the thirteenth century, and who in less than two hundred years had become almost absolute in the peninsula—had long before this maintained factories in Constantinople, and appear to have established an emporium at Soldaya, for which they paid a tribute to the Komans, some years before the Monguls first invaded Europe. When Taurida was overrun by the horde of Toushi, who gave up Soldaya to the flames, and forced the Komans to take refuge in Moldavia, the Genoese hastily embarked with their goods for Byzantium; but about thirty years later again appeared on its shores, and, sailing with a few ships to the bay of Theodosia, landed on the ruined site, where had formerly stood that famous Milesian town, and obtained from the Mongul prince Oran Timur, who reigned at Eski Krim, the cession of a small territory round this spot. In 1280 the first houses were erected of the present town of Kaffa, and it rapidly rose to such importance, that within ten years

* H. D. Seymour's "Russia on the Black Sea," &c.

it was enabled to guard its own port, and send three galleys to the relief of Tripoli, which was at that time straitly besieged by the Saracens.* The colony of Kaffa soon extended its influence, and was succeeded by fresh establishments at Kertch, Taman, and Tana or Azof; the Genoese spread themselves along the coasts of Circassia and Mingrelia, in Georgia, where many of their castles still remain in Trebizond, and to the opposite shores of the Black Sea, and obtained from the Tartars of Russia a monopoly of the export trade in wheat and salt. But in their commerce and privileges they were fiercely opposed by their avaricious and hated rivals the Venetians, with whom they frequently engaged on the waters of Byzantium in long and deadly conflict. In 1295 they massacred all of their opponents who had settled in the suburbs of Constantinople; and the following year, to revenge this deed, a Venetian fleet set sail from the Adriatic, and, defeating the ships of Genoa in a desperate battle on the Bosphorus, darted suddenly upon Kaffa with twenty galleys, and burned and utterly destroyed the town. But the Genoese, not discouraged by this disaster, returned the next year and commenced rebuilding the sacked and ruined city; which rose so speedily from its ashes, that in 1318 it was erected by the pope into a bishopric, and its merchants had founded a fortress at the mouth of the Dniester. All of their establishments in the Black Sea were presided over by consuls, under the government of a podestà, who, appointed by the mother city, resided in the Greek empire at Galatea.

In 1343 a war broke out between the colonists and the Tartars; and a crusade was preached in favour of the Genoese by the Roman pontiff Clement VI., when Zanibeg, the khan of Kipzak, laid siege to Kaffa. He was repulsed after a long blockade; but the inhabitants, fearful of another attack, began to fortify their territories with a stronger and more perfect system of bulwarks, and the magnificent walls, flanked with towers, and surrounded by a deep ditch, whose remains are still clearly seen, were commenced at this period by the Venetian architect Godefrey de Toaglio, and finished in 1386 by Benedict Grimaldi. The southern and finest tower in this rampart was consecrated to the memory of Clement VI. out of gratitude for his exertions in their defence, and

* H. D. Seymour.

bears an Italian inscription to this effect; and it seems probable, that the builders drew their materials for these works from the neighbouring ruins of the ancient Greek city of Kimmericum or Opuk. So Kaffa increased till, according to its historians, it equalled Byzantium in size and population, and surpassed her greatly in its extensive trade and wealth.* In 1365, the Genoese subdued the Greek towns of Soldaya and Balaklava, which were tributary to the Monguls, and obtained a grant from the khan of Kipzak, of all the seacoast between these settlements. Soudak or Soldaya, whose origin goes back to the remotest times, was as early as the eighth century the seat of a bishop; and, although then dependent upon the empire of the East, was ruled by her own princes or dukes. Four hundred years later, the Greek colonies in the Crimea fell before the storm of the Komans, who, after thirty years' dominion, were in their turn subdued by the Monguls, when Soldaya, though it remained tributary to Kipzak, was after a few years restored to the Greeks. It continued with them till the chiefs of the Golden Horde adopted the intolerant Mussulman faith, when the Christians were driven out by the Tartars, and all their churches converted into mosques; though, on the remonstrance of Pope John XXII. with the khan Uzbek, in the year 1323, they received back their former possessions and privileges. But the term of the power of the Greeks in the Crimea was now drawing near to a close: Soldaya with their last settlements on the 18th of June, 1365, were incorporated in the domains of the Genoese, who immediately began to fortify the town with new bulwarks, and built above the rocks overhanging the bay, and which are inaccessible on the side of the sea, an immense fortress in three stages, protected from the valley by a tremendous rampart and ten towers, which still remain in good preservation among the desolate ruins around. Over the entrance gate is a bas-relief representing St. George and the Dragon, with the escutcheon of the doge Adomo; and an inscription beneath states that it was built in the year 1385, when the noble and puissant lord, Giacopo Gorsevi, was the consul and castellan of Soudak. Within the lower castle are the remains of brick cisterns, which, filled by aqueducts of earthen tubes, conveying the rain water from the hills above, were capable

* H. D. Seymour.

of supplying the garrison for many years; and the church, which in the same division is still complete, has five times been changed to suit its possessors of different faiths, having been first erected for a Mongul mosque, then transformed into a Greek church, afterwards accommodated for the Genoese Catholics, again altered to a Tartar mosque, and now in the present day once more consecrated, and devoted to the Greek faith. The middle portion of the fortress is called Katara Koullé, and built in the ledge of the precipitous rock; while the third, the Maiden's Tower, crowns its summit, and here sentinels were formerly constantly posted, as it commands a full view of the entrance to the harbour, of the walled and fortified city, the neighbouring fruitful country, and a vast expanse of sea.*

The Crimea appears to have become separated from Kipzak towards the close of the fourteenth century, after the defeat of the famous Toktamish, to one of whose daughters, Nenekidjan Khanoum, there is a mausoleum erected in the centre of the Jewish town of Tchoufut Kalé, which was then the Mongul seat of government in the peninsula, and was by them called Kirkor. The legend relates that she fell in love with a Genoese nobleman, or, according to some, a Tartar mirza or prince, and her father refusing to consent to their marriage, she fled with her lover to the impregnable walls of Tchoufut Kalé, where they safely remained, till the Genoese was treacherously induced to abandon his place of retreat. He was immediately seized by the emissaries of the angry prince, who commanded him to be put to death; and Nenekidjan in despair, on hearing of his unhappy fate, threw herself down from the precipice, and was dashed to pieces in the fall. Toktamish, bitterly repenting of his harshness, built this beautiful monument to her memory, and caused it to be covered with Arabic inscriptions from the Koran.† When he took refuge in Lithuania, one of his rivals, a son of a former Toushi khan, established himself at Kirkor, and afterwards opposed his army, when united with that of Vitold, on the Vorskla; but a few years later his son, Mahmoud Gerai, succeeded in defeating his father's enemies at Kirkor, and for a year ruled the central districts of the Crimea, though he was ultimately killed in an engagement with the Genoese, and his children taken prisoners.

* H. D. Seymour. † Ibid.

But the conquest of Constantinople, in the year 1453, was a terrible blow to the trade of the republicans in the East. Their rivals, the Venetians, obtained the right of navigating the Black Sea for an annual tribute of 10,000 ducats; and, attempting to gain favour with the new masters of Constantinople, and monopolize their commerce with the West, they soon succeeded in raising differences and hostilities between the Genoese merchants and the Turks. At the same time Mengli Gherai, the heir to the throne of the Crimea, who had been brought up in captivity among the Genoese, finding himself severely pressed by these colonists, while his three brothers were in rebellion against him, requested the assistance of the Ottomans, and offered to hold his throne in obedience to Stamboul. In the year 1475, an expedition, commanded by one of the most celebrated of the Turkish captains, Ahmed, surnamed Kaduk or the broken-mouthed, was despatched by Mahomet II. from the Bosphorus, and arrived before Kaffa, then called Little Constantinople, with a powerful fleet of 482 galleys, and an army of 40,000 men. On the 1st of June, the attack with a formidable range of artillery commenced, and on the 6th the numerous breaches in their fortifications compelled the besieged to surrender at discretion, after they had in vain attempted to capitulate; and Ahmed, a fanatic and intolerant Mussulman, and irritated at their resistance and defence, haughtily accepted their submission, and entered the doomed and ruined town through its blockaded and deserted streets. Taking possession of the consular palace, he disarmed the population, from whom he levied an enormous ransom for the purchase of their lives; and confiscating half the property, both in goods and in slaves, of the inhabitants, which altogether amounted to an immense booty, he sent 40,000 of the citizens in his galleys to Constantinople, where they were established by force in the suburbs of the then depopulated capital, and 1500 of their children, all nobles of the highest rank, were compelled to enter the corps of Janissaries, and profess Islamism. Kaffa had been, for the last two hundred years, a great market for the sale of Circassian, Russian, and Tartar slaves: a tribe of the former people who, in all ages, have sold their children readily for gold had, in 1373, established themselves in Taman and Kertch, and the Monguls found easy purchasers in the Genoese, who disposed of them in their turn to the different nations of the East, for their innumerable Asiatic and Russian prisoners of war. Instead of becoming, like the rest of the Crimea, merely a fief of the Turks, Kaffa was immediately incorporated with their own empire, and in the year 1663, had again attained to great mercantile importance, comprising 4000 houses and more than 80,000 citizens within her walls, and seldom less than 400 ships in her port. Her conquest was soon followed by that of Balaklava and Soldaya, after the latter had sustained a long and vigorous resistance, and had been only compelled by famine to surrender; Mangoup was wrested from a few fugitive Genoese and the Goths, and Mengil Gherai, attempting to obtain the restoration of Kaffa from his allies, who demanded her as a recompence for their assistance, was defeated and taken prisoner to Constantinople. He was replaced on his throne in the year 1478, upon acceding to the following conditions:—

That he should swear for himself and his descendants inviolable fidelity and submission to the Porte, consenting that the khans should be placed on the throne and removed by the Grand Sultan at his pleasure, and that they should make peace and war for the interests of the Ottoman empire. At the same time the sultan conceded that only a prince of the race of Zingis khan should be ever placed on the throne of Little Tartary; that he would never, under any circumstances, put to death a prince of the house of Gerai, and the Gerais should never be compelled to deliver up refugees who had taken refuge in their dominions; that the prayer for the khan should be read in the mosques after that offered up for the Grand Sultan; that the khan should carry five tails on his standard when he went to battle, which was one less than the Grand Sultan himself, and two more than the highest rank of pashas; and that in time of war the Porte should allow 120 purses, or about £12,000 for each campaign, towards the expenses of the khan's guard, and 80 purses, or nearly £10,000 for the Kalipouli mirzas, or the immediate vassals of the khan who were not of noble birth.

The khans of the Crimea drew no revenue from their subjects, but received from the Porte a pension of £160,000 a year; they could not alter the privileges of the nobility, and no noble could be punished without the participation of the beys, or heads of the great houses assembled in council. The second dignitary in the kingdom was the kalga sultan or viceroy of the khan, whose residence was at Akmeshed, the modern Sympherol, where the ruins of his palace, a vast irregular mass of buildings, of which the gardens were once celebrated for their beauty and numerous fountains, still remain on the banks of the Salghir, and where he held a court little inferior to his master's, with a vizier and divan. To the judgment of his tribunal there was an appeal from all the courts of the Kadis, which numbered forty-eight in the peninsula; he was vested with all powers but those of life and death; in the absence of his sovereign he led the armies of Little Tartary to battle, and on the demise of the crown he regulated the affairs of state till a new khan had received his investiture from Stamboul.*

The family next in rank to the Gerais in the Crimea were the Shireens, whose founder had fought by the side of Zingis; they alone could marry the princesses of the royal house, whose sons generally took Circassian or Georgian wives, and near Karasoubazar is a mountain called the Hill of the Shireens, where they were accustomed to hold meetings with their retainers, when they disapproved of the measures of the sovereign, or wished to influence his government. The style of the khan in addressing all foreign powers, except the sultan, was—" Geray, by the grace of God Emperor of all the Tartars, the Circassians, and the Daghestan." All the princes of the reigning family had the title of sultan, and either held offices in the kingdom or lived on lands granted to them by the Porte,† and Circassia, whose allegiance was claimed by the Crimean Tartars, formed a near and certain shelter for all malecontents and political offenders, the mountaineers frequently assisting the khans in their wars with Muscovy and the Cossacks. In the year 1484, Mengli Gerai seized on all the Polish territory between the Bog and the Dniester, with the seaports of Kilia and Bialigorod, or Akerman, a district which had belonged to Lithuania since its conquest by the Grand Duke Olgherd, the son of Ghedemin.‡ He also removed the seat of government to Batchi Serai, and erected the palace ‖ at the entrance of the town, built in the picturesque

---

* H. D. Seymour.   † Ibid.   ‡ Krasinski's "Poland."

‖ A fountain in the midst of the hall of this palace forms the subject of the celebrated poem of the Russian poet Puschkin. It bears this inscription in the Tartar language:—
"Glory to God most high; the face of Baktcheseral is made glad by the beneficent care of the glorious prince Geray Khan. With a prodigal hand he has satisfied the thirst of his country, and he will spread other blessings if God lends him his assistance.

"By care and trouble he has opened this excellent spring of water. If there exist another such fountain, let it come. We have seen the towns of Cham (Damascu-) and

little valley of Djurouk Su, behind which stands the hall of the divan or council-room, in the midst of a terraced garden, well planted and refreshed by numerous fountains. Near this castle, enclosed by trees, is the harem, surmounted by a high tower or kiosk, and on the left side of the palace the mosque terminated by two minarets, and the cemetery, where, in the centre, amidst numerous sepulchres and cypress-trees, stand two domes containing the tombs and monuments of the khans. Thus, Taurida surrendered her rights and independence to Constantinople, and her khans remained for above two hundred and fifty years the vassals and pensioners of the Turks.

Bagdad, but nowhere have we seen such a fountain. The author of this inscription is called Cheiki. If any man, fainting from thirst, reads these words across the water, which escapes trickling from the slender pipe, what do they tell him? Come, drink this limpid water that flows from the purest of springs, it gives health."—Quoted from H. D. Seymour's "Russia on the Black Sea and Sea of Azof.")

CHAPTER VI.

War between Moscow and Poland—Coronation of Demetrius—Death of Ivan III.—Accession of Basil IV.—Prince Glinski—Pillage of Moscow—War with Kazan—Death of Basil—Accession of Ivan the Terrible—Capture of Kazan and Astrakhan—Extinction of the Mongul power in Europe.

> The power and fortunes of the war,
> Faithful as their vain votaries, men
> Had pass'd to the triumphant Czar,
> And Moscow's walls are safe again.—BYRON.

THE war had continued for several years, between Muscovy on the one hand, and Lithuania and Poland on the other, when Casimir, king of the latter country, expired in 1492, and was succeeded by his third son, John Albert, in Warsaw; the eldest, Vladislaf, being already king of Hun-

CONTEMPORARY SOVEREIGNS OF THE SIXTEENTH CENTURY.

MUSCOVY.
Ivan the Great.
1505. Vassili the Courageous.
1534. Ivan the Terrible.

OTTOMAN EMPIRE.
Bajazet II.
1512. Selim I.
1520. Solyman the Magnificent.
1566. Selim II.
1574. Amurath II.
1595. Mahomet III.

GERMAN EMPIRE.
Maximilian I.
1519. Charles V.
1558. Ferdinand I.
1564. Maximilian II.
1576. Rodolph II.

FRANCE.
Louis XII.
1515. Francis I.
1547. Henry II.
1559. Francis II.
1560. Charles IX.
1574. Henry III.
1589. Henry IV.

SPAIN.
Ferdinand V. and Isabella.
1504. Philip I. of Austria, and Joanna.
1506. Joanna alone.
1516. Charles I. of Austria.
1555. Philip II.
1598. Philip III.

PORTUGAL.
Emanuel.
1521. John III.
1557. Sebastian.
1578. Henry the Cardinal.
1580. Portugal united to Spain.

ENGLAND.
Henry VII.
1509. Henry VIII.
1547. Edward VI.
1553. Mary.
1558. Elizabeth.

POLAND.
John Albert.
1502. Alexander of Lithuania.
1507. Sigismand I.
1548. Sigismund II.
1573. Henry of Valois.
1576. Stephen Bathory.
1587. Sigismund III.

SWEDEN.
John II.
1520. Christian II. of Denmark.
1523. Gustavus I.
1556. Eric XIV. deposed.
1569. John III.
1592. Sigismund I.

SCOTLAND.
James IV.
1513. James V.
1542. Mary.
1567. James VI.

DENMARK.
John.
1513. Christian II.
1523. Frederick.
1534. Christian III.
1559. Fredrick II.
1588. Christian IV.

HUNGARY.
Ladislaf VI.
1516. Louis II.
1526. John Sepusius.
1539. John II.
1561. Maximilian.
1573. Rodolphus.

gary, and the second, Casimir, having formerly entered as a priest in the Polish church. The Lithuanians at the same time elected John's younger brother Alexander for their Grand Duke, so that the two nations once more became established under different princes and governments; a separation which, mutually weakening both states, was of the greatest importance and benefit to Russia, where the agents of Casimir had been long secretly and successfully engaged in raising up strife and malecontents in the Muscovite principalities, and constantly urging them, by offers of assistance and remuneration, to revolt. John was hardly established on his throne, when in concert with his two brothers he invaded Moldavia, whose monarch, Stephen, was the ally and relative of Ivan, and the Czar immediately marched 100,000 men upon Lithuania.

In the mean while, the united armies having entangled themselves in the woods of the Bukovina, were surprised and utterly routed by the Moldavians; and Alexander, returning in haste to oppose his Muscovite foe, whom he at first attempted to cut off by poison, was overawed by the enormous force that Ivan had led into the field, and offered to make almost any concessions for peace. A conference was held by the princes, which ended in the arrangement of a marriage between Alexander and Helena, the eldest daughter of the Czar; and her father stipulated that a Greek church should be erected for her use at Vilna, and provided with a suitable attendance of priests. But the terms of this treaty were never faithfully carried into effect; Alexander, a bigoted Catholic, refused to build the chapel for his bride, and, on the contrary, attempted to force those of his subjects who still adhered to the Greek faith to renounce their errors, and conform to the Latin creed;* and, on the death of his brother in 1501, when

---

* The following is a bull of Pope Alexander VI., issued upon this occasion:—
"The bishop Alexander, servant of the servants of God, for a perpetual remembrance. The loftiness of the divine wisdom, which no human reason can grasp, always originating, out of the essence of its boundless goodness, something for the welfare of the human race, produces and brings it into light at that convenient season which God himself, by a secret mystery, knows to be the suitable one, in order that men may know that they can do nothing by their own merits as of themselves, but that their salvation and every gift of grace proceeds from the supreme God himself, and from the Father of light. Truly it is not without a great and lively joy in our mind, that we have heard that some Russians in the duchy of Lithuania, and others living according to the Greek ritual, but in other respects professing the Christian faith, dwelling in the cities and dioceses of Vilna and Kiof, Lukof and Medniki, and other places in the same duchy, have, by the illumination of the Holy Spirit working in them, expressed a desire utterly to reject from their minds and hearts some errors, which, while living in the ritual and custom of the Greeks, they have hitherto observed, and to embrace the unity of the Catholic faith, and of the Latin Roman Church, and to live according to the ritual of the said Latin and Roman Church. But as they have been baptized according to the ritual of the Greeks—namely, in the

he was elected king of Poland in his place, the Poles refused, on account of her religion, to allow his wife Helena to share his crown. The angry Ivan, resenting this affront, and the non-fulfilment of the agreement made by the Lithuanian prince, declared that Polish Russia, as far as the Berezina, had formerly belonged to his ancestors, and should again be his; and, sending three armies by different routes into Lithuania, he wasted the country to the walls of Smolensko,

<small>third person, and some assert that they ought to be baptized anew—the aforesaid, who have hitherto lived and still live under the Greek ritual, refuse to receive baptism again, as though they had been already rightly baptized. We therefore, who in the pastoral office committed to us from above, though insufficiently deserving it, desire to bring every sheep intrusted to us to the true fold of Christ, that there may be one shepherd and one fold, and to the end that the Holy Catholic Church may have no discordant or unsightly members at variance with the head, but all in harmony therewith; and taking into consideration that in the council held at Florence by our predecessor, Eugene the Fourth of blessed memory, at which were present Greeks and Armenians agreeing with the Romish Church, it was decided that the form of this sacrament of baptism should be, 'I baptize thee in the name of the Father, and of the Son, and of the Holy Ghost.' Amen. And also that by the words, 'Let such a servant of Jesus Christ be baptized in the name of the Father, and of the Son, and of the Holy Ghost,' a true baptism is performed; for the main source from which baptism derives its virtue is the Holy Trinity, the instrument is the minister, and the exposition of the sacrament is effected by his ministry in his invocation of the Holy Trinity. We therefore, having maturely deliberated upon the subject with our brethren, declare by these presents, in virtue of the apostolical authority delivered to us and the other Roman pontiffs, by our Lord Jesus Christ himself, through St. Peter (to whom and his successors was committed the dispensation of the ministry), that the repetition of such sacrament thus administered in the third person, is not necessary. We declare that each and all of those who have been baptized in the third person of the Trinity, and wish to leave the Greek ritual, and conform to that of the Latin and Holy Roman Church, are to be admitted in all simplicity, and without any contradiction, obligation, or compulsion, to be rebaptized; it being moreover intended that such rites as they may have been accustomed to observe in the Eastern Church may continue to be observed by them, provided there be no heretical depravity therein, always provided that they first solemnly abjure all errors of the Greek ritual, and such things as differ from the ritual and institutions of the Latin and Roman Church. At the same time, we exhort by the mercy of our God, that each and all of such as are baptized, and who live according to the Greek ritual, repudiating the errors which they have hitherto held according to the custom and ritual of the Greek Church, and contrary to the immaculate and Holy Catholic Latin and Roman Church, and to the approved institutions of her holy fathers, do willingly conform to the said Holy Catholic Church, and to her wholesome doctrines, for the sake of the salvation of their souls, and the advancement of the knowledge of the true God; and that their holy resolution may meet with no hindrance from any one, we now charge and enjoin upon our venerable brother, the bishop of Vilna, by virtue of sacred obedience, that he receive and admit each and all who may be so baptized, and who wish to conform to the unity of the aforesaid Latin Church, and abjure the aforesaid errors, either by themselves or by proxy, or by committing the same abjuration to any of the secular prelates, ecclesiastics, or preachers, or to the learned and worthy professors of the regular observance of the minor orders, or any fitting person to whom such abjuration might be intrusted. And by these presents we grant to all and singular of the aforesaid, full and free liberty to indoct, as often as may be expedient, any such, as aforesaid, who may have in any way incurred the sentence of excommunication, or any other sentence or penalties of the church, on account of the observance of such errors, or any heretical depravity proceeding therefrom, and by the aforesaid apostolical authority to absolve them, and by way of exculpation to inflict a salutary penance, or to adopt any measure which may be deemed necessary in the cases described. But since it might, perhaps, be difficult to convey this our letter to all the places where it may be needed, we will, and by the same apostolical authority decree, that the rescript of this our letter, be recopied by the hand of a notary-public, and sealed with the seal of the aforesaid bishop of Vilna, or some other bishop or ecclesiastical prelate; and that this copy or transcript, shall have as much validity as would be given to the original in every tribunal, and in every place where it shall be exhibited or declared, notwithstanding any apostolical institutions, orders, or ordinances whatsoever. Be it understood, therefore, that it shall not be lawful for any one whatever to infringe, or by any bold act of temerity to contravene this our letter of constitution, declaration, exhortation, commission, mandate, concession, will, and decree; and if any one whatsoever shall dare to attempt this, let him know that he will incur the indignation of Almighty God, and of the blessed apostles Peter and Paul. Given at Rome, at St. Peter's, in the Year of the Incarnation of Our Lord, 1501, 10° Calend., Septemb., in the Ninth Year of our Pontificate."—Herberstein's "Rerum Muscovitarum," edited by R. Major.</small>

possessed himself of Severa, and defeated the Polish field-marshal Ostrofsky near the river Wadrash; where the latter, incautiously relying on the strength and bravery of his own well-armed forces, neglected the commonest precautions, and fell unawares into an ambush of the Muscovites. The city of Brensko, with the other fortresses on the frontier, all fell into the hands of the invaders; and the Lithuanians in a short campaign lost, with the exception of Smolensko, the entire conquests of Vitold, the hard-won fruits of many years of war and bloodshed, while their general was forced to enter the service of Ivan, and was rewarded for his desertion by large estates. But these could not reconcile him to abandon his own monarch, and join the fortunes and campaigns of his enemies; and after having resided for several years in Moscow, where, subject to a strict surveillance, he found himself little more than a slave, on the first opportunity he succeeded in evading his guards in the capital, and made his escape to his own countrymen through the thick and intricate woods.

Alexander, obtaining the assistance of his brother, brought a new and enormous army into the field, consisting chiefly of foreign battalions of Silesians, Bohemians, and Moravians; but the Russians had sent all their plunder into Muscovy, and fortified themselves securely in the captured stronghold; and the Grand Duke, despairing of being able to retake his conquered territories, whose people, having originally belonged to Russia, and being allied to her in customs and faith, had always been hostile to his government, gladly acceded to the proposals of Ivan, and agreed to a truce of a few months. The Czar took advantage of this to march against Livonia, whose masters, the Teutonic knights, in alliance with Alexander, had lately crossed his borders, and plundered the districts about Novogorod; but his armies sustained a most disastrous defeat on the 7th of September, 1502, near Pleskof, and lost above 10,000 men; and though he gained, a few weeks after, some advantages over the enemy, he immediately despatched an ambassador to the Grand Master, Walter Von Plattenberg, and concluded a fifty years' peace. At the same time he requested Von Plattenberg, whose successor ultimately closed his days in a Russian prison, to send one of those iron dragoons to Moscow who had played so valiant a part in the late engagement; and, having gratified his curiosity by examining the soldier's sword and accoutrements, he gave him some valuable presents, and allowed him to return home.*

The following summer the war with Poland was renewed; and Ivan, the Czarovitz, having died six years before, when his physician Leo was beheaded for not having succeeded in saving his life, the Czar sent an army, under the command of his second son Demetrius, with orders to take Smolensko at all risks. The Russian troops remained long, and fought bravely before its walls, but the garrison made a most obstinate resistance; and at length the arrival of the king of Poland with a numerous force, obliged Demetrius to raise the siege, and abandon the attack with his troops; and, shortly after, the Poles concluded a peace with Moscow for six years, on the Russians returning all the prisoners whom they had captured in the former war. Ivan was greatly incensed at this failure, which he entirely attributed to his son's want of skill or courage; and, according to some authors, upon Demetrius first appearing before him when he returned from Smolensko, the Czar flew into a violent passion, and struck him so violent a blow with his possach, that the prince fell dead at his feet. It is also related that Ivan never entirely recovered his son's death, but became from that time a prey to grief and remorse; † but this story, so similar to the more authentic one of his grandson, Ivan the Terrible, rests on merely a slender foundation, though it is certain that Demetrius expired about this period, and that his father scarcely survived him eighteen months.

After the death of the Czarovitz in 1496, Ivan had appointed his only child, Demetrius, the heir to the throne of Muscovy; and in order to secure his succession, which was much opposed by the Czarina Sophia, who wished the crown to be placed on the head of one of her own sons, he caused him to be solemnly inaugurated during his own lifetime, and the ceremony took place on the 4th of February, 1497. It was conducted in the same manner as the ordinary coronations of the Czars. In the middle of the Cathedral of the Assumption three thrones were erected for the Czar, his grandson, and the metropolitan; and opposite to these were placed the imperial crown and regalia, while the church was crowded with the archbishops, abbots, and bishops, and every order and dignitary of the Muscovite ecclesiastics. Upon

* "Universal History." † Lacombe's "Revolutions de la Russie."

the entrance of Ivan and Demetrius, the deacons sang according to custom, "Long live the only Grand Prince and Czar, the great Ivan, may he long reign over us!" This was followed by a prayer to the Holy Virgin and St. Peter, after which the two princes ascended their thrones, and Ivan addressed the metropolitan with these words :—

"Father, according to the custom anciently, and until now observed by our predecessors, our ancestors the Grand Princes have, by the grace of God, consigned the kingdom to their eldest sons, and after their example the Grand Prince, my father, blessed me with the monarchy in his own presence, so also I in like manner blessed my first-born, Ivan, with the kingdom in the presence of all. Since, however, it has happened by the Divine pleasure that my son is dead, but that his only son, Dimitri, whom God gave me in the place of my son, survives; I likewise, in conformity with the same custom, bless him in the presence of all, both now and after my death, with the Grand Duchies of Vladimir, Novogorod, and all else with which I should have blessed his father." The metropolitan then advanced to Demetrius, and, blessing him with the cross, ordered the deacon to read the prayers;* and these finished, two abbots brought the crown and regalia, with which the Czar invested his grandson at the same time that the primate signed him with the cross in the name of the Holy Trinity.† The officiating deacon then commenced the Litany, after which the priests sang from the altar, "Long live the Grand Prince, Ivan, the beloved of Christ, the chosen and honoured of God; long live

---

* PRAYERS READ AT THE CORONATION OF DEMETRIUS.

"O Lord our God, King of kings, Lord of lords, who by thy servant Samuel, the prophet, didst choose David, and anointed him to be king over Thy people Israel, hear now the prayers of Thine unworthy servant, and look down from Thy sanctuary upon Thy faithful servant whom thou hast chosen to exalt to be king over Thy holy nations, and whom Thou hast redeemed with the most precious blood of Thy only begotten Son; anoint him with the oil of gladness, protect him with the virtue of the highest, place upon his head a crown of precious stones, give him length of days, and a royal sceptre in his right hand; place him on a righteous throne, surround him with all the arms of justice, strengthen his arm and subdue unto him all barbarian tongues; let his whole heart be in Thy fear, that he may humbly obey Thee; keep him from the false path, and point out to him the true preserver of the commands of Thy holy universal church, that he may judge the people in justice, and administer justice to the poor, and preserve the children of the poor, and, finally, that he may attain the kingdom of heaven. Even as thine is the power, and thine is the kingdom, so be praise and honour to thee, God the Father, Son, and Holy Ghost, now and for ever."

† Here another followed :—

"O Lord, we pray to Thee, the only King eternal, to whom also is committed the sovereignty of the earth, uphold this prince under Thy protection, continue him in the kingdom, that he may always do that which is good and seemly, make justice to shine in his days, and, in the enlargement and tranquillity of his dominion, let us live quietly and peaceably in all goodness and purity.

"Thou art the King of the world and preserver of our souls; praise be to Thee, Father, Son, and Holy Ghost, now and for ever. Amen."

the Grand Prince and Czar, Ivan Vassilovitz, monarch of Novogorod and all the Russias! Long live the Grand Prince Demetrius, the beloved of Christ, the chosen and honoured of God; long live the Grand Prince and Czar, Demetrius Ivanovitz, monarch of Novogorod and all the Russias!" This chorus was taken up and repeated by the priests scattered over all parts of the cathedral, till the walls and altars resounded with their notes; and, at the same time, the sons of Ivan, and all the princes of the imperial family, came forward and bowed before, and saluted Demetrius.* Then the metropolitan, Simon, addressed this exhortation to the young prince, "O my son, lord Demetrius, by the Divine will the Grand Prince, thy grandfather hath shown thee favour, and blessed thee with the kingdom; do thou also, my son, have the fear of God in thy heart. Love justice and just judgment, obey thy sovereign the Czar, and interest thyself with all thy heart about all the truly faithful. We pray to heaven for thy welfare." The service was concluded with another litany, when the Czar departed for his palace; but his grandson, accompanied by the clergy and princes of the royal family, proceeded to the church of St. Michael the Archangel, to pray before the tombs of his ancestors; after which they returned to the great hall of the Kremlin, and ended the festal day by a banquet, prolonged till past midnight. Among other Russian priests, there were present at the coronation the metropolitan, Simon; the archbishop Tychon, of Rostoff and Jaroslaf; Nyphon, archbishop of Suzdal; Vasian, bishop of Tver; Prothasius, bishop of Riazan and Murom; Afranius, bishop of Columna; and Euphemius, bishop of Sarkel and Podonski; besides Seraphine, prior of the monastery of St. Sergius, and the prior of the monastery of St. Cyril.†

But the career of the young prince, which had begun so auspiciously, was destined to have a brief continuation, and a miserable and tragic close. As Ivan grew old, and the reins of government became feeble and relaxed in his grasp, his ambitious and overbearing Greek wife obtained the most unbounded influence over her husband, and, after much persuasion, induced him, in the year 1502, to consent to the deposition and imprisonment of Demetrius, and the elevation of Gabriel, now their eldest surviving son, to the dignity of heir to the crown. But when the Czar was on his death-bed,

* Herberstein's "Rerum Muscovitarum." † Ibid.

and had reviewed in confession to the archbishop all the stirring scenes and offences of his past life, his heart smote him for this cruelty and injustice, and he commanded that Demetrius should be brought from his dungeon to the room where he lay in the last agonies of death; and, taking his hand, "Alas! my dear grandson," said he, "I have sinned against God and thee, inasmuch as I have afflicted thee with imprisonment, and have deprived thee of thy just inheritance. I beseech thee to forgive me this injury that I have done thee; depart in freedom, and enjoy thy right." Having uttered these words, Ivan fell back and expired; and the young prince, greatly affected by the solemn scene, had scarcely crossed the threshold of the chamber, when he was seized by some of the partisans of his uncle Gabriel, and thrown into a deep and gloomy cellar of the Kremlin, entirely deprived of either warmth or light, where in a very few weeks he perished, according to some writers, from hunger or cold, or, as others state, from suffocation by means of smoke.

Ivan the Great died on the 27th of March, 1505, at the age of sixty-five, after an eventful reign of forty-four years, and was buried with great pomp among his ancestors, in the imperial vault of the cathedral of St. Michael in Moscow. His reign, till towards the end, when it was clouded by the ill success of his troops in both Livonia and before Smolensko, and the revolt of his vassal, the khan of Kazan, had been almost uninterrupted prosperity, and altogether may rank as the most fortunate that the generally disastrous annals of Russia can boast. Though he himself never shone as a soldier, he showed discernment in his choice of able generals, and skill in directing a war; so that Stephen of Moldavia would often say when speaking of him—"Ivan increases his dominions while sitting at home and sleeping, while I can scarcely defend my own boundaries by fighting in person every day." He rather improved the miserable condition of the peasantry, by decreeing that they should be allowed one day in every week for their own occupations when they had hired themselves out to a master, and that every landowner should allow his labourers each a field to cultivate for themselves; and he put a considerable check upon the exactions of the nobility and clergy, when he rendered them liable to the penalties of the law, and for the first time to the terrible punishment of the knout. In 1491, Prince Oukhtomsky, the boyard Khomoutoff, and the Archimandrite of Choudoff, were all publicly knouted for a false title they had forged to some land which belonged to one of the brothers of the Czar. His decrees were often characterized by a most inadequate severity and harshness; "and his aspect," says the Russian historian, "was so fierce, that women, or even the ladies of the court, to all of whom he had a great aversion and contempt, and seldom condescended to speak, had been known to faint when they encountered him in the street or in the palace." In his old age he would often fall asleep during a banquet, when the boyards, fearful of disturbing him and exciting his anger, would long remain silent and almost immoveable; and, though he frequently drank to excess, he would not tolerate intemperance in the nobles of his court. Passionate, harsh, and treacherous, he had few qualities to recommend him to posterity; and his subjects appear to have viewed his decease with little sorrow or regret.

During this reign a census was made for the second time throughout the empire, for the purpose of levying recruits. The first had been ordered by Bereka, the khan of Kipzak, for the sake of exacting a proportionate tribute from each district.

As soon as Ivan was dead, and Demetrius consigned to a close imprisonment, Gabriel assumed the title of regent of the empire for his nephew, as he dared not openly usurp the throne during the lifetime of the rightful heir; and though, some time after the young prince's death, he took the appellation of Czar and Grand Prince,* and changed his name from Gabriel to Bazil, he was never publicly crowned or inaugurated, like his ancestors.

Immediately after his accession, as he was still unmarried, he assembled a council, and desired his ministers to declare which would be most beneficial to his country—to choose a wife from a foreign royal house, or from among his own subjects. They all agreed that it would be far better for their sovereign to marry a Muscovite than a strange princess; as the latter might introduce habits and customs into their country before unknown to Russia, and also many of her

---

* In a Latin letter Bazil addressed to Pope Clement VII., he thus enumerates his own titles:—Clementi Pastoriæ Doctori Romanæ Ecclesiæ, Magnus Dux Basilius Dei Gratiâ Imperator ac Dominator totius Russiæ, nec non Magnus Dux Voldomeriæ, Moscoviæ, Novogradiæ, Plescoviæ, Smolensciæ, Iberriæ, Ingoriæ, Permiæ, Viatkiæ, Bulgariæ, et Dominator et Magnus Princeps Novogorodiæ Inferioris, Terræ Cernigoviæ, Kasaniæ, Volotriæ, Rzeviæ, Bielozeriæ, Jaroslaviæ, Belchiæ, Udoriæ, Obdoriæ, Condiniæque.

countrymen in her train, and would probably belong and persist in adhering to another faith. This council was more particularly urged by Demetrius Trachaniotes, whom Bazil always esteemed as his most faithful friend; and who, having been treasurer and keeper of the seals to Ivan, received, with several other boyards at his death, a gold cross as a token of remembrance, according to a clause in that prince's will. Demetrius is supposed to have chiefly given this advice in the hope that the Czar would choose his own daughter Anna, but his hopes were doomed to disappointment; for an order was sent round to all the nobles, commanding them to follow the common practice of Muscovy, and bring their daughters to the Kremlin, that the Czar might select from among them a suitable bride; and, when fifteen hundred young ladies had been assembled in the palace, Bazil chose Salome, the daughter of the boyard Ivan Saburof, and raised her to a share of his throne.

A year after this, his brother-in-law Alexander expired in Poland from a severe and long protracted illness; and, as soon as he had received the intelligence of his death, Bazil wrote to his sister, the dowager queen, requesting her to use all her influence to induce the general assemblies of Poland and Lithuania to elect him as their king, pledging himself to observe the rights, liberties, and constitution of both states. But his letter only arrived after the appointment of Sigismund, the brother of the late monarch, to the regal dignity; and this prince, who is said by Polish historians to have been a man of great talents and noble character, accordingly ascended the turbulent Polish throne.*

In the last year of the reign of Alexander, the Tartars of the Crimea penetrated into the very heart of Lithuania, but were repulsed, and their forces almost completely extirpated by an army of Poles under Prince Michael Glinski, a noble descended from the family of Rurik, who, during the present reign, had entirely regulated and directed the affairs of that important state. He had been educated in Germany, and served as a youth under the banner of Duke Albert of Saxony, and in Friesland, where he had gained for himself honour and renown among all ranks of warriors and noblemen; and on his return to Poland had acquired the most unbounded empire over its weak and feeble monarch. But

* Krusinski's "History of Poland."

his administration, and the high esteem in which he was held by Alexander, as well as his own haughty and overbearing conduct, had raised many enemies against him, more especially with those bigoted converts in Lithuania who had lately adopted the Latin Church, as Glinski himself adhered to the forms of the Greek. Among these, one of the most dangerous and inveterate was Ivan Zabrzinzscki, grand marshal of Lithuania, whom he had caused, by his influence with the king, to be deprived of his high and coveted office, and who, after the death of Alexander, endeavoured to avenge it by accusing him to Sigismund of treason. Glinski demanded that he should be allowed a fair trial, but the king refused to listen to his request; whereupon the incensed Pole wrote to the Czar of Muscovy, and offered, if Bazil would ensure him safety and independence upon his most solemn oath, to surrender to the arms of Moscow the fortresses that he commanded in Lithuania, with all his soldiers and munitions of war. Upon obtaining a favourable reply to his overtures, he secretly departed for the Russian capital; but first halting on his road at a villa near Grodno, the residence of his adversary Zabrzinzscki, he set a guard of soldiers at night round the house to prevent his victim's escape, and sent a Tartar assassin into his bed-chamber, who attacked the unfortunate Ivan when sleeping, and barbarously cut off his head. After this murder, Glinski escaped with his followers into Russia; and in a war which broke out a few months later between Moscow and Poland, and which was occasioned by the angry remonstrance of the Czar—who, resenting an insult offered to his sister in Poland, also accused Sigismund of having instigated the khan of Kazan to revolt—the Polish renegade was appointed commander-in-chief of the Muscovite army in an attack upon Smolensko, the bulwark of Lithuania and Poland. He had been acquainted with the governor of this stronghold in former days, and believed that he was open to corruption; so Bazil engaged to grant to Glinski the whole city and its district, in perpetuity for himself and his descendants, if he could induce the commander of the fortress to surrender without the tedium and loss of a siege. This the general soon accomplished by his gold; and the treacherous Pole gave up Smolensko without an attempt at defence, and with all his officers, except one who escaped to Poland, deserted to the service of Moscow. The common soldiers, though guiltless of any share in the nefarious transaction, were easily persuaded by their officers that they could not safely return into Lithuania, and accordingly settled in Russia; and, when Smolensko was once in his power, Bazil, ever faithless and treacherous, refused to fulfil his promise to Glinski, but attempted to delude him by fresh hopes of reward if the latter remained sincere in his service. The Polish general, incensed at this conduct, immediately commenced a correspondence with his former sovereign, and offered, if Sigismund would march to the assistance of Smolensko, to deliver it up with his army into the possession of Poland. But a letter in reply from the Polish king, who gladly accepted the proposal, was seized by the Muscovite sentinels at the entrance of the camp, and delivered into the hands of the Czar; and Bazil caused the double traitor to be instantly arrested, and brought bound with chains into his presence. "Ungrateful man!" said he, when Glinski appeared before him, "I will inflict on thee a punishment worthy of thy deserts." To which the general boldly replied, "I do not acknowledge the crime of treason which thou layest to my charge; for, if thou hadst kept faith towards me with respect to thine own promises, thou wouldest have found me a most faithful servant; but when I saw that thou thoughtest lightly of them, and madest it thy chief aim to evade me, it became a heavy grievance to me that I had not been able to accomplish those things which I had conceived in my mind respecting thee. I have always despised death, and will therefore willingly undergo it, but never more let me see thy face, O tyrant!"* Saying this he was led away, though unfettered, by the Czar's order, and conducted to Viezma, where the Muscovite general, in command of a division of the army quartered there, caused a load of heavy chains to be cast down before him, and exclaiming at the same time—"The Czar, as thou knowest, O Michael! honoured thee with the greatest favour whilst thou faithfully served him, but since thou has thought fit to carry on thy treasonable practices with a high hand, he presents thee with this reward as most suitable to thy merits," ordered them to be again fastened upon him. As Gliuski was being conducted through the town on his way to Moscow, he said to the people who crowded round him, "Lest a false rumour

* Herberstein's "Rerum Muscovitarum."

should be spread amongst you as to the cause of my imprisonment, I will briefly unfold to you what I have done, and why I have been taken prisoner, that you may learn from my example what kind of prince you have over you, and what each of you may expect from him." He then began to relate to them all the circumstances of his treason and capture, but was prevented from finishing by the officers who conducted him; and on arriving in Moscow, he was for many years kept in close imprisonment, though some attempts were made for his release, and even the emperor Maximilian wrote several letters to Bazil in his behalf. He at length regained his liberty for a short period, though only to be still more cruelly lost, through several very singular circumstances. In 1526, the Czar, after a union of twenty-one years with Salome, by whom he had no children, assembled a council of boyards to deliberate upon the expediency of a divorce. None daring to differ from their sovereign, they all strongly recommended him to take such a step, though no marriage can legally be dissolved in the Russian Church; and the subservient metropolitan, hoping to gain the favour of his master, promised to declare the alliance void if the Czarina would retire into a convent. Only two monks, a Muscovite named Bassian, and Maximus a learned Greek, who had been brought from Constantinople to correct, by the Byzantine translations, the numerous errors that had gradually accumulated in the Russian Bible and other religious books, were bold enough to declare that it was contrary to all the laws of God and the Eastern Church that the holy bands of matrimony should ever be dissolved; and that, to take another bride during the lifetime of his first wife, would be bigamy and impious sin; but these were rewarded for their courage by being condemned to a perpetual and most rigorous confinement in a monastery. The unfortunate Salome was conducted to her convent sobbing and weeping, and in the greatest distress; and when the primate Daniel began to cut off her hair, and she was presented by the prioress with the ordinary hood of a novice, she indignantly dashed it to the ground, crying, and stamping upon it with her feet. One of the councillors of the Czar, a man called Ivan Schezgona, brutally struck her several times with his staff when he saw this, exclaiming, "Darest thou resist the will of my lord?" upon which she called all who were present to witness that she only consented to take the veil because she was compelled to do so by force, and appealed to the justice and righteous judgment of the Almighty, to revenge her injuries and misfortunes upon the perpetrators.

A month after this event Bazil espoused Helen Glinski, the niece of his imprisoned general, and daughter of Bazil Glinski, another Polish fugitive; and, at the request of his wife, released her uncle from his dungeon, and appointed him, in case of his own death before his heirs had attained their majority, co-regent with Helen of the empire.

But, to return to the Polish war in 1513, which continued for several years with fearful violence. On hearing of the approach of their king, the inhabitants of Smolensko rose up in arms against the Muscovites; but Bazil, who had brought several pieces of cannon from Moscow, caused more to be founded beneath the very walls of the beleaguered city, and battered it almost to the ground; and Sigismund, learning the capture and imprisonment of Glinski, and the final subjection of Smolensko, immediately retired to Borisov. Nevertheless, he sent his army, under the command of Prince Constantine Ostrofsky, the same general who had formerly made his escape from Moscow, to meet the advancing Russians under Prince Ivan Androvitz Czeladin, who were marching from Smolensko upon Orcha or Orsova, a town about thirty miles distant. On the 8th of September 1514, the Polish cavalry crossed the Dnieper at a point near where the Muscovites were encamped; and many of Czeladin's officers earnestly entreated him to charge and overwhelm this division of the hostile army before they were joined by the rest of their force. But the Russian commander would not listen to this proposition, merely replying, "If we were to fall upon this part of the army, the other battalions, to which perhaps more may yet be added, will still remain, and thus great danger would threaten us; let us wait till the whole army has crossed, for our strength is such that without doubt we shall be able, with but little exertion, either to destroy these Poles or to surround them, and drive them like cattle to Moscow, and then it will only remain for us to take possession of the whole of Lithuania." Thus the favourable opportunity was lost, and the entire Polish army, passing the Dnieper, halted within about four miles of their enemies, who, moving their camp, advanced to within a very short distance of Ostrofsky, so that the hostile forces remained facing each other through the whole of a clear and starlight night.

The sun rose bright and glorious upon a cloudless day, and the first rays of the morning had scarcely appeared in the east, when the Russians arranged themselves in order of battle; two wings withdrawing to some distance to the right, to circumvent the enemy in the rear, the main body remaining drawn up in the midst, and a third battalion advancing some paces in front, to challenge the Lithuanians to a combat. The Poles were placed in a long array, standing according to their different nations and principalities, the soldiers of each province being together, and commanded by a captain chosen from among themselves; and they had scarcely formed when the Muscovites, sounding their clarions, furiously commenced the attack. The battle waged long and fiercely without either side appearing to have the advantage, till the Lithuanians feigned a retreat; and the Russian troops, who were encumbered with cuirasses, which hitherto they had not been accustomed to wear, became rather disordered in the pursuit. Upon this, the Poles turned with a sudden charge of artillery, and created frightful slaughter among their ranks. The Muscovites fled in confusion, and escaping in the night, without a knowledge of the country, they came upon a river called Cropivna, within a few miles of Orsova, and so many fell over its steep and slippery banks that the course of the stream was stopped by the heaps of dead.* The old general, Czeladin, whose indolence and apathy had been mainly the cause of their defeat, was taken prisoner in the engagement, with nearly all his officers, and sent in chains to Vilna, where they remained for many years in iron fetters, and reduced to extreme misery, so that they gladly accepted a few dollars from some German travellers who visited them. The greater number ultimately died in captivity. The pope ordered public thanksgivings in the churches for this victory of the orthodox Poles over the Muscovite heretics; and Sigismund, to show his gratitude to the pontiff, sent him an embassy, requesting his acceptance of an accompanying present of fourteen Russian boyards who had been taken prisoners in the late engagement, and were then looked upon as curiosities from a *terra incognita* in Western Europe. But the emperor Maximilian, who was on friendly terms with Mos-

* Herberstein's " Rerum Muscovitarum."

cow, intercepted them at Innspruck, and sent them back with handsome presents to Russia, through Lubeck and Livonia, to the mortification and displeasure of the Polish king, who affirmed that such an act was a violation of kingly faith, and a breach of the established law of nations.*

When Bazil heard of the disastrous defeat of his army at Orsova, he left Smolensko under the command of his generals, and returned to Moscow, having first caused two of his forts in Lithuania to be destroyed, lest they should fall into the hands of the foe. The Poles immediately marched upon Smolensko, but were driven by the Russians from before its walls; and Sigismund only gained three small castles by his victory, as the approach of winter put an end to the campaign. But, four years after, Bazil again invaded Lithuania, laying the country waste with powder, fire, and sword; when his camp was suddenly attacked in the night by a band of the dependants of the waywode, Albert Gastold Polocski. The Lithuanians set fire to several haycocks which had been collected near the Muscovite tents; and as the soldiers rushed out, struck with terror and confusion, half naked, and almost totally unarmed, they slew hundreds, and captured many prisoners. A few Russians escaped to the woods, where they lived for some time by plundering the neighbouring estates, till they were gradually all killed by the inhabitants, though Bazil secured the permanent possession of the province of Smolensko, by removing three out of every four of the people into Russia, and replacing them by Muscovites. Yet he was still surrounded by enemies; the Tartars both of Kazan and the Crimea were plundering the more distant provinces of his empire, and the emperor Maximilian, who had concluded an alliance with Sigismund, sent an ambassador to Moscow, desiring him to put an end to the war. He refused to send any answer to this imperious demand, but informed the Austrian envoy that the emperor had deserted him at a most unseasonable time, and that he could not put so sudden a termination to hostilities, which his imperial majesty himself had encouraged him to commence. Accordingly the campaign was renewed the following spring, as the king of Poland declined to conclude a peace unless Bazil would restore Smolensko, and to this the Czar affirmed that he should never consent; the Poles joined with the Crimean Tartars, and till 1520 continually invaded

* " Universal History."

and harassed Muscovy, but could never retake their important fortress, when, during the summer of that year, they both united with the rebellious Tartars of Kazan.

Kazan, who had revolted against Ivan the Great a few months before his death, and whose khan, seizing upon the persons of fifteen thousand Russians established in the city, had caused them all to be imprisoned or enslaved, and confiscated their houses and goods, followed up this step by marching against Nijni-Novogorod, where the Tartars defeated the Muscovites in a fierce engagement, and secured for a few years the independence of their state. But, in 1519, the same prince, Machmedin VII., having offended his subjects by refusing to lead them against the Muscovites, was deposed and afterwards strangled, and Sheikh Ali, a prince of Astrakhan, who had lived long at the court of Moscow, obtained possession of his throne, and also espoused his wife. However, this khan remained in power for only two years, having during that time brought the Muscovites back to Kazan, and placed them in many of the chief offices of state; for his subjects, displeased at this conduct, sent an embassy to offer the crown to Sahib Gherai, a brother of the khan of the Crimea, and ordered Sheikh Ali to give it up. The latter, finding himself entirely without support, thought it most prudent to obey, and fled to Moscow with his wives and children; while Achmet Gherai, the Crimean prince, conducted his brother with a large and powerful army into Kazan, and, before returning to his own kingdom, crossed the Don and proceeded towards Moscow. Bazil sent an army to oppose them under the general Prince Demetrius Belski, a young officer more distinguished for his birth than for his ability or experience; but it sustained a total defeat near the river Oka from the Tartars of Kazan, who formed a junction with the khan of the Crimea at Columna, and with them entered Moscow. The Czar had left the city under the command of his brother-in-law Prince Peter, and marched himself with a few battalions into Lithuania, to check an inroad of the Poles; but, in the meanwhile, his capital was ravaged and sacked by the invaders, while the immense concourse of people who attempted to take refuge in the Kremlin, caused many hundreds to be crushed and suffocated in the press. Several Polish officers accompanied the Tartars, while a few German artillerymen were shut up in Moscow; but they were unable to bring the unwieldy cannon in the Kremlin to bear upon the enemy, from want of sufficient powder and ammunition, and their immense size,* for it took three days to remove them from the citadel to a commodious spot. Some ambassadors from Livonia, who were also at that time in the city, and contrived to effect their escape, rode thirty-six miles in eight hours without halting, from Moscow to Tver. After two days of confusion and terror, Prince Peter sent an envoy with presents and several barrels of mead to Achmet Gherai, proposing terms of peace, to which the khan agreed, provided that Bazil would consent to pay him an annual tribute for each of his subjects, as had been done by his father and ancestors, and acknowledge himself a vassal of the Tartars, in a written document signed by his own hand.† He at the same time caused a statue of himself to be erected in Moscow, which was broken in pieces by the Russians immediately the Tartars had abandoned the place; and required that the Czar should bring his first payment in person, and prostrate himself before it. Bazil sent the money and written agreement to the khan, but evaded the last stipulation; and Achmet abandoned Moscow with eighty thousand prisoners and an immense booty, and retired upon the province of Riazan, where, in an attempt to take this city, he was beaten back by the Russian governor, Ivan Kowen, and narrowly escaped with life. Here he insolently held an auction, or fair, to dispose to the Muscovites of some of the plunder of their own metropolis, and consented to exchange a few of his innumerable prisoners for an adequate number of Tartar captives. Yet, notwithstanding the two khans of the Crimea and of Kazan carried off, according to Herberstein, the hardly credible number of eight hundred thousand slaves, principally aged men, women, and children; of whom, all who were too infirm for sale were given up to the Tartar youths to be shot or stoned to death, while the rest were sold at Astrakhan on the Caspian, and from thence distributed over Persia and India; or at Kaffa, where they generally became the property of the Ottoman Turks. One of these, a Russian girl, was subsequently transferred to the imperial harem of Constantinople, and became in

---

* "It is constantly the custom," says Herberstein, "with the Russians, to be behindhand with every thing, and never to have any thing ready."
† Herberstein's "Rerum Muscovitarum."

after days the principal wife of the sultan Solyman the Magnificent.

As soon as the Tartars had abandoned Moscow, and her people found themselves once more secure within their walls, a contention arose among the generals of the defeated army, concerning the author of their precipitate flight. The older courtiers accused Prince Belski of neglecting their councils, and allowing the Tartars to cross the Oka through want of sufficient caution and prudence; while he affirmed that it was entirely owing to Prince Andrew, a younger brother of the Czar's, who commanded the central body, and there is not a doubt was the first of the Russians who fled. However, Bazil refused to punish his brother, but contented himself with imprisoning another commander who had joined Andrew in his hasty retreat; and, depriving this officer of his rank and position as governor of a province, allowed further inquiry into the matter to rest.

But the next year the Czar refused to pay the tribute to the Tartars, and prepared for another war with Kazan. He first sent a herald to Achmet of the Crimea, to provoke him if possible to a fair and open fight, saying, "That in the previous summer he had been insidiously attacked without a declaration of war, after the fashion of thieves and plunderers rather than that of bold and honest warriors." To this the king replied, "That in warfare opportunities were of as much importance as arms, and that consequently he made it his custom to choose his own time for fighting, instead of allowing others to choose it for him;" but he made no further attempt to exact the Russian tribute.*

In the June of 1523, Bazil marched towards Kazan, and encamped on Gostinovosero, or the Isle of Merchants, at the confluence of the Volga and the Oka, making it the head-quarters of his forces. From this place he sent out an armed corps in advance, which burned several wooden fortresses around Kazan, and with its cannon made many openings in her walls; but considered that it was not strong enough to mount the hill on which she stands, and storm the town, and therefore waited to commence the siege till it was joined by the rest of the troops. In the meanwhile, Sahib Gherai had sent one of his nephews in disguise to penetrate through the districts occupied by the Muscovites, and rouse

* Herberstein's "Rerum Muscovitarum."

his brother, the khan of the Crimea, in his behalf; but the young prince was unfortunately obliged to pass through an independent territory near Kazan, governed by a hermit or prophet named Said, who was held in such high veneration by the neighbouring countries, that foreign nobles had been known to kiss his feet, and kings to stand uncovered while he sat on horseback; and the old man, though he received him with much apparent kindness, was secretly inclined to favour the cause of Bazil, and, as soon as he found the emissary of Kazan in his power, ordered him to be basely assassinated. Sheikh Ali, the ex-khan, had also brought some rafts up the Volga to assist the Muscovites, who had now assembled all their troops outside Kazan; and despatched a letter to Sahib Gherai at his camp, which he had pitched near the town, desiring him to surrender to himself (Sheikh Ali), his rightful and hereditary sovereign; but Gherai only answered—" If you wish to have my kingdom, take it by the sword. Let him to whom fortune gives it, hold it." He was supported on his side by a large force of Tcheremissian cavalry, a wild Finnish tribe who still inhabit those parts, and who, fighting like the Tartars and Cossacks, greatly annoyed and harassed the Russian camp; and Bazil only waited for a fresh store of provisions, which were being conveyed in a hundred ships up the Volga from Nijni-Novogorod, to reinforce his distressed and starving troops, and commence a bold attack.*

But, though he waited several weeks, his vessels never arrived, and he at length sent out five hundred horsemen to scour the country for provisions, and bring back some intelligence of his fleet. Of these nine only returned, with the news that Ivan Palitzi, the captain of the flotilla, had lost every vessel but ten insignificant rafts, and that their battalion had been attacked by a band of Tcheremissian archers, who had slain all but the nine, who had now made their way to the camp. A few days later, Palitzi himself made his appearance, and confirmed the truth of the report, by stating that ninety of his ships had been captured in an engagement with the Tcheremissians while bound in the river by a thick fog, under cover of which he had effected his escape with the rest; and the Russians, driven to desperation, without food or powder, immediately commenced the siege, but were obliged to raise it after one or two fruitless attempts to force

* Herberstein's "Rerum Muscovitarum."

the gates; and, after suffering a heavy loss, concluded a truce, and commenced a weary march back to Moscow.

Several Tartar ambassadors came with them to the capital, to negotiate the terms of a permanent peace; but they were some years before they could come to an amicable agreement, and the negotiations were ultimately concluded by Kazan freeing herself from her tribute. Bazil attempted to remove the annual fair from the Isle of Merchants, where it had been held for centuries, to Nijni-Novogorod, and imposed a heavy penalty upon any Muscovite who should dare to trade with Gostinovosero; for, as Russia chiefly supplied the Kazanites with salt, he hoped, by depriving them of this article, to induce them to submit; but the prohibition had ultimately an equally injurious effect upon the trade of Russia with the East. Upon the accession of the Emperor Charles V., the Czar sent an ambassador, Prince Ivan Yaroslavski, with congratulations to Vienna, who received many presents from the German court, all of which, according to the custom of Russia, he was obliged to transfer to Bazil upon his return to Moscow. The Czar had also some correspondence wih Pope Clement VII., who despatched an ambassador, Paulus Centurius, to Moscow, to make another though still fruitless attempt, to unite the schismatic Greeks and Russians with the Latin and Western Church; but Bazil, though in the end he refused to comply with this proposal, sent an envoy, Prince Demetrius, to Rome, to observe the service and ceremonies of the Romans, and arrange a regular diplomatic intercourse with the pontiff.* A truce was arranged with Poland for five years, though Sigismund still demanded the

---

* LETTER OF BAZIL TO CLEMENT, ON THIS SUBJECT:—

"To Pope Clement, shepherd and teacher of the Roman Church, Great Bazil, by the grace of God, Lord, Emperor, and Ruler of all Russia, and Grand Duke of Vladimir, &c., &c., &c.

"You sent unto us Paulus Centurius, a citizen of Genoa, with letters, wherein you do exhort us to join in power and counsel with you, and other princes of Christendom, against the enemies of the Christian faith, and that a free passage and ready way may be opened, for both your ambassadors and ours, to go to and fro, whereby, by mutual endeavour on both sides, we may learn the state of things pertaining to the wealth of both. As we have hitherto, by the aid and help of Almighty God, constantly and earnestly resisted the cruel and wicked enemies of the Christian faith, so are we determined to do hereafter, and are likewise ready to consent with other Christian princes, and to grant free passage into our dominions. In consideration whereof, we have sent unto you our faithful servant Demetrius Erasmush, with these our letters: and with him have sent back Paulus Centurius, desiring you also shortly to dismiss Demetrius, with safeguard and indemnity, unto the borders of our dominions. And we will likewise do the same, if you send your ambassador with Demetrius, whereby both by communication and letters we may be better certified of such things as you require; so that, knowing the minds and intentions of all other Christian princes, we may also consult what is best to be done herein.

"Thus fare ye well. Given in our city of Moscow, in the year from the creation of the world, 7300, the third day of April."

restoration of Smolensko, and the Czar as firmly refused to give it up; but on his fifty-first birthday, the 25th of August, 1530, Bazil was at length made happy by the birth of his first child, a long and ardently desired son; and on this occasion he released many prisoners of state, and among others the Polish captives who had lingered in the dungeons of Moscow since the close of the last Lithuanian war. The infant, who in later years gained such fearful celebrity as the Czar Ivan IV., surnamed the Terrible, one of the most cruel and extraordinary monarchs of history, was baptized with great pomp at the monastery of St. Sergius; three monks, one, St. Daniel of Peryaslava, standing as his sponsors, and his father placed him on the tomb of the holy martyr, with a prayer that the spirit of the saint whose ashes it enclosed would guide and protect the child's future life. But the people remembered the curse of Salome, and believed that it would rest upon her husband's son.

But Bazil's own reign was now drawing towards its close, and shortly after this event he fell into a slow consumption, of which he gradually sank during an illness of many months. At length his physicians advised as a cure, that his body should be singed from head to foot with flaming wool; but the remedy proving fatal, he died a few hours after, on the 4th of December of the year 1533, in the fifty-fifth year of his age, and twenty-eighth of his reign. On his deathbed, where he encountered the last enemy with a firmness and resolution worthy of a purer life, he made every arrangement for a council of regency, which he ordered should be composed of the princes Shuiski and Belski, Bazil Glinski, his wife's brother, and the Czarina Helen, and her uncle Michael Glinski, who were also the guardians of Ivan and George his infant sons; as he knew that Simon and Andrew, his only surviving brothers, were already raising partisans in the state to secure their own succession to the throne; and, having given these directions, he desired to be invested, after the custom of his ancestors, with the habit and sanctity of a monk. The boyards who stood around him desiring to lower the power and influence of the church, recommended him to die in peace, and not submit to the fatigue of this ceremony, which had been considered unnecessary by his father and immediate predecessors; but the primate, raising his voice above all, exclaimed—" A vessel of silver is good, but one of gold is better. No one shall steal his soul from me!" And ordained Bazil a priest according to his wish.*

In person, the Czar was tall and handsome, and of a commanding figure, though without possessing his father's immense height and personal strength. Without Ivan's gloomy sternness and cruelty, he was courteous and amiable to all; so that, while treacherous, faithless, and deceitful, he was far more beloved by his subjects; and his body was borne to the imperial vault, in the Cathedral of the Archangel, amidst the tears and lamentations of his people.

Smolensko, with a few fortresses in Lithuania, alone remained as the bare result of his numerous and sanguinary wars, which had almost without exception proved disastrous; "although," says Herberstein, "Prince Bazil is constantly being praised by his courtiers, as if he had brought matters to a happy issue. On occasions when scarcely half his army has returned, they have told him that not a man was lost in battle; and, in the sway which he holds over his people, he surpasses all the monarchs of the whole world." He had scarcely breathed his last, when the Czarina, a most ambitious and dissolute woman, seized the reins of government, and declared herself sole regent for her son; and, upon encountering an open opposition from her brothers-in-law, Simon and Andrew, she caused them to be seized and thrown into a miserable dungeon, where they were tortured by her orders till both perished.

Prince Michael Glinski, though he had been appointed one of the council of regency by Bazil, who, aware of his talents as a general and commander, imagined that he would be the most efficient protector he could choose for the throne of his son, allowed his niece the undisputed government of the empire, till, having associated a favourite named Ovoçina in the imperial power, their oppression and tyranny became so unbearable, and her infamous life so great a scandal to the state, that the old general attempted to remonstrate, but she resented his presumption by causing him to be imprisoned, and barbarously deprived of sight; after which he lingered out a few dreary years in a narrow prison, his sufferings only alleviated by the attachment of his daughter, who nobly obtained permission to share his cell. But Helen had reigned scarcely five years when she was suddenly cut

* Mouravieff's "Church of Russia."

off by poison; and the princes Shuiski, with her brothers, taking possession of her children and the throne, her colleague Ovoçina was torn to pieces by the people; and a contest immediately arose between the regents for the chief share in the government, which filled the streets of the capital with corpses, and, while his education was totally neglected, early accustomed Ivan to scenes of horror and blood. Prince Belski and the metropolitan opposed the influence of the Shuiskis, and had at one time driven them from the palace and from Moscow; but a sudden invasion of the Tartars threw every thing into confusion, and the exiles returning with augmented force, dragged the young Czar from his bed, and carried him to their own castle, while Prince Belski perished at their order by the hand of a hired assassin. The chief of the Shuiskis was killed at length by the fury of a mob, when Prince Glinski established himself as president of the council of the empire; and from this time till Ivan was crowned, in the year 1547, and assumed the entire management of the affairs of state, Moscow was one long scene of terror and combat, while the surrounding provinces were a prey to misrule and Tartar invaders. The Poles made an inroad into the empire, burned several strongholds and the city of Smolensko, though they were unable to capture the citadel of that important fortress; and the fruit of all the wars that had been waged for so long, by Ivan and Bazil, with their eastern and western enemies, appeared about to be irretrievably lost.

The empire of the Golden Horde had become extinct in 1506, on the imprisonment of Achmet its last khan, who, in alliance with Alexander of Poland, had made war upon Mahomet Gherai of the Crimea; but after defeating the Crimean Tartars in a furious battle upon the steppes, the Lithuanians withdrew from the combat, leaving their allies to sustain the war with no shelter but their tents; and the winter commencing with unusual rigour, the soldiers of Achmet endured severe suffering from the deep snow and excessive cold. His wife, who had accompanied him in all his campaigns, after vainly attempting to induce him to break with Poland, deserted with half the army to the Tauridians; and being easily overthrown, with his few remaining followers, by the renovated forces of Mahomet, he escaped with the shattered remnant of his forces, comprising only three hundred horsemen, to Kiof. He was there treacherously seized by order of the ungrateful Polish king, and kept in confinement at the castle of Troki near Vilna, where he died after twenty years' captivity. His dominions were long contended for by the Crimean Tartars and Cossacks, till about fifty years later, after the final fall of Astrakan, the latter drove their rivals across the Don; and, subsequently taking Azof* from the Turks, made that fortress the bulwark of their deserts, and kept the Monguls, till the final conquest of the Crimea, within the limits of their peninsular retreat. After the capture of Achmet, Mahomet Gherai, uniting with Mamai, the khan of the Noghais, besieged and pillaged the city of Astrakhan, then known to the Muscovites as the "Star of the Desert," from its position as an oasis in the midst of the steppe, and both princes occupied the town for some months with their wild and undisciplined shepherd troops; but a dispute arising between them as to who should keep it permanently, Mamai caused his ally to be poisoned at a banquet, and, driving all the Crimeans out of the city, restored it to Bathir, its former monarch.

Years rolled away, and the troubled minority of Ivan IV.† having passed, amidst the hopes and exultations of his subjects he ascended his father's throne, when the khan, Dewlet Gherai of Kazan, who had remained since the reign of Bazil independent of Moscow, marched a large army into Russia, and pillaged the country round the capital. A few battalions, which were sent to oppose them, penetrated into the heart of Kazan; the khan fled precipitately, to take refuge with the Noghais of the steppes, while his queen, Sorimbala, and her children, were made prisoners and brought to Moscow; and the Russians, after placing a governor and a strong garrison

---

* In 1637, Azof was taken by the Cossacks of the Don, and in 1641 a strong army and fleet were sent from Constantinople for its recovery. The expedition was aided by a Tartar force under the khan of the Crimea. The Cossacks bravely defended the place, and after a siege of three months the Turks were obliged to retire with a loss of seven thousand janissaries, and a multitude of auxiliary Moldavians, Wallachians, and Tartars, whom the Ottoman historians do not enumerate. A fresh expedition was sent the next year, and the Crimean khan led one hundred thousand Tartars to assist the Turks. The Cossacks, no longer able to defend the place, set fire to the city, and left a heap of ruins for the Turks to occupy, who rebuilt the city and fortified it anew. The Tartars and Cossacks on the borders of the two empires were continually at war. In 1646, the Tartars pursued the Cossacks into the southern provinces of Russia, and carried off three thousand prisoners, whom they sold for slaves at Perekop. A Russian army advanced against Azof to avenge the affront, but was beaten in several actions by the commander Mousa Pacha and the garrison, who sent four hundred prisoners, and eight hundred Muscovite heads, as trophies to Constantinople. In 1648 the Crimean khan made an incursion into Russia and Poland, and carried off forty thousand of their subjects into slavery.—Creasy's "History of the Ottoman Turks."

† Ivan IV. died March, 1582.

in the city, disbanded the rest of their force. But, two years later, the Kazanites rose up against the Muscovites, who perished in every quarter of the city from poison or the assassin's steel; and, sending an envoy to Astrakhan, they entreated the sultan, Ediger, to come and protect them from their enemies, offering him the crown as the recompence of his assistance. The news of the massacre of their countrymen by Mahometans, was received with the greatest horror and indignation throughout Russia, and a strong body of troops was immediately sent against the rebels, who, after a long campaign of sixteen months, conquered all the territory around the city of Kazan, but failed in every attempt to take that fortress. The besiegers became at length so weary and dispirited, that they loudly clamoured to be permitted to return to their native land; some among them, still determined to persevere, declared that now it would be disgraceful to retreat, and, if they went home with no result after so much toil and bloodshed, they would ever be the mock and scorn of every patriotic Muscovite. Immediately the Czar heard of this outbreak, he hastened with a reinforcement, and the princes Kurbsky, Adasheff, and Serabine, to the scene of action, accompanied by a large fleet of rafts up the Volga, which kept the army supplied during the whole campaign with forage, ammunition, and provisions from Nijni-Novogorod, and transported his soldiers more speedily, and with less fatigue, than by a long and weary march. The Russians had previously built a town on a little river near Kazan, and called it Svielsky, and here they collected all their baggage and stores as they were landed from their ships; cannon, and a battalion of mounted musketeers, introduced into his army by the late Czar, Bazil, formed a most important portion of their force; and their troops were divided, according to their usual custom, into three great wings or divisions, each being separated into companies, with a completely distinct organization—an arrangement very similar to that observed in the enormous armies of Zingis.

As soon as he had arrived at the head-quarters of the Russians before Kazan, Ivan attempted to revive their drooping courage; and an address, written by the metropolitan, was read to them, exhorting the mutineers to obedience. Among other directions in this document, the primate, Sylvester, says, "Observe the commandments of God, and neglect not the service of the church; walk before him honestly and soberly, without intemperance, rebellion, or discontent. Fight bravely against the infidels, armed with the dagger of faith, nor rest till you have expunged them from the earth; and shave not your beards, that ye may attain the favour of the Almighty, the rewards of your sovereign, and the blessings of the Church." But the disaffected soldiers refused to listen either to their sovereign or the priests, and even attacked the more daring of their companions who wished to continue the war. Ivan rushed in between the combatants, and with his officers compelled them to separate; they threatened his life, and no promises of plunder or distinction could induce them to retract from their determination to return to Russia; so that the Czar, to his great mortification, was compelled to remove his quarters and assent to their wish, for the winter was fast approaching, and even the most enthusiastic of his followers declared, that now it would be impossible to continue the siege with their forces diminished, and surrounded by snow and ice.

When Ivan returned to Moscow, another disappointment awaited him; three hundred artisans and mechanics, who had been despatched at his request by the emperor Charles V. to Lubeck, to embark for Russia, had been stopped there by some merchants from Livonia, who gave a frightful description of the empire and its government; and wrote to the German prince, informing him that it would be most dangerous to send workmen to instruct her people, who were so fierce and so numerous, that if they were better armed they might overwhelm not only Livonia but half Europe.* The Czar resolved to revenge this insult at some future period upon Livonia, but for the present was entirely engrossed with the affairs of Kazan.

As soon as he had arrived in his own capital, he invited all the officers of the seditious portion of his army, who amounted to as many as two thousand, to a banquet at the

* In a letter of Sigismund II. of Poland to Queen Elizabeth, he calls the Czar (Ivan IV.) "the Muscovite, the hereditary enemy of all free nations;" and in another letter he says—"We seemed hitherto to vanquish him only in this, that he was rude of arts and ignorant of politics. If so be that this navigation of the Narva continue, what shall be unknown to him? The Muscovite, made more perfect in warlike affairs, with engines of war and ships, will slay or make bound all that shall withstand him, which God defend."
Chancellor says of the Russians—"If they know their strength, no men were able to match with them; nor they that dwell near them should have any rest of them. But I think it is not God's will. For I may compare them to a horse that knoweth not its strength, whom a little child ruleth and guideth with a bridle for all his great strength; that if he did, neither man nor child could rule him."

palace, where, according to the custom then usual in Muscovy, he presented each with a splendid robe. To the ringleaders he gave clothes of black velvet, and then addressing them, he enlarged upon the conduct of the soldiers at Kazan, their refusal to obey his orders, and their attempt to assassinate him; he said, that grieved as he must ever be to find his subjects so rebellious, he was still more so on the discovery, that the promoters of this discontent had been those in whom he had placed implicit confidence, and who were generally called, and ought to be his councillors; and that now, all who hoped for the least mercy had better at once acknowledge their errors, and rely on the benevolence of their Czar. Several threw themselves on their knees and expressed their penitence, others remained stolid and immoveable, while the greater number, terrified and astonished, requested that their lives at least might be spared; but Ivan caused the principal offenders to be immediately seized and executed, the less guilty he absolved with merely a short imprisonment, and the remainder he entirely pardoned, with the condition that they should prove their repentance and faithfulness by their courage before the gates of Kazan.

That same spring Ivan, who was nearly twenty-two years of age, again advanced with an army of three hundred thousand men, and pitched his camp in his old quarters beneath the hill of the Tartar city, where he immediately commenced the siege. His father Bazil had introduced a small body of infantry among his troops; but these, though generally they would have been the most effective in scaling a fortress, were for many years neither serviceable nor popular with the Muscovites, who were unaccustomed to marching on foot, generally rode over the walls of a captured city, and found themselves greatly incommoded by their long robes in a retreat. The strength of the Russian armies in a pitched battle, generally lay in the first tremendous shock of their onslaught. If their opponents stood this, they seldom gained much advantage when face to face with an equal number in the open field.

The daily detail of a blockade is usually monotonous and wearisome, and that of Kazan was protracted and long. A moveable church had been placed next to the tent of the Czar, where service was performed every morning before the soldiers or engineers began their work; and the progress of the siege being slow, and the loss of the Russians heavy, as the Tartars kept up an incessant shower of arrows and stones, Ivan ordered his generals to undermine the walls of the citadel, a form of warfare never previously seen in Muscovy, and quite unknown to the Kazanites. On Sunday, the 2nd of October, 1552, a day still kept as a fast in the Russian church, Prince Kurbsky announced that the mine was complete, and, causing his army to be arranged in order of battle, with himself at their head, the Czar directed the engineer to fire the train, while the priests read and chanted a solemn mass, and as the officiating deacon read the sacred words—"There shall be one fold and one shepherd," * the mine sprung with a tremendous explosion, bringing a quarter of the city to the ground. The Muscovites instantly poured across the ruins, dealing destruction and death all around; the Tartars, horrorstruck and stupefied, thinking an earthquake had caused the shock, and that Heaven had leagued with man to oppose them, first attempted to defend themselves, and then turned and fled across the foaming river Kazanka, and sought shelter in the opposite woods. For several hours confusion and plunder prevailed; till the Russians, like wolf-hounds, were called by their officers off their prey; the banners of Moscow floated from the gilded minarets of the citadel,† the Czar was quartered in the Tartar Kremlin, the palace of the Mussulman khans, and order was at length obtained and secured by the approach of a dark and foggy night.

All those of the Mahometans who consented to receive baptism, were restored to their houses and lands. A bishop was appointed over the city, with directions to employ every means in human power to induce the infidels to embrace Christianity; the Tartar mosques were converted into churches, or ruthlessly razed to the ground; a convent and a monastery were erected by order of the Czar; and the estates and possessions of the Tartar chiefs transferred to the Muscovite soldiers and nobles who had served in the

---

* Mouravieff's "Church of Russia."

† INSCRIPTION IN ARABIC FOUND ON A STONE, PROBABLY A MONUMENT, IN THE MARKET-PLACE AT KAZAN.

"God the holy, the righteous, the great, and the majestic, said—'All those who live in the earth will fade away, but the face of the Lord, clothed in honour and glory, will shine eternally.' Blessings and deliverance be to Mahomet, who declared this world not to be eternal. Also blessings and deliverance to the Lord, who said—'The world is above all kings.' In the year 936 of the Hegira (1520) of Mahomet, in the month of Toulhaghed, the son of Moukhammed Shakia was killed by the hand of the Christian Moukhammed Galal."

war, all the Mussulman peasantry and populace being enrolled as serfs of the crown.

A governor was appointed over the province, and her affairs regulated by a special court, established immediately after its conquest, at Moscow; and this, towards the close of the sixteenth century, was always known as the tribunal of Kazan.

As soon as he had completed the subjection of this kingdom, Ivan turned his thoughts towards the sandy, barren regions of the neighbouring kindred state. Astrakhan, isolated amidst wide and trackless deserts, with a safe and commodious port, and the command of the Caspian, had devoted her energies principally to her Persian and Indian trade; and till her khan, unfortunately for his own freedom and people, had accepted the perilous crown of Kazan, she had joined but little in the policy and dissensions that were at that time distracting both Asia and Europe. But her peacefulness or apathy were of no avail. Ediger and his family had been carried to Moscow, where, to obtain the comfort and freedom of Russian nobles, they consented to embrace Christianity; though, as they were still prisoners, they were totally unable to render assistance to their people, and regretfully abandoned their kingdom to her approaching and imminent fate. Two years after the reduction of Kazan, Ivan with his army embarked on rafts, sailed down the Volga, and by land and water surrounded Astrakhan; twenty thousand Turkish soldiers, sent by Solyman the Magnificent to her assistance, perished beneath the piercing sun of the wild and shadeless steppes; and on the 1st of August, 1554, the city fell before the assault and mines of the Muscovites, and her crown, with that of Kazan and Siberia, now lies amidst the regalia of the Czars.

An attempt was made, a few years later, to wrest her from Russia by the Turks, in order to facilitate the transportation of troops into Persia, with whom the Porte was then at war; and whose forces suffered severely from cold, hunger, and fatigue, during their passage across the snow-capped mountains of Armenia, and the barren windy wastes of Masarbijan. The vizier Sokolli at the same time proposed to his master to connect the Don and Volga by a canal, so that his armies might make the whole journey with less fatigue by water, as in that case they would cross the stormy waves of the Caspian, and effect a landing on the opposite Persian shore; and sending three thousand pioneers and five thousand janissaries to Azof, to secure the entrance, he also despatched thirty thousand Tartars up the Don, to commence this important and difficult work. At the same time, three thousand janissaries and twenty thousand Turkish cavalry marched from Azof to Astrakhan, and straitly besieged the place; but they were repulsed by a vigorous sortie from before the city, by the Russian governor, with immense slaughter, and forced to retrace their steps towards the shores of the Black Sea; while the workmen and janissaries at Azof were defeated by an army of fifteen thousand Muscovites under Prince Serebinoff, and all put to flight. Another force of Turks and Tartars sustained a lost engagement on the Don; and the former, dispirited by this ill success, at length entirely gave up the attempt; and a tempest assailing their fleet as they crossed the turbulent waters of the Euxine on their return, only seven thousand survivors ever reached their destined harbour in the Golden Horn.* "Their Tartar allies," says Creasy, " who knew that the close neighbourhood of the Turks would ensure their own entire subjection to the Sultan, eagerly promoted the distaste which the Ottomans had acquired for Sokolli's project, by enlarging on the horrors of the climate of Muscovy, and especially on the peril in which the short summer nights of those northern regions placed either the soul or body of the true believer. As the Mahometan law requires the evening prayer to be said two hours after sunset, and that of the morning to be repeated at the dawn of day, it was necessary that a Moslem should, in a night of only three hours long—according to the Tartars—either lose his natural rest, or violate the commands of the prophet." The following year an ambassador, Count Nossolitof, arrived at Constantinople from Moscow, to remonstrate with the Porte upon this unprovoked invasion of the dominions of the Czar, and the attack upon Astrakhan; but proposing for the future a peace and alliance between the two empires. In his interview with the Turkish ministers, Nossolitof enlarged upon the toleration with which Ivan treated all the Mussulmen throughout his empire, and affirmed that neither the Czar nor his people were enemies to the faith and followers of Mahomet.†

* Creasy's "Ottoman Turks." † Ibid.

With the conquest and annexation of Kazan and Astrakhan, the last independent kingdoms of the Monguls to the west of the Urals became at length extinct; for the Crimea was now a vassal and tributary province of the Porte. The Tartars—those of Taurida—once more during the reign of Ivan invaded Moscow, and, abandoning the burning city, which they had thoroughly sacked, carried away one hundred thousand captives,* leaving as many dead among the ashes of their homes; but from that time they were forced to be content with plundering the border provinces of the empire; and, as Russia became strengthened and consolidated, she gradually brought the whole of the Crimea beneath her extending sway, though the inhabitants opposed her with a fierce and desperate resistance, and only submitted sullenly and reluctantly to her yoke.† Colonizing and cultivating the fertile shores of the Volga and the Don, the Muscovites kept the Kalmucks, the last remnant of the khanate of the Golden Horde, in obedience to their government. In the seventeenth century these were joined by a few tribes of the same people from China, and served as valuable auxiliaries of the Russians and Cossacks, in their wars both with Germany and the Porte; but in the reign of the Empress Catharine, the celestial immigrants took offence at some new impost, or a slight that had been shown to their chief when fighting against the Muscovite foes, and setting fire to the Russian villages, and to the grass on the steppes as they fled, half a million of their nation escaped over the frozen Volga in the depth of winter, and across the deserts of the Kirghiz, three feet deep in snow, to the protection and dominions of the Chinese Emperor, Kien-long, who gladly received them as his subjects. But their sufferings from cold and fatigue, during a march of two thousand miles, had reduced their number to less than half of its original force; and the Cossacks, who pursued them the following spring, till they were repelled by the army of China on the outskirts of the empire, traced the path that the Kalmucks had followed by the bones of their mouldering dead. A religious solemnity, called the Dalai Lamoi, was instituted,

---

* During the sixteenth century, the corps of the janissaries in Turkey, and that of the Mamelukes in Egypt, appears to have been chiefly recruited with Russian slaves. Paulus Jovius observes that Slavonic was spoken by both.
† The Crimea was first invaded by the Russians in 1736 under Marshal Munnich. The Russians carried barrels of water, fastened to every baggage waggon, on their march, to extinguish the flames which the Tartars had ignited throughout the long dry grass of the steppes. The peninsula was afterwards thoroughly subdued in the reign of Catharine II., by Prince Dolgorouki.

in remembrance of the souls who had perished on this remarkable flight, and a monument of large columns of granite and brass was erected, by order of Kien-long, on the borders of the steppe, which bears an inscription, in commemoration of this event, to the following effect:—

"By the will of God here—upon the brinks of these deserts which from this point begin, and stretch away pathless, treeless, waterless, for thousands of miles, and along the margins of many mighty nations—rested from their labours and from great afflictions, under the shadow of the Chinese wall, and by the favour of Kien-long, God's lieutenant upon earth; those ancient children of the wilderness, the Torgote * Tartars, flying before the wrath of the Grecian Czar, wandering sheep who had strayed away from the Celestial in the year 1616, but are now mercifully gathered again, after infinite sorrow, into the fold of their forgiving Shepherd. Hallowed be the spot for ever, and hallowed be the day. Sept. 8, 1771."†

The grass has grown over the fields that the Monguls once strewed with human bones; the blood has long dried that they shed over a third of the earth; but what vestiges now remain of their influence and dominion in Eastern Europe, except the dye that their despotism has impressed upon the habits, manners, and characters of the inhabitants? No just law, no grand monument, no beneficial institution, they introduced into Russia during more than two hundred years; their power was marked by mere oppression and tyranny, without one virtue to alleviate, or one memorial to leave their names in remembrance; and it has passed away, probably from Europe for ever, without meriting from posterity one feeling of pity or regret for their fall.

But even their ancient territories in Western Asia are now fast being merged within the borders of the immense empire of the Czar; in Persia, China, and at length in Hindoostan, other rulers have supplanted their emperors and chiefs; and, though they still fondly cling to the memories of their former heroes, and every Tartar prince claims descent from Timur or Zingis, the power and fame of the conquering race is now

---

* Torgote, or Kalmuck. "In the original, the inscription gives the year according to the Chinese calendar. The designation of the Russian Emperor is either from some confusion between him and the Byzantine Emperor, or relates to his religion. The account of this emigration was drawn up in the Chinese language by order of Kien-long."—De Quincey's "Revolt of the Kalmuck Tartars."

† De Quincey's "Revolt of the Kalmuck Tartars."

all of the past, and, to use the Persian proverb once quoted by the conqueror of Constantinople—" The spider has wove her web in the imperial palace, and the owl has sung her watch-song upon the towers of Afrasib."*

---

* " Perdi dari mikinned ber kysr Caisar aukebut Burni neubet mizened ber kuimbeti Efrasiyab," was quoted by Mahomet II.—Cantermir's " History of the Ottomans."
Afrasib, an ancient king of the Turanians or Tartars. Vide *ante*, Book I.

APPENDIX.

POEMS DESCRIBING THE PLACES AND MANNERS OF THE COUNTRY AND PEOPLE OF RUSSIA—1568.

"CERTAINE letters in verse, written by Master George Turberville, out of Moscovia. Which went as Secretary thither with Master Thos. Randolp, her Maisties Embassadour to the Emperour, 1568, to certaine Friendes of his in London, describing the Manners of the Country and People."

TO HIS ESPECIALL FRIEND, MASTER EDWARD DANCIE.

My Dancie dear, when I recount within my breast
My London friends, and wonted mates, and thee above the rest,
I feel a thousand fittes of deep and deadly woe,
To think that I from land to sea, from bliss to bale did go.
I left my native soil, full like a reckless man,
And, unacquainted of the coast, among the Russies ran—
A people passing rude, to vices vile inclined,
Folk fitting to be of Bacchus' train, so quaffing is their kind.
Drink is their sole desire, the pot is all their pride,
The soberest head doth, once a day, stand needful of a guide.
If he to banquet bid his friends, he will not shrink
On them at dinner to bestow a dozen kinds of drink:
Such liquor as they have, and as the country gives,
But chiefly two—one called Kwas, whereby the Maijik * lives,
Small ware and waterlike, but somewhat tart in taste,
The rest is Mead, of honey made, wherewith their lips they baste.
And if he go unto his neighbour as a guest,
He cares for little meat, if so his drink be of the best;
No wonder though they use such vile and horrid trade,
Since with the hatchet and the hand their chiefest gods be made;
Their idols have their hearts—on God they never call,
Unless it be Nichola † Bough, that hangs against the wall.
The house that hath no god or painted saint within,
Is not to be resorted to, that house is full of sin.
Besides their private gods, in open places stand
Their crosses unto which they crouch, and bless themselves with hand;
Devoutly down they stoop with forehead to the ground,
Was never more deceit in rags and greasy garments found.

* Maijik, Russian name for peasant.   † St. Nicholas of Bari.

Almost the meanest man in all the country rides,
The woman eke, against our use, her trotting horse bestrides:
In sundry colours they, both men and women, go,
In buskins all, that money have on buskins to bestow.
Each woman, hanging hath a ring within her ear,
Which all of ancient use, and some of very pride do wear;
Their gate is very brave, their countenance wise and sad,
And yet their conduct is most light, their trade of living bad.
Is not the meanest man in all the land but he,
To buy her painted colours, doth allow his wife a fee;
Wherewith she decks herself, and dyes her tawny skin,
She pranks and paints her smoky face, both brow, lip, cheek, and chin.
Yea those that honest are, if any such there be
Within the land, do use the like; a man may plainly see
Upon some women's cheeks, the painting how it lies,
In plaster sort, for that too thick her face the creature dyes.
But such as skilful are, and cunning dames indeed,
By daily practice do it well, yea, sure they do exceed;
They lay their colours so, as he that is full wise
May easily be deceived therein, if he do trust his eyes.
I not a little muse what madness makes them paint
Their faces, waying how they keep the stove by mere constraint;
For seldom when, unless on church or marriage-day,
A man shall see the dames abroad that are of best array.
Thus much, friend Dancie, I did mean to write to thee,
To let thee weet in Russia land what men and women be;
Hereafter, I perhaps of other things will write
To thee, and other of my friends which I shall see with sight;
And other stuff besides, which true report shall tell,
Meanwhile, I end my loving lines, and bid thee now farewell.

To Spencer.

If I should now forget, or not remember thee,
Thou, Spencer, might'st a foul rebuke or shame impute to me;
For I to open shew did love thee passing well,
And thou wert he at parture whom I loath'd to bid farewell;
And, as I went thy friend, so I continue still,
No better proof thou canst than this desire of true good-will.
I do remember well when needs I should away,
And that the post would licence us no longer time to stay,
Thou wrungst me by the fist, and, holding fast my hand,
Didst crave of me to send thee news, and how I liked the land.
It is a sandy soil, no very fruitful vain,
More waste and woody grounds there are than closes fit for grain;
Yet grain there growing is, which they untimely take
And cut, or ere the corn he ripe they mow it on a stake,
And laying sheaf by sheaf, their harvest so they dry;
They make the greater haste for fear the frost the corn destroy,
For in the winter time so glary is the ground,
As neither grass nor other grain in pastures may be found;

In comes the cattle then, the sheep, the colt, the cow,
Fast by his bed, the maijik them a lodging doth allow,
Whom he with fodder feeds, and holds as dear as life ;
And thus they wear the winter with the maijik and his wife.
Seven months the winter lasts, the glare it is so great,
As it is May before he turn his ground to sow his wheat.
The bodies too that die, unburied lie they then,
Laid up in coffins made of fir, as well the poorest men
As those of greater state ; the cause is lightly found,
For that in winter time they cannot come to break the ground ;
And wood so plenteous is quite throughout all the land,
As rich and poor at time of death assured of coffins stand.
Perhaps thou musest much how this may stand with reason,
That bodies dead can uncorrupt abide so long a season ;
Take this for certain truth, as soon as heat is gone,
The force of cold the body binds as hard as any stone,
Without offence at all to any living thing,
And so they lie in perfect state till next return of spring.
Their beasts be like to ours, as far as I can see,
For shape and shew, but somewhat less of bulk and bone they be ;
Of wat'ry taste, the flesh not firm like English beef,
And yet it serves them very well, and is a good relief.
Their sheep are very small, sharp singled, hand full long,
Great store of fowls on sea and land, the moorish reeds among,
The greatness of the store doth make the prices less ;
Besides, in all the land they know not how good meat to dress.
They use neither broach nor spit, but when the stove they heat,
They put their vessels in a pan and so they bake their meat—
No pewter to be had, no dishes but of wood,
No use of trenchers ; cups cut out of birch are very good,
They use but wooden spoons, which hanging in a case,
Each maijik at his girdle ties, and thinks it no disgrace ;
With whittles two or three, the better man the moe,
The chiefest Russians in the land with spoons and knives do go.
Their houses are not huge of building, but they say
They plant them in the loftiest ground to shift the snow away ;
Which, in the winter time, each where full thick they lie,
Which makes them have the more desire to set their houses high ;
No stonework is in use, their roofs of rafters be,
One linked in another fast, their walls are all of tree—
Of masts both long and large, with moss put in between,
To keep the force of weather out, I never erst have seen
A gross device so good, and on the roof they lay
The burden bark, to rid the rain and sudden showers away.
In every room a stove, to serve the winter turn,
Of wood they have sufficient store, as much as they can burn.
They have no English glass ; of slices of a rock
Called Sluda, they their windows make, that English glass doth mock :
They cut it very thin, and sow it with a thread,
In pretty order like to panes, to serve their present need ;
No other glass, good faith ! doth give a better light,
And sure the rock is nothing rich, the cost is very slight.

2 H

The chiefest place is that where hangs the god; by it
The owner of the house himself doth never sit,
Unless his better come, to whom he yields the seat:
The stranger bending to the god, the ground with brow must beat,
And in that very place which they most sacred deem,
The stranger lies—a token that his guest he doth esteem.
Where he is wont to have a bearskin for his bed,
And must, instead of pillow, clap his saddle to his head,
In Russia other shift there is not to be had,
For where the bedding is not good, the bolsters are but bad;
I mused very much what made them so to lie,
Since in their country down is rife, and feathers out of cry;
Unless it be because the country is so hard,
They fear by niceness of a bed their bodies would be marr'd.
I wish'd thee oft with us, save that I stood in fear
Thou would'st have loathed to have laid thy limbs upon a bear,
As I and Stafford did, that was my mate in bed;
And yet (we thank the God of heaven) we both right well have sped.
Lo, thus I make an end; no other news to thee
But that the country is too cold, the people horrid be.
I write not all I know; I touch but here and there,
For if I should, my pen would pinch, and eke offend I fear:
Whoso shall read this verse, conjecture of the rest,
And think, by reason of our trade, that I do think the best.
But if no traffic were, then could I boldly pen
The hardness of the soil, and the manners of the men;
They say the lion's paw gives judgment of the beast,
And so may you dream of the great by reading of the least.

TO PARKER.

My Parker, pen and ink were made to write,
And idle heads that little do, have leisure to indite;
Wherefore respecting these, and thine assured love,
If I would write no news to thee thou might'st my pen reprove.
And since then fortune thus hath shoved my ship on shore,
And made me seek another realm unseen of me before;
The manners of the men I purpose to declare,
And private points besides, which strange and wondrous are.
The Russie men are round, with faces nothing fair,
But brown by reason of the stove and closeness of the air;
It is their common use to shave or else to shear
Their heads, for none in all the land long lolling locks doth wear,
Unless perhaps he have his sovereign prince displeased,
For then he never cuts his hair until he be appeased—
A certain sign to know who in displeasure be,
For every man that views his head will say, " So this is he;"
And during all the time he lets his locks to grow,
Dares no man for his life to him a face of friendship show.
Their garments are not very gay, nor handsome to the eye,
A cap aloft their heads they have, that standeth very high,

APPENDIX.

Which colpack they do term; they wear no ruffs at all,
The best have collars set with pearls, which they rubasca call;
Their shirts in Russia long, they work them down before,
And on the sleeves, with colour'd silks, two inches good and more.
Aloft their shirts they wear a garment jacket-wise,
Called onoriadka, and a sash about his waist he ties;
A pair of yarnen stocks to keep the cold away,
Within his boots the Russie wears, the heels they underlay
With clouting clamps of steel, sharp-pointed at the toe,
And over all a suba furr'd, and thus the Russies go.
Well button'd is the suba, according to his state,
Some silk, of silver other some, but those of poorer rate
Do wear no subes at all, but grosser gowns to sight,
That reacheth down beneath the calf, and that armacka hight.*
These are the Russies' robes; the richest use to ride
From place to place, his servant runs, and follows by his side.
The Cossack bears his felt, to force away the rain,
Their bridles are not very brave, their saddles are but plain;
No bits, but snaffles all, of birch their saddles be,
Much fashion'd like the Scottish seats, broad flacks to keep the knee
From heating of the horse, the panels larger far
And broader be than ours, they use short stirrups for the war;
For when the Russie is pursued by cruel foe,
He rides away, and suddenly betakes him to his bow,
And bends him but about, in saddle as he sits,
And therewithal, amidst his race, the following foe he hits.
Their bows are very short, like Turkey bows outright,
Of sinews made with birchen bark, in cunning manner dight;
Small arrows, crooked heads that fell and forked be,
Which, being shot from out those bows, a cruel way will flee;
They seldom shoe their horse, unless they wish to ride
In post upon the frozen floods, so that they shall not slide.
He sets a slender calk, and so he rides away,
The horses of the country go good fourscore versts † a day,
And all without the spur, once prick them and they skip,
But go not forward on their way; the Russie has his whip
To rap him on the ribs, for though all booted be,
Yet shall ye not a pair of spurs in all the country see.
The common game is chess, almost the simplest will
Both give a check and eke a mate, by practice comes their skill.
Again the dice as fast, the poorest rogues of all
Will sit them down in open field, and there to gaming fall;
Their dice are very small, in fashion like to those
Which we do use; he takes them up, and over his thumb he throws,
Not shaking them a whit, the cast suspiciously,
And yet I deem them void of art that dicing most apply.
At play when silver lacks, goes saddle, horse, and all,
And each thing else worth silver walks, although the price be small;
Because thou lovest to play, friend Parker, other while,
I wish thee there the weary day with dicing to beguile.

* *Hight*, called. † A verst is three quarters of an English mile.

But thou wert better far at home, I wist it well,
And would'st be loathe among these folks so long a time to dwell.
Then judge of us thy friends, what kind of life we had,
That near the frozen pole to waste our weary days were glad;
In such a savage soil, where laws do bear no sway,
But all is at the king his will, to do or else to slay,
And that sans cause, God knows, if so his mind be such:
But what mean I with kings to deal, we ought not saints to touch.
Conceive the rest yourself, and deem what lives they lead,
Where sin is law, and subjects live continually in dread;
And where the best estates have none assurance good,
Of lands, of lives, nor nothing falls unto the next of blood;
But all of custom doth unto the prince redound,
And all the whole revenue comes unto the king his crown.
Good faith! I see thee muse at what I tell thee now,
But true it is no choice, but all at prince's pleasure bow.
So Tarquin ruled Rome, as thou rememberest well,
And what his fortune was at last, I know thyself canst tell;
Where will in common weal doth bear the only sway,
And sin is law, the prince and realm must needs in time decay;
The strangeness of this place is such for sundry things I see,
As if I would I cannot write each private point to thee.
The cold is rare, the people rude, the prince so full of pride,
The realm so stored with monks and nuns, and priests on every side;
The manners are so Turkey like, the men so full of guile,
The women light, and temples stuff'd with idols that defile;
The seats that sacred ought to be, the customs are so quaint,
That were I to describe the whole I fear my pen would faint.
In sum I say, I never saw a prince that so did reign,
Nor people so beset with saints, yet all but vile and vain.
If thou be wise, as wise thou art, and wilt be ruled by me,
Live still at home, and covet not those barbarous coasts to see;
No good befalls a man that seeks, and finds no better place,
No civil customs to be learn'd, where God bestows no grace.
And truly ill they do deserve to be beloved of God,
That neither love nor stand in awe of his assured rod:
Which though be long, yet plagues at last the vile and wicked sort
Of sinful wights, that all in vice do place their chiefest sport.
Adieu, friend Parker, if thou list to know the Russies well,
To Sigismundi's * book repair, who all the truth can tell,
For he long erst in message went unto that savage king,
Sent by the Pole, and true report in each respect did bring;
To him I recommend myself to ease my pen of pain,
And now at last do wish thee well, and bid farewell again.

(Turberville's " Tragical Tales and Sonnets," reprinted
for the Hakluyt Society.)

* Baron Herberstein.

APPENDIX.

The following is a poem founded on the singular mode in which Olég, the ancient Russian prince, is said to have met his death, (see Book I. chap. vi.) translated from the Russian of the celebrated Alexander Pushkin, who was killed in a duel at St. Petersburg, 1837.

THE LAY OF THE WISE OLÉG.

Wise Olég to the war he hath bound him again,
    The Khazars have awaken'd his ire;
For rapine and raid, hamlet, city, and plain,
    Are devoted to falchion and fire.
In mail of Byzance, girt with many a good spear,
The prince pricks along on his faithful destrère.

From the darksome fir forest, to meet that array,
    Forth paces a greyhair'd magician;
To none but Perún did that sorcerer pray,
    Fulfilling the prophet's dread mission.
His life he had wasted in penance and pain,
And beside that enchanter Olég drew his rein.

"Now rede me enchanter, beloved of Perún,
    The good and the ill that's before me—
Shall I soon give my neighbour foes triumph, and soon
    Shall the earth of the grave be piled o'er me?
Unfold all the truth; fear me not, and for meed
Choose among them—I give thee my best battle-steed."

"O, enchanters they care not for prince or for peer,
    And gifts are but needlessly given;
The wise tongue ne'er stumbleth for falsehood or fear,
    'Tis the friend of the councils of heaven.
The years of the future are clouded and dark,
Yet on thy fair forehead thy fate I can mark.

"Remember now firmly, the words of my tongue,
    For the chief finds a rapture in glory;
On the gate of Byzantium thy buckler is hung—
    Thy name shall be deathless in story;
Wild waves and broad kingdoms thy sceptre obey,
And the foe sees with envy so boundless a sway.

"And the blue sea uplifting its treacherous wave
    In its wrath, in the hurricane hour—
And the knife of the coward, the sword of the brave,
    To slay thee shall never have power:
Within thy strong harness no wound shalt thou know,
For a guardian unseen shall defend thee below.

"Thy steed fears not labours, nor danger, nor pain,
  His lord's lightest accent he heareth;
Now still, though the arrows fall round him like rain,
  Now o'er the red field he careereth:
He fears not the winter, he fears not to bleed,
Yet thy death-wound shall come from thy good battle-steed."

Olég smiled a moment, but yet on his brow
  And lip, thought and sorrow were blended;
In silence he bent on his saddle, and slow
  The prince from his courser descended;
And as though from a friend he were parting with pain,
He strokes his broad neck and his dark flowing mane.

"Farewell, then, my comrade, fleet, faithful, and bold,
  We must part—such is destiny's power;
Now rest thee, I swear in thy stirrup of gold
  No foot shall e'er rest from this hour.
Farewell! we've been comrades for many a long year,
My squires, now, I pray ye, come take my destrère.

"The softest of carpets his horsecloth shall be,
  And lead him away to the meadow,
On the choicest of food he shall feed daintily,
  He shall drink of the well in the shadow."
Then straightway departed the squires with the steed,
And to valiant Olég a fresh courser they lead.

Olég and his comrades are feasting, I trow,
  The mead-cups are merrily clashing,
Their locks are as white as the dawn-lighted snow,
  On the peak of the mountain top flashing;
They talk of old times, of the days of their pride,
And the fights where together they struck side by side.

"But where," quoth Olég, "is my good battle-horse?
  My mettlesome charger how fares he?
Is he playful as ever, as fleet in the course,
  His age and his freedom how bears he?"
They answer and say, on the hill by the stream,
He has long slept the slumber that knows not a dream.

Olég then grew thoughtful, and bent down his brow:
  "O man, what can magic avail thee!
A false lying dotard, enchanter art thou,
  Our rage and contempt should assail thee.
My horse might have borne me till now but for thee,"
Then the bones of his charger Olég went to see.

Olég he rode forth, with his spearmen beside,
  At his bridle Prince Igor he hurried,
And they see on a hillock, by Dnieper's swift tide,
  Where the steed's noble bones lie unburied.

They are wash'd by the rain, the dust o'er them is cast,
And above them the feather grass waves in the blast.

Then the prince set his foot on the courser's white skull,
   Saying—" Sleep, my old friend, in thy glory!
Thy lord hath outlived thee, his days are nigh full:
   At his funeral feast red and gory,
'Tis not then 'neath the axe that shall redden the sod,
That my dust may be pleasured to quaff thy brave blood.

" And am I to find my destruction in this,
   My death in a skeleton seeking?"
From the skull of the courser, a snake with a hiss
   Crept forth as the hero was speaking;
Round his legs like a ribbon it twined its black ring,
And the prince shriek'd aloud as he felt the keen sting.

The mead cups are foaming, they circle around,
   At Olég's mighty death-feast they're ringing,
Prince Igor and Olga, they sit on the mound,
   The war men the death-song are singing:
And they talk of old times, of the days of their pride,
And the fights where together they struck side by side.

(Translated from the Russian by T. B. Shaw, B.A., some time Adjunct Professor of English Literature in the Imperial Alexander Lyceum, at St. Petersburg. The reign of Olég was also dramatized by Catharine II., though it is supposed that she was much assisted in her performance by the Russian poet, Derjarvin.)

THE END.

M'CORQUODALE & CO., PRINTERS, LONDON—WORKS, NEWTON.

www.ingramcontent.com/pod-product-compliance
Lightning Source LLC
Chambersburg PA
CBHW051235300426
44114CB00011B/751